D1284523

The UCLA Film
and Television Archive
Studies in History,
Criticism, and Theory

Before
the
Nickelodeon

Edwin S. Porter (1870–1941)

BEFORE the NICKELODEON

Edwin S. Porter
and the Edison Manufacturing Company

CHARLES MUSSER

University of California Press
BERKELEY / LOS ANGELES / OXFORD

University of California Press
Berkeley and Los Angeles, California

University of California Press, Ltd.
Oxford, England

© 1991 by
The Regents of the University of California

Library of Congress Cataloging-in-Publication Data

Musser, Charles.
    Before the nickelodeon : Edwin S. Porter and the
Edison Manufacturing Company / Charles Musser.
        p.   cm. — (The UCLA Film and Television
Archive studies in history, criticism, and theory)
    Includes bibliographical references (p.) and index.
    ISBN 0-520-06080-6. — ISBN 0-520-06986-2 (pbk.)
    1. Porter, Edwin S.—Criticism and interpreta-
tion. 2. Thomas A. Edison, Inc. 3. Silent films—
United States—History and criticism. 4. Motion
pictures—United States—History. I. Title. II. Series.
PN1998.3.P67M87 1991   90-11045
791.43'0232'092—dc20   CIP

Printed in the United States of America

1 2 3 4 5 6 7 8 9

The paper used in this publication meets the minimum
requirements of American National Standard for
Information Sciences—Permanence of Paper for Printed
Library Materials, ANSI Z39.48-1984 ♾

For Eileen Bowser
In Memory of Jay Leyda

Contents

Foreword

By its example, Charles Musser's elegantly argued study of Edwin S. Porter conveys two of the primary goals that the UCLA Film and Television Archive seeks to achieve in sponsoring scholarly publication.

In part we hope to underline the creative role played by film archives in making historical research possible and, often, in helping to set the field's scholarly agenda. The study of early cinema is reliant on the accessibility of films rescued and preserved by institutions such as the Museum of Modern Art, the Library of Congress, the International Museum of Photography, and the UCLA Film and Television Archive. The current worldwide revival of scholarly concern with early film can be traced back to the legendary symposium sponsored by the International Federation of Film Archives in Brighton, England, in 1978.

Our second goal in promoting scholarly publication is to celebrate and promote the renaissance of historical writing currently taking place in the field of film and television studies. After a long period of marginalization to the outer fringes of the discipline, serious historical research is now being rediscovered, redefined, and legitimated by a new generation of young scholars like Charles Musser.

In his writing Musser combines the traditionalist historian's respect for scholarly erudition with the contemporary historian's insistence on methodological self-consciousness, multidisciplinary discourse, and intellectual risktaking. Relying almost entirely on primary archival source materials to construct his arguments, Musser rejects timeworn and reductive explanations of historical causality such as auteurism and technological determinism. His dialectical approach to historical narrative freely crosses disciplinary boundaries to convey the complex interplay of aesthetics with a multifaceted social and industrial context.

In theory, the vast holdings of film and documents available through the nation's archives suggest the possibility of doing historical research that is truly definitive—the "last word" in the field. In practice, the current generation of intellectually expansive scholars are much too aware of the complexity of history to believe that interpretive closure is possible. In his commitment to both exhaustive archival research and audacious interpretation, Charles Musser exemplifies the creative potential in this contradiction.

Robert Rosen
Director
UCLA Film and Television Archive

Acknowledgments

An undertaking such as this can be accomplished only with the assistance of many people. I owe a particular debt to Jay Leyda, who taught my first film course. His advice and example over the intervening seventeen years have been a constant inspiration. My deepest regret is that he is not here to read this book, to which he contributed so generously. Eileen Bowser has sponsored the work of many students of early cinema. Her generosity and understanding have helped to make this project possible. In the process, she has become not only a friend and colleague but a quiet muse. To them, this book is dedicated.

This project began in the fall of 1976 in the context of an independent study with Jay Leyda. Unhappy with the frequently expressed assumption that cinema began with D. W. Griffith, Ismail Xavier and I went to the Library of Congress and looked at a group of early films from the Paper Print Collection. George Pratt taught me how to mine newspapers for information and then made his own research on Porter available to me. Pratt's rigorous, carefully documented articles on early cinema, as well as his thoughtful comments and continued enthusiasm, provided me with models of scholarly diligence. From Tony Keefer of the Connellsville Historical Society, I learned much about researching local history even as he kindly shared information about Porter's early life with me.
Robert Rosen of the UCLA Film and Television Archive and Angelo Humouda of the Cineteca D. W. Griffith in Genoa encouraged me to think of this study as a book from its early stages. The UCLA archive offered crucial assistance to this project at several junctures, and I am most pleased that it appears under its auspices. My own researches were supplemented by discussions and the sharing of information with associates interested in early cinema—

particularly with Noël Burch, Tom Gunning, André Gaudreault, David Levy, Paul Spehr, Pat Loughney, and Jon Gartenberg. Robert Sklar played an important role, providing thoughtful criticism and encouragement as I struggled to give this manuscript coherence and a form others would find useful. William K. Everson, William Simon, John Fell, Kristin Thompson, and Peter Dreyer provided me with thoughtful readings.

Portions of this manuscript have been previously published as articles. I am very grateful to the editors of *Cinema Journal, Film and History, Framework*, and *Iris* for the opportunity to reach audiences with some of these ideas before this study was completed.[1] Such opportunities to participate in the wide-ranging discussions revolving around early motion pictures and the practice of film historiography enabled me to refine my arguments and significantly improve the final manuscript. I am particularly grateful to the Society of Cinema Studies, which awarded the 1978 Student Award for Scholarly Writing to "The Early Cinema of Edwin Porter," the basis for chapter 6. This recognition facilitated the funding of *Before the Nickelodeon*, a film devoted to Porter's Edison career, and encouraged me to keep working on a project that has taken over ten years to complete.

Many people at various institutions went out of their way to assist this project. Pat Sheehan, Emily Sieger, Barbara Humphries, and Kathy Loughney at the Library of Congress; Mary Bowling, Ed Pershey, Reed Able, and Lea Burt at the Edison National Historic Site; John Kuiper and Chris Horak at the George Eastman House; Charles Silver, Ron Magliozzi, Jytte Jensen, and Mary Lea Bandy at the Museum of Modern Art; and David Francis, Roger Holman, and Elaine Burrows at the British Film Institute were all helpful on many separate occasions. Paula Jescavge at New York University's Bobst Library patiently filled many interlibrary loan requests. I am particularly indebted to the Department of Cinema Studies at New York University, where an earlier draft of this manuscript served as a dissertation.

Many other people deserve my thanks. Among them: Warren D. Leight, Rick King, Alexis Krasilovsky, Stephen Brier, John E. Allen, Reese V. Jenkins, Janet Staiger, John Fell, David Bordwell, Judith Mayne, Susan Kempler, John O'Connor, Martin Sopocy, Sam McElfresh, Standish Lawder, Miriam Hansen, Steven Higgins, Kemp Niver, Bebe Bergsten, Jack Miles, Joan Richardson, Anne Richardson, Don Ranvaud, Bob Summers, Porter Reilly, Charles Harpole, Herbert Reynolds, Roberta Pearson, Louise Spence, Richard and Diane Koszarski, Paul Killiam, Noël Carroll, Carol Nelson, Marilyn Schwartz, Pamela MacFarland, Blanche Sweet, and my family and friends. To Lynne Zeavin I and this book owe more than can readily be expressed. Finally, Ernest Callenbach, my patient and supportive editor, deserves particular thanks.

1 Introduction

The first fifteen years of commercial motion pictures were extraordinary: film practices and the films not only differed fundamentally from today's counterparts but also underwent an unparalleled series of changes. During this formative period, Edwin S. Porter emerged as America's foremost filmmaker. Although many books have been written on D. W. Griffith, John Ford, and Orson Welles, not one has been published on the creator of *The Great Train Robbery*. This study is both a biography of the filmmaker Edwin S. Porter and an industrial history of the Edison Manufacturing Company from the beginning of commercial motion pictures through 1909—roughly until the formation of the Motion Picture Patents Company. This double focus is appropriate, for Porter and the Edison Company were associated in one form or another from the spring of 1896, when Porter entered the motion picture industry with a group that owned rights to "Edison's Vitascope," until 1909, when he left Edison's employ. In the interim, he worked for the Edison-licensed Eden Musee and then joined the Edison Manufacturing Company in late 1900. Within a few months he was a key member of the production team operating out of Edison's new motion picture studio. Within another two and a half years, he had become "head of negative production," a position he retained for the next six years.

This dual focus proves efficacious in other respects. This undertaking does not dispute long-held assertions that Porter was the principal American filmmaker of the pre-Griffith era, even though I seek to cast that valorization in a new light. Correspondingly, Thomas Edison and his company were at the center of the industry's activities. In this regard, the commercial practices of the Edison Company were inextricably linked with Porter's creative role as film producer.

1

Each must be seen in light of the other. Porter's departure from Edison, moreover, was not arbitrary but occurred as his methods of film production and representation fell into disrepute and ascendant practices won the strong support of the Edison Company's new chief executive, Frank Dyer. This then is also a study of what has frequently been called "early cinema"—a loosely used term best applied to certain cinematic practices that became antiquated around 1907–8. If—as John Fell suggests—early cinema is pre-Griffith, then this study examines the pre-Griffith modes of representation and production in light of Porter/Edison activities.[1]

Edison's contributions to motion picture history, particularly during the stages of invention and initial commercialization, have been extensively examined by two important figures in film historiography: Terry Ramsaye and Gordon Hendricks.[2] Their assessments are diametrically opposed. Ramsaye's *A Million and One Nights* (1926) is a highly sympathetic account, read by Edison in manuscript and published with his endorsement. Ramsaye's widely read narrative supported—probably knowingly—the inventor's efforts to pre-date his motion picture inventions. These falsehoods were exposed in Hendricks's *The Edison Motion Picture Myth* (1961), which argued that America's greatest inventor was a sometimes grasping and unethical businessman. Angered by this realization, Hendricks developed a highly critical stance toward his subject. While staying close to "the facts," the historian interpreted them so unsympathetically that many of his conclusions must be questioned. Although this present text often relies on Hendricks's and Ramsaye's contributions to film historiography, it seeks to treat Edison and his company's activities in another light, from a perspective that might be called "critical sympathy."

In grappling with Porter's contributions to cinema, most histories have concentrated on two of his productions—*Life of an American Fireman* and *The Great Train Robbery*—offering interpretations of these cinematic milestones rather than an understanding of the road they marked. Limited to a few films, their analyses fail to present a coherent interpretation of Porter's work. Perhaps this was inevitable, since these commentators wrote about Porter within the framework of a larger panorama covering many decades and thousands of extant films. The nature of their enterprise necessarily precluded the time, research, and thinking needed to offer a balanced overview of Porter's work. Moreover, their theoretical framework proved suspect. Writing at a time when it was necessary to emphasize that film was an art, Terry Ramsaye, Lewis Jacobs, and their successors conceived of Porter in romantic terms, as a "primitive artist" whose intuitive insights revolutionized the cinema. "Genius" became a methodological category that obfuscated the need for more critical insight.[3] Even recent overviews often continue to paraphrase Ramsaye's and Jacobs' assessments of Porter ("father of the story film" and "the inventor of editing") until they have become hopeless clichés.[4]

Although Porter has received his share of accolades, he also has his critics.

American historians have often viewed him as a lonely pioneer whose struggles to discover the new medium's untold possibilities were not entirely successful. Not only did they fail to acknowledge the vibrancy and diversity of American early film, but they generally failed to assess Porter's contributions within the context of world cinema, projecting America's post–World War I dominance backwards onto the pre-1912 era, when the French—first Lumière, then Méliès, and finally Pathé—often played more prominent roles. The more international, if still somewhat Eurocentric, outlooks of French historians such as Georges Sadoul have found Porter's place to be much more modest. Comparing *Life of an American Fireman* and one or two other Porter films to the better researched French and English cinemas and ignoring the dynamic of the American's development, Sadoul accuses Porter of imitating James Williamson's *Fire!* with *Life of an American Fireman* and Frank Mottershaw's *Robbery of a Mail Coach* with *The Great Train Robbery*. In so doing, Sadoul passes over the rich contexts of American cinema and popular culture, presenting a narrow, mechanistic analysis of Porter's development.[5] In truth, the observations of Jacques Deslandes and Jacques Richard are the most acute. They refrain from comparative judgments, admitting that one "must recognize one's own ignorance in the area and wait for serious research to be undertaken before one can make statements about the exploitation of the cinema [in America] between 1896 and 1906."[6]

As the field of cinema studies expanded in the early 1970s, superficial overviews of the pre-Griffith period became less and less acceptable. Making a tentative effort to put American early cinema in a larger context, Robert Sklar notes the need for a full-scale study of Edwin S. Porter, an absence this book seeks to fill.[7] More recently, a new generation of scholars has emerged that is interested in early cinema not because it was simply the precursor of classical cinema but because it was a practice with its own logic and integrity. Many of these scholars were working in isolation until the 1978 FIAF (Fédération Internationale des Archives du Film) Conference in Brighton, England, brought them together. There we met, exchanged papers, and saw hundred of films from the 1900–1906 era. Several of the papers dealt with Porter's work.[8]

Since the Brighton conference, an array of articles on early cinema have been written by participants and other historians. Many of these have been excellent, almost all have been provocative and useful.[9] Fewer books, however, have appeared to reflect this new level of interest. Several notable exceptions, Michael Chanan's *The Dream That Kicks* and a series by John Barnes, concentrate almost exclusively on the British cinema.[10] Others have added to the extensive literature already available on Georges Méliès.[11] No full-length study of American cinema prior to 1908 has been published as this goes to press.[12] Yet it is increasingly clear that a series of articles cannot replace sustained, book-length examinations of the period.

This present effort seeks to synthesize research derived from written primary source materials and viewings of films.[13] Writings of the period have been extensively consulted. Trade journals provided indispensable information even as they required painstaking efforts, for the motion picture industry had no specialized publication until 1906. Daily newspapers are another essential resource, one that would need many lifetimes to exhaust. Early motion picture catalogs contribute invaluable assistance, but are scattered across the United States. Collecting catalogs for this study thus led to an important subsidiary publishing project, the six-reel *Motion Picture Catalogs by American Producers and Distributors, 1894–1908: A Microfilm Edition.*[14] Manuscript collections are another key resource. The number of court cases involving motion pictures during this period was staggering. While these suits affected the industry's development, they also document specific cinematic practices. Porter testified often and was routinely asked to establish his professional credentials. Records, correspondence, and other materials at the Edison National Historic Site made possible a systematic study of the Edison Manufacturing Company and the work of its studio manager. There are gaps, however, and one of the most unfortunate was created by a fire that destroyed Porter's personal archive at the Famous Players studio on September 11, 1915.[15]

To balance this substantial reservoir of written materials, there are a large number of extant films. Perhaps 65 percent of the Edison subjects made before February 1908 can still be seen. Only scattered productions from 1894 to June 1897 survive, but the Paper Print Collection at the Library of Congress includes a large number of Edison films made between June 1897 and mid 1905. These films, deposited for copyright purposes as reels of paper photographs, have been restored and rephotographed back onto film by Kemp Niver.[16] The Kleine Collection, also at the Library of Congress, is a much smaller, but still significant, gathering of early, often uncopyrighted Edison films. In an unusually complementary relationship, the Museum of Modern Art has most of the Edison negatives from the period between late 1905 and February 1908. In the early stages of this project I had the opportunity to restore some Porter films, which the museum had already preserved, to their original order. When these were incomplete, surviving frame enlargements were filmed and inserted in their correct places, accompanied by titles taken from catalog descriptions. Very few Edison films made between February 1908 and Porter's departure in November 1909 are extant. There is reason to believe that the negatives for these films were shipped to Gaumont in Paris, where European release prints were made.[17] Perhaps they will one day be rediscovered. For the moment, the films made during this period—coinciding with Porter's loss of status both at Edison and in the industry as a whole—are lost.

This book is focused around three topics: (1) production and representational practices, (2) subject matter and ideology, and (3) commercial methods.

Modes of Production and Representation

My research began as I grappled with the assumptions of an earlier generation of film historians: since the "pioneers" discovered the inherent possibilities
of film editing, the issue as these historians saw it was, who discovered which
techniques, and when did given techniques first appear? It is evident that this
basic perception remains entrenched to this day, albeit without so much of an
individualistic slant. Yet this approach fails to recognize that early cinema's
production methods were radically different from our own. As shown in chapter
5, editing was a routine procedure during the late 1890s. It was primarily performed, however, by the exhibitor, who structured groups of short, one-shot
films into sometimes quite complex sequences. Of course, editing was not as
elaborate a procedure as it would become in later years, but its essential elements were clearly in place.[18] The history of early cinema must therefore consider the manner in which producers assumed control over the editorial function
and the impact that this had on all areas of film practice, particularly the system
of representation.

This history's first line of attention thus examines the dialectical interaction
between cinema's methods of production and its mode of representation. Some
of this seems obvious. When Edison developed a portable camera, new kinds of
subject matter became possible. Conversely, the desire to undertake these new
kinds of subjects encouraged the development of such a camera. Once the camera was in use, however, it allowed for the taking of images that could be
sequenced into multishot stories. While the distinction between production and
representation parallels Marxist distinctions between base and superstructure,
changes in the superstructure clearly do not simply reflect those in the base.[19]
Cinema's production practices have an impact on its representational system
and vice versa.

In the largest sense, cinema production involves three essential processes
or groups: film production, exhibition, and reception (the production companies, the showmen, and the spectators).[20] While the films are a direct result
of the mode of film production, they only have an impact within a changing framework involving the other two operations. The mode of exhibition
comprises the showman's methods of presentation and his relation to the production company's films. The mode of reception or appreciation embraces the
spectators' relationship to the exhibition and the ways in which they understand
and enjoy the films as they are shown. All three processes experienced profound
change and reorganization during the 1895–1909 period. The tendency among
historians to equate film production to the whole of cinema has severely limited
our understanding of motion pictures during the pre-Griffith era.

During its first fifteen years, the cinema's production methods experienced a
series of rapid transformations. Insight into this process is facilitated by Harry
Braverman's *Labor and Monopoly Capital: The Degradation of Work in Twen-*

tieth Century America. Its look at changing modes of production outside the cultural sphere can readily be applied to film practice. According to Braverman, the centralization of work processes under one management is the fundamental step for subsequent transformations of production in advanced capitalism. As he remarks, "Control without centralization of employment was, if not impossible, certainly very difficult, and so the precondition for management was the gathering of workers under a single roof."[21] In the case of early film practice, control over creative decisions was scattered among different groups. Editorial decisions, as already mentioned, were initially the exhibitor's responsibility. Obviously it was not usually possible to bring producers, exhibitors, and spectators under one roof (although this occurred to some extent at the Eden Musee, where Porter worked in the late 1890s). Yet it was not only possible but highly desirable to bring certain practices under the control of a single management. Much of this volume examines the manner in which responsibility for many creative processes was more or less concentrated within the production company. This process of centralization, however, was not fully completed until the introduction of sound films.

As control over essential practices was centralized, the opportunity arose for a division of labor within the production companies. Here again Braverman provides a useful discussion of the economic logic of "the manufacturing division of labor" under capitalism. He is concerned not only with "the breakdown of the processes involved in the making of the product into manifold operations performed by different workers" but with the resulting degradation of work.[22] This division of labor was eventually manifested in the motion picture industry by what has become known as the studio system. Janet Staiger has ably explored this process of the division of labor within a similar theoretical framework, also informed by the work of Braverman.[23] While centralization of creative control was crucial to the formation of the studio system, other factors were simultaneously at play. The rapid expansion of the industry resulted in larger scales of production and created opportunities for dividing labor that capitalism was eager to exploit. The almost constant introduction of new technologies, as well as changes in the larger socioeconomic system, also altered production methods and influenced the reorganization of the workplace.

Porter's role in the process of centralization and specialization was complex and, as Noël Burch has noted, characterized by ambivalence.[24] While helping to concentrate crucial aspects of filmmaking within the production company, Porter opposed most aspects of the manufacturing division of labor. His resistance, in certain respects, is not unlike the worker resistance examined by David Montgomery in *Workers' Control in America*.[25] Although many in the industry— most notably the projectionists—reacted angrily to the rapid degradation of their work life, this volume focuses on the resistance of Edison studio personnel, particularly Porter, to specialization and hierarchy.

From today's perspective, Porter was an extraordinary individual who mastered all phases of film practice. He not only shot a range of news subjects and actualities but produced a variety of successful dramas and comedies. Moreover, he not only directed them, but worked on the scenarios, acted as cameraman, and edited the film—he even developed his own negatives. He designed and built studios, then outfitted them for operation. He devised projectors, perforators, and cameras. He remodeled Edison's projecting kinetoscope, turning it into a first-rate projector, and went on to build prototypes for the Simplex projector, which became the industry standard during the 1920s and is still considered by some to be the best machine of its kind ever made.[26] Yet Porter was not—as one might say of D. W. Griffith, Erich von Stroheim, or Charles Chaplin—a one-man show. Throughout his career and in many different areas, he worked collaboratively and in a nonhierarchical fashion. In short, his whole method of work was incompatible with the studio system.

Initially, the radically different formal structures of pre-1907 films attracted me and other scholars to this era of motion picture practice. The problem of cinematic representation, in recent years one of the focal points of film studies, assumed wider significance in the light of these viewings.[27] Here again, Porter clearly played a central role. He was one of several filmmakers who elaborated the mode of representation that flourished in the early 1900s, only to disintegrate as cinema became a form of mass entertainment. The dialectic between production and representation shaped the Edison films on which he worked. As the production company began to assume control over editing, Porter and his colleagues developed new kinds of continuities between shots. *Life of an American Fireman* (1902–3)—with its overlapping actions, its narrative repetition, and malleable pro-filmic temporality—is particularly illustrative. (The film is analyzed extensively in chapter 7.) Here and in other instances the Edison group applied this new system of continuity in its most extreme form. Such representational strategies proved so successful that they justified and helped to generalize this development. When the viability of these techniques faded, however, Porter refused to give them up. Porter's failure to adopt the emerging proto-Hollywood mode of representation in 1908–9 (embraced by Pathé, Vitagraph, and particularly D. W. Griffith) caused his fall from grace even more than his resistance to the transformation in production.

Although a series of transformations provide the framework for this study, important aspects of early cinema remained relatively stable. In fact, such qualities characterize and define early cinema. Viewers understood and enjoyed screen images in several distinctive ways. Audiences frequently viewed a film in relation to a narrative that they already knew. The narrative might be based on a front-page newspaper item, a play, or a popular song. If spectators were ignorant of the necessary referents, they could make little sense of the film. In other instances, exhibitors facilitated audience understanding of the images with a sound accompaniment—for instance, with a lecture or by speaking dialogue from behind the screen. While some early films required neither special knowledge from spectators nor active intervention by the exhibitor, such situations were neither preferred to other audience-screen relationships nor dominated screen practice. Only in the nickelodeon era did cinema emerge as a cultural practice in which neither the exhibitor's intervention nor special knowledge on the part of the audience was necessary to a basic understanding of the narrative.[28]

Edison films, like early cinema in general, had a recognizable and coherent system of representing the world. As Tom Gunning has pointed out, performers or subjects in front of the lens characteristically played to or displayed themselves for the camera and an imagined audience.[29] Such an approach might involve tableau-like, static compositions or a confrontation with the camera/ spectator (for instance a cavalry charge directed at the lens). Early fiction films likewise more or less adopted a diagrammatic relationship to the real world, one that limited the degree of verisimilitude. Thus depictions of space and time were generally conventionalized and schematic. Sets suggested a locale rather than creating the illusion of a real world. Condensations of time and action within the shot were commonplace. (Perhaps more surprising, many actuality films achieved similar effects through jump cuts or camera stops.) The acting style likewise embodied highly conventionalized gestures that expressed forceful emotions. The periodic reliance on pantomime by early filmmakers further intensified these tendencies. These interrelated elements of a representational system will be called *presentational*, appropriating a term from theatrical criticism that is used to describe similar methods that predominated in the theater during much of the nineteenth century. This presentational approach is, moreover, evident in a wide array of other cultural forms from the same period (painting, photography, comic strips).

If presentationalism usually dominated early cinema, it was not an absolute. Films before Griffith were generally "syncretic": they combined and juxtaposed different kinds and levels of mimesis. Thus verisimilar elements could exist side by side with presentational ones. A real pot hangs on a wall next to another painted on the backdrop. A two-dimensional, pasteboard cabin may be placed in the middle of real woods. Such syncreticism operated between shots as easily as within them. A film like The *"Teddy" Bears* uses a set for one exterior scene and outside location footage for another. Clearly this is different from the consistently represented "seamless" mimetic world of most later cinema.

In examining the interaction between production and representation, it has been advantageous to place early cinema in the larger framework of screen practice. When looking at cinema's beginnings, most histories use some variation of a biological model of development. In its crudest form, this model suggests that the medium was born, grew up, learned to talk, and (having mastered the language of cinema) finally began to produce great works.[30] In any case, cinema moves from the very simple, the naive, and the unformed to the more complex and sophisticated. More recently, a number of historians have seen cinema as emerging out of a diversity of precursors to become a culturally and economically determined form of expression.[31] Both these historical models view the invention of cinema as a starting point. In contrast, a history of screen practice considers projected moving pictures as both a continuation and transformation of magic-lantern traditions in which showmen displayed images on a canvas and accompanied them with voice, music, and sound effects. It is worth noting that this notion of historical continuity was commonplace during the first ten years of cinema. As Henry V. Hopwood remarked in 1899, "A film for projecting a Living Picture is nothing more, after all, than a multiple lantern slide."[32]

The history of projected images and their sound accompaniment has its origins in the mid seventeenth century. The beginning of screen practice does not, however, privilege a moment of technological invention—such as the invention of the magic lantern or the cinematographic apparatus—but rather a fundamental transformation in the mode of production. Screen practice began in the 1640s when the process of projecting images was no longer concealed from the unsuspecting viewer. Instead of being an instrument of terror and magic known only to a select few, the projecting apparatus became an instrument of cultural production that was known to all.[33] The history of screen practice prior to 1896 has been neglected by film historians. Although it remains outside the domain of this study, it provides a necessary framework for understanding the processes of industrial transformation examined in this volume. Pre-cinema exhibitors, for example, were the ones who had ultimate control over the editing process; they acquired slides from a variety of sources (including often making the slides themselves) and juxtaposed one projected image against another. The new technology of motion pictures helped to transform the screen, facilitating a shift in both narrative responsibility and authorship from exhibitors to the production companies.

While the interrelationship between production and representation is key to understanding the changes in editorial and narrative practices, its impact extends beyond these areas. The production of Edison films within a white, "homosocial," male world affected the choice of subjects as well as the ways in which these were depicted.[34] Again and again, when early filmmakers expressed a nostalgia for a lost childhood, it was boyhood they recalled and boyhood that they visualized. Such biases shaped the portrayal of women and blacks in particular. The complex relationships between work and leisure at the turn of the century, which Roy Rosenzweig and Kathy Peiss have astutely explored, finds a profound conjunction in the early film industry.[35]

Subject Matter and Ideology

A second line of attention in this study focuses on subject matter and its treatment in Edison films. Here cinema is related to other cultural texts and practices from which film production appropriated images, gags, and stories. At first they were almost exclusively from the world of masculine amusement, of dancing girls and prize fights. Output was soon adjusted to accommodate "heterosocial" amusement in which women and men participated as spectators. Porter's earliest films, often made with George S. Fleming or James White, served a variety of needs. Some were incorporated into travelogues, perhaps the most popular form of pre-cinema screen entertainment. Others documented vaudeville acts. Most functioned as a visual newspaper. The newspaper in turn-of-the-century America, then one of the few forms of mass communication, had a profound influence on other cultural practices, not least of which was the cinema.[36] Individual films had strong ties to different types of journalistic features: news stories, editorial cartoons, human interest columns, and the comic strip. Even fight films and travel scenes were not inconsistent with cinema as a visual newspaper, for the papers covered both sports and travel. As with the newspapers, the purpose of cinema at the turn of the century was to inform as much as to entertain. By 1902–3, cinema was losing its efficacy as a visual newspaper and was reconceived primarily as a storytelling form. For most production companies, this shift meant that cinema's new role was increasingly to amuse. A significant exception to this pattern involved a group of Porter films made between November 1904 (*The Ex-Convict*) and December 1905 (*Life of an American Policeman*). These had an explicit social concern. Often Progressive in their politics, they presented a complex, sometimes contradictory, and finally conservative vision of the world. Only at the end of 1905, when the nickelodeon era was under way, did Porter accept the notion of cinema as simple amusement—a shift that may well have been influenced by commercial decisions made by Edison executives.

As the proliferation of storefront theaters turned cinema into a form of mass entertainment, traditional guardians of American culture and public morality protested against subject matter they often considered sensationalistic and corrupting. Porter and the Edison Company found that the broader their audience, the narrower the boundaries of acceptable subject matter and its treatment became. While Thomas Edison and his managerial staff actively supported the articulation of certain "standards" in the face of mounting protest, propriety was occasionally violated—at least in the eyes of some critics—even within the Kinetograph Department. The solution that finally won the support of Edison and his executive Frank Dyer was to defuse criticism by supporting a National Board of Censorship. For these entrepreneurs, the issue was not freedom of expression but maximizing profits within a mass communication system.

Films expressed larger social, political, and cultural concerns even as they sometimes served a personal, reparative function for the filmmaker.[37] The ideological orientation of early cinema has been much discussed. Noël Burch has argued that in form and content these films reflected *"the infantilism of the working classes."*[38] Others, such as Robert C. Allen, have seen early cinema as addressing a middle-class audience and presumably reflecting its ideological orientation.[39] Certainly, America has been called a middle-class country, and this is nowhere more apparent than in its cultural products. The middle class, however, was not a single, unified group, but made up of diverse and even contradictory interests. Harry Braverman makes a useful distinction between what he calls the old and the new middle classes.[40] The old middle class was largely outside the labor-capital dialectic in that it neither sold nor bought labor power on an extensive basis. The new middle class of employees, however, functioned within this labor-capital dialectic, assuming in certain respects the position of the working class and at other times that of employer. Although Porter was a member of the new middle class, his attitudes were shaped by his earlier experiences in Connellsville, Pennsylvania, where his family and then Porter himself had been small businessmen. His films reflect a personal distaste for the workings of large-scale, impersonal capitalistic enterprises: particularly *The Ex-Convict, The Kleptomaniac,* and *The Miller's Daughter.* This was not a uniquely personal vision so much as the principal cinematic expression of a more general outlook that then found frequent cultural expression.

In looking at Porter's work, one finds a remarkable ideological unity. The filmmaker's unhappiness with advanced capitalism extended beyond the subject matter of his films and included his resistance to the manufacturing division of labor that arose in the wake of the nickelodeon era. Here again, his approach was that of the old middle class. This did not mean that he wished to work alone, but that he preferred to work with others in an informal, collaborative manner. Finally, the representational system that Porter championed reflected the same old-middle-class orientation, not simply because it embodied a specific set of working methods and prevented the new, impersonal system of mass entertainment from operating effectively, but because it usually depended on audiences sharing his basic cultural frame of reference. Within this framework of production and representation, Porter conducted a far-reaching exploration of cinema's manifold possibilities.

Commercial Methods

Commercial strategies both at Edison and within the industry as a whole constitute a final level of attention. One popular approach to business activities in the film industry has been based on industrial organization economics, "an economic theory of technological innovation, which posits that a product or process is introduced to increase profits in three systematic phases: invention, innovation and diffusion."[41] However, an approach focusing on business strategies provides an insufficient basis for constructing a history of American cinema (or any cultural practice). Moreover, business strategies for the 1895–1909 period were concerned with innovations in many different areas, including subject matter, modes of representation, marketing, and production. It is not clear why the introduction of technology should be privileged in such a history.

Although this study deals extensively with management decisions that had as their goals the maximization of profits, the history of early cinema suggests a more appropriate framework for analysis: the examination of business strategies in relation to changing modes of production and representation rather than simply in terms of technology. This approach is dialectical rather than cyclical, and it rejects the notion of technological determinism implicit in industrial organization economics. Technology is an essential aspect of the mode of production, but it is often not the crucial factor in accounting for change and new economic opportunities. The nickelodeon era was made possible by the production of an increasing number of longer films that could be used interchangeably by theaters. Vitagraph's and Pathé's rapid expansion in film production after 1905 was based on their astute assessment of this new development. In contrast, the Edison Company's failure to respond effectively and quickly significantly weakened its position in the industry. A methodology that translates technological innovation directly into business practices risks patterning information in ways that render it inaccurate.[42]

Relations between film producers and exhibitors are central to an understanding of commercial strategies and disputes within the industry. In the film business, tension has always existed between these two groups as each attempts to achieve dominance within the industry. This conflict has been manifested characteristically in vertical expansion or integration as exhibitors moved into film production or producers into exhibition. Since the advent of the nickelodeons, producers and exhibitors have tried to strengthen their positions by controlling distribution. Sometimes independent distributors have been able to function at this interface. This was the case when the nickelodeon era began— although even then exhibitors and producers owned important exchanges. Within a few years, however, producers were once again seeking to exercise control over this important commercial function. Not surprisingly, distribution has become a key branch of the film industry.

The motion picture industry did not, however, operate as a self-contained entity. One area in which the larger society had a crucial impact on the industry's commercial structure was through the judicial system. Thomas Edison constantly relied on legal action to protect or expand his stake within the industry. Between 1898 and 1902, he had considerable success with this approach and managed to put many competitors out of business. Others were allowed to continue under a commercial licensing arrangement designed to benefit the inventor. Facing setbacks in the courts between 1902 and 1906, "the Wizard of Menlo Park" lost his position as the dominant producer. In 1907, however, his motion picture patents won significant judicial recognition, encouraging the inventor to establish a "trust," a combination of leading production companies subsequently known as "the Edison licensees." The resulting trade association hoped to control the American industry. When it failed to accomplish this, the organization was expanded to include the patents and commercial clout of rival concerns. The resulting Motion Picture Patents Company was formed at the end of 1908 and put into full operation early in 1909. Its goal was to assure a high level of profit and raise barriers against those who would otherwise have entered this profitable field.

The moving picture was only one of several products exploited by Thomas Edison and his executive staff during this era. The Kinetograph Department, where Edison located his film activities, was part of the Edison Manufacturing Company, which also produced batteries, x-ray machines, and dental equipment. Edison's National Phonograph Company, which shared the same top executives as the Edison Manufacturing Company, was more profitable and closer to the inventor's heart. The inventor's storage battery, Portland cement, and iron ore–milling ventures, required large infusions of capital—sapping money from other Edison-operated ventures, including film. (In the case of Portland Cement and iron ore milling, Edison and his investors lost large sums of money.)[43] The motion picture business, while important, was not the sole focus of attention it was for most of Edison's rivals. The inventor's film business also suffered from frequent turnovers in management-level personnel. Porter worked under four different department heads: James Henry White (October 1896 to November 1902), William Markgraf (December 1902 through March 1904), Alex T. Moore (March 1904 through March 1909), and Horace G. Plimpton (March 1909 until August 1915). William E. Gilmore served as vice-president and general manager of the Edison Manufacturing Company from April 1895 to June 1908 and actively participated in all important decisions during that period. He was replaced by Frank Dyer, Edison's chief patent lawyer, who reorganized the Kinetograph Department and the entire film industry, hastening Porter's demotion from studio manager to technical expert in February 1909. These were the people who principally determined Edison business policy, an area in which Porter appears to have had little say.

Business considerations constantly influenced what Porter produced. Economic pressures based on the pattern of film sales were determining factors in the shift from actualities to acted "features." Certain films—for instance, Porter's remake of Biograph's popular hit *Personal*—were first and foremost commercial weapons used to undermine the success of competitors. The decision to rely on "dupes,"[44] calculated on the basis of financial gain, adversely affected the attention paid and resources available to original productions. Edison business strategies were formulated within the framework of the industry's overall development, and it is only within this context that Porter's work can be fully appreciated.

This study is organized in a chronological fashion, broken down into chapters that emphasize important changes from the introduction of cinema as a screen novelty to the establishment of new practices still associated with modern cinema. Deciding upon the precise moment when these changes occurred as the basis for chapter divisions demanded difficult and sometimes arbitrary decisions. Individual chapters often use specific events and circumstances in Porter's work and Edison Company policy as points of division. While a slightly different breakdown could be offered, it is not so much specific dates and divisions that are important as the general pattern of development.

This book is designed to serve several functions above and beyond providing a history of Porter and Edison film activities between 1894 and 1909. It is meant to be used in conjunction with screenings of the films. If, as this study argues, films were often understood within a framework of specific knowledge or with the assistance of a narrator, then today's spectators need that same knowledge readily at hand. If the films are to be fully appreciated, they not only need to be preserved and made available to the public (a function ably performed by the Museum of Modern Art and other institutions), but the context in which they were seen has to be partially reconstituted. Therefore, for example, the song "Waiting at the Church" has been reprinted in its entirety so the reader can see Porter's *Waiting at the Church*, and enjoy the correspondence between the two. Selected catalog descriptions have been included, not only to make available key film narratives—including information that could never be derived from a silent viewing of the film—but to provide descriptions that today's students and historians can use to create their own lectures to accompany the films. This volume also serves as a companion to the documentary film *Before the Nickelodeon: The Early Cinema of Edwin S. Porter*. All the quotations used in the documentary appear in this volume with the appropriate references. A finding aid for these appears in appendix C. In a few cases, recent research has uncovered new information that has made small corrections necessary. The book and the film are designed to complement each other.

This volume also forms part of a larger study, a trilogy of books, I have undertaken on early cinema in America. *High-Class Moving Pictures: Lyman H. Howe and the Forgotten Era of Traveling Exhibition, 1880–1920*, written with the collaboration of Carol Nelson and published by Princeton University Press, looks at the activities of America's traveling motion picture exhibitors, particularly Lyman Howe, and also analyzes cultural divisions within middle-class audiences. *The Emergence of Cinema in America*, a historical overview of American cinema to 1907, published by Scribner's/Macmillan, is the first book in the ten-volume American Film History Project edited by Charles Harpole. Finally, a filmography of Edison films, including extensive documentation, is in preparation. Early cinema, like most cultural phenomena, is not easily grasped in all its complexity. I hope that this body of work, in conjunction with the accomplishments of colleagues and fellow scholars, will enhance people's appreciation for this formative period in motion picture history and contribute to the general knowledge of American culture.

2 Porter's Early Years: 1870–1896

To understand the underpinnings of Edwin Stanton Porter's approach to film-making, we must turn to the world in which he was born and spent the first twenty-three years of his life.[1] As with any individual, his subsequent activities were a complex response to these formative experiences—in his case, one that involved significant continuities. With his films often nostalgically longing for a lost past and a romanticized childhood, a biographical study must reassert the concrete character of that world. Porter grew up in Connellsville, Pennsylvania, a small town fifty miles southeast of Pittsburgh. Its population in 1870, the year of his birth, was 1,292. Despite this modest size, it was not a rural community but a small industrial center.

In the 1870s Connellsville functioned principally as a railroad repair center.[2] By the end of the decade, it was producing large amounts of coke—processed coal used primarily for making steel. Connellsville coke soon became known as the best in the country, and the area depended on this industry for its prosperity. Connellsville more than doubled in size by the 1880 census to 3,615 inhabitants. Although the town had its share of small businessmen, including Porter's father, his extended family, and friends, the environs were dominated by the economic realities of large-scale production. The often-troubled relationship between absentee owners of extensive coke works and a large number of "cokers"—workers who mined the coal and tended the coke ovens—was a fundamental aspect of Connellsville life. Connellsville also boasted various forms of commercial popular culture, in which Porter participated. This environment provided Porter with the experiences, presuppositions, and skills that were to facilitate, shape, and influence his subsequent work as a filmmaker.

The Porter Family

Edwin S. Porter was born on April 21, 1870, to Thomas Richard and Mary (Clark) Porter. His namesake was Edwin M. Stanton, a Democratic politician from Ohio who served as Abraham Lincoln's secretary of war. This name was Porter's own, somewhat later choice, for his parents called him Edward; and as a short chubby boy, he went by the nickname of "Betty."[3] The youngest member of his family for ten years, Ed ultimately became the fourth of seven children, the others being Charles W. (born 1864), Frank (1867), Mary (1868), Ada (1880), John (1883), and Everett Melbourne (1889). His father, Thomas Porter, was one of at least seven brothers who grew up in nearby Perryopolis. Their father, Edward's grandfather, was a stone cutter.[4] After the Civil War, several brothers moved to Connellsville, which was expanding with the growing coke trade. In the 1870s Thomas's older brother Henry, also a stone cutter, became Connellsville's postmaster, a much-sought-after position, which kept his children employed as postal clerks. Through combined financing and partnerships, the Porter clan established or invested in several local enterprises.

Porter's father was a small businessman often dependent on his more successful siblings. When Edward was born, Thomas Porter was working as a cabinetmaker. By the following year he was running Porter & Brother, a furniture store and undertaking establishment owned by his older brothers. The only funeral service in town for the next seven years, Porter & Brother rented furniture for these and other occasions. As Connellsville expanded rapidly in population, the firm began to sell factory-made furniture, for which it also enjoyed a local monopoly. By late 1877 the business was jointly owned by Thomas and John Porter, with John's son Everett Melbourne acting as co-manager. Four years later, John Porter was reportedly worth $50,000, while "Thomas Porter, the managing partner, has very little outside of his investment in firm but is economic, industrious and temperate."[5]

Thomas Porter assumed control of the undertaking business in 1888 when Everett Melbourne, who had been increasingly ill with consumption, died in February, a month after his father. Edward's oldest brother, Charles W. Porter, was soon brought into the family business, renamed Thomas Porter & Co. The local newspaper glowingly described the firm shortly after Thomas had taken full charge:

> ... Of this house it is only fair to say that they have probably done as much toward accelerating the commercial activity of the town by their enterprise as any other concern within its limits. They occupy part of the three-story building of Soisson's Block on Main Street. Their room is of spacious dimensions, being 20 × 70 feet in extent, with a large manufacturing room and other necessary outbuildings in the rear. They unquestionably carry as large a stock as any to be found in the country, including dining-room, reception and drawing room, parlor, library and bedroom suites of every description. In their undertaking department they are equally well equipped, carrying

caskets, coffins, etc. of all grades and sizes. They own two fine hearses, one for children and one for adults, besides a large and beautiful funeral car. Mr. Thomas Porter is especially fitted by nature and practical experience for the delicate duties devolving upon him of the embalming of the dead.

The house was established eighteen years ago under the style of Porter and Brother. This was in a small way, but by diligence in business and energy, fair and honorable dealing, this house now represents the very best class of houses in Western Pennsylvania in the line of fine furniture and funeral directors.[6]

By the early 1890s Charles Porter and his father may have had a falling out: the son set up his own company, eventually forcing Thomas Porter into retirement.[7]

Thomas Porter's success was more modest than his brothers'. Shortly after Edward was born, Samuel, John, and Henry Porter formed a partnership with three other Connellsville men to conduct a general foundry and plow manufactory. The firm added a new branch in 1873 for forgings and machine work. By 1880 some of the partners were bought out and the firm became known as Boyts, Porter & Company. Its most successful product, the Yough pump, captured a substantial market among mining companies across the country. The business flourished and became one of the two major manufacturing establishments in Connellsville during the 1880s.[8]

Edward Porter had other relatives living in Connellsville. His cousin William Porter had a large family and carried on the family trade as a stone cutter.[9] His mother's family was also from the borough. His uncle William Clark sometimes served as justice of the peace, and a great great grandfather, Abraham Clark, had signed the Declaration of Independence. With several aunts likewise living in the area, Edward was related to a significant portion of the population.[10]

Family life was of central importance to the Porters and other Connellsville residents. The disintegration of a family through death or separation was the worst tragedy a person could suffer, according to the *Keystone Courier*, which often featured such incidents on its front page.[11] When Henry Porter learned of his eldest son's death, he suffered a stroke, from which he never fully recovered, dying less than two years later.[12] After Everett Melbourne's death, Thomas Porter named his next child after this deceased nephew. Thomas Porter's role as funeral director meant that death and loss of family constantly impinged on the Porter household. No doubt this left a strong impression on young Edward, most likely shaping his development from an early age. Moreover, loss was something that Porter experienced very directly later in his life, when attempts to start a family would be repeatedly frustrated as his wife suffered a dozen miscarriages.[13] In reaction, the filmmaker became preoccupied with the family unit. Although family-centered dramas were common in early-twentieth-century popular culture, Porter drew on such narratives with remarkable frequency. From *Life of an American Fireman* (1903) to *Rescued from an Eagle's Nest* (1908), it is the saving of the parents' only child (or in the case of *Lost in the*

Alps [1907], their two children) that dominates and brings relief. This perpetually happy conclusion stands in stark contrast to Porter's own life. He was not so fortunate, and his inability to have children contributed to his growing reclusiveness and eccentricity in later years.[14]

While Porter's family was part of Connellsville's community of small businessmen and shopkeepers, the town's merchants are of additional interest in that four of its members eventually purchased the rights to "Edison's Vitascope" in 1896.[15] J. R. Balsley was a prominent builder with a lumber mill. F. E. Markell owned drugstores in Connellsville, neighboring New Haven, and East Pittsburgh. R. S. Paine ran a shoe store and had some additional capital invested in other ventures, including a Florida orange grove. Cyrus Echard worked in the coal trade. These local merchants were a closely knit group. They served together on committees, celebrated each other's birthdays, and hired each other's children to clerk their stores. J. R. Balsley's son, Charles H. Balsley, was Ed Porter's best friend. In 1890–91, both worked for the slightly older J. F. Norcross, who had inherited his father's tailoring establishment. The three bachelors formed a youthful triumvirate, not only at work but in their occasional pursuit of adventure. Work and leisure were interwoven in a single, all-male environment. Their work life, with its informality and equality, was in marked contrast to the coke industry's regimentation and hierarchy. After Norcross married and moved west in the fall of 1892, Porter opened his own business as a merchant tailor.[16]

The coke industry impinged on every aspect of daily life in Connellsville, expanding from 5,000 ovens in 1880 to more than 17,000 by 1893.[17] In 1880 a visitor found his entrance into town "lit up by the lurid glare of coke ovens, while the stars were obscured by the murky smoke."[18] With crowded streets, Connellsville was a "business town where everyone seemed to have an object in view," he observed. "Here and there a drunken man reeled along, and from various drinking houses came the noise of revellers." As he passed along the borough's main thoroughfare he saw "the reflected light of the Pittsburg and Connellsville Gas, Coal and Coke Company's ovens. The ovens number 250, the longest continuous line of ovens in the region." The fumes destroyed nearby vegetation and damaged crops and fruit trees. Industry triumphed over agriculture, and when farmers sought redress through the courts, the justice system finally ruled in favor of the coke operators.[19] Coal mining, tending coke ovens, and running the trains was dangerous work. While the large number of industrial accidents and deaths owing to "consumption" and bad air contributed to the prosperity of the Porter undertaking establishment, the fumes also affected the Porters' health. As a child, Edward suffered bouts of pneumonia aggravated by the bad air.[20]

Although Connellsville's merchants prospered when the coke industry did well and suffered when it did badly, those who owned the industry and those who worked in and around it were removed from many aspects of small-town life. Cokers lived in company housing and bought most necessities from company stores. Their alienation from the local community increased after 1879 when "foreign," that is, Eastern European, labor was brought into the region.[21] The formerly strong kinship and ethnic ties between the cokers and the townspeople began to break down as a result. By 1889 Henry Frick controlled the region's coke trade, and the coke works were owned by distant corporations that had little direct interest in the local communities.[22] For local small businessmen—members of the old middle class—the fundamental opposition was between themselves and mammoth corporate entities represented by the coke industry, not between labor and capital. To a significant extent, these men worked outside the labor-capital dialectic and saw it as a foreign and undesirable intrusion.

Dependent on the coke works for their general welfare, the small-town merchants often felt helpless. Their anxiety increased whenever tension erupted into class warfare. Strikes occurred throughout Porter's youth: in 1877, 1879, 1880, 1883, 1886, 1887, 1889, and 1891.[23] The strikes of 1886 and 1891 were particularly brutal and protracted. The owners sought to break these actions by importing scab labor, thereby forcing strikers to resort to violence to keep the mines closed. The coal operators in turn hired ex-policemen and Pinkertons to protect their interests. In the strike of 1891, cokers were killed and the National Guard was called in. Porter observed a mounting pattern of violence as the coke industry expanded and Frick consolidated his position within it.

The difficult relationship existing between Connellsville's old middle class and the coke industry was apparent in the Democratic *Keystone Courier*, which spoke primarily for the town's small businessmen, its principal advertisers. Its pages contained editorials preaching against strikes—opposing the operators who provoked them as much as the miners who undertook them. The *Courier* constantly called for arbitration and the avoidance of conflicts that disrupted business, not only the coke business but the merchants'. It saw itself as an impartial judge in such situations and felt free to lecture both sides on their responsibilities. The paper and the old middle class saw themselves as representing public opinion and providing a moral weight that should be decisive. In the midst of "the most general strike ever inaugurated here," the *Courier* asserted that "unbiased observers unite in the opinion that if the latter [the workers] return to work, public feeling will compel the former [the operators] to grant the advance asked and remedy the abuses complained of—abuses that even the operators admit do exist."[24] Imbued with this attitude since childhood, Porter later expressed similar desires for the reconciliation of labor and capital. This moral judgment claiming to operate objectively above the conflict is apparent in a number of his films, including *The Ex-Convict* (1904).

Despite being caught in the middle of the labor-capital conflict, Connellsville's merchants generally favored the miners, who were their real or potential customers — and often relations or members of the same church. Certainly it was in their self-interest, for when the coke workers were fully employed and well paid, local business prospered too. During the strike of January and February 1886, a temporary alliance was forged between the miners and many of the merchants. The store owners donated food and clothing, while the miners demanded an end to the "pluck-me's" — company stores that advanced credit to their employees, making money by inflating prices and depriving local merchants of revenues they might otherwise have expected. Significantly, the strike was won by the workers, although the company-store issue was not resolved.[25]

There were limitations and contradictions in the *Courier*'s support for the working class. To retain the paper's support, the coke workers had to stay within the law even if operators brought in scab labor. Attempts by workers to meet these threats with violence or the destruction of company property were strongly condemned. Socialists and other radical elements were anathema. Old-middle-class support for the working class therefore functioned within a limited framework. Within similar limits, Porter's sympathies for the working class are evident in films such as *The Kleptomaniac* (1905).

Growing up in Connellsville, Porter apparently adopted the strong prejudices that his family and friends held against many immigrant groups. During the 1880s the town's native white population developed a deep-seated antipathy for Eastern European immigrants. The first explosion of hostility came in February 1883, when an open letter accused the "Hated Hun" of barbaric acts. "One of the most degrading influences brought to bear on our community is the indiscriminate importation of Hungarian serfs and their employment on public works, in preference to good located citizens who are willing and can perform more and better labor for the same pay," this "Appeal to the Christian Public" claimed.[26] The *Courier*, at first appalled by the vituperative attacks, soon adopted the same terminology. Such hostility focused on the "not overly clean habits and queer customs" of the "Hated Huns." Native workers were disturbed by a common sight: "their women in a state of semi-nudity at work in the . . . blinding dust of a coke yard forking the product of the ovens."[27] By 1886, 25 percent of the cokers were Poles, Hungarians, and Bohemians, while another 10 percent were Germans and Prussians.[28] These workers were initially seen as the tools of the operators who brought them to their mines. During the strike of 1886, however, they proved to be more militant and radical than their domestic counterparts. When they rioted to maintain the effectiveness of the strike, the "Hated Huns" were characterized as lawbreakers and dangerous radicals.

Porter was almost certainly a member of the nativist Order of United Mechanics, which sprang up to challenge the disruptions caused by the protracted, violent strike of 1891. A member of this secret beneficial association had to be a native-born American, of good moral character, believe in a supreme being, favor the public school system, oppose the union of church and state, and be capable of earning a living.[29] Edward Porter's friend and employer, J. F. Norcross, and his best friend's father, J. R. Balsley, sat on the order's financial committee, which organized a parade of its membership in Connellsville on July 4, 1891. The *Courier* announced, "The Biggest Fourth in the History of the Town Promised by American Mechanics, The Red Flag of the Socialists Recently Displayed in the Coke Regions Stirs the Blood of the UAM's. . . . They are anxious to show the foreign rabble who rally under it how well American labor loves the American flag."[30] J. R. Balsley, one of the order's most active members, gave a Memorial Day speech denouncing the troublemakers.

> We are sorry that there is in our land today an element of discontent, but when we know that this class is made up of the scum of foreign nations and a few weak minded of our own land, there need be little [to] fear from this quarter. These men would not be satisfied with any laws that human skill could enact. If it was possible for them to enter heaven, they would at once want to change the ruling of the divine master.[31]

The ethnic stereotypes in Porter's *The Finish of Bridget McKeen* (1901), *Cohen's Fire Sale* (1907), and *Laughing Gas* (1907) were consistent with the attitudes Porter developed in the western Pennsylvania coke region. They had many counterparts in popular culture and reflected the general ethnic and racial prejudices of most native-born whites.

Porter and Connellsville's Cultural Life

Porter has been portrayed by some historians as a naïf who "had no background or experience in art" and so was unaware of the implications of his work.[32] This is certainly inaccurate, for he was an active participant in Connellsville's cultural life at a time when it was being fundamentally transformed. During the 1870s commercial, popular culture had come to Connellsville only infrequently. The churches, public schools, and the local press were the principal cultural institutions. For an evening's entertainment, a minister might deliver a light-hearted lecture on subjects such as "Fashion" or the local debating society argue topics such as "Can the existence of God be proven without the aid of divine revelation?" or "Should foreign immigration be prohibited?"[33] Performances by touring theater groups were rare and not well attended. When Thorne's Comedy Company came to town in April 1880, twenty people were in the audience, and the play was dismissed as "worse than mediocre." This, the first company to be reported in the *Keystone Courier*, did not survive its Connellsville performance and was disbanded.[34] The next troupe to visit the borough, the Stenson Comedy Company, did not pass through town for another eight months. In 1880 residents were dependent on their occasional visits to Pittsburgh for most of their theatrical entertainment.

In September 1881, however, work began on Connellsville's first commercial theater, the Newmyer Opera House, a source of civic pride, "as finely furnished as any in the country."[35] According to one local reporter, "The stage is fitted up with a thousand dollar piano, a five-piece parlor set and Brussels carpet. The drop curtain is one of the prettiest we have seen anywhere, and is supplemented with abundant scenery of various kinds."[36] After opening with a performance of *Camille*, the opera house was frequented by many traveling companies.

Edwin Porter later recalled: "I worked around a local theater of which my brother was manager; acted in the capacity of ticket taker, usher, etc."[37] While the Newmeyer did have a manager named Porter during the 1883–84 and 1884–85 seasons, this was Byron Porter, at most a distant relative.[38] His small orchestra provided visiting theatrical companies with music. It also gave concerts, performing pieces that were arranged, and in at least one instance composed, by Byron Porter himself.[39] Called "the leading artist in this section of the state,"[40] Byron Porter was apparently an important figure in Ed Porter's early life. The two Porter families were closely associated; and, as manager of the opera house, Byron Porter had to maintain links with the town's main undertaker and furniture store in case he needed additional seating. Young Edward was an apparent beneficiary. Byron Porter was also the town's first photographer and ran a photographic gallery and art store. He may have taught Edward the rudiments of photography, an invaluable skill for his subsequent career.[41]

The Newmyer Opera House exposed Porter to a wide range of theatrical experiences. The ever-popular *Uncle Tom's Cabin*, which enjoyed a unique place in American cultural life, was performed there many times during Porter's Connellsville residence. In later years he was said to have acted out the story as a child, assuming the role of slave owner Simon Legree.[42] Other companies gave minstrel shows, melodramas, various works by Gilbert and Sullivan, travesties like the serio-comic *Medea*, Irish plays like *Hibernica* and *Shamus O'Brien*, and even a few tragedies. Performances included *Daniel Boone; or, On the Trail* (a local favorite), *Peck's Bad Boy*, *The Count of Monte Cristo* (minus James O'Neill), and *She*, adapted from Rider Haggard's book and produced by William Brady. The opera house was also used by the Kickapoo Indians, a medicine show; for wrestling matches; and to host a visit by John L. Sullivan, the world's boxing champion.[43] This eclecticism of subject matter would find continuity in much of Porter's own filmmaking career, if only as a result of similar commercial pressures. Certain of his pictures may have also been informed by Porter's early experience in the opera house—for instance, *Uncle Tom's Cabin* (1903), the Irish drama *Kathleen Mavourneen* (1906), *Daniel Boone* (1906), and *She* (1908). His later conception of cinema as filmed theater must have owed something to this as well.

As a successful filmmaker, Edwin Porter recalled other jobs that acquainted him with the mechanical end of the theatrical business. "Later my brother was 'advance' for Washburn and Huntington's circus. I was on the bill car. In that way I came to have a general idea of the circus business. I also traveled with him a part of the season in comic opera."[44] Although these experiences are impossible to verify, they were not unusual for the period. Vaudeville magnate Benjamin Franklin Keith entered the world of commercial amusements after visiting the circus at seventeen.[45] Edward Franklin Albee and Frederick F. Proctor, both prominent vaudeville entrepreneurs, also had early circus experiences.[46] Circuses were the major form of commercial summer amusement in many sections of the United States and frequently came to Connellsville while Porter was growing up. A visit from Barnum's Circus was an important event on the year's calendar, with 20,000 people seeing the main attraction in one day. In 1888 Forepaugh's Wild West Show stopped off and reenacted the holdup of the Deadwood Stage and "Custer's last rally."[47]

Porter also claimed to have been an exhibition skater. Roller-skating became a craze for the first time in the mid 1880s. During the winter of 1884–85 Connellsville had two indoor skating rinks. At their height, the rinks offered recreational skating in which the sexes mingled in casual social contact. Rink managers drew customers by presenting exhibition skaters, bicycle acts, and variety companies. They organized competitions and sponsored "a neck-tie and apron social."[48] Only a few out-of-town performers are mentioned in press clippings, but Porter could have easily been a local demonstrator. Porter thus associated himself with the three major forms of popular culture then making their appearance in Connellsville: the opera house, the circus, and the skating rink.

The emergence of commercial, popular culture in Connellsville during the 1880s produced a cultural split within the town's middle class. The rise of various amusement forms challenged what Alan Trachtenberg has called a virtually official middle-class image of America that was "a deliberate alternative to two extremes, the lavish and conspicuous squandering of wealth among the very rich, and the squalor of the very poor."[49] This Protestant culture sought to enrich people's lives through self-cultivation and self-education. It was centered in the churches, which provided an array of lectures and other educational opportunities. Among these were several examples of pre-cinematic screen entertainment. The lantern shows *Paradise Lost*, *The Customs and Times of Washington*, and *Sights and Scenes in Europe* were given at Methodist, Episcopal, and Lutheran churches.[50] A panorama showing painted scenes of America and Europe was exhibited by Presbyterian and Baptist denominations.[51] In Connellsville, as in most communities outside the metropolitan centers, these two entertainment forms continued to be aligned with religious institutions seeking to educate, inspire, and entertain their mostly middle-class congregations.

The opera house, the circus, and the skating rink did not attempt to educate their patrons; they sought instead to address their desires. They drew middle-class people away from evening lectures. Trying to revive these older forms of community entertainment, some lectures were moved to Newmyer Opera House; attendance, however, did not improve.[52] In frustration ministers and conservative newspapers denounced the skating rinks, but without success. "The louder the denunciations, the more popular the rinks grew."[53] This reaction against secular, comparatively informal forms of amusement was intensified with the appearance of the Salvation Army in 1886. The pro-amusement *Keystone Courier* reported its arrival with derisive headlines, calling the group "a case of misdirected energy."[54] The Young Men's Christian Association, which appeared in Connellsville in late 1884, was a more moderate attempt to maintain or expand the church's position in an increasingly secularized cultural life.[55] In the confrontation between church-oriented, moralizing culture and popular commercial culture, Porter sided with the latter.

Porter's early experiences reflect the extent to which the American middle class participated in the amusement realm. Too often commentators link the "official" cultural programs of churches and elites with the entire Protestant middle classes. Too often informality, camaraderie, and frivolity are located within the working classes. Yet important, probably dominant, elements of the Connellsville middle class did not conform to this Victorian ideal or stereotype. They undoubtedly had strong ties to the plebeian culture described by Francis G. Couvares.[56] Popular entertainment was not segmented by class as much as many historians have suggested. Rather, cultural divisions within classes are at least as important when examining leisure activities.

Porter and Technological Innovation

A poor student who abandoned his formal education at an early age,[57] Ed Porter was inspired by the mythic Thomas Edison, famous stories of whose exploits and childhood were already celebrated in the press. The literature emphasized Edison's natural genius, which flourished without formal schooling, his unequaled instinct for useful inventions, and the assumed benefits of technology.[58] Porter, who would one day call himself Thomas Edison, Jr., sought to duplicate the childhood experiences of his idol. As an adolescent he sold newspapers on a train. In 1884–85, according to a later interview, Edward switched from "news butcher" to telegraph operator, working for the Pittsburgh, McKeesport and Youghiogheny Railroad at Demmler, located between Connellsville and Pittsburgh.[59] These were similar to the first jobs held by Edison. If this interview is correct, Porter began to work as a telegraph operator at the age of fourteen, beating his future employer by a precocious year. In the process he acquired a familiarity with electricity that was to help him enter the motion picture industry.

Connellsville and Porter's family were preoccupied with progress and being "up-to-date." Boyts, Porter & Company sold various mechanical innovations, and the town itself was transformed by basic technological amenities while Porter lived there. After working as a telegraph operator for three or four years, Porter "took up the plumbing trade." A local gas company acquired a franchise for Connellsville in 1886 and by the following year was busy laying pipes to the homes of local residents. In September 1887 plumbers were "busy putting in the pipes."[60] Porter found employment installing this precursor of Edison's electric light. Assuming its resources to be limitless, the gas company left street lamps on twenty-four hours a day, which exhausted its supply of gas within only a few years. No doubt this was a compelling reason for Connellsville to acquire an electric light system in 1889–90.

In September 1889 a group of Connellsville businessmen formed an electric light company and received the local franchise. The generators and equipment used to supply alternating current were purchased from the Westinghouse Company, based in East Pittsburgh. Electric street lights were turned on in Porter's hometown on February 15, 1890. In another few weeks electricity was illuminating stores and residences of Connellsville and neighboring New Haven.[61] By the beginning of 1891 Ed Porter and his friend and fellow tinkerer Charles Balsley had used their spare time to invent a current regulator for electric lamps; this dimmer allowed people to control the intensity of an electric light as they had done with gas light. With this invention, Porter's creativity and his preference for collaborative working methods become apparent; both would continue throughout his working life. The patent application was filed on January 17th and granted on May 5th.[62] Soon after it was approved, the *Courier* announced:

> Charles H. Balsley and Edward Porter received this week letters patent on an Electric Current Regulator, the joint invention of the two young men. It is said to be superior in many respects to any thing yet invented in that line, and can be manufactured almost as cheaply as the ordinary incandescent burners now in use. They have received several flattering offers from manufacturers of electric light machinery, etc. for the right to manufacture and use the appliance on their lamps. The boys, however, are moving with caution in the matter, and have not yet accepted any of the offers. They have also received several orders for the regulator, but as they are not manufacturing the article, they could not fill the orders.[63]

By the following winter J. R. Balsley was selling the device to local residents.[64] Perhaps for this reason, the electric company was soon warning its customers "not to tamper or interfere in any way with any of the poles, wires, converters, conduits or fixtures, etc. controlling or delivering the current made by the Electric Company."[65]

Despite his skills as an electrician and telegraph operator, Porter chose to live in Connellsville and become a merchant tailor. Under other circumstances his early interest in amusements and electricity might have been forgotten and the young small-town businessman would have become a solid, if not stolid, com-

(No Model.)

C. H. BALSLEY, Jr., & E. M. PORTER.
CURRENT REGULATOR FOR ELECTRIC LAMPS.

No. 451,798.   Patented May 5, 1891.

Drawing for current regulator patented by Charles Balsley and Edwin Porter.

munity member. Economic realities, however, intervened. In a town where there were too many tailors, his career choice proved to be a poor one. Dry goods stores (mostly run by Jewish businessmen) were exerting competitive pressures on merchant tailors like Porter by offering ready-to-wear clothing. Here Porter's resistance to a modern industrial system, a fact crucial to an understanding of his later motion picture career and his opposition to techniques of mass entertainment, was already discernible. Nor was this unusual. The U.S. Industrial Commission would soon note the willingness of Jews in the garment industry "to change the mode of production by using the sewing machine and division of labor against which the native tailor has shown a decided aversion."[66] Direct parallels with the motion picture industry can easily be established. People like Carl Laemmle, who managed a dry goods store in the early 1900s, quickly understood the implications and possibilities inherent in the nickelodeon form of entertainment, to which Porter never fully accommodated himself.

In the spring of 1893, Porter's new business, already suffering from excessive competition, was battered by a financial panic and depression. The sales of Connellsville merchants fell precipitately, and Porter's small tailoring establishment was one of the first to close its doors—on June 15th, Edward filed for bankruptcy.[67] Ten days earlier, on June 5th, he had eloped to Cumberland, Maryland, with Caroline Ridinger, whose father was an architect in nearby Somerset, Pennsylvania.[68] Once he had declared bankruptcy, Porter left for Philadelphia. This forced separation from his hometown was an experience shared by many Americans. It undoubtedly fostered a nostalgia for small-town life, which was expressed not only in many nineteenth-century melodramas but in Porter's films *The Miller's Daughter* (1905) and *The "White Caps"* (1905).

In Philadelphia the ex-tailor enlisted in the navy on June 19, 1893, giving his name as Edwin S. Porter and his trade as telegraph operator. His enlistment record continues: "*Eyes*, Brown; *Hair*, Lt. brown; *Complexion*, Sunburned; *Height*, 5 feet 4¾ inches; *Weight (pounds)*, 150."[69] Two somewhat contradictory accounts of his naval career exist, and Porter is the probable source in each instance. After his three-year enlistment was over, the Connellsville boy briefly returned home and provided the local paper with this description of his tour:

> Edward Porter returned last week from a long and interesting cruise on the United States Cruiser New York. He left here the beginning of June, three years ago. Going to Philadelphia, he was assigned on the 18th of the same month to the position of an assistant electrician on the vessel named which went into commission from the Cramp Navy yard on August 1st. His official position was Gunner's mate in the Dynamo Room. The ship was fitted up for a southern cruise at the Brooklyn Navy Yards, leaving for the scene of Brazil's trouble on Christmas day. The New York arrived at Rio on Jan 18th and was one of a squadron of six vessels which forced the demands of United States Admiral Bennett, allowing merchant ships from this country to land their stores on the insurgents' land. After these troubles the New York cruised among the West Indies till the middle of the following June, when she returned to New York

and took out a number of naval reserves for practice. She later performed the same service in Philadelphia for the Pennsylvania reserves, returning to the West Indies and the water of Venezuela for an extensive cruise remain[ing] there till May. The vessel and crew were then recalled to New York to prepare for the opening of the great Kell canal. After joining the review there the vessel made a cruise on the Atlantic seacoast of our country, went into winter quarters at Hampton Roads and in May returned to New York bay where the largest fleet ever gathered in American waters was being concentrated. Our town representative on the crew has had a wide field of experience and has many incidents to relate about the scenes and people of his travels.[70]

This youthful account of Porter's adventures in the navy differs from a much later description in the *Cyclopedia of American Biography*, which claims that Porter "attracted the notice of his superiors by inventing a number of electrical devices to improve the naval communications service. He also assisted Bradley Allen Fiske (q.v.), later a rear admiral, in perfecting the Fiske range-finder."[71]

Porter's naval record offers a more mundane account of these years. The navy gave Porter modest rankings in seamanship (although high points in gunnery) and based him, for the last year at least, in the Brooklyn Navy Yard as a landsman. Although no notice of Porter's contributions to naval technology is to be found in his record, his work in the electrical field is credible, given his earlier accomplishments and later interests. Such work must have kept him in touch with Edison business associates. A cruise to Central and South America may help to explain Porter's later travels in that area as an exhibitor during 1896–97. The navy also altered Porter's personal life and habits. Although he maintained ties with friends and family, he no longer thought of western Pennsylvania as a place to work and live. Financial realities—his bankruptcy and $16 a month in naval pay—meant that Porter had to go where opportunity beckoned. He ended up trusting his future to his boyhood hero Thomas Edison and moving pictures.

3 Edison and the Kinetoscope: 1888–1895

When Porter was eighteen years old and still living in Connellsville, Thomas Edison was contemplating a new invention that would record and play back a series of photographs so as to create the illusion of a moving image. Edison's initial interest was sparked by the photographer Eadweard Muybridge, who presented his zoöpraxiscope in Orange, New Jersey, on February 25, 1888, and stayed on to meet Edison at his laboratory two days later.[1] Muybridge and Edison discussed the possibility of combining the former's projecting machine and the latter's phonograph.[2] "I am experimenting upon an instrument which does for the Eye what the phonograph does for the Ear, which is the recording and reproduction of things in motion, and in such a form as to be both Cheap practical and convenient," Edison wrote in October 1888. "This apparatus I call a Kinetoscope 'Moving View.' "[3] Thinking of a motion picture machine in terms of the phonograph provided a familiar frame of reference for the inventor and those employees working on the project, but the parallels would often prove to be a stumbling block. Edison initially planned to have approximately 42,000 images, each about $1/32$ of an inch wide, on a cylinder that was the size of his phonograph records. These would be taken on a continuous spiral with 180 images per turn. An individual spectator could then look at twenty-eight minutes of pictures through a microscope while listening to sound from a phonograph.[4]

By June 1889 twenty-nine-year-old William Kennedy Laurie Dickson, one of Edison's chief experimenters and a reputable photographer in his own right, was formally assigned to the project.[5] He and Charles A. Brown (Dickson's chief assistant for this project) worked in Laboratory Room 5, where they received

Thomas Edison as photographed by W. K. L. Dickson.

periodic help from Frederick P. Ott, Eugene Lauste, and others. Brown explained their experiments at this stage: "We first took the phonograph and
coated a cylinder and put onto it and had a lens taken out of a microscope and
rigged onto it, and then they had a coarse feed wheel onto it so as to run slower,
and that fed the lens along in front of the coated cylinder; but we made a great
many experiments during that time in trying to see how small pictures we could
get."[6] Vibrations in the nearby machine shops were felt to contribute to their
difficulties. While Edison was away on his European tour in the late summer
and early fall of 1889, Dickson arranged for the construction of a special photographic building for the sum of $516.64. It was in this building, during late
1889 or 1890, that Edison's initial idea was realized in modified form with
larger cylinders of approximately 4½ inches in diameter. Leaves of photographic film were wrapped around the cylinders and a series of tiny images were
taken, spiralling down its length. A few surviving "films" show a man dressed
in white against a black background. He faces the camera and makes strongly

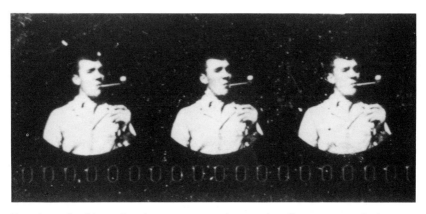

Experimental subject taken by W. K. L. Dickson and William Heise with the 1891 horizontal-feed camera (larger than life-size). The subject is James Duncan, a day worker at Edison's laboratory.

delineated gestures in a presentational style. Some of the frames are blurred, and it is evident that the idea encountered many difficulties.

During his European travels, Edison met Etienne Jules Marey and learned of the Frenchman's successful efforts to photograph a continuous series of images on a film strip that moved along intermittently in front of a single camera lens. Shortly after returning to his laboratory, Edison drew up a new motion picture caveat that reflected these conceptual advances. The successful construction of an instrument based on these principles was postponed, however, as Edison and Dickson devoted most of their time to iron ore milling. Work on the kinetograph revived in October 1890, when Dickson was joined by a new assistant named William Heise. They constructed a new camera that used a ¾-inch strip of film. The film was exposed by using a horizontal-feed system rather than the vertical-feed one that would come to characterize modern motion pictures. A single row of small perforations ran along the bottom edge of the band. Finally, on May 20, 1891, Edison was able to unveil a peep-hole viewing machine.[7] Participants in a convention of the National Federation of Women's Clubs were brought to the Edison laboratory, where they saw "the picture of a man. It was a most marvellous picture. It bowed and smiled and waved its hands and took off its hat with the most perfect naturalness and grace. Every motion was perfect."[8] The man was Dickson. Several additional subjects were taken at this time, including a boxing scene, a full-figure view of a juggler, and a close view of a man with a pipe.[9] All were shot against black backgrounds; in the last two, the subjects faced the camera. That June, Dickson and Edison lawyers began to prepare three patent applications for a motion picture camera (the kinetograph) and a peep-hole viewing device (the kinetoscope). Finally submitted on August 24th to the U.S. Patent Office, these applications initiated a series of legal maneuvers that were to continue for more than twenty years.

Edison and Dickson developed their vertical-feed, 1½-inch (approximately 35mm) motion picture camera during the summer of 1892. Firm evidence of this appeared in October, when frames of motion picture subjects were published in the *Phonogram*, a trade journal for the phonograph industry.[10] Two scenes, of men fencing and boxing, owed much to the subject choices and representational methods evident in Muybridge's serial photography. Another begins with William Heise standing alone in the frame. W. K. L. Dickson enters from behind the camera and shakes hands as both men face an imagined audience. This documentation of celebration and authorship marked the successful completion of Edison's search for a worthwhile motion picture system. These films, while not for commercial exhibition, embodied characteristics that would remain important in the years ahead. The isolation of actions and figures against a black background and the subjects' open acknowledgment of the camera retained the presentational elements evident in earlier experiments. Everyone in front of the camera was male, congruent with the homosocial world of the laboratory. In many instances, laboratory personnel acted as subjects. This approach continued for later experimental films, notably *Dickson Experimental Sound Film* (taken in late 1894 or early 1895). For this, Dickson played the violin into a phonograph funnel while two male employees danced with each other.

Preparations

Construction of a motion picture studio began at Edison's West Orange laboratory in December 1892. The inventor and his secretary, Alfred O. Tate, were making commercial arrangements for the invention's exploitation at the World's Columbian Exposition in Chicago and production facilities were essential. The studio, which became known as the Black Maria, after the black paddy wagons it was said to resemble, was completed the following February at a cost of $637.67.[11] It was approximately fifty feet long and thirteen feet wide. A stage was at one end "entirely lined with black tar paper, giving the effect of a dead black tunnel behind the subject being photographed."[12] The studio rotated on a graphite center and tracks so that sunlight could fall directly on the performers.

The shift from experimental to commercial filmmaking involved many continuities. *Blacksmith Scene*, one of the first motion pictures shot in the new studio, illustrates this. The earliest Edison film to have a commercial life, it was taken before May 1893 by Dickson and Heise. As this suggests, the people immediately responsible for inventing the hardware remained in charge of the kinetograph during this new phase. Characteristically, Edison declined to shift personnel when moving from the phase of invention to that of commercial exploitation. Moreover, the collaborative approach to invention (i.e., Edison-

A Hand-Shake (1892). Dickson and Heise congratulate each other on their invention.

The Black Maria studio (March 1894).

Dickson and Dickson-Heise) was continued as part of the production process. Other continuities are likewise striking: the black backgrounds and the frontal organizations of the mise-en-scène.

Blacksmith Scene depicted a blacksmith and his two helpers hammering an iron forging on the anvil, stopping to pass around a bottle of beer, and then resuming their labors. Although it reworked a subject previously photographed by Muybridge, the activity had become much more elaborate. Edison personnel constructed a fictional workspace within their workspace. Charles Kayser appears to be playing the role of the blacksmith, and the two others are almost certainly Edison employees. The world of the laboratory was transfigured in the blacksmith's shop. A conscious element of play was undoubtedly operating, for the crude smithy contrasted markedly with Edison's sophisticated machine shop. Yet there seem to have been important parallels. The fictionalized workspace has someone "in charge," the head blacksmith; but lines of authority are attenuated by egalitarianism and informality. Work, pleasure, and socializing are interwoven. In terms of American work culture, this scene already presents a nostalgic view, for, as Roy Rosenzweig has remarked, by the late nineteenth century, work and socializing were increasingly separated, with workplace drinking considered part of a bygone era.[13] Nevertheless, this film conveys the interpenetration of work and leisure characteristic of the Edison laboratory environment. The very making of the film seems to have been such an effort. Employees put aside serious undertakings to assume the roles of blacksmiths. If they were expected to work long hours and produce results, discipline was lax

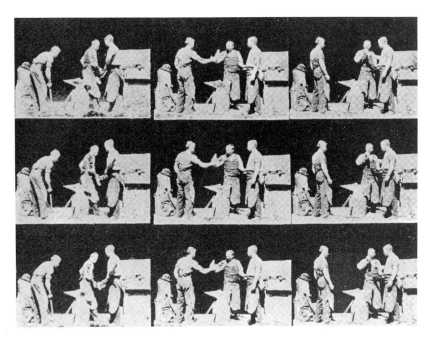

Blacksmith Scene (1893). Work and pleasure are intermixed.

and responsibilities were often loosely defined. The informal lines of authority are also evident in the way that W. K. L. Dickson, the man most responsible for the film, copyrighted the subject even though the films and materials were owned by Edison.[14] Edison was not seeking to conduct an efficient workplace but to establish an environment where creativity could flourish.

Blacksmith Scene served as the centerpiece for the first public demonstration of Edison's new 1½-inch system, at the Brooklyn Institute on May 9, 1893 (see document no. 1). Conducted by George M. Hopkins, president of the institute's Department of Physics, this presentation was remarkable in that it took the form of an illustrated lecture. To explain the principles on which the kinetograph and kinetoscope were based, Hopkins used a magic lantern to project a series of images from a choreutoscope (created in 1866), which created a dancing skeleton. Projected moving images from an instrument similar to Muybridge's zoöpraxiscope were also shown. Edison and Dickson's accomplishments were carefully situated in the general context of efforts being made in "chronophotography." The superior results of their efforts were carefully noted.

Selected frames of *Blacksmith Scene* were then projected onto the screen one frame at a time for inspection by the audience of approximately four hundred scientific people. Hopkins emphasized that the kinetoscope in its complete form was a machine for projecting images on the screen with recorded synchronous

The interior stage area of the Black Maria. Some of the personnel appeared in *Blacksmith Scene.*

sound. Journal formats aside, the first public presentation of modern motion picture frames was done on this screen. Only at the evening's conclusion did those present file by a peep-hole kinetoscope and peer into the machine. With each peep taking half a minute, the last part of the evening lasted more than three hours.

Document No. 1

First Public Exhibition of Edison's Kinetograph.

At the regular monthly meeting of the Department of Physics of the Brooklyn Institute, May 9, the members were enabled, through the courtesy of Mr. Edison, to examine the new instrument known as the kinetograph [*sic*, i.e., kinetoscope]. The instrument in its complete form consists of an optical lantern, a mechanical device by which a moving image is projected on the screen simultaneously with the production by a phonograph of the words or song which accompany the movements pictured. For example, the photograph of a prima donna would be shown on the screen, with the movements of the lips, the head, and the body, together with the changes of facial expression, while the phonograph would produce the song; but to arrange this apparatus for exhibition for a single evening was impracticable. Therefore, a small instrument designed for individual observation, and which simply shows the movements without the accompanying words, was shown to the members and their friends who were present.

Mr. George M. Hopkins, president of the department, before proceeding to the exhibition of the instrument offered a brief explanation, in which he said: "This apparatus is the refinement of Plateau's phenakistoscope or the zootrope, and like everything Mr. Edison undertakes, it is carried to great perfection. The principle can be readily understood by anyone who has ever examined the instrument I have mentioned. Persistence of vision is depended upon to blend the successive images into one continuous ever-changing photographic picture.

"In addition to Plateau's experiments, I might refer to the work accomplished by Muybridge and Anschuetz, who very successfully photographed animals in motion, and to Demeny, who produced an instrument called the phonoscope, which gave the facial expression while words were being spoken, so that deaf and dumb people could readily understand. But these instruments, having but twenty-five or thirty pictures for each subject, could not be made to blend the different movements sufficiently to make the image appear like a continuous photograph of moving things; the change from one picture to the next was abrupt and not realistic. In Mr. Edison's machine far more perfect results are secured. The fundamental feature in his experiments is the camera, by means of which the pictures are taken. This camera starts, moves, and stops the sensitive strip which receives the photographic image forty-six times a second, and the exposure of the plate takes place in one-eighth [*sic*] of this time or in about one fifty-seventh of a second. The lens for producing these pictures was made to order at an enormous expense, and every detail at this end of the experiment was carefully looked after. There are 700 impressions on each strip, and when these pictures are shown in succession in the kinetograph the light is intercepted 700 times during one revolution of the strip. The duration of each image is one-ninety-second of a second, and the entire strip passes through the instrument in about thirty seconds. In the kinetograph each image dwells upon the retina until it is replaced by the succeeding one, and the difference between any picture and the succeeding one or preceding one is so slight as to render it impossible to observe the intermittent character of the picture. To explain in a very imperfect way the manner in which the photographs are produced, I will present the familiar dancing skeleton on the screen. You will notice that the image appears to be continuous, but the eye fails to notice the cutting off of the light, and the image simply appears to change its position without being at all intermittent; but when the instrument is turned slowly, you will notice that the period of eclipse is much longer than the period of illumination. The photographs on the kinetograph strip were taken in some such way as this. I will exhibit an ordinary zootrope adapted to the lantern, which shows the principle of the kinetograph. In this instrument, a disk having a radial slit is revolved rapidly in front of a disk bearing a series of images in different positions, which are arranged radially. The relative speeds of these disks are such that when they are revolved in the lantern the radial slit causes the images to be seen in regular succession, so that they replace each other and appear to really be in motion; but this instrument, as compared with the kinetograph, is a very crude affair."

After projecting upon the screen a few sections of the kinetograph strip, the audience—which consisted of more than 400 scientific people—was allowed to pass by the instrument, each person taking a view of the moving picture, which averaged for each person about half a minute. The picture represented a blacksmith and two helpers forging a piece of iron. Before beginning the job a bottle was passed from one to the other, each imbibing his portion. The blacksmith then removed his white hot iron from the forge with a pair of tongs and gave directions to his helpers with the small hand hammer, when they immediately began to pound the hot iron while the sparks flew in all directions, the blacksmith at the same time making intermediate strokes with his hand hammer. At a signal from the smith, the helpers put down their sledge hammers, when the iron was returned to the forge and another piece substituted for it, and the operation was repeated.

In the picture exhibited in the kinetograph, every movement appeared perfectly smooth and natural, without any of the jerkiness seen in instruments of the zootrope type which have heretofore been exhibited.

The machine in this case was not accompanied by the phonograph, but nevertheless the exhibition was one of great interest. The kinetograph in this form is designed as a "nickel in the slot" machine, and a number of them have been made for use at the Columbian Exhibition at Chicago.

SOURCE: *Scientific American*, May 20, 1893, p. 310.

The Black Maria was rarely used for production during 1893, as the refinement of Edison's motion picture system and the manufacture of kinetoscopes experienced delays. W. K. L. Dickson suffered from nervous exhaustion and was absent from the laboratory between early February and late April 1893. Although this accounts for some of the slowdown, the recession of 1893 may have further impeded this project, as Edison devoted his hard-pressed finances and time to iron ore milling. A new model kinetoscope for films taken with the vertical-feed kinetograph was probably not available until shortly before the Brooklyn Institute demonstration in May. A contract for the manufacture of twenty-five machines based on this prototype was only drawn in late June. Gordon Hendricks indicates that it was given to an Edison employee who had difficulty staying sober. As a result, the machines were not completed until March 1894. Only the prototype was available for exhibition at the Chicago exposition, and this proved too valuable to send.[15]

Initial Film Production

The imminent completion of the kinetoscopes spurred the Edison group into serious film production. *Edison Kinetoscopic Record of a Sneeze* (© 9 January 1894) was a short film made for publicity purposes during the first week of January 1894.[16] By the beginning of March, Dickson and assistant William Heise had shot *The Barbershop* and *Amateur Gymnast*, both full-length subjects. As with most films made during the coming year, these were slightly less than fifty feet long, shot at approximately forty frames per second, and lasted less than twenty seconds. Like *Blacksmith Scene*, *The Barbershop* depicts a homosocial environment where easy comradery is routine. A customer receives a "lightning shave" for five cents—the cost of seeing the film. Since the shave and the viewing of the film take the same amount of time, the subject would seem to gently rib the film spectator, who has been quickly separated from his money. Yet the depiction of a complete shaving cycle highlights the work process (the barber's) and treats the barbershop as both a workplace and a place of leisure.

Amateur Gymnast shows a young man performing a somersault: it was probably one of several films taken of members of the Newark Turnverein, a nearby athletic club. Others show two men on parallel bars and a brief boxing match.[17] These may have been rehearsals for the kinetograph's first famous visitor, the strongman Eugene Sandow. On March 6th Sandow came to the Edison laboratory accompanied by the management of Koster & Bial's, the music hall where he was then performing. For the kinetograph, Sandow stripped to a loincloth and assumed an array of positions that showed off his muscular physique. In cinematography as in photography, Dickson had a well-trained eye. His camera framed Sandow just above the knees. Against the black background, the strongman's physique captured the complete attention of his audience.

Making *Sandow* and other films for this new type of commercial amusement fit easily into the laboratory environment. Although Sandow demanded a $250 fee to pose in the Black Maria unless he could meet Wizard Edison himself, this stipulation was probably unnecessary. Edison, an aficionado of variety entertainment, was delighted to meet the performer. Using a still camera next to the kinetograph, Dickson took several photographs: one caught "Mr. Edison feeling Sandow's muscles with a curiously comical expression on his face."[18] To entertain the inventor, the strongman playfully tossed one of his entourage out the

Amateur Gymnast (1894).

window. The kinetograph added a dash of levity to the laboratory milieu, burdened by discouraging, money-losing efforts in other areas.

The films taken through early March were of men, by men, and principally for men. But this quickly changed. During the second week of that month, the dancer Carmencita pirouetted for the kinetograph—her dress twirling and rising as high as her knees. As the *New York Times* proclaimed, "the vigor, dash, and sinuous movements of Carmencita herself, having long since defied imitation or improvement, were still indefinable and unique."[19] Unfortunately, the few surviving frames of *Carmencita* fail even to hint at the reasons for her reputation. Her rise to stardom occurred under Koster & Bial management at their old music hall on Twenty-third Street. There she attracted unprecedented accolades from critics at all the city newspapers. Whatever her actual abilities, like Edison, she was a larger-than-life creation of the mass circulation dailies.[20] She was soon followed by the female contortionist Mme. Ena Bertoldi, then appearing at Koster & Bial's. Both subjects were meant to appeal to male voyeurs who would soon be peeping into Edison's latest novelty. They were films of women, by men and primarily for men. Sandow, Carmencita, and Bertoldi—all headline attractions—were the first of many variety and vaudeville performers to visit the Black Maria over the ensuing year. The most frequent visitor proved to be Carmencita's chief rival, Annabelle Whitford, who performed her Serpentine,

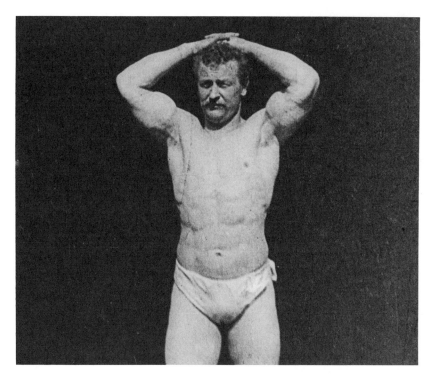

Eugene Sandow.

Sun, and Butterfly dances on numerous occasions between 1894 and 1897. The billowing gauze of her attire was not only sexually evocative but encouraged hand-coloring effects that transcended a strictly masculine appeal. (Hand-coloring work was usually contracted out to the wives of Edison employees, notably the wife of Edmund Kuhn.) However, a large array of dancers came to perform their specialty, including Ruth Dennis (later Ruth St. Denis), who was promoted as "the Champion High Kicker of the World."[21]

These early films functioned within the homosocial amusement world. *Cock Fight*, shot in early March, was an extremely popular subject, for which new negatives would often have to be made. Filmed as a close view, the intimate depiction of this brutal sport was enhanced by the roosters' rapid movements and flying feathers. Its success generated similar types of subjects.

Through a New York professional rat catcher, Mr. Dickson secured a large cage full of dock rats and he has had at the laboratory for some time two pretty little full-brooded rat terriers. It was an extremely difficult task to arrange the ring, which on account of the limitations of the kinetograph could be only four feet square. The first

Carmencita.

contest was with six rats turned loose in the pit at once, and in fifty-two and one-half seconds all had been killed by one of the terriers. A second and a third trial were made with equally good results.[22]

Rat Catcher, the result of this undertaking, was ultimately considered "not good, the rats being too small."[23]

Additional vignettes of masculine daily life also continued to be made. By early April, Dickson had shot *Horse Shoeing*, a simple variation of *Blacksmith Scene*. This highly specialized "genre" also included *A Bar Room Scene*, taken later that spring. Another male-dominated space is depicted, although the emphasis has now clearly shifted toward a distinct leisure realm—from passing the beer bottle in a work context to the saloon. In fact, such all-male environments would frequently support nickel-in-the-slot kinetoscopes in the years ahead. Yet for the first time homosocial space is viewed somewhat critically. Socializing takes the form of a political argument that ends in a fight and requires police intervention. This less than flattering depiction of a saloon suggests a disturbance in the choice and depiction of subjects, a desire to meet the demands (real or imagined) of actual spectators.

The commercial debut of the kinetoscope occurred in mid April with the opening of the first kinetoscope parlor in midtown Manhattan. With a peek costing 5¢ and most patrons expected to see a series of five scenes, viewers had to have disposable income. Most were middle class. At its fashionable location, the kinetoscope drew female as well as male patrons. The masculine appeal needed to be tempered, if not effaced. Three films used for this opening were appropriately desexualized: *Highland Dance*, showing "A 'Lad' and a 'Lassie' in

A Bar Room Scene.

full costume,"[24] *Organ Grinder*, and *Trained Bears*. "The bears were divided between surly discontent and a comfortable desire to follow the bent of their own inclinations," Dickson later reported. "It was only after much persuasion that they could be induced to subserve the interests of science."[25] Made to perform elaborate tricks, the animals evidenced man's mastery of nature while still holding out the potential for violence. Correspondingly, *Organ Grinder* offered a reassuring picture of a happy, harmless Italian street musician, although the perceived threat of the Italian immigrant could not be totally eliminated. Other films made by early summer—for example, *The Boxing Cats*, *The Wrestling Dog*, and *Glenroy Brothers* (a comic boxing routine)—reversed this tension, displaying physical violence induced in the most domesticated of subjects.[26] These subjects parodied and softened the sporting world's manly preoccupations without in any way criticizing them.

These "non-offensive" subjects not only added to the diversity of available images but became essential when the more provocative selections encountered opposition. That summer, for instance, dancing girl subjects were censored by moralistic officials in Asbury Park, New Jersey. Told to close shop or use more

The first kinetoscope parlor at 1155 Broadway, New York City.

acceptable "views," the local exhibitor acquired a print of *The Boxing Cats*.[27] Such comparatively tame views, however, were not the most popular. The kinetoscope gave women a more enticing opportunity: to glimpse the half-hidden male-oriented world of cock fights and risqué women from which they were ordinarily excluded. It encouraged a distinctly feminine voyeurism (in some instances complicated by a narcissistic identification with the women on display), a counterpoint to that motivated by masculine desire. Yet despite the various possible subject positions, every film drew from the world of popular amusement. Sex or violence was at the core of almost every image.

Exploitation of the Kinetoscope

Edison shifted the manufacture and sale of kinetoscopes and films from his laboratory accounts to the Edison Manufacturing Company, which he completely owned, on April 1, 1894. Expenses incurred to that date—for the development of his motion picture system, the building of a photographic building and the Black Maria, the manufacture of twenty-five kinetoscopes, and the taking of various films—totaled $24,118.[28] Henceforth and for the next eighteen years, the Kinetograph Department at the Edison Company (as it was commonly called) was responsible for the inventor's motion picture business. As this new enterprise was starting up, Thomas Edison hired William Gilmore as vice-president and general manager of this and other Edison companies. Gilmore also commenced April 1st, replacing Tate as the Wizard's business chief.

Edison relied on three different groups to market kinetoscopes and films. The first and most prominent was a consortium that included Edison's former secretary and business manager Alfred O. Tate, phonograph executives Thomas Lombard and Erastus Benson, Norman C. Raff, Frank R. Gammon, and Andrew Holland.[29] Through Tate, they had a long-standing order for the first twenty-five kinetoscopes. As soon as these were completed, ten machines were immediately installed at 1155 Broadway, near Herald Square in New York City, where the kinetoscope had its commercial debut on April 14th. A Chicago kinetoscope parlor, using another ten machines, opened in mid May, while the remaining five had a San Francisco premiere at Peter Bacigalupi's phonograph parlor on June 1st.[30] During one thirteen-day period in late June and early July, the San Francisco parlor brought in $961.20 against $249.60 in expenses (including the month's rent of $175).[31] Similar openings followed in other American cities, with consortium members either exhibiting in lucrative territories or making special arrangements with businesses like the Columbia Phonograph Company, which exhibited the machines in Atlantic City and Asbury Park, New Jersey, and later in Washington, D.C. In August the Holland Brothers opened a kinetoscope parlor in Boston and hired James H. White to assist them. White was soon helping them fit up new arcades with the nickel-in-the-slot machines. Among other undertakings, White and fellow employee Charles H. Webster "installed a plant of kinetoscopes in the Flower Show at the Grand Central Palace, New York City."[32] After this four-week November show, the duo bought the machines, and for the next ten months they traveled to different cities exhibiting films.

Edison initially sold kinetoscopes and films on a first-come, first-served basis.[33] Customers included Thomas L. Tally, then based in Waco, Texas, and William Gilmore's brother-in-law, William H. Markgraf. The disorganization that resulted soon forced Edison to rethink this laissez-faire marketing approach. In mid August, he assigned exclusive responsibility for selling regular kinetoscopes within the United States and Canada to the original consortium with Norman Raff and Frank Gammon acting as its principal agents. Through the newly formed Kinetoscope Company they agreed to purchase approximately ten kinetoscopes a week from Edison for $200 a machine. These machines were in turn sold for as much as $350, with discounts of $25 per machine when several machines were purchased. (Sales to consortium members, however, remained at $200 or $225 per kinetoscope.) This contractual agreement could continue in effect for as much as three years.[34]

From its early contacts with customers, the Edison Company developed relations with two other groups that subsequently assumed major roles in marketing its machines. One began its activities in May when Otway Latham, a manager for the Tilden Company, a pharmaceutical firm, ordered a group of kinetoscopes. Joined by his brother Gray Latham, his father Woodville Latham, and Enoch Rector, a fellow Tilden employee, Otway arranged with Edison to show films of prize fights by expanding the kinetoscope's capacity to 150 feet and reducing the camera and projection speed to 30 frames per second. The increased running time of slightly more than a minute enabled them to show abbreviated rounds. Their enterprise, which eventually became the Kinetoscope Exhibition Company, commenced its exhibition activities in late August.[35] Franck Z. Maguire and Joseph D. Baucus, heading the other group, made their first purchase in mid July.[36] By September they had incorporated the Continental Commerce Company and acquired the exclusive rights to sell and exhibit the kinetoscope overseas—so long as they worked the territory to Edison's

Table 1.   Purchases by Edison's Principal Kinetoscope Agents
(Rounded off to the nearest dollar)

	Hollands/ Kinetoscope Co. Raff & Gammon	Lathams Kinetoscope Exhibition Co.	Maguire & Baucus Continental Commerce Co.
May 1894	2,528	1,000	0
June	156	0	0
July	2,978	0	1,275
Aug.	1,215	1,166	2,853
Sept.	5,784	1,724	9,397
Oct.	5,565	2,369	2,678
Nov.	11,288	1,000	11,532
Dec.	9,000	2,134	12,760
Jan. 1895	17,010	2,858	17,186
Feb.	2,012	2,000	14,130
total	57,537	14,271	71,811
Mar. 1895	3,539	1,310	1,230
Apr.	809	800	3,079
May	5,091	212	13,551
June	5,063	90	5,182
July	2,000	92	1,887
Aug.	1,001	0	1,757
Sept.	1,007	810	725
Oct.	0	992	963
Nov.	1,001	66	118
Dec.	1,000	152	294
Jan.	0	150	14
Feb.	0	36	64
total	20,511	4,710	28,864

satisfaction.[37] They were expected to dispose of thirteen machines a week for six months and eight machines a week thereafter.

For the business term from April 1894 through February 1895, the Edison Manufacturing Company had kinetoscope sales of $149,549, film sales of $25,882, and "kinetoscope sundries" sales of $2,416. With motion picture sales totaling $177,847, the three groups were responsible for at least $143,620 or approximately 80 percent of Edison's film-related activities during this period.[38] Corresponding profits totaled $85,338. Although their sales were substantial for the next few months, the companies' purchases slumped badly during the summer of 1895 and never recovered. Their activities were responsible for almost all of Edison's motion picture sales for the 1895–96 business year, when total profits for Edison's film-related business fell to $4,141.

Edison Company expenses included substantial fees for W. K. L. Dickson and William Heise in recognition of their important contributions to the development of Edison's motion picture inventions. Dickson received at least $3,150 and Heise at least $850 between August 1894 and February 1895. Dickson continued to receive about $100 and Heise about $40 a week until the end of November 1895. These substantial sums may have been in addition to their regular salaries.[39] The cost of film stock was not assumed by the Edison Company until July 1894 and totaled more than $6,000 by March 1, 1895.[40] Raw stock purchases amounted to $8,460 for the following business year, with their size falling during the summer and increasing again during the winter. Almost all stock was purchased from the Blair Camera Company; contrary to received opinion, none of it came from George Eastman's company. After having shouldered the financial burden for taking the early subjects, Edison (perhaps with Gilmore's urging) shifted these costs to the three groups responsible for commercial exploitation. Each financed its own subjects, which it alone could use unless proper arrangements were made among the various groups. Both Raff & Gammon and Maguire & Baucus indicated their ownership by including small signs with their initials—R (Raff & Gammon), MB (Maguire & Baucus), and C (Continental Commerce Company)—within the scenes being photographed.

Continued Film Production

The first subject for the Latham-Rector enterprise was a six-round fight between Michael Leonard and Jack Cushing, filmed by Dickson and Heise in the Black Maria on June 15th.[41] A film of men made by men, *The Leonard-Cushing Fight* was meant to appeal to the sporting crowd. Again work responsibilities were forgotten as Thomas Edison happily acted as master of ceremonies and supervised the fistic proceedings. His interest was hardly dispassionate, for he found himself mimicking the boxers' thrusts as the fight intensified. When the legality of the fight under New Jersey law was questioned, Edison's role in the proceedings had to be suppressed. Perhaps this, as much as the time needed for the production of large-capacity kinetoscopes, explains why the Kinetoscope Exhibition Company's storefront arcade on Nassau Street did not open with these films until mid August.

The fruition of Otway Latham's efforts yielded new financing from Samuel J. Tilden, Jr., enabling the group to order seventy-two additional kinetoscopes at $300 a machine.[42] Arrangements were then made for the heavyweight champion James Corbett to fight the New Jersey pugilist Peter Courtney. If he could knock out Courtney in the sixth round, the champion was guaranteed $5,000 against a weekly exhibition fee of $150 (later reduced to $50) for each set of machines on exhibition.[43] On Friday morning, September 7th, four days after Corbett's play *Gentleman Jack* began a Broadway run, the champion arrived in Orange with his entourage.[44] In the meantime,

> Over at the Black Maria, which has been fully described in *The Sun*, several attendants were busy fixing the kinetograph, so that there might be no slips or mistakes in photographing the impending struggle. The Maria, as the building in which Edison's wonderful machine is located is called, reminded everybody of a huge coffin. It was covered with black tar paper, secured to the woodwork by big metal-topped nails, and was the most dismal-looking affair the sports had ever seen. Inside the walls were painted black, and there wasn't a window of any description, barring a little slide which was directly beside the kinetograph and could be opened or closed at the will of the operator. Half of the roof, however, could be raised or lowered like a drawbridge by means of ropes, pulleys and weights so that the sunlight could strike squarely on the space before the machine.
>
> The ring was 14 feet square. It was roped on two sides, the other two being the heavily padded walls of the building. The floor was planed smooth and covered with rosin. All battles decided in this arena must be fought under a special set of rules. A round lasts a little over one minute, with a rest of a minute and a half to two minutes between the rounds. Consequently, the smallness of the ring and the shortness of the rounds necessitate hot fighting all the time.[45]

At 11 o'clock the prize fighters prepared for the ring, but they were delayed another thirty minutes by a technical problem with the kinetograph.

> At 11:45 o'clock everything was ready. The men were first requested to pose in fighting attitudes for an ordinary photograph. Then the chief operator told them to get ready for the fight. John P. Eckhardt of this city was referee and W. A. Brady held the watch. In Corbett's corner were his seconds John McVey and Frank Belcher, with Bud Woodthorpe, bottle holder. In Courtney's corner were John Tracey and Edward Allen, seconds, and Sam Lash, bottle holder. Corbett weighed 195 pounds, he said, and Courtney 190. The men were ordered to shake hands and received instructions as to clinching. Then they went to their corners and waited for the signal to begin the battle. The operators were all ready now, and when the word was given the kinetograph began to buzz.[46]

James Corbett and Peter Courtney pose in the Black Maria before their fight.

Corbett succeeded in knocking out Courtney in the sixth round, and *Corbett and Courtney Before the Kinetograph* (also known as *The Corbett-Courtney Fight*) went on to be a nationwide success. It was shown at Thomas L. Tally's Phonograph and Kinetoscope Parlor at 311 South Spring Street in Los Angeles and in many other large-capacity kinetoscopes across the country. Corbett's contract, however, absorbed much of the profit, and it seems likely that Tilden ultimately lost money on the deal. Moreover, opposition to prize fighting made it difficult to generate additional projects in the months ahead.

After Raff & Gammon and Maguire & Baucus assumed the costs of, and increased responsibility for, making new negatives in September, the same types of subjects continued to be produced. The Kinetoscope Company paid Hornbacker and Murphy to fight a "five round glove contest to a finish" in late September. Each round, however, was limited to fifty feet of film. The

Englehardt Sisters fenced for the kinetograph with both broadswords and foils (*Lady Fencers*). Pedro Esquirel and Dionecio Gonzales performed a Mexican knife duel. In January 1895, with variations on the obvious exhausted, Capt. Duncan C. Ross and Lieut. Hartung fought with broadswords on horseback in the five-round *Gladiatorial Combat*.[47]

Dancers, contortionists, acrobats, and novelty acts also continued to visit the Black Maria from September of 1894 through the following spring. Professor Ivan Tschernoff with his performing dogs, then at Koster & Bial's, appeared in *Skirt Dog Dance* and *Summersault Dog* on October 17th. The following day, Toyou Kichi, "the Marvellous and Artistic Japanese Twirler and Juggler," gave a performance for the kinetograph.[48] Robetta and Doreto, who performed their comic routine "Heap Fun Laundry" at the close of Tony Pastor's vaudeville bill for a week beginning on November 26th, also brought their act out to the Edison laboratory (*Chinese Laundry Scene*).

With the kinetoscope "one of the recognized sights of the town,"[49] performers and amusement entrepreneurs quickly concluded that moving pictures were good publicity and could help their careers. Prof. Harry Welton's Cat Circus was one of several acts that showed improved bookings subsequent to its appearance in the kinetoscope.[50] The manager for James Hoey's upcoming farce announced a new advertising scheme: "Edison's kinetoscope and phonograph are to be combined in a reproduction of the principal spectacular and vocal feature of the new performance, the instrument to be publicly exhibited in the principal cities weeks prior to the play's appearance."[51] Such a response from the public and the theatrical community enabled kinetograph production to continue drawing from diverse elements of the amusement world.

During the fall, various performers from Buffalo Bill's Wild West show, then at the peak of its popularity, came out to the Edison laboratory.[52] Buffalo Bill, his manager, and a group of Indians traveled from Ambrose park in Brooklyn to appear in a series of films on September 24th. These included *Buffalo Bill*, *Sioux Ghost Dance*, *Buffalo Dance*, and *Indian War Council*. This last film consisted of "seventeen different persons" and showed Buffalo Bill addressing the Indian warriors.[53] A small group of Mexicans appeared two weeks later to perform their specialty: the knife duel and lasso throwing.[54] On October 16th, rodeo star Lee Martin rode a bucking bronco in a makeshift corral outside the Black Maria (*Bucking Broncho*).[55] Finally, on November 1st, Annie Oakley demonstrated her rifle-shooting abilities (*Annie Oakley*).[56]

Performers giving specialties in regular New York–based theatrical companies flocked to the West Orange site. On October 6th, Charles Walton and John C. Slavin, from Edward E. Rice's comic opera *1492*, executed their comic boxing routine. That same day Lucy Daly's Pickaninnies of *The Passing Show* tumbled and danced—providing motion pictures with their first images of African Americans. A somewhat later visitor, James Grundy, appearing in *The South Before the War*, executed a cake walk, buck and wing dance, and breakdown.

Band Drill and *Bucking Broncho*. The R at the bottom left of the frame stands for Raff & Gammon.

The Grundy films were then marketed as "the best negro subjects yet taken and are amusing and entertaining."[57] Bertha Waring and John W. Wilson, eccentric dancers from the musical burlesque *Little Christopher Columbus*, and the Jamies from *Rob Roy* added to this long list.

Two of the most ambitious studio productions were taken in December 1894. Early that month members of the *Milk White Flag* company presented the camera with five abbreviated scenes from Charles Hoyt's successful song-and-dance farce. The musical satirizes the part-time citizen-soldiers whose "commanderies" served a purely social function. Its many musical and dance numbers were perfect for the kinetoscope. One filmed excerpt, *Finale of 1st Act of Hoyt's "Milk White Flag,"* had "34 Persons in Costume. The largest number ever shown as one subject in the Kinetoscope."[58] Perhaps the single most ambitious subject of this period was *Fire Rescue Scene*, made for Raff & Gammon. Filmed inside the Black Maria, the production involved elaborate smoke effects and the assistance of a local fire department. The film can be considered an innovative extension of workplace films like *Blacksmith Scene*. Certainly, firemen embodied nineteenth-century manly virtues (courage, strength, etc.), and local fire departments served as centers for many male leisure activities. The homosocial worlds of fire fighting and film production easily converged; they would do so again with much frequency in the years ahead.

Kinetograph activities slowed during the winter months and were then seriously disrupted in April of 1895, when Dickson left Edison's employ. Although this break may have occurred as early as April 2d, it was not made public until late in the month.[59] Dickson's position had become untenable. He had been fighting with Gilmore for control over the motion picture business and for primacy in the inventor's affections. At the same time he was helping two aspiring competitors (the Lathams and the founders of the American Mutoscope Company) develop their own independent motion picture technology. His de-

Fire Rescue Scene.

parture left William Heise responsible for Edison's motion picture business and ended the easy, long-standing collaborative relationship that had produced these films. In the wake of Dickson's departure, Heise proceeded with a handful of additional subjects, perhaps assisted by John Ott. When Barnum and Bailey's Circus stopped in Orange on May 9th, he kinetographed various members of the troupe in the Black Maria before their afternoon performance. Made for the Continental Commerce Company (the circus was soon going to Europe), scenes showed natives of India (*Short Stick Dance*), Samoan Islanders (*Dance of Rejoicing*), a renowned strongman (*Professor Attilla*), and an Egyptian dancer (*Princess Ali*).[60]

By mid June, Edison personnel had taken four scenes from *Trilby: Death Scene, Dance Scene, Hypnotic Scene,* and *Trilby Quartette. Trilby,* the theatrical adaptation of George du Maurier's novel, opened at the Garden Theatre on April 15th and was proclaimed "an instant and deserved success, which swelled at times to the proportions of a triumph."[61] Even before the opening, however, others were quickly presenting excerpts.[62] Although the actor playing the hypnotist Svengali visited the Edison laboratory in May 1896, it is unlikely that members of the cast did so when the show opened. Moreover, the death scene was burlesqued, suggesting the performance of a renegade group. The Edison group had ranged freely through various forms of popular amusement to acquire subjects for their productions. Yet they had not moved outside these well-defined boundaries to make actualities or, with a handful of exceptions, their own original scenes. By spring this lack of diversity, as well as the relatively high cost spectators had to pay to peep, led to declining public interest.

Edison's motion picture business faced slackening demand and other difficulties by the spring and summer of 1895. This decline can be illustrated by an incident that occurred in Asbury Park, New Jersey. For the summer season, six kinetoscopes with *The Corbett-Courtney Fight* were set up inside a building rented from the Asbury Park Amusement Company. This was the second year of kinetoscope exhibitions at the summer resort, but the success of the first season was not repeated. As a local newspaper explained in early August, "The kinetoscopes, although they give wonderful entertainment for those who like that sort of thing, do not seem to have been profitable thus far this summer."[63] Unable to pay the rent, the kinetoscope manager and some cohorts crept into the hall and started to remove the machines under cover of darkness. A night watchman discovered them, called the police, and warned the landlord. In the confrontation that followed the manager was outnumbered and was forced to abandon the attempted removal. The next day a distress warrant was issued turning the machines over to the local amusement company until proper payment was received.[64]

The manager's inability to meet expenses was perhaps not so unusual and symbolizes the wider problems facing kinetoscope entrepreneurs. Overseas, Maguire & Baucus faced serious competition. In London, Robert Paul was making duplicate kinetoscopes and his own original films. Paul's activities, moreover, were safe from legal action, since Edison had failed to take out foreign patents on his motion picture inventions. This severely reduced Edison's potential foreign sales. Domestic imitators also appeared, reducing sales and the price tag within the American market.[65] When the Lathams began to exhibit their crude eidoloscope projector in April 1895, this, too, deflected interest away from Edison's machine.[66] With the urging of Raff & Gammon, Edison began to experiment with projection. According to Terry Ramsaye, Edison sent experimenter Charles Kayser to the Kinetoscope Company's offices in New York, where he pursued these investigations. Nothing useful, however, materialized from these efforts.[67]

One serious effort to bolster the kinetoscope business was made in the spring of 1895: the kinetophone. A phonograph was placed inside a kinetoscope cabinet with rubber ear tubes protruding from a convenient location for the spectator. Recordings and films could then be loosely synchronized. The long-standing promise of a novelty that combined recorded sound and moving image was to be fulfilled. It was hoped that this would not only revive its novelty value but increase the range of available subjects. The local *Orange Chronicle* announced:

An unidentified phonograph parlor boasts a kinetoscope. By 1895 business had slowed.

With this combination wonderful possibilities are opened out before the public. An entire change will be made in the character of the objects and scenes taken by the kinetograph. Previously only scenes were taken in which there was a great variety of action, the element of sound being entirely disregarded. Hence such scenes as prize fights, skirt dances, clog dances and the like were taken. With the new combination, the eye and ear being both concerned, the range of subjects is largely increased, and many things that could not have been effectively taken under the principle of the kinetograph alone will now become available.[68]

This breakthrough was premature and no doubt forced by the onset of declining sales. Efforts to kinetograph and phonograph scenes simultaneously had been made, but without success (*Dickson Experimental Sound Film* and various illustrations testify to these attempts). Thus no new diversity of subject matter resulted. Rather, appropriate music was added to preexisting subjects. The Kinetoscope Company announced, for example, that the kinetophone in its offices was featuring *Finale of 1st Act of Hoyt's "Milk White Flag"*: "as the band is

Looking at and listening to the kinetophone: a pastime that never became popular.

seen coming into view in the Kinetoscope, the music bursts forth with a volume and melody that is truly wonderful and realistic."[69]

The kinetophone was initially marketed in mid April for a cost of $400, $50 more than the kinetoscope. At least one was at Frank Harrison's parlor in Atlanta, Georgia, in May. Although he claimed that they increased business threefold, Harrison had established a special arrangement with the Kinetoscope Company for the upcoming Cotton States' Exhibition, and his endorsement is hardly credible.[70] Within a short time, the price of the kinetoscope fell to $250 and the price of the kinetophone with it to $300. Demand for the kinetophone proved slight, only forty-five being sold.[71] Dickson's untimely departure from Edison must have harmed whatever slight prospects of success the kinetophone enterprise may have initially enjoyed.

As the kinetoscope and kinetophone novelties faded, Raff & Gammon faced fewer and fewer orders for its goods. Seeking to reverse this decline, they assigned employee Alfred Clark the responsibility for making new films. Clark, who looked after film production and sales for the Kinetoscope Company, tried to reorient and broaden the Edison Company's approach to production. That August and September he produced a group of motion picture subjects at the West Orange laboratory that were not tied to popular theatrical amusement, including several historical scenes based on well-known paintings or other iconography.[72] *Joan of Arc*, which showed the French heroine being burned at the stake, and *Rescue of Capt. John Smith by Pocahontas* represented larger-than-life, semi-mythical moments. These films, which were taken outdoors, involved elaborate historical costuming. Only one survives, *The Execution of Mary, Queen of Scots*.[73] Its tableau-like, static quality highlights the moment when the ax descends, cutting off the queen's head. In fact, this effect was achieved using stop-action substitution: the filming was halted, while the actor (Robert Thomae in female garb) was replaced by a dummy; then the action and filming resumed. The camera stop was later cleaned up by splicing the two takes together so that the film appeared to consist of one continuous shot. Other scenes, including *Indian Scalping Scene* and *Frontier Scene* (later retitled *Lynching Scene*), indicate a curious penchant for the gore of murders and executions, subjects regularly depicted in wax at the Eden Musee's Chamber of Horrors.

Demand for Clark's innovative films was modest. In the following months, the handful of new productions returned to tried and true subjects: *Umbrella Dance* and *Acrobatic Dance*, featuring the Leigh Sisters; *Cyclone Dance* and *Fan Dance*, with the Spanish dancer Lola Yberri. The declining kinetoscope business most affected those people who depended on it for their livelihood and resulted in career changes. James White and Charles Webster sold their kinetoscopes in August, with White returning to the phonograph business.[74] Clark likewise sought more secure employment in the phonograph field, with Webster joining Raff & Gammon to take his place.[75] Late in the year, Raff & Gammon went for months without selling a single machine, and the partners considered selling or even liquidating their business. Then they came across a screen machine that was far superior to the Lathams'. It soon returned them to the forefront of motion picture activity in the United States and in the process revived film production at the Edison Manufacturing Company.

4 Cinema, a Screen Novelty: 1895–1897

The first commercially viable motion picture projector in the United States was known as "Edison's Vitascope." This successful adaptation of Edison's films to the magic lantern not only resuscitated kinetographic activities but brought Edwin Porter into the emerging film industry. Unlike the Lathams' eidoloscope, the vitascope had an intermittent action that halted each frame of film in front of the light source, providing the basis for modern motion picture projection. Despite its name, this "screen machine" was the invention of two young men from Washington, D.C., C. Francis Jenkins and Thomas Armat, who originally called it the "phantoscope." The two inventors quarreled, however, shortly after their first commercial exhibitions at the Cotton States' Exposition in Atlanta, Georgia, during October 1895. Acting independently, each tried to maximize his claims and commercial opportunities. In early December, Armat arranged an exhibition for Frank Gammon in the basement of his Washington office.[1]

Raff & Gammon, discouraged over the future prospects of the peep-hole kinetoscope business, greeted Armat's machine like drowning men who had unexpectedly discovered a life raft. Nonetheless, a month of contract negotiations and delays followed the basement demonstration as they sought Edison's blessing for their use of Armat's machine. Edison's control over film production made the inventor's cooperation essential. William Gilmore, vice-president and general manager of the Edison Manufacturing Company, played a key role in these discussions. A hard-headed, if overly aggressive, businessman, Gilmore had little difficulty interpreting the Edison Company's discouraging balance sheets. The Wizard's motion picture business was doing poorly and was increasingly threatened by independent motion picture activities both domestically and overseas. Gilmore was familiar with the Lathams' eidoloscope and possibly with the work of W. K. L. Dickson on the mutoscope (a peep-hole device similar to the kinetoscope). Rumors of the Lumières' film projections in Paris may also have reached the Orange office. Since Edison's half-hearted efforts to develop a projecting machine had been unsuccessful, the phantoscope posed yet another threat. But it was one that the Edison organization now had the opportunity to coopt. Gilmore was therefore predisposed to work with Raff & Gammon. Such a move would not only bolster sales of hardware and film, but maintain a determining presence in the industry and give company machinists valuable experience with the workings of the new apparatus.

At a meeting on January 15, 1896, Raff & Gammon completed negotiations with Edison and Gilmore. The Edison Company would manufacture the vitascope projectors from Armat's prototype and provide the necessary films. Delighted, Raff & Gammon sent a telegram to Armat announcing that the terms of this agreement were "exceedingly favorable for all. Contract will be signed and forwarded tomorrow."[2] This contract gave Raff & Gammon "the sole and exclusive right to manufacture and rent or lease or otherwise handle (as may be agreed upon in this contract or by future agreement) in any and all countries of the world the aforesaid machine or device called the 'Phantoscope.' "[3] In exchange Armat received 25 percent of the gross receipts gained by the sale of exclusive exhibition rights for territories and 50 percent of the gross receipts (minus the cost of manufacture) for other areas of the business, particularly the rental of machines. Raff & Gammon gained the exclusive exhibition rights for New York City, while Armat retained the rights for Washington, D.C.[4] No mention was made of Jenkins in the contract: Armat represented himself as sole owner of the invention.[5]

In mid February 1896 the Armat machine was renamed the "vitascope," perhaps once Raff & Gammon belatedly recognized that Jenkins, who had coined the term "phantoscope," could disrupt their plans and become a potential competitor.[6] Certainly Jenkins had become an active threat by early March.[7] Under such circumstances, extensive publicity was considered essential to the vitascope's success. Raff suggested that "in order to secure the largest profit in the shortest time, it is necessary that we attach Mr. Edison's name in some prominent capacity to this new machine. While Mr. Edison has no desire to pose as the inventor of the machine, yet we think we can arrange with him for the use of his name and the name of his manufactory to such an extent as may be necessary to the best results. We should of course not misrepresent the facts to any inquirer, but we think we can use Mr. Edison's name in such a manner as to keep within the actual truth, and yet get the benefit of his prestige."[8] It was an arrangement that benefited everyone concerned. Raff & Gammon garnered the necessary publicity for their enterprise, while Edison kept his name before the public. Since people simply assumed that Edison must be the inventor, use of his name enhanced the legend of the Wizard's fecund genius. This "biographical legend" was another product of the inventor's "genius." Edison's image as a mythic hero allowed him to acquire financing and manipulate legal and commercial situations in unprecedented ways.[9]

The desire to exploit Edison's name was compelling from a business viewpoint.[10] As Raff & Gammon told Armat: "No matter how good a machine should be invented by another, and no matter how satisfactory or superior the results of such a machine invented by another might be, yet, we find the great majority of parties who are interested, and who desire to invest in such a machine, have been waiting for the Edison machine, and would never be satisfied with anything else, but would hold off until they found what Edison could accomplish."[11] Armat acquiesced. To the public and prospective investors, the vitascope was to be the machine Edison had promised them when the Lathams unveiled their imperfect eidoloscope a year before.[12]

By late March the threat posed by rival machines from abroad had created an urgent situation. As Raff reported: "It becomes more apparent every day that we must take some action with regard to the European machine which is now being exhibited in London, and which we hear is creating a sensation there. If the reports we receive are true, the machine must be quite satisfactory, and we hear of the parties exhibiting the interior of a railway station, with train coming in and going, parties moving about, etc., etc. We also hear of other interesting subjects which they show."[13] The term "chestnuts," which referred to jokes or amusements that had lost their entertainment value through overuse, could be applied to the Edison subjects left over from the peep-show kinetoscope.[14] These would not compete effectively with novel scenes taken abroad. The need for fresh, new subjects had to be added to Raff & Gammon's list of concerns.

For the vitascope group, it was extremely important that their machine enter the entertainment field first. The significance of such a "first" was not one of legal/historical priority. Rather, with projected moving pictures regarded as a novelty, it was essential to be perceived as the first by the amusement-going public, a phenomenon that involved orchestrating one's publicity very carefully. Although moving pictures had been projected in some form within the United States for almost a year, no effort had quite achieved the necessary threshold of recognition. The organization that first achieved this goal would be hailed as the original and its competitors considered imitations. Thus, when Raff & Gammon heard that amusement enterprises in New York were contemplating the addition of the European machine to their shows, the entrepreneurs preempted these plans by quickly preparing for the vitascope at Koster & Bial's Music Hall, continuing a relationship with its management that had earlier provided the kinetograph with a bevy of star performers.

The Edison tie-in was maximally exploited. Several weeks before the Koster & Bial's debut, a press screening was arranged. Although the inventor had a private look at the vitascope on March 27th, this preview was staged at the Orange laboratory on April 3d. The "Wizard" not only attended but played the role of inventor assigned to him. In successive headlines, the *New York Journal* announced:

LIFELESS SKIRT DANCERS.

In Gauzy Silks They Smirk and
Pirouette at Wizard Edi-
son's Command.

Perfect Reproduction of Noted Feminine Figures and Their
Every Movement.

SUCCESSFUL TEST OF THE VITASCOPE.

By it the Great Inventor Will Give Representations of Theatrical Performances with Faces and Forms
In Every Detail.[15]

Like the hypnotist Svengali in *Trilby*, the inventor seemed to command every move and gesture produced by the dancing girls on the screen. They were his creations, objects of desire that he could manipulate to gratify the "bald head row" of older men who sat in the front of the orchestra, the better to eye the Music Hall's female performers. Other newspapers contributed additional accolades to the inventor's genius. Such ballyhoo created anticipation and diverted attention away from the work of the Lumières, the Lathams, and Jenkins.

The Vitascope's Premiere

Raff & Gammon moved quickly forward with their first public exhibitions of Edison's vitascope. They sent Charles Webster to Europe with one screen machine on April 22d.[16] Only when he arrived in London and saw the Lumière cinématographe did it become fully evident that the vitascope would face insurmountable difficulties in foreign markets. To replace their absent employee, Raff & Gammon hired James White, Webster's former associate, in early April for $75 a month.[17] Arrangements were soon finalized for the Koster & Bial's premiere on April 23d. The fee was set at $800 per week, providing Raff & Gammon with a bountiful income during the ensuing four-month run.[18] Thomas Armat acted as moving picture operator (i.e., projectionist) for the first week, after which he was succeeded by his brother. White assumed overall responsibility for the Koster & Bial's showings.[19] Edwin Porter, while still in the navy, may have helped in his off hours to install the electrical system that ran the machine.[20] The opening night response was ecstatic. "WONDERFUL IS THE VI-TASCOPE," proclaimed the *New York Herald*.[21] *The New York Times* enthused:

The new thing at Koster and Bial's last night was Edison's vitascope, exhibited for the first time. The ingenious inventor's latest toy is a projection of his kinetoscope

Koster & Bial's Music Hall at the time of the vitascope premiere.

figures in stereopticon fashion, upon a white screen in a darkened hall. In the centre of the balcony of the big music hall is a curious object, which looks from below like the double turret of a big monitor. In the front of each half of it are two oblong holes. The turret is neatly covered with the blue velvet brocade which is the favorite decorative material of this house.[22]

The *New York Daily News* added:

On the stage, when it was ready to show the invention a big drop curtain was lowered. It had a huge picture frame painted in the center with its enclosed space

Interior of Koster & Bial's. The vitascopes are hidden within their turret-shaped housing in the second mezzanine.

white. The band struck up a lively air and from overhead could be heard a whirring noise that lasted for a few moments; then there flashed upon the screen the life-size figures of two dancing girls, who tripped and pirouetted and whirled an umbrella before them. The representation was realistic to a degree. The most trifling movements could be followed as accurately as if the dancers had been stepping before the audience in proper person. Even the waving undulations of their hair were plainly distinguishable. The gay coloring of the costumes was also effectively shown.[23]

Six films were shown, but only five were made by the Edison Company. The first to be projected was a tinted print of *Umbrella Dance*, with the Leigh sisters. Subsequent views included *Walton and Slavin* (a burlesque boxing bout from 1492), *Finale of 1st Act of Hoyt's "Milk White Flag"* (not listed on the programme), and *The Monroe Doctrine*. Made in preparation for the vitascope debut, *The Monroe Doctrine* offered a new type of subject matter, a comic allegory that was overtly political. Referring to a recent incident in South America, this political cartoon on film showed John Bull and Venezuela fighting. "Uncle Sam appears, separates the combatants and knocks John Bull down."[24] The patriotic audience was delighted and "cheers rang through the house, while somebody cried, 'Hurrah for Edison.' "[25] The final film was of a skirt or ser-

Rough Sea at Dover (1895), taken by R. W. Paul in England. The hit of opening night.

pentine dance. Although the dancer was blonde, none of the reviews indicate she was Annabelle.

Opening night critics were most impressed by the second film to be shown, *Rough Sea at Dover*, of a wave crashing on a shore. This subject, the only one not shot in the Black Maria and the only "actuality," had been sent to Edison by his English competitor Robert Paul:

> The whirr of the machine brought to view a heaving mass of foam-crested water. Far out in the dim perspective one could see a diminutive roller start. It came down the stage, apparently, increasing in volume, and throwing up little jets of snow-white foam, rolling faster and faster, and hugging the old sea wall, until it burst and flung its shredded masses far into the air. The thing was altogether so realistic and the reproduction so absolutely accurate, that it fairly astounded the beholder. It was the closest copy of nature any work of man has ever yet achieved.[26]

Paul's film pointed out the possibilities of aggressively assaulting or confronting spectators with the image rather than simply using the camera for passive display. Patrons in the front rows were disconcerted and inclined to leave their seats as the wave crashed on the beach and seemed about to flood the theater.

Like Edison's peep-hole kinetoscope, the vitascope used a twenty-second loop of film spliced end to end and threaded on a bank of rollers. Raff & Gammon suggested that "a subject can be shown for ten or fifteen minutes if desired, although four or five minutes is better."[27] When, as in most cases, one projector was used, a two-minute wait occurred between films. At Koster & Bial's in New York, however, projectors worked in tandem and there was no wait. Even under these conditions, films still had to be projected for at least two minutes while a new film was threaded on to the other projector. Thus, each subject was necessarily shown at least six times. As one journalist remarked, "The scene is repeated several times, then the click click stops, and the screen is blank. A moment's interval, then a pretty blonde serpentine dancer appeared."[28] Although two projectors eliminated waiting periods between films, they did not reduce the number of times a film was projected at one showing, nor were they customarily used to juxtapose related images. There was little room or concern with editorial techniques in these first exhibitions. Films were usually shown separately and treated as discrete images. In Cleveland, for example, waits were eliminated by alternating films with musical selections by the Chicago Marine Band.[29] Later, some exhibitors filled these interludes by showing "dissolving views" (i.e., lantern slides).

The absence of complex cinematic meanings has sometimes been seen as proof of the screen's primitive qualities, but this simplicity effectively emphasized the novel contribution of moving pictures to screen practice. Audiences, while accustomed to projected photographs that were static and to projected nonphotographic images that could move, were tremendously impressed by animated photographs projected on the screen. "Life-like" motion in conjunction with "life-like photography" and a "life-size" image provided an unprecedented level of verisimilitude. And yet cinema's novelty period involved much more than the exhibition of lifelike images. The rapid diversification of subject matter and the increasingly frequent sequencing of images constantly renewed cinema's ability to intrigue and entertain even regular vaudeville customers during the 1896–97 theatrical season. The first year of projected motion pictures, often called cinema's "novelty period," was one of multiple, successive innovations and not, as some have suggested, an undifferentiated period that simply relied on the new sensation of projected motion pictures.

Producing Films for the Vitascope

Revisionist historians have argued that Edison film production was grossly inadequate.[30] Certainly there were problems, and yet during the summer of 1896, the Edison Company remained the only American-based enterprise that produced a significant number of film subjects. With the Vitascope enterprise preparing for its debut, Raff & Gammon desperately needed new pictures. The recent inactivity was apparent when Frank Gammon took several performers to West Orange on March 24th and found the Black Maria in a dilapidated state. He "had great difficulty in persuading them to go in to the theatre dressed in their thin silk costumes, as it was just like going out into an open field in mid-winter."[31] The raised roof could not be closed to protect the dancers during preparations and rehearsals. Several actors, hearing of these conditions, refused to be filmed. Moreover, the studio was inconveniently located for those working in New York City. Although the vitascope's success and the onset of warm weather improved matters, the rate of production at the Black Maria would never again approach the levels of 1894.

At first the production practices of the kinetoscope era continued. Edison personnel, notably cameraman William Heise, coordinated filming activities, with Raff & Gammon acting as producers. Increasingly, however, James White must have been designated to fill this role. A new collaborative relationship

The May Irwin Kiss. The most popular Edison film of 1896.

was emerging, though this relationship was not yet in effect when *The May Irwin Kiss* was filmed in mid April. While William Gilmore stood by, Heise kinetographed this brief, fifteen-second scene showing the culminating moment of a popular musical farce, *The Widow Jones*. It was made at the behest of the *New York World*, which devoted a full page to "May Irwin and John Rice Posed Before Edison's Kinetoscope—Result: 42 Feet of Kiss in 600 Pictures."[32] The promise of extensive publicity may have induced the two stars to travel to West Orange. The scene was carefully rehearsed and then photographed only once. Perhaps intended for the premiere, the picture was not shown until the second week of the vitascope's New York run. It was immediately hailed as a hit. Several weeks later, Cissy Fitzgerald, the girl with a famous wink, likewise performed her specialty for the Black Maria kinetograph.[33]

Coinciding roughly with the filming of *Cissy Fitzgerald*, the Edison Company completed construction of a new, portable camera. "Our portable taking machine is now completed," Raff wrote Peter Kiefaber on May 6th, "and if tomorrow is a clear day, we expect to secure some every-day street scenes in New York."[34] Yet it was not until May 12th that Heise set to work photographing actualities similar to those that the Lumières were showing in Europe and the Lathams in the United States.

The first Edison street scene was *Herald Square*. The newspaper after which the square was named reported: "The photographers settled down to work at two o'clock yesterday afternoon, when the square was crowded with cable cars, carriages and vehicles of all sorts, while now and then an 'L' train would thunder by. They chose a window on the lower end of the square, where they were within full view of the Herald Building, and at the same time took in Broadway and Sixth avenue for a radius of several blocks."[35] When the film was shown at Koster & Bial's Music Hall, spectators may have had the pleasure of seeing the exterior of the building inside of which they were sitting (assuming, of course, the theater was within camera range). In this play with space, outside became inside—a somewhat disconcerting experience, greatly heightened by the lifelike quality of the image. *Central Park*, showing the main fountain, was taken on the same day. Within a week *Elevated Railway, 23rd Street, New York* was also shot. Six weeks before the American debut of the Lumière cinématographe, Edison actualities were being shown in American theaters. For New Yorkers at least, these were "local views" of locations they encountered in the course of their everyday lives.

Scenes of everyday life significantly diversified the kinds of subject matter that Edison was making. For almost the first time, Edison subjects had no direct ties to popular amusements or leisure activities. Nor did these images have anything to do with either sex or violence. Instead, they recalled the types of photographic images that were routinely presented in lantern shows to religious groups and cultural elites. Of course, these images were familiar, even banal, in terms of subject matter and framing. They would have elicited little reaction— except that they moved. "The Twenty-third street station of the New York elevated was a stirring picture, wherein the train came rushing along at top speed, so realistically as to give those in the front seat a genuine start," remarked one critic.[36] Not only were these films much cheaper and easier to make than those previously taken in the Black Maria, they proved to be at least as popular with audiences.

In late May or early June, Heise and possibly James White took their new portable camera on an ambitious trip to Niagara Falls, long a privileged subject for artists and photographers. Although the Lathams had already made films of this tourist attraction, that did not prevent the vitascope group from treading in their footsteps. The Edison crew shot the falls from a dozen different camera positions using 150-foot film lengths. The results were somewhat disappointing, and only four scenes were finally distributed. The most enthusiasm centered on *Niagara Falls, Gorge*:

> a panoramic picture obtained from the rear end of a swiftly moving train on the Niagara Gorge railway, and one that has never been equalled for completeness of

detail and general effects. In this view the stone bluffs of the gorge, the telegraph poles, rail fences and the waters of the great river go rushing by with incredible swiftness, but yet plain enough for one to note everything in a general way, just as though seated in an observation car. The Whirlpool rapids are in sight one moment and lost to view the next, their whirling eddies and foam-flecked waves sparkling in the sun's rays, forming a very beautiful picture.[37]

Placing the kinetograph on a train was inspired by *Grand Canal, Venice*, a Lumière film in which the camera was situated on a gondola. (A print of this subject had been surreptitiously acquired by Albert Bial in Europe and turned over to Raff & Gammon in late March.) The results helped to establish an association between actuality subjects and a mobile camera that would be strengthened over the next several years. Two other scenes were of the American Falls from the east and west sides. In Boston, these were shown consecutively — the juxtaposition suggesting at least a rough spatial relationship between shots.

The new, portable camera also enabled Edison and Vitascope Company personnel to reconceptualize their filming of performers and sporting activities. Instead of bringing entertainers to the Black Maria, a kinetograph team could now go to amusement locales and capture subjects in their customary surroundings. This new opportunity was exploited in late June while Heise and a Vitascope representative were active in Brooklyn. On June 23d they shot *The Suburban Handicap*, showing Navarre winning the horse race at Gravesend Race Track.[38] *Parade of Bicyclists at Brooklyn, New York* was made four days later. Although participating bicycle clubs still had exclusively male memberships, the bicycle fad had become a way for men and women to socialize together casually.[39] Additional films focused on another site where the codes of social contact had loosened — Coney Island.[40] Taken at Bergen Beach, where the vitascope was being shown, these included *Shooting the Chutes*, *Ferris Wheel*, and *Streets of Cairo*. The Ferris wheel, almost 200 feet high, was a local landmark that provided visitors with a magnificent view of Jamaica Bay. *Streets of Cairo* (later retitled *Camel Parade*) was taken at the Egyptian Encampment.[41] Paul Boyton's "Shooting the Chutes" was a hit amusement ride (imitations were springing up everywhere). Two shots of this attraction were taken, "the first showing the shoot down the incline and the other the dash into the water."[42] These separate views may have been part of a single 150-foot subject, making it one of the first instances in which the producer assumed an editorial role, juxtaposing two spatially and narratively related shots.

Recognizable, if highly specialized and ephemeral, "genres" were established and/or developed during the summer months. *The Haymakers at Work* and *Carpenter Shop* recalled the first workplace films. One subject continued the filming of burlesque boxing matches by depicting a male-female duo. It combined sexual suggestiveness with violence in a single motion picture subject for perhaps the first time. *Bathing Scene at Coney Island*, taken in early July, not

Shooting the Chutes, showing the descent down the incline.

only continued the documentation of that popular amusement resort but provided a variation on the popular *Rough Sea at Dover*. All these films were taken with either 50-foot or 150-foot rolls of films. While 50-foot sections of the longer films were often sold, these remained the two standard lengths.

The Lumière influence on Edison production was wide-ranging and strong. Short comedies, reminiscent of the Lumières' *The Gardener and the Bad Boy*, (*L'Arroseur arrosé*) appeared. These included two variations on that prototypical gag in which the bad boy plays a trick on the gardener and gets spanked for his prank. In one Edison version the gardener was male, in the other female. In *The Lone Fisherman* a man casts for fish from a plank cantilevered off a bridge. His friends come and upend the plank, sending him into the water. Street scenes continued to abound (*Street Sprinkling and Trolley Cars, Deadman's Curve*, etc.). Lumière military scenes, which had taken the vaudeville circuit by storm, were quickly and consciously emulated. Heise and his crew photographed *Firing of Cannon at Peekskill by the Battery of Artillery* and at least one other subject at the New York State militia encampment by the end of July.[43]

The production of news film was spurred by the screening of the Lumières' attention-gathering *The Coronation of the Czar of Russia* at Keith's Union

Square Theater in late July. A month later the kinetograph team took *The Arrival of Li Hung Chang*, depicting the Chinese viceroy at New York's Waldorf Hotel. Li Hung Chang having arrived on the S.S. *St. Louis*, they also filmed several scenes related to the ship's departure (*Steamer "St. Louis" Leaving Dock, Baggage Wagons*). Moreover, the quotidian *Ferryboat Leaving Dock, New York* suddenly enjoyed a second life as the timely news subject *Steamer "Rosedale"* when that ferryboat sank in New York harbor.

The paucity of surviving films makes it difficult to characterize the results of all this activity in very great detail. Terry Ramsaye reports that the portable camera was placed on the roof of the new Raff & Gammon headquarters at 43 West Twenty-eighth Street. At this makeshift studio, performers and small fictional scenes could be conveniently photographed. Although dancers may have dropped by the midtown location to appear in scenes such as *Couchee Dance*, it is not known which scenes were shot there. Candidates include *Irish Way of Discussing Politics*, a reworking of *A Bar Room Scene*, and *Watermelon Contest*, shot against a plain background and showing two "darkies" guzzling watermelon. So too are three scenes of cartoonist J. Stuart Blackton performing lightning sketches, each taken in mid August with 150-foot loads of film. The most successful, *Edison Drawn by "World" Artist*, was often used to conclude a film program on "Edison's Vitascope."[44] When shown at Proctor's Pleasure Palace in mid September, it was declared "the most curious and interesting of the new views" and was kept on the bill in subsequent weeks.[45]

A number of Edison films were designed to elicit political reactions from theatrical audiences; the theater was then a site where partisan political opinions could be expressed through shouts of approval or disdain. That *The Monroe Doctrine* was one of the first films made for projection was not, therefore, fortuitous but a calculated attempt to find favor with Koster & Bial's patrons. Its success was followed by *Blackton Sketches, No. 2 (Political Cartoon)*, in which Blackton rapidly draws likenesses of President Grover Cleveland and candidate William McKinley (rather than his Democratic-Populist rival, William Jennings Bryan). The film begins with a patriotic image of America's commander in chief, then moves on to suggest McKinley as his likely successor. With pro-Republican audiences predominating at the Music Hall and other New York theaters, the response must have been electric. *Irish Way of Discussing Politics*, in which two Irishmen discuss politics over a glass of whiskey, lampooned the Tammany Hall crowd. Likewise, in *Pat and the Populist*, the bricklayer Pat is approached by a Populist office seeker and "shows his displeasure by dropping bricks on the politician."[46] Not all images were resolutely anti-Democratic. When Bryan was campaigning in New Jersey, Heise took a news/political film—*Bryan Train Scene at Orange*. Yet such a film was not necessarily meant to be pro-Bryan. Rather it could be exhibited ambiguously and elicit both cheers and catcalls, generating an informal opinion poll from an audience.

Throughout the summer and into September, Edison retained a virtual monopoly over the production of American subjects. Lumière films were not taken in the United States until September and not shown here until November. W. K. L. Dickson and the American Mutoscope Company photographed American subjects during the summer, but did not begin their exhibitions until September. Only the Lathams competed in this regard; but their limited number of subjects, inferior projection system, and internal squabbles hindered their effectiveness. With the Edison Manufacturing Company producing an adequate number of new subjects during the summer and early fall, the problems encountered by the Vitascope group occurred principally in other areas.

The Vitascope Group

In a number of crucial respects, the Vitascope organization was typical of film companies as the novelty era began. It manufactured its own equipment and made its own films. In addition, it retained control over exhibition as well as production. In fact, the four leading rivals had incompatible technologies—the vitascope, eidoloscope, cinématographe, and biograph—and thus each company had to operate in a self-contained fashion. However, the Vitascope organization was uniquely burdened by a loose affiliation of individuals and groups, whose interests often did not coincide. At the center was the Vitascope Company, incorporated by Norman Raff, Frank Gammon, and James White (as the third member of the board of directors, with one share of voting stock) in early May.[47] (This was one indication that the stockholders of Raff & Gammon's old Kinetoscope Company were not to play a part in this new enterprise. In fact, it was soon liquidated.) Raff & Gammon acted as a clearing house for the entrepreneurs, who had bought exclusive exhibition rights at considerable expense. As these owners were desperately trying to recoup their investment, they had little sympathy for, or understanding of, the company's problems. Raff & Gammon, moreover, did not control the Edison Company's activities and could only plead for quick action. Thomas Armat and T. Cushing Daniel, with their patent applications, were yet another affiliated organization. Although the coordination of these groups sometimes presented awkward problems, vitascopes served as the principal purveyors of moving pictures in the United States throughout the summer of 1896. The number of available machines, the comparative variety of films, the Edison name, and the hard work of the states rights owners assured a rapid, nationwide diffusion of this novelty.

Raff & Gammon's principal commercial strategies worked on two levels. First, they sought an immediate windfall by selling off the exclusive exhibition rights for specific territories (known as "states rights") to entrepreneurs, with publicity generating interest and raising the price. The sale of rights then bound these investors to the Vitascope enterprise. As Raff explained to Armat, "After our territory is once sold, we need have but little fear about future business. After the purchasers of territory have their money invested, nothing will prevent their going ahead, and they will co-operate with us against all possible competitors and against untoward conditions and circumstances."[48] Thus, long-term profits would be achieved by renting machines to the states rights owners for $25 to $50 per month and through the sale of films.

States rights was considered a particularly effective way to deal with the threat presented by competing machines. This long-term strategy, however, was premised on controlling the exhibition field through Armat's patents—on which applications had been made but not yet granted. At best, such aid was in the distant future. During the interim, the goodwill and cooperation of the Edison Manufacturing Company were crucial.

In a long, often redundant, letter to William Gilmore, Raff outlined those areas in which Edison Company assistance was sought: good workmanship in the manufacture of vitascopes, prompt service, easy access to a camera and operator, exclusive ownership of films that they financed (so continuing an already established arrangement), and a promise not to sabotage the Vitascope Company by marketing a competing machine.[49] Raff's deference of tone, his frequent reference to moral obligations, and his eagerness to share profits with Edison and Gilmore all underscore the Edison Company's crucial role. This obeisance must also be placed against the background of Edison's business dealings in the closely related phonograph industry where he had just (February 1896) forced the North American Phonograph Company into bankruptcy. The investors in the old company plus the various owners of states rights either folded or, as in the case of the Columbia Phonograph Company, lost the special benefits of their investment. Edison then replaced the defunct company with the new National Phonograph Company under his immediate ownership. As Robert Conot has remarked, such activities gave Edison the worst image in this associated industry.[50] Moreover, if Edison chose to assume direct control over the phonograph, why not over moving pictures? Raff & Gammon never explicitly asked this unsettling question in their correspondence, but it was obviously on their minds. Nor did they apparently receive any reassurances. For the moment, Edison cooperated because Raff & Gammon were extremely useful and served both his reputation and pocketbook. In the longer term, Edison self-interest would prevail.

In the end, vitascope rights were sold for virtually every state outside the Deep South. Owners of these states rights came from a variety of backgrounds. Many had exhibited the phonograph and/or kinetoscope and were anxious to continue a profitable association with Edison. Others had a background in electricity and were ready to continue their Edison association but move into the entertainment field. A few had either theatrical experience or been otherwise

William E. Gilmore.

active in the field of popular amusement. A significant number of the Vitascope entrepreneurs had no relevant background, however, but were small business-men hoping to strike it rich on Edison's latest novelty.

States rights owners had several ways to make a return on their investment. Typically, owners acted as exhibitors, providing a selection of films, a projector, and an operator. This package was commonly offered to theaters for a fee, usually several hundred dollars a week. In other circumstances, these exhibitors either rented a vacant storefront and kept any profit above expenses or pre-sented films at a hall and divided receipts with its manager. A few leased subterritories to amusement managers who wanted complete control over their shows. Several historians have offered useful overviews of the experiences of these "pioneers," but focusing on the activities of one group of individual en-trepreneurs is another way to understand the opportunities and difficulties faced

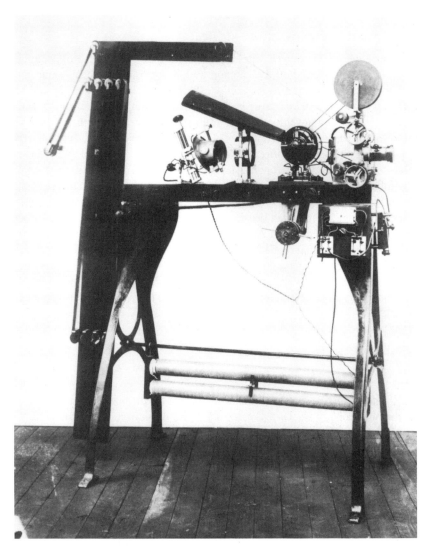

One of the first vitascopes.

by these early exhibitors.[51] What were their backgrounds? How did they come to acquire the rights? How did they try to exhibit this novelty and what kind of reception did it enjoy? The next section will address these questions by looking at the group based in Connellsville, Pennsylvania, with which Edwin Porter was deeply involved.

The Connellsville Entrepreneurs
Acquire States Rights

As production on the vitascopes moved forward at the Edison works during March and April 1896, Raff & Gammon were busy promoting the machine and selling territories to entrepreneurs. Edwin Porter, then approaching the end of his naval enlistment and pursuing his interest in electricity, came in contact with this latest of Edison novelties. Perhaps seeing a demonstration in their office, he informed his friend Charles H. Balsley of this new invention and the commercial opportunities it seemed to offer. On March 30th, Raff & Gammon received two pieces of correspondence from Balsley asking about territory in Pennsylvania. The following day they responded, explaining that Pennsylvania had been sold and offering other territories.[52] Balsley's father, J. R. Balsley, and several other Connellsville merchants then decided to purchase the rights to the neighboring state of Ohio. A telegram on April 4th, however, informed the potential investors that Raff & Gammon had agreed to hold Ohio for "an interested party," Allen F. Rieser, who ultimately bought the rights.[53] Members of the consortium then traveled to New York and purchased the rights to Indiana for $4,000 — an acquisition soon announced in the Connellsville newspaper[54] (see document no. 2).

DOCUMENT No. 2

THEY OWN INDIANA

The exclusive rights for the state of Indiana for the new Edison marvel, the Vitascope, have been secured by J. R. Balsley, R. S. Paine, F. E. Markell and Cyrus Echard of Connellsville.

The vitascope is an improved kinetoscope by which moving life size figures of men, women and animals are thrown on a screen by means of bright lights and powerful lenses. A feature of the new machine which astonished the gentlemen named who recently witnessed a private exhibition in New York, for it is not ready for public view, was the almost entire absence of vibration in the pictures as they appear on the screens. The machine is said to be the wonder of the age. A vast money making field is opened up by it, as exhibitions can be given in theatres and halls, reproducing scenes and views with all the realism of life.

The four Connellsville men struck while the iron was hot, and secured the exclusive territory of Indiana. No one can exhibit the machine in Indiana without first securing the right from the gentlemen who control that state. They will probably sell the rights by counties and cities and will doubtlessly realize handsomely on their investment. The vitascopes will not be sold, but remain the exclusive property of their maker, Raff and Gammon of New York, who will lease the machines for a nominal sum monthly. This will enable purchasers of states rights to control their states absolutely. Messrs. Balsley, Paine, Markell and Echard have not disposed of any territory yet, but will place it on the market in a short time. There are great possibilities for the vitascope. The rights to Allegheny county, Pennsylvania were sold to Harry Davis by the syndicate for only $1,000 less than they paid [for] the rights for the whole state. There's money in it.

SOURCE: *Connellsville Courier*, April 17, 1896.

These four Connellsville men were, like many other Vitascope investors, small-time businessmen ready to risk hard-earned capital on the latest invention of America's folk hero Thomas Edison. J. R. Balsley had left the lumber business and retired to part-time inventing. In February 1896 he was selling a thread cutter and holder, "an ingenious little invention that everyone using spool thread will be glad to have."[55] Although Richard S. Paine, shoe store owner, had nearly gone bankrupt in the late 1870s and 1880s, he was prospering in the mid 1890s and owned stock in the local electric company.[56] He was ready to take another chance on the man who predicted the world would soon be run on electricity. F. E. Markell, a pharmacist with several drug stores, was prospering and six years later would become the first president of the Citizens National Bank.[57]

Appropriately, but coincidentally, a stereopticon lecture was given in Connellsville a few days after the group purchased their vitascope rights. As they were about to become entertainers, the local entrepreneurs surely attended. The program, called "The Secret of Success," illustrated the life and work of Thomas A. Edison and ended "in a grand concert by Edison's latest, loudest and best, the Auditorium Phonograph."[58] Certainly these small businessmen dreamed of succeeding on Edison's coattails.

Enthusiastic about their purchase, Paine and J. R. Balsley were ready to risk still more capital. Interest centered on several territories, particularly California, a state for which Raff & Gammon received many inquiries, including one from Thomas L. Tally, who operated a kinetoscope parlor in Los Angeles.[59] Having purchased Indiana, Balsley obtained a brief option on California. A telegram sent April 11th told him: "Price twenty-five hundred. Can hold till Monday no longer."[60] If Balsley was unwilling to invest additional capital, Paine seemed ready to buy the California rights alone. "We will be glad to let you have California if we can do so," Raff & Gammon wrote Paine on April 18th. "There are several parties after it and we have rather obliged ourselves to Mr. Balsley although we shall ask him to decide the matter today." A handwritten note at the bottom informed Paine that "Mr. B has taken Cala." and offered him other states as alternative investments,[61] but Paine was satisfied and the Connellsville entrepreneurs stopped there.

Balsley sent the down payment of $833.34 for California to Raff & Gammon on April 20th. It was acknowledged on the eve of the vitascope's premiere at Koster & Bial's:

> You will find the receipt is in a little different form from the one given you on Indiana but we think you will agree with us that it is more specific and better for you. Since giving you a receipt on Indiana, we have adopted this regular form for all future sales of state rights as we want all receipts to be as uniform as possible.
>
> We are promised fifteen machines on the 7th of May, and of that number we have put you down for one for Indiana. If we possibly can, we will save another for your use in California, but we cannot promise positively. However, we are confident that we can deliver you one or more machines before the first of June and possibly considerably before that date.
>
> We note your remarks as to securing the Vitascope view of Coke Works, and we will probably make our arrangements to secure the same at the proper time. We thank you for your kind offer, and shall be glad to take advantage of it when the time comes.
>
> The Edison Works have secured their first lot of what we call "clear stock" for films and we are counting on producing splendid results by use of the same. In fact, the outlook is very bright and we think the machine is going to create a sensation at our exhibit tomorrow night at Koster & Bial's.
>
> Very truly yours,
Raff & Gammon
>
> We enclose letters referring to California rights. Please return letters to us.[62]

As Raff had written to Edison's general manager, William Gilmore, the new contract made it clear that Raff & Gammon could not be held responsible for rival machines. It was this increased burden of risk that the Connellsville group found unsettling—particularly once amusement notices announced the imminent arrival of competing machines. Four days before the vitascope's debut, ads for Proctor's vaudeville organization reassured its patrons: "Coming very Soon to Proctor's Pleasure Palace—the Photo-Electric Sensation that all London is now flocking to see—The Kintographe."[63] Writing Raff & Gammon on April 25th, Paine worried about rival organizations and quoted a negative review of the vitascope's performance. Raff, with the Koster & Bial's premiere just behind them, countered with a reassuring and self-assured letter that offered to refund their money and sell the territory to another interested party. He dismissed potential competitors, insisting that "Information which we have received satisfies us, beyond doubt, that we not only have a superior machine but that we have such tremendous advantages over any similar machine that is now in existence or could be constructed hereafter, that there is but little [to] fear in way of competition." As Raff later added, "There never was a good, big-paying thing which has not been imitated."[64] Another letter of assurance was sent to J. R. Balsley two days later.[65] The Connellsville group wavered but decided to stay in.

The vitascopes being manufactured at the Edison works were not ready as quickly or in the quantity that Raff & Gammon had hoped for and led others to expect. On May 9th the completion of the first three or four machines was still a week away. Owning the rights to Illinois, Massachusetts, New Jersey, and Maryland, P. W. Kiefaber was given two of these for an exhibition at Keith's in Boston. He insisted, with considerable justice, that two machines were necessary for a good show: certainly two were being used at Koster & Bial's.[66] The Boston premiere came on May 18th. On that same day, Paine and Charles Balsley also left Connellsville for New York to pick up their equipment and to learn how to operate the machine.[67] Within a week, other openings had occurred in Hartford, Philadelphia, and Atlantic City. The Connellsville consortium were forced to delay their debut, for they took their first projector to San Francisco, the cultural capital of the West, rather than to Indiana as originally planned. Gustave Walter had agreed to show the vitascope at his vaudeville theaters in San Francisco and Los Angeles. Porter remained behind in the New York area, waiting for his enlistment to run out.

Rival Novelties:
The San Francisco Opening of the Vitascope

As Balsley and Paine were about to arrive in San Francisco, William Randolph Hearst's *San Francisco Examiner* devoted a full-page article to the Lathams' eidoloscope with its "Instantaneous Photographs of a Bull Fight." The article, profusely illustrated with line drawings based on film frames, informed readers that the bullfight "was arranged by Mr. Gray Latham for the purpose of taking Eidoloscope pictures now being thrown on the screen" in New York.[68] No equivalent coverage was devoted to the Connellsville entrepreneurs either before or during the vitascope's San Francisco debut. Its effect was to partially undermine perceptions of the vitascope as the original screen machine. Twelve days before the eidoloscope article, the *Examiner* had run a story on the vita-scope, but it focused on the predictions of Charles Frohman, one of the theater's leading impresarios, who sent road companies to San Francisco from his New York base. The vitascope, he believed, was "destined to substitute for stock scenery actual representations of scenes with all the human agents necessary, sitting, standing, moving about, chatting, in short, fulfilling the ordinary every-day duties and occupations of the ordinary individual."[69]

Once in San Francisco, Balsley and Paine encountered difficulties in setting up their machine—a common problem for the first vitascope showmen. In this instance, their lens gave too large an image for the distance from the Orpheum Theater's balcony to the screen and a new one had to be purchased from George Beck for $55.[70] There may have been further complications as well, for the *New York Clipper* listed the vitascope's West Coast debut as June 1st,[71] though it was not until June 7th that the local press, after many promises that the vitascope was coming, could announce the novelty's opening for the following day. In doing so the papers presented moving pictures as one of several novelties competing for the attention of vaudeville patrons. The *Examiner* informed its readers:

> The Orpheum announces a strong string of novelties. Of these great stress is laid on the engagement of Edison's latest wonder, the vitascope. This wonderful machine, if it may be termed a machine, has been the sensation of the East for the past two months and has been secured by the Orpheum circuit at great expense, it is claimed. "Wizard" Edison has named the latest product of his remarkable genius the "vitascope" from the fact that it projects apparently living figures and scenes upon a screen or canvas before the audience. Another novelty announced is of a troop of Marimba players from Guatemala.[72]

Still other novelties like the dancer Papinta were holdovers from the previous week.

Balsley and Paine opened the vitascope on June 8th, projecting five films with an intermission of two minutes between each film.[73] Perhaps because San Franciscans had read such glowing reports of the machine's feats in New York, the novelty proved a mild disappointment. While declaring that the vitascope was "well worth seeing," the *San Francisco Chronicle* only gave it a brief two-line review.[74] Since most of the films had been or were available at Bacigalupi's Kinetoscope, Phonograph and Graphophone Arcade at 940 Market Street, the critic felt "the selection of pictures had not been the most interesting so far."[75] San Francisco clearly expected to see the best films available. Other newspapers did not feel compelled to comment on the machine's debut at any length. The *Examiner* reviewed the Orpheum's program only in passing. "The presentation of fine pictures by Edison's vitascope will be a pleasing feature of this week's program," it reported.[76] To most it did not seem to be the "Sensation of the 19th Century," as Walter suggested in his ads.

The blasé attitude that greeted the vitascope has to be understood in the context of rival novelties, particularly rival forms of screen entertainment, which converged on the West Coast during the spring of 1896. Alexander Black's picture play *Miss Jerry*, a "novel form of entertainment," had its debut in San Francisco on June 8th at the Metropolitan Temple.[77] It presented an entire play on the screen using a large number of photographic slides that followed each other in rapid succession. Dialogue for the various roles was mimicked by a narrator, in this case Miss Carrie Louis Ray. The *San Francisco Call* described the picture play as "a most exquisite treat."[78] A lengthy review in the *Chronicle* was more impressed with Black's picture play than with the vitascope, to which it was indirectly compared. "The photographer has done his work so admirably that it only needs a bit of imagination to make it all seem real, even to a nineteenth century audience. The idea is from Edison, but the love story is so daintily and prettily told and so full of humor withal that it would be a captious audience that was not pleased."[79]

The illustrated song was yet another novelty. Lantern slides, projected onto the screen, offered a visual interpretation of the song's lyrics as they were performed. On the day the *Examiner* announced the vitascope opening, it ran a half-page article on the illustrated song calling it "the Latest Novelty of the Stage." After excerpting a song and describing the slides that accompanied it, the newspaper concluded with a brief quote from the proprietor of a vaudeville theater:

> The day for ordinary ballad and sentimental singers on the vaudeville stage is rapidly passing away. Recent advancements along electrical and photographic lines have added so much to the pictorial advantages of the stage that the camera has been brought into active requisition in this particular. During the past few months pictures instinct with life, vivid with color and clear in characterization have been associated with a song so that while the verbal description and harmony come from the throat of a singer, the eye is satisfied with the mimic portrayal of the scene. Not only does the song thus presented gain at least 50% in the estimation of the audience, but it also enhances the salary of the singer in equal proportions.[80]

At approximately the same time, moving pictures, the picture play, and the illustrated song jointly refocused the public's attention on the entertainment possibilities of projected images. Only during the course of time was it to become apparent that moving pictures were to dominate the commercial screen to the virtual exclusion of other formats.

The greatest photographic novelty during much of 1896 was not moving pictures but the x-ray. This newest discovery received constant newspaper attention between March and June, with Hearst's *Examiner* featuring stories in which bullets embedded in Civil War veterans were discovered after thirty years of unsuccessful probing. Edison himself received considerable front-page attention as he worked on "perfecting the x-ray."[81] Americans were even more impressed by the ability to reveal something no one could see than to capture and "reproduce" what could be seen every day. The vitascope, viewed as the logical extension of Edison's peep-show machine, was outclassed by this impressive scientific discovery.

Despite initial disappointment with the vitascope, the *Chronicle* reassured its readers that subjects closer to their initial expectations were to be offered during the second week: "There are many films coming and the sensational one of the Wave, which has been so much written about, will be worth seeing especially."[82] The following week *Sea Waves* (i.e., *Rough Sea at Dover*) was heartily praised: "Those who have not seen the wave should see it. It is such a thrilling realistic thing that the people in the front seats involuntarily get up afraid they will get wet."[83] Since James Corbett was about to fight Tom Sharkey in San Francisco on June 24th and since Corbett was the home-town hero, *The Corbett-Courtney Fight* was added during the second week as a timely subject with hometown appeal.[84] Boxing fans were able to examine their hero's technique with a life-sized image, and Corbett dropped by to watch himself fight.[85] This coup, however, had to compete with the x-ray. On June 18th, the world boxing champion "submitted to the most searching of all photographic processes for the first time in his life and when it was over Corbett said that the experience had been both interesting and enjoyable." After examining various parts of his skeletal structure, Dr. Phillip Jones made an x-ray of his right forearm—a process that took twenty minutes. The result was then published in the *Examiner*.[86] Once again the vitascope had been preempted by a rival novelty.

The vitascope's third week at the San Francisco Orpheum featured *The May Irwin Kiss*, which finally reached the West Coast two months after it had been taken. While the response at the Orpheum was not reported in the press, the film was given an enthusiastic reception almost everywhere. According to one review, "the hit of the show, so far as marvellous lifelike effects and mirthful results with the audience go, was the amusing, much-prepared-for kiss—the May Irwin kiss from the 'The Widow Jones.' In this the effect was wonderful. The figures were so large that one could almost tell by the motion of the lips what Rice was saying to May Irwin and what Miss Irwin was replying. The facial expression was the widow to a T, and ditto Rice, and the real scene itself never excited more amusement than did its vitascopic presentment, and that is saying much."[87] In the middle of the third week, it was announced that "new views have arrived for the vitascope and this week will be the last one that the wonderful work of this machine will be seen."[88] The vitascope's run ended on a happier note than it began.

The vitascope was a "novelty"—a term applied to oddities, scientific innovations, ingenious demonstrations of strength and coordination, or displays of beauty and sexual allure with which vaudeville managers tried to amuse their patrons. Shortly after the vitascope's departure, the *Chronicle* remarked, "Vaudeville novelties are appearing in such rapid succession at the Orpheum that it would seem as if the supply must soon be exhausted. Papinta, the vitascope, Black Patti, Blondi and Macart's dog and monkey circus have all appeared in rapid succession and now comes another novelty in the way of Herr Techow's cat show, which by reason of its oddity ought to attract attention."[89]

The importance attached to novelty was particularly significant at this moment in American history. The United States was coming out of a major depression (the one that had bankrupted Porter's tailoring establishment), spurred on by the introduction or successful commercialization of a wide array of products and technical improvements: the automobile, the phonograph, electric trollies, and electric light—as well as cinema. This emphasis on novelty celebrated innovation and the changes transforming American life. Vaudeville confronted this transformation and often expressed it by emphasizing not only novelty but variety. As one journalist explained,

> To those interested in the secret of the great success of vaudeville upon the stage, it must be obvious that the clue to the whole thing lies in the nervousness and desire for change that is characteristic of nineteenth century mankind. Sitting in a theatre for three hours at a stretch, looking at the same faces, hearing the same voices and waiting for the denouement of a play, is apt to become monotonous to most people. They prefer a constant change, both of actors and acts, and this they get in a theatre where vaudeville is presented.[90]

From this perspective, the vitascope was *the* vaudeville novelty of the nineteenth century, for cinema was to transform America's cultural life in the years ahead.

Despite its need for novelty, popular culture also relied on familiarity. Late nineteenth-century theater, particularly as it was performed in America's small towns, brought back the same plays year after year to be seen by the same audiences. In vaudeville successful acts were held over so that the spectators could see them again the following week and experience the same pleasure. Vaudeville acts themselves were rigorously defined by categories that were repeated over the course of time in an almost ritualistic formula.[91] The obverse side of variety was repetition. The acceptance of repetition can be seen in the projection strategies adopted for the vitascope, with its film loops, and in the exhibition of both new films and holdovers. It is also evident in the redundancy of subject matter that immediately followed the first films. A myriad of "kiss films" followed the Irwin/Rice novelty. Given the cultural framework in which they were shown, it would be too easy for the cultural historian simply to dismiss these imitations as derivative. Vaudeville and the vitascope valorized tradition and continuity as well as change and innovation.

Porter Joins His Connellsville Friends in Los Angeles

Porter was discharged from the navy on June 18, 1896.[92] Later he testified that his career as a motion picture operator began in June 1896, and he may have stayed briefly in New York City to operate the vitascope at Koster & Bial's.[93] At the end of the month, he was in Connellsville, but he soon "went to California to operate the first Vitascope machine exhibited there."[94] If the former naval electrician left Connellsville quickly, he could have reached Los Angeles just as the vitascope was opening at Walter's Orpheum Theater in that town.

After a week's hiatus while Balsley and Paine moved from San Francisco to Los Angeles, the Connellsville entrepreneurs resumed their film projections on

July 6th. The *Los Angeles Times* heralded the machine's imminent debut with enthusiasm greatly exceeding that of the San Francisco press:

> The vitascope is coming to town. It is safe to predict that when it is set up at the Orpheum and set a-going, it will cause a sensation as the city has not known for many a long day.
>
> The vitascope is Edison's latest and most shining triumph. It is a miracle of human ingenuity in the realms of electricity and photography. It is on the same order as the kinetoscope, with the difference that in the kinetoscope one person at a time peeps into a hole and sees a tiny moving picture while in the vitascope, the picture is thrown upon a screen and shines forth . . . life-size, so that the entire audience can see the picture at once. The vitascope was first publicly exhibited only about two months and a half ago.
>
> The things shown by the vitascope are of many different kinds. A bit of Broadway in New York is very striking. The audience can see the swarms of people hurrying along, the jostle of horses, carriages, trucks, etc., in the street, all moving and changing and so real one almost expects to hear the street noises. A snowstorm, a skirt dance and a sea beach scene are some of the things shown. The life-like reality of the pictures is said to be startling. In San Francisco and elsewhere, one of the most popular scenes was a reproduction of the famous bit of acting in which May Irwin is kissed by John C. Rush [sic]. The changing expression of their faces, their graceful movements, the play of hand and lip and eye, are said to be faultlessly reproduced.[95]

The *Los Angeles Herald* felt it necessary to describe the novelty and how it worked, suggesting that Balsley, Porter, and Paine were the first to project moving pictures in the city that was to become the center of the film industry.[96] Once again there were competing novelties. *Miss Jerry* opened on the same night, this time at the Los Angeles Theater. Inquiries for tickets to Black's picture play indicated that "any novelty will take well in Los Angeles."[97] Another "novelty" reported in a *Herald* article ran opposite the paper's blurb on the vitascope: a French scientist claimed that thoughts could be photographed.[98] In this context, projected moving pictures did not seem quite so "marvelous." Anything, however extraordinary, now seemed possible. As the *Los Angeles Herald* was to comment on the vitascope, "Can genius go farther? We have been made to hear the voices of our distant friends and now we are enabled to see them move and act. Truly it is enough to make Franklin turn in his grave with wonder of it and yet, so attuned are we to the marvelous in this day and age of the world that we are scarcely decently surprised."[99] Nevertheless, the vitascope headlined one of the Los Angeles Orpheum's best programs in its three-year history.

News of the vitascope's arrival had packed the 1,311-seat Orpheum.[100]

> Every seat in the theatre was sold ere the box office window was opened for the evening's business. Standing room only was sold, and the purchasers of it formed a fresco around the entire circuit of the walls from box to box in addition to which some hundreds who applied for seats left, to come again later in the week. So much for what

was expected of the management, and it can be said but in a few words, the immense audience was not disappointed.[101]

The *Los Angeles Times* provided readers with a clear description of the show's format, the protracted screening of the "endless band" of film and the interruptions that occurred while these films were changed:

> The theatre was darkened until it was as black as mid-night. Suddenly a strange whirling sound was heard. Upon a huge white sheet flashed forth the figure of Anna Belle Sun [*sic*], whirling through the mazes of the serpentine dance. She swayed and nodded and tripped it lightly, the filmy draperies rising and falling and floating this way and that, all reproduced with startling reality, and the whole without a break except that now and then one could see swift electric sparks. Then the picture changed from the grey of a photograph to the color of life and next came the fairy-like butterfly dance. Then, without warning, darkness and the roar of applause that shook the theatre; and knew no pause till the next picture was flashed on the screen. This was long, lanky Uncle Sam who was defending Venezuela from fat little John Bull, and forcing the bully to his knees. Next came a representation of Herald Square in New York with streetcars and vans moving up and down, then Cissy Fitzgerald's dance and last of all a representation of the way May Irwin and John C. Rice kiss. Their smiles and glances and expressive gestures and the final joyous, overpowering, luscious osculation was repeated again and again, while the audience fairly shrieked and howled approval. The vitascope is a wonder, a marvel, an outstanding example of human ingenuity, and it had an instantaneous success on this, its first exhibition in Los Angeles. A representation of Niagara Falls is now on its way [from the] East, where it was first exhibited only two weeks ago, and this will be added to the bill on Thursday evening.[102]

The opening night performance suffered from minor deficiencies, which were probably owing to inadequate power, since the Connellsville group was running its machine on batteries, an uncommon practice at the time.[103] The vitascope, unlike traditional magic lanterns or the Lumières' cinématographe, ran on electricity, which often created problems. The first vitascope exhibition in Worcester, Massachusetts, for example, was marred by electrical problems. As a result, "Cissy Fitzgerald's wink was invisible owing to insufficient speed and light, and the boxers struck with dreamy sluggishness."[104] Here Porter's background as an electrician and telegraph operator provided expertise that could correct the problem. After one critic returned to the Orpheum, he was able to report that the vitascope "scored even a greater success than on its first appearance, for there had been time to remedy all slight defects caused by the hurry in which it had been necessary to set it up."[105]

The vitascope program at the Los Angeles Orpheum was changed in midweek and reviewed the following day:

> The announced change of programme of the Vitascope at the Orpheum last evening was well received, though some of the plates [*sic*] which had just arrived from New

York were broken in transit and could not be presented. The view of the whirlpool
rapids of Niagara Falls was a most realistic picture showing the rushing, roaring,
whirling foam-beaten waves and splashing spray true to nature. Another view presented was that of the Atlantic Ocean beaches rolling up to the shore in the vivid way
peculiar to the breakers of that turbulent pond. The picture of the female equilibrist
doing a difficult act was appreciated, but the sympathies of the audience went out to
the two performers in the kissing scene, and the graceful woman who danced in
skirts.[106]

During the first week of moving pictures, at least 20,000 attended the Orpheum,
while as many as 10,000 others were turned away. This encouraged the theater
to plan a Sunday matinee.[107] Suggesting the city's enthusiasm for the novelty,
a *Los Angeles Times* reporter speculated on the vitascope's future. "Wonderful
as it is, the vitascope is as yet surely in its infancy," he wrote. "It is hard to say
to what proportions it may yet be used in the amusement field with the development of color photography and the combining together of the vitascope and
the phonograph, both of which are probably not so very far away."[108]

The most successful films shown on the vitascope were those that isolated a
specific characteristic or representational technique to achieve a novel effect: the
close view of a kiss, the forward-moving wave assaulting the spectator, even
scenes of busy street life "vitascopically" presented inside a theater (breaking
down the separation of indoors and outside). These images were non-narrative,
pure examples of what Tom Gunning has called the cinema of attractions.[109]
The May Irwin Kiss, for example, was excerpted from a musical, but audiences
did not need to know the story or the situation in which the kiss occurred to
enjoy the film. In fact, as we shall see, the film could easily be attributed to an
entirely different play. With the couple placed against a black background, the
kiss was isolated in time and space. Even to the extent that the kiss had a
beginning, middle, and end, this progression was undermined by the scene's
rapid repetition during the exhibition process. Films like the wave were particularly effective when shown as loops, the repetition of the scene mirroring the
repetitive nature of the ocean waves breaking on the shore. In the process these
loops drained the image of temporal and spatial meaning.

During the second week, Porter and his associates offered another set of
films. "The vitascope came last and the audience applauded every one of the
magic pictures rapturously," reported the *Los Angeles Times*. "The new pictures
were Amy Fuller's famous skirt dance, ending with a hand spring; a picture of
three pickaninnies, patting, juba and cutting up capers, and a weird Oriental
thing, 'the India short stick dance' in which half a dozen natives figure."[110]
Ending their Orpheum engagement after the second week, Balsley, Paine, and
Porter had toured the California vaudeville circuit as it then existed. Their options were limited by their dependency on electricity. As another vitascope exhibitor wrote Raff & Gammon, "To enable us to make money we have to so
remodel the machine that it can be worked with hand power when we cannot

Tally's Phonograph Parlor on Spring Street in the summer of 1896.

get electricity and construct new travelling cases so that the breakable parts can be safely and rapidly packed for shipment. I believe there is plenty of business to be obtained in the country once we are prepared to work it, but it is worse than folly undertaking it in our small towns until we are ready to meet a three night's business and then pack up and get out to the next town."[111] Visits to California's smaller cities and towns were neither practical nor financially justified, particularly in the middle of the summer.

After the Orpheum run was over, R. S. Paine returned to Connellsville, leaving Porter and Charles Balsley to manage the machine. The two friends stayed in Los Angeles and reopened their show at Tally's Phonograph and Kinetoscope Parlor. Tally, who was eventually to become a major West Coast exhibitor and an important executive at First National during the late 1910s and early 1920s, promoted his move into cinema with blurbs in the local papers:

> Tonight at Tally's Phonograph Parlor, 311 South Spring St, for the first time in Los Angeles, the great Corbett and Courtney prize fight will be reproduced upon a great screen through the medium of this great and marvelous invention. The men will be seen on the stage, life size, and every movement made by them in this great fight will be reproduced as seen in actual life.
>
> New York and London went wild over this wonderful invention and last week the Orpheum was packed to the walls with people anxious to see the wizard's greatest wonder, the vitascope. Come tonight and see the great Corbett fight. From this date on the fight will be exhibited every evening.[112]

Tally's Phonograph Parlor as it would appear in 1898. Thomas Tally appears behind the kinetoscopes.

The next day it was reported that "great crowds flocked to see the greatest wonder of the world, the vitascope, Mr. Edison's latest invention. Performances will be given regularly every afternoon and evening and the programme will be changed daily."[113] Admission was ten cents. After a successful run, the Connellsville entrepreneurs sold their rights for California to Tally and returned home. Tally's machine was destroyed by fire shortly thereafter—or so, at least, it was said—perhaps as a way for Tally to free himself from any royalty requirements.[114]

The Vitascope Faces Increasing Difficulties

Purchasers of vitascope exhibition rights faced steadily rising competition throughout the United States. Gray Latham surreptitiously examined the vitascope at Koster & Bial's and added an intermittent mechanism to the eidoloscope.[115] The Lathams' improved machine then opened at Hammerstein's Olympia in New York City on May 11th and had a successful five-week run. Subjects included *Whirlpool Rapids, Niagara Falls*; *Fifth Avenue, Easter Sunday Morning*; and *Bullfight*. All "were excellently produced and won storms of applause."[116] During July they were "hot competition" for the vitascope in

Atlantic City.[117] By mid May, C. Francis Jenkins had found a backer for his phantoscope—the Columbia Phonograph Company—and was beginning to market his machine.

The Lumière cinématographe premiered at Keith's Union Square Theater in New York City on June 29th. It was soon evident that "nothing has ever before taken so strong and lasting a hold on the patrons of this house as the cinematographe."[118] Although only three cinématographes were in the United States by mid August, thereafter Lumière machines arrived from France with greater rapidity. Since the cinématographe did not use an endless band, people had to return to the theater to see the same subject again. Relying less on the mere novelty of lifelike images than vitascope entrepreneurs, the cinématographe operators were beginning to explore ways to sequence films as early as July, when they showed various scenes of the coronation of the czar and czarina in Russia.[119] A less well known competitor was the kineopticon, which played at Tony Pastor's theater in New York City from late August to mid October. Among its European views were *Paris Street Scenes*, *Boxing Kangaroo*, and *Persimmons Winning the Derby*.[120] The vitascope's "monopoly" was challenged by an array of competing machines, many of which were technically equal or superior to Armat's projector. The only way for Raff & Gammon to block them effectively was through court action based on patent infringement. This was impossible since Armat's disputed patent applications had not yet been granted. Competition was a reality that the vitascope entrepreneurs had to endure from the outset.

Despite Raff & Gammon's best efforts, vitascope entrepreneurs faced many difficulties.[121] In Canada the Hollands could only give vitascope exhibitions in Toronto and Montreal, where the cinématographe and eidoloscope provided direct competition.[122] The Edison Manufacturing Company was also producing films of poor technical quality. The raw stock used during the summer was still manufactured by the Blair company. Although Blair's semi-opaque product had been excellent, the emulsion peeled away from the base of its clear stock.[123] "I enclose you a sample of a film 'Herald Square', that has been run through just seven times. We have at least six films (amongst them 'Annabelle') in as bad a condition," wrote an unhappy Andrew Holland. "It simply means that we are working for the [Edison] Laboratory—paying our own expenses and doing the chores for nothing. For my part, I would rather pitch the business to the dogs than to continue it under such circumstances."[124] The films' photographic quality was often poor, too. Edmund McLoughlin, who owned the rights to most of New York State, was unhappy that his films were "very gray" and discussed the problem with people at the Eastman Kodak Company. They suggested that Edison was not using the proper emulsion.[125] In mid September the Edison Manufacturing Company shifted its purchases of film stock from the Blair Camera Company to Eastman, inaugurating a customer-supplier relationship that was to endure for many years.[126] The Edison Company, however, was not as quick to correct these failings as Raff & Gammon and the vitascope owners would have liked. The problem of quality was further exacerbated by the high price of Edison goods, which gave the inventor a healthy profit but left the states rights owners unremunerated.

Owners of exhibition rights felt their efforts were often compromised by a shortage of new, exciting subjects—particularly when competing against rival machines. Kiefaber demanded "good humorous, startling features to keep public turned towards us; with good live scenes we can keep our people attached to us."[127] This need was underscored when the Lumière organization arrived with a large backlog of subjects, all unfamiliar to American audiences. Keith manager E. F. Albee only reinforced this impression when he complained to Kiefaber that "the last two weeks, the films have been of such poor material and the views so indistinct that instead of the machine being a feature, it has become a farce."[128] But subject matter and technical excellence were not the only factors at play. Since Keith had acquired the American rights to the Lumière machine for the first months of its exhibition in the United States, it was inevitable that the cinématographe supplanted Kiefaber's vitascope at Keith's Boston and Philadelphia theaters.

Although the cinématographe, with its technically superior system and diversity of unfamiliar scenes, was the exhibition service of choice for most vaudeville managers, sufficient demand existed to support several moving picture companies. During the summer those few Lumière machines in the United States were located in the large cities, where diverse venues could accommodate the offerings of rival exhibition services. Although the Lumières harmed the vitascope entrepreneurs, this competition was far from fatal in its results. Yet competition quickly moved beyond a vitascope/cinématographe rivalry, as is well illustrated by the Connellsville group's experiences in Indiana.

Indiana

While R. S. Paine, Charles Balsley, and Edwin Porter were busy exhibiting the vitascope in California, Cyrus Echard and J. R. Balsley traveled with the vitascope through Indiana, showing films in Terre Haute and perhaps a few other towns. One problem with Indiana was the absence of large cities. Even Indianapolis (1900 population: 169,164) was oriented toward three-night stands by traveling road companies. The vitascope was ill suited for such conditions, and the entrepreneurs must quickly have realized that it would be impossible to recoup their $4,000 investment. By mid July they had returned to Connellsville disappointed.[129]

A week-long engagement for the Connellsville group came about by chance. Harry Clark, A. F. Rieser's business manager, was in Ohio when he ran off with his employer's vitascope. He had booked an exhibition at the Empire Theater in Indianapolis when Rieser's electrician caught up with him. Rieser later reported:

"They [the theater's management] have now arranged with the owner of Indiana to run a vitascope there next week."[130] Charles Balsley and perhaps Edwin Porter, having returned from California, were enlisted to show their films for this October engagement.[131]

In a city like Indianapolis, with more than one amusement house, theater managers routinely competed with each other by booking the season's most popular novelty—projected motion pictures. Thus, a phantoscope opened at English's Theater on September 14, 1896, simultaneously with the state fair. It was shown before each performance and between acts of the spectacular melodrama *Sinbad*. "Its pictures will create the same sensation here that they have been doing in New York and elsewhere," predicted the *Indianapolis Sentinel*.[132] Two days later, the evening was enthusiastically reviewed by the *Indianapolis Journal*:

"SINBAD'S" SUCCESS AT ENGLISH'S

The life and color of "Sinbad" as presented by David Henderson's famous American Extravaganza Company has a never-failing charm. It opened its week at English's last night and was welcomed by a large audience. . . .

One feature of the performance altogether new to the audience and which took the people by storm was the phantoscope. The pictures were shown between the acts. The first was the "May Irwin Kiss" a burlesque on the famous Nethersole kiss in "Carmen." It was received with roars of laughter and is certainly very lifelike. The second picture shown was a surf scene at Dover, England, and this was remarkably well done. The bathers, the waves of the ocean, the spray and all were shown to life. The Corbett-Courtney fight was the last picture and it was as if the audience sat at the ringside. A Sioux ghost dance, the great national bicycle parade, "Trilby" burlesque and other pictures will be shown in addition to those seen last night.[133]

The phantoscope had become a particularly serious problem for Raff & Gammon and their affiliates because the Columbia Phonograph Company had gained access to the Vitascope Company's exclusive subjects. Under these circumstances the use of Edison's name and the well-publicized New York opening were the vitascope's only unique assets, and even their value was beginning to fade.

To the public, the vitascope was becoming just one of several screen machines. When the *Indianapolis Journal* announced the forthcoming appearance of the Connellsville group at the Empire Theater in conjunction with Charles Frohman's road show of *The Lost Paradise*, it was not certain what to call the machine. It reported that "a dozen or more pariscopic views will be shown between acts. The pariscope, vitascope, cinematograph or whatever one calls it is the reigning sensation of the year in theatricals."[134] The *Sentinel* also referred to the films as "parascopic illustrations"—perhaps the name that Clark had intended to use for his runaway show. Immediately below the *Sentinel*'s announcement of the vitascope, an ebullient notice informed readers that the

eidoloscope, "the most costly feature ever introduced in any theatrical performance," would soon be in town, too. "The bullfight which it reproduces in the
last act of Rosabel Morrison's production 'Carmen' is the most startling incident
ever seen under similar conditions."[135] Having been preempted by the phantoscope and outpromoted by the eidoloscope, Porter and Balsley might have expected a cool reception. The reviews of their opening night, however, suggest
that Porter's skills as a mechanic, electrician, and showman were already apparent (see document no. 3). The *Sentinel* felt that "to say it was a success is
putting it lightly."[136] When *The Lost Paradise* left the Empire at midweek, the
vitascope remained behind, teaming up with the American Vaudeville Company
for another week. The vitascope was again declared a success and a crowd
pleaser, all the more so since some of the pictures were hand tinted.[137] Despite
the good press, however, attendance was light.[138]

Document No. 3

Empire—"The Lost Paradise"

It would have been hard to choose a better time for the revival of
[Henry Churchill] DeMille's melodrama "The Lost Paradise," than the
present. The play teems with doctrines, speeches and situations bearing on
the alleged conflict between capital and labor, the action centering on a
strike in a great factory. A love story is woven in and a tale of sacrifice
for love, but the parts of the story in touch with the spirit of industrial
unrest abroad these days are those that elicit the most applause. . . .

Between the second and third acts is given an exhibition of the original
Edison's vitascope. The same series of pictures is given that received such
favorable mention on its presentation at Koster & Bial's, in New York.
The vitascope is an expansion of the kinetoscope. If the name had not
been already appropriated, "living pictures" would be the most applicable
term. The best of the series are Loie Fuller's dance, the view of Herald
Square, in New York, in which the spectator sees cable cars, trucks and
carriages passing, people crossing the street and moving along the side-
walks, and the view of the breakwater at Southampton which shows the
waves rolling in one after another and breaking on the beach. The illusion
is almost perfect, the effect being produced by so rapid a succession of
pictures that before the eye has dropped the one the next has appeared,
producing an effect of motion. Six in all are given, including the amusing
long-drawn-out "Widow Jones kiss." "The Lost Paradise" will appear
only to-day and to-morrow, with the usual matinees, a new company
coming the last half of the week.

SOURCE: *Indianapolis Journal*, October 20, 1896.

Soon after the Indianapolis showing, the Connellsville group disposed of their rights to Indiana—presumably at considerable loss.[139] Balsley returned to Connellsville, where he spent the rest of his life, at one point serving as a cameraman/stringer for Pathé News, but otherwise pursuing a career outside the film industry.[140] Porter, however, went back to New York: he was in the moving picture industry to stay.

The Connellsville group's fate was similar to that of many fellow states rights owners. Lacking experience in the amusement field, they may have been wise to quit before losing more money and while their exhibition rights could be sold for anything at all. During their short career, they had exhibited in a diversity of circumstances. Vaudeville theaters had provided their most lucrative engagements, but the entrepreneurs had also exhibited in an arcade and between the acts of a play. J. R. Balsley and Echard may also have exhibited the vitascope at a summer park in Terre Haute. This diversity of venues well illustrates the eclectic nature of pre-nickelodeon motion picture exhibition as it was to be practiced for the following ten years.

The Vitascope Company in Disarray

By October 1896 Raff & Gammon were locked in a competitive battle that pitted their machine against many others. In New York City during the week of October 12th, moving pictures peaked as a vaudeville novelty, appearing in at least six theaters.[141] Raff & Gammon were exhibiting Edison's vitascope at Proctor's Pleasure Palace and Proctor's 23rd Street Theater, where it had been since September 14th. Lumière's cinématographe was into the fourth month of its run at Keith's Union Square Theater, where it still headed the bill. The kineopticon continued to show American and English views at Pastor's Theater. The centograph was "shown to good effect" at Miner's Bowery Theater.[142] The American Mutoscope Company, having premiered its biograph in Pittsburgh on September 14th, had its "official" New York debut at Hammerstein's Olympia on October 12th. Although advertised modestly, the biograph was greeted with enthusiasm.[143]

The American Mutoscope Company, often referred to as the Biograph Company because of its projector, had developed its own motion picture system using 70mm gauge film that had four times more surface area per frame than the Edison standard. The Biograph founders, moreover, had created a camera that worked on a different mechanical principle than the kinetograph. Film was moved forward by a friction feed and the camera created its registration sprockets as each frame was exposed; these frames were, therefore, not equally spaced along the film. Although the final results were effectively the same, Biograph was able to take out patent applications on its system. The biograph was best suited for protracted stays at first-class houses and produced a higher-quality image than either the vitascope or Lumière cinématographe. With the resulting demand for its exhibition service, Biograph quickly expanded its operations and dominated vaudeville exhibition for the rest of the 1890s.

The Vitascope Company and its affiliated entrepreneurs were adversely affected, of course, by the competition offered by the Lumière Agency and the Biograph Company. The vitascope's rapid decline and eventual demise, however, was largely owing to the rapid proliferation of independent manufacturers that sold films and projectors to small-time exhibitors without restricting the territory in which they could operate. Charles Webster left Raff & Gammon and formed the International Film Company with Edmund Kuhn. By October they were manufacturing and selling a variety of film subjects.[144] Their initial film offerings were dupes of Edison subjects that had not been copyrighted. These dupes, therefore, were perfectly legal. By September the Columbia Phonograph Company was not only selling phantoscopes but offering films for sale at half the Edison price.[145] Many of these films were also dupes of Edison subjects.

While the biograph was designed for the top end of the market, other manufacturers developed projecting machines that were better adapted to the needs of traveling exhibitors than the vitascope. By September, Edward H. Amet's magniscope was for sale.[146] A few months later, the International Film Company began to sell its projectograph. Both machines possessed features that made them superior to the vitascope and were sold outright without territorial restriction or royalty requirement.[147] A dozen other projectors were on the market by the end of 1896.[148]

The Edison Manufacturing Company Breaks Away from Raff & Gammon

While the Edison Company's commitment to Raff & Gammon was never very deep, commercial pressures soon encouraged the inventor and Gilmore to distance their enterprise from the Vitascope Company. In late September, Edison began to sell films through Maguire & Baucus for 25 percent less than states rights owners could buy them from the Vitascope Company.[149] One infuriated exhibitor asked Raff & Gammon, "Is this monopoly on the Vitascope broken up or what is the matter?"[150] The only honest answer to this question would have been in the affirmative. Edison thus played one of its old kinetoscope agents off against the other. Yet as Raff & Gammon feared almost from the outset, it was never likely that Edison executives would have permitted their operations to remain under the Vitascope Company's umbrella for very long.

The Edison Company had built only seventy-three of eighty vitascopes called for in its contract with Raff & Gammon.[151] By October 1896 additional orders were extremely unlikely: the vitascope was an outmoded machine. The Edison Company, therefore, chose to ignore Armat's pending patents and constructed its own screen machine. Called both the "projectoscope" and the "projecting kinetoscope," it was first tested at the Bijou Theater in Harrisburg, Pennsylvania. Its November 30th premiere was lauded on the front page of the *Harrisburg Telegraph*:

> After ... a select audience of city and county officials, newspaper men and their friends ... witnessed a test exhibition of "Wizard" Edison's projectoscope (improved vitascope), at the Bijou Theater this morning, the "Telegraph's" representative is prepared to state that the invention will do until the greatest inventor of the age springs something new and still more startling in its effects on an amusement-loving public. The private exhibition was arranged by manager Foley and was a thorough success. This newest wonder of the electrical age will be here for several weeks or more in charge of G. J. Weller, one of Mr. Edison's representatives, who is under instructions to allow no one to see portions of the machine, for which patents are now pending. It is a great improvement on the vitascope in that it makes the object thrown upon the canvas larger and more distinct.[152]

The projectoscope was soon called "the greatest attraction ever presented at any amusement place in this city."[153]

Additional projectoscope prototypes were used for exhibitions in the eastern states over the next few months. On February 16th a preliminary circular announced that "Edison's Perfected Projecting Kinetoscope" was on the market for $100.[154] The machine was well received. Early purchasers included Lyceum entertainers J. Stuart Blackton and Albert E. Smith. Nonetheless, film equipment was no longer where the Edison Company was making substantial sums of money. Sales of screen machines for the business year ending February 28, 1897, totaled $21,159, but they produced only a modest profit of $1,534. Since Edison suffered a loss of $447 on his cabinet kinetoscopes, the profit from sales of hardware came to just over $1,000.[155]

Edison motion picture profits were now coming principally from sales of film, not equipment. For the business year ending February 28, 1897, film sales more than quintupled over the previous year to $84,771 and yielded a profit of $24,564.[156] With film sales becoming the key to profitability, much greater attention had to be placed on this area of the business. Heise and the kinetograph were removed from Raff & Gammon's control even as the Edison Manufacturing Company hired one of the Vitascope Company's key employees, James White, to head its Kinetograph Department in late October. His salary was $100 a month plus a 5 percent commission on all film sales.[157] At the same time, Thomas Edison began to copyright his company's most important films in an effort to protect them from the widespread duping that had sprung up (the first films reflecting this change in policy were copyrighted on October 23d). White, still relying on William Heise as camera operator, embarked on an ambitious production schedule.

James White's formal assumption of leadership of the Kinetograph Department precipitated few shifts in subject matter or treatment. Among the first of the new copyrighted subjects were *Streets of Cairo* ("four Egyptian Girls in full

Streets of Cairo.

native costumes executing the fascinating 'Midway' dance") and *Feeding the Doves* ("a beautiful girl and her baby sister dealing out the morning meal to the chickens and doves").[158] The fluttering of birds in the latter scene exploited the cinema's ability to show subtle motion, while the farm setting evoked nostalgia for a simpler, earlier time (as with *Blacksmith Scene* and other films). Although these represented two contrasting depictions of women, the reliance on display differed from the aggression evident in *Mounted Police Charge* and *Runaway in the Park*. For these last two, the action rapidly approached the camera, threatening to penetrate the imaginary dividing line between space in front of the camera and space behind it (between performer and spectator or between representation and reality). Following the many Lumière films of cavalry charges, White was using a simple, but effective, way to symbolically convey masculine activity.

Edison production was increasingly oriented toward turning out an array of related subjects that exhibitors could organize into sequences. Within a week of being hired, Edison's new motion picture head was filming the New York police. Accompanying the two just mentioned scenes, *Park Police Drill—Left Wheel and Forward* and *Park Police Drill—Mount and Dismount* showed a battalion of mounted officers drilling in preparation for the Annual Horse Show. The drill was performed for the camera; it was a conscious creation of spectacle, a display of discipline and state power that was sure to impress audiences. In November,

Mounted Police Charge. The frame suffers from nitrate deterioration.

White and Heise took four films that elaborated on *Fire Rescue Scene.* Three were photographed on November 14th, with the cooperation of the local Newark Fire Department.[159] These showed the fire engines leaving headquarters (*A Morning Alarm*), a fire run down Broad Street (*Going to the Fire*), and a final scene of fire fighting (*Fighting the Fire*). Within a few weeks, exhibitors such as Lyman Howe were combining these into elaborate sequences.[160]

White's energy, captivating personality, and sense of the popular allowed for commercial success. It was these qualities more than his official position that enabled him to dominate the collaborative relationship he had with Heise. They also facilitated ties with prominent companies like the Lehigh Valley Railroad. Undoubtedly, this alliance was based on mutual interests. The American Mutoscope Company, which was rapidly emerging as Edison's chief rival, was enjoying immense success whenever its biograph showed *The Empire State Express.* One night at Hammerstein's Olympia, the New York Central Railroad bought two hundred seats to show off its vaunted train, suggesting that such films were not only seen as excellent publicity but as an inspirational symbol of corporate power.[161] It was in the interest of both parties to counter the Biograph–New York Central alliance with an Edison–Lehigh Valley one.

By early December, White and Heise were filming along the Lehigh railroad, accompanied by prominent corporate officials. On December 1st, near Lake Cayuga, New York, they took *The Black Diamond Express.* This scene, in

The Edison camera crew ready to film *The Black Diamond Express*. James White rests his arm on the camera. William Heise is to the right. They are accompanied by employees of the Lehigh Valley Railroad.

which the train comes at the camera placed by the side of the track, proved to be one of the Edison Company's most popular subjects and was remade several times over the next six years. Many other railway scenes were also shot, but few of the resulting films were copyrighted or placed in Edison's catalogs. This trip then brought the cameramen to the Buffalo area, where they made a second and more satisfactory attempt to photograph Niagara Falls. Seven of these subjects were eventually copyrighted and sold, including *Rapids Above American Falls* and *American Falls—From Incline R. R. Buffalo Horse Market* and several horse-related scenes at the Buffalo Country Club were also taken. On December 23d a party of Lehigh Valley Railroad executives visited the Edison Laboratory and were treated to a screening of films taken on the company-sponsored trip, beginning with the Buffalo Country Club and concluding with Niagara Falls. The choice of subjects seemed designed to encourage tourism and use of the Lehigh road. This mutually beneficial relationship between film and transportation companies would be further developed in the coming years.[162]

The Kinetograph Department's wish to avoid expenses whenever possible was again evident in a series of films taken in and around Harrisburg, Pennsylvania, at Christmas time. Although Bijou Theater manager J. G. Foley continued to enjoy packed houses with Edison's projectoscope in mid December, the Waite Comedy Company was threatening to curtail this success by showing films between play acts at the nearby Grand Opera House.[163] Foley, not wanting to be outdone by a rival theater, arranged for White and Heise to take a

The Black Diamond Express.

series of local views. When *Police Patrol Wagon* was made on Christmas Eve, "a large crowd assembled on Market Street, near Third, to watch the projectoscope people take a picture of two drunken men engaged in a fight and their arrest by Sergeant McCann and a couple of officers. The police patrol wagon dashed up and hustled the men off to the county jail."[164] Other views included *Market Square, Harrisburg, Pa.*, "with all the holiday shoppers, electric cars, Commonwealth hotel and many familiar figures and faces passing by."[165] In *The Farmer's Troubles*, "a wagon driving up Market street meets with several misadventures which attracts general attention." *First Sleigh Ride* was "taken after the first fall of snow and shows an exciting race along the river road."[166] On Christmas Day, *Pennsylvania State Militia, Double Time* and *Pennsylvania State Militia, Single Time* were photographed on or near the Capitol Grounds. All were copyrighted on January 8th and then offered for sale.

Before the Harrisburg views could be shown at the Bijou Theater, another exhibitor acquired the local scenes (as well as a new projectoscope) and secretly arranged to show the films at the rival Grand Opera House on January 13th and 14th. Once the screenings were announced, the distraught Bijou manager went to court in an attempt to block the Opera House screenings, but his plea for an

Receding View, Black Diamond Express.

injunction was refused.[167] Threats, promises, and appeals for a boycott appeared in various papers, but these simply increased people's curiosity. By the time Foley's Bijou began to show the pictures on the 15th, a large percentage of the city's amusement goers had seen the especially commissioned views. Only a scene of a local fire run, which had not been offered for sale, enjoyed its debut at the Bijou.

Another major filming expedition involved President McKinley's inauguration. The Edison team made a preliminary visit to Washington, D.C., in late January (*Pennsylvania Avenue, Washington, D.C.* [© February 11, 1897]). They returned for the March 4th event and took eleven subjects, including *McKinley and Cleveland Going to the Capitol* and *McKinley Taking the Oath*. The cinematographers stayed on, filmed the new president attending religious services and ultimately accumulated more than a dozen views related to this quadrennial event. They received little attention in the nation's media capital, since with the breakup of the Vitascope operations, a large-scale, Edison-affiliated exhibition service no longer existed. Rather, the biograph at Keith's enjoyed the lion's share of publicity for presenting these subjects. Although Lumière cinématographes were in three New York venues (two Proctor houses and the Eden Musee), they could not handle Edison perforations and had to wait until similar subjects made the round trip to Lyons, France, for developing and printing.[168]

In April, White and Heise returned to the lines of the Lehigh Valley Railroad

Cock Fight.

and shot a group of subjects. Two were additional negatives of the onrushing Black Diamond Express. For *Panoramic Scene, Susquehanna River,* "the camera was placed on the rear of a moving train as it steamed along at the high rate of speed."[169] This receding view returned to a technique used to film Niagara Falls. It differed in only one minor, but significant, aspect from *The Haverstraw Tunnel,* a Biograph film made only a few months later. Biograph's camera was placed on the front rather than the rear of the train. The resulting bold penetration of space (including the entrance into a tunnel) was more shocking, more daring, than the backward-looking, nostalgic view that had almost become Edison's trademark.

Receding View, Black Diamond Express was "the first picture ever taken of a receding train . . . as the passengers are seen in the windows and on the rear end of the train, waving their handkerchiefs, hats, etc."[170] Edison and its sales agents then promoted the film as "a very clear, sharp picture which will be found pleasing and interesting, particularly if shown immediately after the approaching view of the same train."[171] Exhibitors were urged to purchase the two separate films and juxtapose them to create a spatial world, with the second shot acting as the reverse angle of the first. Temporally, continuity was suggested but not specified. Certainly one cannot assume that this juxtaposition implied a linear progression of action across the cut. However fundamental the temporal relationship between these separate scenes is to the sequence, it re-

Making Soap Bubbles.

mains difficult to define precisely. Independent, self-contained units that stand on their own, the two films together yield the impression of repeated action and a temporal overlap. It is this tension—between scenes perceived as self-contained wholes, on one hand, and their potential as part of a more complex sequence, sometimes involving spatial and temporal connections, on the other—that provides a framework for understanding early cinema and its editorial strategies. In fact, this nonspecificity could be resolved by the exhibitor (through narration or perhaps sound effects) or by the spectator's own subjective interpretation. Thus, by early 1897 editing—the arrangement of selected shots—was already becoming crucial, not simply for the construction of narrative but for the creation of spatial and temporal worlds.

As cinema quickly lost its value as a technological novelty, it was being reintegrated into screen practice. The possible spatial relations between these three subjects taken of or on a train were hardly novel—they appeared almost routinely in nineteenth-century travel lectures. The issue of temporality, however, was practically a new one. Using photographic slides, the screen had presented a series of frozen moments. Now images unfolded in time, creating new issues, new problems that were beginning to be explored.

White and Heise made two more series of related films in April. One was of Barnum and Bailey's Circus, then performing in New York City (*Chas. Wertz, Acrobat; Trick Elephant No. 1*). In contrast to two years earlier, the camera now visited the circus rather than the circus visiting the camera. The other

Mr. Edison at Work in His Chemical Laboratory. Staged in the Black Maria but modeled after a well-known photograph of the inventor in his laboratory.

series focused on Grant Day, April 27th, when Grant's Tomb on Riverside Drive, New York City, was dedicated with a parade (*Grant Veterans—G.A.R.*) and speeches (*McKinley's Address*). In part because they were so easy to film, parades would become extremely popular news subjects.

During the winter and spring of 1897, the Kinetograph Department continued its production of simple, one-shot vignettes intended to stand on their own within a variety programming format. However, the Edison Company's initial reliance on preexisting forms of popular amusement was all but reversed. *The Little Reb*, a scene from *Winchester*, was virtually the only filmed excerpt of a play or musical taken during the 1896–97 theatrical season. *Making Soap Bubbles* and *Children's Toilet* continued Lumières' quotidian views of infants and small children (*Baby's Dinner*; *Children at Play*). Established genres were elaborated. *Husking Bee* was a kiss film shot by a barn door: a man discovers a red ear of corn and his reward—a kiss—is exacted. *Cock Fight*, the remake (© December 24, 1896), now has two bettors active in the background. In *Chicken Thieves*, African Americans raid a chicken roost and are then pursued by angry white farmers with guns. The image of African Americans as happy-go-lucky petty thieves, common to the minstrel show and the Sunday supplement of most newspapers, was unfortunately, if predictably, being broadened.

A few films of dancers were still made. *Parisian Dance* showed "a dance in costume by two young ladies,"[172] and Annabelle returned in late April or early May to perform her Serpentine and Sun dance specialties to replace worn-out negatives. Yet more oblique ways of displaying female sexuality were being developed. *Pillow Fight*, which imitated a Biograph Company hit, is one example. It revealed "four girls in their night dresses, engaged in an animated pillow fight."[173] Here the sexuality was young, innocent, and unselfconscious.

One of the most intriguing Edison films from this period is *Mr. Edison at Work in His Chemical Laboratory*. Recalling *Blacksmith Scene*, a fictional workspace was created in the studio, and the inventor went through a mock experiment. Facing the camera, but apparently absorbed in his work, the "Wizard" flits from bottle to bottle, filling a vial that appears ready to divulge some secret discovery. Hokum of a type that Barnum would have appreciated, the film was able to reinscribe the inventor into the cinema process. A year earlier, "Edison's Vitascope" had had a virtual monopoly in its field. This not only involved a projection technology but an output of subjects. As projector models and non-Edison films proliferated, his place became less and less obvious, less and less visible. It was no longer hailed in newspaper publicity and only rarely mentioned in amusement advertisements. The film thus provided a means for reasserting his presence in a new way (on the screen), but one that recalled earlier Lumière subjects (*The Messers Lumiere at Cards*) even as it played with the inventor's legend.

Edwin Porter, Itinerant Exhibitor

Edwin Porter, who had come to New York City to work for Raff & Gammon during the fall of 1896, followed White and Webster in the general exodus from the Vitascope Company. He was soon running a projectograph for Harry J. Daniels and a man named Dowe of Hamilton, Ontario.[174] Daniels was a specialist in ventriloquism and catch-as-catch-can showmanship. Undoubtedly he provided a lecture to accompany the pictures Porter was responsible for projecting. Together they traveled the Caribbean, which Porter may have known from his naval stint. In March they were reported to be exhibiting in Barbados.[175] Porter was one of many independent exhibitors crisscrossing the North American continent and the world, showing films to people for what was more often than not their first time. Far from Edison's New Jersey base, the show was sometimes promoted by introducing Porter as Thomas Edison, Jr.[176]

5 Producer and Exhibitor as Co-Creators: 1897–1900

The Eden Musee, a New York amusement center that regularly showed films, was licensed by Thomas Edison under his motion picture patents in February 1898. Just as important for our purposes, the Musee provided Edwin Porter with his principal form of employment—that of motion picture operator—during this same period. Projecting the Musee's films, Porter was involved in the creation of elaborate, high-quality programming that gave the Musee its excellent reputation. In the process, he and the Musee staff performed a crucial creative function that was as important as that of the production companies. They selected and acquired short films and frequently edited these subjects into programs with complex narrative structures. They were also responsible for the sound accompaniment: a lecture, music, sound effects, and even voices from behind the screen. These programs were very different from those that Porter and the Connellsville group had presented in the summer of 1896. The exhibitor was no longer presenting a novelty but had reintegrated motion pictures into the well-established practices of screen entertainment. By focusing on the production activities of the Edison Manufacturing Company and the exhibitions at the Eden Musee, new insight can be brought to the little-understood motion picture practices of the late 1890s.

The Peripatetic James White and Edison Film Production

Shortly after the 1896–97 theatrical year had ended and just as cinema's novelty period had come to a close, the Edison Company inaugurated a practice of great consequence for anyone interested in this era of history. When copy-

Suburban Handicap, 1897. The event shown in four different shots. As with many films from this period, this one only survives in a poor-quality, grainy paper print.

righting films, Edison began to submit complete paper prints to the U.S. Copyright Office. This would remain company policy for the next eight years. Nitrate films would decompose or be destroyed, but these invaluable records survived.[1] Moreover, they have remained virtually untouched and certainly unaltered for more than fifty years, while the handful of surviving nitrate prints were frequently subjected to commercial exigencies, including modernization and other forms of textual modification. Once these paper strips were rephotographed back onto film in the late 1950s and 1960s, they provided a unique resource, which even now has not been fully appreciated.

The earliest paper prints include *Buffalo Police on Parade*, taken June 10, 1897, and *Free-For-All Race at Charter Oak Park*, taken near Hartford, Connecticut, on July 5th. They not only document the kinetograph team's summer travels to Chicago and various points in the eastern United States, but enable us to understand the Edison Company's limited, but important, editorial role. *Suburban Handicap, 1897*, taken June 22d, was a four-shot, 150-foot film of the prestigious horse race at Sheepshead Bay, Long Island. In chronological order, it offered glimpses of the pre-race parade, the start, finish, and weighing out. The individual scenes may have been too short to sell on their own, and it was assumed that a purchaser would want as complete an account of the event as possible. In any case, White and Heise kinetographed and constructed a simple narrative. The shots lack camera movement (there was no attempt to follow the action), but are serviceable, if distant, views of the events. In the third shot, two heads are in the left foreground, lending depth perspective and the sense of being a participant. Whether or not intentional, such framings began to provide the basis for a news/actuality aesthetic. Other films taken that summer were not so ambitious. *Philadelphia Express, Jersey Central Railway* consisted of two takes. In the first, a train comes under an overpass and past the camera. The kinetograph was then halted and not restarted until another train approached the overpass. Edited together, these "takes" appear to be a single shot, with one train quickly following another. Time was elided, much as it was in the nineteenth-century theater when a character's off-stage (and therefore usually incidental) activities were radically condensed (the actor exited and then immediately reappeared).

The Edison Company employed a single production unit through the summer of 1897. As we have seen, this unit was collaborative in nature, as William Heise routinely acted as camera operator between 1892 and mid 1897, first with W. K. L. Dickson and then with James H. White. This phase of the Edison Company's history concluded shortly after the Monmouth County Horse Show in Long Branch, New Jersey, during mid August. This was probably the last joint White-Heise venture for many months, as the photographers took six copyrighted films of the event. These one-shot films (*Judging Tandems, Exhibition of Prize Winners*, etc.) reaffirmed the customary practice of selling individual scenes to exhibitors for use in more complex sequences. Edison's kinetograph and prestige served as a pass to this stylish, mid-August event.[2] The cameramen's attendance, however, is explained less by the horse show's newsworthiness than by the continued opportunities it provided the filmmakers for interweaving work and leisure.

By the following spring, the Kinetograph Department had at least three discrete film production units operating under Edison auspices. Immediately after the Monmouth County Horse Show, White embarked on a tour that ultimately lasted ten months and sent him halfway around the world. The 25-year-old Kinetograph Department head was joined by photographer Fred W. Blechynden. Since William Heise could not be spared for this ambitious trip, Blechynden assumed the veteran's customary role in the collaborative pairing. Heise remained at the laboratory to supervise developing and printing of negatives as well as to take occasional films.

James White's tendency to combine work and play (with film production

Philadelphia Express, Jersey Central. Two takes spliced together to form one shot.

often subordinated to manly adventure and enjoyment) was nowhere more apparent than on this trip, which ultimately produced over 130 copyrighted subjects. By August 22nd White and Blechynden were in the San Francisco Bay
area, where they took a group of films at the famous glass-enclosed Sutro Baths.
Some were simple quotidian shots of the baths. In *Cupid and Psyche*, however,
the Leander Sisters were performing on the stage for a large group of male
spectators, casually dressed in bathing suits. The camera was behind the two

Cupid and Psyche. The female performers dance for the male customers and the male cameramen.

women, who danced for the spectators and then turned and pranced for the lens and the all-male camera crew.

The Edison Manufacturing Company probably purchased the motion picture camera equipment used on this world tour (or used equipment supplied by Blechynden).[3] Unlike previous Edison cameras, this one did not operate on electricity—bringing Edison into line with common industry practice. Its new, if still crude, panning capabilities are evident in the seven-film "Pacific Coast Life Saving Service Series," taken near San Francisco. The pictures were "illustrative of the work being done by the Life Saving Corps of the United States Government, and show the methods in vogue at one of the most important stations on either side of our Continent."[4] A very quick, jerky camera move reframes the boat for *Launch of Surf Boat. Return of Lifeboat* consists of three shots, all taken from the same spot: between each take, the camera framing shifts in an effort to follow the boat. In the final shot, however, as the boat comes through the breakers, the camera pans to keep it in frame. Lack of control over the action required this responsiveness from the camera crew, producing new elements of a nonfiction aesthetic. Other films were shot from a single camera position but involve two or more takes. In some cases, as with *Boat Wagon and Beach Cart*, these cuts are virtually invisible and eliminate dead spots in the

Return of Lifeboat. In the final shot, as a wave takes the boat down the beach, the camera pans to keep it in frame.

action. In contrast, *Launch of Life Boat* utilizes a jump cut to show two important moments of a process, but without attempting to disguise or soften the transition. Although these films of practices and demonstrations were not fictional (i.e., seeking to create the illusion of an actual rescue), they were often advertised as such.

James White continued his reliance on subsidies from transportation companies. On September 2d, the photographers took three films of the S.S. *Coptic* leaving its dock. This ship was owned by the Occidental and Oriental Steamship Company, which later provided the pair with passage to and from the Far East. The following day White and Blechynden began to tour the lines of the Southern Pacific Railroad Company; they filmed accommodations and sites that were part of the package tours then being offered by the railroads (*Hotel Vendome, San Jose, Cal.* and *Surf at Monterey*).[5]

While in San Francisco, White apparently met William Wright, whose animatographe was playing at the Chutes, a local amusement park. Wright, the leading West Coast motion picture man, possessed crude production capabilities. He had been in Seattle, Washington, just after news of the Alaskan Gold Rush broke.[6] Between August 6th and 9th, he took films related to the Klondike excitement (*S.S. "Williamette" Leaving for Klondike* and *First Avenue, Seattle, Washington*). White apparently either purchased these negatives or worked out a royalty arrangement and eventually sent them back to the laboratory. Wright may have subsequently taken other films on the West Coast for the Edison Company.

By early October, White and Blechynden were in Denver, Colorado, where they photographed events centered around the Festival of Mountain and Plain, celebrated during the first week in October. This included a parade on the 4th (*Masked Procession* and *Cripple Creek Floats*) as well as an Indian encampment (*Wand Dance, Pueblo Indians* and *Buck Dance, Ute Indians*).[7] The intrepid

Wand Dance, Pueblo Indians.

cameramen then apparently returned with the Utes to their reservation (*Serving Rations to Indians*), after which they headed south to Mexico.

White and Blechynden spent mid October to mid December in Mexico. Once again, their subjects were made with the active support of the railways. As the Edison catalog remarked:

> The *open-sesame* of a general manager's pass, issued to Mr. Edison's photographers, has enabled us to lay open before the public views taken in the heart of our great Sister Republic. The Mexican Central to-day is a great railroad system, managed by capable and courteous officials. It is due to their interest in our work and the liberal assistance proffered to our artists, that they obtained such excellent and characteristic pictures of Mexican life.[8]

Several films were taken at the Hacienda de Soledad, in Sabinas, Mexico (*Cattle Leaving the Corral*). Scenes of Mexico City included *Las Vigas Canal, Mexico City* and *Sunday Morning in Mexico*. Perhaps the most notable films of the entire trip were taken of a bullfight in Durango. The three-shot *Bull Fight, No. 1* has a close view/far shot/close view structure. The middle shot contains a slight camera move. It is also possible that the shots were taken at two different locations and then combined to create the appearance of a single incident. *Bull Fight, No. 2* consists of two shots: in both the camera follows the action. *Bull*

Bull Fight No. 1.

Fight, No. 3 shows three scenes from a single camera position, including the bull's collapse. Although the production company made a significant editorial intervention, the three brief films remained separate elements for the exhibitor's construction of a larger program.

White and Blechynden returned to the United States shortly before Christmas 1897. Once again they traveled under the auspices of the Southern Pacific Railroad, arriving in San Diego on December 20th (*Street Scene, San Diego*). Vast expanses of orange groves were filmed from the front of a train moving in Riverside (*California Orange Groves, Panoramic View*). Checking into a Los Angeles hotel on New Year's Eve, they shot *South Spring Street, Los Angeles*, the first film to be taken in the country's future motion picture capital. Along the way, a diverse group of railway scenes were added to their collection. Again these scenes of everyday occurrences and annual events were well suited to an evening-length travel lecture combining slides and film.

The itinerant cameramen were reensconced in San Francisco by January 22d when they visited the Union Iron Works and took *Launch of the Japanese Man-of-War "Chitose"* and several related scenes. Two days later, they filmed

S.S. "Coptic" Running Against the Storm.

a parade celebrating the 50th anniversary of the discovery of gold in California (*Native Daughters*). At this point White made a momentous decision. Having toured for six months, the photographers nonetheless left for the Far East aboard the S.S. *Coptic* on February 3d—less than two weeks before the sinking of the U.S. Battleship *Maine*. Again the Occidental and Oriental S.S. Company subsidized their way. Buffeted by a typhoon that damaged the ship and prolonged their passage by several days, they filmed *S.S. "Coptic" Running Against the Storm*.[9] The camera was strapped to the deck as a mountainous sea burst over the bow, precariously extending a procedure begun when a Lumière operator put a camera on a gondola moving through Venice.

White and Blechynden arrived in Yokohama, Japan, on February 24th. Over the next eight weeks, they traveled to Shanghai, Hong Kong, Canton, Macao, Nagasaki, and finally back to Yokohama. Twenty-five films made during this circuit were eventually copyrighted, including *Street Scene in Hong Kong, Canton River Scene, Shanghai Street Scene No. 1*, and *Theatre Road, Yokohama*.

Japanese Sampans and *Theatre Road, Yokohama.*

White also tried to establish an Edison agency in the Far East and later claimed to be looking for materials that his employer could use in experiments.[10] Returning home on the S.S. *Doric* (*Game of Shovel Board on Board S.S. "Doric"*), White and Blechynden arrived in Hawaii on May 9th. Films taken the next morning included *Honolulu Street Scene* and *Kanakas Diving for Money.*[11]

On May 16th, four weeks after the United States declared war on Spain, White and Blechynden again reached San Francisco. War films, not travel scenes, were in demand, and the fruits of this trip never received the attention White must have originally expected. Responding to these new circumstances, the collaborators tooks a few scenes of American troops departing for the Philippines (*California Volunteers Marching to Embark*) and finally headed home. As was often the case with Westerners visiting Asia, White had become seriously ill.[12]

During White's ten-month absence, William Heise produced approximately twenty-five copyrighted subjects, all taken either at the Black Maria or in the Orange-Newark environs. In some instances at least, he worked closely with John Ott. On two occasions, the photographer took films in close cooperation with local civic organizations. At the request of the Ambulance Fund, Heise shot five negatives in downtown Orange on October 8, 1897.[13] Two were of the vehicle racing from its stable. Three others showed a man hit by a trolley and then picked up and rushed off by the ambulance. A local theater employee played the victim. *Ambulance Call* and *Ambulance at the Accident*, the best depictions of each scene, were copyrighted and sold separately, but commonly promoted and shown together (for example, at benefits for the Ambulance Fund).[14] Other films were made with the help of Gatling Gun Company A, a popular group of citizen soldiers whose armory served as their social club. On Thanksgiving morning, the crews gathered and performed their evolutions for the camera.[15] These included *Gatling Gun Crew in Action* and *Mount & Dis-*

Ambulance Call and *Ambulance at the Accident.*

mount, Gatling Gun. Shown at a benefit for the Company's Athletic Fund, they were also copyrighted and sold.[16]

Heise took winter scenes of sleighing, sledding, snowballing, and ice hockey during early February 1898. Other miscellaneous scenes included an April snowstorm in Llewellyn Park (Edison's residential neighborhood) and a May game of minor league baseball between Reading and Newark. That spring the Black Maria was used for several comedies. *The Burglar* was based on a well-known scene in Evans and Hoey's farce *A Parlor Match*: A burglar struggles to open a safe, but his task is interrupted when the office boy enters the room and reveals that the safe is used as a coal bin. *The Telephone* spoofed a new and increasingly common communication technology:

> Posted on the wall is the startling sign, DON'T TRAVEL. USE TELEPHONE. YOU CAN GET ANY-THING YOU WANT. Man comes in, rings up, takes telephone, talks, then waits a moment; opens little door at the bottom of receiver, and takes out—a glass of beer! Blows off the foam, takes a deep draught, and telephones for a cigar. Waits for a moment; gets impatient and calls again, when out comes a blast of flour, plastering his face and clothes so that he looks like a miller.[17]

Both one-shot scenes were awkwardly handled, suggesting why Heise never assumed a more prominent role in film production.

The most successful comedy made during White's absence was undoubtedly *What Demoralized the Barbershop*, which Heise shot in the Black Maria with the help of John Ott.[18] The set for this reworking of *Barbershop Scene* was more elaborate, but the key shift was in the introduction of a new element—women. This all-male milieu is located in a cellar, with a set of steep stairs leading to the sidewalk. Here two women, presumably prostitutes, stop in the doorway and raise their skirts to reveal white-stockinged legs. Neither the customers nor the camera glimpse their upper torsos and faces. The men, who can see but not be

What Demoralized the Barbershop. The all-male world of the barbershop is disrupted as two prostitutes try to drum up some business.

seen (except by the film spectators!), lose their composure and scramble to get a better view. The camera, likewise, is low enough to provide an upward look. The film thus inscribes male voyeurism within its simple gag narrative. It also suggests the superiority of cinematic voyeurism: film spectators can look from the unhumiliating comfort of their seats. In the darkened theater, they can see but not be seen. If the film provides a laugh at the male customers' expense, it also offers the spectator the titillation of their view.

Heise's output discloses basic problems with subject matter that paralleled White's. His response to the inflamed patriotism sparked by the *Maine* sinking was limited to *American Flag* and *Old Glory and the Cuban Flag*. The first example of flag-waving remade an earlier subject, while the second offered a modest variation appropriate for the current circumstances. Two versions were taken of each, the ones against a black background apparently intended for hand coloring. None, however, depicted events relevant to the Cuban crisis.

Edison on the Legal Offensive

Although Thomas Edison copyrighted and marketed over 130 films during 1897, his enterprise was competing against several other motion picture manufacturers. Among the most prominent were the American Mutoscope Company (i.e., Biograph) and the International Film Company in New York; Edward Amet in Waukegan, Illinois; and Sigmund Lubin in Philadelphia. As a result, the volume of Edison's film-related sales changed little. For the year ending March 1, 1898, film sales were down 11 percent to $75,250, while film profits remained virtually unchanged at $24,439. The marketing of Edison's projecting kinetoscope had gone fairly well, but projector sales of $27,802 only yielded profits of $4,826. If Edison hoped to regain his dominance of the motion picture industry, patent litigation seemed to offer the most promising route.

Edison filmmakers at ease on the set for *What Demoralized the Barbershop.* William Heise in barber chair; possibly John Ott behind him.

As Gordon Hendricks has shown, Edison had difficulty acquiring patents for his motion picture camera, since his innovations had been anticipated in almost every respect by previous inventors. On February 21, 1893, Edison was finally issued patent no. 491,993 on application no. 403,535 for his method of steadily advancing the film. The process of revising application no. 403,534 took even longer owing to excessive claims and the delaying tactics of Edison's lawyers.[19] (Since patents were only good for thirteen years, delaying their date of issue was often an effective strategy for extending the patentee's control over an industry.) Finally on August 31, 1897, Edison was granted his motion picture camera patent, no. 589,168.

In December 1897 Edison lawyers launched a legal offensive against a number of producers and exhibitors. Edmund Kuhn's and Charles Webster's International Film Company was the first target.[20] Rather than fight the case in court, International closed its doors. Maguire & Baucus, one of Edison's principal selling agents, but one that also sold Lumière and International Film Company subjects, was sued at the same time. They did not contest the suit either. While F. Z. Maguire continued working with the Edison organization and sold its films during much of 1898, the partners gradually moved their activities to England.[21] Lubin was sued on January 10th and Biograph on May 13th: both contested these suits and remained in business.[22] Over the year, Edison sued a

The Eden Musee.

number of other "infringers." Some of these acknowledged the inventor's patents and became licensees. With licensing arrangements characterizing Edison's commercial practices during the late 1890s, we now turn to look closely at Edison's first motion picture licensee—the Eden Musee.

The Eden Musee

The Eden Musee, an imposing stone structure on the south side of Twenty-third Street west of Madison Square, was located in a fashionable New York entertainment and shopping district. When a group of Frenchmen opened the Musee on March 28, 1884, the amusement center featured waxworks, often of a topical character, and musical concerts, along with an occasional specialty—lantern shows, marionettes, and so forth.[23] The Musee's catalog described its purpose:

> The founders of the EDEN MUSEE had a higher object in view than that alone of establishing a profitable commercial enterprise. It was their intention to open a Temple of Art without rival in this country, affording to all an opportunity for instruction, amusement and recreation, without risk of coming into contact with anything or any-

body that was vulgar or offensive. For children and young people, particularly, the Eden Musee will prove a constant source of enjoyment and instruction. A child will learn more from a plastic representation of events and persons than a book can teach. Illustrated newspapers, giving pictorial views of incidents and scenes of today, have already a great advantage over the ordinary journals which give us only the dead letterpress; and from the cold, colorless engravings of an illustrated newspaper to the life-like plastic groups of the Eden Musee is an immense step towards a realistic representation of nature and life.[24]

Through ticket price and programming, the Musee appealed to a middle-class audience whose sense of cultural propriety included a strong dose of moralism.

By the mid 1890s the changing world of New York amusements had left the Musee in a tenuous situation. To compete with the rising tide of vaudeville, it often featured dancers, singers, and other performers. Yet these worked against the image outlined in its catalog and were not apparently successful. Musee president Richard G. Hollaman solved the crisis by making moving pictures an important third element in the house's programming. On December 18, 1896, the Lumière cinématographe began to show films in the Winter Garden, which could accommodate 2,000 people.[25] According to the *Mail and Express*, one of New York City's smaller afternoon newspapers:

> The Cinematographe is having a successful run at the Eden Musee. This is due mainly to the new views that have been taken especially for the Musee. One of the latest and most interesting is that of Li Hung Chang's march into Fifth Avenue from Washington Square. Li Hung Chang can be readily recognized, as can many of the officials who accompanied him. Along each side of the avenue there is a great crowd of people waving their handkerchiefs and applauding. The thirty-five or more other views are equally lifelike and interesting. The views are all well chosen and occasionally a peculiar effect is produced by reversing the view. When this is done everything is entirely opposite from the first effect. The views are shown each hour during the afternoon and evening.[26]

There was a close affinity between the Eden Musee's waxworks and its moving pictures, both of which strove toward "a realistic representation of nature and life."

Although Hollaman chose to use the French cinématographe rather than the vitascope or projectoscope, he nonetheless added a wax figure of Thomas Edison to his collection in February 1897. Edison, who was sketched in his studio and donated a suit of clothes to cover his likeness, was shown "seated at a table on which are the drawing of the phonograph and one of the completed instruments. Edison is holding the tubes to his ears, listening to the first complete message ever inscribed on a phonograph cylinder."[27]

The Lumière cinématographe lasted only two months at the Eden Musee. On February 22d, a week after the Lumière service opened at Proctor's Pleasure

Palace, Hollaman introduced the cinématographe Joly as a "permanent feature" at his house. The new exhibition service was owned and operated by German emigré Eberhard Schneider. Musee publicity announced that the new machine "reproduced long scenes without noise and flickering of light on the screen. Many of the scenes take from three to five minutes, and each detail is strikingly exact."[28] A lecture and music accompanied the opening night performance, with views primarily from France.[29] In mid April the Musee shifted its emphasis to American views and renamed Joly's apparatus the "American Cinematograph."[30] By May, groups of American and foreign films were being shown on alternating hours.[31] Two or more films in a program often contained related subject matter, which was frequently noted as the principal or headline attraction.

Although New York had a population that was nearing three and a half million in 1897, the Eden Musee was the only amusement center in the city that committed itself to motion pictures on a full-time basis. Vaudeville managers thought of moving pictures as a popular turn that had to be replaced more or less frequently to keep the bill fresh and lively. Even B. F. Keith, whose organization evidenced the greatest enthusiasm for films, did not keep motion pictures on his Union Square theater bill all the time. After the Lumière cinématographe's five-month stay ended in late November 1896, manager J. Austin Fynes allowed seven weeks to go by before bringing in Biograph for a fifty-week run. Then the theater was once again without motion pictures. At the other extreme, Pastor's Theater had seven different motion picture engagements between mid January 1897 and early February 1898. These kept motion pictures on his bill for twelve of the sixty-five weeks. Other vaudeville theaters, including the Proctor theaters and Huber's 14th Street Museum, showed films periodically as well.[32] This gave the Eden Musee a unique role in New York City and, because New York was the center of motion picture activity, in the United States as a whole.

When a problem arose at the Eden Musee in mid 1897, Richard Hollaman increased his commitment to moving pictures when other managers might have backed away. On June 14th, Schneider's cinematograph started a fire that sent 1,500 patrons stampeding to the exits. The Musee's publicist minimized the narrowly avoided catastrophe, which came just over a month after the infamous Charity Bazaar fire in Paris, also started by a cinématographe Joly. Schneider lost his contract, and Hollaman brought back the Lumière cinématographe.[33] At the same time, Hollaman hired Frank Cannock to build a projecting apparatus for the Musee's use. This machine was installed at the Musee in August. "For months a skilled inventor has been working upon models and a new cinematograph will be placed on exhibition today," reported the *New York Times*. "It is a wonderful machine and the vibration is reduced to a minimum."[34] The *Mail and Express* added, "The new machine is superior to any that has been shown before. It projects with the least flicker and looking at the picture does not weary the eyes."[35] Cannock worked with William Beadnell, who handled publicity for the Eden Musee, and with Edwin Porter, who joined the project in the summer of 1897 while he was projecting films in New York City.[36]

Hollaman's move may have inaugurated the American Cinematograph Company, an exhibition service based at Room 205, 5 Beekman Street, New York City. Although the nature of its relationship with the Musee remains somewhat hazy, the service must have been at least partially owned and controlled by the amusement enterprise.[37] As the Musee prospered, so too did this exhibition service.

Porter Operates and Builds Projectors

Having returned from his Caribbean tour after the theatrical season ended, Edwin S. Porter projected advertising films in Herald Square during the summer of 1897.[38] Although his name was not mentioned, the exhibition was reported in a trade journal for the motion picture and phonograph industries, the *Phonoscope*:

> A very interesting and novel advertising exhibition is now being given on the roof of the building at 1321 Broadway, facing Herald Square.
> Animated films are shown illustrating advertisements. The pictures were all by the International Film Co., 44 Broad Street, and are attracting the attention nightly of thousands of people. As an instance of the enterprise and hustle of the International Film Co., the Democratic Mayor was nominated on Thursday night and on Friday his picture was on the screen at 34th Street.[39]

Since this job for the International Film Company was performed at night, Porter helped with the construction of the Musee's cinematograph during the day.

After spending the summer months in New York, Porter and his former partner Harry J. Daniels joined with Professor V. W. Wormwood's Dog and Monkey Circus and toured Quebec and Nova Scotia in September and October (see document no. 4). Porter showed Lumière films of Queen Victoria's 1897 jubilee on a projectograph acquired from the International Film Company.[40] Showing a number of films that dealt with a single subject, Porter had to sequence these scenes into an order that gave a clear account of the ceremonies and maintained the audience's maximum interest. Harry Daniels undoubtedly provided a running commentary with the films. With people coming to see images of a significant event that had occurred on the other side of the Atlantic, the simple novelty of projected motion pictures was clearly in the past.[41] Porter and Daniels also helped to amuse patrons with pictures unrelated to the royal jubilee and illustrated songs. Although it was called "an unqualified success" and played to large audiences, the troupe was short-lived.[42] By mid November Wormwood was on the vaudeville circuit and Porter was without a job.[43]

DOCUMENT No. 4

Wormwood's Monkey Theatre

Wormwood's Monkey theatre will play at the academy of music one week commencing September 27, and will give daily matinees, commencing Tuesday afternoon at 2:30. This company of unique entertainers consist of 31 monkeys and 24 dogs, who execute tricks that are highly amusing. They ride bicycles, turn somersaults, act as waiters, barbers, jugglers, fencers, comedians, and do many surprising and pleasing acts. These sober faced little animals are dressed like little old men and women, and understand and obey at the word of command. The scene at the races is very amusing. The dogs are harnessed to small sulkies and the monkies act as drivers; they make things lively as round the stage each one goes, trying to win the race. Another scene is the "Pardon Came Too Late," and is acted out in most human manner. As an extra attraction the management will present the latest projecting machine with new and startling views, including the Queen's jubilee parade and the Colonial and Indian troops. See the grand jubilee procession and the Queen in her carriage drawn by eight horses, and you will witness a sight of a life time and be as well pleased as though you were there at the time. Another attraction will be H. J. Daniels and his wooden family of talking children who never fail to please.

SOURCE: *Halifax* [Nova Scotia] *Morning Chronicle*, September 25, 1897, p. 5.

The Eden Musee Moves into Production— *The Passion Play*

During the fall, the popular Eden Musee was turning away potential patrons for the first time in several years. On Sunday, October 3d, five thousand people were admitted and filled every seat in the Winter Garden.[44] With tickets 50¢ for adults and 25¢ for children, the box-office must have approached or exceeded $2,000 for one day. This was attributed to the fact that the Musee had begun to move into film production. "The popularity of the Cinematograph at the Eden Musee is as great as ever," reported the *Mail and Express*. "The fact that four times as many views are shown there as elsewhere is another reason for its popularity. In addition the Musee pictures are taken especially for the Musee and reproduced on the most perfect machine made, which was also perfected by the Musee."[45] To take its subjects, the Musee hired William Paley, a former x-ray exhibitor who had moved into the motion picture field after suffering the adverse effects of radiation.[46] As the Musee's commitment to film expanded, other new employees were also needed.

Porter, who returned to New York after his Canadian tour, used his connection with Beadnell to get a job at the Musee as a motion picture operator.[47] It seems likely that he toiled on projector improvements reported early in 1898. In February refinements made the pictures "as perfect as possible." A month later further exertion reduced vibration and sharpened the image.[48] The image quality provided by different projectors varied widely during the 1890s, and specific improvements could substantially contribute to an exhibitor's success. Porter's mechanical flair was an important asset, giving him access to companies and situations unavailable to the average operator.

Hiring Porter roughly coincided with the Eden Musee's production of *The Passion Play of Oberammergau*. Late in 1897, after attending the opening film exhibition of *The Horitz Passion Play* in Philadelphia,[49] Musee president Richard Hollaman resolved to produce a filmed reenactment of the famous *Passion Play* in Oberammergau, Germany. He enlisted the aid of Albert G. Eaves, who had the costumes and script from Salmi Morse's thwarted theatrical production of the Passion Play. Henry C. Vincent, a stage director at Niblo's Garden Theater, was employed to select the actors, paint the scenery, and supervise the production on the rooftop of Grand Central Palace.[50] According to Terry Ramsaye, "One of the major difficulties encountered arose from the fact that the director, the aged and authoritative Vincent, believed that he was making a series of lantern slides for stereopticon presentation. All efforts to explain to him that the camera recorded motion continuously failed entirely. It was Vincent's practice to put the company into rehearsal and when a striking moment arrived to dash out before the camera and scream 'Hold it!'"[51] Filming took six weeks. Using subterfuge, the Musee's cameraman William Paley and the actors finally shot twenty-three scenes, totaling approximately 2,000 feet. These were projected at approximately thirty frames per second, giving roughly nineteen minutes of screen time.[52]

The films, which were recently found and preserved by the George Eastman House, were taken with a distant, static camera. Frontal compositions, while often effective, seem to derive from a stage performance. The bare sets and narrative simplicity at least evoke the reputed folk culture of the Oberammergau peasants. Although the Eden Musee implied that the films showed that famed *Passion Play*, critics quickly dismissed the ruse, since it had last been performed in 1890, well before Edison's kinetograph had been invented. "Nor do these pictures even approach a close imitation of the Oberammergau play," remarked one knowledgeable reviewer. "Of the twenty-three scenes shown yesterday seven do not occur at all in the play of Oberammergau, which begins with the entry of Christ into Jerusalem."[53] Similarities to the Morse *Passion Play*, never successfully produced in New York, were noted.[54]

The Musee's films were only one element in an extensive, complex program. According to the *Phonoscope*, the addition of lantern slides in keeping with the subject produced an entertainment of approximately two hours.[55] These images were accompanied by a lecturer who stood next to the screen and by an unseen organist and vocalists. The results were shown publicly for the first time on January 28, 1898, though its official premiere came three days later.[56] Reactions and reviews were more positive than anticipated.[57] The *New York World*, for instance, praised the production:

PASSION PLAY AT EDEN MUSEE

SACRED DRAMA SHOWN BY MEANS OF THE CINEMATOGRAPH

A series of Passion Play pictures is now being presented at the Eden Musee by the cinematograph. The scenes have been reproduced from sketches at the time of the last presentation of the biblical drama given at Oberammergau. The motion pictures were secured from a representation given in this country by actors garbed in the costume drawn from these designs and drilled in the various tableaux. Twenty-three scenes are shown, beginning with the shepherds watching their flocks and ending with the ascension. The best of them were the flight into Egypt, the raising of Lazarus, the crucifixion and the descent from the cross. The exhibition made a decidedly favorable impression and will doubtless be the means of attracting many visitors to this popular place of amusement.[58]

The Passion Play was shown twice a day—at 3 in the afternoon and 9 in the evening—for the following three months and periodically thereafter. Over 30,000 people saw it during the first three weeks, with ministers and church people making up the bulk of the audience.[59] The program thus attracted the types of culturally conservative, middle-class patrons that the Musee had always publicly courted.

The Musee's *Passion Play* was an extension and revitalization of a lantern show that was familiar to most Americans. The typical illustrated lecture on the Oberammergau *Passion* had, since John Stoddard's first lectures in 1880, shown the events surrounding the play as well as the play itself.[60] The simple life of the Oberammergau woodcarvers who assumed roles in the production, the arrival and accommodation of the tourists, and views outside the theater, all provided a context for the presentation of the play. The Musee's *Passion Play* continued this tradition. While the play was shown using motion photography, heightening the intensity and realism of the theatrical experience, it was embedded in a static world of stock travel slides. Later, after the 1900 performance of the play, four scenes filmed in the village were sold with the Passion Play films: *Trains Loaded with Tourists Arriving at Oberammergau, Opening of the Great Amphitheatre Doors for Intermission, Street Scene in Oberammergau,* and *Anton Lange's House.*[61] These films were undoubtedly meant to supplement or replace some of

The Passion Play of Oberammergau. Two scenes "re-enacted" on an open-air stage in New York City. The train scene was taken in Oberammergau at the time of the 1900 performance.

the slides used in earlier programs. In 1898 the different materials—slides and film—emphasized the different pro-filmic elements: films/theatrical reenactment versus slides/nontheatrical actualities.

The combining of slides and films was a common exhibition practice during this period. The Musee's *Passion Play* well illustrates the reasons for these choices.

1. *Visual pleasure.* The technology for projecting moving pictures was still sufficiently primitive to strain the eyes. A combination of "flicker" and "shakiness" quickly reduced the viewer's satisfaction. In *Animated Photography*, Cecil Hepworth felt, "the best plan is to show one or two slides between each animated photograph. The still photograph is a great relief to the eyes and a thorough rest after the more or less tiring living photographs."[62]

2. *Cinematic effect.* The contrast between static and moving photo-

graphs could be dramatically effective and "relieve the monotony of a simple stereopticon entertainment with the interesting features of a moving picture."[63] At the same time, the larger photographic slides had more detail and allowed for skillful tinting.

3. *Diversity of images and supply.* The exhibitor had many more photographic slides to choose from in comparison to films. Many types of images were only available as still photographs or even as drawings mechanically transferred to glass.

4. *Cost.* Films were extremely expensive and few exhibitors could afford a program consisting exclusively of moving pictures. By combining slides and films, C. Francis Jenkins suggested, an exhibitor could "occupy an entire evening and at the same time present the attractiveness of a moving picture entertainment, but at much less expense."[64]

The little that has been written about cinema during the late 1890s often focuses on the distinction between a few longer, important films, of which *The Passion Play* is a prime example, and the many short films that are generally considered less significant.[65] This analysis creates a false distinction. *The Passion Play* was not a single film but a program composed of as many as twenty-three discrete scenes, each of which was its own "film," and an unknown quantity of slides. Such confusion equates the films that were produced with what was shown—an equation arising in part because the Musee was both the producer and the best-known exhibitor of these films.

The functions of film production and exhibition were independent: programs were by no means fixed but could be altered in their length, order, narration, or format. On February 18th, for instance, the Musee added a choir of boys chanting anthems to its program. By late March the accompanying lecture by Professor Powell had been extended and the choir boys were singing new anthems.[66] Moreover, the success of *The Passion Play* led the Musee to send out at least two touring companies in early March to give exhibitions in other theaters. These had different lecturers, performers, and formats to facilitate moving from town to town.[67]

When Hollaman's *Passion Play* films were later offered for sale by the Edison Company, they could be purchased individually or as a group.[68] Sigmund Lubin and William Selig subsequently produced rival film versions of the Passion Play that were also sold on a scene-by-scene basis. Selig actually suggested five different programs using either 25, 20, 15, 12, or 9 films.[69] Exhibitors who could not afford the entire series made a selection based on their resources and preferences. They could purchase additional films at a later date and/or combine films from different companies. The exhibitor was dealing with two different units: (1) the short individual film that paralleled the slide as a primary unit subject to editorial manipulation, and (2) the program constructed out of these slides and films, which was never standardized. There was no "definitive" version, and in this sense never a finished, complete work that achieved permanent closure.

The Passion Play was a major cinematic event and one that quickly turned the Eden Musee into an Edison licensee. With the program appearing shortly after Edison's legal offensive had begun, the inventor brought suit against Richard Hollaman and the entertainment center for patent infringement on February 7th.[70] An accommodation was reached two weeks later, not only with the Musee, which turned its *Passion Play* negatives over to the Edison Manufacturing Company, but with William Paley. On March 7th, Paley received a contractual letter from William Gilmore outlining arrangements under which he was to take films (see document no. 5). With James White still in the Far East, the Edison Company placed this experienced cameraman under contract. His first assignment was to make films relating to the Spanish-American War.

DOCUMENT NO. 5

Orange, N.J., March 7, 1898.

Wm. Paley, Esq.,
  c/o Eden Musee
    23rd St., New York

Dear Sir:-

    With further reference to the subject of the arrangement to be made with you, the conclusions reached between us are as follows: It is our idea that you will continue to take original negatives of animated pictures for us, such an arrangement to cover a period of one year from February 21, 1898, the necessary negative stock to be furnished by us, punched ready for use, without charge, in our regular standard lengths, which for the first strip is about 50 feet, and longer strips multiples thereof, up to about 150 feet, we to allow you an upset price for such negatives of Fifteen Dollars ($15.00) net on all accepted by us. All positives made from such accepted negatives are to be sold by us in the open market at regular rates, we undertaking to list the subjects in our regular catalogues from time to time as they are issued, and to have them listed whenever and wherever possible in any catalogues gotten out by our various agents or representatives. Where a special subject is to be taken, requiring an additional amount of money over and above the $15.00 above referred to, to cover actual traveling or other similar expenses, in addition to furnishing the negative stock we would of course be perfectly willing to confer with you and agree upon an amount to be paid in addition for any such expenses.

    In consideration of your giving us a portion of your time and services in the furnishing of satisfactory negatives as above outlined, we agree to pay you a royalty of Thirty Cents (30 cents) on each positive strip sold by us, either directly or indirectly, from each 50 (about) feet negative, the longer strips to be paid for on the same basis at a proportionately higher rate, such royalties to be paid monthly, we submitting a sworn statement as to the number of films sold from the negatives furnished by yourself. It is of course mutually understood between us that this arrangement is not exclusive in any way, we reserving the right to make similar arrangements with other parties should it be deemed by us wise to do so. It is also understood that the royalty so paid you does not apply in any way to negatives taken by ourselves or by others for our account, and it is further understood that the royalty is not to be paid on the so-called "Passion Play" pictures which we are now making under arrangement with Messers. Richard G. Hollaman and Albert G. Eaves, or to the subjects taken from the "Second Act of Martha."

This arrangement can be terminated by either party upon ninety days' written notice. In event of the arrangement being terminated by either party at any time, it is understood that the negatives in our possession shall so continue, and as long as there is any demand for positive strips from such negatives by you, we shall continue to pay you the royalty, just the same as if the contract was in full force and effect.

I believe the above covers the understanding in full between us. If you have any further suggestions to offer, please let me know at once; otherwise let us have your approval in writing.

Yours very truly,

(Signed) W. E. Gilmore
General Manager

Source: NjWOE.

The Spanish-American War

The sinking of the *Maine* and the Spanish-American War were a boon to the American film industry, as cinema regained a wide audience. Prior to these events, New York exhibitors were suffering through yet another period of underutilization. Even Keith's had let the Biograph service go after a year-long run. Once again, the Eden Musee was the only amusement center advertising a film exhibition in local papers.[71] When Biograph opened at Proctor's Pleasure Palace on February 14th, this situation would not have changed significantly—except that the *Maine* was blown up in Havana Harbor the following day.

Within a week after the explosion, Pleasure Palace audiences were seeing "the ill-fated Battleship Maine"—actually a film of her sister ship—on the screen. The Musee, which had previously highlighted developments in Cuba, may have hired Biograph to show similar films when the Musee's cinematograph was not showing *The Passion Play*.[72] By mid March, the "wonderful Biograph" was arousing patriotic enthusiasm with scenes related to the *Maine*, views of the Spanish ship *Vizcaya*, which had recently visited New York harbor, and "counterfeit presentments" of Consul General Fitzhugh Lee, who headed the inquiry into the "Maine" explosion, and of Charles Sigsbee, the ship's captain. Such inflammatory subjects were deemed "highly instructive."[73]

As President McKinley wavered between war and reconciliation with Spain, the "new" or "yellow" journalism of William Randolph Hearst's *New York Journal* and Joseph Pulitzer's *New York World* worked hand in hand with the music halls and theaters to incite Americans' warlike spirit. During the early part of the day, many New Yorkers read detailed descriptions of the latest Spanish atrocities and perused *Journal* editorials that declared, "A war would show first of all, what sort of stuff this country is made of, and what kind of men it has produced in the last thirty years."[74] Later in the day, these people might attend the theater, where patriotic songs encouraged group demonstrations. Biograph's exhibitions often provoked loud applause or hisses (depending on the subject). A film of the American flag at the conclusion of each program guaranteed long, hysterical cheers. The press gave such outbursts extensive coverage, and the *World* claimed that they indicated "the temper of the people in the present crisis."[75] Audience enthusiasm encouraged the Biograph Company to send cameramen to Havana, where they photographed noteworthy scenes. At the end of March, these films were being shown at the Pleasure Palace. These "Life-Motion Views" presented "the Wreck of the Maine, Divers Ascending and Descending, Consul General Lee at His Residence, The Reconcentrados, etc."[76] A week later, the Eden Musee was showing the same Biograph views. "The workings of the divers are plainly seen," reported the *Mail and Express*. "These views aroused much enthusiasm, and when a fluttering United States flag was shown nearly everyone present, including women, cheered."[77]

Neither the Edison Company nor the Eden Musee could afford to tolerate the Biograph Company's monopoly of war films. Biograph was Edison's major commercial rival, while the Musee had few war subjects for its cinematograph and was forced to spend substantial sums on the Biograph service, which nonetheless first exhibited its films elsewhere. These organizations and Edison's selling agent F. Z Maguire accordingly made arrangements with Hearst's *New York Journal* and dispatched William Paley to Florida and Cuba.[78] Hearst not only made his news yachts available to the Edison cameraman for transportation and as a platform for taking films, he paid for Paley's trip.[79] His was "the journalism that acts."[80]

Paley, still recovering from an illness, left his sickbed in mid March and headed for Key West, Florida.[81] There he worked closely with Karl C. Decker, a Hearst journalist, taking one-shot films related to the crisis. On the 27th he filmed *Burial of the "Maine" Victims*. For *War Correspondents*, the two staged

Burial of the "Maine" Victims.

a good-natured foot race among reporters, who were supposedly taking "war copy" to the telegraph office. Decker followed up the rear in a carriage, coming in last. (The *Journal*, failing to see the humor in this arrangement, described the scene by asserting that Decker beat his rivals.) Another film depicted Decker on the decks of the *Journal*'s despatch yacht *Buccaneer*. Paley and Decker also used the despatch yacht's decks for filming views of Admiral Sampson's fleet in the Dry Tortugas, southwest of Key West (*U.S. Battleship "Iowa"*).[82] Although the cameraman and journalist made three attempts to film in the vicinity of Havana Harbor, only two scenes were successfully taken: *Wreck of the Battleship "Maine"* and *Morro Castle, Havana Harbor*.[83] In fact, with the sole exception of *Burial of the "Maine" Victims* (150 feet), all the films were only 50 feet in length—ideally suited for the active editorial intervention of the exhibitor (see document no. 6).

Wreck of the Battleship "Maine."

DOCUMENT NO. 6

JOURNAL PICTURES OF WAR CHEERED.

Crowd at Proctor's Theatre
Shows Its Approval of Enterprise.

A TRAGEDY OF MOVEMENT.

Funeral of the Maine Victims Enrages the Big Audience.

At Proctor's Theatre last night enthusiastic crowds cheered the Journal to the echo as they watched the War-graph throw upon the giant screen the pictures which the Journal's correspondents had secured of the scenes attending the prosecution of the war in Cuba.

In these days of excitement it takes a good deal to stir a big theatre audience to any great display of feeling unless applause is drawn from it by patriotic songs and a liberal waving of flags, but the people last night showed that they appreciated the service the Journal has done for humanity by giving to the simple black and white depiction of the War-graph the same outburst of applause that greeted the National anthem.

There were pictures of all sorts, the grave, the gay and the grewsome [*sic*]. The battle ship Maine was shown as she steamed serenely into Havana harbor and then, later, there were thrown upon the screen the Journal's own picture of the wreck, the skeleton arms of the wrecking derricks stretched above her and the buzzard like fleet of Spanish patrol boats circling about that which was once a ship of the United States Navy.

It may have been accident or design that made the operator slip in a slide that threw the banner of Spain on the screen, but the hisses that assailed it fluttered the curtains and caused a man who had tucked a wide brimmed hat under his chair to make a suggestive move toward his hip pocket. Then there followed upon the screen the title: "Funeral of the Victims of the Blowing Up of the Maine."

When the glitter of the wargraph shone out again it showed a scene familiar enough, in its crystallized state, to the readers of the Journal, but which, when shown as it was at Proctor's Theatre last night, gained a significance and a reality that no newspaper could produce.

The orchestra hushed and a bugler behind the scenes began to play that sad, last call, "Taps," as a company of blue jackets swung around the corner of the pictured scene. In the midst of them could be plainly distinguished a dingy, one-horse landau, with a crepe-draped coffin within it.

"One," said the spectators. Next second it was "Two," and so the grim count went on. There seemed to be miles of that awful procession of the dead, which the Journal's camera had caught. It was not mere photographic repetition: the crowd soon saw that. It was the real thing, and as the full horror of that cowardly murder swept through the theatre a sigh went up that not even the lighter pictures which followed could change to a smile.

During an interval James Thornton, the comedian, read from the stage some of the Journal's bulletins of the progress of the war, and more cheers were given for American successes.

Then followed more pictures: The race of the newspaper correspondents in Havana to catch the outgoing boat with a red-hot piece of news; General Lee descending the steps of the American Consulate; the distribution by the Journal of supplies and medicines to the starving reconcentrados, and a picture of the President.

General Lee seems to be the popular hero of these days. He gets every bit as much cheering as the President, if not a little more. Another thing that the crowd at Proctor's Theatre showed was that not even the fever of war can take the innate chivalry out of the American people. It is the custom to announce every picture before it is thrown on the screen, and the advance sign said "The Queen Regent of Spain."

There were some scattering hisses, but when the projector threw upon the canvas the pictures of a woman—a woman who looked as if she had suffered—the hisses died away. Once again there was a flicker and the sign said "The King of Spain." Again came the hisses, but when there was shown out on the screen the picture of a little boy in knickerbockers, sitting in a chair that looked several sizes too large for him and wearing a distinctly pathetic appearance, the hisses vanished in a flutter of actual applause and a feminine murmur of "Oh, pshaw, he's only a little bit of a boy."

SOURCE: *New York Journal and Advertiser*, April 26, 1898, p. 13. This exhibition was almost certainly mounted by the American Cinematograph Company, with which Porter was associated. Several things may be noted about this account. Some films, for instance *War Correspondents*, were given a different context (Havana rather than Key West). The exhibition included as many slides as films: not only title slides but photographs of the Spanish flag, queen and king. Although the presentation reveals only a tentative narrative progression, the program was devoted to a single subject around which the audience's emotions were skillfully manipulated.

Less than a week after Paley's return, his pictures had been copyrighted by Thomas Edison and prints were being sold to impatient film exhibitors. The demand was so great that Paley, who had returned to New York on April 15th, returned to Florida on April 21st in anticipation of a declaration of war, which came four days later. Maguire advanced $500 to Paley against the cameraman's future royalties and may have provided him with film stock, but he told Gilmore: "As Mr. Paley is practically spending his own money, you can readily understand that this is a very good arrangement for us. The trip will practically cost us nothing."[84]

On his second trip, Paley went to Tampa, Florida, and photographed scenes of military preparations (*10th U.S. Infantry Disembarking from Cars*) and everyday scenes of military life (*9th Infantry Boys' Morning Wash*). Several views of Cuban refugees were also taken (*Cuban Refugees Waiting for Rations*). Camp scenes became more and more common as Paley waited for the invasion of Cuba to commence (*Blanket Tossing a New Recruit* and *9th and 13th U.S. Infantry at Battalion Drill*). On June 8th, the patient cameraman took *Roosevelt's Rough Riders Embarking for Santiago* and other scenes of troops boarding transports. The soldiers baked for a week under Tampa's ferocious sun; it was not until June 22d that they landed at Baiquiri, Cuba (commonly spelt "Daiquiri"). Paley along with other correspondents probably accompanied the convoy on the *Olivette*. *U.S. Troops Landing at Daiquiri, Cuba* and *Mules Swimming Ashore at Daiquiri, Cuba* perhaps taken from this ship, were said to be of the first American soldiers to reach Cuban soil.[85]

Once Paley reached Cuban soil, transporting the portly cameraman and his equipment proved a nightmarish task, particularly with the shortage of horses. Aided by an army teamster, he finally reached general headquarters and photographed *Major General Shafter*, showing the obese commander astride his horse. Paley took only a few additional subjects (*Troops Making a Military Road in Front of Santiago*; *Packing Ammunition on Mules, Cuba*) before disaster struck. The wagon carrying his baggage broke down, exposing photogra-

71st N.Y. Volunteers Embarking for Santiago.

pher and apparatus to a night-long rainstorm. The camera stopped working, Paley came down with a fever, and his Cuban expedition was ended. With the assistance of Charles E. Hands of the *London Daily Mail*, he reached a resupply point and went home dangerously ill.[86]

By April 18th, Paley's films were being shown at the Eden Musee, which acted as a center for war news and patriotic demonstrations:

> The Cuban wax works attracted much attention there last evening and the new figure of General Lee was continually surrounded by his admirers. The orchestra gave a concert of patriotic selections, including the battle hymns of civilized countries. The cinematograph exhibited new pictures taken in and about Havana Harbor by the Musee's artist and also pictures of American battleships at anchor and in movements, cavalry dashes, sham battles and National Guards on the march. Frequently the patriotism of the audience would rise to such an extent that there would be cheering.[87]

Enjoying its own supply of war films (via Paley), the Musee ended its *Passion Play* performances on May 4th, after two hundred exhibitions. Henceforth, all its energies were concentrated on sustaining the bellicose mood of New Yorkers. On May 7th, a week after Commodore George Dewey's victory in Manila Bay,

Advertisement for Edison "War Films."

his wax figure was on display in the Musee foyer. Meanwhile, Porter and his immediate boss, Eugene Elmore, showed "scenes from Havana, of the American warships, the sunken Maine, the Maine crew, burial of the Maine sailors and other views taken in and about Havana harbor and Key West. In addition are views of sham battles, infantry maneuvers and target practice."[88] Exhibitions devoted exclusively to the war were given hourly. Some focused on a particular aspect of the struggle, while others were more eclectic. New views were shown on a weekly basis into the summer. Many "were taken by the Musee's own artist, and are different from those shown at other places."[89]

The Cuban crisis and Spanish-American war brought moving pictures into an unprecedented number of metropolitan theaters.[90] One week after war was declared, the Eden Musee was one of at least seven Manhattan theaters showing war films—one more than at the novelty highpoint a year and a half earlier.[91] Porter and his associates at the American Cinematograph Company operated one of several exhibition services that took advantage of the resulting demand for film programs. In a later interview, Porter stated that he and William Beadnell supplied several vaudeville houses with film turns. "We had machines in the Eden Musee, in the Proctor houses and also some of Percy Williams."[92] Spring programs at Proctor's 23rd Street Theater were consistent with the supply of films available down the street at the Eden Musee, but the American cinematograph was replaced by Blackton and Smith's burgeoning American

Developing motion picture film in 1898–99.

Vitagraph Company toward the end of June. Blackton and Smith had developed a secret reframing device that improved their exhibitions. They had also established their own production capabilities. Since the American Cinematograph Company had to give preferential treatment to the Musee, the switch was a logical one.

Porter and Elmore were partially responsible for the addition of American Vitagraph to the Edison stable of licensees.[93] Perhaps they visited Blackton and Smith's offices to gather evidence of illegality that would enable them to regain their old outlet at Proctor's. Or perhaps they hoped to purchase some of Blackton and Smith's original productions to enhance their collection. Instead, they and other potential purchasers found dupes of Paley's war films. Thomas Edison soon sued Vitagraph for copyright and patent infringement, with Elmore and Porter providing depositions to support the case. Caught red-handed, Blackton and Smith reached an agreement with William Gilmore whereby they would not contest Edison's suit, but would work under a licensing arrangement similar to that made with the Eden Musee and William Paley.

Programs at the Musee were being constantly updated and changed, a challenging task for Porter and Elmore, who had to experiment with novel combinations of subjects. In June moving pictures were exhibited while a soloist sang national airs.[94] Later in the month, with the largest collection of war films in the city, the Musee began to show them all on Sundays at 3 and 9, giving "an opportunity to thousands to see these remarkable pictures at a slight cost."[95] The Musee's motion picture operators arranged the films as a chronology of the war: "The Maine sailors on parade are shown and then the Maine sailing into Havana harbor. Following is the burial of the Maine sailors, General Lee at Havana, other scenes in and about Havana, the various camps, soldiers at drill, battleships at anchor and in action, troops leaving Tampa for Santiago and other equally vivid scenes up to the storming of Santiago."[96] Audience response to the films was so enthusiastic that many of the pictures had to be shown a second time.[97]

The Eden Musee generally used its screen as a kind of patriotic news service. In August the entertainment center was showing one new war view each day. With over one hundred films in its collection, the motion picture operators showed twelve views each hour during the week, changing subjects each hour so visitors could stay as long as they liked and see different views.[98] By the end of August, their collection had swelled to nearly two hundred.[99] As soldiers returned from war in September, the Musee enjoyed a special kind of status:

> The Eden Musee is becoming a headquarters for the soldiers in this city. Since they returned scarcely a day passes that at least 500 do not visit the Musee. The majority of the Rough Riders have been there. They praise the war groups and take the greatest interest in the war pictures. The pictures taken in and about Santiago are cheered, and often have to be shown again. The other visitors take almost as much interest in the soldiers as in the attractions at the Musee. Little groups frequently surround the soldiers and question them about the war, and there is not an attendant in the house who has not a choice collection of souvenirs given him by the soldiers. On Wednesday Gen. Wheeler dropped into the Musee. He was recognized almost instantly and received cheers and greetings from the soldiers and visitors. One of the Musee's artists made sketches, and a figure of the popular hero will soon be on exhibition.[100]

The Eden Musee was thus dedicated to heroicizing the United States' imperial adventures and those who implemented its policy—not least of whom was Col. Theodore Roosevelt, soon to be elected governor of New York.

By November, Porter and Elmore had responded to the fading popularity of war views by taking a more documentary-like approach to their subject matter.[101] As the Musee announced,

> Since the beginning of the war with Spain cinematograph war views have been shown at the Eden Musee. The Musee's own artist took the pictures, and as fast as they were developed, they were shown. A genuine novelty in these pictures has now been arranged. It is the nature of a panorama of the whole war. The moving picture scenes begin with the arrival of soldiers at Tampa and include various important movements that followed, up to the surrender of Santiago. Over twenty views are shown. Among them are the Red Cross upon the field, Colonel Astor setting out to meet General Toral, artillery practice, Rough Riders landing, battle of San Juan, troopships in a storm, the surrender of General Toral, the raising of the Stars and Stripes over Santiago

and many other important scenes. All the pictures are accompanied by ingenious effects, including martial music, firing of guns and wind and rain.[102]

The Musee staff moved toward an increasingly elaborate, narrative account of the war. While it is impossible to ascertain Porter's precise contribution to the construction of program-length narratives such as *Panorama of the War*, as the Musee's chief motion picture operator he must have been intimately involved in the editorial process. Although this creation of complex film programs with extended narrative sequences was then common,[103] the Musee's unique position encouraged experimentation with film structures. The institution not only had a diverse selection of films, but regular customers who had to be entertained with new film combinations within this repertoire. The continual restructuring of programs was facilitated by the mechanics of exhibition. Films were not spliced together on a single reel, but threaded individually onto the projector (otherwise it would have been impossible to show the same subject twice in response to audience demand). While detailed programmes of these exhibitions do not survive—if they ever existed—documentation for similar programs is suggestive. Although the Musee may have had two moving picture machines, allowing one film to be juxtaposed against another, slides were a popular, though typically unmentioned, part of these programs. Vitagraph and Eberhard Schneider showed slides taken by *New York Herald* photographers as well as films.[104] Producers and distributors, including Sigmund Lubin and the Stereopticon & Film Exchange, urged exhibitors to purchase films and slides of the war and to combine them into an evening-length program with lecture.[105] A lecture may well have continued to be part of the Musee's programs as well.

Panorama of the War is comparable in many respects to more recent documentaries using silent stock footage—though the modes of production and exhibition are radically different. At the Musee, post-production was located in the projection booth and achieved on the screen rather than in the editing room and on the projection print. With showmen responsible for post-production, creative contributions were made by both cameramen and exhibitors. Paley's films from the war zone turned the motion picture photographer into a vaudeville hero, but the editorial arrangement of scenes and the live sound accompaniment were created in places like the Musee. Drawing from the same material, exhibitors produced their own distinctive programs—priding themselves on the quality and originality of their individual exhibitions. Not only did each have creative responsibility, they often claimed authorship of their programs—assertions that had much validity.

Both *The Passion Play* and *Panorama of the War* demonstrate that cinema in the late 1890s had the capacity to convey information and to affect its audiences both emotionally and intellectually in ways that were far more sophisticated than acknowledged in existing film histories. These histories, based on naive readings of a few catalogs and vaudeville programs, have virtually ignored

Ringling Brothers Circus showed war films, organizing them into a longer narrative called "The Story of Cuba."

the crucial role of the exhibitor. Rather than being isolated units within a miscellaneous collection of subjects, these short films were often elements of a larger, integrated program. While these programs were generally dependent on a lecture, this does not mean they lacked effective and comparatively elaborate visual structures.

During the late 1890s, there was a dialectical tension between unified programs built around a single event, theme, or narrative and the variety format, with its emphasis on novelty and diversity. The Eden Musee favored the former. The New York exhibitor Eberhard Schneider was at the other extreme, often emphasizing variety to the point of separating films that had a thematic relationship. In one program, for instance, Schneider placed *Snowballing* between *Spanish Attack on an American Camp* and *Charge of American Cavalry*; then *Storm at Sea* between *Execution of a Spy, Turco-Grecian War* and *Defense of a House, Turco-Grecian War*.[106] American Vitagraph, in contrast, fluctuated between these two extremes and often offered its audiences a middle ground. One point seems evident. Porter received a very particular kind of training at the Eden Musee, training that sensitized him to the possibilities inherent in the significant juxtaposition of related images. The use of editorial procedures was arguably most advanced at the Eden Musee, and it should not surprise us that one of its graduates was to continue to make strides in this area when he moved into production with the Edison Company at the beginning of 1901.

Porter and the Eden Musee After the War

Once the Spanish-American War ended in early August 1898, the number of Manhattan theaters showing moving pictures steadily declined. During the last week of August, films were still advertised for five theaters, in October for only four. By early November Proctor's Pleasure Palace had dropped its exhibition service, "much to the relief of the regular patrons."[107] Only Keith's and the Eden Musee were still boasting moving pictures in mid December. The Musee remained the sole Manhattan venue offering 35mm motion pictures as a permanent part of its programming. With audiences tired of war films, the Eden Musee began to show different kinds of subject matter, including views of foreign lands.[108] Elmore and Porter continued to feature *Panorama of the War*, but alternated it with a program of comic scenes early in December, a series of Christmas views during the holidays, and "illusions and reproductions of fairy tales" in mid January.[109] Even when not seeing war films, the Musee's patrons enjoyed thematically structured programs, which made its exhibitions distinctive.

New material relating to the American occupation of Cuba provided occasionally popular attractions. "For several days an artist of the Musee has been in Havana gathering interesting scenes," announced the Musee at the beginning of the new year. "He will remain there for several weeks and when the U.S. takes formal control on January 1st, he will make pictures of the stirring scenes, including the novelty of the flag over Morro Castle. The Govt. has given the artist permission to use forward positions."[110] Two surviving films, *General Lee's Procession, Havana* and *Troops at Evacuation of Havana*, show American troops marching through the streets of the former colonial capital.

The Opera of Martha, which Paley had shot almost a year earlier, was also presented for the first time in January. The Castle Square Opera Company, which had performed the opera at New York's American Theater early in 1898, probably provided the actors and even the sets.[111] With *The Passion Play of Oberammergau* and then the war films drawing large crowds, the Musee had delayed its exhibition. Publicity announced that "The entire second act of 'Martha' will be reproduced by the moving picture machine. As the pictures are shown the music is sung from behind the screen."[112] The picture "consisted of five scenes about 1,300 feet in length: 1. Duet outside the Inn, 2. Quartette in- side the Inn, 3. Spinning Wheel Chorus, 4. Martha singing 'Last Rose of Summer,' and 5. Goodnight Quartette. The film shows a quartette of well-known opera singers acting and singing their parts in this ever popular opera."[113] *The Opera of Martha*, like *The Passion Play*, was an extended effort at filmed theater. The exhibitor's sound accompaniment, however, was not presented in front of the screen by a lecturer explaining the images, but from behind the canvas to heighten the illusion of reality by synchronizing voice to the image. Today it can be considered an early form of dubbing. In July 1899 Richard Hollaman sold this film, along with *The Passion Play*, to Thomas Edison for $1,000.[114]

During the winter and spring of 1899, the Musee revived old programs and showed news films of noteworthy events. Travel scenes, humorous vignettes, and historical subjects were exhibited in programs grouped by genre, with two different groupings exhibited alternately during a week. By the spring, "mysterious" films were receiving extensive press attention. These trick films, particularly Georges Méliès' "Houdin films,"[115] were the perfect antidote for a year of war topicals. Many gave "an illusionary or supernatural effect," while others were declared to be "exceedingly humorous."[116] Méliès' creations remained popular at the Eden Musee throughout the year, culminating in *Cinderella*, which was shown over the Christmas holidays.

While working at the Eden Musee, Porter continued to manufacture motion picture equipment. During the summer of 1899, he built "the cameras, the printing machines and projecting machines for the Palmer-McGovern Fight."[117] These were made for the American Sportagraph Company, which carefully emulated the Veriscope organization. The Veriscope Company had filmed the Corbett-Fitzsimmons fight in March 1897 using a special-sized film that required its own cameras, printers, and projectors.[118] This gave the Veriscope Company absolute control over its exhibitions and generated large profits from its numerous road shows. The American Sportagraph Company hoped for the same good fortune, and Porter's equipment was well suited to the challenge. The sportagraph had a special large-size film that yielded a superior image. It could run on either direct or alternating current, weighed only thirty pounds, and could be set up in less than an hour.[119] Porter's experience as a traveling exhibitor and his knowledge of various projecting machines enabled him to produce a sophisticated instrument that avoided many of its predecessors' shortcomings.

The sportagraph's main attraction was the fight between "Pedlar" Palmer, the bantamweight champion of England, and Terry McGovern, the bantamweight champion of America. They were to meet on September 11, 1899, at the Westchester Athletic Club in Lake Tuckahoe, New York—a convenient fifteen miles by railroad from midtown Manhattan. The fight was expected to be "one of the greatest boxing matches ever engaged in."[120] With the fight as its headline attraction, the American Sportagraph Company also planned to show "photographic reproductions of noted horse, Bicycle, foot and yacht races, sculling matches, wrestling contests and other outdoor exercises and amusements with the stars of the sporting world as contestants."[121] Between the various moving pictures, high-class vaudeville acts were to be given "to make one of the strongest two and a half hour shows on the road."[122]

When the weather on September 11th was overcast, making it impossible to take pictures, the organizers postponed the fight. "Now, we have contracted to show the pictures in all parts of the world, and you can realize what a loss it would mean to go on without them," promoter Gray explained. "I am sure the public will rightly see how I stand in the matter."[123] The dispirited, but surprisingly understanding, crowd left, only to return the following day, when the cameras and eight thousand people watched Terry McGovern, "the pride of

South Brooklyn," defeat his opponent in two minutes and thirty seconds, less than a round. The fight was a major disappointment to boxing aficionados. Lacking its headline attraction, the American Sportagraph Company fell into oblivion. The Palmer-McGovern pictures, with their odd-sized film gauge, received no commercial distribution whatsoever. Philadelphia filmmaker Sigmund Lubin usurped the limited market for this subject by marketing a "reproduction of the fight showing the introduction, full fight and knockdown" in less than 400 feet.[124] If, as seems likely, Porter and the American Cinematograph Company were financially involved in this venture, they suffered a serious setback.

Porter had little time to ponder the sportagraph's failure, since the Eden Musee was preparing for Admiral Dewey's triumphal arrival in New York City on September 27th:

> The Eden Musee will add much to the Dewey celebration. For months its artists and sculptors have been at work arranging pleasing surprises. The interior of the Musee has been changed in many respects, and new war groups and war scenes in wax will cause the Musee to look like the interior of an arsenal. The Cinematograph will give hourly exhibitions of moving pictures taken in Cuba, Porto Rico and the Philippines. The whole front of the Musee Building will be arranged in the form of a mammoth battleship. From the top of the front will arise a mast similar to that of a warship. Nearly forty feet above the building will be a turret, in which will be two sailors with rapid-firing guns. At the sides of the top will be other sailors, apparently on deck. On each side of the front will be a mammoth gold eagle. In the center will be a still larger eagle which will measure thirty feet from tip to tip. Over 10,000 yards of flags and bunting will assist in carrying out the form of the battleship. Each entrance to the Musee will be arranged as the gangway of a battleship. Over each door will be the name of the warship represented.[125]

This coordinated programming, built around a particular event, was characteristic of the Musee, distinguishing it from the more common vaudeville format of entertainment, with its emphasis on variety.

James White, having long ago returned from his Far Eastern voyage, organized the Edison licensees so they could effectively cover the celebration. Altogether the Edison Company put eight camera crews in the field.[126] White reserved for himself the honor of filming Dewey on board his ship. The resulting pictures, *Admiral Dewey Receiving the Washington and New York Committees* and *Admiral Dewey Taking Leave of Washington Committee on the U.S. Cruiser "Olympia"* (taken on September 28th), were shown the following day and given special attention:

> As a compliment to Thomas A. Edison, Admiral Dewey gave permission for taking Cinematograph pictures of the visit to the Olympia of the Reception Committee and Gov. Roosevelt. The picture is shown at each of the performances at the Eden Musee to crowded audiences, and has elicited storms of applause. Admiral Dewey is seen pacing the deck awaiting the committee and the Governor. The clearness of the picture

brings the spectator side by side, as it were, with the hero of the day. His every movement is as clearly defined as is his greeting of the committee and the Governor as they step on the deck of the Olympia from the ladder swung by the side of the vessel.[127]

"Interesting views of the land and naval parades" were added later in the week.[128] The Musee, like the Edison Company, recognized that flag-waving and a sympathetic treatment of America's imperial adventures reaped rewards at the box-office.

The end of the Dewey celebration merged with the beginning of the America's Cup races, as the *Columbia* easily retained the cup in a three-race sweep. This testament to American know-how received daily front-page coverage by the newspapers. Correspondingly, films of these races were thrown on the Musee's screen shortly after the sailing duels were over. "Instead of the whole race being shown at once, it is shown in a series of four pictures of several minutes length each," reported the *Mail and Express*.[129] Some historians have suggested that Porter took these films of the America's Cup as well as other subjects while he worked at the Eden Musee.[130] Yet Porter, who frequently acknowledged his activities as a moving picture operator and camera builder, never mentions working as a moving picture photographer at this time. It is possible, even probable, that he participated in filming such major news events as the Dewey celebration, but if Porter worked as a cameraman, it must have been sporadically and of little importance. Attributions of film authorship to Porter during 1898–1900 are, for this reason, highly suspect. Two other possibilities seem more likely. Paley, in his continuing association with the amusement center, may have taken the pictures, or the Musee may have made special arrangements to acquire copies of the subjects being taken by American Vitagraph.

In the second half of 1899, motion picture exhibition underwent a significant change that had serious implications for both the Eden Musee and the Edison Manufacturing Company: 35mm moving pictures became a permanent feature at many Manhattan vaudeville houses. Biograph had remained on the bill at Keith's since the Spanish-American War, but that situation was unique. Then in mid June, Vitagraph began to show films at Tony Pastor's, where it would remain for the next nine years. The exhibition service presented its own exclusive films of the boxer James Jeffries in training and the Dewey celebration. "The American Vitagraph has been excelling in enterprise during the past week," reported the *New York Clipper*. "Several views were taken of the Olympia and projected here the evening of the same day, and the Dewey land parade was seen on Saturday evening, five hours after the views were taken."[131] This practice continued with the America's Cup races.

Proctor's theaters did not have films on their bills. For the Dewey celebration, they showed lantern slides of the events. For the America's Cup races, the positions of the boats were reported to Proctor's theaters by wireless and charted on immense maps between acts. Such maps were useless in the evenings, when most patrons attended the theater, since the viewers already knew the outcome. Responding to commercial pressures from both the biograph at Keith's and the vitagraph at Pastor's, F. F. Proctor hired Edison licensee William Paley to provide his theaters with an exhibition service. Possessing several theaters, the vaudeville entrepreneur offered Paley inducements that the Eden Musee could not match. On October 9th Paley premiered his kalatechnoscope at Proctor's 23rd Street Theater, a few doors away from his old employer. Two weeks later he was exhibiting at Proctor's Pleasure Palace on Fifty-eighth Street. There the cameraman set up an office and production facility, enabling him to process film and get it on the screen with maximum speed. *The Burning of the "Nutmeg State,"* taken on October 14th, was shown on the very day of the disaster. Within a month the kalatechnoscope was also at Proctor's theater in Albany, New York, and in Philadelphia. In the trades, Proctor manager J. Austin Fynes announced that Paley's film service was booked for an indefinite run, and it remained at Proctor's houses into the nickelodeon era.[132]

The most prominent vaudeville managers had recognized that film companies needed steady commercial outlets if they were to retain the necessary staff and resources to cover important news events. By late 1899 New York papers were advertising film showings in seven or more theaters, at least six of which presented vaudeville.[133] These changes had an enormous impact on the Eden Musee, which was deprived of its role as the only permanent exhibition venue for 35mm film in New York. Furthermore, the Musee no longer possessed its own production capabilities. Meanwhile, the leading vaudeville exhibition services—Biograph, Vitagraph, and Paley's kalatechnoscope—were establishing reputations by exhibiting their own exclusive films in a timely fashion.

Not long after these developments, Porter left his position at the Eden Musee to become a traveling motion picture exhibitor. In a later deposition Porter observed: "In the summer of 1900 I went on the road with a show of my own."[134] This may well have been motivated by the realization that the Musee's role was no longer as central as when Porter had arrived. In any case, traveling with a black tent, playing carnivals and fairs, culminated Porter's career as an exhibitor.[135] With a selection of films and some slides, he tested his abilities as a showman against many different kinds of audiences. As he had done for the previous four years, Porter saw what people enjoyed and learned to get the most out of his modest resources. Yet now at the age of thirty, his apprenticeship in this area was about to end.

The Edison Manufacturing Company and Its Licensees

The Edison Company's sales and profits for films and projecting kinetoscopes were generally lower from 1898 through 1900 than they had been in the previous two years. Film sales were reduced by almost half, from $75,250 in 1897–98 to $41,207 in 1898–99, $38,991 in 1899–1900, and $49,756 in 1900–1901. Sales of projecting kinetoscopes also fell.[136] This reflected competition from several sources. Biograph contested Edison's suit for patent infringement and dominated film exhibition in first-class vaudeville houses. In the fall of 1898 it had projectors in twenty theaters across the United States.[137] In addition, its mutoscopes were quickly replacing kinetoscopes, being a more efficient peep-hole individual viewing device for moving pictures. Edison also failed to close down Sigmund Lubin, whose films were sold for less than Edison's on a per-foot basis. Moreover, Lubin shot his films at fewer frames per second. Purchasers, therefore, could show a Lubin film of equivalent length for a longer period of time. Such competition forced the Edison Company to reduce its sale price from 30¢ per foot in January 1897 to 24¢ per foot in May 1898 and 15¢ per foot by July 1898.[138] Meanwhile the quantity of footage sold remained constant or increased only slightly, resulting in a rapid falloff of gross income.

Much Edison-related film business was conducted by licensees, who captured a large share of the revenues. From 1898 to 1900, Edison was heavily dependent on these companies for new film subjects. Approximately half of the Edison-copyrighted films from this period were made by American Vitagraph and William Paley. The first Vitagraph films to be copyrighted by Thomas Edison and sold by his company were of the naval parade of August 20, 1898 (*The Fleet Steaming up the North River*). These nine films were taken from a yacht and provided some of the best pictures of the flotilla. Thereafter, Blackton and Smith supplied Edison with many comedies, for example *The Burglar on the Roof* (made by late September but not copyrighted by Edison until December 12, 1898) and *Willie's First Smoke*, as well as trick films such as *Vanishing Lady* and *Congress of Nations*. They also took news films of Admiral Dewey's visit to New York (*Presentation of Loving Cup at City Hall, New York*) and Washington (*Presentation of Nation's Sword to Admiral Dewey*), the America's Cup, the Galveston flood (*Bird's Eye View of Dock Front, Galveston*), and lesser events.

Fewer Paley films entered Edison catalogs (which does not necessarily mean that the cameraman made fewer films than Vitagraph). *Automobile Parade*, which he shot on Saturday, November 4, 1899, was copyrighted by Edison on February 6, 1900. *Dick Crocker Leaving Tammany Hall*, taken on November 18th, was copyrighted on February 9, 1900. A comedy, *An Exchange of Good Stories*, taken of Chauncey Depew and Marshall Wilder in early November may have entered the Edison catalog as *Two Old Pals*, but was never copyrighted. *The Burning of the "Nutmeg State"* and a news film of Sir Thomas Lipton's departure from New York on November 1st were neither copyrighted nor promoted by Edison's Kinetograph Department.[139]

While the Edison Manufacturing Company gained possession of its licensees' negatives and offered them for sale, it had little control over the selection of subject matter, the manner in which these subjects were turned into films, and even the time at which a film might be available for marketing. Vitagraph and Paley made films for use in their vaudeville theaters. Many of these were timely subjects that soon lost their commercial value. Yet these licensees generally retained original subjects for several months—as exclusives for their own exhibitions—before turning them over to Edison for copyright and sale. The Edison Company's relations with these affiliated enterprises was decentralized and informal.

The licensing arrangement perhaps benefited the licensees more than the licensor. Under the constant encouragement of William T. Rock, the third Vitagraph partner, Thomas Edison sued such unlicensed exhibitors as Eberhard Schneider and seriously disrupted their business.[140] While Edison generated some publicity that may have encouraged showmen to buy his company's products, Vitagraph acquired many of the victims' exhibition venues. Ironically, very little money from these exhibitions ever reached Edison coffers. Vitagraph took many of its own films and acquired other subjects directly from European producers. Its purchases from Edison were small and apparently did not even cover the royalties that Edison owed Vitagraph for the sale of prints from its negatives.

Edison tried to shift the commercial balance in his favor when he licensed the Klondike Exposition Company, organized by Thomas Crahan of Montana. In a contract dated March 14, 1899, Thomas Edison was to receive 20 percent of the net receipts derived from the company's exhibitions.[141] The contract also reveals the extent to which Biograph's activities were judged superior, as Edison made a commitment to a large-format motion picture system. For this venture, the "Wizard" agreed to construct two kinetographs, which took pictures 2″ high and 3″ wide, at the cost of $1,000. With these machines in hand, Crahan left for Alaska on June 8th.[142] He was accompanied by an Edison-designated photographic specialist, Robert Kates Bonine (1862–1923), a well-known stereo-view and lantern-slide photographer, originally from Altoona, Pennsylvania. Bonine, who established his reputation taking photographs of the Johnstown flood in 1889 and the Chicago World's Columbian Exposition in 1893, had done some work for Edison in 1898.[143] Bonine also carried a still camera for lantern slides and a regular 35mm motion picture camera.[144]

The two men traveled through Alaska to Dawson City in the Yukon and then into the gold fields. Surviving films from the expedition include *White Horse Rapids*; *Washing Gold on 20 Above Hunker, Klondike*; and *Packers on the Trail* (all submitted for copyright in April 1900 or May 1901). Upon their return in late October, Crahan and Edison discovered that the large-format films had poor registration. "When we project them on the screen the whole picture moves up a foot, then down six inches then up and so on," Edison explained to John

Charles Kayser at work.

Ott before asking him to make "a corrector for correcting negatives so that although the negative prints vary on the film the positives are equidistant."[145] Edison's staff tried to make such a device, but Eberhard Schneider later suggested that they were unsuccessful: "Kayser, one of Edison's inventors, made an intermittent printer, the size of a steam roller such as is used today by the New York Paving Company. The thing would not work at all, and I had to do some printing on certain films for Jim White, Edison's laboratory expert and manager in 1900."[146] By mid January the Klondike Exposition Company had expended $7,385, run out of cash, and still needed projectors and films. Edison was forced to negotiate a new arrangement, under which he supplied the necessary equipment and films. This enabled Crahan to put together three illustrated lectures entitled *Artistic Glimpses of the Wonder World*.[147] By June 1900 any hope Crahan had of recouping his investment and going to the Paris Exposition had ended. The Klondike Exposition Company therefore sold its equipment and film to Edison for $2,500 in cash and $2,500 in Edison goods (phonograph records, etc.).[148] The venture was a financial failure—not only for Crahan but also for the Edison Company, which posted its smallest film profits of any year in the era of projection.

James White
and the Kinetograph Department

Given the often problematic, if large-scale, activities of the Edison licensees, production under James White continued to be of importance. One difficulty in discussing the Kinetograph Department and its accomplishments, however, is determining what White produced and what was produced by the licensees. This is complicated by irregular copyright practices, little production information, and lack of a regular Edison-affiliated exhibition outlet through much of 1899. By early August 1898 the Edison Company had adopted a practice espoused by Sigmund Lubin and was staging reenactments of military actions for the camera. This may have begun with *Shooting Captured Insurgents* and *Cuban Ambush* (both © August 5, 1898), which featured Spanish atrocities and cowardice. Both were somewhat perfunctory and used the same location and camera setup. Although White may have been too ill to participate in these efforts, he had recovered by early October. Perhaps for this reason, William Heise withdrew from filmmaking that month (he left Edison's employ only to return a year later in a nonfilm role).[149] White was responsible for *Battle of San Juan Hill* and *Charge of the Rough Riders at El Caney*, made in late 1898 or early 1899. These were not copyrighted, however, and do not survive. White was soon focusing on America's counterinsurgency in the Philippines, staging and filming such pictures as *Advance of Kansas Volunteers at Caloocan* (© June 5, 1899) and *Capture of Trenches at Candabar* (© June 10, 1899). These avoided the expense of sending a cameraman to the Far East and allowed White to show the heroic actions of American soldiers—something unlikely to be filmed in the midst of a guerrilla war. These one-shot scenes, often shot through underbrush or from a camera position low to the ground, used more credible staging and smoke effects to heighten the scene's realism. The practice of using National Guard units to play the American soldiers likewise added credibility. These films, too, could be sequenced into a series.

The Edison policy of filming reenactments continued in 1900 with the Boer War. By now the scale and level of spectacle had increased—along with the accompanying risks. On April 11th, White was taking a series of these films, including *Boers Bringing in British Prisoners* and *Charge of Boer Cavalry*. While filming *Capture of Boer Battery*, the cannon fired prematurely and wounded the Kinetograph Department manager (see document no. 7). A few days later, White returned to complete the series with Mason Mitchell, an actor who had fought with Roosevelt's Rough Riders during the Spanish-American War, organizing the battle scenes. The participants, said to number two hundred, were primarily members of a local militia. They received $2 each for the day's work (after briefly striking for a 75¢ raise), a $400 investment by the Edison Company.[150]

Filipinos Retreat from Trenches (© June 5, 1899).

DOCUMENT NO. 7

INJURED IN SHAM BATTLE
Two Men Wounded in a Reproduction
of the Engagement at Spion
Kop, in South Africa

Brick Church, N.J., April 11— Two men were injured this afternoon in West Orange at a sham battle in reproduction of the famous engagement at Spion Kop, in South Africa. James H. White, General Manager of the Edison projecting kinetoscope business, had arranged it. The scene was on the rocky side of the eastern slope of the second Orange Mountain, near the Livingstone line. About 200 men had been engaged, half of them in Boer costume posted on the top of the crest, while the remainder attired as British stormed the heights. A good sized cannon was used to heighten the effect and the kinetoscope was placed in position to take the moving pictures. Through some blunder the cannon was discharged prematurely, and Mr. White and one of the men, William McCarthy of 33 South street, Orange, were struck by the wad and burned by the powder. McCarthy's injuries were trivial, but Mr. White was badly lacerated as well as burned, and his condition tonight is reported as serious.

SOURCE: *Philadelphia Ledger*, April 12, 1900, clipping, NjWOE.

White improvised another group of one-shot, acted films over the course of 1899 and 1900, the "Adventures of Jones Series." The first were shot in Llewellyn Park shortly after a February snowstorm. *Jones' Return from the Club* and *Jones and His Pal in Trouble* show the inebriated protagonist (possibly played by White)[151] wrestling with a policeman. In one, Jones is the victor, in the other the cop is. Exhibitors had a choice of alternative endings in which either the law or pleasure would prove triumphant. Subsequent films were shot in the Black Maria. In *Jones Makes a Discovery*, Jones's pal consoles the drunkard's wife with intimate affection—only to be discovered by Jones and tossed out the window. Later subjects include *Why Mrs. Jones Got a Divorce* (© January 17, 1900), in which Mrs. Jones finds irrefutable evidence that the cook has been embracing her husband (telltale handprints on his jacket). Frustrated by his continued denials, she covers him with a panful of flour and discharges the help. Clearly, all is not as it should be in a proper Victorian household, as pleasure and desire exceed their proper boundaries.

By the latter part of 1899 James White and the Kinetograph Department were offering exhibitors multishot subjects in a few unusual circumstances. *Boston Horseless Fire Department* (© September 15, 1899) showed "the entire horseless fire department of Boston accompanied by the old style apparatus which is drawn by horses running at terrific pace down Batterymarch Street." The Edison catalog then noted: "Another view on the same film shows a portion of the Boston fire department making a quick hitch in the engine house and the running out with the horses on a gallop."[152] These linked scenes suggest a thematic relationship: the horseless carriage is on its way to the rescue while the horsedrawn engines are still coming out of the firehouse. This contrast, which is only implicit in the film and would have had to be drawn out by the exhibitor's lecture, apparently justified selling the two scenes as part of the same film.

Shoot the Chutes Series (© September 23, 1899) was called "positively the most wonderful series of pictures ever secured by an animated picture camera." It looks at the same subject from three different vantage points:

The first scene is taken from the pond of the chutes, and shows a number of boats laden with gay Coney Island pleasure-seekers coming down into the water in rapid succession. The next scene is taken from the top of the incline, showing the boats being loaded, starting away, running down the chutes and dashing into the water. The next

Shoot the Chutes Series.

and most wonderful picture was secured by placing the camera in the boat, making a panoramic view of the chutes while running down and dashing into the water. 275 ft.[153]

The camera explores and penetrates the space of this "attraction"; moreover, it was the spatial relations between shots—the ability to introduce multiple perspectives—that provided the necessary justification for the selling of these scenes as one film. As with the proposed combination of *The Black Diamond Express* and *Receding View, Black Diamond Express*, the spatial world portrayed is complex, while the temporality remains imprecise or underdeveloped. (Was this supposed to represent the same action repeatedly from three different perspectives or simply similar actions?) Other multishot actuality films were unfortunately not copyrighted. This includes *Foot-ball Game*, which was taken in Orange on November 30, 1899, and "shows many exciting plays, kickoffs, touchdowns, rushes, etc."[154]

The Edison Company's appropriation of editorial responsibility is also evident in two fiction films: *The Astor Tramp* (© October 27, 1899) and *Love and*

The Astor Tramp. The tramp climbs into a millionaire's bed and then reads about his escapade in the newspapers.

War (© November 28, 1899). White, a singer who made several records for Edison's National Phonograph Company, used his position as head of Edison's Kinetograph Department to produce these "Picture Songs," which were then billed as part of Edison's ongoing efforts to synchronize sound and image. "We have at last succeeded in perfectly synchronizing music and moving pictures," declared Edison catalogs. "The following scenes are very carefully chosen to fit the words and songs which have been especially composed for these pictures."[155] Similar efforts to adapt motion pictures to the song-slide format had already been tried at the Eden Musee and elsewhere. In White's case, the production company provided the narration/song as well as an editorial construction.

The Astor Tramp was a "side splitting subject, showing the mistaken tramp's arrival at the Wm. Waldorf Astor mansion and being discovered comfortably asleep in bed, by the lady of the house."[156] In the second scene, which the Edison catalog does not mention, the tramp is back on the street: he grabs a paper from a newsboy and reads about his recent escapades, gesturing to the audience as he struts around the stage-like set. In fact the film was based on an incident that had received widespread newspaper attention five years earlier.[157] Adopted by popular culture, the episode spawned a skit at Tony Pastor's entitled "The PAstor Tramp." Despite this notoriety, the Edison catalog urged exhibitors to use some kind of verbal clarification to motivate the character's actions and the relationship between the shots: "The music and words accompanying are explanatory and can be either sung or spoken."[158]

The catalog description for the 200-foot, six-scene *Love and War* also reveals a narrative coherence not apparent from simply watching the film. It was "an illustrated song telling the story of a hero who leaves for the war as a private, is promoted to the rank of captain for bravery in service, meets the girl of his choice, who is a Red Cross nurse on the field, and finally returns home triumphantly as an officer to the father and mother to whom he bade good bye as a private."[159] Here again, the title and story line were familiar ones.[160] Only four scenes were copyrighted under this title, but two other films, including the concurrently made *Fun in Camp*, were apparently added to *Love and War* to fill out its advertised length. For both "song films" the careful fit between words and picture required the production company to exercise a high degree of creative control. However, both films lacked the spatial and even temporal complexity of the multishot actualities.

These precocious, though still tentative moves toward multishot films coincided with important developments in motion picture practice. First, the technology of projection was improving. The Edison Company had incorporated Albert Smith's reframing device into its projecting kinetoscope.[161] This enabled the projectionist to reframe the image when it jumped out of registration without having to stop the projector and manually reposition the film. In the past, this problem had been reduced by showing short lengths of films interwoven with slides. Projection quality was also improving, encouraging longer subjects. Secondly, it coincided with the move toward permanent exhibition outlets in vaudeville and the emergence of more established exhibition companies. Commercial stability encouraged longer subjects, in part because larger units were more efficient to work with. Production efficiency was matched by representational innovation. Subjects shown from multiple viewpoints, picture songs, and narrative sequences were often operating within narrowly defined genres. The 1899 *Shoot the Chutes Series* treated the same subject as the 1896 *Shoot the Chutes* (and its many imitations)—but in a new way. *Boston Horseless Fire Department* was likewise an elaboration of the overused fire run.

During the spring of 1900, White and the Kinetograph Department made a bona fide attempt to produce synchronized sound motion pictures. This was for New York City's Board of Education under the supervision of Associate Superintendent Alfred Theodore Schauffler. The resulting program lasted an hour and included the following scenes:

1. A ride through the Ghetto.
2. School assembly, foreign children.
3. Dismissal to the class rooms.
4. Kindergarten games.
5. Recess games, boys.
6. Recess games, girls.
7. A workshop in full operation.
8. Classroom gymnastics.

A Storm at Sea. The cameraman changed lenses or positions to give a "cut-in."

    9. Grace hoop gymnastics drill.
  10. Rapid dismissal to the street.
  11. Ballgames. Foot ball, etc.
  12. Assembly in an uptown school.
  13. Rhythmic ball drill to music.
  14. Cooking class in operation.
  15. Marching salute to the flag.
  16. Indian club swinging, High School Girls.

Accompanying these films were phonograph recordings of the children performing recitations and songs, as well as of the music to which they executed their exercises.[162] According to a member of the Schauffler family, these films were made on the roof of a New York high school so that the scenes could be filmed in sunlight. The superintendent's greetings, the pledge of allegiance, the national anthem, and piano music were recorded first, with people speaking and performing directly into the big horn attached to a phonograph. Then the cylinders were played back and the students and teachers executed their activities to the recordings, mouthing their parts when appropriate.[163] White then traveled to the Paris Exposition, where he was present at the rehearsals for the display that opened at the Social Economy Palace on June 29, 1900.[164]

    A Storm at Sea, taken by White in mid June on his way to the Paris Exposition, shows a storm from the bridge of the *Kaiserina Maria Theresa* in two shots—an establishing view and a close view notable for its visual heightening of the storm's violent effect. A cut-in like this one or a cut-out like the one in *Razing a Factory Chimney,*[165] which was made in England at about the same time, continued earlier screen practices with their well-developed spatial relationships. It would be a mistake, however, to consider this cut-in as an attempt at a match cut: temporality was a difficult and persistent problem in early cinema. Its underdeveloped nature can be explained in large part by the severe limitations on temporal specificity in traditional lantern shows. Significantly, from their first appearance such two-shot constructions were listed and sold as a single scene. Cut-ins and cut-outs were the type of editorial strategies over which producers had easy and relatively uncontested control.

While in Europe, White (along with an as yet unidentified colleague) filmed Paris and the 1900 Exposition, using a riotous array of camera movements. *Panoramic View of the Champs Elysees* was taken from the front of a moving vehicle and *Panorama of the Paris Exposition, from the Seine* from a boat. For *Panorama from the Moving Boardwalk*, the camera was placed on a "Platform Mobile." Either on their way or shortly after arriving in Paris, the photographers acquired a more sophisticated panning mechanism, which allowed their camera to follow action more smoothly. This is evident in *Champs de Mars*, in which the camera plays cat and mouse with two women. Panning right to left, the camera follows them until they move behind an arch. It tries to pick them up again, but the women foil the operators' expectations. For *Panorama of Eiffel Tower*, the camera tilts vertically, moving up the tower and then back down—at which point the American showman Lyman Howe peers into the lens and smiles broadly. These subjects proved popular with a large number of exhibitors (including Howe, who appeared more discreetly in other scenes) and were usually combined into sequences that gave American audiences a rich impression of the event.[166] When *Panorama of the Moving Boardwalk*, for example, was followed by *Panorama from the Moving Boardwalk*, one the reverse angle of the other, a clear spatial world was constructed, although the temporal relationship between shots was only proximate and nonspecific.

On his return to the United States, White quickly employed the mobile tripod head to shoot sweeping panoramas of well-known locations. His peripatetic lifestyle continued with *Circular Panorama of Atlantic City, N.J.*, *Circular Panorama of Mauch Chunk, Penna.*; *Circular Panorama of Niagara Falls*; and *Panoramic View of the White House, Washington, D.C.* These films revelled in the camera's newfound ability to present spectacle on an unprecedented scale. In the process, narrative concerns appear temporarily forgotten. Such pictures can be contrasted to earlier "panoramas" which involved the camera moving through space, usually on the front of a conveyance. These earlier efforts were easily incorporated into the narrative flow of a travel program and so proved popular. Even if included in longer programs, White's circular panoramas tended to interrupt any narrative progression. Although there were some exceptions, this technique was used most frequently to represent awe-inspiring

Panorama of Eiffel Tower. The camera could now tilt smoothly up and down.

scenery or large-scale devastation (*Panorama of Wreckage of Water Front, Galveston*). The new panning capacity, however, was perfect for following action and keeping subjects in frame when making news films.

The Edison Manufacturing Company Reaches Its Commercial Nadir

Edison's film business was in dire straits by 1900. Despite White's production of a significant number of commercially attractive films, the Edison Company lacked strong photographic skills. Eberhard Schneider would later claim that White "knew nothing whatever as to the composition of developer and its effects. He made up hypo developer in quantity (fully mixed) for weeks ahead and many good negatives . . . were spoiled in this ink solution."[167]

Biograph, moreover, was vigorously contesting the inventor's patent suit. Tensions between licensees and licensor were high. When the Edison Company failed to turn over the money it owed Vitagraph, the unhappy licensees threatened to sue for an accounting. They had forgotten who held the trump cards, and William Gilmore obligingly reminded them by cancelling their contractual relationship in January 1900. A series of stormy exchanges followed, which threatened to send Blackton and Smith to jail. Although Gilmore eventually worked out a new arrangement with the Vitagraph group in October 1900, thereby acquiring a fresh influx of films for Edison catalogs, relations remained uneasy and depended on legal coercion. If Edison lost his court case against Biograph, his commercial "allies" would obviously become commercial enemies.

The Edison Manufacturing Company also faced uneasy relations with its selling agents. Although providing a large outlet for Edison goods, Frederick M. Prescott's New York office had begun to sell Lubin films. In June 1899 Edison brought suit against Prescott and forced another American entrepreneur out of the film business.[168] Two individuals, who were to play important roles in the industry and effectively promote Edison products in the years ahead, appeared to sell Edison goods on the exclusive terms Edison demanded. The first of these was George Kleine, whose Kleine Optical Company in Chicago started to purchase Edison films in June 1899.[169] The second was Percival Waters, who had worked with White at the Vitascope Company and was then a small, New York-based jobber of Edison films.

In November 1899 Waters formed a silent partnership with James White and John Schermerhorn, Gilmore's brother-in-law and assistant general manager of the Edison Manufacturing Company since 1896.[170] Their partnership, called the Kinetograph Company, was to act as an exhibitor and selling agent of Edison films. Waters was to run the business, while White and Schermerhorn promised to arrange several thousand dollars worth of credit, to send customers to the Kinetograph Company whenever possible, and take "such picture subjects as would tend to increase their business to suit their special customers in the various theaters."[171] Although Gilmore was almost certainly aware of the arrangement, it involved obvious conflicts of interest. As Waters' attorney later asked, did White and Schermerhorn act in the best interests of the Kinetograph Department or the Kinetograph Company when these interests diverged? Yet White and Schermerhorn were simply taking advantage of a commercial opportunity in a manner consistent with the business practices then prevalent at the Edison works.[172]

The Kinetograph Company filled a need that had become apparent not only with the demise of Prescott's agency but because the Edison Company needed its own vaudeville exhibition outlet. One of the new company's first actions was to establish a permanent working relationship with Huber's 14th Street Museum. Edison had already sued George Huber earlier in the year for hiring Lubin and others to exhibit non-Edison films in his theater.[173] With rival vaudeville theaters making motion pictures a permanent attraction, Huber's museum contracted for the Kinetograph Company's exhibition services in November

1899.[174] Increasingly the Kinetograph Company acted as Edison's exhibition arm, acquiring the first copies of completed films and showing them in its programs. Unlike the licensees who took subjects for their own use, Waters arranged with White to provide their company with special films for its exhibitions. Along with Kleine and Peter Bacigalupi in San Francisco, the Kinetograph Company became an Edison selling agent with special discounts. Perhaps because of these compromised origins, Waters' Kinetograph Company developed a complementary relationship with Edison's Kinetograph Department that flourished long into the future, outlasting White's tenure as department manager and the constitution of the company as a silent partnership.

Edison, embattled on various fronts early in 1900, came close to selling his motion picture business. In March the Biograph and Edison companies were close to a "union of interests in the moving picture field."[175] After further meetings, according to Terry Ramsaye, Biograph secured an option to buy Edison's motion picture interests for half a million dollars, paying $2,500 for the option on April 12th.[176] Perhaps this helps to explain the decision to incorporate the Edison Manufacturing Company on May 5, 1900. The new corporation was activated three days later when Thomas Edison turned over "all rights, title and interest in and to the business heretofore conducted by me and known as the 'Edison Manufacturing Company' with the exception of the Projecting Kinetoscope, Kinetograph, Kinetoscope and Film business and everything pertaining thereto."[177] Since the film interests were about to be sold, they were not assigned to the new corporation.

The financing of the Edison-Biograph deal, however, fell through—if it had not, the history of American cinema would undoubtedly be quite different. Although Edison retained his personal control over moving pictures and so continued to pursue patent infringement and to copyright films in his own name, the corporate and privately owned parts of the business were effectively merged. With Biograph's option unexercised, Edison and his associates reassessed their motion picture business and decided to increase their own commitment to the field rather than renew negotiations with Harry Marvin and other Biograph executives. William Gilmore began to shift the Edison Manufacturing Company's commercial strategies in light of the difficulties encountered during the previous few years. Edison had to depend less on his licensees. This meant investing in a new studio and hiring additional personnel. The employment of Edwin Porter was part of this renewed commitment.

6 The Production Company Assumes Greater Control: 1900–1902

Creative responsibilities were rapidly centralized within the production companies during the first years of the new century. Nowhere was this more evident than with the shift of editorial control from exhibitor to producer. Responsibility for narrative construction accompanied this shift, ultimately making possible and valorizing the production company's claims to authorship. This far-reaching transformation was taking place in the film practices of other countries as well, notably of England and France. In the United States, the Edison Manufacturing Company not only led the way in this process but struggled with these complex issues in particularly revealing ways.

Porter Becomes an Edison Employee

By the fall of 1900 the Edison Company was reorganizing its Kinetograph Department and upgrading its technical system. Edwin Porter, with his mechanical ingenuity and experience, was the appropriate person to hire for the latter effort. The experienced operator had his own reasons for joining the Edison staff. His small factory for manufacturing projectors had recently been wiped out by fire.[1] Since traveling motion picture exhibitors were suffering through a difficult period, Porter was not eager to pursue such a commercial venture if other options were available. The exhibitor's admiration for Edison was undoubtedly another influential factor. In the end, Porter was added to the inventor's payroll a few days before Thanksgiving 1900. He was employed to "improve and redesign moving picture cameras, projecting machines and perforators," based on the superior equipment he had built and used at the Eden Musee.[2]

Edison Laboratory in West Orange, ca. 1900. Black Maria is in center.

According to Porter, "Mr. White, also Mr. Gilmore, recognized the superiority of my machine over theirs and they engaged me more as a technical man to improve their machine."[3] Edison advertisements described the 1901 Model Projecting Kinetoscope, which benefited from Porter's improvements, as "a complete revolution in projecting machines."[4] Besides the customary claims to a steady, flickerless image, the Edison machine "is equipped with the only perfect take up device which has ever been constructed to reel up 1,000 ft. of film without hitch or failure. Shows both stereopticon slides and animated pictures. One person can work the whole machine. It has a new adjustable arc lamp which is a marvel in itself. The lamp house is adaptable to any kind of illuminant known to the profession." By 1901, after having incorporated improvements from Albert Smith's vitagraph and the Eden Musee's cinematograph, Edison's projecting kinetoscope was among the best in its field. At a cost of $375 in labor and materials, Porter also constructed a new printing machine in January and early February.[5]

By the fall of 1900 the Edison Company had decided to build a new studio that would ensure a steady supply of films and improve its competitive position. The evident stabilization of exhibition outlets through vaudeville theaters made this appropriate. Because the demand for film programs had fluctuated between 1896 and 1899, relying on licensees to produce films and locate exhibition opportunities had kept expenses and risk low. Now that moving pictures were a permanent feature and exhibitors required a consistent supply of films, a new approach was merited. The result was the nation's first indoor, glass-enclosed film studio where pictures could be produced year-round—a definite improvement over both the Biograph and Vitagraph companies' open-air rooftop stages.

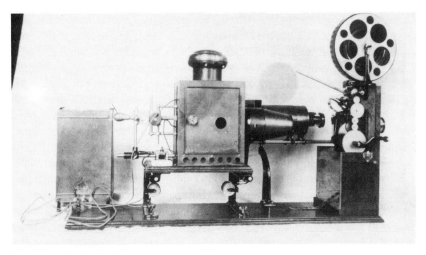

The Edison Projecting Kinetoscope, ca. 1901.

Unlike the Black Maria, the new studio was to be located in the heart of New York's entertainment district. All the personnel and materials needed for regular film production were at hand.

In October 1900 the Kinetograph Department rented the top floor and roof of 41 East Twenty-first Street for $150 a month. The Hinkle Iron Company was hired "to furnish, deliver and erect complete and in good substantial and workman-like manner a photographic Studio on roof" at a cost of $2,800.[6] The first expenditures for the New York studio were dispersed in December for "Pay Roll—Photo Gallery"—a total of $95.77. Another $10 was spent "hoisting 3 drums and shafting." On January 12, 1901, E. E. Hinkle announced that the building was complete after a mason had pointed up all the front and rear fireproof blocks at the studio. By mid February the studio was in working order.[7]

The Edison Company shared its space with Percival Waters' Kinetograph Company, which moved from offices across the street even before construction was completed. According to Waters, the space was

approximately 90 feet by 20 feet and on the roof above this floor there was a large studio occupying substantially the entire roof, fitted up especially for the purpose of taking moving pictures. . . . The proposition was made to me, and I accepted it, by which I was to pay the agent of the building monthly in advance $150., the entire rent for the top floor and the studio and I was to receive credit at the end of each month on my account with the Edison Company for $110, making my rent $40. The Edison Company was to have the exclusive use of the studio on the roof and a room approximately 8 × 10 feet lighted by a sky light and another room approximately 25 feet by 10 feet electrically lighted which was used as a dark room and dressing room and access to these two rooms through my place of business and the privilege of using the front rooms on my floor as dressing rooms. The company was also to have the use of

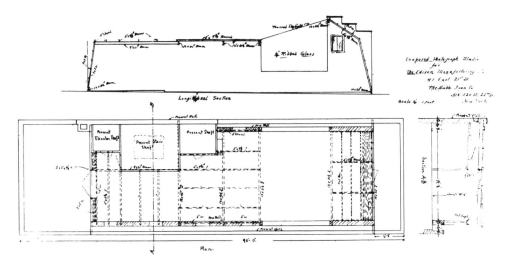

Blueprint for Edison's new motion picture studio on Twenty-first Street, New York.

the telephone, have such electric light as was needed and the use of my shop which I fitted up with a complete set of tools which they did use from time to time in connection with repairs to machines and cameras in connection with their operation of the studio and the producing of pictures there. They also had the use of my projecting machines for the purpose of exhibiting and testing their films.[8]

Porter recalled that "after being with [the Edison Company] a short time and as they were in need of a cameraman and producer, I was given charge of the first skylight studio in the country."[9] Porter actually had little experience as a cameraman; he was hired because of his considerable knowledge of cinematic practices and because his background as an electrician and machinist enabled him to put the studio in working order and to keep it that way. On staff, he was available to further improve the projecting kinetoscope and Edison's cameras. In addition, Edison executives needed someone who would not desert the studio if the inventor's patents suffered setbacks in the courts. Many of the more experienced cameramen could not have been trusted precisely for this reason. Porter's self-effacing manner, his emulation of Edison, and his lack of conflicting business interests all suited him to the company's needs. Also, studio productions did not then have the same importance—vis-à-vis news films and other actualities—that they were later to assume.

Porter's move into filmmaking occurred, moreover, within what might be called a collaborative system of production. Collaboration was, as already shown, familiar in the early years of film—whether between Porter and Charles H. Balsley, Dickson and Heise, White and Blechynden, or J. Stuart Blackton and Albert E. Smith. Now Porter shared his new responsibilities with George S.

Fleming, an actor and scenic designer who started working for the Edison Company on January 13, 1901. Fleming earned $20 per week, while Porter received only $15. This relationship with Fleming would provide Porter with a model for subsequent organizations of film work. In the years ahead, whether with Wallace McCutcheon, James Searle Dawley, or Hugh Ford, Porter would seek out a similar collaborative working method. Porter would feel most secure dealing with the filmic issues (camerawork, editing, special effects, camera tricks, etc.) and look to others to handle the actors. Although the stories and scripts for these subjects came from many sources, Porter would customarily shape them to his own sense of the commercially popular.

Although this collaborative system typified pre-Griffith film production, it has been little recognized. Janet Staiger has articulated the general historical consensus in characterizing pre-1907 filmmaking as relying on the "cameraman system." In the cameraman system, a single individual is responsible for the production of a given film.[10] The notion of a single cinematographer improvising short skits, or, more typically, traveling about the country taking actualities, resonates with the concept of early cinema as simpler and more "primitive."

The cameraman system was indeed employed during the pre-Griffith era, but then it was used in later years as well. The collaborative approach, with its informal exchange of ideas and sharing of roles, was more characteristic of the early period. Although this working method typically involved two key individuals, others also made contributions. Thus, James White assisted Porter and Fleming on such studio productions as *Execution of Czolgosz* and *Life of an American Fireman*. Collaboration, however, frequently went beyond Porter, Fleming, and White to include members of the staff whose contributions would never be expected (or even tolerated) in later, more hierarchical and labor-specialized organizations. While filmmakers of this period, including Porter, did occasionally have to work alone, this collaborative approach was preferred.

The new studio changed the balance of power between the Edison Company and its licensees. On January 10th, White and Gilmore terminated their licensing agreement with the talented, but difficult, American Vitagraph Company, after Blackton and Smith claimed that they were unable to pay a 10 percent royalty on exhibition income.[11] In the future, the Vitagraph owners were theoretically restricted to showing only Edison films. Though exhibiting European subjects in order to keep their business afloat, they ceased virtually all production activities. Only William Paley continued to operate under formal Edison auspices.

By mid February, Porter and Fleming were turning out short films; one of the first, *Kansas Saloon Smashers*, was the occasion for a rare publicity still. Excepting a few winter scenes (*Ice-Boat Racing at Red Bank, N.J.*) and news films of McKinley's second inauguration (*President McKinley and Escort Going to the Capitol*), most Edison subjects from the winter of 1901 were shot in the studio. Full-scale production of short comedies continued at Edison, while

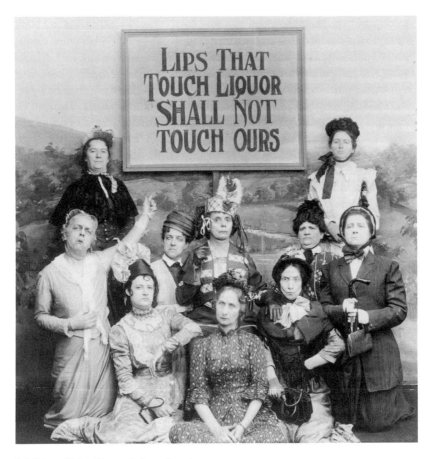

Publicity still for *Kansas Saloon Smashers*.

Biograph, with its outdoor facilities, suspended most production. Edison's investment was already paying off.

The Cinema as a Visual Newspaper

Until recently, historians looking at turn-of-the-century American cinema have generally dismissed it as naive, primitive, and unformed. Next to the consistent photographic realism of Lumière and the theatrical artifice of Méliès, American subjects have seemed eclectic, derivative, "literal and unimaginative," and "significant today mainly as social documents."[12] A more sympathetic and careful examination, however, reveals a unifying principle behind much American film production. As Robert C. Allen has pointed out, the screen was often described and conceived of as a "visual newspaper," where news items, human interest material, political satires, short cartoon-like sketches, and the sports page could all be combined within a variety format.[13] As *Leslie's Weekly* observed of Edison's rival, "The Biograph goes hand in hand with the daily press in presenting to nightly audiences events which they have seen during the day or read of in the evening papers."[14] This came about, according to Harry Marvin, Biograph's vice-president, in response to audience demand:

> In building up our business we were of the opinion at first that what the public would desire would be a series of finished and artistic pictures representing a scene or event of historic interest or artistic value. At first we followed such a course, but we soon found that the public demanded of us the prompt and reliable service of the daily newspaper rather than the artistic or aesthetic finish of the weekly or monthly magazine. That is to say, the public has expected us to gather the news in a pictorial way and disseminate it at once.[15]

If Biograph offered the visual newspaper par excellence, Edison subjects also owed much to this philosophy of production.

As the first form of mass communication and mass entertainment, newspapers profoundly influenced many cultural forms, including cinema. The mode of representation used by these papers included, at one end of the spectrum, the "objectivity" of the *New York Times* and the *New York Tribune*, which treated the reporter and the camera as recorders of reality and arranged the resulting stories hierarchically, based on their newsworthiness. The primary function of these papers was to inform and, through their editorial pages, to instruct their readership. At another extreme was the variety format of the Hearst papers, which were as interested in entertaining as in informing, preferring the sensational to the dry. In many instances, of course, the *Journal* did provide its readership with photographs and "objective" accounts of important happenings, but the comic strip suggests that amusement was also an important function.

The front page of the *New York Journal* was an excellent indicator of events considered worthy of the Kinetograph Department's attention throughout 1901–2. *Kansas Saloon Smashers*, first advertised as *Mrs. Carrie Nation and Her Hatchet Brigade*, portrayed the prohibitionist and her followers on a saloon-wrecking rampage that received front-page coverage.[16] The film was both reenactment and burlesque. While the set was based on a *Journal* photograph of a destroyed saloon in Wichita, Kansas, the characters and their actions owed much to the satirical cartoons appearing on the paper's editorial page.[17] Lubin's exhibition service showed the film at Bradenburgh's Ninth and Arch Street Museum, where the pictures were "declared to be genuine ones" and headed the entire bill.[18] This popular subject was promptly remade by both Lubin and Biograph. Later, when Carrie Nation's husband demanded a divorce, news reports inspired Edison's *Why Mr. Nation Wants a Divorce*.[19]

Terrible Teddy, the Grizzly King, a burlesque on Teddy Roosevelt, then vice-president-elect, who was shooting mountain lions in Colorado, was based on a political cartoon series also running in the *Journal*. In a panel printed on

Kansas Saloon Smashers. A stop-action, concealed edit as Carrie Nation destroys the saloon.

February 4th, the cartoonist showed Teddy perched heroically on a pile of animals while two men wearing small tags labeled "my photographer" and "my press agent" record the event in the background. The second scene was inspired by a panel that appeared on February 18th. As with the Carrie Nation film, Porter and Fleming were playing with a subject that enjoyed frequent satirical treatment. To offer but one example, Dumont's Minstrels were performing the burlesque "Teddy Roosevelt, the Bear Hunter" the very week that this film was made.[20]

"My Photographer" and "My Press Agent" watch Teddy shoot a cat in the first scene of *Terrible Teddy, the Grizzly King*.

Short screen comedies shared much with comic strips in the Sunday papers. The Happy Hooligan series, started by Blackton and Smith and continued by Kinetograph personnel, were indebted to the various cartoon strips depicting tramps ("Burglar Bill," "Happy Hooligan," and "Weary Willie") and appeared almost as regularly. The simple one-shot gags of *Happy Hooligan April-Fooled* (© April 6, 1901) and *Tramp's Strategy That Failed* (© May 15, 1901) are closest in their narrative structure to the Sunday strips. In these films, the humor revolved around the conflicts between constituted society and the outcast, with most situations ending with the tramp receiving an almost ritual beating.

The rube was another comic strip character who appeared in Porter/Fleming films. In *Another Job for the Undertaker, The Hayseed's Experience at Washington Monument, Rube's Visit to the Studio, Rubes in the Theatre*, and *How They Do Things on the Bowery*, this country hick encounters the modern mysteries of city life with costly naivete. In one comic strip, Uncle Reuben's unfamiliarity with "moving staircases" causes the loss of his bag and the "brick of gold" he has already been conned into purchasing.[21] In *Another Job for the Undertaker*, the rube's inability to read and his unfamiliarity with gas lighting cause him to blow out the flame, resulting in his asphyxiation and death. In *How They Do Things on the Bowery*, he is duped by a woman con artist, one of the many fast-talking city types to take advantage of his gullibility.

TERRIBLE TEDDY, THE GRIZZLY KING.

CHAPTER XI.

"Our hero stood transfixed with horror. A bear, a mountain lion, a deer and a pack of other wild beasts were advancing madly upon him in solid phalanx, bent upon his destruction.

"From another direction marched a squad of fierce photographers to take snap-shots of his last moments, to picture him in his mortal defeat.

"Before the maddened beasts could do their work of vengeance upon our hero sixteen shots rang out in sixteen seconds. The animals fell writhing on the greensward, dying one by one.

"Striking a heroic attitude upon the piled up corpses Terrible Teddy, the Grizzly King, waited for the photographers to unlimber their cameras.

"But before they could move another step an awful shout was heard.

"Die, Terrible Teddy," said the shout, "your last moment has arrived."

(To be continued in our next.)

Cartoons provided the storyboard for *Terrible Teddy, the Grizzly King*.

Hearst's papers also combined information and amusement in ways disquieting to the journalistic standards of the highbrow press. The *New York Journal* published artists' sketches of news events, particularly when appropriate photographs were unavailable. What was lost in accurate reporting was gained in romantic melodrama. Sketches of battles were more visually dynamic than photographs of the trenches during periods of inactivity. Likewise a battle enacted for the kinetograph in the New Jersey hills provided a romantic realism that William Paley never matched when he photographed U.S. troops in Florida or Cuba. Artists' sketches appearing on the front page of the *New York Journal* dramatized the sensationalistic aspects of the Biddle brothers' escape from prison.[22] These were subsequently used by Porter and Fleming for the production design of *Capture of the Biddle Brothers.*

Perhaps the *Journal*'s most distinctive use of visuals was the composite illustration that combined both drawing and photographic material. Such a syncretic amalgamation of disparate mimetic materials was at odds with the concept of a consistently represented, and therefore coherent, world that was then on the ascendency in the bourgeois theater and press.[23] Certainly it was inimical to the *New York Times*, which in any case continued to put far more faith in the word than the image. The representational strategies in Hearst's papers have parallels in much of early cinema, particularly in Porter's work at Edison. In *Terrible Teddy, the Grizzly King*, the natural, wooded location coexists with the cartoonist's tags still attached to the actors. The carefully constructed authenticity of the set for *Kansas Saloon Smashers* is seemingly contradicted by the painted mirrors and props along the back wall and with the stop-action photography of trick films used each time Mrs. Nation smashes a mirror. This syncretism, which has been denigrated as immature by historians accustomed to viewing Hollywood realism as a teleological endpoint, thus had its equivalent in long-standing cultural forms (e.g., theater, newspapers, the magic lantern).

Editorial Strategies

Most Porter/Fleming productions from the winter of 1901 were single-shot acted films between fifty and one hundred feet in length. These depicted a simple gag with a clear, though brief, Aristotelian construction—a beginning, middle, and end. In *The Old Maid Having Her Picture Taken*, the woman is so unattractive that when she looks into a mirror, it cracks and falls to the floor. When

Capture of the Biddle Brothers.

Exhibitors were urged to show *Old Maid Having Her Picture Taken* and *Old Maid in the Drawing Room* as a larger unit.

she poses for a picture and looks into the lens, the camera explodes. This comedy featured Gilbert Saroni, a well-known vaudeville performer and female impersonator who specialized in playing unattractive old maids in vaudeville sketches like "The Giddy Girl."[24] *The Old Maid in the Drawing Room* (copyrighted as *The Old Maid 'in the Horse Car*) was a facial expression film with Saroni photographed in close-up as he talked to the camera. "Her facial expressions are extremely humorous," declared one Edison catalog, "and when this picture was first shown in New York City, the audience was convulsed with laughter."[25] It was suggested that the old maid was busy talking about her adventures at the photo gallery. Thus, if an exhibitor desired, he could combine these two single-shot films to create a more elaborate subject. By giving the audience a better view of a face that was capable of destroying a camera, the exhibitor could introduce a self-reflexive element that only added to the farce.

From the outset, however, Porter and Fleming produced a significant number of multishot acted films, thus assuming control over the editorial function in select circumstances. The first scene of *Terrible Teddy, the Grizzly King* is described in an Edison catalog:

A burlesque on Theodore Roosevelt hunting mountain lions in Colorado and taken from the New York Journal and Advertiser. The scene opens in a very picturesque wood. Teddy with his large teeth is seen running down the hill with his gun in hand, followed by his photographer and press agent. He reconnoitres around a large tree and finally discovers the mountain lion. He kneels on one knee and makes a careful shot. Immediately upon the discharge of his gun a huge black cat falls from the tree and Teddy whips out his bowie knife, leaps on the cat and stabs it several times, then poses while his photographer makes a picture and the press agent writes up the thrilling adventure. A side splitting burlesque.[26]

In the next scene, unmentioned in the Edison catalog, the hunter and his retinue

Biograph's *How Bridget Made the Fire.*

No. 1497
Title *How Bridget Made the Fire.*
Length 142 ft.
Code Word *Gageiro*

The Finish of Bridget McKeen.

are shown coming down a path: visual continuity and narrative coherence between the first and second shots are disrupted by the sudden appearance of a new pro-filmic element—Teddy's horse. Although Kemp Niver has suggested that there is continuity of space, time, and action between these two shots,[27] the inspiration for the scenes—two cartoon panels printed two weeks apart—offers contextual evidence that indicates this is unlikely. Not strong enough to stand alone as a separate subject, this second shot became commercially viable as a tag to the opening scene.

The Finish of Bridget McKeen, another two-shot comedy made in February, may have been inspired by Biograph's single-shot *How Bridget Made the Fire,* produced in June of the previous year. Other possible antecedents also existed. Like *The Finish of Michael Casey,* which Porter made a short time later, this ethnic joke was made at the expense of the "thick-headed" Irish. The first scene was filmed against the backdrop of a kitchen (including the far edge of the ceiling), with a stove, table, and chair as the only real objects on the set. The decor is a schematic, two-dimensional suggestion of a kitchen, just as Bridget, played by a male employee, is a burlesque of a maid rather than a believable portrayal. Using stop-action procedures, Porter replaced the actor, who is using a can marked "kerosine" to start the stove, with a dummy. After an explosion expels the dummy upward out of the scene, pieces of the body/dummy fall to the earth after an abnormally long time.[28] It is this distension of time that provides the scene with one of its key comic elements. The second scene is simply a static, painted backdrop showing Bridget's tombstone, on which is written the well-known ditty "Here Lies the Remains of Bridget McKeen Who Started a Fire with Kerosine." The relationship between the two scenes is easily understood, particularly for English-speaking audiences. Not only is the first shot the cause of the second, but the ditty recounts the previous scene even as it works as an effective punch line.

Another Job for the Undertaker, made two months after *The Finish of*

Bridget McKeen, has a similar narrative structure. Shot 1 is a typical trick film: when a rube enters his hotel room, its contents and his clothes quickly vanish. "He then walks up to the gas jet and in direct disregard of the sign (which reads 'Don't Blow out the Gas') proceeds to blow out the gas. Three vigorous breaths are consumed in extinguishing the light, when the Rube faces the foreground of the picture with a satisfied look and tumbles into bed. The scene instantly changes to a funeral procession, headed by Reuben's hearse and followed by carriages of his country friends."[29] The second shot was filmed outside using procedures associated with actualities. The editorial combination of disparate mimetic elements is consistent with Porter's use of painted and real pro-filmic elements within a single scene. The syncretic mode of representation is simply taken to another level, utilizing editorial strategies that Porter had learned well as an exhibitor.

Terrible Teddy, the Grizzly King, The Finish of Bridget McKeen, and *Another Job for the Undertaker* share many characteristics. The first scenes are self-contained narratives constructed like many single-shot films of the period. The only significant difference is the addition of a tag, a short fragment that gained its value in reference to the principal scene. Each tag also represents a shift in representational methods, from narrative to non-narrative, from theatrical to painterly, from trick to actuality, or from movement to stasis. The photographer's editorial prerogatives were still confined to specialized situations. Within these limited possibilities, the films lack phenomenological continuity from one shot to the next: their relationships are aspatial and atemporal. Continuity is restricted to a narrative or thematic level. Porter had not begun to explore the spatial and temporal relations that were to become fundamental to later narrative cinema.

Two multishot films made early in 1901 are significant for yet another reason: they made use of a dissolve. In *The Finish of Bridget McKeen,* Porter dissolved between the main narrative gag in the kitchen and the tombstone tag. In *Why Bridget Stopped Drinking,* made about the same time but not copyrighted, Porter used a single camera position for both shots—the dissolve smoothing and clarifying the jump in time. The dissolve, a common screen technique developed in the mid nineteenth century, was executed by exhibitors during the course of projecting slides.[30] It was considered a particularly elegant way to move from one image to the next, preventing sudden jumps when scenes changed. In the late 1890s exhibitors occasionally dissolved from film to film or film to slides, but with mixed success.[31] The technique was not only tricky but required good timing, considerable equipment, and an extra assistant. In transitions from film to film, it was possible and much more practical for dissolves to be made in the motion picture camera or during the printing process. Méliès' *Cinderella,* which Porter projected at the Eden Musee, was perhaps the first film to contain dissolves: this technique was soon adopted by Blackton and Smith for *Congress of Nations.* Porter then employed it regularly during 1901–2, concluding with *Life of an American Fireman*. If nothing else, it gave the production company new opportunities to assume control over the editorial process.

A group of studio films in late April and early May featured the dog known as "Mannie," who appears with his owner, Laura Comstock, in *Laura Comstock's Bag-Punching Dog*. The film begins with a close view of the duo and then cuts to a vaudeville-type routine probably taken from their act then being performed at Keith's Union Square Theater. Prospective purchasers were told that Mannie's "high jumps and lightning-like punches are remarkable and cause one to marvel at the amount of patience that must be necessary to teach a dog such tricks."[32] The introductory portrait functioned much like the facial expression film in the suggested combination of two Gilbert Saroni comedies discussed above. Here the producer asserted editorial control because the portrait was not strong enough to be sold on its own. It was also placed at the beginning of the picture rather than at the conclusion. Both uses of "emblematic shots" are innovations that can apparently be attributed to Porter, and yet here again caution and qualification are essential. Lantern-slide portraits of Spanish-American war heroes had often been exhibited in conjunction with related scenes. Thus, a portrait of Captain Sigsbee might have preceded the film of his ship, the *Maine*. Porter, therefore, applied his expertise as an showman to new material and a new situation. It was a significant achievement, but hardly an unexpected departure from previous practice.

Norman H. Mosher—Laura Comstock's husband, her manager, and Mannie's trainer—developed a relationship with Porter that would endure for over five years, during which time Mannie appeared in many Edison productions.[33] At the outset of this association, Mannie played the tramp's nemesis in several Happy Hooligan films. *Pie, Tramp and the Bulldog* consists of one "shot" of three separate camera takes (or subshots): (1) the tramp indicates to the film spectators that he is hungry, but that the bulldog prevents him from getting to the pie cooling on a nearby window sill, and so he exits the frame; (2) the tramp immediately returns on stilts to outsmart the dog and eat the pie on the ledge; (3) the dog gets the tramp by jumping out the house window, and the two exit with the dog holding onto the tramp's pants. Here Porter spliced together a succession of takes taken from a single camera position to give the illusion of a single, uninterrupted continuity. Rather than using this procedure to create a "trick," he used it for pacing purposes and to construct a narrative that would have been difficult to execute during a single take. (The time occupied by the tramp's off-screen acquisition of stilts was condensed in a way that obeyed theatrical convention.) *Pie, Tramp and the Bulldog* was praised in a subsequent Edison catalog: "This we believe to be one of the funniest pictures ever put on exhibition. It has had a run of five weeks at Proctor's New York Vaudeville Theatres and the audiences never seemed to tire of it."[34] With the studio in operation only a few months, Porter and Fleming were proving themselves adept producers of short comedies.

The Tramp's Dream, another film in this series, meticulously imitated a Lubin picture of the same title made in late 1899.[35] (Clearly Edison personnel were as ready to "borrow" from their contemporaries as vice versa.)[36] The picture has a more complex shot structure than Porter's previous films: shot (1) the tramp goes to sleep on the park bench; shot (2) the dream—the usual confrontation between the tramp, who wants a free meal, and the dog, which grabs the tramp by his pants; shot (3) a return to shot 1, the tramp is being hit on the foot and shaken by a passing policeman. The last shot explains why the dream ends and also reinforces the parallelism of the tramp being attacked by the dog and the patrolman: he gets no rest in either his dream world or his real world. Not only is there temporal continuity (although its precise nature is not defined), but a movement into and out of the tramp's mind. Subjective images, whether dreams, visions, or a character's subjective "point-of-view," were among the first instances in which cameramen employed sophisticated editorial strategies that created spatial and temporal relations between shots.[37]

Spring 1901

That spring, Edison production moved back outside the studio. Porter probably took *Buffalo Bill's Wild West Show Parade*, which "shows Buffalo Bill and his family of Rough Riders on their triumphal entry in New York, April 1, 1901."[38] Over the following weeks, Wild West Show performances in Madison Square Garden included "the hold-up of the Deadwood Stage."[39] This may have inspired or even provided the necessary actors and props for another Edison film made that spring—*Stage Coach Hold-up in the Days of '49*:

> This scene will give you a good idea of the desperate "Hold-Ups" that occurred on the plains when the rush was made to the new gold fields in '49. It shows the desperadoes coming from ambush, covering the driver of the stage with Winchester rifles and ordering him to halt. The occupants of the coach are compelled to dismount from their places, and are lined up in a very realistic manner with their hands thrown up. The outlaws get all the booty they can, and are just departing when an armed Sheriff's posse arrives. They pursue the bandits and after a desperate chase and a brutal conflict, capture them and return to the scene of the robbery. The bandits are then forced at the points of revolvers to ride in front of the coaching party to Dad's Gulch, a mining town, where they are safely landed in the lock-up. This picture will joyously intoxicate any audience, and deafening applause for an encore will be certain. Length 150 ft.[40]

Stage Coach Hold-up might answer several historical questions even as it raises others. It is a possible model for the British film *Robbery of a Mail Coach* (September–November 1903) as well as a precursor of Porter's later *The Great Train Robbery*.[41] While the description may be a somewhat expansive version of what was actually shown on the screen, the picture could have contained as many as four shots. Unfortunately it is a lost film and the catalog description

A Trip Around the Pan-American Exposition makes use of the viewer-as-passenger convention.

provides no certain answers to its possible construction. The historian must look elsewhere to trace the development of film narrative at Edison.

After the success of its Paris Exposition subjects, the Edison Company spent considerable energy securing films of the Pan-American Exposition in Buffalo, New York. Again a mobile camera was heavily employed. A camera crew, probably including James White as producer and Edwin Porter as photographer, took the two-shot *Opening, Pan-American Exposition*, showing a parade of dignitaries and soldiers, on May 20th. This was soon followed by *A Trip Around the Pan-American Exposition*, a 625-foot subject photographed from a launch making a tour of the exposition's canals. The camera was assigned the role of privileged passenger and took in all the sights. This popular subject was also sold in 200, 300, 400, or 500-foot strips, depending on the desires of the exhibitor. For *Panoramic View of Electric Tower from a Balloon*, the camera caressed the electric tower with a vertical tilt up and down, recalling White's earlier treatment of the Eiffel Tower in *Panorama of Eiffel Tower*. The title and catalog description, however, urged exhibitors to test their patrons' imagination—or gullibility: the camera, it was suggested, had been in a captured balloon that moved up and down next to the tower. By the beginning of June they had accumulated over twenty films, including *Johnstown Flood*, *Aerio-Cycle*, and *Trip to the Moon*—short scenes taken of specific attractions.[42] Once again, these were designed for longer, theme-oriented programs in which exhibitors asserted an authorial role. To facilitate these efforts, the Edison firm published a "Pan-American Supplement" that provided full descriptions of each film as material for the showman's live narration.[43]

A significant group of photographers were associated with the Edison Company by early 1901. Although William Paley was the only surviving licensee on the East Coast, William Wright or some other Edison-affiliated cameraman must have filmed President McKinley launching the battleship *Ohio* in San Francisco before a crowd of 50,000 cheering people.[44] Since late 1898 James White may occasionally have served as his own cameraman, but more typically he worked with Porter or Alfred C. Abadie when producing news films and actualities. Porter may have emerged as the only close to full-time Edison camera operator. The extent to which his collaboration with George S. Fleming continued outside the studio is unknown. Two Edison production units were active on May 30th, Decoration Day: Porter was probably in Ithaca, New York, taking *Cornell–Columbia–University of Pennsylvania Boat Race*, while another unit was at an amusement park filming *Shooting the Chutes at Providence, Rhode Island*.

While Edison cameramen were filming actualities all over the northeastern United States, Porter spent much of his time producing short comedies and trick films at the Edison studio and in nearby locations. *Building Made Easy, or How Mechanics Work in the Twentieth Century* (85 feet) used stop and reverse action to show a bricklayer and carpenter working effortlessly, constructing a building in ways that defied gravity. The building of New York's subway was the premise for *The Finish of Michael Casey*, yet another explosion film. *Little Willie's Last Celebration*, made to commemorate the Fourth of July, likewise ends with Willie in smithereens. Unfortunately these pictures were not copyrighted and do not survive.[45]

Edison Attains a Virtual Monopoly

On July 15, 1901, a decision recognizing Edison's patent claims was handed down in the U.S. circuit court for the southern district of New York. Judge Hoyt Henry Wheeler's tentatively worded opinion concluded: "The defendant appears to have taken the substance of the invention covered by these claims and the plaintiff, therefore, appears to be entitled to a decree."[46] While the defendant, the American Mutoscope & Biograph Company, appealed to a higher court, it was allowed to continue operating under certain restrictions.[47] Yet even before Edison's victory, Biograph was struggling with financial adversity. That

New York Clipper, July 27, 1901, p. 480.

spring, the company had begun to lose money, a situation that continued well into 1902, if not beyond.[48] Its moving picture service was becoming less profitable and popular because the company was limited by its 70mm film format. Whereas exhibitors such as Vitagraph and George Spoor's Chicago-based Kinodrome Service could show European imports like Méliès' *Cinderella* on their 35mm projectors, Biograph could not do so. Biograph's logical move was to switch to a 35mm format, but its executives dared not do this, as their special-sized film could have provided a decisive distinction between the Edison and Biograph systems from a legal standpoint. The cost of litigation and the impact of Judge Wheeler's decision only furthered Biograph's decline.

Other "disruptive" elements within the industry were also affected by Judge Wheeler's decision. The Edison Company had hired Sigmund Lubin's chief photographer, Jacob (James) Blair Smith, starting July 14th. Smith, who assumed William Heise's old role, enjoyed a high weekly salary of $25 a week ($10 more than Porter's) because he could testify concerning Lubin's infringement on Edison's patents. As a result, after consulting with his lawyers, Lubin relocated to Germany.[49] With Lubin knocked out of competition, Vitagraph reduced to the role of exhibitor, and Biograph locked into a large-format film and on the commercial defensive, the Edison Company was on the verge of controlling the motion picture industry in America.

Edison's victory in the courts encouraged other holders of motion picture patents to negotiate a settlement. Thomas Armat, whose Armat Moving-Picture Company held important projection patents, was anxious to form a combination. To Thomas Edison, he argued that

> Years have gone by and your proper profits in the business have not yet I believe materialized. The same is true of me. Every year cut off from my enjoyment of the fruits of my toil is a matter of loss. In looking over the field I am more and more convinced that the situation can be made to bear the <u>full</u> success of our hopes in but one way—by the formation of a trust into which you will throw your film patent, the Armat Company the Armat patents, and the American Mutoscope and Biograph Company its Mutoscope patents, together with a withdrawal of all further appeal on your film patent.
>
> This combined action would establish a real monopoly, as no infringer would stand against a combination of all these strong elements. The way things are now the woods are full of small infringers who are reaping that which belongs to yourself and ourselves. . . . There is big money in <u>all ends</u> of this business if properly conducted and little in it otherwise.[50]

Armat's proposal revived earlier attempts at consolidation by Biograph and anticipated the combination of forces that eventually formed the basis for the Motion Picture Patents Company late in 1908. The trust Armat envisioned would, however, have centralized all activities within a single production office and hobbled the American industry for years. Although Armat and T. Cushing Daniel held meetings with Edison and Biograph, they could not agree on the terms. Armat tended to view the projection patents as paramount, while Edison felt the same about his own position. The actual formation of a patents trust was to wait another six years until similar circumstances once again presented themselves.

When Edison's lawyer Howard W. Hayes learned of Edison's court victory, he sent Gilmore his congratulations from Europe and then asked:

> Will it not be worth while to spend a little more money now in getting out a better class of films? I was surprised to find what good films they have here in Paris, they are very clear and with no jumps. Whenever any important even[t] happens like the Henley Boat Race, the films are on the market within two days afterwards.[51]

J. B. Smith, for one, helped to address some of these concerns. As foreman of the Edison film plant, Smith soon "made many improvements in the machinery and methods of taking and making pictures. At that time it required an hour to perforate 200 feet of film on a step punch which time has reduced to just one-third; it took 20 minutes to print the same length of film on what was known as continuous printers, which were succeeded by stop motion printers, which accomplished the same task in from six to seven minutes according to the density of the negative."[52] Smith, like Porter, was not only a cameraman but a mechanical expert.

The Edison Company continued active production in the wake of its court victory. *Soubrette's Troubles on a Fifth Avenue Stage* and *What Happened on Twenty-Third Street, New York City* appear to be ordinary street scenes at first, but each shows a woman unexpectedly revealing a significant portion of her undergarments. Both films featured A. C. Abadie as the swell and Florence Georgie as the unfortunate woman. In the latter picture, her dress is blown up when she steps over a Herald Square blow hole (anticipating Marilyn Monroe by fifty years).[53] Again, as Judith Mayne has pointed out, this is a film that appealed explicitly to male spectators.[54] Georgie's giggles reassure the spectator and authorize his look. Likewise the use of theatrical display and the performers' acknowledgment of the camera were perhaps necessary means of allaying the spectators' discomfort at an unexpected encounter with a forbidden, voyeuristic pleasure. Tom Gunning has called early cinema an exhibitionist cinema rather than a voyeuristic one as Christian Metz defines it. While this may be true, historically this rupturing of a self-enclosed fictional world usually mediated the spectators' experiences in ways that facilitated their voyeurism, not undermined it.[55] This is evident in *Trapeze Disrobing Act*, made that fall. The performer in this studio production was probably Charmion, whose "risque disrobing act on the flying trapeze" was popular at the turn of the century.[56] Although her striptease was performed for the camera and cine-viewers, the two male spectators inside the mise-en-scène authorized the film spectators' voyeurism. Such pictures were so "hot" that the Victorian males' repressive psychic mechanisms had to be allayed if these patrons were to find the intended pleasure rather than

Trapeze Disrobing Act.

unpleasure in their voyeurism. Produced for burlesque houses and "smokers," these films were by male filmmakers and for male spectators.

In contrast, one-shot comedies such as *The Tramp's Miraculous Escape* and *The Photographer's Mishap* were suited for "polite" vaudeville with its mixed-sex audiences. Both were photographed along train tracks, using stop-action techniques to simulate a train colliding with its victim.[57] *Weary Willie and the Gardener* and *The Tramp and the Nursing Bottle*, part of the tramp series, were shot in a park or in someone's backyard. Each recycled an earlier film gag. All of these comedies were made quickly and at minimal expense.

During their first six months, Porter and Fleming assumed editorial control only in highly circumscribed situations, chiefly by adding dependent tags as endings to one-shot comedies. Two films made in August and September 1901 suggest that they were moving beyond these constraints: *Life Rescue at Long Branch* and *Sampson-Schley Controversy*. *Life Rescue at Long Branch*, retitled *Life Rescue at Atlantic City* for the Edison catalog, presented a two-shot, staged rescue by lifeboat. It was a popular subject that Sigmund Lubin had filmed in Atlantic City during 1899. Lubin's *Life Rescue* was "the most wonderful picture ever taken. Two people went out too far in the ocean to bathe; the gentleman was drowned, the lady saved by the life guards, who can be seen swimming out to her."[58] The Edison film shows two different parts of a rescue, and connects

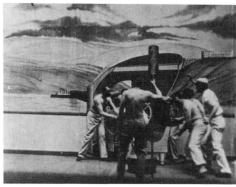

Sampson-Schley Controversy.

them with a dissolve. The major distinction between *Life Rescue at Long Branch* and earlier rescue films such as *Ambulance Call* and *Ambulance at the Accident* is the dissolve that ties the shots together and the corresponding assertion of editorial control by the cameraman/producer. It moved beyond the limitations of earlier Edison acted films as two shots of equal weight told a simple linear narrative. The film was more modest than James Williamson's *Fire!* made in England two months earlier, but it represented a minor advance in the Kinetograph Department's approach to filmmaking.

Sampson-Schley Controversy was based on an argument between two naval officers that had erupted onto the front pages of the popular press. The controversy concerned a naval battle in Santiago Bay during the Spanish-American War, the actions of the two principal American officers, and the question of who ultimately was in command. A political cartoon in Hearst's *New York Journal* provided Porter with a sketch for his film.[59] Since the cartoon reflected his own political sentiments, Porter probably found it an attractive subject to adapt.[60]

Sampson-Schley Controversy was first copyrighted as a two-shot film on August 15th and offered for sale. It was puffed in Edison advertisements as:

> The greatest naval and dramatic Production ever attempted in animated pictures. Admiral Schley is depicted on the bridge of the "Brooklyn" commanding the American Fleet which is engaged with the Spanish fleet. A portion of Schley's crew appears in the immediate foreground of the picture furiously working a 13 inch gun and giving a dramatic demonstration of the famous picture "The Man Behind the Gun."[61]

The scene of Winfield Scott Schley on the bridge, which conforms to the first panel of the cartoon, is enhanced by the second shot, in which one member of the gun crew is killed. This illustrated a well-known incident of the battle in Santiago Bay, when Boatswain Ellis was killed and Schley insisted that his body remain on deck until it could be given a proper Christian burial.[62] Schley's conduct is associated with the actions of these courageous common sailors, while William T. Sampson was well known for his aristocratic pretensions.[63] Although mentioned in the title, Sampson was never shown in this version of the film. George Kleine thought that a more appropriate title would be *Schley on the Bridge and Man Behind the Gun*; certainly it reflected the film's two-shot structure.[64] The sets were similar in both shots and used extreme theatrical foreshortening, with model boats in the far background representing the Spanish enemy.[65] The camera's framing of an identical background is slightly different in each shot, suggesting that the two scenes occur on different parts of the ship. The temporal relation between the two shots is vague, but potentially significant in light of Porter's later films: the relative positions of the model boats and the characters' behavior in each shot suggest a temporal repetition. It appears that these two aspects of the same battle occur simultaneously, but are shown successively on the screen.

Three weeks after its initial release, Porter added a final scene to *Sampson-Schley Controversy*. This was based on the second panel of the cartoon: "The conclusion of the picture shows Admiral Sampson at an afternoon Tea Party, the center of an admiring group of old maids. Length 200 ft."[66] A dissolve between the last two shots was achieved in the printing. The cartoon strip points out that Schley's actions on the *Brooklyn* occurred while the admiral was at a tea party. Contextual information thus indicates that all three shots of the *Sampson-Schley Controversy* represented actions occurring at the same time. The film raised the problem of depicting simultaneity, which Porter would confront again in later work. In the *Sampson-Schley Controversy*, however, this temporal simultaneity is only implicit. Audiences familiar with the cartoon or the controversy may have made the connection, or it may have been made for them by the showman. While temporal relations between shots were implied within the film itself, it was the exhibitor's or the spectator's task to define them more explicitly.

In expanding *Sampson-Schley Controversy* to three shots, Porter used his experience as a showman to produce a simple contrast: the man behind the gun/the man behind the tea cup. The use of contrast was an editorial strategy often employed by exhibitors. In an earlier Biograph program the operator showed a series of "couplets," including *Blizzard in New York City/A Little Ray*

A political cartoon in the *New York Journal* inspired *Sampson-Schley Controversy*. Captions established the temporal relationship between scenes.

of *Sunshine* and *Cremation/Hatching Chickens*.[67] Similar combinations had also been suggested by slide producers for pre-cinema lantern shows. Clearly Porter had appropriated editorial responsibility formerly within the domain of the exhibitor to make a political comment. The acceptance of this new role was still limited: Kleine, for instance, was a Republican who may have sympathized with

Sampson and so chose not to sell the last scene—essentially registering an editorial veto. Although the film could still be used by showmen either within a variety format as a political editorial or as part of a larger program on the Spanish-American War (such programs continued to be popular), the tension between cameraman/producer and showman/exhibitor with regard to editorial responsibility had emerged as a central issue.

McKinley Pictures

When President McKinley went to the Pan-American Exposition early in September 1901, James White and an Edison camera crew were present to take advantage of their special photographic concession. On September 5th they took a simple one-shot film of McKinley delivering a speech that praised American business, competition, and the tariff. The next day, while holding a reception in the Temple of Music, the president was shot in the chest and abdomen by Leon Czolgosz, a Cleveland anarchist. The Edison crew, waiting outside, took a "circular panorama" of the anxious crowd soon after the assassination was announced. Suddenly, the Edison Manufacturing Company had a moving picture exclusive on the biggest news event of the new century: "Our cameras were the only ones at work at the Pan-American Exposition on the day of President McKinley's speech, Thursday September 5th and on Friday September 6th, the day of the shooting. We secured the only animated pictures incidental to these events."[68] Three films, fewer than first announced, were offered for sale: *President McKinley's Speech at the Pan-American Exposition*, *President McKinley Reviewing Troops at the Pan-American Exposition*, and *Mob Outside the Temple of Music at the Pan-American Exposition*.[69] Shortly thereafter, frame enlargements were published in the *New York World*, along with a brief article featuring White's role and mentioning several anonymous employees, almost certainly including Edwin Porter and J. Blair Smith.[70]

When President McKinley died a week after the shooting, Edison employees filmed the funeral ceremonies as they moved from Buffalo to Washington to McKinley's hometown of Canton, Ohio. Eleven films were offered for sale. These were no longer simple, single-shot subjects comparable to those the Edison Company had sold during the Spanish-American War. Most scenes, such as *Taking President McKinley's Body from Train at Canton, Ohio*, consisted of several shots that were too brief to be easily sold or exhibited individually. With the Edison Company anxious to get these groupings of moving snapshots on the market, they released unedited camera rushes that included flash frames.

When purchasing the McKinley films, exhibitors had two basic choices: they could either acquire single subjects for their programs or purchase a prearranged selection of subjects joined together by dissolving effects. *The Complete Funeral Cortege at Canton, Ohio* (675 feet) is one example of this second option. The order given by the Edison Company was:

McKinley's last speech.

Arriving at Canton Station (40 feet)
Body Leaving Train at Canton, Ohio (60 feet)
President Roosevelt at Canton Station (90 feet)
Circular Panorama of President McKinley's House (80 feet)
President McKinley's Body Leaving the House and Church (200 feet)
Funeral Cortege Entering Westlawn Cemetery at Canton, Ohio (200 feet)[71]

Dissolving from scene to scene, the production company was able to give the exhibitor a standardized program with a little something extra.

Many, perhaps most, exhibitors chose not to abdicate their editorial role. A programme from the Searchlight Theater in Tacoma, Washington, shows that a different selection was made for its display of McKinley films. The traveling exhibitor Lyman Howe also devoted a substantial portion of his semi-annual tour to films of the Pan-American Exposition and McKinley's funeral, but presented yet another selection and ordering.[72] Although a programme does not survive for John P. Dibble's presentations, this New Haven–based traveling showman began with films of the Pan-American Exposition, included McKinley's last speech, and ended with the funeral ceremonies.[73]

Exhibitors enjoyed a financial windfall as people flocked to see the

Pan-American Exposition by Night goes from day to night as the camera makes a sweeping pan of the exposition.

McKinley/Exposition films. Edison likewise benefited. From October to December 1901, when these films were in greatest demand, the Kinetograph Department set a sales record unmatched during any three-month period between 1900 and 1904.[74] Porter and his associates continued to exploit this trend with *The Martyred Presidents* (© October 7, 1901), a film indebted to nineteenth-century magic-lantern subjects like *Our Departed Heroes*.[75] In the film's opening scene, photographs of Lincoln, Garfield, and McKinley fade in and out, framed by the static image of a monument. The second shot, a brief tag, shows the assassin kneeling before the throne of justice. The dissolving on and off of photographs, once done by the exhibitor in lantern shows, was now done by the moving picture photographer. While the catalog considered the film "most valuable as an ending to the series of McKinley funeral pictures,"[76] the question of its placement in a program was a decision left to the exhibitor.

Kinetograph personnel invested further energies in the Buffalo area during mid to late October. Shortly after making *The Martyred Presidents*, Porter photographed *Pan-American Exposition by Night*.[77] While Porter and subsequent historians referred to this film for its early use of time-lapse photography, its two-shot construction is also noteworthy. There is a pan in the first shot taken during the day that is continued from the same point, in the same direction, and at the same pace in the second shot filmed at night. Here Porter combined two common stereopticon procedures. The temporal relation between the two shots is characteristic of day/night dissolving views, a popular genre of lantern show entertainments: the image of a building during the day gradually dissolved to the identical view at night (the second view was often produced by using a day-for-night technique). The panorama as a genre pre-dated the cinema by more than a hundred years and found its way into many forms of popular culture, including lantern shows, for which long slides were slowly moved through the lantern. In 1900 it was adapted to moving pictures as the "circular panorama," with the photographer rather than the projectionist responsible for the speed and direction of the movement. The combination of day/night dissolving views with a panorama in moving pictures was a visual tour de force. "This picture is pronounced by the photographic profession to be a marvel in photography, and by theatrical people to be the greatest winner in panoramic views ever placed before the public," declared the Edison catalog.[78]

The principle of multi-camera coverage, which the Edison Company had applied to important news events in the late 1890s, continued, not only with the McKinley funeral pictures but for *Captain Nissen Going Through Whirlpool Rapids, Niagara Falls*, photographed on October 10, 1901. As an Edison description explained,

> Captain Bowser is shown embarking in his boat at Niagara Falls, Ontario. After he carefully embarks, the 'Fool Killer' is taken in tow by a rowboat and towed out into the stream. Here the captain is seen to go below the whaleback deck and close the hatch. Then the trip through the Rapids begins. One of our cameras, which was operated by a second photographer, was in waiting on a trolley car, and the progress of the 'Fool Killer' is followed on its entire trip through the mad waters.[79]

Here the advantages of having two cameras focus on two different aspects of a single situation were apparent. Just prior to the closing of the exposition, the photographers shot their last Pan-American films, including another night view of the exposition (*Panorama of Esplanade by Night*). They also took two short panoramas of nearby Auburn State Prison on October 29th, the morning that Czolgosz was executed inside.[80]

Executions, still considered a form of entertainment by some turn-of-the-century Americans, had been popular film subjects during the novelty phase of cinema. Audiences had been impressed that the image of someone who was demonstrably dead could appear so lifelike.[81] With sensationalistic newspapers detailing the steps leading to Czolgosz's death and the *New York Times* noting the large number of applicants who hoped to watch McKinley's assassin die, it was hardly surprising that the Edison firm chose to make *Execution of Czolgosz, with Panorama of Auburn Prison*.[82]

The *New York World* reported that "the owner of a kinetoscope telegraphed that he would pay $2,000 for permission to take a moving picture of Czolgosz entering the death chamber."[83] If White and Porter hoped to film Czolgosz on his way to being executed, they had to be content with filming the exterior of the prison and making "a realistic imitation of the last scene in the electric chair." This studio reenactment, "faithfully carried out from the description of an eye witness" was based, one can be sure, on newspaper reports.[84] Edison production personnel took roles in the film, and James White can be seen signaling "cut" to the cameraman (Porter) just before the film ends. (According to Iris Barry, the Edison Company also tried to recreate Czolgosz's assassination of McKinley, but finally thought better of it.)[85]

Execution of Czolgosz.

Although *Execution of Czolgosz, with Panorama of Auburn Prison* contains only four shots and "three scenes," the resulting film has a surprisingly sophisticated structure. According to the Edison catalog:

> The picture is in three scenes. First: Panoramic view of Auburn Prison taken the morning of the electrocution. The picture then dissolves into the corridor of murderer's row. The keepers are seen taking Czolgosz from his cell to the death chamber. The scene next dissolves into the death chamber, and shows State Electrician, Wardens and Doctors making final test of the chair. Czolgosz is then brought in by the guard and is quickly strapped into the chair. The current is turned on at a signal from the Warden, and the assassin heaves heavily as though the straps would break. He drops prone after the current is turned off. The doctors examine the body and report to the Warden that he is dead, and he in turn officially announces the death to the witnesses. 200 ft.[86]

The film's longer, copyright title acknowledges that it is a hybrid that combined two genres: the panorama and the dramatic reenactment. An exhibitor could buy the narrative portion with or without the opening panoramas. Thus the editorial decision of the producers could be disregarded if the exhibitor so desired. The film, however, was not simply two separate subjects held together by a dissolve and a common theme: it also made use of a spatial, exterior/interior relation between shots that was beginning to be employed by other filmmakers.[87] The dissolve between the first two scenes not only linked outside and inside, but actuality and reenactment, description and narrative, a moving and a static camera.

The panoramas at the beginning provide the narrative with a context, a well-constructed world in which the action can unfold. Photographed on the day of the execution, the first shot pans with a train as it approaches the prison and then reveals an empty passenger car.[88] It was such a car that brought the witnesses to the prison and led to the final stages of the execution.[89] The second shot shows a more foreboding portion of the facade. These shots distinguish this reenactment film from its contemporaries by heightening the realism. At the same time, they are part of a drama that leads the audience step by step to a vicarious confrontation with the electric chair and a man's death.

The temporal/spatial relation between the second and third scenes is more complex than a casual viewing would suggest. For a modern audience, schooled in the strategies of classical cinema, the pause before Czolgosz's entrance in the last scene facilitates the illusion of linear continuity by allowing time for the prisoner to move from one part of the prison to another. The *New York Times* noted, however, that "Czolgosz was confined in the cell nearest to the death chamber, so that when he entered the execution room this morning he had only to step a few feet through the stone arch."[90] This spatial relation between the two rooms was known by Edison personnel and most spectators: it suggests the kind of temporal overlap occasionally found in theater. The narrative event was not structured like the descriptions in the *New York Times* and *New York Journal*. These started with (1) the activities in the death chamber prior to Warden Mead's signal to have the prisoner brought in—including the testing of the chair, (2) then moved to Czolgosz's cell and his march down the corridor, and (3) shifted back to the death chamber with a description of the execution. The *Times* maintained a rigorous chronological account of events, while moving freely from a description of activities in one space to activities in another. Porter, in contrast, maintained individual scenes intact by manipulating early cinema's flexible pro-filmic temporality.

Execution of Czolgosz is remarkable for its control of pro-filmic elements. There is a purposeful elaboration of plot in the dramatic portion of the film: Czolgosz is not simply led off and executed. At the beginning of the second scene, the prisoner is at the doorway of his cell. After a few moments, the guards enter from the right, and he withdraws from the doorway. The guards open the cell door, go in and bring him out. He is brought from his cell reluctantly but without resistance. Acting and gesture are restrained, motivated by the desire to reenact the execution in as realistic a manner as possible, in marked contrast to Porter's comedies, which were indebted to burlesque and the comic strip. Deviations from the norms of classical cinema in acting style and schematic set construction have sometimes been attributed to the naivete of early cinema, a lack of control over pro-filmic elements and insensitivity to "the demands of the medium." In *Execution of Czolgosz*, control and sensitivity are not the issues. This affirms the fact that Porter's comedies were "crude" because he was working within a genre where crudity was expected—burlesque and realism being fundamentally at cross-purposes. Yet despite the reliance on reenactment in *Execution of Czolgosz*, the two interior scenes are photographed against sets that show a single wall running perpendicular to the axis of the camera lens. As with *The Finish of Bridget McKeen*, the images lack almost all suggestion of depth—flattened not only by the sets but by the actors, who move parallel to the walls.

Edison's Conservative Business Strategy

From mid July 1901 to mid March 1902, a period of eight months, the Edison Manufacturing Company had a virtual monopoly in film production and sales within the United States. Rather than anticipating a possible reversal in the higher courts and parlaying this potentially short-term legal windfall into a long-term business advantage, Gilmore and White pursued a conservative, shortsighted business policy. Rather than investing in expensive productions that might yield lasting benefits, they produced inexpensive actualities and duped European spectacles to avoid high negative costs. Thomas Edison needed money for his other business schemes and was clearly unwilling to allocate funds for the Kinetograph Department. As he wrote in mid December 1901, "I am putting all my ducats in the storage battery."[91] Underfinanced, the Edison Company directed revenues toward attorney fees rather than into uncertain production ventures.

While producing McKinley films, Porter paused to photograph the America's Cup races off Sandy Hook in late September and early October, including "*Columbia*" and "*Shamrock II*," *Start of Second Race*, and *Panoramic View of the Fleet After Yacht Race*. This group of eight short films was also offered to exhibitors as a complete set, with dissolving effects melding them into a single program totaling 775 feet.[92]

During this period, filling special orders was an important part of the Kinetograph Department's business. James White later explained that the Edison Company "took pictures for people at special prices per foot for the negative and a special price per foot for the positive printed therefrom. These negative films remained in possession of the Edison Manufacturing Company but were the property of the people for whom they were exposed. The positive films were issued from them only on written order and in accordance with the price agreed upon at the time the negatives were taken."[93] Since the resulting pictures were neither copyrighted nor entered into Edison catalogs, the full dimensions of these activities remain unknown. However, in early November, White took a moving picture from the rear end of a train "to be used by 'Dare Devil' Schreyer in his sensational 'mile-a-minute ride behind a train' on the stage of Keith's Theatre, New York."[94] Many orders were made by or executed through the rapidly growing Kinetograph Company with the help of silent partners White and Schermerhorn. In October 1901 "the largest contract ever known in the moving picture business" had the Kinetograph Company exhibiting special films for Mayor Richard Crocker's reelection campaign. Projected images played prominent roles on both sides as Seth Low's Fusion ticket fought Crocker's Tammany Hall gang.[95] A typical Kinetograph Company exhibition occurred on a large canvas covering the front of a saloon run by James J. Dowling, brother of the local Democratic district leader. One selection was "a cartoon representing Seth Low standing in a waste[basket] and showered with Tammany votes."[96] As several hundred people watched, the machine burst into flames, terminating the exhibition—an appropriate denouement, for Low was soon victorious. Afterwards Waters offered to sell fifty projecting machines "which have been used less than one month; complete and guaranteed in every part."[97]

Soon after the Crocker contract, the Kinetograph Company engaged White to film *The Jeffries and Ruhlin Sparring Contest at San Francisco, Cal., November 15, 1901* and undoubtedly hoped the results could be toured like *The Corbett-Fitzsimmons Fight* or *The Jeffries-Sharkey Fight*. White's expenses for taking the pictures totaled $457.[98] Although the Edison manager later claimed to have traveled across the country alone, the inactivity of the Edison studio during November and December suggests that Porter may have accompanied him. Certainly Porter's experience as an electrician would have been valuable in lighting the indoor event, a difficult task, at which the Vitagraph and Edison companies had failed two years earlier.[99] Immediately before the fight,

> The attendants began to stretch new canvas on the ring and a dozen men with ladders and a whole tool shop began to pull and haul at a great square of boards and canvas that hung over the squared circle. It was the kinetoscope apparatus, eighty powerful arc lights and four Navy searchlights. For ten minutes the electricians swung through the rafters getting everything in readiness. On the Grove street side of the Pavillion a temporary booth with glaring red peep holes held the business part of the machine.[100]

These powerful lights produced extreme heat, which the combatants felt from the very beginning.[101] The fight only lasted five rounds, limiting the film's commercial usefulness. As White later recalled, "the pictures were not long enough in themselves to form a complete exhibition, and therefore they had to be put in vaudeville as a short act. A bull fight would be, I think, fifteen or twenty rounds. The film I took would take about twenty minutes to exhibit at the usual rate of speed."[102] After selling a copy of the fight film to someone on the West Coast, the Edison Company assumed ownership of the subject and credited Waters' account. The sales price on this subject was raised to 25¢ a foot, with the added fee serving as a royalty and presumably going to the fighters.[103] The Kinetograph Company still showed the fight film at Miner's Eighth Avenue Theater during the first two weeks of December; it was then copyrighted and offered for sale to the general public.[104]

The West Coast expedition turned into a reprise of White's 1897–98 tour of the West and Mexico. Soon after the fight, he was in British Columbia taking films for the Canadian Pacific Railroad (*Panoramic View, Kicking Horse Canyon*). These later views of dramatic scenery were taken from the front of a moving train near Golden and Leanchoil. Back in the Bay Area, White produced numerous films for travel lectures (*Fishing at Faralone Island, Chinese Shaving Scene*). He then visited Southern California (*Ostrich Farms at Pasadena*) before heading south to Mexico City, where he filmed *The Great Bull Fight* on February 2, 1902.[105] This 1,000-foot film was sold in whatever lengths the exhibitor might desire.

During White's three-month absence, East Coast production was slight. On November 16th, an Edison cameraman shot *Automobile Parade on the Coney Island Boulevard* with "perhaps 100 machines in line, big and little, old and new, steam, electric and gasoline."[106] The parade, sponsored by the Long Island Automobile Club, was part of the preliminaries to a series of races in which Frenchman Henri Fourier, "the King of Chauffeurs," drove a "lightning mile" in 51⅘ seconds. These races, which made the front page of New York papers, were delayed, and lack of light probably prevented them from being successfully kinetographed. The new year began with the filming of the Mummers Parade in Philadelphia. James Smith may have been responsible for both productions.

With few new studio productions to sell, the Edison Company used its legal position to acquire original negatives from former competitors. A group of Vitagraph subjects from 1900 were acquired and copyrighted in Edison's name in mid December. These included *The Mysterious Cafe, Harry Tompson's Imitations of Sousa, Roeber Wrestling Match, The Artist's Dilemma,* and *The Fat and Lean Wrestling Match.* Edison's sales listings were also enhanced by "dupes." Méliès' *Little Red Riding Hood* and other Houdin trick films were added to the Edison catalog in the later part of 1901.

Production at the Edison studio resumed in January 1902, coinciding with Porter's increase in salary to $20 a week. From this point forward, the former exhibitor turned cameraman assumed firmer control over studio production. While collaborations with George Fleming and others continued, Porter was at the center of these activities. This new situation began with a series of trick films, some of which were remakes of foreign subjects.[107] In *Uncle Josh at the Moving Picture Show,* a rube confuses the projected image with real life and, trying to interfere with events shown on the screen, disrupts the show. Though this gag was as old as projected moving pictures, Porter's comedy was indebted to an earlier film by Robert Paul, *The Countryman's First Sight of the Animated Pictures.*[108] Porter's remake substituted Edison scenes and titles for the films within the film. Since the comedy's production required mattes and optical reduction, it posed a technical challenge Porter must have found intriguing. *The Twentieth Century Tramp; or, Happy Hooligan and His Airship* was indebted to Ferdinand Zecca's *A la conquête de l'air*.[109] It used a split screen image: the top half showed a tramp on a bicycle pedaling his balloon-airship against a plain background, while the bottom half is a "circular panorama" of the city. In the pre-cinema lantern world, such images had been achieved by the use of multiple projections, allowing each slide—each part of the image on the screen—to unfold independently in time. It is easy to conceive of a lantern show similar to *The Twentieth Century Tramp*, in which a mechanical slide of a tramp was projected onto the top half of the screen and a moving panorama on the bottom. Practically, the new technology of moving pictures required that such composites be executed on the film rather than on the screen, and they were one element in the gradual consolidation of creativity within the production company.

Upon his return to New York, manager James White spurred East Coast production, revitalizing the concept of cinema as a visual newspaper. Edison personnel photographed Paterson, New Jersey, shortly after its devastating fire on February 9th (*Panorama of the Paterson Fire*). Cameramen had arrived too late to shoot any actual firefighting. As a result, the films emphasized spectacle and landscape, displaying the devastation with sweeping panoramas. No effort was made to show how the fire affected people's lives. On February 15th *The Burning of Durland's Riding Academy* was taken at Central Park West between Sixty-first and Sixty-second streets in New York City. The panning camera captured firemen hosing down the still smoldering remains. Since the film was only of local importance, it was renamed *Firemen Fighting the Flames at Paterson* and sold as footage of the better-known event. Relabeling films to increase their commercial potential was neither unusual nor "naive" but consistent with the highly opportunistic business ethics of Edison and other film producers.

On February 17th, the Kinetograph Department photographed *New York City in a Blizzard*.[110] Immediately after the snowfall, Porter and his associates made *Capture of the Biddle Brothers*, reenacting the sensational shoot-out between the Biddle brothers and law officers. This one-shot film of a newsworthy event was executed in the cool, controlled style of *Execution of Czolgosz*. The Edison catalog informed potential purchasers:

CAPTURE OF THE BIDDLE BROS.

The public throughout the world is acquainted with the sensational capture of the Biddle Brothers and Mrs. Soffel, who, through the aid of Mrs. Soffel, escaped from the Pittsburg jail on January 30th, 1902. Our picture, which is a perfect reproduction of the capture, is realistic and exciting. It shows the sheriffs in two sleighs coming down the hill on the snow covered road. Mrs. Soffel and the Biddle Brothers appear in the foreground going toward the sheriffs. Immediately the sheriffs are seen by Ed. Biddle, he stops the sleigh, and rising, begins firing at the sheriffs with a shotgun. He is the first to be shot and falls to the ground in a snow bank, but, game to the last, he rises

on one elbow and fires shot after shot with his revolver. Mrs. Soffel and the second
Biddle then begin firing. When Mrs. Soffel sees that their capture is certain, she attempts to take her own life by shooting herself with the pistol. The sheriffs are finally
victorious and the two convicts with the unfortunate woman are loaded into the sheriffs' double sleigh. Class A. 125 ft.[111]

In late February and early March, the Kinetograph Department filmed Prince
Henry of Prussia's visit to the United States. Edison cameramen photographed
the royal visitor's arrival in New York City and followed him to Cambridge,
Massachusetts, where the prince met the German-American psychologist and
philosopher Hugo Münsterberg at Harvard. Porter was even sent to Chicago to
photograph *Prince Henry at Lincoln's Monument, Chicago, Illinois.*[112] The
most noteworthy films were of the christening of Kaiser Wilhelm's yacht *Meteor*
at Shooter's Island, taken on February 25, 1902. In this last situation, Edwin
Porter and Jacob Smith filmed the *Meteor* entering the water simultaneously
from their two different camera positions. When these two films, *Christening
and Launching Kaiser Wilhelm's Yacht "Meteor"* and *Kaiser Wilhelm's Yacht
"Meteor" Entering the Water* were shown together, what had been filmed simultaneously was shown successively. Exhibitors could present the same event
from two different points of view, offering their patrons a double perspective
that might be described as a novelty.

Edison films taken in the winter of 1901–2 were principally actuality subjects. Like *Cutting and Canaling Ice*, taken in Groton, Massachusetts, most
consisted of several shots taken at approximately the same time and place. These
single, but elaborated, scenes were still small enough for showmen to incorporate into larger sequences, but allowed the producer to perform an editorial
function as well. The few studio films made in early 1902 included *Facial Expression*, which showed "one of the most talented lady facial expression artists
in the world, executing the most amusing facial gyrations."[113] Two others of the
same genre followed. *Burlesque Suicide, No. 1* and *Burlesque Suicide, No. 2*
were medium shots of a despairing man putting a gun to his head. In one version
he takes a drink instead of pulling the trigger; in the other he points his finger
at the camera and laughs.[114]

While comedies and fairy-tale films were popular with audiences, the lack of
competition meant that the Kinetograph Department did not have to cater extensively to this demand. Many could be imported and duped. Edison's New
York studio was used less during the winter of 1901–2 than when it first
opened. Unnecessary expenses (actors' salaries, sets, etc.) could thus be avoided.
The shift toward story films then taking place in Europe was delayed in the
United States by legal and business factors.

William Paley, who remained an Edison licensee into 1902, continued to take
actualities that ended up in the Edison catalog. *Montreal Fire Department on
Runners*, taken in March 1901 for the opening of a Proctor theater in that
city, showed a fire run that demonstrated the Canadians' use of sleighs for

firefighting purposes. Two months later, Paley took local views of the trolley car strike in Albany, New York. These, too, were shown in the local Proctor theater. "Paley's kalatechnoscope will blossom out this week by displaying several moving pictures incidental to the big trolley car strike of last week," reported the *Albany Evening Journal*. "A picture of the Third Signal Corps escorting the repair wagon down State street will be shown, also the first car that was run down State street with militiamen as passengers, besides other interesting incidents."[115] These were greeted by loud rounds of applause from the predominantly anti-union audience at Proctor's and then offered for sale as *The Great Albany Car Strike*.[116] Paley took more films in or near Montreal during 1902. These included *Skiing in Montreal* (© February 10, 1902), *Coasting Scene at Montmorency Falls, Canada*, and *Arrival of the Governor General, Lord Minto, at Quebec* (© February 17, 1902).[117] These served as a modest supplement to Edison's own output.

Histories of early cinema often refer to a decline in the popularity of moving pictures around the turn of the century, particularly in vaudeville theaters, where motion pictures were the last act on the bill and large portions of the audience left when the films were shown. These programs were often known as "chasers," and for this reason these years have often been called "the chaser period." Disfavor has generally been attributed to a jaded audience tiring of actuality scenes and news footage. Although at least one recent historian has dismissed this as a myth perpetuated by gullible scholars, data from different branches of the film industry indicate that cinema did experience a period of retrenchment and even contraction early in the twentieth century.[118] The Edison Company's near monopoly contributed to these difficulties. The Kinetograph Department would have had to expand its production levels rapidly if other branches of the industry were to have remained unaffected by the court decision. Instead, as the preceding section has shown, the Edison corporation pursued a self-serving business policy. As one might expect, Edison film sales (and profits) increased significantly during the 1901–2 business year—roughly 68 percent, from $49,756 to $82,108. This increase, however, was not equivalent to the sales lost by the inventor's competitors. Sales of projecting kinetoscopes, moreover, remained the same as the year before the Edison monopoly.

While Edison's legal actions contributed to difficulties in the motion picture industry, evidence also suggests that the concept of cinema as a visual newspaper needed to be rethought. Actuality subjects were losing much of their appeal. As long as the Edison Manufacturing Company was the only American business selling news films, this decline was not an immediate problem, since it controlled the entire market. Only when Edison's competitors reentered the moving picture field in the spring of 1902 did the Kinetograph Department have to rethink its production patterns.

Defeated in the Courts,
Edison Faces Renewed Competition

The circuit court decision upholding Edison's patents was reversed on March 10, 1902, by the court of appeals. The lower court was instructed to dismiss the bill of complaint against Biograph with costs. In his closely analyzed opinion, Judge William James Wallace wrote:

> It is obvious that Mr. Edison was not a pioneer, in the large sense of the term, or in the more limited sense in which he would have been if he had also invented the film. He was not the inventor of the film. He was not the first inventor of apparatus capable of producing suitable negatives, taken from practically a single point of view, in single-line sequence, upon a film like his, and embodying the same general means of rotating drums and shutters for bringing the sensitized surface across the lens, and exposing successive portions of it in rapid succession. Du Cos anticipated him in this, notwithstanding he did not use the film. Neither was he the first inventor of an apparatus capable of producing suitable negatives, and embodying means for passing a sensitized surface across a single-lens camera at a high rate of speed, and with an intermittent motion, and for exposing successive portions of the surfaces during the periods of rest. His claim for such an apparatus was rejected by the patent office, and he acquiesced in its rejection. He was anticipated in this by Marey, and Marey also anticipated him in photographing successive positions of the object in motion from the same point of view.
>   The predecessors of Edison invented apparatus, during a period of transition from plates to flexible paper film, and from paper film to celluloid film, which was capable of producing negatives suitable for reproduction in exhibiting machines. No new principle was to be discovered, or essentially new form of machine invented, in order to make the improved photographic material available for that purpose. The early inventors had felt the need of such material, but, in the absence of its supply, had either contented themselves with such measure of practical success as was possible, or had allowed their plans to remain upon paper as indications of the forms of mechanical and optical apparatus which might be used when suitable photographic surfaces became available. They had not perfected the details of apparatus especially adapted for the employment of the film of the patent, and to do this required but a moderate amount of mechanical ingenuity. Undoubtedly Mr. Edison, by utilizing this film and perfecting the first apparatus for using it, met all the conditions necessary for commercial success. This, however, did not entitle him, under the patent laws, to a monopoly of all camera apparatus capable of utilizing the film. Nor did it entitle him to a monopoly of all apparatus employing a single camera.[119]

Edison's patents were rejected, and the inventor had to seek patent reissues with new, narrower claims.

Biograph revived its business and began to merchandise Warwick films, duped Méliès subjects, and 35mm reduction prints of its own large format films.[120] Biograph thus had a two-pronged business strategy, in which the company produced pictures exclusively for its own exhibition circuit, but eventually sold the subjects after their "first-run" potential was exhausted. As we have seen, this approach was similar to Vitagraph's during the 1890s. The transition to 35mm films was difficult for Biograph and took over a year to complete. Company executives initially straddled the problem by offering two services: the old, 70mm Biograph service and the new, 35mm "Biographet" service.[121] The large-gauge projectors at Keith theaters could only show Biograph's own productions. The 35mm service used imported films, but did not receive sufficient attention to make it fully competitive with Vitagraph or the Kinetograph Company. Biograph was hampered by the technological incompatibility of its two services.

Judge Wallace's decision freed all American film producers from immediate legal constraints. Vitagraph resumed the production of news topicals and other subjects for use on its expanding exhibition circuit. Chicago producer William Selig, who had remained relatively unaffected by the eastern court battles, resumed advertising in the *New York Clipper*.[122] Sigmund Lubin returned from Europe and reactivated his business. He not only resumed production but sold duplicate copies of copyrighted Edison productions, notably those of Prince Henry's American tour. In a quid pro quo, Lubin was disrupting Edison's business just as Edison had disrupted his. The "Wizard" promptly challenged Lubin with a lawsuit, but was denied a preliminary injunction, leaving the Philadelphia optician free to pursue these activities while the case worked its way through the courts.[123]

Renewed competition forced the Kinetograph Department to reassess its business policy. In some areas, Gilmore and White refused to change. With Lubin consistently underselling Edison's rate of fifteen cents per foot for prints by three cents, Gilmore did what he had done with the National Phonograph Company. He refused to lower prices and insisted that Edison's product was the standard against which all competitors should be judged:

SPECIAL NOTICE TO EXHIBITORS

We have no cheap films to offer, but we will give you the finest subjects procurable at a fair price; films that are worth owning and that will cultivate the public's taste for motion picture shows instead of disgusting them.[124]

The Edison Company also announced an increase in the size of its photographic staff and the number of picture-taking operators.[125] By midsummer it was employing three active photographers. In the United States, Porter remained based in the New York studio and also took some actualities, while J. Blair Smith traveled along the East Coast taking news and travel films. In Europe, the Lebanese-American cameraman Alfred C. Abadie was responsible for supplying the Kinetograph Department with his own original subjects as well as prints of the best European releases. In addition, James White and one or two others occasionally photographed new subjects.

White left for Europe in April to arrange for the importation of film subjects and to photograph the coronation of Edward VII.[126] Although the crowning was postponed owing to Edward's poor health, the department manager was able to shoot films of his trip. Among those copyrighted and offered for sale in June were *The S.S. "Deutschland" Leaving the Dock in Hoboken*, *The S.S. "Deutschland" in a Storm, No. 1* and *Shuffleboard on S.S. "Deutschland."* White may have been accompanied by Abadie, who then remained in Europe to represent Edison's interests. By August, Abadie was sending back coronation films to be duped at West Orange. One of these was hand-carried by Edison lawyer Howard Hayes. On shipboard, Hayes sent notice of his imminent arrival:

> U.S.M.S. "Philadelphia"
> Friday, August 22, 1902
>
> My dear Gilmore:
>
> We get in early tomorrow morning, probably about 9 o'clock. I will telegraph you to that effect from quarantine where we are due about mid-night. I have a new film of the coronation taken by another company which Abadie gave me to give to White for him to "dub." I shall get to my house not later than noon, so if no one comes to the wharf for it you had better send a messenger to my house for it any time after twelve. The negative of the coronation Naval Review will arrive about next Wednesday. Abadie [said] he could not get them off earlier than Wednesday the 20th. . . .[127]

The timely importation of English and French subjects would continue to concern Gilmore and White for the next several years. Edison was increasing its duping of foreign films for the American market and attempting to acquire these before Biograph, Vitagraph, or Lubin.

While actualities and short comedies still provided Edison with the bulk of its original productions, longer studio-made films began to play a key role as the company sought to maintain commercial dominance. This development, which put new emphasis on the studio where Porter was in charge, was reflected in the production of four "story" films: *Appointment by Telephone* (© May 2, 1902), *Jack and the Beanstalk* (© June 20, 1902), *How They Do Things on the Bowery* (© October 31, 1902), and *Life of an American Fireman* (© January 21, 1903).

Appointment by Telephone is a simple, three-shot comedy in which Porter achieved a smooth narrative progression from one scene to the next.[128]

APPOINTMENT BY TELEPHONE

> Two young men are seated in a broker's office. A young lady calls one of them on the telephone and makes an appointment to meet him at a certain restaurant. The scene dissolves to the outside of a restaurant, and the young man appears waiting for the young lady, who soon comes along and they go inside. The scene dissolves again and shows the interior of the restaurant and the young couple coming in and taking their seats at a table next to the window. The young man's wife happens to pass the window just as they get seated, and looking in recognizes him. She confronts the pair in the restaurant in a state of great anger just as the waiter is serving champagne; then the trouble begins. The table and chairs are wrecked, and the husband and young lady

Appointment by Telephone.

are severely horsewhipped by the enraged wife. A very fine photograph, full of action from start to finish, and a subject that will appeal to everyone. 100 ft.[129]

It was a remake of a two-part Edison subject from 1896:

AN APPOINTMENT BY TELEPHONE—First Scene—

A gay young man in a Wall Street broker's office, with wicked intentions makes an engagement with a pretty typewriter. The sequel brings about his discomforture and the triumph of the typewriter.

SUPPER INTERRUPTED—Second Film—

The gay young man with the wicked intentions, from his Wall Street broker's office, hies himself to the place of appointment and meets the pretty typewriter. Just as they are sitting down to supper his irate wife appears upon the scene and there is a denouement. The wicked young man is exposed and disgraced by his wife's explanation.[130]

Not only was the 1902 remake sold as a single subject, but Porter added another shot, taken outside the restaurant. The three-shot film isolates a beginning (the appointment), a middle (the meeting), and an end (the confrontation with the wife). The second shot establishes the space from which the wife spies her husband's infidelities. The film employs not only an exterior/interior spatial relationship between shots 2 and 3 but a reverse angle to show overlapping space. This construction of a fictional world is achieved as the young man and his female companion exit in shot 2 and enter in shot 3 and is reinforced by the movement of the wife from the sidewalk to the interior of the restaurant in the final scene. Temporal continuity is established between these two shots, although it remains imprecise: the set in the third shot is constructed and filmed in such a way that even the possibility of matching action is excluded. Unlike earlier Edison films, the sets have corners and additional walls: they are no longer simple flats erected parallel to the camera. The elaboration of space both in terms of editorial strategy and set construction occurs simultaneously.

Appointment by Telephone can be seen as a sketch, an experiment in cinematic representation, which Porter immediately employed in *Jack and the Beanstalk*, a ten-shot narrative more than twice the length of any previous studio-made film. Porter was assisted by James White's brother, Arthur.[131] "It was a matter of great difficulty, and required great artistic skill to arrange all the different scenes, pose the various subjects and take the views successfully," claimed Porter in a deposition. "It took in the neighborhood of six weeks in the spring of 1902 to successfully make this photograph."[132]

Fairy tales had gripped the romantic imagination at the beginning of the nineteenth century, providing a vision that combined innocence, myth, and age-old tradition, which were rapidly being undermined by a capitalist economy. They lent themselves to either radical interpretations of a lost equality and harmonious past, or conservative memories of contentment, ignorance, and piety on the part of the folk.[133] Porter, however, turned to a version of *Jack and the Beanstalk* that had been bowdlerized so as to provide a moral justification for Jack's robbing of the giant. The result, in the words of Bruno Bettelheim, makes the film "a moral tale of retribution rather than a story of manhood achieved."[134]

By the end of the century, fairy tales had been largely relegated to children, who were entertained and socialized by such lantern shows as *Cinderella*, *Robinson Crusoe*, *Bluebeard*, *Gulliver's Travels*, and *Jack and the Beanstalk*. These subjects briefly regained an adult audience as Georges Méliès and G. A. Smith revitalized this screen staple, making fairy-tale films an important genre of early cinema. The theatrical tradition of pantomimes, which generally used fairy tales as a narrative premise, also provided an important model for films of this genre, particularly in respect to acting style. (But less often a narrative model. Pantomimes customarily sacrificed narrative for spectacle. With the exception of Méliès' *Cinderella*, these films seem consistent with the narrative elaboration found in lantern shows.) To cite merely one instance of stage and lantern show traditions converging in cinema, the depiction of dreams and vi-

Jack and the Beanstalk. Scene 1: Jack departs after having sold the cow for a hat full of beans.

sions in *Jack and the Beanstalk* was done using devices common to both media. The extremely close interrelationship between theater and screen is particularly apparent in *Jack and the Beanstalk.*

Jack and the Beanstalk is ignored by Terry Ramsaye and Lewis Jacobs, no doubt because its subject matter and techniques are indebted to Méliès (particularly *Bluebeard*, 1901), suggesting that Porter was an imitator rather than an originator. This quiet dismissal does the film a disservice, for it contains all the elements that historian A. Nicholas Vardac sees in *Life of an American Fireman*: the pictorial development of two lines of action, spectacular devices such as the vision that introduces the second line of action, dissolves between scenes, and a change in camera position showing interior and exterior as the action moves from one space to the next.[135] The cinematic innovations cited by Vardac had become common techniques and strategies for filmmakers by 1901 and can be found much earlier in lantern shows.

Porter's first use of an increasingly elaborate and integrated narrative can be located in May and June 1902. Obviously this does not mean that *Appointment by Telephone* and *Jack and the Beanstalk* were among the first narrative films. With earlier subjects, however, individual scenes had functioned as self-contained units that could be selected and organized at the discretion of the exhibitor, who thus maintained a fundamental relationship to the narrative as it was constructed and projected on the screen. In films like *Jack and the Beanstalk*, the exhibitor's role was reduced to one of secondary elaboration. Dissolves had given the production company a degree of editorial control, and the simple progression of a story from shot to shot tended to concentrate creative contributions in the hands of the producer. What is under consideration, then, is a shift in the character and function of the narrative, not its first application to either cinema or the screen. Under these new circumstances the exhibitor was increasingly reduced to the role of programmer and narrator.

The catalog description for *Jack and the Beanstalk* (see document no. 8) had a dual purpose: to sell the film and provide material for a potential lecturer. Although "every scene [was] posed with a view to following as closely as possible the accepted version of *Jack and the Beanstalk*," an exhibitor's running commentary could clarify the story line, add characterization, and enrich the film's psychological dimension. The benefits derived from such an intervention are readily apparent after checking this description against a silent viewing of the film. It assigns a narrative significance to the last tableau that it otherwise lacks. In scene 5 Jack's conflict between obeying his mother and following the dictates of his dream is played up in the description. Likewise the fairy's revelation that the giant killed and robbed Jack's father must either be conveyed as part of a narration or assumed to be part of the audience's previous knowledge.

DOCUMENT No. 8

Jack and the Beanstalk

SCENE 1.—TRADING THE COW.

Jack's mother, being very poor, has dispatched him to the market to sell her only cow that they may not starve. The good fairy meets the village butcher at the bridge and informs him that Jack will pass that way with a cow which he can doubtless purchase for a hatful of beans, Jack being a very careless and foolish lad. The fairy vanishes, and Jack appears upon the scene leading the cow. The bargain is struck, and Jack runs away to show his mother what he considers a very gratifying price for their beautiful animal.

SCENE 2.—JACK RETURNS WITH THE BEANS.

Shows Jack's return to his mother's cottage, bringing the beans in his hat, and showing them to her in great glee, his mother's disappointment and scolding, which ends in Jack being sent supperless to bed, and the mother throwing the beans in the garden in great anger.

SCENE 3.—GROWING OF THE BEANSTALK.

A night scene in the garden, with beautiful moonlight and cloud effects. The good fairy appears, and waving her magic wand, commands the beanstalk to grow; and, lo and behold, from the hatful of beans that has been so ruthlessly thrown into the garden, a beanstalk of great size is seen to grow in a few moments, and to climb up the cliff above the clouds.

SCENE 4.—JACK'S DREAM.

Showing the interior of Jack's bedroom with the moonlight streaming through the window. The good fairy appears and stands beside Jack's cot directing his dream. Jack dreams of the growing beanstalk and the award that awaits him who dares to climb it. Next he sees a vision of the Horn of Plenty, bags of the giant's gold and the talking harp, which dances before him in a weird manner. One by one these articles appear and disappear in the picture, coming as if from the dim distance, and as quickly and silently fading away. The climax of this scene is reached when the hen which lays the golden eggs walks into Jack's chamber. An egg is left on the floor, which suddenly grows to an enormous size, breaks in two, and there appears in its centre Jack's little fairy, who is afterward to make him happy for life.

SCENE 5.—CLIMBING THE BEANSTALK.

Jack awakes in the early morning, and looking out from his window, finds the enormous beanstalk which has grown above the clouds. Remembering his dream of the night before, he believes he can climb it with ease; but also remembering his mother's scolding for trading the cow for the beans, he is prompted to be cautious, and concludes to consult his mother. She protests vigorously against his climbing the beanstalk, but Jack sending her into the house on a pretext, starts up the beanstalk without her knowledge. The mother returns and is frantic when she finds Jack has gone up beyond her reach. She scolds and commands him to return, but the dauntless boy only laughs and continues to climb. His playmates, who are calling for Jack on their way to school, witness Jack's start on his perilous journey, and joining hands, they dance about the beanstalk in great numbers, cheering and waving their hats at the brave boy.

SCENE 6.—JACK ABOVE THE CLOUDS.

Here we dissolve the view and show Jack two-thirds up the beanstalk, far above the clouds, with his mother's cottage and the hilltops a great distance below him. He is still tirelessly climbing his ladder of bean vines, and pauses as he reaches a dizzy height to wave his hat to his playmates and mother.

SCENE 7.—ARRIVAL AT THE TOP OF THE BEANSTALK.

Jack arrives at the top of the beanstalk in what appears to be a fairyland. He is very tired and sleepy and lays down in a bed of moss to rest.

He soon falls asleep, and his good fairy again appears and tells Jack the story of the giant, who, many years ago, killed and robbed his father (who was a knight residing in a castle), and drove his mother from their home. She then causes a vision of the giant's castle to appear before Jack, and commands him to go to the giant's house where great fortunes await him. Jack's enthusiasm is fired by the story of his father's wrongs, and he immediately sets out to obey the commands of the fairy.

SCENE 8.—THE GIANT'S KITCHEN.

Shows Jack's arrival at the giant's house, and being admitted to the kitchen by the giant's wife. The giant suddenly enters, and in great fear lest he kill and eat the little boy, the good wife hides Jack in a large kettle. The giant comes in and roughly demands his supper, then his harp, bags of gold and the hen which lays the golden eggs. He finally falls asleep from the playing of the harp. Jack creeps from his hiding place in the kettle and steals the hen and as many of the bags of gold as he can carry away. Just as he leaves the kitchen door the giant awakens, and, seizing his great cudgel, chases our little hero, who is now thoroughly frightened.

SCENE 9.—JACK DESCENDING THE BEANSTALK AND DEATH OF THE GIANT.

The chase to the beanstalk has been very close, but Jack reaches it a little ahead of the giant. He throws the bags of gold down into his mother's garden and quickly scrambles down with the precious hen hanging over his shoulder. Reaching the ground first, he hastily commands his mother to bring him the ax, and vigorously chops at the beanstalk until it falls in a heap, bringing the giant to the ground with a mighty crash, breaking his neck and instantly killing him. Here the good fairy again appears and informs Jack that he has acted like a brave knight's son and that he deserves to have his inheritance restored to him. She waves her magic wand, and, lo! Jack's costume is changed from that of a peasant boy to a young knight, and his mother is likewise transformed from a peasant woman to a lady.

CLOSING TABLEAU.

A most beautiful scene, showing Jack and his mother seated in the fairy's boat, which is drawn by three beautiful swans, proceeding on their way to the castle which is to be their future home. The good fairy is seen to be flying through the air, guiding Jack and his mother on their way.

In introducing this novel tableau, giving as it were an entirely new version to the ending of the story, we believe we are adding a feature which will be most pleasing to every child who witnesses the performance. It is certainly most gratifying and comprehensive, and will at once be recognized as the beginning of the journey to the castle which, in accor-

Jack and the Beanstalk. The cut from interior (end of scene 4) to exterior (beginning of scene 5) is not a match cut.

dance with the good fairy's promise of the reward to him who dares to climb the beanstalk, she is restoring to Jack and his mother.
Sold in complete length only. Class A. 625ft.

SOURCE: *Edison Films,* September 1902, pp. 116–17.

Since the film was designed so that "the audience finds itself following with ease the thread of this most wonderful of all fairy tales," the showman's spiel remained optional. If the exhibitor so wished, he could let his patrons rely on their own familiarity with the story, since it "is known to every child throughout the civilized world" and "appeals to every man and woman because they remember it as one of the most pleasant illusions of their childhood."[136] A lecture, however, enabled the exhibitor to make his own creative contribution to the cinematic story. *Jack and the Beanstalk* only lacks an adequate cinematic language if the film is expected to act as a self-sufficient narrative—a misreading of its institutional context.

Intimately tied to the development of a more elaborate narrative was the creation of a fictional world with spatial and temporal relations between scenes. With scenes 3, 4, and 5, Porter cuts freely from the cottage exterior to the interior of Jack's room and back to the exterior. Scenes 5, 6, 7, 8, and 9 are carefully constructed with entrances and exits, glances, set cues, and narrative continuities that give spectators information from which to deduce the approximate spatial relationships between the various shots. Temporality remains more problematic, still unspecified and at moments perhaps even confused: the cut between scenes 4 and 5, which is open to different interpretations, may serve as an example. In scene 4, after Jack ends his dream, he wakes up and walks to the window in his nightgown. Scene 5 begins with Jack at the window, but fully clothed; a moment later he disappears from view and comes out the front door. The catalog confuses the issue by inaccurately describing this portion of the film,

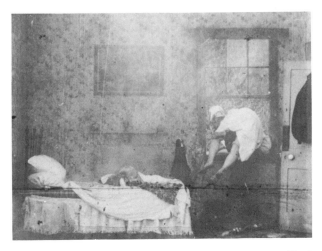

Fire! Williamson also cut from interior to exterior.

but at least two interpretations seem possible. Porter could have intended a temporal match cut on action while simply ignoring an element of continuity (clothing); or, he may have intended something we might call a temporal abridgment, although the term suggests a precise awareness of temporal continuities that the filmmaker and his audience did not enjoy. A similar cut occurs between the last two shots of James Williamson's *Fire!* in which the camera "follows the rescue out the window." Here the fireman is never actually shown climbing through the window as he carries the victim from the burning bedroom to safety outside. This could be seen as a match cut that is awkwardly executed or again as a kind of temporal abridgment (excluding roughly the time it took the fireman to climb through the opening).

The problem highlighted in these two cuts is one that faced all filmmakers of this period—temporality. Whereas the spatial relations employed in lantern shows could readily be adopted by cinema, the temporal dimension was only implied with static slides, primarily via a narration. Film, which is presented unfolding in time, demonstrates a tendency to make temporal relationships explicit. Continuity of action, embryonic at best in lantern shows, likewise became a central problem for early cinema. The mechanistic prejudice of film historians in the past has been to assume that early filmmakers were attempting to match action, just doing it badly. The problem is then seen as one of execution and manipulation of pro-filmic elements. The reverse is more likely: early filmmakers like Porter and Williamson had adequate control over pro-filmic elements, but their major problem was conceptual. Across both cuts there is strong narrative continuity that is translated into something that to our modern eyes approaches a match cut: but neither Porter nor Williamson was attempting to match action between contiguous spaces.[137]

Jack and the Beanstalk was a success even before it was released. No other American production company had the resources and the ambition to make a comparable film. Edison lawyers had to make special efforts to prevent competitors from selling duped copies. This postponed its release, for *Jack and the Beanstalk* was advertised as completed and ready for sale in late May.[138] According to subsequent Edison announcements,

> We have purposefully delayed the delivery of our great production, "Jack and the Beanstalk," until the production could be adequately protected by law, in as much as pirates have been copying our films and have been waiting until the production could be put on sail [sic] so that they could duplicate and offer it to the public. We have taken steps to protect our film both as a theatrical production and as a picture, and the film will be ready for delivery July 15.[139]

After motions for a temporary injunction against Lubin's duping activities were denied on June 25th, the film was eventually released without any legal protection for Edison's ownership.

General Manager William Gilmore remained determined to win courtroom recognition for Edison's method of copyright. "I do not want to give up the fight if there is a possible way of getting around it," Gilmore wrote to an Edison lawyer, "as this man Lubin is continuing to duplicate films that cost us a great many hundreds of dollars to obtain and one particular film that we have just gotten out has cost us pretty near a thousand dollars to get the negative, and he simply goes ahead and copies same, making a negative and issuing positive from same indiscriminately, so you see that he is doing our business a great deal of harm and we, apparently have no redress."[140] Lubin's tactics forced the Edison

Company to adopt a new pricing system in July 1902. Class A films, usually recently copyrighted Edison productions, were sold at 15¢ per foot, while Class B subjects, mostly older Edison films and dupes, went for 12¢. Edison announced:

> To counter the effect of cheap films, duplicates, worthless subjects and short length films that are being offered in the market, we are listing our genuine Edison films in two classes. Some of our subjects cost us large sums of money to obtain while others are procured at a nominal cost. Therefore the films of inexpensive subjects, we shall list as Class B at the net price of $6.00 per 50 feet.[141]

Judge Dallas's refusal to enjoin Lubin from duping virtually ended Edison's practice of submitting paper prints for copyright purposes. As a result, few films taken in the summer and fall of 1902 have survived.

After completing *Jack and the Beanstalk*, Porter worked on a series of short films, including imitations of popular Biograph comedies. While Biograph was showing these pictures on its programs, it was not selling them to independent exhibitors. Edison's competing versions were made available to the trade. Biograph's *A Jersey Skeeter* (filmed by Arthur Marvin on July 26, 1900) was reworked as *Smashing a Jersey Mosquito*; its *She Meets with Wife's Approval* (sometimes called *The New Typewriter*, taken by R. K. Bonine on July 21, 1902) was redone as *Smith's Wife Inspects the New Typewriter*; and *Shut Up!* (Bonine on August 4, 1902) became *Oh! Shut Up*. Porter also continued his ongoing series of tramp films with *Hooligan's Fourth of July*.

While Porter and Fleming were busy in the studio, J. Blair Smith was sent to Martinique, where he covered the aftermath of the Mount Pelée eruptions of May 8 and 20, 1902, which killed more than 30,000 people.[142] The Edison Company announced: "One of our special photographers was dispatched to Martinique on the first steamer sailing after this great catastrophe, and we will have the first genuine films that will be offered to the exhibitor. Do not bother with unscrupulous film makers who will offer pictures of dilapidated, blown down buildings or some other fakes as scenes from Martinique."[143] By mid July Edison's Orange factory was selling a dozen subjects taken by Smith on his trip and three shots of a studio model of Mount Pelée in various stages of eruption, taken by Porter. The Edison catalog suggested that the combination of Porter's faked and Smith's genuine films "will make a complete show in themselves."[144]

Throughout the summer and fall, Edison photographers were busy filming news topicals, incidents of human interest, and travel scenes. One cameraman visited the summer city of Chautauqua, New York, and filmed *The Annual Circus Parade* on August 9th, *Chautauqua Aquatic Day* on August 14th, and many quotidian scenes like *Swedish Gymnastics at Chautauqua, No. 8*.[145] *Fat Man's Race* and *Sack Race* were shot at an outing of St. Cecil's Lodge on Long Island. News films included *C. D. Graham Swimming the Lower Rapids*, taken on August 31st, *Mrs. Taylor Going over the Horseshoe Falls in a Barrel*, and *Trial Run of the Fastest Boat in the World, the "Arrow,"* on September 6th. In Europe, A. C. Abadie was filming *French Army Maneuvers*, *Panoramic View of the Streets of Paris*, and *Santos Dumont's Airship*.

The largest group of films in Edison's February 1903 catalog were taken by a freelance cinematographer, perhaps Walter Parker.[146] After filming numerous scenes in the Yukon around Dawson City during the winter and spring of 1902, he worked his way down to Seattle, Washington, where he took a group of scenics. From there he traveled to Denver, Colorado, and filmed *Broncho Busting Scenes, Championship of the World* at the Fall Carnival on October 9 and 10, 1902.[147]

"Telling a Story in Continuity Form"

In Paris, Alfred C. Abadie attended the opening of Méliès' *Le Voyage dans la lune* at the Théâtre Robert-Houdin and then quickly purchased a copy to send back to Edison for duping.[148] Since Méliès knew Edison would dupe his films and so was unwilling to make a direct sale, Abadie's purchase had to be quite devious. According to Arthur White, "through a certain Charles Gershel, a French photographer, 23 Boulevarde des Capuchines, Paris, who had a brother-in-law in Algiers, who had a theatre, Abadie was enabled to buy prints of the latest Melies pictures, among them 'The Trip to the Moon.'"[149] By the beginning of October, Edison was selling copies of Méliès' burlesque space fantasy as a Class A subject.[150] Years later Porter recalled, "From laboratory examination of some of the popular films of the French pioneer director, George Melies — trick films like 'A Trip to the Moon'—I came to the conclusion that a picture telling a story in continuity form might draw the customers back to the theatres and set to work in this direction."[151] A key moment must have been the rocket landing on the moon. One shot ends after the rocket hits the Man-in-the-Moon in the eye, making him wince. In the succeeding shot, the rocket lands on the surface of the moon and its passengers disembark. The event is seen twice from different perspectives. While Méliès' double depiction of the landing had legitimate storytelling reasons, the overlap emphasized the continuities of action and narrative from one shot to the next. It is this kind of continuity that Porter examined, conceptualized, and applied in many of his subsequent films.

How They Do Things on the Bowery could be called an experiment in editorial principles. Its simple, comic narrative had been presented in Biograph's earlier, one-shot *Uncle Si's Experiences in a Concert Hall* (photographed by F. S. Armitage on April 13, 1900).

HOW THEY DO THINGS ON THE BOWERY

Scene Bowery. Young woman drops her handkerchief while passing a Rube. He picks it up and gives it to her. She induces him to go into a side door of a saloon.

How They Do Things on the Bowery.

Second scene, saloon. Rube and woman enter, take seats at table and order drinks. While the Rube is paying for same, woman puts knock-out drops in the Rube's glass. They drink and the Rube falls asleep. Woman takes all his valuables and leaves. Waiter wakes him up. He discovers his watch gone, fights with waiter, and is thrown out. Third scene, outside of saloon. Police patrol drawn up. They put Rube in and drive off. Length 125 feet.[152]

In the second shot of the film, the prostitute and Uncle Josh sit at a table in a saloon and have a drink: she slips him a Mickey Finn, steals his wallet, and leaves. When the waiter finds Uncle Josh asleep, he kicks the rube out and throws his suitcase after him. In the third shot, a paddy wagon comes down the street and parks outside a building. The waiter dumps Uncle Josh into the gutter and again throws the suitcase after him.

The spatial and temporal relations between shots 2 and 3 are determined by the continuity of action as the waiter throws Uncle Josh out of the saloon. These actions, coming as they do at the end of both shots, reveal the relationship between the two scenes only in the final moments of the picture. Shots 2 and 3 are finally shown to take place in contiguous spaces, inside and outside the saloon. Shot 3 repeats the same time period shown in shot 2, employing a temporal repetition from a different camera position. This temporal construction, which was implicit in *Sampson-Schley Controversy* and *Execution of Czolgosz* and was an exhibition possibility when two cameras simultaneously filmed the christening of Kaiser Wilhelm's yacht *Meteor*, was now made explicit by the producer's assumption of editorial responsibility and the repetition of specific actions in contiguous shots. It is this concept of continuity that Porter would elaborate in *Life of an American Fireman* and many subsequent Edison films.

In *How They Do Things on the Bowery*, Porter also used a panning camera to follow action in the final shot, as the paddy wagon backs up to the saloon. For the first time Porter applied the mobile camera associated with actuality production to fiction filmmaking. Heightening a sense of realism for spectators, this procedure to some extent departed from early cinema's presentationalism. And yet the cinema's syncretism easily incorporated and contained these changes. The use of a panning camera established a much stronger sense of off-screen space. To use an insight of André Bazin's, the edges of the picture were perceived much more as a mask and much less as a frame or proscenium arch.[153] This heightened sense of a spatial world thus coincided with the introduction of a new editorial technique that specified the spatial as well as temporal relations between shots. Such camera pans would remain a key element in Porter's cinematic repertoire over the next six years. *How They Do Things on the Bowery* laid out the representational system that Porter would use during his years at Edison. Yet it was with *Life of an American Fireman* that this was elaborated, refined, and ultimately found its first large-scale, successful realization.

7 A Close Look at
Life of an American Fireman:
1902–1903

Life of an American Fireman is a landmark film as much because of its role in film historiography as because of its remarkable manifestation of early cinema's representational practices. Many past claims for its importance, however, are unfounded. The picture represents a consolidation of Edwin Porter's development as a filmmaker, not the qualitative leap Terry Ramsaye, Lewis Jacobs, A. Nicholas Vardac, and Porter himself have suggested by calling it "the first story film."

Although copyrighted on January 21, 1903, *Life of an American Fireman* was produced many weeks earlier. On November 15th, the *Newark Evening News* announced:

TO SAVE WOMAN AND PUT OUT FIRE.

AND WHILE EAST ORANGE FIREMEN
PERFORM KINETOSCOPE MACHINE
WILL RECORD SCENE.

There will be a fire on Rhode Island Avenue, East Orange, this afternoon, or at least the East Orange firemen will be called out and go through the motions of extinguishing a fire and rescuing a woman from the upper story of a house for the benefit of the Edison Kinetoscope Company, which will have one of its chainlightning cameras there to reproduce the scene.[1]

The picture might also be called *Life of an American Filmmaker*, for this scene, and probably others, featured James White as the daring fireman (see document no. 9). Ultimately, the Edison Manufacturing Company enlisted the assistance of fire departments from four different localities.

212

Despite the elaborate nature of this production, shooting was almost certainly completed before the end of 1902. Ramsaye offers one explanation for a possible two-month delay between production and release: "White cast himself for the lead in this picture. When W. E. Gilmore, general manager for Edison, screened the picture he ordered retakes to eliminate White on the grounds that it was subversive of corporate policy for an executive to be an actor."[2] The retakes, if there were any, may have been filmed while White was away, or even delayed until his return, for he married Pauline Dede on November 30, 1902, and went on a month-long honeymoon.[3] Yet it seems more likely that Edison executives were hoping for a favorable resolution to their copyright case. When this failed to materialize, they went ahead with their sales. The film was finally offered for sale at the end of January (see documents nos. 10 and 11).

DOCUMENT No. 9

RESCUE FROM FIRE
WAS HUGE SUCCESS

Lightning Cameras Took Pictures While
East Orange Firemen Perform
a Realistic Scene.

HOUSE APPEARED TO BE ALL AFLAME

Hemmed in by dense clouds of suffocating smoke, that belched forth in volume, a woman, with a babe in her arms, stood in the window of a tenement house on Rhode Island avenue, near Crawford Street, East Orange yesterday afternoon. No help was near, and the woman and child seemed doomed to an awful death, when Hook and Ladder No. 1 of the East Orange Fire Department dashed up. Manager James H. White of the Edison Kinetoscope Company, of West Orange, was the "Old Sleuth" of the occasion, and, swinging himself off the vehicle before it came to a stop, scrambled up the ladder, which was quickly raised by Firemen Judd and Stasse, and carried woman and child down to safety just as the men of Hose Co. No. 5 ran a line of hose into the building. It was a stirring scene, and it will be witnessed by many thousands, for the kinetoscope company had one of its machines there, and a series of moving pictures was taken.

The fire, though not exactly incendiary, had been planned many hours before it occurred. Mr. White, whose business it is to arrange details, such as the "Battle of San Juan Hill," the sinking of an ocean steam ship, a collapsing warehouse, and similar scenes not witnessed in every-day life, had secured the partially dismantled tenement. It is owned by a man by the name of Lanzillo, and was partially destroyed by the fire a year ago, so that it was in first-class shape for the demonstration. Cans filled with salt hay, tar and other substances calculated to produce a dense smoke were placed in every room, and at the proper moment, when a woman used to such things and regularly employed by the company for the purpose, had taken her place in the window, the contents of the cans was fired.

Were Stationed Around Corner.

Hose Co. No. 5 and the-hook and-ladder company were stationed in Halsted street and at the tap of the bell the two companies raced for the fire. Driver Flynn, Fireman Judd, Fireman Stasse and Mr. White were abroad the truck and Firemen Ohiman, Dobbins, Markfield and Dech were with the hose wagon, and while the laddermen were attending to the rescue, the latter crew coupled on to a hydrant and ran their line of hose up to the building in record time. Chief Engineer Blair, of the East Orange Fire Department and Chief Hodgkinson of Orange were interested onlookers.

Mr. White, who dressed himself in the togs of a fireman for the occasion, has figured in several striking scenes before. When the battle of Spion Kop was fought in West Orange a year or so ago, Mr. White, who is six feet tall and of massive frame, got in the way of cannon about the time it went off. After awhile he "woke up" and the surgeons at Orange Memorial Hospital picked wadding out of his chest. It was some time before he was able to be about. He is lieutenant of Company H, N.G.N.J. of Orange, and will shortly go to Berlin, Germany, to look after Mr. Edison's interests in the kinetoscope business. He is well known throughout the Oranges and has been head of the Kinetoscope department for several years.

SOURCE: *Newark Evening News*, November 16, 1902, p. 4.

DOCUMENT No. 10

LIFE OF AN AMERICAN FIREMAN

Is the Greatest Motion Picture Attraction ever offered to the Exhibitor! It is thrilling and dramatic, replete with exciting situations, and so crowded with action, interest and spectacular effects, that an audience witnessing it is simply SPELLBOUND. It shows:

First—The Fireman's Vision of an Imperiled Woman and Child.

Second—The Turning in of the Alarm.

Third—The Firemen Leaping from their Beds, Dressing and Sliding Down the Poles.

Fourth—Interior of the Engine House, Horses Dashing from their Stalls, and Being Hitched to the Apparatus.

Fifth—Men Descending on Poles, and Rushing to their Places on the Fire Apparatus.
Sixth—The Apparatus Leaving the Engine House.
Seventh—Off to the Fire (a Great Fire Run)
Eighth—The Arrival at the Fire, Showing an Actual Burning Building, the Firemen Coupling the Hose, Raising the Ladders, the Rescue Scene from the Interior and Exterior. Great Smoke and Flames Effects. 425 feet. Class A. $63.75

This film is sold in one length only. Send in your complete order quick, Get the film and Get the money. This is the only complete fire scene ever attempted where the men are shown leaving their beds, and A Genuine hitch taken inside the engine house. A Money Getter is what this film has been pronounced. You need it in your business because it will be the strongest card on your bill. Catalogue #168 Describes this and Over One hundred other New Subjects.

SOURCE: Edison advertisement, *New York Clipper*, January 31, 1903, p. 1100.

DOCUMENT NO. 11

Life of an American Fireman

In giving this description to the public, we unhesitatingly claim for it the strongest motion picture attraction ever attempted in this length of film. It will be difficult for the exhibitor to conceive the amount of work involved and the number of rehearsals necessary to turn out a film of this kind. We were compelled to enlist the services of the fire departments of four different cities, New York, Newark, Orange, and East Orange, N.J., and about 300 firemen appear in the various scenes of this film.

From the first conception of this wonderful series of pictures it has been our aim to portray "Life of an American Fireman" without exaggeration, at the same time embodying the dramatic situations and spectacular effects which so greatly enhance a motion picture performance.

The record work of the modern American fire department is known throughout the universe, and the fame of the American fireman is echoed around the entire world. He is known to be the most expert, as well as the bravest, of all fire fighters. This film faithfully and accurately depicts his thrilling and dangerous life, emphasizing the perils he subjects himself to when human life is at stake. We show the world in this film the every movement of the brave firemen and their perfectly trained horses from the moment the men leap from their beds in response to an alarm until the fire is extinguished and a woman and child are rescued after many fierce battles with flame and smoke. Below we give a description of each of the seven scenes which make up this most wonderful of all fire scenes, "Life of an American Fireman."

Scene 1.—The Fireman's Vision of an Imperilled Woman and Child. The fire chief is seated at his office desk. He has just finished reading his evening paper and has fallen asleep. The rays of an incandescent light rest upon his features with a subdued light, yet leaving his figure strongly silhouetted against the wall of his office. The fire chief is dreaming, and the vision of his dream appears in a circular portrait upon the wall. It is a mother putting her baby to bed, and the inference is that he dreams of his own wife and child. He suddenly awakes and paces the floor in a nervous state of mind, doubtless thinking of the various people who may be in danger from fire at the moment. Here we dissolve the picture to the second scene.

Scene 2.—A Close View of a New York Fire Alarm Box. Shows lettering and every detail in the door and apparatus for turning in an alarm. A figure then steps in front of the box, hastily opens the door and pulls the hook, thus sending the electric current which alarms hundreds of firemen and brings to the scene of the fire the wonderful apparatus of a great city's fire department. Again dissolving the picture, we show the third scene.

Scene 3.—The Interior of the Sleeping Quarters in the Fire House. A long row of beds, each containing a fireman peacefully sleeping, is shown. Instantly upon the ringing of the alarm the firemen leap from their beds and, putting on their clothes in the record time of five seconds, a grand rush is made for a large circular opening in the floor, through the center of which runs a brass pole. The first fireman to reach the pole seizes it and, like a flash, disappears through the opening. He is instantly followed by the remainder of the force. This in itself makes a most stirring scene. We again dissolve the scene, to the interior of the apparatus house.

Scene 4.—Interior of the Engine House. Shows horses dashing from their stalls and being hitched to the apparatus. This is perhaps the most thrilling and in all the most wonderful of the seven scenes of the series, it being absolutely the first motion picture ever made of a genuine interior hitch. As the men come down the pole described in the above scene, and land upon the floor in lightning-like rapidity, six doors in the rear of the engine house, each heading a horse-stall, burst open simultaneously and a huge fire horse, with head erect and eager for the dash to the scene of the conflagration, rushes from each opening. Going immediately to their respective harness, they are hitched in the almost unbelievable time of five seconds and are ready for their dash to the fire. The men hastily scamper upon the trucks and horse carts and one by one the fire machines leave the house, drawn by eager, prancing steeds. Here we dissolve again to the fifth scene.

Scene 5.—The Apparatus Leaving the Engine House. We show a fine exterior view of engine house, the great doors swinging open, and the apparatus coming out. This is a most imposing scene. The great horses leap to their work, the men adjust their fire hats and coats, and smoke begins pouring from the engines as they pass our camera. Here we dissolve and show the sixth scene.

Scene 6.—Off to the Fire. In this scene we present the best fire run ever shown. Almost the entire fire department of the large city of Newark N.J., was placed at our disposal and we show countless pieces of apparatus, engines, hook-and-ladders, horse towers, horse carriages, etc., rushing down a broad street at top speed, the horses straining every nerve and evidently eager to make a record run. Great clouds of smoke pour from the stacks of the engines as they pass our camera, thus giving an impression of genuineness to the entire series. Dissolving again we show the seventh scene.

Scene 7.—The Arrival at the Fire. In this wonderful scene we show the entire fire department, as described above, arriving at the scene of action. An actual burning building is in the center foreground. On the right background the fire department is seen coming at great speed. Upon the arrival of the different apparatus, the engines are ordered to their places, hose is quickly run out from the carriages, ladders adjusted to the windows and streams of water poured into the burning structure. At this crucial moment comes the great climax of the series. We dissolve to the interior of the building and show a bed chamber with a woman and child enveloped in flame and suffocating smoke. The woman rushes back and forth in the room endeavoring to escape, and in her desperation throws open the window and appeals to the crowd below. She is finally overcome by the smoke and falls upon the bed. At this moment the door is smashed in by an axe in the hands of a powerful fire hero. Rushing into the room he tears the burning draperies from the window and smashing out the entire window frame, orders his comrades to run up a ladder. Immediately the ladder appears, he seizes the prostrate form of the woman and throws it over his shoulder as if it were an infant, and quickly descends to the ground. We now dissolve to the exterior of the burning building. The frantic mother having returned to consciousness, and clad only in her night clothes, is kneeling on the ground imploring the firemen to return for her child. Volunteers are called for and the same fireman who rescued the mother quickly steps out and offers to return for the babe. He is given permission to once more enter the doomed building and without hesitation rushes up the ladder, enters the window and after a breathless wait, in which it appears he must have been overcome by smoke, he appears with the child on his arm and returns safely to the ground. The child, being released and upon seeing its mother, rushes to her and is clasped in her arms, thus making a most realistic and touching ending of the series. Length 425 feet. Class A. $63.75.

SOURCE: *Edison Films*, February 1903, pp. 2–3.

While documentation of early showings is sparse, *Life of an American Fireman* was treated as a headliner in New York theaters. Probably first shown at Huber's Museum by the Kinetograph Company, it was soon appearing on Vitagraph programs with *The Fireman's Children; or, Chips off the Old Block* (apparently an uncopyrighted Edison film made in late 1902 or early 1903).[4] When the Chicago Novelty Company, a small traveling troupe that featured motion pictures and vaudeville, showed the film in Reading, Pennsylvania, they promoted it with the claim that it featured Pennsylvania fire departments in action.[5]

As with *Jack and the Beanstalk* and earlier Edison films, Porter and his colleagues chose a subject that was in the mainstream of popular culture and screen practice. *Bob the Fireman*, a twelve-slide lantern show, made in England before the advent of cinema, was still being sold in the United States in 1902–3. It was sufficiently popular to have survived in considerable numbers, with lectures in at least two different languages.[6] Maxwell and Simpson, illustrated song singers, made hits with such titles as "Fire, Fire and Smoke."[7] The narratives and highly conventionalized imagery of these innumerable shows were transferred to the cinema largely intact. As already discussed, the commercial potential of fire rescue films was established by November 1896 when White produced *A Morning Alarm*, *Going to the Fire*, and *Fighting the Fire*. Edison's September 1902 catalog listed ten fire films under one heading, while others were scattered through its 120 pages.[8]

By early 1902 several multishot films of firefighting had been produced. William Selig had made the 450-foot *Life of a Fireman* by the end of 1900 and considered this to be his most important negative.[9] Sigmund Lubin's multishot, 250-foot *Going to the Fire and Rescue* was probably made sometime in 1901:

This is a new film and it is safe to assume that it is an only one of its kind ever made. When the alarm is given the horses are seen to run from their stalls and place themselves in their accustomed places at the wagons. The harness is adjusted, the firemen jump on, and they dash out of the fire house and down the street. The picture changes and the entire apparatus is seen coming at full gallop toward the audience down a long lane. The picture again changes and the fire laddies are again seen rescuing women and children from a burning building, after which, in another change of the picture they are seen to arrive at the fire house, unharness the horses and back the apparatus into the house. This film is animated throughout and the photography is perfect. This is an extraordinary picture of an interesting subject.[10]

Four slides from the lantern show *Bob the Fireman*. Numbers read backwards to guide projectionist.

As Georges Sadoul has argued, James Williamson's four-shot, 280-foot account of a fire rescue, *Fire!*, may have provided Porter with a particularly direct source of inspiration.[11] Yet Sadoul's accusation of imitation seems overstated. While the last two scenes of both films share many similarities, Porter's "debt" tended toward the pro-filmic elements of set construction and gesture, which were themselves highly conventionalized and hardly originated with Williamson. With *Life of an American Fireman*, Porter was working within a genre that was among the most advanced in cinema. The popularity of the subject, the very frequency with which it was filmed and the constant search for novelty were important factors influencing this film's production. By 1901–2, several production companies were already selling multishot fire films. In *Life of an American Fireman*, Porter exploited this tentative shift toward centralized control and produced a more elaborate and effective story.

One of the most spectacular, if rigid, genres in turn-of-the-century popular culture, the fire rescue cut across many different cultural practices. In 1855 Currier and Ives published a series of prints under the rubric "Life of a Fireman." The same year John E. Millais painted "The Rescue," a narrative painting later appropriated for the lantern show *Bob the Fireman* as the ninth of twelve slides.[12] "Fighting the Flames," a popular outdoor spectacle first produced for the Paris Exposition of 1900, appeared at Coney Island in 1904, when it was filmed by the Biograph Company.[13] The basic story of *Life of an American Fireman* found subsequent articulation in *A Fireman's Christmas Eve*, a theatrical spectacle copyrighted a month after Porter's film and staged at Proctor's 23rd Street Theater that October (see document no. 12). Like everyone else, Porter was working within a well-established genre. It was not narrative as such, but the execution of narrative to achieve novelty, spectacle, and suspense that was of import. At his best, Porter's strength lay in his ability to rework previous formulas in innovative and novel ways. Certainly this was the case with *Life of an American Fireman*.

DOCUMENT No. 12

Novel Act at Proctor's

"A Fireman's Christmas Eve" Shows Thrilling Scene
of the Fire Fighters' Experience.

The 'life of a New York fireman' is shown in a capital novelty introduced at Proctor's Twenty-Third Street Theatre yesterday. It may be described, for want of a better name, as a pictorial drama, with the title "A Fireman's Christmas Eve," suggesting the incidents of the principal scenes.

When the curtain rises a street is shown and the passers-by reflect the varying elements that enter into Metropolitan life. Newsboys, shopmen, and shopgirls go to and fro. Then a little colored newsboy seats himself on the doorstep and falls asleep. The snow falls and night comes on. The policeman on the beat sees the sleeping boy, and taking one of the papers from his bundle, covers him with it to keep off the cold.

Then the scene changes, showing the interior of the fireman's home. The fireman is singing while his wife plays his accompaniment on the organ. The fireman's child plays about the room. The clock strikes the time of departure and the fireman kisses his wife and child good-bye and goes to his duties. The mother undresses the little one, who now toddles off to bed, after having hung up a stocking for the goodies Santa Claus is to bring.

Now the scene again changes, showing the interior of the fire house. Both the main floor and the sleeping room of the men are shown. The fireman comes in, bearing in his arms the little black boy whom he has saved from freezing to death. The boy is revived and at once takes out his dice and begins to shoot craps. Then he 'obliges' with a song and dance, and the firemen, engaged in polishing up their machine, join in the chorus. After bidding the Captain good-night the men ascend to their sleeping room and once again the scene changes.

The fireman's wife is now lighting candles on the Christmas tree. There is a sudden blaze, a shriek, then the cry of fire.

Now the interior of the firehouse is again shown. Down the pole slide the easily awakened fire fighters, the horses come rushing pell mell into their places underneath the suspended harness, and in a twinkling everything is ready for the rush to the fire.

In the next scene the horses and engine are seen apparently on the way to the place of need. The effect is thrilling, a treadmill being used, and the bustle, hurry, and excitement of a run to the fire being admirably suggested. Finally, the burning house is revealed, a fireman rescues the child from an upper room, the net is spread, and the mother leaps to safety, and the blaze is extinguished.

The audience yesterday was stirred to such enthusiasm as might have resulted if they had been witnessing a real fire and real rescues.

The big engine is finally drawn from the stage by the horses, a difficult turn being made completely around the stage. It is a most interesting act and should prove decidedly popular.

SOURCE: *New York Times*, October 25, 1903, p. 22C. George Pratt, who brought this text to my attention, believes *A Fireman's Christmas Eve* was written after its author, Claude Hagan, saw *Life of an American Fireman*. The play was copyrighted February 21, 1903.

The intertextual framework in which this film was made and seen has been briefly sketched. Yet it is at least as important to understand the film within a more general social framework, notably in relation to local fire departments. In his insightful study of Pittsburgh, Francis G. Couvares has discussed the central role that volunteer fire companies played in nineteenth-century "plebeian culture."[14] These organizations drew their membership from the working and middle classes (usually skilled workers, clerks, independent artisans, and shopkeepers). Firefighting was only one aspect of their activities. More generally, they were a part of the informal network of institutions that catered to male sociability—the saloon, tobacco shops, and sporting clubs. Fire companies, moreover, routinely provided entertainment and spectacle for their neighborhoods and cities. Band concerts, dances, picnics, parades, and Fourth of July celebrations were some of the occasions when the local fire department assumed prominent positions in neighborhood and even citywide activities. Representing their town or neighborhood, they often functioned as a symbol of civic pride. Fire engine races and other competitive events between departments both locally and regionally were routine. These departments thus sustained a homosocial, egalitarian environment that was the heart of plebeian culture. Given their crucial position at the intersection of social and cultural activity, and of public and private spheres, fire departments predictably played prominent roles during cinema's early years.

The move from volunteer companies to a professional fire department in the later decades of the nineteenth century tended to undermine the plebeian nature of this institution. Inter-class sociability broke down and institutional ties to the community were inevitably weakened. In the face of increasingly large-scale commercial amusement, the fire department's cultural role lost ground. Nonetheless, a figure like Kansas City fire chief George Hale, the creator of "Fighting the Flames" and then Hale's Tours, reminds us that this tradition was not simply marginalized but simultaneously transformed from within, a process in which cinema actively participated. Hence all those fire films. Motion pictures inevitably involved a loss of control over the image by those being represented. This loss, while slight in the case of local views meant principally for hometown consumption, grew with the ambition of the project. With *Life of an American Fireman*, local firemen still performed for the camera, demonstrating their skill and manly courage. Yet this spectacle belonged to someone else. The ideology of the picture itself had not shifted (for its filmmakers shared similar values and structures of feeling), but the image was now an alternative to (and ultimately challenged) the mode of production on which plebeian culture relied. A local fire department could not compete with this spectacle, but had to accept more modest aspirations. As a result, its efforts at spectacle become an echo, a pale imitation, of that which it had originally helped to create. Cinema incorporated and then supplanted those efforts. And yet this process was hardly obvious to people appearing in or watching these films. Perhaps it became clearer in the 1910s and 1920s when volunteer fire departments became the focus of denigrating comedies such as *The New Fire Chief* (Independent Moving Picture Company, 1912) or were subsumed by a larger narrative as in *Foolish Wives* (1921).

By 1902 the volunteer fire department was excluded from major cities where professional forces operated. Yet even in these metropolitan areas, the fire department remained a symbol of societal cohesion. The urban firefighter was a working-class hero par excellence, an individual who risked his life to save others. He could be admired by fellow members of the working class while presenting a reassuring image to the bourgeoisie as the savior not only of lives but of property. Bridging class divisions at a time when the social framework was under great stress, *Life of an American Fireman* and other films of this genre were popular in part because they successfully transcended class and urban/rural divisions, echoing a plebeian sensibility. In heroicizing the American fireman as "the most expert, as well as the bravest, of all fire fighters,"[15] the filmmakers also appealed to American patriotism. Thus the use of four fire departments becomes important, not simply because two were volunteer (Orange, East Orange) and two professional (New York, Newark), but because localism was superseded.

Life of an American Fireman, moreover, allowed for a wide variety of interpretations through the exhibitor's lecture. The *Clipper* description suggests a simple story in which a fireman thinks of an imperiled woman and child, whom he and his fellow firemen subsequently rescue. The catalog, however, offers a more elaborate account, in which a fire chief dreams of his wife and child, who are in danger. Nor was this perceived simply as coincidence, for the fire chief was a favorite target of deranged "firebugs" (see document no. 13). A fire chief had every reason to envision his family in danger, and every respectable family man could identify with his situation. Depending on the emphasis of his spiel, the showman could privilege either the working-class hero or the chief, a hero of America's new middle class. In either case, *Life of an American Fireman*, like many of Porter's later films, foregrounded the family and the need for a cohesive society.

DOCUMENT No. 13

INCENDIARIES AFTER FIRE CHIEF.

Make Three Attempts to Burn His House in Jersey City.

Two attempts were made last night to burn a three-story frame house at 54 Ferry Street, Jersey City, owned by John Conway, Chief of the Fire Department.

The house is occupied by three families. One of the tenants at 6 o'clock found some oil-soaked waste burning in the cellar. Kerosene had been poured on all the stairs from the cellar to the top of the house. The fire was extinguished but an hour later more paper was found burning in another part of the cellar. This also was extinguished.

An attempt was made to fire the same house in March last.

SOURCE: *New York Times*, September 6, 1901, p. 12.

Representational Practices in *Life of an American Fireman*

A full appreciation of *Life of an American Fireman* requires a shot-by-shot analysis. In shot 1, a dream balloon shows the fire chief thinking of a mother

Frames from *Life of an American Fireman*—two per shot—except for shot 5 (one frame), shot 6 (3 frames), and shot 7, which is not represented.

and child (a composition with religious overtones), possibly his family. The dream balloon fades away and the fire chief exits. This shot is spatially and temporally independent from the rest of the film. Shot 2 is a close view of a hand pulling down the arm of the fire alarm. There is a temporal overlap at the end of shot 2/beginning of shot 3 as the firemen, at first asleep, jump out of bed in response to the alarm. The firemen, on the second floor of the firehouse, put on their clothes and jump down the fire pole until only one is left. Shot 4, the interior of the engine house with its vaunted interior hitch, was actually filmed in an elaborate outdoor set: the floor is mostly grass. The scene begins as the horses are quickly harnessed to the engines. After a few moments, the firemen come down the fire pole. Here, a more substantial temporal overlap with a redundancy of action is employed between shots 3 and 4. The end of shot 4/ beginning of shot 5 employs yet another overlap. Shot 4 ends with the fire engine racing off forward right. Shot 5 begins with the firehouse doors opening and a fire engine exiting off right. In shots 3, 4, and 5, Porter shows everything of dramatic interest occurring within the frame. This results in a redundancy of dynamic action—the slide down the pole, the start to the fire—effectively heightening the impact of the narrative. At the same time, the repeated actions clearly establish spatial, temporal, and narrative relationships between shots. It is, as Porter realized, a kind of continuity, but one radically different from the continuity associated with classical cinema.

Shot 6, "Off to the Fire," is a conventional rendering of the fire run and relies on the quantity of fire engines to impress its audience. Narrative consistency is sacrificed to spectacle. In shot 7 a fire engine races by a park. As the fire engine approaches, a pan follows the action, focusing on James White, who jumps off the vehicle in front of a burning building. Again, the moving camera suggests the immediacy of a news film. Convention and narrative continuity rather than continuity of action establish the relationship between shots 7 and 8. Shot 8 shows a bedroom interior as the woman gets out of bed, staggers to the window, and is overcome by smoke. The fireman breaks in the door, enters, and then breaks out the window, where a ladder appears. After carrying out the woman, he immediately returns for the child hidden in the bed covers. The fireman leaves with the child, but quickly returns again with a hose and douses the flame.

Shot 9, using virtually the same camera position as the concluding section of shot 7, shows the same rescue from the outside. The woman leans out the window (in shot 8 she does not lean out the window; however, the gesture is identical) then disappears back inside; the fireman brings her down the ladder; she tells him of her threatened child; he races back up the ladder and returns with the child. As the mother and child embrace in a tableau-type ending, the fireman again ascends with the hose. Shots 8 and 9 show the same rescue from two different perspectives. The blocking is carefully laid out, and continuity of action is more than acceptable. The activities in shot 8 have their counterparts in shot 9 as people move back and forth from inside to outside: the succession of complementary actions tie the two shots together—something Porter did only twice in *How They Do Things on the Bowery*. While on one level these two shots create a temporal repetition, on another level they each have their own distinct and complementary temporalities, which together form a whole. When the interior is shown, everything happening inside unfolds in "real" time while everything occurring outside is extremely condensed. The reverse is true when showing the rescue from the exterior. In keeping with theatrical conventions, whenever actions take place off-screen, time is elided.

This complementary relationship between shots is a kind of proto-parallel editing involving manipulation of the mise-en-scène instead of manipulation of the film material through decoupage, and manipulation of time over space. While *Life of an American Fireman* uses familiar spatial constructions, its temporal construction differs radically from matching action and parallel cutting, which audiences would see only six years later in such Griffith films as *The Lonely Villa* (1909). *The Lonely Villa* utilizes a representational system dominated by the linear flow of time, an accomplishment made possible by fragmentation of the mise-en-scène and a rapid shift in shots as the narrative moves back and forth between locations. *Life of an American Fireman* remained indebted to the magic lantern show, with its well-developed spatial constructions and an underdeveloped temporality. By showing everything within the frame, Porter was, in effect, making moving magic lantern slides with theatrical pro-filmic elements. Shots are self-contained units tied to each other by overlapping action. Ironically, *Life of an American Fireman* has frequently been praised for its fluidity and the way it condenses time through editorial strategies. The reverse is often true: the action is retarded, repeated.

Life of an American Fireman contains a series of fascinating contradictions. The frontal organization of pro-filmic elements occurring in most scenes is briefly broken in shot 7 by the sweeping camera, which momentarily reveals a "continuous" off-screen spatial world that exists outside the static rectangle of the camera frame. The pervasive presentationalism, indebted to traditional stage practices, is again contradicted by the "omniscient" camera, which views the same actions from two (and if two, why not three, four, or five?) different perspectives. Shots are constructed as discrete, independent units even as they are made subservient to an overall narrative. Having developed strategies that superseded the exhibitor's role as editor, Porter continued to draw upon his own background as an exhibitor by combining scenes of four different fire departments (just as an exhibitor might show a *Passion Play* using films from four different producers). This syncretic film is caught somewhere between the presentation of simulated reality and a fictional story. This story, which exists to the extent that the fire chief and his vision of wife and child resonate throughout subsequent scenes, is periodically sacrificed to spectacle. The tentative story, therefore, could either be ignored or developed by the showman as he was inclined. As if to compensate exhibitors for their lack of editorial opportunities, the film offered them great latitude in presenting the film. Contradictions such as these inspired Noël Burch's description of Porter as a two-faced Janus who looks backward and forward in time.

The narrative and temporal organization that Porter made explicit in *How They Do Things on the Bowery* and *Life of an American Fireman* can be found in many of his later films, including *Uncle Tom's Cabin* (1903), *The Great Train Robbery* (1903), *The Ex-Convict* (1904), *The Watermelon Patch* (1905), *The "Teddy" Bears* (1907), and *Rescued from An Eagle's Nest* (1908). Other filmmakers, notably those working at Biograph, followed Méliès' and Porter's lead in films like *Next!* (photographed November 4, 1903), *A Discordant Note* (June 26, 1903), *The Burglar* (August 21, 1903), *Wanted: A Dog* (March 1905) and *The Firebug* (July 1905). English films like G. A. Smith's *Mary Jane's Mishaps*

(1903) and Cecil Hepworth's *Rescued by Rover* (1905) have similar temporal constructions, while Méliès continued to use overlapping action in *Le Voyage à travers l'impossible* (1904) and *Le Mariage de Victorine* (1907). Porter and his contemporaries were working within a cultural framework that made this mode of narrative organization intelligible, even "natural," to their audiences.

The narrative procedures in *Life of an American Fireman* involve structures occurring in different cultural forms at different times. Sergei Eisenstein used brief overlaps in *October* (1927), but these broke the "seamless" linear continuity of shots that had become part of classical narrative cinema. The procedure may be similar to Porter's, but its function was completely different, for Porter's strategy was to create a greater degree of continuity than had theretofore existed.

The parallels between *Life of an American Fireman* and medieval French poetry—*chanson de geste*—are extremely provocative. Erich Auerbach, in examining *Chanson de Roland* and *Chanson d'Alexis*, notes that "in both we have the same repeated returning to fresh starts, the same spasmodic progression and retrogression, the same individual occurrences and their constituent parts."[16] The description of Roland's death (*laisses* 174–176) is one example of this narrative technique:

174

2355 Roland feels that death is overcoming him,
It descends from his head to his heart.
He ran beneath a pine tree.
He lay down prone on the green grass.
He places his sword and his oliphant beneath him.
2360 He turned his head toward the pagan army:
He did this because he earnestly desires
That Charles and all his men say
That the noble count died as a conqueror.
He beats his breast in rapid succession over and over again.
2365 He proffered his gauntlet to God for his sins.

175

Roland feels that his time is up,
He is on a steep hill, his face turned toward Spain.
"Mea culpa, Almighty God,
2370 For my sins, great and small,
Which I committed from the time I was born
To this day when I am overtaken here!"
He offered his right gauntlet to God,
Angels from heaven descend toward him.

176

2375 Count Roland lay beneath a pine tree,

He has turned his face toward Spain.
He began to remember many things:
The many lands he conquered as a brave knight,
Fair France, the men from whom he is descended,
2380 Charlemagne, his lord, who raised him.
He cannot help weeping and sighing.
But he does not wish to forget prayers for his own soul,
He says his confession in a loud voice and prays for God's mercy:
"True Father, who never lied,
2385 Who resurrected Saint Lazarus from the dead
And saved Daniel from the lions,
Protect my soul from all perils
Due to the sins I committed during my life!"
He proffered his right gauntlet to God,
2390 Saint Gabriel took it from his hand.
He laid his head down over his arm,
He met his end, his hands joined together.
God sent His angel Cherubin
And Saint Michael of the Peril,
2395 Saint Gabriel came with them.
They bear the Count's soul to Paradise.[17]

The *laisse* is the primary unit of production for *chansons de geste*; its equivalent is the shot in turn-of-the-century cinema. Just as Porter showed the same
rescue from two different perspectives, so the author of *Chanson de Roland* used
laisses similares to describe the manner in which Roland dies. Certain actions
are reiterated: Roland feeling that his time is up (lines 2355 and 2366), beating
his breast (2364 and 2369) and offering his gauntlet to God (2365 and 2373).
Other actions or speech in *laisse* 174 are omitted in 175 and new ones added.
Both Porter and the *chanson*'s author made use of this technique at climactic
moments in their narratives.

Overlapping action, which Porter used throughout *Life of an American Fireman*, is frequently encountered in *chanson de geste* as well, for instance at the
end of *laisse* 164 and beginning of 165:

He [Count Roland] suffered such pain that he could no longer Stand,
Willy-nilly, he falls to the ground
The Archbishop said: "You are to be pitied, worthy knight!"

When the Archbishop saw Roland faint,
He suffered greater anguish than ever before.[18]

These congruencies are not simply representational coincidence, but are intimately related to parallel modes of production. Jean Rychner has explored the
complex relationship that existed between the performers who sang the epic

poems and the surviving *chansons*. He concludes that "all the good singers are also improvisers; they created their songs themselves, and, when they did not create them properly speaking, they knew how to combine the songs of others, how to condense several poems into one, how to modify, complete and amplify."[19] The *chanson de geste*, like the early film program, was an open work, subject to the jongleur's manipulation—with the manipulation of *laisses* the primary level on which this was accomplished. New *laisses* could be added or whole sections could be omitted. Elaboration of narrative was not achieved within a simple linear time line but through repetition. Furthermore, with such a system of production, overlapping narrative was an effective way to relate a new or different *laisse* to the existing narrative.

There are other parallels. Audiences for *Chanson de Roland* and *Life of an American Fireman* already knew the story they were seeing and/or hearing. Much of their enjoyment came from relating the individual presentations to the known narrative: appreciation was based on the audiences' ability to judge skill of execution and effectiveness of representation in comparison to previous presentations. Correspondingly, the film producer or jongleur relied on iconographic images, gestures, and phraseology in the creation of scenes and *laisses*.[20] Images and forms of expression were both highly conventionalized from the perspective of the producer as well as of the audience.

Chanson de Roland and *Life of an American Fireman* occupy similar places in the respective developments of European literature and the American screen to the extent that both forms were moving toward a new mode of production in which a work had closure and there was a single "author." This was achieved in literature, of course, by a movement toward the written text. Both works are exceptions within their respective forms because of "the unity of subject and internal cohesion,"[21] which placed them at the forefront of these developments. This exploration of convergences, however, is not an attempt to elevate *Life of an American Fireman* to the status of *Chanson de Roland* as a work of cultural significance. *Chanson de geste* developed over a period of centuries and was a major form of cultural expression. The cinema in 1903 was still only one of many forms of popular culture, and the circumstances that conditioned this kind of narrative structuring were short-lived. The Edison Manufacturing Company bore little resemblance to a medieval court: cinema, driven by fierce competition, continued its rapid transformation, quickly developing strategies more consistent with narrative techniques found in other contemporary media, particularly the use of a linear time line. The mode of representation used by Griffith only ten or fifteen years later would be compared to that of Charles Dickens.[22] Yet *Life of an American Fireman* is emblematic of a crucial moment in film history. It signaled a further shift in the editorial function from exhibitor to production company and a tendency toward producing larger units (i.e., longer and therefore more complex films). Although this can be attributed in some degree to industrial efficiency, maximizing profit, and the structure of American industry, such pressures were increased exponentially by a new level of narrative organization, often called "the story film." Because story films could be more effectively produced by an organization having greater creative control, the role of the filmmaker was fundamentally constituted as we conceive of it today.

Life of an American Fireman in Film History

Film history is an emerging discipline. It began early, in manuals like Cecil Hepworth's *Animated Photographs* (1897) and in courtrooms where legal proceedings valorized priority and the myth of the first time. By the 1910s, with the films of the pre-nickelodeon era unavailable and unknown to most people working in the industry, the film pioneers laid claim to various "firsts." Perhaps one of the most enduring has been the assertion that *Life of an American Fireman* was "the first story film." Porter had this claim presented in the May 1913 issue of *Theatre Magazine*:

> Mr. Porter was the first man to tell a complete story with moving pictures. That was in 1900 when he made the film of *Life of an American Fireman* for the Edison people. This original story-telling moving-picture reel began with the fireman's home, where he was seen kissing his wife and baby good-bye. Then successively the pictures showed his arrival at the firehouse, sitting at the chief's desk later at night, dozing off and having a vision of his wife and child, the child saying her prayers at the bedside; the fireman awakens and there is a shift to the bedroom, showing the mother putting the child to bed; shift, lamp upset; shift fire alarm box pulled at the street corner; shift inside the firehouse, showing the firemen sliding down the poles and hitching the horses; shift to the bedroom mother unconscious from the smoke; shift fire engines tearing through the street; shift arrival at the chief's own home; putting ladder up with rescue of wife and then the child. This was the first complete story ever told in moving pictures just thirteen years ago.[23]

This article was not simply a case of hazy memory but a calculated attempt to elevate Porter's stature to a level consistent with his position at Adolph Zukor's Famous Players Film Company, where he was head of production. It rewrote history to make Porter's role intelligible—and primary. The revision had two vectors. First, it pushed the film's production date back to 1900, to the time of his arrival at Edison and the first American screenings of Méliès' *Cinderella*. Second, it described a group of cinematic techniques that could be found only in the most advanced films of 1908–9. While arguing for his place as "a father of the story film," Porter equated it with the highly developed technique of parallel editing and linear continuity that he had never employed at Edison. This fantastic description reveals an embarrassing case of Griffith envy, obscuring the true significance of the film and renouncing the mode of representation on which Porter's Edison films were based.

Terry Ramsaye, consistent with his sympathetic portrayal of Thomas Edison, valorized Porter's claim in *A Million and One Nights* (1926):

> There have been tiny, trivial efforts to use the screen to tell a story, exemplified by Cecil Hepworth's *Rescued by Rover*, the adventures of a little girl and a dog, photographed in London, and *The Burglar on the Roof* made by Blackton and Smith of Vitagraph. They were mere episodes.
>
> Now in the Edison studios, where the art of the film was born, and also where it was best bulwarked against the distractions of the fight for existence, came the emergence of the narrative idea.
>
> James H. White was in charge of Edison's "Kinetograph Department" and Edwin S. Porter, becoming a cameraman, was the chief fabricator of picture material. Between them evolved a five hundred foot subject entitled *The Life of an American Fireman*.[24]

That *Rescued by Rover* (1905) is said to precede *Life of an American Fireman* is only one of many failings in this brief account.

Lewis Jacobs' work on this subject is impressive when placed against Ramsaye's claims. Jacobs unearthed primary source material for *The Rise of the American Film* (1939), reprinting the catalog description and photographs taken for copyright purposes. The stills, however, were rearranged to conform to modern notions of linear continuity—and to Porter's assertions in this area. Jacobs never tried to resolve the discrepancy between the catalog description and the more elaborate intercutting suggested by his rearrangement of stills. Instead, he praised Porter's contributions in a manner that finally extended Ramsaye's assertions:

> If Georges Méliès was the first to "push cinema towards a theatrical way," as he claimed, then Edwin Porter was the first to push cinema towards the cinematic way. Generally acknowledged today as the father of the story film, he made more than fictional contributions to movie tradition. It was Porter who discovered that the art of motion pictures depends on the continuity of shots, not on the shots alone. Not content with Méliès' artificially arranged scenes, Porter distinguished the movies from other theatrical forms and gave them the invention of editing. Almost all motion picture developments since Porter's discovery spring from the principle of editing, which is the basis of motion picture artistry.
>
> By 1902 Porter had a long list of films to his credit. But neither he nor other American producers had yet learned to tell a story. They were still busy with elementary one-shot news events ... , with humorous bits ... , with vaudeville skits ... , scenic views ... and local topics. ... None of these productions stood out from the general. Literal and unimaginative, they are significant today mainly as social documents.
>
> ... Porter therefore concocted a scheme that was as startling as it was different: a mother and child were to be caught in a burning building and rescued at the last moment by the fire department.
>
> Tame though such a plot sounds to us today, it was then revolutionary.[25]

Georges Sadoul, in his *Histoire générale du cinéma* (1948), agrees with Jacobs' "logical" rearrangement of copyright photographs but points out that this gave a total of "eleven shots in the film rather than eight."[26] By breaking the last scene down into five shots, Sadoul presents a clear case of intercutting back and forth between two scenes.

Although Sadoul disagrees with Jacobs over who was "the inventor of editing," both had the same conception of early cinema, one similar to that offered in *Theatre Magazine*. The Jacobs/Sadoul description of the film was modified in detail rather than principle by the first copy of the film to be recovered, the one at the Museum of Modern Art (MoMA). The intercutting was even more elaborate than Jacobs or Sadoul had imagined. As Jean Mitry notes in his *Histoire du cinéma* (1967), "seven scenes decompose into fifteen." From this he concludes:

> One may say with more objectivity that if the English have discovered continuity and montage, Porter was the first to understand that the act of cinema depended on this continuity. In effect, the action is followed across several successive shots. This is a contribution which can't be overestimated. With Porter the continuity becomes genetically linked to the drama, at least to the dramatic emotion.[27]

Much film history was written using the Jacobs/Sadoul analysis buttressed by the MoMA print.

A whole generation of historians had become publicly committed to this print when the paper print project at the Library of Congress uncovered a different version of the film. Both versions are essentially identical except for the last scene—scene 7. Scene 7 in the MoMA print makes use of parallel editing and matching action, while the Library of Congress (DLC) version uses a temporal repetition similar to the one in *How They Do Things on the Bowery*. It is obvious that someone, at some point, intercut the last two shots of the DLC version, following the action as it moves back and forth between interior and exterior, and matching action each time the fireman goes through the window.[28]

Kenneth Macgowan in *Behind the Screen* (1965) and Gerald Mast in *A Short History of the Movies* (1976) laid out both versions of the film, favoring the MoMA print but refusing to make any definitive judgments:

> It is obvious from the copyright print that the director took just exactly the scenes he needed for intercutting. If he hadn't intended to intercut elaborately, why would he have shot the firemen returning through the window and rescuing the child as well as other firemen entering to put out the fire with the hose? And yet a doubt remains. In the rest of his short films, Porter never used such intricate intercutting again.[29]

> There are two conflicting versions of this rescue scene: one of them using the one-shot, cutless method of Méliès, the other using a more complicated editing plan. The rescue scene tells its story from two set-ups: from inside the house (point of view of the wife and child awaiting rescue) and from outside it (point of view of the firemen

making the rescue). In one of the extant versions of the film, the audience sees the whole rescue first from inside the house and then repeated again from outside the house. This method, in the stock tradition of sticking with the focal character throughout, makes little narrative sense. The fireman could not possibly go through the entire rescue operation twice; such games with time would await Alain Resnais's *Last Year at Marienbad.*[30]

Jacques Deslandes and Jacques Richard dismiss the MoMA version in *Histoire comparée du Cinéma* (1968), but they do not offer the kind of exhaustive reasoning that might convince others.[31] Some historians, such as William Everson in his *American Silent Film* (1978), simply avoid the sticky issue by not referring to the film. It is only in the last few years that careful examination and methodology have established the authenticity of the paper print version at the Library of Congress. In 1978 the Museum of Modern Art itself showed the paper print version at the FIAF conference on early cinema in Brighton, England.

The adulteration of *Life of an American Fireman* was not an isolated case. The copy of Méliès' *A Trip to the Moon* at the British Film Institute, for example, lacks the overlapping action in which the rocket lands on the moon, conforming instead to more modern notions of linear continuity. In the process, a self-validating system was created. The "modernized" versions of these films supported historians who projected classical cinematic strategies backwards to the origins of a "natural cinematic language" and vice versa. Today it is clear that the DLC paper print version is internally consistent, is consistent with Porter's own development as a filmmaker, and with the development of international cinema during the 1901–7 period. If any doubt remained, the discovery of a print of *Life of an American Fireman* in northern Maine by the American Film Institute confirmed the authenticity of the paper print version.[32]

Life of an American Fireman was based on a familiar story; its narrative elements occurred and reoccurred across many forms of popular culture. Porter was hardly the father of the story film. The film deserves our attention for its rich accumulation of cinematic techniques. Working within a genre, Porter presents the familiar material in a new and interesting way. The film, however, does not present the world with "the principles of modern film editing"—quite the reverse. It has a special place in film history: it is a coherent, elaborate film that uses cinematic strategies outside the repertoire of later classical cinema. The film shows us that cinema did not develop in a simple, linear direction. It presents a mode of representation that was unstable, transitory, a direction in narrative cinema that was briefly explored, gradually discarded, and then quickly forgotten.

Porter's and White's development as filmmakers through *Life of an American Fireman* reveals with particular clarity a series of changes taking place within screen practice. The introduction of moving pictures made possible and even encouraged shifts and transformations within the interrelated modes of exhibition and image production as editorial control and narrative responsibility were increasingly centralized in the production company. These changes in film production and exhibition both helped to produce and were generated by a changing mode of representation with specific strategies for depicting spatial and temporal relations between shots. Obviously these shifts and the subsequent transformation that made them permanent did not happen on a national or international level overnight. As the next chapters make clear, even within the Edison Company itself, A. C. Abadie and then R. K. Bonine continued to shoot short travel scenes that could be bought by lecturers and incorporated into their shows.[33]

The centralization of editorial procedures was gradual and centered on acted story films where the production company needed maximum control over filmic and pro-filmic elements. There was, of course, a real economic incentive for the rationalization of production and exhibition. Not only was it more efficient to manufacture longer, standardized prints than to handle brief scenes that had to be selectively purchased, but most exhibitors were more interested in profits than in retaining or developing their skill as storytellers. Many showmen preferred the production companies to make editorial decisions for them. Yet in certain forms like the travelogue, which did not require continuity of space, time, and action, editorial control remained in the hands of exhibitors for many years to come. Traveling lecturers like Burton Holmes and Dwight Elmendorf continued to create their own shows and remained popular into the 1910s, dominating what would now be called the documentary market. Their travelogues/documentaries lacked precisely those characteristics that made *Jack and the Beanstalk* and *Life of an American Fireman* important moments in Porter's development as a filmmaker and in the history of the American screen.

8 Story Films Become the Dominant Product: 1903–1904

The shift to story films at the Edison Manufacturing Company was a gradual, but uneven, process that began in 1902 and proceeded in fits and starts through late 1904. By the conclusion of that year, this type of picture had clearly become the dominant product, both for Edison and throughout the motion picture industry. It was a development occurring on different levels. By the second half of 1903, Edison's "duping" of foreign pictures clearly privileged story films. As might be expected, this corresponded to the embracing of fictional headline attractions by most vaudeville exhibition services. Not until the later part of 1904, however, did Edison personnel focus the bulk of their own production efforts in this area. Between January 1903 and October 1904 output of staged/acted films remained irregular, as the Edison Company sought to avoid undue negative costs and was thwarted by legal and personnel problems. Ambitious, commercially successful story films were made, yet they were usually followed by much more modest productions, if not an outright hiatus in filmmaking.

Disruptions

The completion of *Life of an American Fireman* coincided with important changes within Edison's Kinetograph Department. On February 5, 1903, James White left for Europe to become Edison's new European sales manager.[1] White's new position was important for Edison's phonograph and film businesses, and William Gilmore was not sure whether he could handle the responsibility. As he wrote Thomas Edison from Europe shortly after White had taken the job:

> It would seem to me that the proper way to take hold of things here is to have one good man to look after the business in the different countries as a whole the same as I do in America but the point is who is the man. I am not prepared to say that White is big enough to swing it. I hardly think he has the experience necessary. Then again I find that he lacks nerve, which to my mind is very essential. However, as we have given him the opportunity I suppose we must let him go for the present.[2]

Gilmore also felt that White required close supervision to curtail his more impulsive schemes.[3] White's charm and entrepreneurial spirit were better suited to a producer or salesman than a ledger-conscious manager.

White's position as head of the Kinetograph Department was filled by William H. Markgraf, another of Gilmore's brothers-in-law, who had been working elsewhere in the Edison Manufacturing Company. Although he had obtained his job through nepotism, the new department manager did not receive a percentage of film sales as had James White. Nevertheless, his $30 weekly salary was raised on January 1st to $40—twice Porter's. Markgraf acted as a middle-level executive—a member of the new middle class—whereas White had functioned as a quasi-independent entrepreneur under the umbrella of Edison's corporation. Markgraf's hiring introduced a differentiation in managerial function. The department head was no longer a film producer, salesman, cameraman, and film actor. He oversaw production activities, but did not participate directly in them. Yet this was not management as Frederick Taylor envisioned it. Markgraf lacked the expertise to challenge or even guide his staff's working methods. This left Porter more firmly in control of production, since he alone had the requisite knowledge and experience.

As the Kinetograph Department was preparing *Life of an American Fireman* for release, Edison suffered two judicial defeats that affected company sales of films and projecting kinetoscopes. Although both setbacks were eventually reversed on appeal, at the time they were highly disruptive, bringing into question the company's future within the industry. The first involved Thomas Armat, who, through the Animated Photo Projecting Company and its successor, the Armat Moving-Picture Company, had sued the American Mutoscope Company for infringement of his projection patents. He brought suit on the last day of 1898 and, after considerable delay, won a circuit court decision favoring his patent in October 1902.[4] Reluctant to have either the patent's scope or his ownership tested in a higher court, Armat came to an agreement with Biograph. Biograph agreed to recognize the patent if he "would not insist upon the payment of the license fees . . . until the Armat Company had secured a permanent injunction against the Edison Company."[5]

In November Armat sued the Edison Company. A preliminary injunction was filed on January 19th, prohibiting the company from selling projectors. Edison lawyers appealed for a stay, and the injunction was vacated a week later. The reprieve occurred primarily because Armat's control of the patent was in doubt owing to his earlier conflicts with Jenkins.[6] Nonetheless, the Edison Company was threatened with substantial damages and a realignment of the American motion picture industry around Armat. Armat, still anxious to avoid further testing of his patents, renewed his suggestion for a combination involving Edison, Biograph, and the Armat Moving Picture Company. In a letter to Gilmore, he pressed his case, pointing out that "the Armat Moving Picture Company has <u>never sold a machine</u>, therefore any monopoly that may be built up under its patents is <u>absolutely intact</u>."[7] He attempted to play on the Edison Company's concurrent difficulties with Lubin by suggesting that "in fighting us you are in effect fighting for Lubin and the others who have contributed nothing to this art, and if you succeed in defeating us, you will throw this country open to the kind of competition that obtains in Europe, where the biggest fakir, such as Lubin, makes the money at the expense of legitimate business." Edison's lawyers, unmoved by Armat's anti-Semitic appeal, decided to await the outcome of the suit. Armat, however, chose not to pursue it. In June 1903 the Edison Company altered its projecting kinetoscope, replacing its one-third shutter with a half-shutter. The new shutter allowed less light to be projected through the film and onto the screen, but seemed to protect the company from any future outcome of the suit, since Armat's patent had been poorly worded.[8] Notwithstanding these commercial disruptions and slight curtailment in the projector's quality, sales of projecting kinetoscopes for the 1903 business year increased less than 10 percent over the preceding year—to $36,651 with profits of $15,637.

The second decision involved the Lubin copyright case and directly affected Edison film production. On January 22d, one day after *Life of an American Fireman* had been copyrighted, Judge George Mifflin Dallas ruled that Edison's method of copyrighting motion pictures was unacceptable. Since 1897 Thomas Edison (via his secretary) had been sending paper prints of his company's films to the Library of Congress, where each was duly copyrighted as a single photograph. Edison lawyers argued that this procedure was adequate: "Each view is not sold by itself, but are sold in numbers together, being printed on one strip of film for the foregoing purpose (of showing successive views of the same object that give the appearance of actual motion) and constituting one photograph."[9] Lubin denied that "such photographic representations constitute one photograph and that the same can be copyrighted as one photograph or protected by a single copyright and avers that such photographic films are the result of joining together distinct and independent photographic exposures each requiring a separate copyright for securing an exclusive right to such original intellectual conception as it may contain."[10] Judge Dallas agreed with Lubin, ruling that:

> It is requisite that every photograph, no matter how or for what purpose it may be cojoined with others, shall be separately registered, and that the prescribed notice of copyright shall be inscribed upon each of them. It may be true, as has been argued, that this construction of the section renders it unavailable for the protection of such a series

of photographs as this; but if, for this reason, the law is defective, it should be altered by Congress, not strained by the courts.[11]

Edison appealed.

Edison executives, while waiting for a review, drastically curtailed their company's output of original subjects, anticipating that these would be copied by Lubin and other "infringers." Little or nothing was produced at the Edison studio over the next three months, although a few new films taken by Abadie in Europe were offered for sale. A small fire ravaged the Kinteograph Department's darkroom on February 9th, injuring William Jamison and further disrupting production. The company's February and particularly its May catalogs featured dupes of foreign productions: Méliès' *Joan of Arc*, *Robinson Crusoe*, and *Gulliver's Travels*; Urban Trading Company news films of the Durbar celebrations in Delhi, India; Pathé's *Ali Baba and the Forty Thieves* as well as Williamson and G. A. Smith pictures.[12]

Deeply concerned with the many legal problems that threatened the future of his enterprises, Edison had his principal patents lawyer, Frank Dyer, move into his laboratory on April 1, 1903.[13] Soon after, Edison's legal fortunes in the motion picture field were revived. On April 21st, in a landmark decision, Judge Dallas's ruling was reversed by the U.S. court of appeals. Judge Joseph Buffington, writing the opinion, asserted that:

> The instantaneous and continuous operation of the camera is such that the difference between successive pictures is not distinguishable by the eye and is so slight that the casual observer will take a very considerable number of successive pictures of the series, and say they are identical. . . . To require each of numerous undistinguishable pictures to be individually copyrighted, as suggested by the court, would in effect be to require copyright of many pictures to protect a single one.
>
> When Congress in recognition of the photographic art saw fit in 1865 to amend the Act of 1831 (13 Stat 540), and extend copyright protection to a photograph or negative, it is not to be presumed it thought such art could not progress and that no protection was to be afforded such progress. It must have recognized there would be change and advance in making photographs just as there have been in making books, printing chromos and other subjects of copyright protection."[14]

A year after bringing his copyright suit against Lubin, Edison had finally won. Although films had been copyrighted in Edison's name for six years, the threat of legal action had always been enough to intimidate potential dupers less determined than Lubin.[15] Judge Buffington's decision was the first actually to recognize the validity of Edison's method of copyright. If the court had done otherwise, it would have discouraged American motion picture production still further. Howard Hayes, Edison's lawyer for the case, greeted the decision with enthusiasm. "It is a strong one and will be followed I think in other courts," he wrote Gilmore. "Now that copyrighting the films has become of importance I want to arrange a plan by which the copyrighting can be done correctly and evidence of it kept so that it will be available in any suit on a moments notice."[16] As a result of Hayes' directive, copyright files were subsequently kept at West Orange; today they provide the historian with essential information about most Edison productions.[17]

The series of legal battles and injunctions between 1901 and April 1903 left the American industry in shambles. Uncertainties had discouraged investment in plant and negatives. Although Biograph had won its court case against Edison in March 1902, it remained a weakened competitor during the following year. The subjects and representational practices for its large-format service were increasingly antiquated. A typical program relied on a miscellaneous collection of short actualities with a few trick films and comedies thrown in for relief.[18] In contrast, Vitagraph had recognized the value of "headline attractions all of which are long subjects lasting from 10 to 20 minutes each."[19] This enabled Vitagraph to take over the Keith circuit from Biograph during the first week of April. Afterwards one trade journal observed that the new Vitagraph program was "the best series of films seen here in many weeks."[20] George Spoor's Chicago-based exhibition service made a similar shift toward story films, a key element in the reviving popularity of vaudeville film programs.

Edison, Vitagraph, Lubin, Spoor, and Selig—all relied heavily on European imports. Like Edison, many took local, inexpensive films that could not be provided by European producers. To a remarkable degree, Edison's competition with its rivals revolved around the rapidity with which newly released European story films could be brought to the United States, duped, and sold. The original prints that Edison acquired for these purposes were then purchased by Waters' Kinetograph Company, while dupes were marketed to other exhibitors. An urgent telegram from Gilmore to White in England underscored the importance of this business practice:

> White: Vitagraph Co. getting foreign films ahead of us. They have received poachers, deserters, falling chimney and others at least ten days ahead of us. This very embarrassing. Unless can have your assurance that arrangements can be made for immediate shipments will send someone to take charge this end of the business. . . . Gilmore.[21]

Edison executives had adopted a business strategy that largely ignored the production capabilities of its film department. By duping foreign films on a massive scale, the department could limit its investment primarily to the cost of negative stock.

The easy money Edison and other American producers had been making from dupes was threatened in March 1903, when Gaston Méliès arrived in the United States to represent his brother Georges. In June he opened a New York office and factory to print and distribute Méliès' "Star" films and to secure the economic benefits for their creator. His first catalog chided American manufacturers, announcing

> GEORGE MELIES, proprietor and manager of the Théâtre Robert-Houdin, Paris, is the originator of the class of cinematograph films which are made from artificially arranged scenes, the creation of which has given new life to the trade at a time when it was dying out. He conceived the idea of portraying comical, magical and mystical views, and his creations have been imitated without success ever since.[22]

He also announced, "we are prepared and determined energetically to pursue all counterfeiters and pirates. We will not speak twice, we will act." Star films were then considered "the acme of life motion photography,"[23] and Georges Méliès was using a double camera to take two negatives of each subject, shipping one to New York. Henceforth, these were copyrighted, putting an end to the duping of future Star films.[24] Edison and other American companies found different makes to dupe, but they now had to face competition in the domestic market from the world's foremost manufacturer.

Production Resumes at Edison

When Edison filmmaking resumed in late April, the Kinetograph Department's organization and personnel had substantially changed. Not only was Markgraf the new manager, but Arthur White and George S. Fleming had left in early April. Fleming was promptly replaced by William Martinetti, a scenic painter who earned $20 per week—the same sum as Porter. With these disruptions, film sales for the 1903–4 business year advanced 20 percent to $91,122—a modest increase given the general industrywide revival and the impact of *Great Train Robbery* sales late that business year. Production and related film costs, moreover, increased still faster, and film profits fell 13 percent to $24,813.

Although Edison ads ballyhooed *Life of an American Fireman*, nothing of equal ambition was immediately undertaken. The next sixty-two copyrighted Edison films were brief scenes made for the exhibitor-dominated cinema. Most were part of the popular travel genre. Twelve had been shot by James White in the West Indies during his December 1902 honeymoon (*Native Women Coaling a Ship and Scrambling for Money*). With White's arrival in Europe, Abadie was free to tour the Mediterranean basin with his camera. He started out at the Grand Carnival in Nice (*Battle of Confetti at the Nice Carnival*); traveled to Syria, Palestine (*A Jewish Dance at Jerusalem*) and Egypt (*Excavating Scene at the Pyramids of Sakkarah*); then went through Italy, Switzerland, and Paris before reaching England on May 10th. Abadie then returned to the United States, where his films were developed and thirty-four submitted for copyright.

Edison's New York–based cameramen resumed production on April 29th, eight days after Judge Buffington's decision. Over the next two weeks, Edwin

Documenting "the other half": *New York City "Ghetto" Fish Market*.

Porter and James Smith shot at least fifteen travelogue-type subjects in and around Manhattan. The series included panoramas of the skyline; staged activities by the fire department, police, and harbor patrol (*New York Harbor Police Boat Patrol Capturing Pirates*); parades (*White Wings on Review*), and scenes of New York's underbelly (*New York City Dumping Wharf*). For *New York City "Ghetto" Fish Market*, Smith placed his camera at a window or on a low rooftop. Looking down on an open air market, it panned along the street as one or two individuals in the crowd stared into its lens.[25] Soon afterwards, Porter stopped off in Sayre, Pennsylvania, and took *Lehigh Valley Black Diamond Express*, a replacement negative of that still popular subject, on May 13th. Perhaps the cameraman was on a visit to Connellsville; in any case, he had returned to New York City by May 30th, Decoration Day, when he filmed *Sixty-Ninth Regiment, N.G.N.Y.* as the unit marched up Fifth Avenue. Three weeks later he photographed *Africander Winning the Suburban Handicap*. Such subjects had been taken for the past six years and had become routine.

Méliès' entry into the American market and the resolution of various court suits encouraged U.S. film companies to produce more ambitious films with American locales and subject matter. If *Jack and the Beanstalk* and *Life of an American Fireman* were part of nonspecific urban/industrial genres found in all major producing countries, American story films made in the second half of 1903 tended to be more nationalistic. Biograph's first dramatic headliners, *Kit*

Carson and *The Pioneers*, as well as Edison's *Uncle Tom's Cabin, Rube and Mandy at Coney Island*, and *The Great Train Robbery*, all used American myths and entertainments as a source.[26] Certainly this made sense, since less nation-specific pictures could be acquired from overseas.

Uncle Tom's Cabin

Harriet Beecher Stowe's anti-slavery and anti-capitalistic novel *Uncle Tom's Cabin* (1851) remained immensely popular throughout the North as an affirmation and retrospective justification of the Civil War. Its spectacular story, more than its political content, was kept alive by theatrical adaptations that numerous acting troupes performed in America's opera houses.[27] When the Kinetograph Department returned to production during spring 1903, it arranged for one of these itinerant companies to stage the play's highlights in the Edison studio. This decision may have been influenced by Biograph's May release of *Rip Van Winkle*, a 200-foot compendium of scenes from the *Rip Van Winkle* play, showing "the various events beginning with Rip's departure for the mountains and ending with his awakening from his 20 years' sleep."[28] Porter's *Uncle Tom's Cabin*, which totaled 1,100 feet, was much more ambitious. The play was condensed rather than excerpted. A race between the steamboats *Natchez* and *Robert E. Lee* was done in miniature, and a few effects, like the double exposure used to show Eva's ascent to heaven, were reworked to take advantage of the motion picture camera's capabilities.

Porter's *Uncle Tom's Cabin* has often been criticized for its lack of "cinematic" qualities and viewed as a disappointing regression after *Life of an American Fireman*.[29] Such criticism feels the absence of a coherent spatial/temporal world as an absolute loss. It valorizes narrowly progressive tendencies in Porter's work, isolating filmic strategies felt to have contributed to the development of Hollywood cinema. While *Uncle Tom's Cabin* does not fit into a simple linear pattern of development from *Life of an American Fireman* to *The Great Train Robbery*, it does represent a sustained exploration of the filmed theater genre that remained an important aspect of Porter's filmmaking career—whether *Parsifal* (1904), *The Devil* (1908), or James O'Neill in *The Count of Monte Cristo* (1912).

A relatively unadulterated record of nineteenth-century theater, *Uncle Tom's Cabin* displays the presentational elements of this practice that exerted often determining influences on the screen: acting techniques (codified gesture, the playing to an audience), spatial construction (set design, the use of frontal compositions, the maintenance of a proscenium arch), and a nonrealistic, but highly serviceable, temporality. For traveling theater companies, portable sets had to suggest or symbolically represent the locale for a drama. Since changing scenery was difficult, action that moved to a different locale generally had to wait until

Uncle Tom's Cabin. Eliza escapes while Uncle Tom is sold into slavery.

the completion of subsequent actions in the current scene before it could be played out.

The same time frame is shown successively in the last two scenes of *Uncle Tom's Cabin*. In scene 13, Uncle Tom is beaten on the veranda by Simon Legree's minions and then carried off; George Shelby, Jr., arrives to buy back Tom, then leaves in search of him; and finally Marks—an officer of the law and symbol of the state—kills Legree *to revenge the death of Uncle Tom*. As the final scene begins, Uncle Tom is still alive in the woodshed and George Shelby, Jr., arrives in time to witness his death. Although Tom's death is shown last, the intertitles and action clearly suggest that it precedes the killing of Legree. Temporality, as in the closing scenes of *Life of an American Fireman*, is manipulated for emotional and thematic purposes determined in part by a religious interpretation of events. This reordering of events, which violates the linear logic of later narrative cinema, can easily appear naive or inept to modern audiences. For turn-of-the-century audiences, it allowed the emotional highpoint, the death of Uncle Tom, to come last where it belonged.

Viewing the film today, audiences are faced with fundamental problems of comprehension—identifying characters and following narrative development. At the turn of the century, however, the story was part of American folklore and native-born Americans were as familiar with the melodramatic incidents portrayed on the screen as with the mechanics of a fire rescue. As with *Jack and the Beanstalk* or most news films, the narrative was not presented as if the audience was seeing it for the first time, but existed in reference to a story assumed to be already present in the audience's mind.[30]

Porter's *Uncle Tom's Cabin* reveals its reliance on audiences' preexisting knowledge in various ways. Following the example of G. A. Smith's *Dorothy's Dream*, each scene is introduced by a title that does not explain the next scene but labels it to prime the viewer's preexisting knowledge.[31] General familiarity with the narrative was reflected in most Edison ads and promotional materials, which simply listed the scenes, as if that would adequately define their contents. Even the reprinted description assumed that the reader already knew the various characters. *Uncle Tom's Cabin* was a ritual reiteration of a common heritage and could trigger deeply felt emotions that audiences already associated with the narrative. But even allowing for this a priori knowledge, the exhibitor could still use a lecture to help audiences follow the on-screen narrative and identify characters whose dress sometimes changed from one scene to the next. For immigrants and those otherwise unfamiliar with the film's frame of reference, additional cues must have been essential.[32]

Uncle Tom's Cabin was heralded by George Kleine as "the most elaborate effort at telling a story in moving pictures yet attempted," and subsequently described as "the largest and most expensive picture yet made in America."[33] By employing an established Uncle Tom's Cabin theatrical company, Porter made a film that looked expensive yet required much less investment than a truly "original" production like *Jack and the Beanstalk*. Certainly its scale did not intimidate Edison's competitor Sigmund Lubin, who immediately remade it.

Lubin had reacted to Edison's victory in the copyright case with his customary flair: he copyrighted over thirty popular titles without bothering to make the films. These included *Three Little Pigs*, *Old Mother Hubbard*, and *Jack and Jill*.[34] Hearing that Edison intended to film *Uncle Tom's Cabin*, Lubin copyrighted that title as well, a fact that was shared with customers. As the traveling exhibitor N. Dushane Cloward, informed the Orange laboratory:

> While in Lubin's Philada. office yesterday one of his assistants volunteered some information regarding a matter in which I know you people are interested.
> It may not be a fact or it may not be news to you or if both it may be of no importance but i [sic] feel that the statement passed on to you would be of no injustice to Lubin and may be of guidance to you. The conversation was on new film subjects. The party asked me how Edison people were getting along with U/T/Cabin. I having told him that I had been dealing with Edison. I replied that I had heard some talk of the subject being prepared last Spring but knew nothing of it whatever. The representative remarked that Lubin had a copyright for the title of Uncle Tom's Cabin in motion pictures and had it several years.[35]

Cloward's information delayed the film's release from late July to early September while Edison's lawyer investigated. "I learned that Sigmund Lubin has copyrighted a photograph under the title 'Uncle Tom's Cabin' on May 1st 1903," Howard Hayes reported, after consulting the Library of Congress. "That copyright, however, does not give him a monopoly on the title. The copyright applies to the picture itself, regardless of the title, so, unless you copy his picture, he cannot interfere with the use of the title."[36] The following week, Edison finally advertised its film in the trades. The week after, Lubin announced the imminent release of his *Uncle Tom's Cabin*.[37]

Edison executives thought Lubin might try to sell their film on the basis of his earlier copyright. Lubin, in fact, simply waited for the picture's release before making his own meticulous imitation. By dropping a cakewalk sequence, increasing the pacing and filming at fewer frames per second, Lubin reduced the length of his version from 1,100 feet to 700 feet. His brochures for the film even lifted entire descriptions from the Edison catalog.[38] With Lubin's pictures underselling Edison's by a penny per foot, his *Uncle Tom's Cabin* offered substantial savings to exhibitors.

Summer Fun

Following the solemnity of *Uncle Tom's Cabin*, most Edison productions taken during the summer months involved elements of play. Both before and behind the camera, the spirit of Coney Island frequently prevailed.[39] *Little Lillian, Toe Danseuse* brought "the youngest premiere danseuse in the world" before the camera and made skillful use of stop-action photography to combine four separate dances into one continuous "shot," with "her beautiful costume changing mysteriously after each dance."[40] *Subbubs Surprises the Burglar*, the first of several comedies made in rapid succession, was shot on July 16th. Featuring a popular cartoon character, this single-shot film otherwise imitated Biograph's *The Burglar-Proof Bed* (shot June 27, 1900). When a burglar enters Subbubs' bedroom, "The man awakes and pulls a lever, closing himself up in the folding bed, the bottom of which is iron-clad, with guns and portholes. The burglar is dumbfounded, and cannot move. Subbubs turns his battery loose, blowing the burglar to pieces. He then raises an American flag on a staff on top of the bed as a signal of victory. The bed opens up again and Subbubs goes to sleep."[41] In *Street Car Chivalry*, an attractive young lady is offered a seat by every man in the trolley. A stout woman with an arm full of bundles, however, is ignored until she loses her balance and collapses on top of a "dude." The narrow limits of male gentility are spoofed, and the different ways each woman claims a seat provide comic repetition. The film was sufficiently popular for Lubin to remake it that fall.[42]

The Gay Shoe Clerk, a brief comedy shot on July 23d, was inspired by at least two films: either Biograph's *Don't Get Gay with Your Manicure* or *No Liberties, Please*[43] (shot July 10, 1902) and G. A. Smith's *As Seen Through a Telescope*, which Edison distributed as *The Professor and His Field Glass*:

NO LIBERTIES, PLEASE.

A young man in a manicure parlor attempts to kiss the pretty attendant but has his ears soundly boxed for his trouble.[44]

THE PROFESSOR AND HIS FIELD GLASS.

An old gentleman is shown on a village street, looking for something through a field glass. Suddenly, he levels the glass on a young couple coming up the road. The girl's shoe string came loose, and her companion volunteers to tie it. Here the scene changes, showing how it looks through the old man's glass. A very pretty ankle at short range. Scene changes back again and shows the old fellow tickled to death over the sight. The couple, who, by the way, caught "Peeping Tom," come toward him, and as the young man passes behind him, he knocks off his hat and kicks the stool on which he is sitting, from under him, making the old chap present a rather ludicrous appearance, as he sits in the street. Length 65 feet.[45]

THE GAY SHOE-CLERK.

Scene shows interior of shoe-store. Young lady and chaperone enter. While a fresh young clerk is trying a pair of high-heeled slippers on the young lady, the chaperone seats herself and gets interested in a paper. The scene changes to a very close view, showing only the lady's foot and the clerk's hands tying the slipper. As her dress is slightly raised, showing a shapely ankle, the clerk's hands become very nervous, making it difficult for him to tie the slipper. The picture changes back to former scene. The clerk makes rapid progress with his fair customer, and while he is in the act of kissing her the chaperone looks up from her paper, and proceeds to beat the clerk with an umbrella. He falls backward off the stool. Then she takes the young lady by the arm, and leads her from the store. Length 75 feet.[46]

Porter's film inverts one gender position in the Biograph narrative (in which the manicurist's lover-husband boxes the man's ears). Likewise, it dispenses with Smith's matte and explicit point-of-view motivation but keeps the "very close view" of the woman's ankle. It is the man behind the camera (and presumably the male viewer) instead of the man behind the telescope whose attention is focused on the woman's ankle, motivating the cut to a closer view. Such simple shifts and recombinations suggest the variations that frequently characterized "originality" in this period.

The Gay Shoe Clerk valorizes the spectator's position in a manner that recalls *What Demoralized the Barbershop* (1897). True, the young man not only sees but touches and even kisses the young lady, but his transgression is promptly greeted by a bash on the head from the chaperone. Meanwhile, the male spectator enjoys the woman's ankle *and* the shoe clerk's chastisement. In fact, both pictures suggest that cinema, by removing the spectator's physical presence from the scene, allows the (male) viewer to take pleasure in what is otherwise forbidden. The close view of the young lady's ankle is shown against a plain background to further focus the viewer's attention, suggesting the subjective nature of the shot and abstracting it from the scene. Not only does this second shot have a different background, but the female customer probably had a stand-in. Her dress, at least, is different: the far shot does not reveal the white petticoats, which are prominently displayed in the closer view. Porter and other

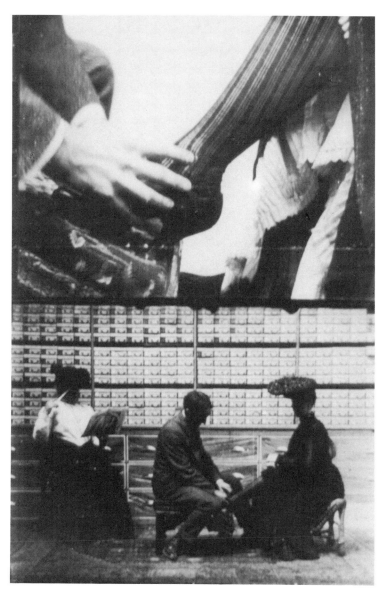

The Gay Shoe Clerk. The cut from a very close view back to establishing shot.

No. 2364 S.

Title "Don't get gay with your Manicure."

Length 47 ft.

Code Word Garrouil.

early filmmakers obviously anticipated the editorial principles of the artificial woman articulated by Lev Kuleshov.[47] The ankle is also isolated in an abstracted space. While Porter seems to have been concerned with matching action, the cut did not involve a seamless "move in" through a spatially continuous world but functioned within a syncretic representational system.[48]

Playfulness was plentiful at the Edison studio. Thinking up skits and pulling them off was fun even if work weeks were long. One can imagine Abadie's leg—or that of some other assistant—filling the young lady's stocking in *The Gay Shoe Clerk*. Tasks were manageable and varied. The integration of work and play was particularly evident during August, when the cameramen chose activities that took them to resort areas and the seashore. Informal supervision and the quotidian nature of many films enabled these employees to sneak away from the hot city and relax.

On several occasions, Edison personnel took their cameras to Coney Island, where they produced actualities such as *Shooting the Rapids at Luna Park* and *Rattan Slide and General View of Luna Park*.[49] There, Porter made the "headliner" copyrighted as *Rube and Mandy at Coney Island*, but listed in Edison's catalog under a slightly different title:

RUBE AND MANDY'S VISIT TO CONEY ISLAND.

> The first scene shows this country couple entering Steeplechase Park. They proceed to amuse themselves on the steeplechase, rope bridge, riding the bulls and the "Down and Out." The scene then changes to a panorama of Luna Park, and we find Rube and Mandy doing stunts on the rattan slide, riding on the miniature railway, shooting the chutes, riding the boats in the old mill, and visiting Professor Wormwood's Monkey theatre. They next appear on the Bowery, where we find them with the fortune tellers, striking the punching machine and winding up with the frankfurter man. The climax shows a bust view of Rube and Mandy eating frankfurters. Interesting not only for its humorous features, but also for its excellent views of Coney Island and Luna Park. Length 725 feet.[50]

Rube and Mandy at Coney Island can be compared to exhibitor-constructed programs of the period that combined travel views or scenics with short comedies—a programming idea suggested by William Selig. One can imagine a program on Coney Island consisting of *Shooting the Rapids at Luna Park* and similar films, but laced with studio comics for variety.[51] Working within such a syncretic framework, Porter integrated comedy and scenery, maintaining a consistent tone from one shot to the next even as he perpetuated this dichotomy within the individual shots.

In *Rube and Mandy at Coney Island*, two country bumpkins experience the marvels of New York's famous amusement park. While the vaudeville actors did their bits in stage costume with exaggerated gestures, Porter treated Coney Island for its scenic value with a highly mobile camera (five shots contain significant camera movement) still associated with actuality material. In several

We see Prof. Wormwood and his Dog and Monkey Theater over Rube and Mandy's shoulders in *Rube and Mandy at Coney Island*.

scenes the performers' improvisations forced Porter to accommodate the unexpected by following the action with his camera. In another scene, the actors' movements about the amusement park enabled the camera to photograph a "circular panorama." The performers are often subservient to a scenic impulse, not only with the panorama but at Professor Wormwood's Dog and Monkey Theater, where the film viewer looks over the actors' shoulders to see the animals perform. The couple mediates the audience's experience of the amusement park and ties together a series of potentially discrete views as they move from one ride to the next. At other moments, Coney Island serves as a setting for the comedians' business. The scenes are arranged through an association of analogous situations: Rube and Mandy's arrival in an absurd carriage is followed by rides on wooden horses and a cow; "Shooting the Chutes" is followed by a ride in a love boat. Although the film has little narrative development, it achieves a degree of closure, opening with the couple's arrival and ending with an apotheosis-like "bust view" of the two eating a hot dog against a black background. This final scene repeats the preceding one while abstracting it from the Coney Island setting and reducing it to a "facial expression" shot.

Porter spent mid August in the popular seaside resort of Atlantic City, making at least one film during his working vacation. *Seashore Frolics*, staged using cooperative vacationers, ends with a persistent still photographer (Porter's assistant?) being dumped into the ocean by good-natured bathers. The cameraman closed his summer season of filming at the New York Caledonian Club's 47th annual festival of sports on Labor Day.

That August, A. C. Abadie was at Coney Island (*Orphans in the Surf* and *Baby Class at Lunch*), then retreated to Wilmington, where he filmed outdoor scenes for N. Dushane Cloward. Cloward, a traveling exhibitor who played churches and noncommercial venues during the theatrical season, opened a motion picture show in Brandywine Springs Park for the summer of 1903.[52] He arranged with the Edison Company to take local views that would attract patrons to his theater. Cloward had Abadie photograph a baby review and a Maypole dance on August 21st.[53] Together they organized the filming of *Turning the Tables* and *Tub Race* at the local swimming hole. In the former, a policeman tries to chase a group of boys out of a forbidden swimming hole, but finds himself pushed into the water instead. The naughty boys break the law; but the law, rather than the boys, has to pay.

Cameraman J. B. Smith, although principally confined to the Orange laboratory, where he remained in charge of print production, spent part of August photographing the America's Cup races between the *Reliance* and Sir Thomas Lipton's *Shamrock III*. This news event, however, was not given the amount of attention it had received two years earlier. Only three films were offered for sale: two covered the start and finish of the first race on August 22d. The third film, taken midway through the second race, was not considered worth copyrighting. The films were offered as individual topicals rather than a complete series worthy of headliner status.

The Porter-Abadie-Smith trio continued to be the responsible photographers during the fall. After Labor Day, Porter returned to his New York base, where he filmed *Eastside Urchins Bathing in a Fountain* and *New York City Public Bath* as part of his continuing documentation of the city's ghetto life. In a sweeping panorama, the 150-foot *Tompkins Square Play Grounds* documents a supervised playground with basketball and boys forming a human pyramid for the camera. Porter followed his Lower Eastside shoots with various short comedies. *Two Chappies in a Box* is set in a vaudeville theater, where two male spectators respond to a female performer on the stage. For today's viewer, the humor comes from a simple psychoanalytic reading. A phallic wine bottle stands between the two men on the railing of their box, and they become so excited over the woman's singing that they spill the contents and ruin the draperies. For this offense they are quickly expelled. As with many of these short comedies, an obscene joke lurks just below the surface of a film that seems to be teaching a moral lesson—that rowdy behavior will not be tolerated. Between such minor comedies, Porter filmed *The Physical Culture Girl*, a vaudeville-type turn that

Two Chappies in a Box.

featured the recent winner of the Physical Culture Show at Madison Square Garden. Two months earlier, Biograph had made a similar subject with the same title. Porter's *Heavenly Twins at Lunch* and *Heavenly Twins at Odds*, of baby twins, appealed to Americans' love for small children (the *New York Journal*, for instance, consistently ran pictures of babies, playing to its readers' sentiments).

Smith spent most of the fall working as a foreman at the West Orange film plant, while Abadie traveled along the East coast taking films of floods, fire ruins, parades, and the Princeton-Yale football game. Like Porter, they were expected to perform multiple tasks. Abadie, in particular, functioned as a roving cameraman sent on special assignment (i.e., the cameraman system). Many of these short Edison films, particularly the topicals, were done in a perfunctory fashion, perhaps because similar subject matter had been shot so frequently. After seeing films of the Galveston disaster in 1900, audiences might be expected to find *Flood Scene in Paterson, N.J.*, photographed by Abadie in mid October, somewhat anticlimactic. The law of diminishing returns seemed to operate and Markgraf, like other American film executives, failed to mobilize his cameramen to mount the elaborate and timely coverage that might have kept alive White's vision of a visual newspaper. Interest was shifting to the cinema's capacity as a storytelling form. This was particularly apparent at Biograph.

In March 1903, after losing the Keith theaters as an exhibition outlet, the Biograph Company reassessed its business strategies and placed new emphasis on fictional narratives. By June, Biograph had opened an indoor film studio with electric lighting at its newly acquired offices on Fourteenth Street.[54] If the Edison Company's glass-enclosed studio had had advantages over Biograph's old rooftop facility at 841 Broadway, the competitive edge returned to Biograph, since filming was no longer affected by weather and winter hours. In the months immediately following the studio's completion, Biograph cameramen shot many multishot fictional subjects. Most were not offered immediately for sale but used as exclusive headliners for Biograph's revived exhibition service. Biograph's resurgence in production and its commitment to a 35mm format revived the company's fortunes. By August, Biograph had regained its position on the Keith circuit and was again competing seriously with Edison.

The move toward story films had accelerated by the latter half of 1903. Lubin made *Ten Nights in a Bar-Room* (700 feet) in October.[55] Although fairy-tale films like Méliès' *Fairyland* and Hepworth's *Alice in Wonderland* continued to be popular, English story films depicting crimes and violence began to appear and found receptive audiences. Sheffield Photo's *A Daring Daylight Burglary*, British Gaumont/Walter Haggar's *Desperate Poaching Affray* and R. W. Paul's *Trailed by Bloodhounds* were duped and sold by Edison, Biograph, and Lubin between June and October 1903.[56] Such films provided inspiration and competitive pressures that help to explain the production of Porter's most famous subject, *The Great Train Robbery*.

The Great Train Robbery

In late October, Porter began working with a young actor, Max Aronson. Earlier that month, the thespian had toured with Mary Emerson's road company of *His Majesty and the Maid*.[57] The engagement did not work out, and he returned to New York in need of employment. After changing his name to George M. Anderson, Aronson found work at the Edison studio, thinking up gags (*Buster's Joke on Papa*, shot October 23d) and appearing in pictures (*What Happened in the Tunnel*, photographed on October 30th and 31st). Porter continued to collaborate with Anderson on numerous subjects over the next several months, including *The Great Train Robbery*.

The Great Train Robbery was photographed at Edison's New York studio and in New Jersey at Essex County Park (the bandits cross a stream at Thistle Mill Ford in the South Mountain Reservation) and along the Lackawanna railway during November 1903.[58] Justus D. Barnes played the head bandit; Anderson the slain passenger, the tenderfoot dancing to gunshots, and one of the robbers; and Walter Cameron the sheriff. Many of the extras were Edison employees. Most of the Kinetograph Department's staff contributed to the picture: J. Blair Smith was one of the photographers and Anderson may have assisted with the direction.[59]

The film was first announced to the public in early November 1903 as a "highly sensationalized Headliner" that would be ready for distribution early that month.[60] Since the Edison Manufacturing Company urged exhibitors to order in advance and the film was not ready until early December, the delay probably explains why the Kinetograph Department submitted a rough cut of the film for copyright purposes. It avoided distribution snags once the release prints were available. The paper print version of the film, copyrighted by the Library of Congress, is longer than the final release print by about fifteen feet. Over the years, surviving copies of the film have been duped and offered for sale. Although a few have suffered extensive alteration, most have their integrity fundamentally intact. One of the most interesting versions was hand tinted.[61]

The Great Train Robbery had its debut at Huber's Museum, where Waters' Kinetograph Company had an exhibition contract. The following week it was shown at eleven theaters in and around New York City—including the Eden Musee.[62] Its commercial success was unprecedented and so remarkable that contemporary critics still tend to account for the picture's historical significance largely in terms of its commercial success and its impact on future fictional narratives. Kenneth Macgowan attributes this success to the fact that *The Great Train Robbery* was "the first important western."[63] William Everson and George Fenin find it important because "it was the first dramatically creative American film, which was also to set the pattern—of crime, pursuit and retribution—for the Western film as a genre."[64] Robert Sklar, viewing the film in broader terms, accounts for much of the film's lasting popularity. He points out that Porter was "the first to unite motion picture spectacle with myth and stories about America that were shared by people throughout the world."[65] Little more has been said about Porter's representational strategies since Lewis Jacobs praised the headliner for its "excellent editing."[66] Noël Burch, André Gaudreault, and David Levy are among the few who have discussed the film's cinematic strategies with any historical specificity; their useful analyses, however, can be pushed further.[67] *The Great Train Robbery* is a remarkable film not simply because it was commercially successful or incorporated American myths into the repertoire of screen entertainment, but because it presents so many trends, genres, and strategies fundamental to cinematic practice at that time.

Porter's film meticulously documents a process, applying what Neil Harris calls "an operational aesthetic" to the depiction of a crime.[68] With unusual detail, it traces the exact steps of a train robbery and the means by which the bandits are tracked down and killed. The film's narrative structure, as Gaudreault notes, utilizes temporal repetition within an overall narrative progression. The robbery of the mail car (scene 3) and the fight on the tender (scene

EDISON FILMS

PATENTED AND COPYRIGHTED.

Replete with Thrilling and Exciting Incidents in Fourteen Scenes,

THE GREAT TRAIN ROBBERY

Was shown to enthusiastic houses during Xmas week in New York at the following theatres :

Hurtig & Seamon's
Circle Theatre
Proctor's 125th St.

Keith's 14th St.
Harlem Opera House
Tony Pastor's
Eden Musee
Huber's Museum
Orpheum, Brooklyn
Comedy Theatre
Orpheum Music Hall

SEND FOR FULLY
ILLUSTRATED
AND
DESCRIPTIVE
PAMPHLET.

LENGTH, 740
FEET.
PRICE, $111.
CODE WORD,
VACUNABAN.

Edison Exhibition Kinetoscope, $115.00. Edison Universal Kinetoscope, $75.00.

MAIN OFFICE and FACTORY, Orange, N. J.

EDISON MANUFACTURING CO., NEW YORK OFFICE: 83 Chambers St.

OFFICE FOR UNITED KINGDOM : 52 Gray's Inn Road, Holborn, London, W.C., England.
EUROPEAN OFFICE : 32 Rempart Saint Georges, Antwerp, Belg

SELLING AGENTS:

THE KINETOGRAPH CO...................................41 E. 21st St., New York
KLEINE OPTICAL CO..................................52 State St., Chicago, Ill.
PETER BACIGALUPI....................933 Market St., San Francisco, Cal.

THE ORIGINAL AND ONLY

4) occur simultaneously according to the catalog description, even though they are shown successively. This returning to an earlier moment in time to pick up another aspect of the narrative recurs again in a more extreme form, as the telegraph operator regains consciousness and alerts the posse, which departs in pursuit of the bandits. These two scenes (10 and 11) trace a second line of action, which apparently unfolds concurrently with the robbery and getaway (scenes 2 through 9), although Porter's temporal construction remains imprecise and open to interpretation by the showman's spiel or by audiences through their subjective understanding. These two separate lines of action are reunited within a brief chase scene (shot 12) and yield a resolution in the final shoot-out (shot 13).

The issue of narrative clarity and efficiency is raised by *The Great Train Robbery*. At one point, three separate actions are shown that occur more or less simultaneously in scenes 3, 4, and 10. How were audiences, even those that understood the use of temporal repetition and overlap in narrative cinema, to know that scenes 3 and 4 happened simultaneously, but not scenes 1 and 2? How were they to determine the relationships between shots 1–9 and 10–11 until they had seen shot 12? There are no intertitles, and much depended on audience familiarity with other forms of popular culture where the same basic story was articulated. Scott Marble's play *The Great Train Robbery*, Wild West shows, and newspaper accounts of train holdups were more than sources of inspiration: they facilitated audience understanding by providing a necessary frame of reference. While *The Great Train Robbery* demonstrated that the screen could tell an elaborate, gripping story, it also defined the limits of a certain kind of narrative construction.

The common belief that *The Great Train Robbery* was an isolated break-through is inaccurate. While Porter was making his now famous film, Biograph produced *The Escaped Lunatic*, a hit comedy in which a group of wardens chase an inmate who has escaped from a mental institution.[69] On the very day that Thomas Edison copyrighted his celebrated picture, Biograph copyrighted a 290-foot subject made by British Gaumont, *Runaway Match*, involving an elaborate car chase between an eloping couple and the girl's parents. Eleven days later the film was offered for sale as *An Elopement a la Mode*.[70]

A Daring Daylight Burglary, which the Edison Company had duped and marketed in late June, was particularly influential in creating the framework within which Porter produced *The Great Train Robbery*,[71] even though American popular culture provided the specific subject matter. Edison's 1901 *Stage Coach Hold-up*, a film adaptation of Buffalo Bill's "Hold-up of the Deadwood Stage," served as one source. The title and initial idea for the film were suggested, however, by Scott Marble's melodrama. The *New York Clipper* provides a story synopsis:

> A shipment of $50,000 in gold is to be made from the office of the Wells Fargo Express Co. at Kansas City, Mo., and this fact becomes known to a gang of train robbers through their secret agent who is a clerk in the employ of the company. The conspirators, learning the time when the gold is expected to arrive, plan to substitute boxes filled with lead for those which contain the precious metal. The shipment is delayed, and the lead filled boxes are thereby discovered to be dummies. This discovery leads to an innocent man being accused of the crime. Act 2 is laid in Broncho Joe's mountain saloon in Texas, where the train robbers receive accurate information regarding the gold shipment and await its arrival. The train is finally held-up at a lonely mountain station and the car blown open. The last act occurs in the robber's retreat in the Red River cañon. To this place the thieves are traced by United States marshals and troops, and a pitched battle occurs in which Cowboys and Indians also participate.[72]

The play premiered on September 20, 1896, at the Alhambra Theater in Chicago, and soon came to the New York area, where it was well received.[73]

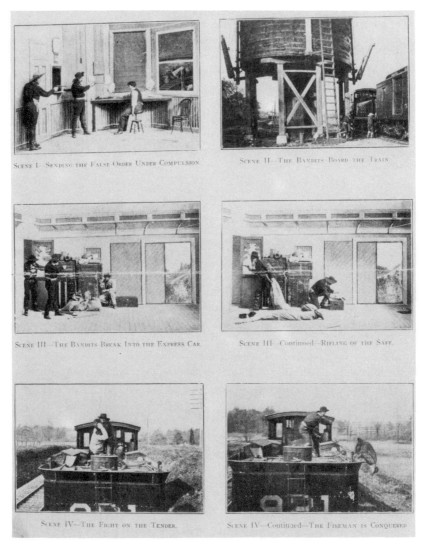

One page of Edison's illustrated catalog for *The Great Train Robbery*. The operational aesthetic at work: the film details the robbery of a train step by step.

Periodically revived thereafter, the melodrama played at Manhattan's New Star Theater in February 1902. Porter could have easily seen it on several occasions.

The Great Train Robbery was advertised as a reenactment film "posed and acted in faithful duplication of the genuine 'Hold-ups' made famous by various outlaw bands in the far West."[74] News stories of train holdups, like the ones appearing in September 1903, may have encouraged a more authentic detailing of events (see document no. 14). Eastern holdups, also evoked in Edison ads, took place in Pennsylvania on the Reading Railroad in late November—after the film was completed. A telegraph operator was murdered and several stations held up by "a desperate gang of outlaws who are believed to have their rendezvous somewhere in the lonely mountain passes along the Shamokin Division."[75] It was hoped that such incidents would make the film of timely interest. *The Great Train Robbery* continued to be indebted to at least one aspect of the newspapers, the feuilletons in Sunday editions, with their highly romanticized, but supposedly true, stories of contemporary interest.

DOCUMENT NO. 14

KILLS HIGHWAYMAN

Express Messenger Prevents
Robbery—Bullet Wounds Engineer.

Portland, Ore. Sept. 24.—The Atlantic Express on the Oregon Railroad and Navigation line, which left here at 8:15 o'clock last night, was held up by four masked men an hour later near Corbett station, twenty-one miles east of this city. One of the robbers was shot and killed by "Fred" Kerner, the express messenger. "Ollie" Barrett, the engineer, was seriously wounded by the same bullet. The robbers fled after the shooting, without securing any booty. Two of the highwaymen boarded the train at Troutdale, eighteen miles east of here, and crawled over the tender and to the engine, where they made the engineer stop near Corbett station.

When the train stopped two more men appeared. Two of the robbers compelled the engineer to get out of the cab and accompany them to the express car, while the others watched the fireman. The men carried several sticks of dynamite, and, when they came to the baggage car, thinking it was the express car, threw a stick at the door. Kerner heard the explosion, and immediately got to work with his rifle. The first bullet pierced the heart of one of the robbers and went through his body, entering the left breast of Barrett, who was just behind. Barrett's wound is above the heart, and is not necessarily fatal.

After the shooting the other robbers fled, without securing any booty, and it is supposed that they took to a boat, as the point where the hold-up occurred is on the Columbia River.

The robbers ordered Barrett to walk in front while approaching the baggage car, but he jumped behind just before the express messenger fired. The body of the dead robber was left behind on the track, and the wounded engineer was brought to this city. Sheriff Story and four deputy sheriffs went on a special train to the scene of the robbery, where one of the gang of outlaws was found badly wounded from a charge of buckshot which he received in the hand. He said that his name was James Connors, of this city, but refused to tell the names of any of the other bandits or the direction in which they went. The Oregon Railroad and Navigation Company offers a reward of $1,000 for the arrest of the highwaymen.

SOURCE: *New York Tribune*, September 25, 1903, p. 14.

As David Levy has pointed out, it was within the genre of reenactment films that Porter exploited procedures that heighten the realism and believability of the image.[76] *Execution of Czolgosz* and *Capture of the Biddle Brothers* provided Porter with an approach to filming the robbery, chase, and shoot-out. In *Execution of Czolgosz* he had intensified the illusion of authenticity by integrating actuality and reenactment, scenery and drama. In *The Great Train Robbery* he took this a step further, using mattes to introduce exteriors into studio scenes. On location, Porter used his camera as if he were filming a news event over which he had no control. In scenes 2, 7, and 8 the camera is forced to follow action that threatens to move outside the frame. For scene 7 the camera has to move unevenly down and over to the left. Since camera mounts were designed either to pan *or* tilt, this move is somewhat shaky. This "dirty" image only adds to the film's realism. The notion of a scene being played on an outdoor stage was undermined. Biograph described the desired effect when advertising *The Escaped Lunatic*: "Fortunately there were a number of . . . cameras situated around the country . . . and this most astonishing episode was completely covered in moving pictures."[77]

The Chase

The chase became a popular form of screen narrative in 1903; *The Great Train Robbery* and Biograph's *The Escaped Lunatic* were the first American productions to reveal its impact. The chase appeared early in cinema history: an Irish cop chases a "Chinaman" through a revolving set in *Chinese Laundry Scene* (1894), and a mad dash lasting a split second ends G. A. Smith's *The Miller and the Sweep* (1898). James Williamson's *Stop Thief!* (1901) isolated the provocation, the chase, and the resolution in three different camera setups. These remained isolated occurrences. Porter's *Jack and the Beanstalk* (1902), for instance, ignored the dramatic potential of the chase as the giant climbs down the beanstalk after Jack. According to American catalogs and trade journals from the early nickelodeon era, the two English imports *A Daring Daylight Burglary* and *Desperate Poaching Affray* initiated the craze.[78] The chase provided a new kind of subject matter, a new narrative framework that would be elaborated and refined in succeeding years until one-reel pictures such as Griffith's *The Girl and Her Trust* (1912) and Mack Sennett's comedies had seemingly exhausted its possibilities within their allotted one thousand feet.

Although the chase is implied throughout most of *The Great Train Robbery*, it only becomes explicit for a single shot (scene 12). *The Escaped Lunatic*, in contrast, makes the chase the dominant element of the film, as it would be for subsequent Biograph subjects such as *Personal* (June 1904) and *The Lost Child* (October 1904). As used by Biograph, the chase encouraged a simplification of story line and a linear progression of narrative that made the need for a familiar story or a showman's narration unnecessary. These chase films locate the redundancy within the films themselves as pursuers and pursued engage repeatedly, with only slight variation, in the same activity. Rather than having a lecture explain images in a parallel fashion, rather than having the viewer's familiarity with a story provide the basis for an understanding, chase films created a self-sufficient narrative in which the viewer's appreciation was based chiefly on the experience of information presented within the film. This had, of course, been true for certain types of films since the 1890s, most particularly trick films and some actualities. The chase, however, greatly expanded the domain and the means by which this relationship between audience and screen subject could operate.

While *The Escaped Lunatic* and its English predecessors pointed the way to a more modern form of storytelling by presenting a self-sufficient narrative, they did not inaugurate a full-scale transformation of the representational system, which was necessary before this modern viewer/screen relationship became the dominant mode of reception. Although historians usually place *The Great Train Robbery* at the cutting edge of cinema, noting correctly that it was often the first film to play in an opening nickelodeon, Porter's work can already be seen as moving at a tangent to cinema's forward thrust. Porter's initial use of the chase was not to create a simple, easily understood narrative but to incorporate it within a popular and more complex story.

The Railway Subgenre: Spectator as Passenger

To be fully appreciated, *The Great Train Robbery* must be situated within the travel program's railway subgenre. The railroad and the screen have had a special relationship, symbolized by the Lumières' famous *Train Entering a Station* (1895) and half a dozen other films. Both affected our perception of space and time in somewhat analogous ways. Describing the shift from animal-powered transportation to the railroad, Wolfgang Schivelbusch has remarked: "As the natural irregularities of the terrain that were perceptible on the old roads are replaced by the sharp linearity of the railroad, the traveler feels that he has lost contact with the landscape, experiencing this most directly when going through a tunnel. Early descriptions of journeys on the railroad note that the railroad and the landscape through which it runs are in two separate worlds."[79] The traveler's world is mediated by the railroad, not only by the compartment window with its frame but by telegraph wires, which intercede between the passenger and the landscape. The sensation of separation that the traveler feels on viewing the rapidly passing landscape has much in common with the theatrical experience of the spectator. It is not surprising, therefore, that an important subgenre of the travelogue centered on the train. This equation of train window with the screen's rectangle found its ultimate expression with Hale's Tours.

In the 1890s illustrated lectures, often known as "lantern journeys," featured railroads as the best way to reach and view American scenery. These frequently created a spatially coherent world with views of the train passing through the countryside, of the traveler/lecturer in the train, of scenery that could be seen out the window or from the front of the train, and finally of small incidents on sidings or at railway stations. The railroad, which carried its passengers through the countryside, was ideally suited for moving the narrative forward through time and space. John Stoddard and other lecturers presented these journeys as alternatives to travel for those who lacked the time, money, or fortitude for such undertakings.[80] Offering personal accounts of their adventures, these professional voyagers were figures with whom audiences could identify and from whom they could derive vicarious experience and pleasure. Audience identification with showman Burton Holmes took place on three levels—with the traveler shown by the camera to be within the narrative—a subject of the camera; with the showman as the cameraman—the producer of images of a certain quality; and, finally, as a speaker at the podium—with a certain voice and narrational perspective. The point-of-view shot out the window or from the front of a train was privileged in such a system because it conflated camera, character, and narration.

The introduction of moving pictures reinforced the parallels between train travel and projected image. "According to Newton," observes Schivelbusch, "'size, shape, quantity and motion' are the only qualities that can be objectively perceived in the physical world. Indeed, those become the only qualities that the railroad traveler is now able to observe in the landscape he travels through. Smells, sounds, not to mention the synesthetic perceptions that were part of travel in Goethe's time, simply disappear."[81] This new mode of perception, which is initially disorienting, then pleasurable, is recreated as the moving pictures, taken by a camera from a moving train, are projected onto the screen.

The epiphany of going through a tunnel likewise found a prominence in this subgenre that matched its significance in train travel. An early review of such a film begins by contrasting the resulting effect to an earlier moving picture novelty derived from pre-cinema lantern shows—the onrushing express:

> The spectator was not an outsider watching from safety the rush of the cars. He was a passenger on a phantom train ride that whirled him through space at nearly a mile a minute. There was no smoke, no glimpse of shuddering frame or crushing wheels.

What Happened in the Tunnel. Outwitted and humiliated, the "masher" tries to hide behind a newspaper.

There was nothing to indicate motion save that shining vista of tracks that was eaten up irresistibly, rapidly, and the disappearing panorama of banks and fences.

The train was invisible and yet the landscape swept by remorselessly, and far away the bright day became a spot of darkness. That was the mouth of the tunnel, and toward it the spectator was hurled as if a fate was behind him. The spot of blackness became a canopy of gloom. The darkness closed around and the spectator was being flung through that cavern with the demoniac energy behind him. The shadows, the rush of the invisible force and the uncertainty of the issues made one instinctively hold his breath as when on the edge of a crisis that might become a catastrophe.[82]

As this novelty wore off, phantom rides became incorporated into the travel narrative, enabling the showman to literalize the traveler's movement through time and space.

The railway subgenre soon incorporated short scenes for comic relief. G. A. Smith made a one-shot film of a couple kissing in a railway carriage—a gag that had comic strip antecedents. He suggested that showmen insert *Kiss in the Tunnel* into the middle of a phantom ride, after the train had entered the tunnel. Unlike the structuring strategies suggested by Selig,[83] comedy and scenery were contained within the same fictional world. Ferdinand Zecca's *Flirt en chemin de fer* (1901) was intended for the same use, but rather than require the entrance

A Romance of the Rail. Not only does Phoebe Snow wear a white gown on the Lackawanna Railroad, but tramps ride the rails in their evening dress and decline a dusting off from the astounded conductor.

of the train into a dark tunnel, Zecca matted in a window view of passing countryside. A Lubin film, *Love in a Railroad Train* (1902), depicts a male traveler's unsuccessful attempts to sneak a kiss from a woman passenger. When they emerge from the tunnel, it turns out that he is kissing her baby's bottom.[84] Porter combined a variation on Lubin's gag with Zecca's use of a matte to make *What Happened in the Tunnel.* A forward young lover (G. M. Anderson) tries to kiss the woman sitting in front of him when the train goes into the tunnel but ends up kissing her black-faced maid instead. The two women, who anticipate his attempt and switch places, have a laugh at his expense. The substitution of a black maid for a baby's bottom suggests the casual use of demeaning racial stereotypes in this period. *What Happened in the Tunnel* was the last film Porter made before *The Great Train Robbery*: its matte shot served as an experiment for similar efforts (scenes 1 and 3 of the headliner).

A Romance of the Rail, filmed in August but not copyrighted until October 3, 1903, elaborated on the comic interlude. To counter its image as a coal carrier, the Lackawanna Railroad, known as "The Road of Anthracite," developed an advertising campaign in which passenger Phoebe Snow, dressed in white, rode the rails and praised the line's cleanliness in such slogans as:

> Says Phoebe Snow, about to go
> Upon a trip to Buffalo:
> "My gown stays white from morn till night
> Upon the Road of Anthracite."[85]

A Romance of the Rail lightheartedly spoofs not only the slogans but the advertisements' photographic illustrations. Like *Rube and Mandy at Coney Island,* the film combines scenery and comic relief. The narrative is clearly paramount as Phoebe Snow meets her male counterpart (also dressed in white) for the first time at a railway station. They fall in love and marry in the course of a brief ride, spoofing romantic associations with train travel. Scenery is pushed into the background, except in the fourth shot, where the camera framing gives equal emphasis to the scenery and the couple, who are, like the spectator, watching the scenery. Although *Romance of the Rail* has a beginning, middle, and end, it lacks strict closure since exhibitors often inserted the film into a program of railway panoramas. The ratio and relative importance of scenery to story were left to their discretion.

Audiences for these films continued to assume the vicarious role of passenger. One moment they would be looking at the scenery from the train; at another they would be looking at the antics of fellow passengers. Hale's Tours made this convention explicit by using a simulated railway carriage as a movie theater, with the audience sitting in the passenger seats and the screen replacing the view from the front or rear window. This theater/carriage came complete with train clatter and the appropriate swaying. The superrealism of the exhibition strategy was adumbrated by bits of action along the sidings and in the train, which contradicted the suggestion of a fixed point of view. Coherence was sacrificed in favor of variety and a good show. Whether *What Happened in the Tunnel* or *A Romance of the Rail* were used in the first Hale's Tour Car at Electric Park in Kansas City during the summer of 1905 is not known, but such use would seem logical.[86] When Hale's Tours became a popular craze in 1906, however, these films were advertised again in the trades as "Humorous Railway Scenes" with this purpose specifically in mind.[87]

The Great Train Robbery brought the railway subgenre to new heights. During the first eight scenes, the train is kept in almost constant view: seen through the window, as a fight unfolds on the tender, from the inside of the mail car, by the water tower, or along the tracks as the cab is disconnected and the passengers are relieved of their money. Although the film was initially shown as a headliner in vaudeville theaters with its integrity intact, it was also introduced by railway panoramas in Hale's Tours–type situations. The spectators start out as railway passengers watching the passing countryside, but they are abruptly assaulted by a close-up of the outlaw Barnes firing his six-shooter directly into their midst. (This shot was shown either at the beginning or end of the film. In a Hale's Tours situation it would seem more effective at the beginning, in a vaudeville situation at the end as an apotheosis.) The viewers, having assumed the role of passengers, are held up. The close-up of the outlaw Barnes reiterates the spectators' point of view, brings them into the subsequent narrative, and intensifies their identification with the bandits' victims. Since this shot is abstracted from the narrative and the "realistic" exteriors of earlier scenes, the title that the Edison catalog assigned to this shot—"Realism"—might at first appear singularly inappropriate.[88] Yet the heightening of realism in twentieth-century cinema has been associated not only with a move toward greater naturalism but with a process of identification and emotional involvement with the drama. It is this second aspect of realism that the close-up intensifies.

The process of viewer identification with the passengers in a Hale's Tour presentation of *The Great Train Robbery* was overdetermined: introductory railway panoramas, reinforced by the simulated railway carriage and the close-up of Barnes, turned viewers into passengers. These strategies of viewer identification coincided with the viewer's social predisposition to side with responsible members of society being victimized by lawless elements. The second portion of the film, however, breaks with the railway subgenre and this overdetermination and becomes a chase. The presence of the passengers is forgotten. Music or simulated gunshots, rather than railway clatter, became the appropriate sound effects.[89] The breakdown of the viewer-as-passenger strategy, always just below the surface of the railway genre, was complete by the end of the film. This breakdown subsequently occurred on an entirely different level as well. Adolph Zukor, who would work with Porter ten years later, managed a Hale's Tours car in Herald Square during the early stages of his motion picture career. After the venture's initial success, he began to lose money until the customary phantom rides were followed by *The Great Train Robbery*. Although this combination revived his customers' interest and his own profits, Zukor eventually replaced the simulated carriage with a more conventional storefront theater.[90]

Another Change in Personnel

Early in 1904 the Edison Manufacturing Company was forced to find yet another manager for its Kinetograph Department. Shortly after the release of *The Great Train Robbery*, William Markgraf went to England on motion picture business. Once there, he went on a month-long drunken binge. In the midst of his alcoholic haze, he bought at least 200,000 feet of Lumière film stock without proper authorization.[91] Gilmore was forced to call his brother-in-law back to the United States and ask for his resignation. Although Markgraf's salary was terminated in late March, he had been effectively removed from any position of responsibility somewhat earlier. Perhaps because Porter assumed extra responsibilities as a result—and could claim credit for *The Great Train Robbery*—the studio manager's salary, which had been raised to $25 per week in October, was increased again to $35 per week. Moreover, an M. Porter, undoubtedly Porter's youngest brother Everett Melbourne, was hired at $4 per week—an office boy's salary—early in the year.

Few promising candidates appeared to fill the position Markgraf was vacating. Alex T. Moore, who had known Gilmore since their mutual employment by Edison electric light companies, applied for the job sometime in January.

Gilmore, uncertain of Moore's qualifications, sent him to be interviewed by Percival Waters at the Kinetograph Company. As Waters later recalled,

> Moore came into my office one day with a card of introduction from Mr. Gilmore. He stated to me that he had applied to Mr. Gilmore who was an old friend of his for a position with the Edison Manufacturing Company. Mr Gilmore said to him that he might have an opening in the film manufacturing department, but thought that he would require a man experienced in the moving picture business and suggested that he call upon me and talk over the requirements of that business. I told Moore that I would be very glad to give him any information which I had and went over my experience and what I thought would be required of a manager of such a department. He said that he believed he could easily pick up the details. He thanked me for the information I had given him and I told him that if he should secure the position he must feel that he could call upon me at any and all times and that I would do my best to acquaint him with the business. Afterwards, said Gilmore asked me if I had seen Moore and I told him that I had and that he seemed to have a good appearance and I didn't question but that he could operate the department satisfactorily.[92]

Waters' ties with the Edison Company had developed sufficiently for him to exercise an indirect veto over the hiring of key personnel. The exhibitor may have even been pleased at the prospect of working with an inexperienced manager, since the novice would frequently be dependent on him and his knowledge of the industry. Moore's assumption of the position in late March inevitably strengthened Waters' ability to make Edison's Kinetograph Department serve the interests of his Kinetograph Company.

Moore was conditionally hired at $50 per week. After a two-month trial, his salary was raised to $75 per week, including retroactive pay. One of Moore's first orders of business was to dispose of Markgraf's legacy of Lumière film, which had proved defective. When the stock was run through a projector, the emulsion stripped off the base. It could only be used as leader. (No wonder Eastman Kodak dominated the industry!) Joseph McCoy, Edison's undercover agent, later reminisced about the disposal of the unsatisfactory material:

> Moore wanted to get clear of the Lumiere Company film. I was to sell the film to other manufacturers of films and the Edison Company was not to be known in the transaction.
>
> I sold some of the film to the Edison Company at 4¢ a foot. Other manufacturers said if it was good enough for the Edison Company to use, they would buy some of the film.
>
> I sold 160,000 feet of the Lumiere film. Geo Melier [sic] of East 38th Street [sic] bought 10,000 feet. Smith of the Vitagraph Company bought the film and Lubin of Philadelphia. They all had the same trouble with the film stripping from the celluloid base.[93]

McCoy's practical solution typified the business ethics often practiced by Edison, his associates, and American industry. Today it would be called fraud.

Although *The Great Train Robbery* caused Edison film sales to surge in December 1903, such "headliners" were still considered only one dimension of Porter's production responsibilities. The producer thus turned his attention to making short comedies, including the timely Christmas subject *Under the Mistletoe*, and filming winter scenery, for example *Crossing Ice Bridge at Niagara Falls* and *Ice Skating in Central Park, N.Y.* Multishot comedies like *Casey's Frightful Dream* (January 1904) and *Little German Band* (February 1904) were increasingly typical. The latter film required three different studio sets—one for each shot. A small band plays music outside a saloon, and the owner invites them inside, generously giving each a glass of beer. They drink up and after one musician surreptitiously fills his tuba with brew from a conveniently located keg, they depart. Outside the band share the spoils, using their instruments as drinking vessels. The suspicious saloon keeper, however, catches them in the act. If children can be naughty and escape retribution in most early films, men who act like boys are rarely so lucky. In these comedies, punishment of adults usually involves social or sexual humiliation.

During early 1904, Porter continued to work closely with G. M. Anderson who appeared in such productions as *Wifey's Mistake* and *Halloween Night at the Seminary*. In the latter film, Anderson spies on a group of young girls in pajamas who are dunking for apples and playing other Halloween games. When the girls discover the Peeping Tom, they dunk him in the tub of water, an overly large vagina-like container (the scene cries out for a simple psychoanalytic reading). The film's play with pleasure and voyeurism, transgression and punishment is similar to *Two Chappies in a Box*, *The Gay Shoe Clerk*, and other Edison comedies, suggesting both the popularity of this theme and the way repetition and slight, but clever, variation can be used to comic effect.

Anderson's contributions included the story idea for *The Buster Brown Series*, the first Edison "feature" to appear after *The Great Train Robbery*. Its seven scenes were taken in February and early March, except for *Buster's Joke on Papa*, which had been made and released as a separate short. These were listed as follows:

R. F. Outcault Making a Sketch of Buster and Tige

Buster's Revenge on the Tramp

Buster and the Dude

Buster Cleans a Bargain Counter

Buster's Joke on Papa

Tige to the Rescue

Buster and the Balloon Vender.[94]

This comedy was made with the assistance of the comic strip's creator, Richard F. Outcault, who had worked for Edison as a draftsman and made some early

Outcault sketches for Porter's camera; the bargain counter shortly before Buster and Tige arrive.

sketches of the Black Maria before becoming a cartoonist. Eager to help his nephew Will Rising, who sometimes worked at the Edison studio as an actor, Outcault appeared in a scene making a lightning sketch of his cartoon characters. The cartoonist had sold the theatrical rights for his Buster Brown characters, however, and a musical based on the comic strip was then being previewed out of town.[95] Outcault's enthusiastic participation in the Edison film was halted when Mellville B. Raymond, who owned the theatrical rights, threatened to sue the sketch artist for violation of his contract. As a result, Outcault tried to get the film off the market and finally sued Waters and the Edison Company in the U.S. circuit court.[96] Edison sought to ease Outcault's embarrassment by delaying the picture's distribution; in mid May, however, the Buster Brown films were put on the market.[97]

The legal paperwork for the Outcault case reveals much about the production of *The Buster Brown Series*. A memo for Porter's deposition describes the film's evolution and suggests the ways in which their collaborative working method functioned (see document no. 15). Anderson suggested the original idea. Norman Mosher brought in "Mannie," the trained dog, and a group of scenes was made. Actor Will Rising, trying to better his position, suggested filming his uncle, the cartoonist. The picture evolved casually, through the collective effort of the studio staff. Porter may have supervised and shaped the process, but clearly he tended to think and operate in nonhierarchical terms.

Each scene in *The Buster Brown Series* was conceived separately and treated as the analogue of a cartoon strip. Each had its own title. Although, as was done with *Buster's Joke on Papa*, scenes could have been sold separately as shorts, The Buster Brown Series was offered for sale "in one length only." Yet unlike *Jack and the Beanstalk* or any of Porter's previous "feature"-length films, *The Buster Brown Series* lacks the narrative development and complexity that previously justified the producer's control of the editing process. In constructing his

The once successful actor, undone by alcohol and down on his luck, works for the Edison Company.

The comic strip as storyboard.

subject, the studio manager assumed a responsibility that had once been the exhibitor's—as with the Happy Hooligan series of 1901–2.[98] Whereas the showman had formerly acquired individual scenes, Porter and his crew now created and combined these vignettes until the larger film contained the elements Porter desired. By 1904 the motion picture producer's editorial control had grown to the point where narrative continuity was no longer a necessary basis for his intervention. He now combined a series of potentially self-sufficient scenes that had only a main character in common. As with other Porter films, however, the influence of exhibitor-dominated cinema continued to be felt within the production house itself. The scene of Outcault doing his lightning sketch was placed at the head of the film when it was first released, but by 1906 it had been moved to the end.[99] This casual rearrangement of scenes reflected the influence of Porter's experiences as a showman in the 1890s.

DOCUMENT NO. 15

Memo for Affidavit of Mr. Porter

The idea first originated by a man named [G.M.] Anderson suggesting a scene of a boy stealing jam (Buster not thought of). Then Mosier [Norman Mosher] came along with a trained dog; assembled boy and dog into jam scene. This led up to assembling a series of these pictures on different subjects. Dyer was consulted to see if there was any infringement in this. Advised later by Dyer that no infringement was made and they could even use the title. Porter had carefully abstained from copying any of the original "Buster Brown" cartoons in his subjects. About five subjects in the series up to that time. Some time the latter part of February or first of May [sic; it was March], Rising said to Porter, "Dick Outcault is a nephew of mine, and I think I could get his permission to use the name 'Buster Brown' (This idea had never occurred to Porter before this time). I stated to Rising, 'All right' and that if he could secure permission from Outcault to use the title, I would make it worth his while. I gave him money to go to Flushing to pay car fare and expenses. Rising, I think went over that afternoon or the following day, returning with the letter of March 2nd from Outcault, and said everything was all right." This is the only letter Porter had ever received from Outcault. Porter knows writing to be Outcault's because he has compared it with Outcault's signature on his cartoons.

"I told Rising I was very anxious to wind up a series of pictures and that waiting until the following Monday or Tuesday would delay getting them out and I suggested that I go to Flushing, take my camera and take the picture of Outcault making a sketch of 'Buster Brown,' Outcault himself having suggested that he pose for that, as stated by Rising."

Within a day or two Rising and Porter went over to Outcault's house and found he was very busy. "We had quite a chat with him in general and he spoke of the 'Buster Brown' show and Raymond, and that there was my first knowledge that there was a 'Buster Brown' show in existence. He spoke of the business they were doing, and during our conversation he said the great trouble with the show was there was not enough 'Buster' in it to please the children and ladies; that the success of the 'Foxy Grandpa' show was that it was confined to the boys and grandpa. He mentioned at the time a vaudeville turn that they used in the play, the six Cuttys; that they were paying $600 a week for, and it had no bearing on the 'Buster Brown' show. I suggested why wouldn't it be a good idea if the pictures were a success to have Mr. Raymond put a machine on showing 'Buster Brown.' He thought it was a very good idea and said he would suggest it to Mr. Raymond. He then said, 'I am very busy, there is a gentleman upstairs for whom I am making a sketch' and he suggested that I come up with him and wait for Rising who was talking to some member of the family; Outcault said he could not pose for us that day, but when Rising returned he said, 'Now, I have an engagement with Pach, the photographer on Broadway, to pose for a picture on Sunday morning; why can't I kill two birds with one stone and stop in your place Sunday?' The following Sunday he came there and posed for the picture. After securing his sanction for using the title, we thought it would be a good idea to put in one more scene, one of his own, the Bargain Counter. This is the reason the 'Bargain Counter' scene was added. At this time and at other times there were conversations with Outcault in which it was thoroughly understood that defendants were going to market these goods as they saw fit."

"In talking about Rising on the day we called at Outcault's home, he said, 'Will is in hard luck' and that he was merely doing this for Will's benefit; that anything Will got out of it he would be satisfied with." Outcault made practically the same statement when he called on Mr. Waters. After the receipt of the first Sanger letter by the Edison Company, Outcault called at Waters office and Porter was present, and Outcault made, in effect, the same statement that he did this solely for Rising's benefit in the hope that he might get some benefit out of it. Only the three named were present at that time.

SOURCE: Edwin S. Porter, memo for affidavit of Mr. Porter, n.d. [May 1904], NjWOE. Outcault's letter, addressed to "Mr. Ed Porter, Manager Kinetograph Co.," informed him: "You have my permission to use Buster Brown on the machine—and I will be in early next week and pose for you in the act of drawing Buster if you like" (R. F. Outcault, March 2, 1904, NjWOE).

Skirmish Between Russian and Japanese Advance Guards, reenacting Biograph's reenactment, *The Battle of the Yalu*.

The Russo-Japanese War

War films had proven their popularity almost from the beginnings of cinema. When the confrontation between Russia and Japan in the Far East became the Russo-Japanese War in February 1904, film companies happily seized the opportunity. Although the Charles Urban Trading Company in England sent cameramen to cover the war, Edison and other American producers were content to film mock battles in New York and New Jersey based on dispatches from the front. The Biograph Company scored the first success with *The Battle of the Yalu*, photographed in Syracuse, New York, on March 16th and 17th. It was "running at all the leading Vaudeville Houses. Cheered by Audiences from start to finish."[100] The Edison Company was sufficiently impressed to remake the film for its own commercial purposes in Forest Hill, New Jersey. On Saturday, April 2d, Porter photographed *Skirmish Between Russian and Japanese Advance Guards* using members of the local National Guard. The result was a four-shot picture, with each scene prefaced by a simple title ("Japanese Outpost on the Yalu River," "The Attack," etc.).

Porter quickly followed *Skirmish Between Russian and Japanese Advance Guards* with *Battle of Chemulpo Bay*, taken on April 8, 1904. It was based on an actual incident, which had taken place in February:

BATTLE OF CHEMULPO BAY. This picture shows the crew of a Japanese Man-of-War working a gun during the engagement of Chemulpo Bay. The Russian cruiser "Variag" and gunboat "Korietz" are shown coming from the port. Immediately they are attacked by the Japanese fleet and after sustaining much damage from the enemy's guns, both are seen to sink before reaching the bay. 150 feet.[101]

The film was shot in the Edison studio; the battleship set, with its extreme foreshortening, was similar in construction to the one Porter had used in the first scenes of *Sampson-Schley Controversy*. This picture is more elaborate, however, for Porter cuts from an establishing view of activities on the deck to a masked point-of-view shot—as if taken from the binoculars of the officer on deck—of the Russian flag being hit by the Japanese gunfire. To one knowledgeable observer, the film recalled the miniature warships then being exhibited at the St. Louis Exposition.[102] It was extremely popular, selling 109 copies during 1904–5, as compared to 56 copies of *Skirmish Between Russian and Japanese Advance Guards* and 34 copies of *The Buster Brown Series.*

To help meet the demand for Russo-Japanese war films while avoiding any undue expense, the Kinetograph Department also duped English news films and purchased a group of travel films taken in Russia, China, and Japan from Thomas Armat—which he had acquired previously from Burton Holmes.[103] Edison was offering its customers a mixture of studio creations, comparatively realistic reenactments using American military personnel, and scenes actually filmed in the belligerent countries. This disparate array of mimetic techniques reflected the way many American newspapers, notably Hearst's *New York Journal*, covered the war.[104]

Dupes, Remakes, Copycatting, and Cheap Productions

During the spring and summer of 1904, the Kinetograph Department avoided production of narrative "features," just when such activities were increasing at other studios. Duping foreign subjects not covered by copyright continued to be viewed as a less expensive and surer way to provide customers with dramatic headliners. When, as sometimes happened, an American competitor put out a popular film protected by copyright, Porter was asked to imitate it. Whatever the reasons—objective business analyses of costs and sales, changes in management, disorganization, complacency, or Porter's lack of a collaborator—the Kinetograph Department became inordinately derivative.

Porter and his associates turned out a mixture of short comedies, human interest films, and news topicals. *Dog Factory*, photographed in the studio on April 15th, was a simple variation on the often used circus gag (filmed by Lumière and others) in which dogs were turned into sausages. Porter gave the gag a new twist: sausages were turned into dogs. The subject sold forty-two prints during the 1904 business year. The following week Porter remade Biograph's *A Farmer Who Can't Let Go* (shot May 3, 1900):

HOLD-UP IN A COUNTRY GROCERY STORE

Several farmers are discussing politics in a country store. A bunco man enters and takes an electric battery from a bag. He induces the Rubes to join hands and take hold of the handles. The current is turned on and they go through some very funny stunts, while the bunco man goes through their pockets, taps the till, and makes a hasty exit. 160 feet.[105]

Here a swindler uses modern, urban technology to outwit naive farmers. In this simple variation on the rube's visit to the large city, the countryside is now invaded by dynamic and dangerous modernity. The subject, however, sold only a dozen prints during 1904.

One comedy, to which Terry Ramsaye has devoted much printer's ink,[106] was commissioned by Lew Dockstader for his minstrel show. Never intended for the Edison catalog, it was neither copyrighted nor appears in records at the Edison National Historic Site. Our knowledge is based on the fortuitous: something went wrong. Dockstader's short film, shot in Washington on the morning of May 19, 1904, was to be inserted into his show, following a scene in which a black-faced minstrel surveyed the countryside from a balloon and made amusing observations. At a crucial moment Dockstader was to fall out of the balloon, and the film would begin with him, in minstrel shoes and outfit, sprawled on the Capitol steps. One witness to the event explained,

> I saw this made-up negro walk off and chalk a place on the asphalt, within range of the camera, I suppose, then fall down. Up drives the other carriage and the fellow dressed as the President steps out, and with his coachman lifts Mr. Negro into the carriage. There is a great deal of bowing and hat tipping, and the exchanging of cigars, and of course the picture machine kept on taking it in. The act was done over, so as to make sure, I suppose.[107]

The event created grave concern and front-page news in New York and Washington. Roosevelt, who was facing reelection, had recently had lunch with Booker T. Washington at the White House, to the distress of southern whites. Many were concerned that Dockstader's film would be used to exploit the incident for political purposes.[108] Washington police looked for laws under which they might arrest the minstrel man. Investigators were sent to New York, where they confronted Porter and demanded the film be turned over. Porter handed them a roll, which the law officers promptly exposed to the light. While the police believed that they destroyed the undeveloped negative, the ruined film was actually a blank: the subject was saved until Edwin Porter's personal archive burned in a fire at the Famous Players' studio ten years later.[109]

A week after the Dockstader escapade and ten days after Coney Island's Luna Park opened for the summer season, Porter photographed *Elephants Shooting the Chutes at Luna Park*, showing a new amusement considered by many to be "more wonderful than any of the other new features at Coney Island from a spectacular standpoint."[110] The subject may have been extraordinary, but Porter had taken that type of film many times before. On May 28th he shot *Inter-Collegiate Athletic Association Championships, 1904* in Philadelphia with A. C. Abadie. Intertitles were used to introduce the various track and field events. This and *Inter-Collegiate Regatta—Poughkeepsie, New York, 1904*, which he filmed alone between June 25th and 28th, attracted little interest, selling only two copies each.

Abadie, who had been inactive during the winter, resumed work in early May

Table 2.   Edison Film Production, March–July 1904

Subject type	Number in category	Negative feet	Print feet	Print to neg. ratio[a]
Actualities	40 (82%)	5,045 (68%)	42,915 (38%)	8.5
Staged/fiction	9 (18%)	2,335 (32%)	69,560 (62%)	29.8
Total	49	7,380	112,475	15.2

[a]Includes only sales of prints for the 1904 business year (March 1, 1904, to February 29, 1905).

by taking a series of scenes at the 101 Ranch in Bliss, Oklahoma Territory. Acts seen in Wild West shows were filmed in natural surroundings. *Bucking Broncos* sold almost fifty prints over the next two years. Other films, such as *Brush Between Cowboys and Indians*, did not sell nearly as well. During July he filmed topicals including *Pollywogs, 71st Regiment, N.G.S.N.Y., Initiating Raw Recruits* in Peekskill, New York, and *Parade, Mystic Shriners, Atlantic City, New Jersey*. These were hardly novel additions to the Edison catalog.

In August 1904 Porter filmed *Fire and Flames at Luna Park, Coney Island*, a simple one-shot film of the spectacle "Fire and Flames." Biograph had earlier photographed a similar spectacle at a rival amusement park, Dreamland. Of the two, Biograph's *Fighting the Flames—Dreamland* is the more elaborate.[111] Porter's film did little more than meet the requirements of Edison executives, who saw the film as an effective means of competition. Despite its limitations, the Edison film sold thirty-six copies over the next two years.

The composition and distribution of Edison productions for the March–July 1904 period can be analyzed using a surviving survey of Edison film sales during the years 1904–6. The data are given in table 2. Two features (*The Buster Brown Series* and *Skirmish Between Russian and Japanese Advance Guards*) sold 45,595 feet struck from 1,275 feet of negative, for a print/negative ratio of 35.8 to one. These two films, listed above in the staged/fiction category, were 4 percent of the listed subjects and 17 percent of the negative footage but accounted for over 40 percent of total film sales. This statistical analysis would be significantly altered if information about dupes was available. Such a revised analysis would reinforce what is already clear from the table: staged/fiction "headliners" were the most popular (and potentially profitable) types of productions.

By the summer of 1904, the Edison Company had abdicated its position as America's foremost motion picture producer to the American Mutoscope & Biograph Company. Biograph had recognized the importance of fiction headliners and had begun regular "feature" production by mid 1904. With Wallace McCutcheon acting as producer, Biograph's staff made *Personal* in June, *The*

Moonshiner in July, *The Widow and the Only Man* in August, *The Hero of Liao Yang* in September, and *The Lost Child* and *The Suburbanite* in October.[112] These headliners were all enthusiastically received by the vaudeville-going public. They were not offered for sale, however, but kept for exclusive use on the company's exhibition circuit. Biograph was perhaps the first company, certainly the first company in America, to make regular "feature" production the keystone of its business policy.

The French Threat:
Pathé Enters the American Market

The commercial threat that Méliès posed when he entered the American market in June 1903 never fully materialized. The opening of Star Films headquarters in New York coincided with Edison's distribution of *A Daring Daylight Burglary* and the waning of Méliès' dominant position in the international film industry. In England, James White still had a wide assortment of European subjects he could send to the United States for duping. Of the thirty-four pictures listed in Edison's January 1904 catalog, nineteen were dupes. In the September 1904 catalog thirty-six of fifty-two were dupes. Many of these were dramatic headliners and many also were made by Pathé Frères of Paris. The Edison Company's attitude toward this underhanded business was articulated by lawyer Frank Dyer. "I understand that personally you are averse to the copying of our competitors' films," he wrote Gilmore, "but at the same time there must be a good profit in that business as it does away with making an original negative."[113]

This profitable state of affairs began to unravel in mid July 1904, when Gilmore received a letter from Pathé announcing its intention to open a New York branch:

> For more than a year we have watched the methods employed by your company, who copy all our Films which they think interesting, in defiance of our rights of ownership.
>
> We know that under the present laws of your country, aside from the special precautions we have taken, we are unable to legally put a stop to same, but as we are about to establish an agency in New York for the sale of our products, and we desire to come to some agreement with you, in order to avoid that in return we will not copy your Films.[114]

Pathé's request was considered unacceptable. To stop duping would be to curtail a profitable venture, and such an arrangement might also be construed as an informal licensing arrangement under Edison's patents. More to the point, the establishment of a branch office in New York City posed a threat to Edison's position in the American industry. Pathé, like the Edison Company, but unlike Méliès, supplied exhibitors with a wide variety of subjects. It was a modern business organization, with substantial working capital and experience accumulated from its phonograph operations. As a film producer, Pathé was growing rapidly and establishing an international network of offices that fostered maximum distribution of its product.

Frank Dyer formulated a response to the French company's letter, suggesting

> that possibly a desirable solution of the difficulty might be secured by calling Pathe's attention to our patent on the moving picture film (reissued Jan. 12, 1904, No. 12192), stating that this patent covers all film now in use, and that in the event of their establishing an agency in New York that they contemplate, we will promptly bring suit for infringement. The suggestion might then be made that we would make an agreement with them under which they would give us the option of copyrighting and duplicating their films in this country, paying them a royalty per foot on all films which might be duplicated. . . . The advantages of the arrangement suggested are that we would keep Pathe Freres out of this country and would be in a position to legitimately copy their films, which, I understand from Mr. Moore are of excellent quality. If the arrangement is not made, and Pathe Freres establish themselves in New York, we would encounter a more active competition on their part and would have to undergo the uncertainty of a suit against them on our patent.[115]

Pathé ignored Edison's warning and opened its branch office with Jacques A. Berst as manager. Making all its prints in Paris, the French concern began to supply its New York office before London. By the time White's purchases arrived in the United States, Pathé had filled much of the demand.[116] Films still considered worth duping were purchased in New York City by Edison's industrial spy, Joseph McCoy.[117] Visiting the Pathé office in November 1904 and using information provided by Berst, McCoy reported that "they opened up for business in this country about two months ago and they have had so much business that they have been unable to supply the demand for their films."[118] Pathé had not only established itself as a major competitor, but had undermined one of Edison's major profit strategies—the making of inexpensive dupes.

George Kleine and the Edison Company Go Separate Ways

Shortcomings in film production had serious commercial consequences for the Edison Manufacturing Company. It undermined a long-standing relationship with George Kleine, Edison's able Chicago selling agent, who had been responsible for approximately 30 percent of Edison's film sales.[119] Friction between Kleine and William Gilmore developed in February 1904 when West Orange allowed Biograph to acquire the exclusive concession for films of the Louisiana Purchase Exposition.[120] Kleine, who already had the exposition concession for lantern slides, wanted to sell his slides in combination with motion pictures. In April he wrote Gilmore: "It is distasteful enough to me to be compelled to sell films made by the Biograph people, but what else is left? I have spent time and money on this matter and will be compelled to sell World's Fair Films in connection with my slides; you will agree with me that it would be idiotic to throw away any advantages that may offer themselves."[121] Faced with the rise of Pathé and Biograph, Kleine began to distribute Biograph and original Pathé films (rather than Edison dupes) on a regular basis in August. Gilmore reacted angrily to Kleine's "betrayal." "Of course, as I told you when you were here, you are at perfect liberty to make any arrangement that you like with other manufacturers," he blustered, "but I cannot see how I can consistently continue to have all communications and inquiries sent to you, nor do I consider it wise or judicious that we should continue to permit you to advertise as the 'General Western Selling Agents' for our goods."[122] Kleine pleaded with Gilmore for a better understanding of his situation. Others simply filled the void, he explained, weakening his own commercial position. His company always favored the Edison trademark and sold only small quantities of rival makes. Kleine then concluded:

> We have been so closely identified with the Edison Mfg. Co. for years, that any disturbance of our relations would affect the welfare of our concern seriously, and it would probably require a year or two for matters to readjust themselves. You see that I do not hesitate to admit it. There are certain obligations involved on both sides, considering the past. The advertising of which you complain was voluntary on my part, and not involved in any agreement. I can therefore drop it without disturbing the peace with others; or eating crow, which I hate.[123]

Gilmore, however, seemed determined to break with Kleine. One key issue was Kleine's refusal to distribute Edison dupes of Pathé films.[124] The disagreement came to a head at the end of September, when Gilmore revoked Kleine's special discount effective October 1, 1904. The Edison organization quickly set up a Chicago office under John Hardin, who had entered the industry in 1898 as motion picture department manager of Montgomery Ward, then a Chicago-based mail-order house.[125] Kleine sent out a form letter to his customers explaining the break.[126] A few days later Kleine publicly blasted Edison's duping policy. His advertisement began by noting: "There are various kinds of 'Dupes.' The dictionary describes one kind as a 'Victim of deception.' " Urging customers not to be duped, the manufacturer concluded: "In no case will 'Dupes' be delivered to our customers when the original can be obtained. In some instances the originals can be purchased at the same prices as the 'Dupes' in others at a slightly advanced price."[127] Kleine's position pleased European producers, and he was gradually to become the U.S. representative for many English and French firms. His stand further dramatized the Kinetograph Department's weaknesses, the bankruptcy of its duping policy, the increased competition from Pathé and Biograph, and the need for Edison to expand its production of headliners.

Edison versus Biograph:
The Remaking of *Personal*

Remaking a popular American film was the counterpart to duping foreign productions. Since 1896 the Kinetograph Department had intermittently pursued this practice. Now, in August and September, it remade Biograph's two biggest hits: *Personal*, which was retitled *How a French Nobleman Got a Wife Through the New York Herald Personal Columns* (photographed August 1904) and *The Escaped Lunatic*, which became *Maniac Chase* (September 1904). Culminating with these two features, the Kinetograph Department's legal piracy destroyed Biograph's structure of exhibition and sales. Ironically, it was precisely this two-tiered structure, of initial distribution on Biograph's circuit and subsequent sales to non-Biograph exhibitors, that made these remakes so profitable for Edison.

Waters' Kinetograph Company, American Vitagraph, and Biograph were locked in a business struggle for domination of vaudeville exhibition in the east. All three companies had exclusive films for their circuits. While Biograph generally withheld its films from independent exhibitors long after (in some cases nine months after) their first appearance on its programs, Percival Waters had no such advantage. Although occasionally commissioning a specific subject, Waters usually had to make do with the first Edison print to be sold. His exclusives varied from several days to two weeks.[128] To compensate, Waters began to rent films to theaters and train their electricians to run a projector (which Waters was happy to sell them). He could rent a reel of film for approximately $25 a week, while the Biograph and Vitagraph services, which still included a projector and operator, were almost twice as expensive. The reel of film had become the commodity.[129] The Kinetograph Company was no longer an exhibition service but a renter, a distributor. Waters' money-saving offer, however, was not adequate inducement for many vaudeville managers to switch suppliers: they wanted first-run hits like Biograph's *Personal*.

Personal is a comedy about a Frenchman who tries to arrange a rendezvous at Grant's Tomb with prospective American brides by placing an ad in the *New York Herald*'s personal column. Besieged by a large crowd of American working-class women, he panics and makes his escape. The chase scenes that follow are essentially the same: the Frenchman runs toward and past the camera with the women in pursuit. Variation in each scene is created by a different obstacle the pursuers have to overcome—a stream, a fence, a ditch, and so forth. The denouement comes with the European hiding in the bushes, only to be discovered by a "determined Diana" with a gun.[130] The film's none too subtle lampooning of the fashionable marriages between impoverished European noblemen and the daughters of rich Americans accounted for its immense popularity.

After Waters tried unsuccessfully to purchase a copy of *Personal*, he induced the Edison Company to make a comparable version. For Waters the business maneuver had its desired effect: Biograph, which promoted *Personal* as an exclusive, was embarrassed. According to Waters: "Keith opened a theatre in Cleveland and used the Biograph film as one of his principal attractions and advertised that no one else could exhibit this film, but a rival theatre got one of the Edison films and exhibited it much to Keith's chagrin. Keith evidently went to the Biograph Company and raised a rumpus."[131] In July of the following year, Keith's circuit permanently abandoned Biograph for the Kinetograph Company.[132] Biograph's exhibition circuit did not survive the blow.

The Edison Company made a handsome profit on its remake. *How a French Nobleman . . .* was on the market before the original Biograph production and, according to Waters, exhibitors often considered Porter's film superior.[133] In the end, *How a French Nobleman . . .* was the most successful Edison headliner in 1904, selling eighty-five complete prints during 1904–5. The eventual addition of the Keith circuit to Waters' list of customers also meant the Kinetograph Company was in a position to buy more Edison films in the future.

The Edison remake forced Biograph to put *Personal* on the market at a reduced price. To recoup its losses and prevent similar remakes in the future, the company also initiated a suit for copyright infringement against the Edison Co. and claimed damages of $3,000.[134] Edison lawyers defended the legality of the remake on several levels. First they pointed out that their client had not made a dupe and so had not violated the copyright in a narrow sense. Second, they argued that a photograph's content was not copyrightable and that Biograph had failed to copyright its pantomime as a dramatic production, placing the story in the public domain. (After the court case, Biograph would copyright its productions twice—as photographs and as dramas.) Looking for a loophole, Edison lawyers also argued that *Personal* had been photographed from several different camera positions and on several different strips of film; therefore, Biograph's single copyright offered inadequate protection for what were in fact several different series of photographs.[135] If the court had accepted this argument, it would have invalidated most of Edison's copyrights as well. As a precaution, the inventor thus started to copyright new productions one scene at a time.[136]

Edison lawyers also suggested that the idea for the film had come from a comic strip. An actress working at both Biograph and Edison had seen a copy of such a strip lying on the desk of Biograph's production chief, Wallace McCutcheon. "We have not as yet been able to get any clue as to the comic paper from which the idea was obtained by McCutcheon," wrote Delos Holden to Edison's lawyer Melville Church, "but this may not matter much as I shall endeavor to make the statement in the Porter affidavit so positive as to throw the burden on the defendant to produce the publication."[137] According to Edison lawyers, the question was over two different interpretations of a story

Porter's remake of *Personal*. In a new opening scene, his French nobleman preens for the mirror. For the next, the filmmaker used the same location as Biograph—Grant's Tomb—as women pursue their male quarry.

that did not originate with either party. Therefore, they slanted Porter's deposition to emphasize the artistic differences between the two productions.[138] Although several of these arguments were ignored by the judge, Edison won the case in the lower courts and again on appeal because Biograph had failed to copyright the film as a dramatic production. When the Kinetograph Department followed *How a French Nobleman . . .* with *Maniac Chase*, Edison's rival finally recognized that it would have to offer its films for sale soon after they were first shown.

By mid October 1904 Edison's policy of duping and remaking the films of his competitors was no longer profitable. His company had to take the risk of investing in original productions, and its output for the second half of its 1904 business year reflected the demand for "feature" story films and acknowledged increasing competition from Biograph and Pathé. Edison sales records for the August 1904–February 1905 period yield the statistics in table 3. The commercial importance of staged/acted films is obvious (even exaggerated in this instance, since there were no major news films to boost actuality sales). Feature

Table 3.   Edison Film Production, August 1904–February 1905

Subject type	Number in category	Negative feet	Print feet	Print to neg. ratio
Actualities	8 (38%)	1,525 (16%)	7,610 (3%)	5.0
Staged/acted	13 (62%)	7,790 (84%)	214,705 (97%)	27.6
Total	21	9,315	222,315	23.9

Table 4.   Edison Film Production, 1904–1906

March 1904–February 1905

Subject type	Number in category	Negative feet	Print feet	Print to neg. ratio
Actualities	48 (69%)	6,570 (39%)	50,525 (15%)	7.7
Staged/acted	22 (31%)	10,125 (61%)	284,265 (85%)	27.6
Total	70	16,695	334,790	20.0

March 1905–December 1905

Subject type	Number in category	Negative feet	Print feet	Print to neg. ratio
Actualities	21 (48%)	6,940 (36%)	60,580 (14%)	8.7
Staged/acted	22 (52%)	12,382 (64%)	365,060 (86%)	29.5
Total	43	19,322	425,640	22.0

February 1906–February 1907

Subject type	Number in category	Negative feet	Print feet	Print to neg. ratio
Actualities	49 (80%)	7,715 (47%)	118,438 (14%)	15.4
Staged/acted	12 (20%)	8,750 (53%)	741,490 (86%)	84.7
Total	61	16,465	859,928	52.2

acted films had become the Kinetograph Department's principal source of income. A statistical analysis for the 1904–6 period shows a steady relationship between actuality and fiction films in terms of negative production and prints sold (see table 4).

Film historians have tried to pinpoint the moment when narrative acted "features" of approximately 500 to 1,000 feet in length began to dominate the cinema. Robert C. Allen, for instance, has located the shift in 1907 and ties it to the need for greater control over the rate of production. He argues that "the spurt in narrative film production cannot be attributed to a sudden drop in public interest in the documentary film," but occurred despite it.[139] Allen and others have relied on raw quantitative data of titles copyrighted to reach this conclusion. This methodological approach has a fundamental weakness, which tables 3 and 4 demonstrate. Quantification by subject titles offers little insight into what spectators are likely to be watching. Furthermore, during 1905 and 1906, the bulk of print sales for actualities came from three major news events: Roosevelt's inauguration, the Russo-Japanese Peace Conference, and the San Francisco earthquake. In many cases, no prints of an actuality subject were sold. Except for a few comparatively rare events of national import, the public had generally lost interest in nonfiction subjects.[140]

From the summer of 1904 onward, acted headliners were made in substantial quantities and consistently outsold actualities. Excepting occasional "hits," actuality material continued to be manufactured primarily because (1) local news footage was desired by vaudeville houses renting films from the Kinetograph Company and it was considered expedient to accommodate them; and (2) such films were so inexpensive to make that a small profit could be gained on a local subject if two or more prints were sold. The shift to acted "features" was not, as Allen has suggested, a result of the nickelodeon era but a precondition for it. Significantly, story films became the dominant industry product just as the rental of films was replacing the letting of an exhibition service to the theaters. Both were key preconditions for the nickelodeon era.

The Legacy of Exhibitor-Dominated Cinema

Although Porter was manager of the Edison studio and a successful film-maker, he continued to project films at Edison charities and other special occasions.[141] This residual role was manifested on another level: the legacy of exhibitor-dominated cinema continued to influence the methods of production and representation inside the Edison Manufacturing Company. Tension continued to exist between the shot and the complete subject as the basic unit of film production, although the larger unit was primary in an increasing number of instances.

The rapid shift in responsibility for exhibition from distributor to theater further reinforced the decline of the exhibitor's editorial role. Editorial control was centralized principally in the production companies, while exchanges purchased predominantly longer subjects and programmed them with a few additional shorts to fill a 1,000-foot reel. While exchanges and most exhibitors were happy to purchase *How a French Nobleman* ... in its entirety, the Edison firm also offered prospective purchasers the opportunity to buy individual scenes. In 1905 showmen purchased four shots of the premise-establishing scene at Grant's Tomb, five of the denouement, and fewer copies (one, two, or three) of the chase scenes—indicating that a few exhibitors, even in 1905, were still resisting the trend toward standardization and editorial control by the production companies.[142] Although showmen bought the entire film in the vast majority of cases, the *How a French Nobleman* ... narrative was constructed in such a way

Spoofing the travelogue: *European Rest Cure*.

that the film could be expanded or contracted by the simple addition or elimination of chase scenes. Such a structure continued earlier methods of filmic organization.[143]

The legacy of exhibitor-dominated cinema also affected the making of *European Rest Cure*. Begun in July 1904, but not copyrighted until September 1st, *European Rest Cure* was an elaborately produced film with many studio sets. This spoof on the travelogue follows an American tourist across Europe and the Middle East on a "rest cure" in which one physically or emotionally wrenching disaster follows another. Foreign locales were actually pasteboard sets of pyramids, Roman ruins, and a French cafe, while additional scenes were shot at the docks as the tourist leaves and returns. Porter combined this original material with footage of *S.S. "Coptic" Running Against the Storm*, taken by James White on his Pacific voyage in 1898, and *Pilot Leaving "Prinzessen Victoria Luise" at Sandy Hook*, taken by White in late 1902. Another shot was excerpted from *Sky Scrapers of New York from the North River*, which James Smith had filmed in May 1903. The short films incorporated into this longer feature could still be purchased individually: one or two were used by Lyman Howe for a program he assembled, *Detailed Scenes of a Trans-Atlantic Voyage from New York to Southampton*.[144]

As with *A Romance of the Rail*, *European Rest Cure* evolved out of the travel genre and was part of the shift toward filming dramatic material. Once again, Porter took a "documentary" genre and reworked it as a comedy "feature" with a character other than the narrator/tour director to act as a unifying element. The film parodies the format of many nineteenth-century travel lectures, which used materials from different sources and combined scenes taken on location with others photographed in the comfort and artifice of the studio. Fun is poked at the romantic aura of travel perpetuated by exhibitors who

Capture of "Yegg" Bank Burglars: the "Yeggs" shoot it out and escape across a lake.

were themselves often beholden to railroad and shipping companies. As before, Porter was working effectively within a well-established genre. In this case, however, the continuing popularity of the traditional form may have created audience resistance to the spoof and resulted in modest sales, for the title sold only twenty-three prints in the year and a half after its release.

Following *European Rest Cure,* Porter worked on *Capture of "Yegg" Bank Burglars,* another production in which the exhibitor's former editorial role remains apparent. Filmed between August 15th and September 10th, this headliner was motivated by Lubin's *The Bold Bank Robbery,* first advertised in the *New York Clipper* on August 13th. Thus it continued the pattern of imitating other companies' successes.[145] Porter's film reenacted "the Criminal life and methods of the 'Hobo' Bank, Vault and Safe Burglar as described in paper read by William A. Pinkerton of Pinkerton's National Detective Agency before the Annual Convention of the International Association of Chiefs of Police, St. Louis, MO.; June 6 to 11, 1904."[146] Using the speech as a foundation, along with additional information and suggestions by Robert A. Pinkerton and G. S. Doherty of the Pinkerton agency, Porter produced a film within the crime genre he had first explored with *The Great Train Robbery.* Compared to the earlier film, Porter simplified the narrative construction and generally avoided the problematic returning to earlier points in time and the shifting back and forth between different lines of action.[147] At the same time, additional elements were added: the robbery is planned and scouted before it is put into action, and the chase elaborated.

There are two different versions of *Capture of "Yegg" Bank Burglars,* however. The first survives in the Library of Congress Paper Print Collection. On August 27th, Porter and Abadie (in his last documented appearance as an Edison cameraman) filmed *Railroad Smash-up* outside of Boston. While this human-interest news film of a planned train collision was soon released as a separate subject, Porter also used it to end his bank burglary film in a spectac-

Parsifal: Sets came from a theatrical production, but the film was intended to be accompanied by a lecture.

ular fashion. In a transitional scene, the burglars were shown mounting a locomotive and making good their escape. The next scene is the smash-up shot at Revere Branch, Massachusetts. The camera pans with a quickly moving locomotive, which collides with one coming from the other direction. As with *European Rest Cure*, actuality footage was put into a narrative context and given a new meaning.

The second version, the one eventually advertised in the Edison catalog, replaced the train collision and transitional scene with four scenes copyrighted separately as *Rounding up the Yeggmen*. They showed the burglars' capture by undercover police agents. Although the Library of Congress ending is more spectacular, its radical departure from Pinkerton's speech may have been unacceptable. Nevertheless, some prints of the earlier version were almost certainly sold.[148] It seems possible that some customers had a choice of endings. The integration of news material into a dramatic subject, the use of different endings: these syncretic procedures were influenced by Porter's experiences as an exhibitor.

Porter's next film was copyrighted as *Nervy Nat Kisses the Bride*, then sold as *"Weary Willie" Kisses the Bride*.[149] In this three-shot comedy, which recalls Porter's *What Happened in the Tunnel*, a tramp takes advantage of a spat between bride and groom to sneak a kiss—and be thrown off the train for his efforts. Set in a train station, inside a train, and on the tracks, this film could either be integrated by the exhibitor into a program of railway scenes or shown in a variety format. Here the exhibitor's editorial role was still implicitly acknowledged.

Parsifal

In early October, after making *Maniac Chase*, Porter ventured to Brooklyn for the filming of *Parsifal*. "Specifically posed and rehearsed," it had the "identical talent, scenery, and costumes used in the Original Dramatic Production."[150] Although the play was condensed and Porter resorted to stop-action photography in a few instances, restaging appears minimal. Each scene was a single shot taken by a distant camera that took in the entire set and made the actors small in the frame. Frontal compositions preserved the feeling of a proscenium arch. Looked at silently without a detailed knowledge of the story, the film is and was unintelligible: it was sold with a lecture and treated as a "sacred" film similar to *The Passion Play of Oberammergau*. A Kleine catalog, listing *Parsifal* with its other religious films, observed that "some critics have objected to its pagan elements but these serve to bring out the purity and splendor of the Christian Faith."[151] Certainly its static style and dearth of entertaining features made it appropriate for the holy day. Robert Whittier, who played the role of Parsifal, subsequently used the films as part of an illustrated lecture entitled *Wagner from Within and Without*.[152]

The opening of Richard Wagner's opera *Parsifal* at the Metropolitan Opera House on Christmas Eve 1903 was preceded by much controversy, as Wagner's widow went to court in a vain attempt to stop the performance. Its debut was reported on the front pages of New York newspapers. According to the *New York World*, "It was elevating and inspiring beyond words to express, but it was not entertaining."[153] A dramatic version followed in which "Mr. Payton in Brooklyn merely put the Corder translation of Wagner's libretto on the stage, with scenery as near like Mr. Conreid's [producer of the Metropolitan Opera House version] as he could afford to make."[154] This would appear to be "the original dramatic version" for another, by Marion Doran, appeared at the West End Theater in May 1904.

On March 1, 1904, Harley Merry acquired the motion picture rights for the dramatic version from Chase and Kennington:

> In consideration of Harley Merry having loaned us the sum of Eighteen Hundred dollars ($1800) receipt of which is hereby acknowledged, we hereby give said Harley Merry the sole rights to negotiate with whomsoever he may desire to produce in moving pictures etc. our play "Parsifal," said Harley Merry to have and to hold all the profits arising from the same.
>
> We also agree to give said Harley Merry our aid and that of our company at all times, and in every possible manner, to produce said moving pictures.[155]

With Porter actively involved, a contract was signed between the Edison Manufacturing Company and the Merry Scenic Construction Company on June 9th: it gave Merry a royalty of 2¢ per foot on every print sold. The film was shot four months later and totaled the extraordinary length of 1,975 feet (approximately thirty minutes). To accommodate the royalty without reducing Edison's profit margin, the film was sold for 17¢ per foot: one complete print cost $335, of which $39.50 went to Merry. *Parsifal* was elaborately advertised with several full-page ads in the *New York Clipper*, but sales were modest. The Kinetograph Department informed Merry that it had sold five prints of the film as of November 30th and another print in December—yielding a royalty of $237.[156] Other records indicate that sixteen prints were sold by February 1905, suggesting that Merry may not have received a full accounting.[157] Whatever the figure, *Parsifal* was a financial disappointment given Edison's expensive promotional campaign.

Porter made four additional films in October 1904: all sold comparatively few prints. In midmonth, he visited the state fair in Danbury, Connecticut, where he shot *A Rube Couple at a County Fair* (seven copies sold in 1904–5) and *Miss Lillian Schaffer and Her Dancing Horse* (five copies sold). Returning to New York, he produced a topical comedy to herald the opening of the city's subway system: *City Hall to Harlem in 15 Seconds via the Subway Route* (twenty-five copies sold), which showed "Casey's first trip through the Subway. Rapid Transit no longer a dream."[158] Casey's trip was hastened by an explosion that sent him hurtling through the tunnel at a much faster speed than the average traveler's: the new subway system only boasted that it could get one from City Hall to Harlem in 15 *minutes*. Shortly thereafter, Porter and his new assistant William Gilroy photographed *Opening Ceremonies, New York Subway, October 27, 1904*; it was quickly developed and sent to Percival Waters by special messenger so that it could play at Huber's Museum. A news film of local interest, it sold only six prints.

During the first ten months of 1904, the Edison Company had relied heavily on dupes even as it produced four imitations of Biograph subjects and a fifth inspired by a Lubin "feature." One picture was ersatz theater and another cribbed from a comic strip. Three films recycled footage. While Edison-produced headliners increased in quantity after mid August, they did not do so in originality.[159] The resulting erosion of Edison's commercial standing was reflected in a letter that William Gilmore sent to Frank Dyer. After complaining about the progress being made in several patent suits against Biograph and Lubin, the general manager remarked:

> The competition that we have to meet in this line of business, not only on the part of these people but particularly on the part of a lot of small operators, is becoming so great that I feel that some action must be taken in these cases at once. Selig is becoming very active in the West, and from such information as I have been able to gather he is evidently backed up by a lot of small dealers, and the character of the work that he turns out is bad in the extreme. On the other hand, the Mutoscope Company does not seem to hesitate to do everything they can to hurt the trade in general, and the only way I can see to get it on some sort of satisfactory basis is by pushing the suits and endeavoring to obtain a decision either one way or the other.[160]

Gilmore, however, was not foolish enough to rely solely on a possible legal solution. He finally recognized that Edison had to produce its own "original" productions if the Kinetograph Department was to attract customers in large numbers. As a result, Porter was given new resources, additional staff, and considerable discretion in his choice of subject matter and production methods.

9 Articulating an Old-Middle-Class Ideology: 1904–1905

Late in 1904 the Edison Manufacturing Company began to produce films closely tied to trends in American popular and mass culture, but they seldom followed in the immediate paths of rivals. This commitment to the risks and rewards of producing original narrative "features" coincided with the hiring of William J. Gilroy in late October. Gilroy, who had worked intermittently for the Kinetograph Department since at least September 1902, served as Porter's trusted assistant and received $15 per week.[1] In mid January 1905, moreover, the Kinetograph Department hired Robert K. Bonine, who had worked for Edison in the late 1890s and then for Biograph in the early 1900s. Replacing Jacob B. Smith, who had left two weeks earlier, he received $35 per week—the same salary as Porter. While Bonine was in charge of the Edison film development facilities at the Orange Laboratory, he took a significant number of actualities during the two and a half years of his Edison employment, beginning with *President Roosevelt's Inauguration* on March 4th.

The Edison staff was further strengthened by a talent raid on the Biograph Company. A. E. Weed, an experienced Biograph cameraman, and Wallace McCutcheon, the Biograph production chief, joined Edison in mid May. Weed, probably a replacement for A. C. Abadie, was paid $18 per week. *Drills and Exercises—Schoolship "St. Mary's,"* shot on May 31st, was his first official production. Hiring Wallace McCutcheon, the producer of *Personal* and other Biograph hits, was a major coup. McCutcheon perhaps expected to start another production unit for fiction films, but he found himself acting as Porter's chief collaborator. Since the new co-producer/co-director garnered a $40 per week salary, Porter's income had to be raised to the same figure. Both men received the same pay for the next two years—suggesting the equality of their professional relationship. (How these two leading American filmmakers collaborated will be considered in the following chapter.) This talent raid both hurt Biograph and helped Edison. The revitalization of production did not wait for McCutcheon's arrival, however, but began with *The Ex-Convict* (November 1904). In the six months until McCutcheon's arrival, actor Will Rising may have worked most closely with Porter.

American Themes and Values: Family and Society

Historians since Terry Ramsaye have remarked on Porter's articulation of social problems in *The Ex-Convict* and *The Kleptomaniac* (January 1905).[2] These two features were part of a larger group of films, made between November 1904 and December 1905, that directly and indirectly confronted significant social issues in American life. Despite a shift away from actualities, Porter continued to conceive of cinema as a form that could inform and instruct as well as entertain. His films were still linked, albeit less directly, to the concept of a visual newspaper, for he focused on problems raised in the antitrust editorials and political cartoons of the *New York Journal-American* and the *New York World*. These pictures, which represented one of several ideological positions evident in American popular and mass culture, were the most ambitious cinematic expressions from this period.

Although several Porter/Edison films, if viewed separately, are ideologically consistent with then emerging trends of Progressive thought, as a body of work they express the often contradictory worldview of the old middle class and small-town America confronted with an era of large-scale manufacturing and monopoly capital.[3] In short, these films remained consistent with Porter's own experience of America while growing up in Connellsville, Pennsylvania, and with a viewpoint expressed twenty years earlier in his hometown newspaper, *The Keystone Courier*.

The Ex-Convict, advertised as "a beautiful pathetic story in Eight scenes,"[4] quickly and simply depicts a former criminal who is forced to return to a life of crime because he cannot escape the stigma of his past. A member of the working class, he is sympathetically portrayed as a good family man driven to despair by the plight of his sick child. Dismissed from his job because of his past, the ex-convict cannot find work and is soon forced to return to a life of crime. He tries to rob a wealthy home but is caught and seems certain to return to prison—a development that will completely destroy his family. Instead, it turns out that his captor is the father of a girl whom he has recently saved in an earlier scene. When the daughter appears and is reunited with her saviour, the father relents and sends the police away. In the final scene, the rich man befriends the ex-convict, bringing food and presents to his garret apartment.

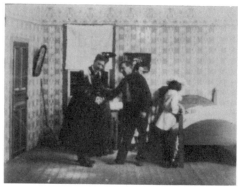

A young girl is embraced by her wealthy family after the ex-convict has rescued her from an onrushing automobile. Later, the fathers shake hands when they visit the poor man's home.

This film was based on a vaudeville one-act, *Number 973*, by Robert Hilliard and Edwin Holland. It previewed at Keith's Union Square Theater on March 27, 1903, and was enthusiastically received (see document no. 16). When the playlet, which Hilliard and Holland also co-directed, headed a bill at the same theater on August 31st, the *Dramatic Mirror* felt that

> the piece is strong, concise and well-written and the situations are dramatic without being overdrawn. Mr. Hilliard did excellent work as the rough malefactor with the right sort of heart, and his scene with the little girl was played with much delicacy and feeling. Mr. Holland as the District-Attorney was dignified and forcible, and little Jane Pelton as the child was very sweet indeed. The setting and light effects were admirable in every way.[5]

Hilliard, once a leading actor in the legitimate theater, was an established vaudeville star of the first magnitude. The one-act thus generated unusual attention. A short review in the *New York World* remarked that the "pathetic little playlet . . . stirred a deeper feeling than vaudeville sketches usually allow."[6] A critic with a sharp memory, however, noted that the Hilliard-Holland script was itself heavily indebted to the play *Editha's Burglar*.[7] Like Hilliard, Porter was reworking a well-known story.

Starting from the Hilliard-Holland playlet, Porter visualized the information into seven additional scenes. Unlike *Uncle Tom's Cabin* or *Parsifal*, *The Ex-Convict* was not filmed theater, but an adaptation that took advantage of the filmmaker's ability to place a scene in an appropriate location (outside a store, home, or factory and on the street) and to move quickly from one setting to the next. The naturalistic locales and the accelerated pace heightened the emotional intensity of the viewer's reaction to the pathetic story, achieving a level of realism impossible on the stage. Titles at the beginning of each shot in some cases provided lines of dialogue spoken by the character within the scene. In the process of adaptation, Porter also added an important new element: the ex-convict's family. This reflected Porter's own preoccupations and made the film more complex.

The Ex-Convict thus represents a major breakthrough in stage-to-screen adaptation. First, it opened up the play, situating the action in many more locations. Second, it reworked and altered the story itself, making it the filmmaker's own. These creative moves soon became standard practice in American cinema. Examples in silent film include Porter's *The Miller's Daughter* (1905) and *The Prisoner of Zenda* (1913), Cecil B. DeMille's *Male and Female* (1919), and Griffith's *Way Down East* (1920) and *Orphans of the Storm* (1921), but they continue to this day.

DOCUMENT No. 16

HILLIARD TRIES A NEW PLAY

The admirers of Robert Hilliard had a chance on Friday afternoon to see him in two widely different characters. At half-past two he appeared as the debonair van Bibber in The Littlest Girl and at four o'clock he showed that he could be just as effective in shabbier make-up as the principal person in a new one-act play called Number 973, written by himself and Edwin Holland. The scene of the sketch is laid in the home of Thomas Campbell, District Attorney of New York. Thither comes a burglar who is caught in the act by the District-Attorney who recognized in him the man he had sent up some ten years before for alleged manslaughter. The lawyer promptly telephones for the police, and while he is waiting listens to the burglar's interesting story. Later during the temporary absence of the lawyer the little daughter of the house appears. She had a narrow escape from death the day before under the hoofs of a runaway horse and, it transpires that the man who had saved her was none other than the burglar, who had been driven to his rash act by starvation. The father overhears the conversation between his child and the unfortunate fellow and when the police come in he dismisses them. The inference is that he will not prosecute the preserver of his baby, and the curtain falls on a very pretty picture. The piece made a decided hit at this trial performance and Mr. Hilliard made a neat little speech, expressing his thanks at its very cordial reception. The play is decidedly more effective for the average audience than The Littlest Girl and is a welcome addition to Mr. Hilliard's repertoire.

SOURCE: *New York Dramatic Mirror*, April 4, 1903, p. 18.

The Ex-Convict focuses on two central institutions whose structures and values concerned Porter throughout his career — family and society. In his many family-centered dramas, parents are constantly threatened with the loss of a child through sickness, fire, or some bizarre act of nature. Again and again they are driven to despair and either through some bold act (the fireman's daring rescue in *Life of an American Fireman* or the father's battle with a bird in *Rescued from an Eagle's Nest*) or simply good fortune, the child is saved and the family reunited. As mentioned in chapter 2, child-centered dramas were not rare in turn-of-the-century America, but Porter's own films reveal an emotional urgency and personal preoccupation that reflected his own loss of progeny. Although the family was often romanticized in American culture of this period, Porter's systematic idealizations reveal a longing for a way of life he found increasingly unattainable. The loss of the child is his own loss.

The Ex-Convict places family and society in conflict, but family values are given primacy. The love and intimacy within the ex-convict's and wealthy attorney's families are contrasted to the impersonality, selfishness, and class antagonism of the social system. The ex-convict is forced to break the law in an attempt to save his daughter's life because society, controlled by the rich, fails to protect its more vulnerable members. The ex-convict's desperate decision to steal is viewed sympathetically, if not actually condoned. When the ex-convict is finally caught, it appears that his family will be destroyed and his child allowed to die once he goes to jail. Family ties become a mechanism for reconciling class differences. If the rich man can forgive the would-be burglar because the ex-convict's daring rescue saved his daughter's life, he can empathize with the poor man's plight because the attempted burglary was motivated by his own child's sickness. In *Uncle Tom's Cabin*, the death of Eva precipitates the destruction of the family, and the selling of Uncle Tom foreshadows America's internal strife, culminating in the Civil War. *The Ex-Convict* presents a parallel situation, in which class rather than racial antagonisms are on the verge of spinning out of control. Here, both children (childhood representing innocence and hope for the future) are saved by the good works of the opposing classes and a last-minute reconciliation becomes possible.

In the United States, where Social Darwinism was widespread, Progressives argued that the working class was being forced into a state of destitution and "the great middle class" into one of dependency and genteel poverty. In expressing a longing for a world with greater social justice, for the reduction of class conflict and for a heightened consciousness of the well-to-do vis-à-vis the real grievances of the working class, *The Ex-Convict* articulated a central concern of the Progressive movement.[8] During the year Porter made this film, Robert Hunter, a journalist of Progressive persuasion, examined the plight of family men in situations similar to the ex-convict's. "The mass of working men on the brink of poverty hate charity," he wrote. "Not only their words convey a knowledge of this fact, but their actions, when in distress, make it absolutely undeniable. When the poor face the necessity of becoming paupers, when they must apply for charity if they are to live at all, many desert their family and enter the ranks of vagrancy; others drink themselves insensible; some go insane; and still others commit suicide."[9] As Porter's film points out, they might also turn to crime.

The state plays a key, if peripheral, role in *The Ex-Convict*. One of its representatives, a policeman, undermines the ex-convict's honest, modest, and happy way of life by informing his employer of his past. Another patrolman engages the rich child's nurse (whose nurturing role is the female counterpart of the policeman's) in conversation, causing (or failing to prevent) an accident that would have killed the child if the ex-convict had not intervened. In each instance, the policeman is not intentionally bad—he is merely warning the employer or flirting with the nurse. The consequences of their actions are nonetheless catastrophic, and in both cases it is the ex-convict who suffers. Porter suggests that the state must be more thoughtful and aware of its responsibilities. Its actions (or its failure to act) have consequences in modern society, which is faced with new technology (the automobile that almost runs over the child) and impersonal class relations (the warehouse owner who fires his employee, presumably because he has no personal relationship with him and cannot vouch for his character).

The Ex-Convict was not the first film to deal with class conflict and idealize a reconciliation of labor and capital. In Pathé's *The Strike*, produced in the summer of 1904, a walkout leads to violence and the deaths of a worker and the factory owner. Eventually the owner's son, who had sided with the workers, and the dead worker's wife, who killed the owner in a moment of rage, reconcile their differences. The film ends "in an apotheosis [where] Labor as a Workingman and Capital as a Rich Man, unite their power to give happiness and fortune to every man. Justice appears and ratifies this alliance."[10] It is quite possible that a viewing of this and similar European imports encouraged Porter to raise social concerns in his films. Despite many parallels between the Edison and Pathé films, Porter chose to situate the conflict between labor and capital not within the work place but within the home. He tended to foreground the social rather than the economic dimensions of the conflict.

The Kleptomaniac, which Porter photographed in the second half of January 1905, continued to explore the themes examined in *The Ex-Convict*. Condemning the class bias of government and justice, it is Porter's most radical film. The details given in the Edison catalog are not always evident when the film is viewed silently—for instance, there is no reason to suppose the kleptomaniac is a banker's wife (see document no. 17). Many of the specifics, however, could have been articulated in a showman's lecture. Reliance on the exhibitor's mediation is also suggested by Porter's camera framing and composition. As William Everson has observed, "the interior shot of the department store is so 'busy,' with so many identically dressed women bustling around in a protracted long shot, that the audience is given no guidance at all as to where to look or what is going on."[11] The exhibitor could relieve some of this confusion, perhaps basing his lecture on the catalog description. In this particular scene, a commentator might have reminded viewers that their frustrating efforts to detect the kleptomaniac were not unlike the task of the store detective (recalling the viewer identification with passengers in *The Great Train Robbery*).

DOCUMENT NO. 17

THE KLEPTOMANIAC
Two Acts—Ten Scenes and Tableau.

The Kleptomaniac (Mrs. Banker)	Miss. Aline Boyd
Store Detective	Mr. Phineas Nairs
Female Detective	Miss. Jane Stewart
Superintendent Department Store	Mr. George Voijere
The Thief	Miss. Ann Egleston
Police Court Judge	Mr. W. S. Rising
Justice	Miss. Helen Courtney

Shoppers, Salesladies, Cash Girls, Policemen, Prisoners

ACT I.

Scene I.—Leaving Home.

The opening scene shows a beautiful residence in a fashionable residential section of New York city. A handsome and richly gowned lady is descending the steps, while a stylish victoria, with coachman and footman in full livery, is waiting at the door. She enters the carriage, gives the footman his orders and drives off. All the surroundings indicate wealth and fashion. *Mrs. Banker* is going on a shopping tour.

Scene II.—Arrival at Department Store.

The next scene shows a well-known department store at Herald Square, New York city. A stylish turnout is coming down Broadway and stops in front of the main entrance. The footman jumps from the box and *Mrs. Banker* alights and enters the store.

Scene III.—Interior Department Store.

The interior of the department store is shown. Shoppers are busily engaged making purchases at the different counters. Cash girls are running about in all directions and a floor walker is busy giving orders and directing and attending to the wants of customers. Presently *Mrs. Banker* is seen approaching the hosiery counter. The saleslady waits on her and shows her the different styles, but none appear to suit her. While the saleslady's back is turned for a moment, *Mrs. Banker* quickly conceals a pair of hose in her muff and then passes on to the glove counter. In the meantime, her actions have excited the suspicion of a female detective, who now shadows her from counter to counter. At the glove counter she purchases some gloves and orders them sent home, and at a favorable moment adroitly slips a pair into her muff. The lynx-eyed female detective, however, has detected her in the act, informs the floor walkers, and then leaves to find the store detective, and both soon return to the scene. *Mrs. Banker* is now at the silverware counter, closely watched by the detective. To distract the clerk's attention she requests to be shown some article in a rear case, and while the clerk's back is turned she seizes the opportunity to take a silver flask from the counter and secrete it in her muff. As she turns to go the female detective steps up and accuses her of the theft, which she indignantly denies. The store detective now approaches and conducts *Mrs. Banker* away through a throng of curious shoppers, who have been attracted by the excitement and commotion.

Scene IV.—Superintendent's Office.

The scene shows the interior of the superintendent's office. He is occupied at his desk while the stenographer is transcribing on the typewriter. The female detective enters and explains the situation. Presently *Mrs. Banker* enters accompanied by the store detective. The female detective boldly accuses her of shoplifting. *Mrs. Banker*, in a most haughty manner, denies the charge, whereupon the female detective quickly snatches her muff and withdraws the stolen articles. *Mrs. Banker* then breaks down and confesses and pleads for mercy. The superintendent is deaf to her entreaties, and the store detective leads her away.

Scene V.—Under Arrest.

The scene now returns to the exterior of the store. The carriage is still waiting. *Mrs. Banker* and the detective enter the carriage and drive away.

Scene VI.—Police Station.

The exterior of the police station house is shown. A carriage drives up to the door, and the occupants alight and enter the building. We recognize *Mrs. Banker* and the store detective.

ACT II
Scene I.—The Home of Poverty.

A scantily furnished room. Poverty and hunger are plainly in evidence. A poor woman is seated at a table with her face buried in her hands. Her youngest child is seated on the floor crying with hunger. Presently a young girl enters. She is evidently the older daughter, who has been out begging in the streets but has returned empty-handed. In desperation the mother throws a shawl over her head and rushes from the room.

Scene II.—The Thief.

A street scene. An errand boy is coming out of a grocery store with a basket on his arm. The proprietor rushes out and sends him back to the store for some things he has forgotten. The boy leaves his basket at the door and goes back into the store. At this moment a poor woman comes along, takes a loaf of bread from the basket and hides it under her shawl. The proprietor, who has watched her, rushes out, seizes her and calls for the police. An officer soon appears and drags the woman off to the patrol wagon.

Scene III.—In the Police Patrol.

The scene shows the exterior of a police station house. A patrol wagon is being rapidly driven up the street and stops in front of the station house in the middle of the street. The snow is piled high up on both sides, making it impossible to drive up to the sidewalk. A poor woman is taken from the wagon by an officer and led into the station house.

Scene IV.—Police Court.

A court room seat. The judge enters and takes his seat. He raps for order and opens the court. Among the motley crowd of prisoners the judge discerns *Mrs. Banker*. He calls a court attendant and instructs him to give *Mrs. Banker* a chair away from the other prisoners. The clerk then proceeds to call the case.

The first prisoner before the bar is a tough. His blackened eye and battered condition tell their own story. He is quickly sentenced. Vagrancy and larceny cases follow and no time is lost in disposing of them. The next case is one of disorderly conduct. A flashily dressed woman appears and tries to flirt with the judge. She is quickly given an extra sentence "on the island" for her impertinence, and as she is led away by the officer she raises her foot and dress and waves ta-ta to the judge.

The next case is petty larceny. We recognize the poor woman in the two preceding scenes. The officer who arrested her, as well as the groceryman, appear against her. She pleads for mercy. Her little daughter rushes to her side and falls on her knees and pleads to the judge for her mother. But the judge is deaf to all entreaties, and the poor woman is sentenced and led away.

The next case is shoplifting. *Mrs. Banker* is led to the bar. Her husband, accompanied by a lawyer appears in her defense. The female detective gives her evidence, but the judge ignores her testimony and discharges the prisoner, who falls weeping into her husband's arms.

The Kleptomaniac. Mrs. Banker goes on a carefully planned shoplifting spree at Macy's; the desperate mother spontaneously steals bread for her children. The courtroom, where, as the final tableau suggests, justice favors the wealthy.

Tableau—Justice
A tableau of the figure of Justice. On one side of the scale is a bag of gold, and on the other a loaf of bread. The balance shows in favor of the gold. The bandage on the brow of Justice, however, discloses one eye. Fully described and illustrated in Circular No. 233. 670 ft.

Source: *Edison Films,* July 1906, pp. 55–56.

In *The Kleptomaniac* Porter juxtaposes the situations of two women.[12] The impoverished woman is shown at home, in the context of her family. Important details are shown that elicit the viewer's understanding and sympathy: the barren room, the absence of a husband/provider, and the weighty responsibility of children who need care and are still too young to work. Mrs. Banker is never shown inside her home, although the brownstone from which she emerges

An editorial cartoon on the front
page of the *New York World*.

clearly indicates her social status. Porter denies her the sympathetic context of
family life. She, as the title indicates, has no motivation for shoplifting other
than the thrill. Mrs. Banker goes *inside* a high-class emporium (Macy's) and
steals some expensive, nonessential baubles under the noses of sales personnel.
Her actions are clearly premeditated. The poor woman is overwhelmed by temp-
tation, stealing food left *outside* and unattended. Her actions are spontaneous.
Although she left home determined to help her family, her specific actions are
far from certain. Finally, once arrested, the wealthy kleptomaniac is treated
with a courtesy and leniency denied the more deserving mother.

The media during this era frequently criticized and visualized the inequities
of a judicial system that favored the rich and lacked understanding for the
circumstances of the poor. In June 1896 the *New York World* ran a front-page
political cartoon that anticipated Porter's closing tableau in *The Kleptomaniac*
in all its details.[13] Similar examples of this iconography were undoubtedly produced during the intervening nine years. Porter offered exhibitors the opportunity of extending this criticism still further by identifying the kleptomaniac with
the banks. The depiction of Mrs. Banker stealing in Macy's reflected indirectly
on her husband, suggesting that he stole as well, but on a grander scale and with
the same tacit support and "understanding" of the government. The banking
community, which played a key role in the emergence of monopoly capital and
the trusts, was frequently attacked by the Progressive movement, which held it
responsible for reducing members of the middle and working classes to impov-
erishment. Thus the poor woman steals to alleviate her family's destitution,
which Mr. Banker's accumulation of wealth had helped to create. On this level,

The "White Caps." Rural justice may be harsh, but it is the guilty who are punished.

the simple dualism of rich and poor approaches a more profound, more dialectical relationship between the two central figures.

In *The Ex-Convict* and *The Kleptomaniac*, the impoverished parents' crimes
are motivated by the needs of their children and are not condemned. Rather, a
socioeconomic system in which two essential social values—familial responsibility and honesty—are in conflict is itself in need of reevaluation. *The Kleptomaniac*, however, does not have the requisite happy ending evident in *The
Ex-Convict*. The personal interaction that makes this possible in the former film
is absent in the latter.

Edison's *The "White Caps"* (August 1905) looks at a troubled nuclear family
and the community's eventual intervention in its problems outside the established channels of justice. In 1905 White Cap vigilante groups were active in
rural areas of the border states and the Midwest. Members, generally faced with
declining income and political power, acted as agents of social control, punish-
ing offenses that the state and local governments failed to address adequately.
In this Porter/McCutcheon production, a husband comes home drunk and beats
his wife and daughter. To punish him, relatives and neighbors of the beaten
woman form a squad of white-hooded vigilantes. After a struggle, the drunkard
is tarred, feathered, and drummed out of town on a rail. The film offers a view

of small-town America in which a wayward member is taught a lesson without the formalities of a legal system.[14] The rural community acts as an extension of the family.

A pro-vigilante view of these events was offered in Edison advertisements:

> During the rapid march of civilization in America, covering the past fifty years, certain social conditions developed which had to be regulated and controlled by unusual methods. A lawless and criminal element almost invariably accompanied the advance guard of civilization and to keep this element in check the law abiding citizens were compelled to secretly organize themselves for their own protection.
>
> The "Vigilantes" during the gold excitement of '49 in California and the "White Caps" of more recent years in Ohio, Indiana, and other Western States, are well-known organizations which dealt summarily with outlaws and the criminal classes in general.
>
> We have portrayed in Motion Pictures, in a most vivid and realistic manner, the method employed by the "White Caps" to rid the community of undesirable citizens.[15]

The Progressive perception of corrupt justice in *The Kleptomaniac* could be easily perverted in a different setting, particularly in a rural one.

The "White Caps" had at least two theatrical antecedents. The first was Owen Davis's play *The White Caps*, which appeared in various cities a few months before the Porter film was made.[16] Despite the similarity in name, however, their narratives had little in common. Rather the tone and narrative of the Porter film owed more to Thomas Dixon, Jr.'s adaptation of *The Clansman*, which the playwright was rehearsing—amidst considerable publicity—as *The "White Caps"* went into production.[17] In *The Clansman*, villainous blacks are sponsored by corrupt carpetbaggers, while the Klan is presented as a force for regeneration. If the Edison film avoids the overt racism of Dixon's novel, it depicts and even accepts a pattern of alternative justice that supports it.

The methods used to influence spectators in *The "White Caps"* can be compared to Griffith's approach in *The Birth of a Nation*, which was based on *The Clansman*. Porter assumed that the viewers' moral outrage at the husband's behavior would lead them to condemn the drunkard and condone his punishment. (In fact, the brutal treatment of the husband usually leads present-day audiences to recoil from his fate.) Griffith, anxious to convert people to his beliefs in white supremacy, did not assume shared attitudes and effectively used parallel editing to force his audience into identifying with the Klan. The Edison film maintains a psychological distance from its subject matter, not because Porter attempted to be objective but because he relied on the audiences' pre-established attitudes to elicit their reactions.

Family was also a subject that Porter addressed in his comedies. *The Strenuous Life; or, Anti-Race Suicide* (December 1904), lightheartedly spoofs family life and fatherhood. President Roosevelt, who had just won reelection, believed Americans had to lead "the strenuous life" (it was the title of one of his books)

The Seven Ages: William Shakespeare via *The May Irwin Kiss*.

if the United States was to retain its position of world leadership. He also declared that married women of northern European stock had a responsibility to produce at least four children to prevent "race suicide."[18] Porter combined and burlesqued these two elements: the father returns home as his wife gives birth and soon finds himself caring for quadruplets. The father's expression of pride as he weighs the first baby motivated Porter to cut in to a close shot of his face. (By late 1904, the interpolated close-up of a character's face had been used in well-known films like Biograph's *The Lost Child* and G. A. Smith's *Mary Jane's Mishaps. The Strenuous Life* signaled its entry into Porter's repertoire of cinematic strategies.) The father's expression quickly changes to distress as one infant after another is brought in by the nurse. Roosevelt's stock phrases are lampooned in a manner that recalls *Terrible Teddy, the Grizzly King* (1901).

The centrality of family can also be seen in Porter's treatment of romance and sexuality. In *The Seven Ages* (February 1905), Porter photographed a series of short vignettes reminiscent of kiss films such as *The May Irwin Kiss* (1896). These were structured on the premise provided by Shakespeare's "seven ages of man"—a theme often illustrated in nineteenth-century lantern shows. Beginning with toddlers and concluding with old people, the film shows couples kissing. Each of the first seven scenes contains two shots. These scenes open with an establishing shot and conclude with a medium close-up that gives a better view of each kiss. A final tableau for the eighth scene shows an old maid alone, introduced with the title "What Age?" To emphasize her solitude, Porter broke with the structure of earlier scenes and refrained from cutting in. The repetition and diversity of age groups undermines the kiss's exclusively sexual dimension. For Porter, sexuality is expressed within the context of the recurring life-cycle made possible by the family. Without a person to kiss and the family structure Porter associated with it, a woman becomes sexless, ageless, and eccentric while a man (like Jack in *Jack the Kisser*, which Porter made in September 1907) becomes unstable.

The Country and the City

The rural America of The *"White Caps"* contrasts sharply with the impersonal city of *The Ex-Convict, The Kleptomaniac,* and *Life of an American Policeman.* These urban dramas focus on the breakdown of community relations and their replacement by an unfeeling and often corrupt class structure. *The Miller's Daughter* (September–October 1905) contrasts this sinful, decadent city to the simple, honest country in a fascinating reworking of Steele MacKaye's melodrama *Hazel Kirke.* MacKaye's play was first performed at the Madison Square Theater on February 4, 1880, and ran for 486 performances. It pioneered theatrical realism by dispensing with mustachioed villains[19] and subsequently became a standard number in the melodrama repertoire of traveling theatrical troupes.[20]

Hazel Kirke is set in the British Isles, where Hazel, the daughter of miller Dunstan Kirke, is expected to marry Aaron Rodney, a member of the local gentry, who has rescued Kirke's mill from insolvency. But she falls in love with Arthur Carringford, whom Dunstan Kirke has saved from drowning and Hazel has nurtured back to health. He is young, while Rodney is old. The passion of youth triumphs, and Hazel and Carringford elope. Dunstan Kirke banishes her from his home despite Rodney's intervention on Hazel's behalf. Carringford, we now learn, is also a member of the nobility and is defying his mother's wish that he marry a woman of his own class. Lest he break his ill mother's heart and kill her, Carringford and Hazel keep their marriage a secret and live on a small country estate. In time the couple are separated by the machinations of Arthur's mother, who knows her son faces destitution if he does not marry the woman she has selected. Hazel learns of her husband's predicament, returns home, is again rejected by her father, and tries to commit suicide by jumping into the rushing waters below the mill. The blind father, unable to rescue her, realizes what he has caused and raves incoherently. Then Hazel appears with the now penniless Arthur Carringford, who has, it turns out, jumped into the millrace and rescued her from death. Given another chance, Dunstan Kirke forgives, and a family reconciliation occurs.

Porter's extraordinary adaptation begins by juxtaposing Hazel with each of the two suitors, whose social positions, age, and character have been transformed. The discrepancy of age has disappeared. Instead, Arthur Carringford is a suave, citified, well-to-do artist, while his rival Aaron Rodney is a plain, dependable young farmer. Although Hazel prefers Carringford's surface attractiveness and sophistication, her father, the old miller, intuits his perfidy. When Hazel elopes with Carringford, the artist's villainous intentions are revealed: his real wife appears and stops the wedding by producing proof of their marriage. Hazel's refusal to abide by her father's wishes, her violation of family unity, has caused her disgrace: she is exiled to the distant, anonymous city. Like Eve, Hazel has offended a wrathful father and is banished from the bountiful countryside (later in the film a vision of her father looms on the church wall to make this

The Miller's Daughter. The miller disowns his daughter, but finally forgives her when she presents him with a grandchild.

religious connection explicit). Living in city slums, "Hazel now realizes the full meaning of her disgrace" as she suffers the meager existence of the working poor. Exposed to the realities of class society, she is left destitute after her sole source of livelihood, a sewing machine, is repossessed. In despair, she returns to her father, pleading for forgiveness, which is again refused. It is Rodney, her once spurned but honest suitor, who rescues her from attempted suicide in the millrace. Through his act of courage, they are united and create their own family. The old miller's earlier judgment of Rodney has been confirmed and his wishes finally recognized, paving the way to a reconciliation with his daughter. The family, once fragmented, is reunited and linked to the next generation with the birth of a child. God, family, and country triumph over city, class society, and duplicity.

This film adaptation is unusual in many respects. For instance, there is a brief mention in MacKaye's *Hazel Kirke* that Carringford is going to give Hazel a drawing lesson, providing a cue for the reconceived character. In Porter's film the father-miller becomes the moral center of the film, whereas it is Hazel who best understands her own interests in the play. In *Hazel Kirke* it is Dunstan who misjudges Carringford and refuses to acknowledge his daughter's love and happiness until it is almost too late. In Porter's adaptation, Hazel is fooled by Carringford. She must learn the role of dutiful daughter, wife, and mother. The father assumes a godlike role. The change in title from the woman's name to her designated relationship to her father corresponds to this essential repositioning. It also suggests the extent to which the film industry at this time continued to be a male-privileging institution in comparison to the theater.

This screen adaptation shares many parallels with Porter's adaptation of *The Ex-Convict.* The mechanism for family reconciliation—the child—is a Porteresque touch. Porter also reverts to melodramatic, good-versus-evil stereotypes, but increases the realism by making the characters ordinary people, filming on location and avoiding the pastoralism of MacKaye's play. Many offstage occurrences are shown in the Porter film, including Hazel's suicidal jump and her rescue. Class differences are banished from rural life (Rodney is just an average farmer) and located in the city. The portrayed conflict between small-town America and large-scale capitalism articulated the beliefs and fears of many native-born Americans. It reflected not only Porter's early experiences but the major demographic shifts of the 1880s and 1890s that had pushed Americans, including Porter and Griffith, out of small towns and into the metropolitan centers. The poverty of the urban slums, the conspicuous consumption of the wealthy, the antagonisms between classes, and the apparent corruption of local government deeply distressed city dwellers who recalled a romanticized and untroubled small-town childhood. Correspondingly, those still living in rural areas feared for a future shaped by distant, urban forces.

The opposition between rural and urban America provided the framework for a modest chase comedy, *Down on the Farm*, which Porter shot in October 1905, immediately after the completion of *The Miller's Daughter*. A group of boarding school girls, daughters of wealthy urbanites, steal apples from a farmer. The farmer chases them across fields and over fences (in a reversal of the women chasing the French nobleman in Biograph's *Personal*) until they turn on the exhausted rube, throw him into the lake, and pelt him with apples. The country is clearly at the mercy of the city.

Edison films consistently highlight the city-country opposition. The rube or Uncle Josh character who comes to the city and is puzzled and overwhelmed by urban life is a theme Porter absorbed from the self-confidently urban culture of newspapers and vaudeville. From *Another Job for the Undertaker* (1901) to *Down on the Farm* and *Stage Struck* (July–August 1907), his comedies lampoon the country as unsophisticated and old-fashioned, whereas the dramas, derived from a romantic-realist tradition, usually idealize the countryside and criticize city life. *The Ex-Convict* and *The Kleptomaniac* focus on impersonal social and legal injustices of the city, while *The "White Caps"* shows a much more intimate community, where transgressions are punished quickly, surely, and pointedly. The conflicting views of city and country in Porter's dramas and comedies, which would be given more elaborate expression in the films of Griffith (*The Country Doctor*, 1909) and Mack Sennett (*Tillie's Punctured Romance*, 1914), reflect the transformations and conflicts in American life, particularly in a middle class torn between the traditional values and certainties of an increasingly outmoded way of life and the sophistication, convenience, and higher living standards of economically advanced urban centers. It was the middle class whose members contributed most extensively to American cultural life and articulated this conflict in particularly intense form.

The police, as representatives of the state, are a presence in many of Porter's films. The state and the family work hand in hand when constituted society is confronted by outsiders. But when Porter looks at the difficulties of urban life,

Life of an American Policeman: helping a child lost in the large, impersonal city (a scene appearing in both versions) and chasing a speeding, wealthy motorist who has almost run over a child (in neither version but available for separate purchase).

the police and the state often assume more complex roles. Porter's *Life of an American Policeman* is a sympathetic portrait of the agents of the law. Photographed with the cooperation of the New York Police Department in the fall of 1905, the subject was first shown at two vaudeville benefits for the Police Relief Fund in early December.[21]

Porter focuses on the daily routine of policemen without reference to their superiors, the higher courts, or the larger system of justice of which they are but a part. The emphasis is on good deeds and the ways in which the police benefit the community in which they live. The opening scene, which presents a policeman at home with his wife and child, identifies the police with the institution of the family. The policeman's role in maintaining community values in the impersonal city is shown when policemen help a lost child and rescue a would-be suicide from the river. Their courage is demonstrated as one policeman controls a runaway horse and others risk their lives capturing a desperate burglar. The latter scene, also sold separately as *Desperate Encounter Between Burglar and Police*, reenacts a robbery and the killing of a policeman as he tries to make the arrest. The actual incident took place on Manhattan's Upper East Side on the morning of March 20, 1904. News reports reveal significant discrepancies between the film sequence and what probably occurred,[22] suggesting that the film exaggerates the heroic actions of the police and the cowardice of the burglar.

In the film's last scene, a cop takes an unscheduled rest period, then skillfully circumvents the roundsman—emphasizing the policeman's humanity by showing his petty foibles in the context of real courage.[23] The film, a portrait of common people, avoids grandiose heroics that would reduce it to simple propaganda. Of all Porter's films, *Life of an American Policeman* comes closest to fulfilling the demands of nineteenth-century realism.[24] The focus on common people, the portrayal of real situations (even to the point of returning to the original location and using actual participants to recreate the event), the refusal to subject the film to a single narrative, and the inclusion of the home life all make this a remarkable film.

From an editorial standpoint, the tension between the individual shot, the various sequences, and different possible programs is particularly striking in the case of *Life of an American Policeman*, with its 1,000-foot, full-reel length. Yet Porter in fact had 1,500 feet of usable subject matter, composed of nine discrete sequences. To solve this problem Porter (or the Edison Company) made two different 1,000-foot versions—one with "Desperate Encounter Between Burglar and Police" and the other with "River Tragedy," a sequence in which the police rescue a woman who has jumped into the Hudson. *Bicycle Police Chasing Auto* was in neither version but only sold separately. In addition several of the sequences appearing in the features were offered for sale as individual shorts. The subject reveals a conflict between one single order (the "preferred" version that included "River Tragedy") and possible alternative orderings, either the producer's alternate version or others that renters or exhibitors could create themselves. Thus *Life of an American Policeman* is an open or reversible text. Even within sequences like "Desperate Encounter between Burglar and Police," shots were conceived as discrete units linked together by overlapping action and temporality. Although Porter had largely, though not exclusively, assumed the role of editor, he continued to work under the strong influence of exhibitor-dominated cinema. The product lacked standardization. Porter's freedom to work in this way would, however, rapidly be curtailed by the demands of the nickelodeon era that was just beginning. The 1,000-foot restriction on a picture's length was already an industry standard, creating problems that Porter would seek to avoid in the future. On one hand, *Life of an American Policeman* can be considered Porter's last film of the pre-nickelodeon era; on the other, it already reflected the transition to this new exhibition form.

The Ex-Convict, The Kleptomaniac, Life of an American Policeman, The Miller's Daughter, and *The "White Caps"* offer an elaborate view of American life that acknowledges important social issues yet yearns for the simple solutions that once seemed so effective in the small-town environment out of which Porter had originally come. The films express the same middle-class concerns that the Progressive movement spoke to on a political level. The middle class was itself in transition: the old middle class that was outside the labor-capital dialectic was rapidly giving way to a new middle class that was part of this dialectic, shading into the working class at one end and the large capital-owning class at the other. Given the heterogeneity of the American middle classes, the political movement that they produced was predictably far from unified in its programs and in its alliances with other social groups. Porter's films best articulate the views of the older, more rural middle class—the petite bourgeoisie whose members were neither employers nor employees. The political radicalism of specific films, when viewed in a larger context, had an underlying conservative basis. They articulated an angry response to a loss of power as government and the socioeconomic system became less responsive to this group's expectations and needs. Vigilantism of a certain sort became emotionally, if not intellectually, attractive.

Porter's subject matter and treatment differed substantially from the films being made by other American production companies. Biograph leaned toward comparatively sophisticated sexual comedies, such as *Personal*. Love triangles with clear references to infidelity, often involving a pretty "typewriter," were common in headliners like *The Story the Biograph Told*. Porter rarely dealt with sexuality in this way, and then only when imitating previous successes. Biograph subjects consistently offered entertainment rather than moralism. Its films celebrated the urban culture on which they were based—lampooning the city man who moves to the suburbs in *The Suburbanite* (October 1904) or summers in the rural countryside in *The Summer Boarders* (July 1905). Biograph dramas, moreover, commonly saw the country as a source of poverty and violence (*A Kentucky Feud*, 1905).

J. Stuart Blackton and Albert E. Smith, the two English-born producers of the Vitagraph trio, were also anxious to portray the excitement and dynamism of the city, to valorize the speed and mobility of the automobile. In Vitagraph's *The 100 to One Shot; or, A Run of Luck* (1906), a young man goes to the city, where he stumbles onto a hot tip at a race track and wins the money needed to save his family home from foreclosure. In a Porter film, gambling would never provide the means to salvation; but for Blackton and Smith, urban culture, even its more sinful manifestations, was a fount of opportunity and good fortune. Even Vitagraph's *A Midwinter Night's Dream* (1906), about a waif who dreams he is taken into the home of a wealthy family, owes much more to a sentimentalism derived from Charles Dickens than to contemporary American concerns.

The German-Jewish immigrant Sigmund Lubin was content to entertain moving picture audiences with comedies based on his competitors' successes (*A Dog Lost, Strayed or Stolen*; *I. B. Dam and the Whole Dam Family*; *Meet Me at the Fountain*), fight reproductions, and films of crime (*Highway Robbery*, *The Counterfeiters*). William C. Paley and William Steiner with *Avenging a Crime; or, Burned at the Stake* as well as William Selig with *Tracked by Bloodhounds* also featured violent confrontations. Many Selig films, however, used Colorado as a background for their dramas, increasingly romanticizing the frontier rather than the city. Porter's films aside, the exploration of social issues on the screen was primarily a European phenomenon, with Pathé's *The Strike* (*La Grève*, 1904), *Scenes of a Convict's Life* (*Au Bagne*, 1905), *Le Cuirassé Potemkine* (1905), and *Mining District* (*Au Pays Noir*, 1905) providing a few surviving examples. Porter was the only filmmaker directly to confront American social concerns during this period.

Society and Its Outcasts

Not all Porter/Edison films from this period explored conflicts within the social structure. The staples of the industry in the pre-Griffith period, as today, concentrated on dramatic conflict between constituted society and those living on its fringes or completely outside it. The tramp, a frequent subject of Edison comedies, was one of society's outcasts. While Porter was growing up, tramps were customarily seen as a dangerous menace. As a result of an attempt to control their pilfering, many ended up in the Connellsville town jail.[25] Almost twenty years later, the tramp and his relationship to society were often viewed in more romantic terms.

> The nearer these refugees from modern society can approach the habits of their primeval ancestors the greater appears to be their satisfaction. Many of them boast not only that they no longer need to work, but that they can live without begging. They tell you they are perfectly independent of the laws which govern the rest of the world.
> ... Is stealing to the man or boy who has abandoned human society for that of nature a crime? Stealing is the first law of nature by which all animals not subdued by man and all plant life obtain subsistence.[26]

This perception of the tramp's predicament begins to explain his status as the single most popular figure in turn-of-the-century culture. In "Happy Hooligan," "Burglar Bill," "Weary Willie," and dozens of other comic strips, plays, and short films, the tramp is generally portrayed as an annoying, but relatively harmless, scavenger, whose petty thievings and inevitable punishment provide numerous situations for comedy. The ritual beatings he receives at the hands of the law or outraged citizenry humorously define proper society's boundaries in terms of the outcast. They conform to Henri Bergson's assertion that the comic lies in an individual's inability to adapt to society, and that comedy functions as a kind of social ragging.

The Burglar's Slide for Life (March 1905) elaborates on Porter's earlier *Pie, Tramp and the Bulldog* (1901) as the bulldog protects the home. He is man's (*socialized* man's) best friend. The tramp burglar, looking for a free lunch, prowls an apartment building. He hides in a vapor bath when the mistress of the house enters the room. Porter's familiar overlapping action is used as the tramp is discovered, flees through a window, and is chased down the clothesline by the family dog (Mannie). In his desperate effort to escape, the fleeing burglar thus mimes a then popular daredevil stunt ("the slide for life"). Reaching the courtyard, he is beaten by other apartment dwellers and bitten by the dog.

The tramp avoids his ritual beating in *Poor Algy!* (September 1905) by

Poor Algy has in error received the tramp's customary punishment.

switching clothes with the young lover, Algy. When Algy, dressed as a tramp, tries to approach his girl, she fails to recognize him and retreats. Algy chases after her. The girl soon passes a pugilist doing roadwork for an upcoming fight. He administers the tramp's traditional beating—to poor Algy. Once again Porter played with a well-established genre and its codified relationships between characters: minimal variations gave the piece a freshness not always apparent to present-day viewers.

"*Raffles*"—*the Dog* (June 1905) was another Edison comedy involving a thief. The original *Raffles* started out as a series of short stories by E. W. Hornung about a gentleman safecracker of elderly years who wins readers' amused tolerance more than their condemnation.[27] By June 1905 *Raffles* had been made into a play and a comic strip. In "*Raffles*"—*the Dog*, "Raffles," once again played by Mannie, is a charming, innocent thief directed by conniving masters. After the thieves rob several upright citizens, a chase ensues that concludes with their capture. The dog's asocial behavior is like that of other petty thieves in Edison comedies: the tramps in *Poor Algy!* and *The Burglar's Slide for Life*, the juvenile delinquents in *The Terrible Kids* (1906), and the shiftless "darkies" of *The Watermelon Patch* (1905).

Porter, like other filmmakers of the pre-1908 period, often portrayed outlaws who threaten society as members of fringe or outcast groups, with such characterization serving as motivation for their illegal activities. This is the case with the racial humor and black stereotyping in Porter and McCutcheon's *The Watermelon Patch* (October 1905). Their happy-go-lucky thieves, who "seem to think eating watermelon is the only pleasure in the world"[28] are comedic counterparts to the ruthless, scheming lovers of white women in *The Clansman*. *The Watermelon Patch* begins as an absurdist comedy: a number of "darkies" steal watermelons and flee, pursued by redneck farmers dressed in skeleton costumes. Losing their pursuers, the darkies reach their destination, where they dance and

The Watermelon Patch. Inside and outside: spatial distortions reduce fun-loving "darkies" to pygmies.

enjoy their watermelon until the rednecks arrive. When the whites board up the exits and seal the chimney, the darkies are soon covered with soot, another racial "joke." (In 1905 many Negro performers still went on stage in black face—as did white actors impersonating blacks. This joke played with the "childish" belief that black skin is black because it is covered with soot.)

In the film's last three shots, Porter alternated exterior and interior scenes using an editorial construction similar to the ending of *Life of an American Fireman.* After showing the rednecks sealing the chimney, Porter cut to the interior, where the "darkies" hear the intruders, grow quiet, and slowly feel the ill-effects of the smoke. Realizing what is happening, they make their escape. The final shot, once again of the exterior, returns to the moment when the darkies begin to make their escape. It shows them coming out of the house and receiving the blows of the amused rednecks. What is fascinating, both cinematically and perhaps as an example of unconscious racism, is the contrast between the exterior scenes in which the handful of rednecks dwarf the tiny shack and the interior scenes in which the shack comfortably holds twenty "darkies"—reducing them to the size of pygmies.

The Watermelon Patch is as revealing of the state of American cinema in 1905 as it is of American racism. Earlier Edison films depicting African Americans include *Chicken Thieves* (1897), in which "darkies" raid a chicken coop; *Watermelon Eating Contest* (1896), a one-shot facial expression film of happy blacks eating watermelon; and *The Pickaninnies* (1894), showing three Negro youths doing a jig and breakdown. These often-used motifs are integrated into Porter's later film. The dancing and watermelon contest are treated as self-contained scenes, which interrupt the *Watermelon Patch* narrative. The isolated images of blacks presented in these earlier films are unified and elaborated.

They are superstitious, petty thieves, good dancers, and love watermelon. They like to have a good time, but their inherent laziness must be subsidized by pilfering.[29]

The Watermelon Patch owes much to Biograph's *The Chicken Thief* (1904), in which darkies steal chickens and bring them home for a party of eating and dancing. On their next outing, the two thieves are chased and caught by angry rednecks.[30] The many parallels between the two films are partially explained by McCutcheon's involvement in both projects. Sigmund Lubin's somewhat later *Fun on the Farm* (November 1905) makes the lighthearted tone of these two films even more explicit: tarring and feathering the local pumpkin(!) thief is shown to be one of the many amusing ways to pass the time down on the farm. In all these films, whites chasing blacks is shown to be good, clean fun. African Americans are portrayed as childlike and unsocialized. Whites, as responsible members of society, are obliged to chastise them and maintain discipline.

Although many early films (comedies as well as dramas) used made-up whites to play the roles of blacks, the Edison Company assured prospective buyers of *The Watermelon Patch* that "all the watermelon thieves are genuine negroes."[31] Not surprisingly, this and most other motion pictures did not make a "sure hit" in the black communities. As storefront theaters began to appear across the country in late 1905 and 1906, those intended for black audiences were among the few to fail. According to one amusement manager, "When a negro goes to a show, it pleases him most to see black faces in the performance. But no pictures are made with Senegambian [*sic*] faces."[32] The few films that did use black performers must have alienated these audiences even more.

While those outside proper society are undersocialized in Edison comedies; outsiders in Edison dramas are antisocial. They threaten society's very fabric, often by directing their attacks against the family. In *Stolen by Gypsies* (July 1905), gypsies abduct a well-to-do family's child, who has been left momentarily unattended by a nursemaid. This film belongs to a popular kidnapping genre that emerged in 1904. Porter's first effort was the three-shot *Weary Willie Kidnaps a Child* (May 1904), but the genre was made popular by such English imports as *The Child Stealers* (1904).[33] Illustrious examples of this family-centered genre eventually included Cecil Hepworth's *Rescued by Rover* (1905) and D. W. Griffith's directorial debut, *The Adventures of Dollie* (1908). All have remarkably similar narratives. A gypsy or some other outcast steals and then abuses the young child of a respectable, upper-middle-class family. The parents experience a range of emotions—anguish, guilt, remorse—over their loss. As in *Stolen by Gypsies*, the situation is usually more poignant because the victim is an only child. In the inevitable happy ending, the child is rescued and the nuclear family restored.

By October 1904 the genre was well enough established for Biograph to turn

In *Stolen By Gypsies*, parents mourn the loss of their only child, whose portrait dominates their home.

it inside out and make a comedy, *The Lost Child*. When the child disappears into a dog house, the mother assumes the worst and chases an innocent passerby, whom she believes to be the kidnapper. Societal paranoia and the family-centered drama are spoofed, although the irony is softened because the generic form defines it as an amusing exception. For the first half of *Stolen by Gypsies*, Porter and co-director Wallace McCutcheon, who had been partially responsible for *The Lost Child*, took the popular Biograph success and gave it another twist. As before, the wrong people are chased. They are no longer innocent pedestrians, however, but chicken thieves. Moreover, the child is actually stolen. Although sometimes humorous, the first part emphasizes the vulnerability of the family to assault. The second returns to the conventional formula: the child is found and reclaimed by the parents, reuniting the family, while the police perform the subsidiary function of backing up their action with force.

Porter considered *Stolen by Gypsies* an important film and sent the following note to West Orange with the undeveloped negative:

The Train Wreckers. The outlaws capture the switchman's daughter; later her lover, the engineer, kills her tormentors.

July 6th

Dear Sir:

Am sending you today undeveloped negative complete with announcements of "Stolen by Gypsies". Have made tests of same and found them photographically perfect. In as much as this has been a quite expensive production kindly see that every care is taken with them. Have instructed Mr. Bonine to develop them in "Pyro."

Very truly yours,
E. S. Porter

P.S. Please return negative to me after they are developed and I will trim same and forward to you immediately.[34]

Stolen by Gypsies, shown with Edwin Arden's play *Zorah* at Proctor's 5th Avenue Theater, was lauded by the *New York Sun*. The review was promptly reprinted in an Edison ad:

Yesterday between the second and third acts there was a wait of over half an hour, during which the audience was treated to an intensely interesting motion picture drama, entitled "Stolen by Gypsies." There was so much human interest in this little story and its climaxes came so thick and fast, as it followed the child from the moment that it was stolen up to the hour of its rescue a year later in the gypsies' camp that it made "Zorah" by comparison seem rather stilted and stagy.[35]

Despite the praise, the feature sold a modest 59 prints over the next year and a half (compared to the more than 300 copies sold of Hepworth's *Rescued by Rover*, which was released in the United States at about the same time).

The Train Wreckers (November 1905) includes Porter's most violent expression of the conflict between constituted society and its outsiders. The outlaw band, with its apparently irrational desire to destroy all social order, is finally eliminated by a combined force of railroad personnel and select passengers.

From the Lumières' *Train Entering a Station* (1895) to Ilya Trauberg's *China Express* (1929), the train is one of the central iconographic figures in silent cinema, and Porter, perhaps more than anyone, made it so. Trauberg's train is divided into first, second, and third class compartments, with the principal conflict between the workers in third class and the imperialists and their Chinese associates in first. Porter's train has no such differentiation. Although the film's principal characters are skilled members of the working class, the conflict is not between classes or different social groups, but against an external threat, a cause around which society can rally all its members. With order finally restored, a romance between the engineer and the switchman's daughter, introduced at the beginning of the film, resumes. Society is able to return to its proper preoccupations.

The Train Wreckers effectively demonstrates the need for social cohesion in a way that could serve as a prototype for future good-guy-versus-bad-guy conflicts. It was extremely successful, selling 157 prints during 1905–6, and its narrative would be reworked six years later in one of D. W. Griffith's most successful Biograph films, *The Girl and Her Trust* (released March 28, 1912). Films like *The Train Wreckers* and *Stolen by Gypsies* see the social order as continually threatened from without. In articulating this conflict, Porter used the chase as a central narrative strategy: the bulldog chases the tramp down the clotheslines; the rednecks pursue the watermelon thieves; the railroad passengers overtake the train wreckers; and constituted society defeats its enemies. In films where Porter examined the inner workings of society, this is much less likely to be the case.

The Edison Comedies

Although Porter took serious looks at American society, comedies were the mainstay of Edison production. Generally they worked within well-defined genres, like *Poor Algy!* and *The Burglar's Slide for Life,* or adapted narratives from fads and hit songs that had wide audience recognition. Many completely avoided any reference to societal concerns. Porter made one technical breakthrough that elevated several of his comedies from this period to the status of "novelties": it was a special form of object animation. As Porter applied the technique, a hodgepodge of letters moved against their black backgrounds until they formed the intertitles for the succeeding scene.[36] This was done for *How Jones Lost His Roll* (March 1905), *The Whole Dam Family and the Dam Dog* (May 1905), *Coney Island at Night* (June 1905), and *Everybody Works but Father* (November 1905).

When Edison's advertising manager, L. C. McChesney, sent out copy for *How Jones Lost His Roll,* he did not find it necessary to mention the film's narrative.

The Whole Dam Family

Postcard art was the source for *The Whole Dam Family and the Dam Dog*.

This film has already created a decided sensation in numerous Vaudeville Theatres, Moving Picture Entertainments, and among Exhibitors both in this country and abroad. There is not a dull or uninteresting moment throughout the entire picture while at several points the audience breaks into rounds of applause and laughter. From beginning to end the audience is kept in one continual state of expectancy. The illustrations which are reproduced from the film itself show "HOW JONES LOST HIS ROLL," while the letters after much effort and manoeuvering disentangle themselves at intervals and tell the story in words. . . . Everyone wants to know how it is done.[37]

The story, about Jones who is systematically cheated of his money by a so-called friend, is told twice, in words and pictures, with the "jumble announcements" making the intertitles more important than the pictures they illuminate, inverting the normal relationship between image and title.

The humorous subversion of conventional narrative strategies was also an important aspect of *The Whole Dam Family and the Dam Dog*. Many films of this period (Biograph's *The Firebug*, Vitagraph's *The Servant Girl Problem*, and Edison's *How a French Nobleman Got a Wife . . .*) are introduced by a close-up of the main character(s) "so that his make-up, costume . . . , facial expression and bearing may be appreciated by the audience."[38] Sometimes, as with Biograph's *The Widow and the Only Man*, name cards at the bottom of the frame identify the individual. In *The Whole Dam Family and the Dam Dog*, each family member is introduced with a close-up and a name card—"Mr. I. B. Dam," "Miss U. B. Dam," and so on—at the bottom of the frame. These are followed by an abbreviated one-scene narrative as the Dam dog (Mannie) interrupts a family meal by pulling the tablecloth and all the dishes onto the floor. As Tom Gunning points out, the normal relationship between the introduction of characters and the development of narrative is reversed. Not only wordplay but playing with the audience's expectations of cinematic form contributed to the comedy's humor.

Edison advertising announced that *The Whole Dam Family and the Dam Dog* continued "a popular fad which has been widely advertised by lithographs and souvenir mailing cards and has recently been made the subject of a sketch in a New York Vaudeville Theatre."[39] Production records indicate that this film

The Whole Dam Family and the Dam Dog: a family portrait.

was shot in late May 1905, a month before the theatrical production had its debut at the Aerial Gardens in New York.[40] The Edison film was not indebted to the theatrical production for its conception; publicity merely referred to it as a general indication of the subject's timeliness and popularity. Rather it took the postcard caricatures and realized them in a series of facial expression "films." A group portrait follows, formally reprising the family panorama on the postcard. The dog's initial appearance in the final, narrative segment remains consistent with a left-to-right reading of the postcard as well as its place outside the enveloping dark background. If the subject was familiar, the company claimed to have used its "usual up-to-date methods" to illustrate "this popular subject in a most novel and original way." Narratization that gave new and special meaning to the designation of the family pet as "the Dam dog," the Edison dog itself, animated titles, and close-ups: all brought original elements to a popular fad, enabling Edison to sell 136 copies of the film during 1905–6. On the eve of the nickelodeon era, this combination of novelty and familiarity was the formula for commercial success.

Everybody Works but Father (November 1905) "opens with a laughable 'Jumble' Announcement—a new feature, exclusively Edison, mysterious and novel to a degree."[41] Its narrative was based on a song of the same title popularized by Lew Dockstader. Biograph had already made a similar film a month earlier, but without the animated intertitles. The Biograph film was advertised as "a decided novelty for Illustrated Song Singers," and a surviving program urged the audience to join in the chorus, a strategy of exhibition not suggested in Edison promotional material.[42] Another Edison animated title from this period survives in the George Kleine Collection at the Library of Congress. This fragment reads "23 Skidoo," but has no accompanying picture. In any case, the Edison Company must have felt that the novelty of animated titles had been exhausted. Perhaps because *Everybody Works but Father* sold only forty-seven copies in the fifteen months after its release, the procedure was abandoned. J. Stuart Blackton, in contrast, soon applied the technique to new situations when he animated his sketches in *Humorous Phases of Funny Faces* (April 1906) and various stuffed animals in *A Midwinter Night's Dream* (December 1906). Porter was one of the first filmmakers to use animation techniques, but others were to see their broader possibilities.

Porter and his contemporaries frequently turned hit songs into comedies. In May 1905, a few months before making *Everybody Works but Father*, Porter photographed *On a Good Old Five Cent Trolley Ride*. This "burlesque on street car service"[43] was based on a song of the same title with the following chorus.

> When speeding along on the trolley
> I feel like a big millionaire.
> A ride on the Trolley is jolly,
> Whatever you give up is fare.
> The Trolley's a hummer in summer
> If you've got a girl at your side.
> To tease in the breeze while you're stealing a squeeze,
> On a good old five cent trolley ride.[44]

The Kinetograph Department suggested that "it greatly adds to the effectiveness of the picture if the music of the well-known popular song 'On a Good Old 5¢ Trolley Ride' is played while the picture is shown. The words and music of a portion of the chorus complete the picture."[45]

The Little Train Robbery (August 1905) was indebted to another well-known hit—this time in cinema. Porter burlesqued his own *The Great Train Robbery* by substituting children for adults and using a miniature railroad and playhouse as sets. The young robbers don't take money but candy and dolls. Their getaway replicates the escape in *The Great Train Robbery*, except that the delinquents are finally captured by full-grown policemen. The bandit queen who has organized the robbery, however, escapes. The film's stance was intended to be nostalgic. The Edison Company hoped that "while the young folks are enjoying themselves their elders can find equal enjoyment in recalling their own youthful days, when their highest ambition was to become a 'Jesse James,' or a 'Bandit Queen.' "[46] The film was nostalgic for another reason. Porter made the film at Olympia Park while visiting his hometown of Connellsville.[47] Released as the nickelodeon era was beginning, *The Little Train Robbery* must have

Boarding School Girls. The car wiggles down the road. The scene suggested too much exuberance and was removed.

disturbed literal-minded critics who saw storefront theaters as schools for crime. Such a film would have provided undesirable role models for the young. Even worse, it suggests that these children were modeling themselves on the bandits in a film "universally admitted to be the greatest production in MOTION PICTURES." If the Kinetograph Department honestly expected the new film to "meet with the same unqualified approval and unprecedented success as *The Great Train Robbery*,"[48] it was disappointed. The picture sold a meager thirty prints during 1905–6, when most of Porter's comedies sold two or three times that number.

Another Edison comedy, *Boarding School Girls* (July–August 1905), followed the students of Miss Knapp's Select School to Coney Island. As with *Rube and Mandy at Coney Island* (1903), the film enabled audiences to vicariously enjoy the famous resort through characters who were there on an outing. Although made only two years later, *Boarding School Girls* integrates narrative and spectacle, as well as performers and environment, in a much more seamless fashion. A remarkable traveling shot of the girls being driven to the amusement park, photographed from another moving vehicle, was removed after the first prints were made.[49] The scene can be found in the paper print version, but not in the otherwise complete negative at the Museum of Modern Art. Perhaps the playfulness appeared too dangerous (the car wiggles back and forth across the road) and bad for the school's image. Once the group arrives at the amusement park, "they take in everything in sight. Passing through Creation they capture the 'Miniature Railway' and 'shake' their governess who endeavors to overtake them. 'Shooting the Chutes,' 'Riding the Camels,' 'The Dew Drop,' 'Steeplechase' and 'Carousel' are all visited. A parade on the beach in bathing costumes is followed by a visit to the 'Flying Swings' and a dip in the surf. 'The Trolley,' 'Razzle Dazzle,' 'Moving Stairway,' 'The Twister' and 'Barrel of Love' are next visited in turn, until finally overtaken and captured by their governess they start for home."[50]

Another Porter comedy, produced in the fall or winter of 1905, was *Minstrel Mishaps*, which survives in the Kleine Collection at the Library of Congress. It was "conceived and produced by America's Only Minstrel Star, LEW

DOCKSTADER,"[51] showing his "late arrival on the special, his dash to the theatre in the only cab in town, the great make-up scene, the minstrel band and the Biggest Knock-out Finish with Lew Dockstader himself in every scene." The film was toured as part of Dockstader's Minstrels in the spring of 1906 and "caused most laughter and applause."[52] By the end of 1907, Dockstader was selling the picture to film exchanges. A year later, the Edison Company bought the negative and sold the comedy as a regular release.

Actualities and Short Subjects

Although the production of narrative features had increased dramatically by early 1905, Edison cameramen continued to generate a diverse selection of films. Porter photographed news and sporting events like *President Roosevelt's Inauguration* (with Robert K. Bonine); *Play Ball—Opening Day, NYC* (April 1905), which showed the baseball game between John McGraw's New York Giants and the Boston Braves;[53] *Opening of Belmont Park Race Course* (May 1905); and *Start of Ocean Race for Kaiser's Cup* (May 1905). *Spectacular Scenes—N.Y. City Fire* (December 1905) showed "the destruction of the Lackawanna and Jersey Central Railroad Ferry Houses."[54] *Scenes and Incidents, Russo-Japanese Peace Conference* was photographed on August 8, 1905, in Portsmouth, New Hampshire—the setting for President Roosevelt's mediated settlement of the Russo-Japanese War. It offers an interesting case study in the production of newsworthy actuality subjects in 1905.

Scenes and Incidents, Russo-Japanese Peace Conference, Portsmouth, N.H. sold thirty-one copies, or 24,800 feet of film—almost 40 percent of Edison's actuality footage for 1905. It also provoked a court case. The story begins in mid July, when George H. Keyes of the Portsmouth Observation Company arranged for an Edison photographer to come to Portsmouth, New Hampshire. Porter arrived a week later and took a 220-foot subject of a dynamite explosion that widened the Piscataqua River. Total cost to Keyes:

220 feet negative @ 40¢ per foot	$88.00
220 feet positive @ 12¢ per foot	26.40
Porter's expenses	25.90
	$140.30[55]

The negative was held at the Edison lab and prints sold to Keyes. Keyes was eager to have Porter return the following week and film the ceremonies surrounding the Russian-Japanese Peace Conference. He thus brought the most popular news subject of 1905 to the Kinetograph Department's attention.

Once Edison executives were informed of the event, they decided that the subject should be marketed commercially rather than made for a commission. Moreover, the Kinetograph Department wanted an exclusive and so appeared to cooperate with Keyes without actually committing itself to his request. When

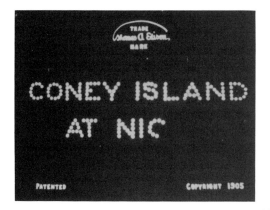

Porter complemented the fantasy world of lights that was Coney Island at night with animated titles.

Porter returned to Portsmouth on August 6th, Keyes learned that the cameraman would not be in his employ. Duped, Keyes angrily contacted the Biograph Company, which agreed to supply a motion picture photographer, who arrived the following day. Fortunately for Keyes and Biograph, but unfortunately for Porter, the ceremonies that had been scheduled for August 7th were delayed until August 8th.[56] Keyes now tried to turn the tables by initiating a suit against Edison, so that Porter's camera equipment was attached an hour before the festivities. Fast work enabled Porter to reach a bondsman, free his equipment, and still photograph the pageantry. Without Keyes, neither Edison nor Biograph would have filmed this historic event.

During 1905 the Kinetograph Department also produced a few human interest films like *Steamboat Travel on the Long Island Sound* (August 1905) and *Firemen's Parade, Scranton, Pa.* (September 1905).[57] Neither was considered important enough to copyright. Coney Island had been a favorite locale for this type of subject, and the Edison Manufacturing Company acquired "the exclusive privilege for the season of 1905 at Dreamland, one of the principal parks."[58] For *Coney Island at Night* (June 1905), Porter's camera caressed the lit-up amusement center with long sweeping pans, producing an eerie beauty. Other subjects made under this arrangement included *Hippodrome Races, Dreamland, Coney Island* (June 1905), *Mystic Shriners' Day, Dreamland, Coney Island* (July 1905), and *June's Birthday Party* (July 1905), as well as *Boarding School Girls.*

In June an Edison photographer took several short films in Bliss, Oklahoma, with Lucille Mulhall's Wild West Show. Such films as *Lucille Mulhall Roping and Tying Steer, Great Buffalo Chase,* and *Western Bad Man Shooting Up Saloon* sold between one and six prints.[59] Short comedies from 1905 included *Unfortunate Policeman* and *Digesting a Joke.* In the latter film comedian James T. Powers cuts out an amusing article from a paper, swallows it, and seems to find its contents amusing as he digests it.[60] (None of these subjects were copyrighted, although descriptions can be found in Edison's July 1906 film catalog.) The Edison Company was able to offer many more short comedies by selling individual scenes from its longer films. In 1905–6, the company sold nine copies of "Burglar and Bulldog" from *The Burglar's Slide for Life*, eight copies of "Sneezing" from *The Whole Dam Family and the Dam Dog*, seven of "Girls and the Bumpety Bumps" from *Boarding School Girls*, and five of "Old Sweethearts" from *The Seven Ages*. This did not mean that Porter conceived of each scene as an independent film. The Kinetograph Department's sale of these separate scenes recognized that some exhibitors still wanted to purchase short subjects, even though such films could no longer be profitably produced for that purpose alone.

Miscellaneous subjects showed the sharpest decline in popularity and production. Among the handful to be photographed were *Blowing Bottles* and *The Kilties Band*: neither sold a single print. Sales figures and copyright practices make it clear that by 1905–6 all forms of motion picture production other than "feature"-length narrative films had become marginally profitable at best. The shift to longer story films was not a "choice" made by producers: it was a necessity determined by the tastes and demands of exhibitors and their audiences. Edison's variety approach to film production was in its final stages of decline as the nickelodeon era arrived; the rise of storefront theaters simply completed its demise.

10 Elaborating on the Established Mode of Representation: 1905–1907

Between December 1905 and May 1907, filmmaking practice at the Edison Manufacturing Company changed very little even as motion picture exhibition was undergoing a fundamental upheaval. As before, there were two production units. One was headed by the solitary, itinerant cameraman Robert K. Bonine, who toured the United States and its possessions, taking travel subjects as well as some news films and industrials. While the cameraman system was used for actualities, a collaborative system of production remained in effect at the studio as Edwin Porter and Wallace McCutcheon continued to explore the rich possibilities of cinema within the already established representational system of fiction film. With the nickelodeon era beginning, the Kinetograph Department enjoyed enhanced profitability and spent more time working on each subject. That this response to the proliferation of storefront motion picture theaters was commercially inappropriate is evident from a brief look at the emerging new era of exhibition.

A Transformation in the Realm of Exhibition

The rapid proliferation of specialized storefront moving picture theaters — commonly known as nickelodeons (a reference to the customary admission charge of five cents) — created a revolution in screen entertainment. In retrospect the ten-year period between 1895 and 1905 witnessed the establishment and finally the saturation of cinema within preexisting venues. Reviewing vaudeville in late 1905, the new publication *Variety* declared that "in the present day when a special train is hired and a branch railroad tied up for a set of train robbery or wrecking pictures, the offerings are really excellent and those who remain

Early nickelodeon theaters such as this one transformed the film world.

and watch them, get sometimes what is really the best thing on the bill. The picture machine is here to stay as long as a change of film may be had every week."[1] Regular Sunday motion picture shows were being given in many eastern cities, and traveling motion picture exhibitors prospered and increased in numbers. Penny arcades and summer parks boasted of numerous picture shows by 1904–5. Such success pointed to the potential viability of specialized picture houses.

Nickelodeons transformed and superseded these earlier methods of film exhibition. They were more than simply specialized motion picture theaters—a common, if often ignored, venue for film exhibition since 1895. The new exhibition mode was made possible by a large and growing, predominantly working-class, audience; the existence of rental exchanges, which facilitated a rapid turnover of films; the conception of the film program as an interchangeable commodity (the reel[s] of film); a "continuous" exhibition format; a sufficient level of feature production to meet demand for frequent program changes; and the relative independence of film exhibition from more traditional forms of entertainment. The nickelodeon phenomenon developed first in the urban, industrial cities of the Midwest, beginning in Pittsburgh, where Harry

An Edison Exhibition Projecting Kinetoscope, ca. 1907–8.

Davis opened his first Pittsburgh storefront theater in June.[2] With the area's working classes enjoying unprecedentedly high wages, Davis's experiment was a success and was quickly imitated in Pittsburgh, Chicago, Philadelphia, and elsewhere. The "nickel madness" of motion pictures spread outward from its midwestern, urban base in an uneven pattern, taking almost two years to reach all parts of the United States.

Although nickel theaters were being recognized as important exhibition outlets by early 1906, New York City, the nation's production capital, did not feel their presence until that spring.[3] Within six months New York was assumed to have "more moving picture shows than any city in the country."[4] In Manhattan the largest concentration was on Park Row and the Bowery, where at least two dozen picture shows and as many arcades were scattered down a mile-long strip. Their principal patrons were Jewish and Italian working-class immigrants.[5] While these groups made up the hard-core moviegoers, middle-class shoppers from the Upper East and Upper West sides helped to support the theaters along Fourteenth Street and Sixth Avenue. When members of the elite or leisure class saw films, they did so at travel lectures like those given by Burton Holmes or at vaudeville performances, not in dingy storefronts.

As newspaper editorials soon made clear, the "better classes" viewed the nickelodeons with contempt and alarm.[6] The sense of farce and anarchistic play in the comedies and the condemnation of the rich, not only in social message films like *The Kleptomaniac* but in more conventional melodramas, could be reinterpreted in ways that might threaten the status quo. Both the appeal to sexual desire and pleasure and the depiction of violent and transgressive acts (robbery, murder) encountered strong condemnation from conservative religious groups. Moreover, nickelodeons facilitated ideological slippages or disjunctions in the reception of films: audiences tended to appropriate pictures for their own purposes, which were often quite different than those intended by the filmmakers and production companies.

Nickelodeons created "the moviegoer"—a new kind of spectator who did not view the pictures in vaudeville formats, as one of many offerings at the local opera house, or as part of an outing to the summer park. To attract these often devoted patrons, storefront theaters found it profitable to change their offerings with increasing frequency. New programs were being offered twice a week in July 1905, and three changes each week were becoming common by late 1906.[7] During the following year, many nickelodeons began to change programs every day but Sunday.[8] The lateral expansion of motion picture houses across the country and this vertical increasing frequency of changing programs caused a tremendous demand for films.

Immense opportunities were created not only for exhibitors and producers but for film renters, who operated at the interface between production companies and exhibitors. In the historical model offered here, distribution is not seen as a fundamental aspect of cinema's production, like film production, exhibition, and viewing. The point at which film production and exhibition meet, however, becomes of central importance in a capitalist system. It can be likened to a fault line where two tectonic plates confront each other, creating large quantities of energy. Screen history suggests a "law": significant changes in either the mode of exhibition or the mode of film production will create new commercial opportunities at this interface. The nickelodeon boom was a revolution in exhibition on an unprecedented scale. Those who took advantage of this golden, fleeting opportunity were to later control the industry—William Fox, Marcus Loew, Carl Laemmle, and the Warner brothers. The rise of a new generation of film exchanges proved to be a crucial moment in the industry's history.

Chicago became the first and largest center for new film exchanges. Eugene Cline, Max Lewis's Chicago Film Exchange, and Robert Bachman's 20th Century Optiscope had become active film renters by 1905.[9] They were joined by William Swanson in the spring of 1906.[10] William Selig, who did not enter the rental business himself, aided Swanson financially. Carl Laemmle became unhappy with the high-handed treatment he received when renting films for his two Chicago theaters in mid 1906.[11] Rather than open more nickelodeons, Laemmle started his own exchange in October and attracted customers by offering "service" as well as a reel of film.[12] The film rental business in New York was at least six months behind Chicago. The new generation of exchanges did not appear until early 1907. Nickelodeon manager William Fox, for example, only opened his Greater New York Film Rental Company in March 1907.[13] Increasingly renters appeared in cities outside the traditional centers of New York, Chicago, and Philadelphia.

Thriving exchanges were hampered by a shortage of new pictures. When Laemmle listed popular subjects for rent in May 1907, he included some that were almost two years old—for example, Edison's The "White Caps" and The Watermelon Patch.[14] The demand for films encouraged several groups of film veterans to move into production. Vitagraph recognized the shifting realities of exhibition and greatly increased its fiction film production. It began to sell prints of these original subjects to other renters in September 1905.[15] In early January 1907 George Kleine joined with Samuel Long and Frank Marion, both of Biograph, to form the Kalem Company, which was incorporated in May and began to sell films in June.[16] At about the same time, George Spoor, who owned the Kinodrome Film Service and National Film Renting Bureau, joined with Gilbert M. Anderson, who was then directing for William Selig, and formed Essanay.[17] The large demand for film not only created incentives to start new production companies, it benefited established manufacturers such as Edison.

Edison Benefits from the Nickelodeon Craze

The Edison Manufacturing Company derived enormous profits from modest investments as the moving picture shows proliferated: sales of projecting kinetoscopes grew rapidly as new exhibitors purchased equipment. Gross income on equipment, which had increased 42 percent for 1904 and 52 percent for 1905, leaped 131 percent for 1906—to $182,135, with $87,228 profit, and jumped another 130 percent for 1907 to $418,893, with $220,622 profit. The Edison machine was known for its durability; its high quality and popularity owed much to Porter's technical improvements. The pattern for projector sales stood in marked contrast to film sales, which in 1906 grew 64 percent to $191,908, with $96,527 in profit, but stabilized in 1907, edging up only 7 percent to $205,243, with $116,912 profit.[18] The increase in 1906 was achieved by selling more copies of each subject. Not only did the Kinetograph Department fail to respond to mushrooming demand by increasing the production rate of new negatives, the number of new fiction narratives actually declined. During 1906 Porter and McCutcheon produced only ten features that were copyrighted and offered for sale through the Edison organization. The same pace continued into the following year, as only another four features were released onto the open market through July 1907, when Porter and his production staff moved to Edison's new indoor studio in the Bronx.

Sales on a per-film basis approximately doubled in 1906 over the previous year. The most popular film of 1905, *The Whole Dam Family and the Dam Dog*, sold 92 prints during the year of its release, but *Dream of a Rarebit Fiend* sold 192 copies the following year. Other features sold between 52 and 146 copies. Older films continued to do well, their sales buoyed by the nickelodeons' need for product. With exchanges constantly complaining about the lack of new subjects, "it was necessary for a number of renters to purchase from manufacturers older subjects in order to supply the demands of the trade."[19] As a result, films made by Edison in 1904 sold more prints in 1906 than they had the previous year.[20] In April 1906 *The Great Train Robbery* was still considered the most popular film in distribution, showing the longevity of its appeal.[21]

Detailed records of the Kinetograph Department's finances survive for the 1906 business year, during which the cost of talent, properties, expenses, traveling, and so forth totaled $12,235, with negative costs averaging 81¢ per foot ($810 for a full 1,000-foot reel of film). The cost of producing a positive foot of film came to $.036, excluding negative costs, and $.0427 with the cost of negatives. The Edison Company produced 1,839,042 feet of finished film, which it sold at an average price of $.1027 per foot. Gross income from sales was $188,870. The potential profit margin, before deducting for general expenses such as advertising, salaries for the sales force, long-term investment, and general overhead, was exactly 6¢ per foot.[22]

The increase in Edison film sales for 1906 was remarkable, since the company continued to sell its product at a premium, giving an edge in pricing to competitors. As John Hardin, Edison's Chicago representative, told the home office: "Our 12¢ (per foot) price to the trade of course operates to a certain extent against our selling a large number of prints in competition to Pathe's and Vitagraph's prices, but at the same time if we have a sufficient supply to fill first orders when the new films first come out, we can dispose of a pretty fair number of prints, say from ten to twenty of a good subject at any time."[23] Although strong demand in the face of higher prices testifies to the continued popularity of Edison films, it also resulted from an industrywide product shortage.

Booming film sales kept Edison's factory for the manufacture of positive prints running at capacity. This allowed Porter to spend more time on individual films, to reduce his rate of production and thus to contradict the typical profit-maximizing response, which called for a rapid increase in production. Instead, Porter put greater emphasis on the elaborately wrought image, partially justifying the premium charge. Edison advertisements conveyed this attitude to potential purchasers:

> Edison films are perfect in detail and action. No effort or expense is spared to produce THE BEST. The strictest attention is paid to details, situations, action and surroundings. We realize that Desperate Escaping Convicts and Pursuing Guards do NOT usually laugh; that Police Officers, after making an arrest, do not leave their clubs and helmets

Kathleen Mavourneen's house was
burned in miniature.

behind them on the sidewalk, and that a Gale of Wind does not usually blow through
private bedrooms.[24]

This ad from January 1906 compared Edison's carefully constructed, "realistic"
films to several popular Vitagraph subjects. Vitagraph's "slapdash" methods
often contributed vitality and spontaneity to the films, however, while also allowing for more rapid production.

Edison's new emphasis on the perfectly made, handcrafted image is apparent
in Porter's *The Night Before Christmas* (December 1905), for which "the photographic and mechanical difficulties encountered and finally overcome if detailed would seem incredible." A panoramic view of Santa Claus driving "his
reindeer over hills and mountains and over the moon" was done in the studio
using miniatures of the sleigh and reindeer, an elaborately painted moving backdrop, and mechanical effects.[25] A copy of the film survives with different tints,
allowing one to appreciate the complete visual impact. *Dream of a Rarebit Fiend*
(February 1906), in which "some of the photographic 'stunts' have never been
seen or attempted before,"[26] also reflected this new emphasis. Porter needed
eight weeks to execute the array of special effects in this 470-foot, eight-minute
film.

Porter's films grew more ambitious. Miniatures were also used for *Dream of
a Rarebit Fiend* and for *Kathleen Mavourneen* (July 1906) when the heroine's
house was burned for the camera. For *Daniel Boone* (December 1906) a log
cabin set was built in Bronx Park, and Porter handpainted sections of the negative to create a fire effect. *The "Teddy" Bears* (February 1907), following the
example of Vitagraph's *A Midwinter Night's Dream*, contains a sequence of
object animation using stuffed bears: Porter worked eight-hour days for a full
week to shoot the necessary ninety feet of film.[27] Not all releases were produced
with such attention to visual detail, but some—including *Life of a Cowboy*
(May 1906), *Kathleen Mavourneen*, and *Daniel Boone*—presented complex narratives and large casts that required extensive preproduction.

Despite publicity, some Edison productions were made quickly and inexpensively, including *Winter Straw Ride* (March 1906), *How the Office Boy Saw the Ball Game* (July 1906), and *Honeymoon at Niagara Falls* (August 1906). A few others—for example, *The Terrible Kids* (May 1906), *Waiting at the Church* (July 1906), and *Getting Evidence* (September 1906)—were made with care but without unusual effects, large casts, or far-off locations. Although the goal of the Kinetograph Department was to maximize sales on a per-film basis by offering a quality product, film sales indicate that the expense of "quality" could not be equated with popularity or high sales. *The Night Before Christmas* had sold 59 copies by March 1, 1907; *Winter Straw Ride* sold 57; *Waiting at the Church*, 52; and *How the Office Boy Saw the Ball Game*, 59. Exchanges and exhibitors purchased 72 copies of *Kathleen Mavourneen*, 75 of *Honeymoon at Niagara Falls*, and 79 of *Getting Evidence*. Although the Edison Company sold 192 prints of *Dream of a Rarebit Fiend* and 109 of *Life of a Cowboy*, it also sold 146 copies of *The Terrible Kids*. A film's success had more to do with conception, timeliness, and ties to other kinds of popular and mass culture than to expenditures of time and money.

The Kinetograph Department altered some of its other practices in response to changing conditions in the industry. Porter's slow, if steady, move away from exhibitor-dominated cinema continued. The Kinetograph Department no longer sold individual scenes from acted subjects as it had done with *How a French Nobleman Got a Wife . . .* nor alternate combinations of scenes as with *Life of an American Policeman*.[28] Editing had become one of several procedures firmly integrated within the producers' repertoire. Efficiency was certainly one determinant in this development, since nonstandardization inhibited rapid print production at Edison's already overworked West Orange plant. The concept of film subjects as an interchangeable commodity also made such custom work inappropriate. Films were no longer sold to exhibitors—that is, to single users whose preferences might wisely and profitably be taken into account. Renters and exchanges now purchased the prints, rapidly circulating them to a variety of theaters. With purchasers no longer showing the films, the direct relationship between producer and exhibitor that had existed during the first ten years of the cinema was severed.

The Night Before Christmas also inaugurated a shift away from the socially relevant films that Porter had produced during 1904–5. The Edison films of 1906–7 were generally light entertainment, as the company favored subjects that had sold well during the previous year. Ten of the fourteen features made between December 1905 and June 1907 can be classified as comedies. Of the remainder, *Life of a Cowboy*, *Kathleen Mavourneen*, and *Daniel Boone* owed much to theatrical melodrama, while *Lost in the Alps* was a child-centered drama of a kind that had already proved its popularity. Regarding subject matter, Porter was probably working within limits imposed by his superiors, even though he retained considerable freedom within those limits.

Edison executives failed to capitalize fully on new opportunities within the industry. Rather than using all of its resources to respond to the nickelodeon's demand for product, the Edison Company continued to make films sponsored by outside firms. In January 1907 the popular singer Vesta Victoria was photographed in New York for the Novelty Song Film Company. That April Porter made a motion picture for the Colonial Virginia Company to be exhibited at the Jamestown Exposition. The film, which depicted the founding of Jamestown, required ten days of studio time, for which the client was billed $25 a day. For the entire production, the Kinetograph Department received $1,866.24.[29] In contrast, *Life of a Cowboy* generated over $11,000 in sales. Edison production efforts were further hampered in 1906 when Percival Waters' growing rental business expanded its Twenty-first Street offices at the expense of Porter's already cramped studio space.[30] Increasing the output of story films did not become a concern until the spring of 1907, in part because executives had not anticipated the high demand for prints and did not sufficiently enlarge their manufacturing capacities.[31] Nonetheless, R. K. Bonine, who was in charge of print production, worked as a traveling cameraman and was absent during much of 1906 and 1907. (His protracted absences, however, meant William Jamison usually assumed de facto responsibility.) In many areas of the Kinetograph Department, specialization was resisted and cost-efficiency studies were either not undertaken or ignored.

Edison's legal activities may have allayed any urgent desire to reorganize the company's production practices. After his motion picture patents case against the Biograph Company was dismissed in March 1902, Thomas Edison quickly applied for a patent reissue, which was granted on September 20, 1902.[32] One week later, Edison instituted new suits against Biograph, Selig, and Lubin.[33] Edison subsequently sued Georges Méliès, William Paley, Pathé Frères, and Eberhard Schneider on November 23, 1904.[34] Suit was also brought against Vitagraph in March 1905.[35] A year later Judge George W. Ray declared that the feeding device of the widely used 35mm Warwick camera was "different in principle and mode of operation from complainant's" and dismissed Edison's complaint against Biograph.[36] Edison lawyers appealed and won an important, if partial, victory in the court of appeals on March 5, 1907. Justices William J. Wallace, E. Henry Lacombe, and Alfred C. Coxe ruled that Edison's patents covered the standard camera used by most production companies but did not cover the special biograph camera used by the American Mutoscope & Biograph Company.[37] A complete victory either way would have sent the case to the U.S. Supreme Court, but this partial victory gave both sides what they needed most—a recognition of their patents. Biograph was finally freed from Edison's legal harassments, and Edison had a ruling that strengthened his clout over other infringers. The *New York Times* assumed that this would enable Edison to soon eliminate most of his competitors (see document no. 18). The possibility that Edison might be able to dominate the industry through patents encouraged company executives to neglect other commercial opportunities.

DOCUMENT No. 18

MOVING PICTURE MEN HIT.
COURT DECISION FAVORING EDISON COMPANY
MAY CLOSE SOME PLACES.

The moving picture business of the whole United States, which has grown to enormous proportions in the last few years, is affected by the decision of the United States Court of Appeals in deciding on March 6th that the moving picture apparatus of all the numerous companies in this country, with one exception, is an infringement on the patents covered by the Edison Co..

For over four years litigation has been in progress over the use of the special sprocket movement of the Edison apparatus, which is the vital part of the moving picture machine. This allows the film that is being drawn through a machine to stop for a small fraction of time, say a thirty-fifth of a second, and no other means has yet been discovered that will answer the purpose.

It is said that many of the concerns making moving pictures will have to go out of business by reason of the decision. Owing to the demand, it is said that companies left in control of the field will be utterly unable to supply the wants of houses exhibiting moving pictures. Until they can catch up on their orders the exhibition houses will have to go out of business.

SOURCE: *New York Times*, March 9, 1907, p. 2.

Since the late 1890s Edison's legal activities had created a high level of uncertainty throughout the American industry and so discouraged investment. As this continued into the nickelodeon era, underfinanced American film manufacturers could not keep up with the demands for new product. Nonetheless, they responded more effectively than Edison. Once Vitagraph began to sell films in September 1905, production averaged about two headliners a month—more than twice the Edison rate. In March 1907 Vitagraph expanded to three and soon four important subjects a month. Sigmund Lubin increased production in mid 1906. By the summer of 1907 he, too, was approaching one new subject a week. Selig was releasing about one feature a month by the second part of 1906. By mid 1907 the Chicago filmmaker had doubled that rate.[38] Although Biograph's legal position was the strongest, the firm faced financial difficulty. Filmmaking was seriously disrupted when Wallace McCutcheon departed for the Edison Company in spring 1905. After its new production head, Frank Marion, resumed regular production that July, Biograph averaged two features a month. Marion's departure for Kalem in January 1907, however, sent Biograph reeling. Although the firm still managed to turn out film subjects, few were popular, and Biograph was unable to pay interest on its loans.[39]

Since Edison's patent litigation threatened American producers more than their foreign competitors, it greatly facilitated foreign domination of the American screen. Films made by Pathé, Méliès, Gaumont, Urban-Eclipse, Nordisk, Italian "Cinès," and many other European companies poured into the United States, where they were purchased by product-hungry exchanges. In a statistical analysis of films released in the United States during the last ten months of 1907, Lawrence Karr found only 364 of 1,092 to be of American make.[40] While sales for some foreign imports were small, most films projected in American theaters were European. Moreover, Pathé firmly established itself as the dominant force in American cinema during 1906–7.[41]

Edison's desire to control the growing deluge of foreign, particularly Pathé, films, in conjunction with Pathé's anxiety over Edison's strong legal position, encouraged active negotiations between the two concerns early in 1907. As F. Croydon Marks, Edison's Paris-based negotiator, wrote to general manager Gilmore in April, Pathé Frères "are so busy at their works that they would be glad (if they could see themselves making the same money and with the same prospects of business) to be relieved of the control of the American territory."[42] Although the Pathé brothers did not make a formal offer, they expected to receive ten dollars per meter of negative and an additional royalty on prints. Finally they insisted that Edison "must undertake to buy one of all their films they now produce leaving it to us [Edison] whether we would make any positives or reproductions from them or not."[43] Since the cost of Pathé negatives was more than three times what Edison was then paying to produce its own films, Pathé's offer was not greeted with much enthusiasm.

Edison's March court victory may have convinced Gilmore that there were more effective ways for Edison to gain control over the American industry. His counter offer was simply to pay Pathé a per-foot royalty on prints sold.[44] Pathé felt that they had been led astray and that Edison had never intended to conduct serious negotiations. As Charles Pathé wrote in May,

> Although we are glad of the opportunity we have had of making your personal acquaintance, you will allow us to express our regret at the want of commercial courtesy which the Edison Company has shown towards our company.

> We cannot withhold from you that the refusal you have intimated to us might have been made a month and a half earlier, which would have prevented our Company from losing through it some hundred thousands of francs.[45]

Negotiations delayed Pathé's plans to open American printing facilities that would have reduced their costs approximately two cents for every foot of film sold.

When Gilmore tried to reopen negotiations, Pathé refused. Subsequently writing from Europe, Edison's general manager claimed to be relieved:

> I find that the conditions are even worse than we ever suspected. They are putting out on the continent pictures that are not only nude but absolutely prohibitive from our standpoint. . . .
>
> What we want to do is go ahead with our own lines. As Mr. Edison has well said, these outside entanglements do not prove to be of value, and I am firmly convinced that he is right in the conclusion. What Mr. Moore wants to do now is to push ahead the new studio, get out our own subjects and I am satisfied that we will be able to hold our own, not only in the American field but elsewhere.[46]

Whatever Gilmore may have truly felt about Pathé, the Edison Manufacturing Company found itself on the commercial defensive by spring 1907. Other companies had taken better advantage of the rapidly changing conditions within the motion picture industry.

Production Practices at Edison

Edison production practices remained the virtual antithesis of the studio system that would develop in response to the nickelodeon boom. The informal, sometimes haphazard collaboration that had characterized the making of *The Buster Brown Series* (1904) continued as Porter and McCutcheon produced *Daniel Boone; or, Pioneer Days in America* in December 1906. Florence Lawrence, who played Boone's daughter in her first screen appearance, subsequently detailed the production process and underscored these continuities (see document no. 19). Rather than having a continuous production schedule, the Edison staff geared up for each new undertaking. The Kinetograph Department lacked a stock company and hired actors on a per-film basis. Porter frequently relied on traveling theatrical troupes to supply performers who had worked together and could contribute costumes and props. In the case of *Daniel Boone*, actors were not from Buffalo Bill's Wild West Show, as Lawrence recalled (it was then in Europe), but from the spectacle *Pioneer Days*, which opened at the Hippodrome on November 28, 1906, and ran through December and into January.[47] This meant that they had other commitments: on matinee days, filming was precluded. Other actors, such as Lawrence, were hired through casting calls. Production personnel also continued to be used in bit parts, for which they

Daniel Boone. Boone's daughter (Florence Lawrence) befriends an Indian maid in the first scene. Later, Daniel Boone and his companion swear vengeance in front of the hero's burned house.

received double pay as a bonus. Appearing in a picture was a way for everyone to pick up some extra cash: it was not a primary commitment. Production schedules were dictated by the availability of performers rather than the reverse.

DOCUMENT NO. 19

My mother heard that Edwin S. Porter, then the chief producer and manager at the Edison studio on Twenty-first street, was engaging people to appear in an historical play. I decided to see him at once. My mother accompanied me to the studio.

The news of intended activity on the part of the Edison people must have been pretty generally known, for there were some twenty or thirty actors and actresses ahead of us that cold morning. I think it was on December 27th, 1906. At least it was during the holidays. Everybody was trying to talk to Mr. Porter at one time, and a Mr. Wallace McCutcheon, who was directing Edison pictures under Mr. Porter, was fingering three or four sheets of paper, which I found later were the scenario.

Mr. Porter and Mr. McCutcheon conferred together and Mr. Porter announced that only twelve people were needed for the entire cast, and that some of these had been engaged. He next read off some notes he had made during his conference with Mr. McCutcheon, about as follows:

One character man who can make up to look like Daniel Boone.

One character man to play Daniel Boone's companion.

One middle aged woman to play Mrs. Daniel Boone.

Two young girls about sixteen years old to play Daniel Boone's daughters.

One young girl who can make up like an Indian maid.

Six men who can make up as Indians.

The part of Daniel Boone, his companion, the Indian maid and a couple of the bloodthirsty savages, he announced, had been filled. That left the parts of Mrs. Boone, the two Boone girls, and four Indians open. As I remember, Col. Cody's Buffalo Bill show was then in New York City and the people selected to play the parts he announced as "filled" were from the show.

Mr. McCutcheon looked at me, then at Mr. Porter and I was told that I was engaged as one of Daniel Boone's daughters. I must have said something to mother almost instantaneously, for one of the men, I forget which, asked, "Is this your mother?" I replied that she was, and Mr. Porter thereupon engaged her to play the part of Mrs. Daniel Boone.

Our names and addresses were taken and we were told "that was all" for the time being, and that we would be notified when to report at the studio. We were to receive five dollars a day for every day that we worked.

There was none in the cast who knew the title of the play until we reported for work on January 3, 1907. At this stage of the motion picture industry the producers were very secretive about such matters. "Daniel Boone; or Pioneer Days in America," was announced as the name of the play. We began work on the exterior scenes first.

Besides mother and myself, others who were playing the principal roles were Susanna Willis, and Mr. and Mrs. William Craver. Mr. Porter and Mr. McCutcheon were the directors. It was during the production of this picture that I learned that the photoplay "Moonshiners," which I had witnessed some three or four years previously, was the first dramatic moving picture ever made in America, and that Mr. McCutcheon was the man who directed it.

All of the exterior scenes for the Daniel Boone picture were photographed in Bronx Park. As one of Boone's daughters I was required to escape from the Indian camp and dash madly into the forest, ride through streams and shrubbery, until I came upon Daniel Boone's companion. As a child I was fond of horses and had always prided myself on being able to handle them, but the horse hired by Mr. Porter was evidently of a wilder breed than the ones I knew. I couldn't do anything with him and he ran off no less than five times during the two weeks we were making the exterior scenes. I was not thrown once, however.

During all this time the thermometer stood at zero. We kept a bonfire going most of the time, and after rehearsing a scene, would have to warm ourselves before the scene could be done again for the camera. Sometimes we would have to wait for two or three hours for the sun to come out or get it just right for the taking of a scene which required certain effects. The camera was also a bother being a great clumsy affair.

One afternoon we didn't pay sufficient attention to the bonfire and permitted it to spread. The fire department had to be called out to prevent its burning and ruining all the trees in the park. While beating the blaze away from a tree Mr. Porter discovered a man who had committed suicide by hanging himself, probably while we were working on the picture. We did not do any further work that day.

All the interior scenes were made at the Edison studio, on the roof, where the stage space would accommodate but one set. We could only work while there was sunlight as arc lamps had not then been thought of as an aid to motion picture photography. Three weeks were required to complete the picture.

SOURCE: *Photoplay*, November 1914, pp. 40–41. Tom Gunning generously brought this article to my attention. Florence Lawrence's dates are incorrect: the completed film was copyrighted on January 3, 1907. William Craver had supplied the horses for Porter in the somewhat earlier *Life of a Cowboy* (May 1906), and he probably did so for this film too, as well as appearing in it (*Moving Picture World*, December 7, 1912, p. 961).

A lack of efficiency was evident in several areas. The decision to film *Daniel Boone*, ill suited for winter production, suggests an absence of careful planning. But whatever Porter chose to make, productivity slowed each winter when the days grew short. Stormy weather would also have precluded shooting. Unlike the Biograph studio, Edison's Twenty-first Street facilities lacked electric lights, not because Porter was indifferent to the technology, but because the small, glass-enclosed studio could not accommodate them. Despite such obstacles, the three-week shooting schedule for *Daniel Boone* was still extremely protracted. (Two years later, Griffith would handle the same type of story in a few days.) Characteristically, Porter focused on visual details rather than the major thrust of the narrative. With only a few daylight hours available for filming, time spent on achieving photographic effects was costly and not always successful. Rather than reconceive the more time-consuming setups, Porter adapted the production schedule to his filmmaking goals.

Porter and McCutcheon relied on collaborative, nonspecialized working methods. Although Porter was studio manager, he worked with the sets and operated the camera, while McCutcheon was in charge of the actors. America's top two filmmakers from the pre-nickelodeon era thus worked in tandem rather than establishing separate production units or a clear hierarchy. Decisions were made laterally rather than vertically. Both men, in fact, were accustomed to operating in this manner. Porter had collaborated with George S. Fleming, James White, and G. M. Anderson, while McCutcheon had worked closely with Frank Marion.

The *Daniel Boone* scenario was a joint responsibility and reflected the Porter-

McCutcheon partnership. Like many films, it emerged from a melange of pre-cursors. Only part of the film's title and not the plot was taken from the Shubert spectacle. The picture was an adaptation of *Daniel Boone: On the Trail*, one of several Daniel Boone plays written and produced in the late nineteenth and early twentieth centuries.[48] At the same time, *Daniel Boone; or, Pioneer Days in America* owes much to two McCutcheon/Biograph films: *The Pioneers* and *Kit Carson*. The focus on family, not as central to McCutcheon's earlier dramas, places *Daniel Boone* squarely within Porter's family-centered orientation.

Porter's old middle-class predilections remained as apparent in his produc-tion methods as in the themes and subject matter of his earlier films. Although the New York studio was called a factory, the manufacturing division of labor was not in evidence. Porter insisted on acting as producer, scenarist, camera-man, and editor. Beyond this he was also involved in refining the projecting kinetoscope and the construction of Edison's new Bronx studio. (Bronx Park was chosen as a location for *Daniel Boone* because it was nearby.) As George Blaisdell defined Porter's role, "During this period he made all the pictures, built and designed the cameras, wrote many of the scenarios, staged all the produc-tions and operated the camera. He did in fact produce the pictures."[49]

The Issue of Narrative Clarity— Audience Familiarity

The Edison Manufacturing Company's continued reliance on pre-nick-elodeon production practices was not confined to filmmaking as such, but in-cluded the ways that viewers were expected to understand the resulting subjects. Methods of reception or appreciation remained much as they had been since the late 1890s. Representational practices fell into three basic categories, with the basis for comprehension centered either in the spectator, the exhibitor, or the film itself. None of these dominated or was necessarily preferred. In fact, they were complementary and often interdependent. All involved redundancy in dif-ferent forms.

Porter and his contemporaries continued to rely on audience awareness of hits, crazes, and well-known stories within popular culture. This meant a dif-ferent relationship between audience and cultural object than in more elevated culture, where narratives were usually presented with the assumption that au-diences were encountering them for the first time. *The Night Before Christmas* (December 1905) "closely follows the time honored Christmas legend by Clem-ent Clarke Moore, and is sure to appeal to everyone—both old and young."[50] Lines from the poem were used to introduce several scenes, helping the audience to maintain a conscious correspondence between the screen drama and the book, continuing a representational practice evident in *Uncle Tom's Cabin*. Relying on the audience's previous knowledge of Moore's poem, Porter estab-lished the necessary narrative clarity even while instilling a degree of nostalgia for lost childhoods. The film's success depended primarily on the spectacle and

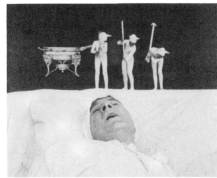

Dream of a Rarebit Fiend, scenes 2, 4, and 6.

novelty of Porter's execution—on the way he told a familiar story, not on the novelty of the story itself.

The next Edison film, *Dream of a Rarebit Fiend*, was partially inspired by Winsor McCay's comic strip "Dream of the Rarebit Fiend," which had appeared in the *New York Telegram* since 1904.[51] Porter not only borrowed the title but shared McCay's dream-based narrative structure, elements that had already figured in Biograph's somewhat earlier *Dream of the Race-Track Fiend* (September 1905). Likewise, the Edison film convincingly realized McCay's surreal imagery on the screen using a variety of photographic tricks—an achievement not attempted in the earlier Biograph film. Although such visuals had many antecedents, Porter may have found another McCay strip, "Little Nemo in Slumberland," a useful point of departure. The basic story line and some of the film's visuals, however, can be found in an earlier Pathé film made by Gaston Velle—*Rêve à la lune* (1905):

> A brave drunkard is surrounded by gigantic bottles in human form, with which he executes a wild, disorderly quadrille. Next he sleeps. . . . He fancies himself in a public square under the kindly gaze of the moon, with which he immediately falls in love.

He wishes to reach it and, to do this, grabs onto a lamp post. But the moon is still too far away. Our man does not hesitate but jumps the wall of a nearby house. . . . Not without several pitfalls, he reaches the roof of the house, on which he has difficulty maintaining his balance, for there are several close calls when he could have been hurled down into the void. He falls while crossing an attic window and disturbs the neighbors.

But our obstinate drunkard still wants to catch the moon. He leans against a chimney-flue, which wobbles on its base. Suddenly a hurricane appears and carries our man into space, always riding the flue. He covers many miles, crossing the clouds while the storm rages around him. He is in outer space, about to catch the object of his desire. The moon itself awaits his efforts, approaches him and extends its hospitality to him. He resolutely enters the brilliant star and penetrates its mouth. But the moon does not seem to take warmly to the visitor, for after several expressions of distaste, it spits the poor drunkard into space, and we see him rapidly tumble toward earth to end up finally in his bed, where he immediately awakens from his strange dream.[52]

Porter's use of the McCay title not only provided a frame of reference that helped audiences understand the dream transitions but obscured his borrowings from the Velle narrative. Familiarity with the McCay comic strip was not as necessary to audience understanding of the narrative as it was for many other films. In this respect, *Dream of a Rarebit Fiend* conforms to more modern expectations of adaptation.[53]

The film begins with a medium shot of the fiend consuming large amounts of alcohol and Welsh rarebit. For subsequent scenes, Porter employed a different special effect for each shot, keeping the spectator off balance and making it impossible for the average viewer to figure out how the photographic stunts were achieved. The second shot was a double-exposure, superimposing the fiend and a swinging white lamppost against rapidly panning, zigzagging camerawork of New York City streets. It suggested the subjective sensation of the fiend's predicament without being a point-of-view shot. When the man enters his bedroom (scene 3) invisible strings drag his shoes across the floor and stop action causes the furniture to disappear. The fourth scene uses a split-screen effect— juxtaposing a close-up of the sleeping fiend with a far shot of people in devils' costumes, making it appear that they are hitting him on the head with forks and shovels. When Porter cuts back to the room, it is a miniature that allows the filmmaker to manipulate the bed in astonishing ways. The sixth scene uses another type of split screen as the fiend's bed travels across the skyline of New York. Scene 7 uses a drawn background and cut-outs. Scene 8 is a studio close-up of a steeple on which the fiend is skewered. The final scene returns to the bedroom as the dreamer crashes through the roof and wakes up. The changing tricks and discontinuities disorient the spectators in ways analogous to dream, particularly the dreams portrayed in Winsor McCay's comic strips.

The Terrible Kids (April 1906) was part of the widespread comic depiction of undersocialized youth. In the cinema, the popular bad boy genre would soon

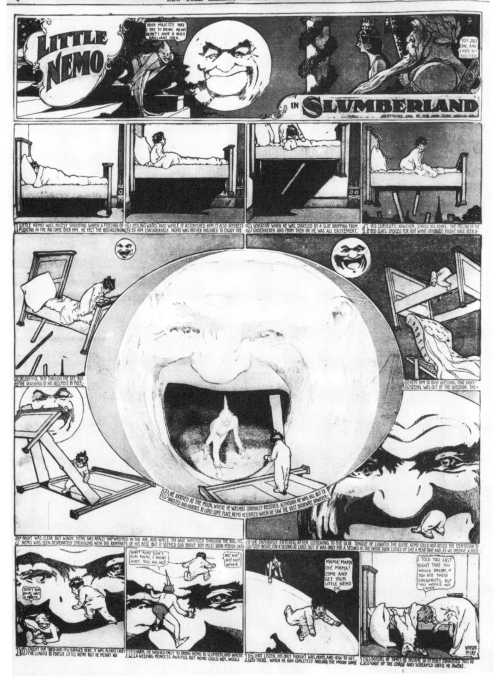

This Winsor McCay cartoon strip shares many similarities with *Dream of a Rarebit Fiend*. Little Nemo's dream, however, is caused by too many donuts.

The "terrible kids" and their faithful dog wreak havoc on the adult world.

come under heavy criticism for providing young viewers with undesirable role models. Porter's comedy shows two boys disrupting a neighborhood's routine with the help of their dog, played by Mannie. Every scene is a variation on a mischievous prank: Mannie "jumps onto the Chinaman's back, seizes his queue and drags the poor chink to the ground"; when they encounter a billposter on a ladder, the dog "grabs the billposter by the leg of his trousers and he falls to the ground with the ladder on top of him while the kids enjoy the billposter's predicament."[54] Several women and an Italian apple vendor with a push cart are also victims. Eventually these annoyed adults turn pursuers and capture the two pranksters with the help of the police. As the boys are driven off in the police van, Mannie opens the van door, and the kids escape as the film ends.

Delinquent kids appear constantly in early film comedies. James Williamson's *The Dear Boys Home for the Holidays* (1903) and *Our New Errand Boy* (1905), Biograph's *The Truants* (1907) and *Terrible Ted* (1907); Pathé's *Les Petits Vagabonds* (1905), and Porter's own *The Little Train Robbery* (1905) are just a few additional examples of the bad boy genre. Others such as Biograph's *Foxy Grandpa Series* (1902) and Edison's *Buster Brown Series* (1904) had comic strip antecedents and also became plays. The Amusement Supply Company offered a full program of five films and fifty-two "life model" stereopticon slides on *Peck's Bad Boy and His Pa*, which were meant to illustrate the best-selling book of the same title.[55] In all of these films one or two boys disrupt staid adult life and undermine authority. While Foxy Grandpa outwits the boys on their own terms (showing that the child exists in all of us and that Grandpa is entering a second childhood), more often than not the adults are easily fooled.

The relationship of *The Terrible Kids* to similar films (and to the bad boy genre in other popular forms) was an essential part of the film's meaning. Since the boys in these films were anonymous, intertextual and intratextual redundancy were essentially of the same kind. The audience's frequent encounters with similar texts provided the reassurance of familiarity. Audiences were expected to identify and sympathize with the kids, suggesting a nostalgic desire for a simpler, less regimented past. According to the catalog description of *The Terrible Kids*, "The antics of the kids, the almost human intelligence of 'Mannie' and the narrow escapes from capture, are a source of constant amusement and are sure to arouse a strong sympathy for the kids and their dog."[56] The genre savors the rejection of authority even as it offers a momentary release from the increasingly regimented workplace. The bad boys escape at the end of both *The Terrible Kids* and *The Little Train Robbery*—as if to appear in some other film.

While scanning the newspapers of this period, one constantly stumbles across antecedents for American films. This suggests that virtually every film functioned within a well-established intertextual context. Even a film with as simple and obvious a narrative as *How the Office Boy Saw the Ball Game* conformed to a popular stereotype. Released in July 1906, much of the subject was recycled from *Play Ball*, a topical film Porter had shot the previous year on opening day of the National League baseball season. A week after that game, the *New York World* published a full-page photograph of the crowd with the caption, "If your office boy or any of your clerks had sudden calls to the funerals of grandmothers or uncles on that memorable Saturday perhaps you might shed a little light on the matter by a close scrutiny of this picture."[57] This caption articulated the premise of Porter's film. In a small office, the lady stenographer writes a note for the office boy that reads "Dear Teddy: Come home at once. Grandma is dead." The boss accepts the excuse and the office boy has a free afternoon to see the game. The young lady stenographer faints in disbelief when the boss falls for the explanation. The bookkeeper is told to escort her home. Left alone, the broker also decides to take the afternoon off and see the game. The remainder of the film intercuts Teddy on a telephone pole looking through a spyglass with masked point-of-view shots of the game—including a view of the boss discovering the stenographer and bookkeeper in the stands (the matte, as was customary, was added at the printing stage). For a short time they are all kids again, playing hooky from adult responsibility. Unlike Teddy, whose skylarking remains undetected and hence unpunished, the stenographer and bookkeeper are reprimanded by authority. They play by some rules (they pay to see the game) but not others. Teddy, safe on his distant perch, does not pay to see the game (either with money or by suffering the boss's wrath). Like the "terrible kids," he can disregard societal rules and get away with it—something adult characters seldom succeed in doing.

In *How the Office Boy Saw the Ball Game*, Porter celebrates baseball as a unifying activity that cuts across age and class barriers. Movie patrons are encouraged to recall their childhoods nostalgically, for they see the game through

The office boy sees not only the ballgame but his boss lecturing the bookkeeper and stenographer for attending the game.

the office boy's spyglass—from his point of view. The spectator, however, regresses nostalgically to *his* childhood. Gender is presumed to be male—like the filmmaker and the office boy. As Adrienne Harris has pointed out, "Baseball is centrally a place without time and without women."[58] In 1906 the game reflected the male-dominated world in which and about which Porter and others made their films. Whether the stenographer is in the office or at the ballgame, her position is in the margins. She never speaks in her own voice. She writes Teddy's note—signing someone else's name, and her main job is to record the male boss's words. Even when she faints, it only becomes an excuse for the bookkeeper to escape as well. Likewise in baseball, if a woman speaks, Harris suggests, it will be as "a false mock male self."[59] In *How the Office Boy Saw the Ball Game*, the boy's point-of-view shots of the game reproduce the male-fetishized close-up of the woman's ankle in *The Gay Shoe Clerk*, but in an appropriate latency-age form. Women spectators of both *The Terrible Kids* and *How the Office Boy Saw the Ball Game* are likewise forced to assume the role of a false mock male self to enjoy the films in the spirit in which they were made.

Obadiah Binks tries to elude his family, and his jilted bride is left "waiting at the church."

While *The Terrible Kids* conformed to a genre diffused throughout Western popular and mass culture and *How the Office Boy Saw the Ball Game* was based on a generalized, urban American witticism about office boys and ballgames, *Waiting at the Church* (July 1906) required spectators to be familiar with the lyrics of one specific song, a hit popularized by Vesta Victoria (see document no. 20). As one vaudeville manager noted, "to those who know the song, this is extremely funny."[60] The film itself was described in *Views and Film Index*:

WAITING AT THE CHURCH

Obadiah Binks is sitting on a bench in the park. A young lady strolls along and finally seats herself very comfortably on the same bench. Before long they engage in conversation and Obadiah proposes. At first she is surprised by the very sudden announcement of his love for her, but she suddenly falls upon his neck and hugs and kisses are mutual. He declares his love for her and they agree upon a date to get married.

Obadiah's home is then shown. Finally the young lady is seen waiting at the church for Obadiah. He does not come but sends a messenger with a note in which he states, "Can't get away to marry you today: my wife won't let me."[61]

This brief trade description passes over Porter's elaboration of the song's simple story. Porter did more than merely illustrate the song. Although the original lyrics are from the woman's point of view, the film shifts the focus to Obadiah Binks. No longer a con artist who robs a naive, sexually frustrated woman of her money, Obadiah is portrayed as a zany bigamist trying to outwit one wife so that he can marry a second. The discrepancy between the lyrics and the film narrative is an essential part of the picture's humor. The film's farcical tone is retained, but the story is explored from a new perspective.

DOCUMENT NO. 20

WAITING AT THE CHURCH

Written by Fred W. Leigh
Composed by Henry E. Pether
Published by Francis, Day and Hunter [New York, 1906]

1. I'm in a nice bit of trouble
   Somebody with me has had a game
   I should by now be a proud and happy bride
   But I've still got to keep my single name

   I was proposed to by Obadiah Binks
   In a very gentlemanly way
   Lent him all my money so that he could buy the home
   And punctually at twelve o'clock today

Chorus:
   There was I waiting at the church
   Waiting at the church,
   When I found he'd left me in the lurch
   Lor, how it did upset me!

   All at once he sent me round a note
   Here's the very note
   This is what he wrote
   Can't get away to marry you today
   My wife won't let me.

2. Lor, what a fuss Obadiah made of me
   When he used to take me to the Park
   He use to squeeze me till I was black and blue.
   When he kissed me he used to leave a mark.

   Each time he met me he treated me to wine
   Took me now and then to see the play
   Understand me rightly when I say he treated me
   It wasn't him but me that use to pay.

3. Just think of how disappointed I must feel
   I'll be going crazy very soon
   I've lost my husband the one I never had
   And I dreamed so about my honeymoon!

> I'm looking for another Obadiah
> I've already bought the wedding ring
> There's all my little faltheriddles packed in my box
> Yes, absolutely two of everything.

With *Waiting at the Church*, Porter used redundancy in several different ways. The song's familiarity was incorporated into the psychology of the characters as well as the narrative. When Obadiah is chased by his wife and children, they seem to have gone through this routine before. Determined to keep the family together and knowing what to expect, they prevent him from reaching his would-be bride "waiting at the church." Actions and situations are also repeated through the use of similar chase scenes. Like the chorus of the song itself, redundancy is the central organizing principle of the film.

The "Teddy" Bears was not only one of Porter's personal favorites but serves as a rich, revealing example of the filmmaker's work in the early nickelodeon era.[62] Advertised as "a laughable satire on the popular craze,"[63] Porter and McCutcheon's first film of 1907 was completed in late February. The juxtaposition of two different referents is an important element of *The "Teddy" Bears'* humor and success. It starts out as an adaptation of "Goldilocks and the Three Bears" and works within the framework of the fairy-tale film. For the first two-thirds of its running time, the life-sized teddy bears (actors in costume) are the subject of an endearing children's film. Suddenly the picture moves outside the confines of the studio, changing moods and referents. The bears chase Goldilocks across a snowy landscape until "Teddy" Roosevelt intervenes, kills the two full-grown pursuers, and captures the baby bear.

The sudden appearance of "Teddy" was based on a well-known incident when President Roosevelt was on a hunting expedition in Mississippi and refused to shoot a bear cub. This was in November 1902. Shortly thereafter Morris Michtom, a Russian immigrant who ran a small toy store and would eventually start the Ideal Toy Corporation, began to make and sell "Teddy's bear"—a stuffed version of the spared cub. The novelty had become a craze by 1906–7, when thousands of toy bears were being sold each week and music such as "The Teddy Bear March" (copyrighted 1907) was popular.[64] Unless audiences appreciated the shift in referents, the killing of the two endearing bears seemed bizarre and at odds with the earlier part of the film. Sime Silverman missed the point in his *Variety* review when he wrote:

> Probably based on the fairy tale of "Goldielocks and the Three Bears," *The Teddy Bears* series at the Colonial this week is made enjoyable through the mechanical acrobatic antics of a group of fluffy haired little hand-made animals. The closing pictures

The *"Teddy" Bears* unexpectedly shifts moods from animated stuffed animals in the first part to the killing of anthropomorphic bears in the second. Porter also juxtaposed location shots with exterior scenes set in the studio.

showing the pursuit of the *child* by the bear family is spoiled through a hunter appearing on the scene and shooting two. Children will rebel against this position. Considerable comedy is had through a chase in the snow, but the live bears seemed so domesticated that the deliberate murder in an obviously "faked" series left a wrong taste of the picture as a whole.[65]

Not everyone agreed with Sime.[66] The shift in referents revealed to the audience that *The "Teddy" Bears* was not simply a children's film, but was also aimed, like Lewis Carroll's *Alice in Wonderland*, at adults. By judging the film from the viewpoint of a child, who could not be expected to grasp a range of contemporary references, Sime postulated a relation between viewer and cultural object that would be more applicable to later cinema. In fact, his review is one of several indications that criteria for assessing films were changing and that subjects relying on an audience's prior familiarity with narrative elements were being received with less sympathy.

The "Teddy" Bears is a political burlesque on Teddy Roosevelt, reminiscent of *Terrible Teddy, the Grizzly King* and *The Strenuous Life; or, Anti-Race Suicide*. As Sime noted, the bear family's anthropomorphic activities have endeared the animals to the audience by the time the Roosevelt hunter appears on the scene. Audiences then tend to react unsympathetically to his shooting of the two adult bears. The liberal press sometimes expressed a similar viewpoint. After Roosevelt killed a she bear in 1907, the *New York World* responded with a front-page column devoted to the critical remarks of nature writer Dr. William J. Long. Headlines read: "Calls Roosevelt Bear Killing Pure Brute Cowardice."[67]

Porter's continuing commitment to pre-nickelodeon representational strategies is also evidenced in the shot construction of The *"Teddy" Bears*. The film has eighteen shots: the first thirteen and the last were taken in the studio, while the four chase scenes were photographed outside in a city park. Although Griffith was to shoot interiors in the studio and exteriors on location on a regular basis by 1909, Porter never developed this convention of consistent mimetic realism, at least in his Edison films. From our post-Griffith perspective, studio scenes of the bear-house exterior are at odds with those photographed in the park. Although this syncretism can feel misplaced or naive today, Porter's studio work was generally motivated by a desire for greater control over the mise-en-scène. Correspondingly, Porter's frequent reliance on the chase encouraged location shooting and prevented films from becoming claustrophobic.

Shots continued to be conceived as discrete units in The *"Teddy" Bears*, even though editorial control was firmly in Porter's hands. As before, each scene has its own self-enclosed temporality, which is related to outgoing and incoming shots by repeated actions and the unfolding story. Goldilocks' exit through a hallway (shot 7) is followed by an entrance into the bedroom (shot 8), another example of Porter's familiar uses of the temporal overlap. There is no matching action or linear continuity. Mismatches in screen direction and conflicting entrances and exits further reveal the discrete nature of individual scenes. The *"Teddy" Bears* makes rich and effective use of a representational system Porter had explored and developed since his arrival at Edison. Within this system, he continued to mature as a filmmaker.

Porter drew on the same repertoire of techniques in *Cohen's Fire Sale* (June 1907), which focuses on a Jewish milliner whose merchandise is inadvertently taken away by a garbage man and ends up in the city dump. The shopkeeper recoups his investment by starting a small fire in his store and covering the damage through insurance. He benefits still further by a fire sale, which quickly clears the store of imperfect goods. The story is based on the stereotypical Jewish businessman for whom fire was "our friend" and the fire company was "our enemy" — a view rendered in iconographic form on a comic postcard of the period. The story itself is quite simple and clearly depicted; but character motivation, narrative logic, and audience comprehension of a few key pieces of information — for instance that a piece of paper is an insurance policy — relies on this highly specific anti-Semitic stereotyping. Here redundancy reinforces those ethnic prejudices that audiences initially relied on to understand the film.

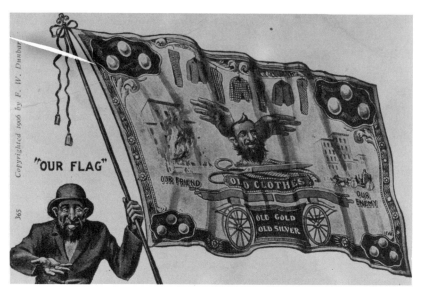

An anti-Semitic "comic" postcard of the period.

Cohen's Fire Sale integrates pasteboard representations and actual objects in extreme ways. Hats in the foreground of Cohen's display are real—those in the background are painted. Cohen's sleeping cat suddenly becomes a pasteboard animal when its tail is tied to the kerosene lamp. Though these syncretic juxtapositions differ little from Porter's set-design strategies in *The Finish of Bridget McKeen* (1901), the quality and detail of execution have improved. Again the exterior of Cohen's store is a set, while other scenes were filmed on New York City streets. Scenes of a fire truck coming out of the station and of the firefighting are actuality material, taken of a fire company in action. Like Porter's previous work, *Cohen's Fire Sale* incorporates a diversity of mimetic representations and undercuts any notion of a seamless continuity. Shots continue to act as self-contained units of representation in other ways as well. Chase scenes integrate narrative elements like the pursuing shopkeeper with superfluous incidents that had appeared in turn-of-the-century, one-shot films. In one scene, for instance, street gamins wear some of Cohen's misplaced hats and dance a cakewalk until Cohen arrives to take away the headwear.

Porter's construction of shots and his frequent reliance on audience familiarity with a film's subject were part of the same representational system. If one shot did not follow clearly after another or if extraneous elements were introduced, audiences had a frame of reference that allowed them to fill in gaps or follow the narrative's main line. If spectators lacked the necessary frame of reference, they missed the joke or could not follow the story line. Novelty of

Cohen tries to sell his damaged goods.

execution and familiarity of subject matter were the basis of this approach. Although Porter's reliance on the audience's prior knowledge was extreme for the period, it nonetheless characterized and crystalized the distinctive elements of this period's representational system.

Self-sufficient Narratives and Intratextual Redundancy

Narrative clarity was often achieved through intratextual redundancy. Two common structuring principles proved especially efficacious in this respect: first, discrete scenes could be gathered around a unifying theme or character; second, as a corollary, scenes could be built around a chase. Redundancy of situation, which Porter had used in *The Buster Brown Series* and *The Seven Ages*, was also utilized for comedies like *The Nine Lives of a Cat* (July 1907) and *The Rivals* (August 1907). After evoking the age-old adage about cats with its title, *The Nine Lives of a Cat* proceeds to show nine unsuccessful attempts to eliminate an uncooperative feline. *The Rivals*, based on a comic strip by T. E. Powers that ran in the *New York American*,[68] showed two male rivals fighting over the attentions of a desirable woman. In one scene Charlie escorts Tootsie, only to have her stolen away by George. In the next scene George escorts the girl, only

The Rivals (left): a romantic triangle that soon self-destructs. It was based on a cartoon series (above).

to have her stolen away by Charlie. This continued until Porter had the desired number of scenes. To achieve closure, he had the woman leave both rivals for a third. The organizing principle of such films was indebted to the repetitive structures of daily and weekly comic strips. (The strip alternated combinations each week.) Repetition with slight variation is the basis for their comedy. Similar structures occur in somewhat later Porter/Edison films like *Laughing Gas* (November 1907) and *The Merry Widow Waltz Craze* (April 1908).

While the chase also utilizes a repetitive structure, it achieved added levels of clarity by setting up a simple opposition between pursuer and pursued that could be expressed compositionally by foregrounding first one group and then the next, and through movement, as the pursued and pursuers come toward and past the camera. Although Porter made a few simple chase films such as *From Rector's to Claremont*, he soon combined the chase with other forms of intratextual redundancy, as in *"Raffles"—the Dog* (June 1905), *The Terrible Kids*, and *Getting Evidence*.

In *Getting Evidence* (September 1906), a jealous husband visits the Hawkshaw Detective Agency (a redundant naming device in its own right) and asks the detective to obtain evidence of his wife's supposed infidelities. Only a photograph is deemed acceptable evidence and the private eye's attempts to secure it provide a series of comic incidents. The detective becomes a surrogate authority figure with the right to pry. Soon he is pursuing a woman he believes to be the man's wife. Each time he takes a picture of the woman and her lover, his camera is destroyed and he is roughed up. He is run over by a car; when posing as the couple's waiter, he is doused with seltzer. When the determined photographer sneaks up on the romantic couple at night and uses a flash, his subjects destroy the camera once again. At the seashore he takes a successful picture, hides the negative and then "is pursued by a crowd, caught and ducked thoroughly in the surf."[69] When the black-eyed, limping detective finally presents his evidence to the husband, his photograph is of the daughter rather than the wife.

Rather than providing evidence against the wife, the photograph exposes the detective's incompetence and the husband's unfounded suspicions. As Alan Trachtenberg points out, the authority of the patriarch and his surrogate eye is mocked and loses some of its authority.[70] As Biograph's films of the Westinghouse works in East Pittsburgh (taken in 1904) clearly show, surveillance was commonly directed against the working class in factories. Such people, who provided the nickelodeons with a majority of their patrons, undoubtedly were amused to find someone like their boss and his delegated representative in such a predicament. As with *The Terrible Kids*, this suggests that films could be appropriated by working-class audiences in ways never anticipated by Porter and yet consistent with his own opposition to a regimented workplace. The humor touches on an important issue of American life without dealing with it directly as Porter did in *The Kleptomaniac* and *The Ex-Convict*.

Porter's use of intratextual redundancy was simple and effective; it allowed for the production of one-reel films without complex narratives. Similar films were made by other producers in considerable quantity. Many of these can still be seen, including Biograph's *Mr. Butt-In* (February 1906) and *If You Had a Wife Like This* (February 1907), Vitagraph's *The Jailbird and How He Flew* (July 1906) and *Liquid Electricity* (September 1907), Hepworth's *The Fatal Sneeze* (June 1907), Urban's *Diabolo Nightmare* (October 1907), Eclipse's *A Short-Sighted Cyclist* (1907), and Gaumont's *Une Femme vraiment bien* (1908).

Getting Evidence. The disguised detective takes a snapshot.

The titles of all films played an important naming function, either defining the central concept or suggesting the referent viewers needed to interpret the film even before the narrative began. Redundancy, one of the defining characteristics of "low" popular culture as opposed to "high" art[71] was essential to the narrative cinema of 1906–7, as it had been to the films Porter produced in earlier years.

Severe limitations were placed on other kinds of self-sufficient narratives in pre-1908 films. If a story was unfamiliar, how was the spectator to know if a succeeding shot was backwards or forwards in time? The temporal, spatial, and narrative relations between different characters and lines of action were often vague or, worse, confusing. Visual cues like repeated action were helpful, but not always possible. Occasionally the producer used intertitles, but this practice was not universally accepted and was rarely used at the Edison studio during 1906–7. One limited solution was to tell simple stories. This is what Porter did with *Lost in the Alps* (March 1907), a family-centered drama of twenty-four shots (see shot-by-shot breakdown on page 358).

The family unit established in the opening two shots is quickly threatened as the children wander through a snowstorm and succumb to the elements (shots 3–5). The worried parents are the focus of the next four shots and their rescue

(text continued on p. 359)

Lost in the Alps, Shots 1, 2, 7, 19.

Shot 23.

Lost in the Alps: a shot-by-shot breakdown.

shot 1. exterior of house (set) — mother sends son and daughter off right with lunch basket.

shot 2. sheep's meadow — children come from deep left and give lunch to father, a shepherd.

shot 3. children staggering home through woods — snow falling.

shot 4. children struggling through snow — girl struggles off right carrying younger brother as snow falls.

shot 5. children collapse.

shot 6. mother working at home (interior, set) — she looks at clock, is very worried and goes outside.

shot 7. exterior (same as shot 1) — mother comes outside, she goes off right and returns discouraged, then reenters house. After a brief moment, the father comes on right and enters the house.

shot 8. interior of house (same as shot 6) — mother is waiting and husband enters; he hears the news and quickly leaves.

shot 9. interior of monastery — father enters from right and explains the situation to monks, who go off and reenter with two Saint Bernard dogs.

shot 10. dogs race through the snow.

shot 11. dogs race through the snow.

shot 12. dogs race through the snow.

shot 13. dogs race through the snow.

shot 14. dogs race through the snow.

shot 15. dogs race through snowy countryside.

shot 16. pan from stream to dogs going down path.

shot 17. dogs race through snow, downhill, and across stream.

shot 18. dogs race across snowy fields.

shot 19. dogs race down steep slope.

shot 20. dogs sniff where children were last shown collapsing (shot 5), but the children cannot be seen.

shot 21. father and monks come down snowbank and are greeted by one Saint Bernard.

shot 22. same location as shot 20, but children are now in the snow; monk and father enter frame, embrace children, and wrap them in blankets.

shot 23. home, same set as shot 6 — mother at home, father and men return with children, who are slowly revived.

shot 24. emblematic shot of dog/hero.

efforts are continued by the Saint Bernards in shots 9–19. Only in the last two shots of the narrative (22–23) is the family reunited. The extent to which the mother's worrying, shown in shots 6 to 8 and 23, overlaps with the children's struggle in the snow is uncertain, but implicit to the story's construction. The repeated actions of mother and father leaving and entering their house in shots 6 to 8 clearly establish temporal relationships between these three scenes, however, while time is condensed within them. In shot 7, when the mother goes off-screen right and then quickly returns to the house, the spectator understands that she has searched for her children over a longer period of time than she is out of frame. Although the mother's return is followed immediately by that of her husband, considerably more time has presumably elapsed between these events. There is a major discrepancy between real time and screen time within a single shot; and the nature of this discrepancy must be determined by the viewer. It was a combination of representational strategies that Porter had used since *Life of an American Fireman*.

The narrative is, by later cinematic standards, radically distended as the Saint Bernards romp through the snow for eleven successive shots. For Porter, the scenic beauty of these scenes was paramount, and the narrative was pushed into the background. This emphasis on scenery is consistent with earlier Edison films like *Rube and Mandy at Coney Island* where the comedy was interrupted by scenic display. The limitations endemic to the construction of a story in Porter's representational system made these nondiegetic digressions all the more important. Slightly more than a year after *Lost in the Alps* was made, last-minute rescue films were to have a very different construction. Advanced filmmakers like Griffith would take similar material and intercut the children, parents, and dogs in a way that heightened the dramatic intensity of the film. The mother's worrying would have punctuated the rescue rather than appearing before and after it. Under such circumstances the scenic value of the snowy landscape would have become secondary to the suspense generated by the narrative.

Complex Narratives

Porter did periodically rely on complex, unfamiliar narratives. The frequency with which exhibitors facilitated their viewers' comprehension of these films through sound effects, a lecture, behind-the-screen dialogue, and/or informal comments during the screenings is impossible to determine with any accuracy. Although this assistance was offered in some circumstances, it was certainly not offered in all. Porter's most ambitious projects must therefore be looked at from this double perspective. On the one hand, some exhibitors intervened to make complex narratives more intelligible; on the other hand, the films were often exhibited without such assistance and were not readily understood by their audiences. This problem, which faced many filmmakers, was underscored by the *Film Index*:

MOVING PICTURES—FOR AUDIENCES, NOT FOR MAKERS

Regardless of the fact that there are a number of good moving pictures brought out, it is true that there are some which, although photographically good, are poor because the manufacturer, being familiar with the picture and the plot, does not take into consideration that the film was not made for him but for the audience. A subject recently seen was very good photographically, and the plot also seemed to be good, but could not be understood by the audience.

If there were a number of headings on the film it would have made the story more tangible. The effect of the picture was that some people of the audience tired of following a picture which they did not understand, and left their seats. Although the picture which followed was fairly good, the people did not wait to see it.

Manufacturers should produce films which can be easily understood by the public. It is not sufficient that the makers understand the plot—the pictures are made for the public.[72]

With films such as *Life of a Cowboy*, *Kathleen Mavourneen*, and *Daniel Boone*, it is difficult to determine whether Porter and McCutcheon misjudged their audience's knowledge of these stories, wanted the films to be shown with a commentary, or failed to achieve the level of self-sufficient clarity they originally intended. Certainly the gap between the filmmakers' ambitions and what an audience might reasonably be expected to understand without an exhibitor's lecture is apparent either by contrasting a silent viewing of *Life of a Cowboy* (May 1906) to a reading of the Edison trade description or comparing this description to a review that appeared in *Variety* (see documents nos. 21 and 22). For all his praise, *Variety*'s Sime Silverman viewed the first part of the film as a series of discrete incidents like *Life of an American Policeman* rather than as a unified narrative. While many of the individual situations were immediately recognizable from Wild West shows, the story that held these situations together was not easily discernible.

DOCUMENT NO. 21

LIFE OF A COWBOY

The opening scene shows the interior of the "Big Horn" saloon. A Mexican greaser is standing at the bar drinking. An old Indian enters and walks over to the bar. Upon being refused a drink he walks away and sits down on a box. The greaser now orders a drink and is about to hand it to the old Indian when an Indian girl who is evidently the old Indian's daughter rushes in and knocks the glass out of the greaser's hand. As the greaser is about to strike the girl a cowboy, who is the hero, appears on the scene, knocks the greaser down and kicks him out of the saloon.

An English tourist, with his valet, now enters. While they are looking round the saloon, a Salvation Army lass comes in and asks for a donation, but they pay no attention to her. At this moment several cowboys ride into the saloon and begin shooting, and compel the tourist and valet to give up their money and valuables to the girl. When the girl leaves they make the tourist and valet dance to the music of their revolvers and then make them buy drinks for the entire crowd. After a few parting shots, they ride out of the saloon.

The next scene is on a ranch. The ranchman's daughter comes out of the house, sees a stage coach, in which are the tourist, his wife and valet, also a young lady who becomes the heroine of the story coming up the road. A number of cowboys now dash down the road to meet the stage coach, and are welcomed in true Western style. The young lady and the cowboy hero are old friends. The greaser, who has been paying marked attention to the young lady, is roughly pushed aside by our hero, which adds to the bad blood already between them.

The next scene shows the ranch owner, with his family and guests, enjoying some cowboy sports. One of the sports is the lassoing of a woman while riding at full speed, and some other wonderful tricks with the lariat. The English tourist, who is present becomes greatly interested. Presently the lariat falls over his head, and he is dragged round the yard to the great amusement of everyone. A wrestling bout is also shown.

The next scene shows the stage coach leaving the ranch with the entire party. The greaser mounts his pony and rides after the stage. The occupants soon discover that they are being followed by the greaser and a band of Indians. The driver lashes his horses into a wild gallop. The Indians overtake the coach and ride alongside of the horses, and bring the stage to a stop and compel the passengers to get out. The stage driver is shot and falls off the coach. The greaser now seizes the young lady and places her on a horse, while the rest of the gang compel the rest of the passengers to run before them at the point of their guns.

The wounded stage driver is seen galloping up the road. He reaches the house and is met by our cowboy hero who catches him as he falls exhausted from his horse. The news soon spreads and a dozen cowboys are soon in hot pursuit after the greaser and his gang. After a terrific ride they overtake one of the Indians, who is shot and falls to the ground. Our cowboy hero rides along side of our heroine's horse while both horses are galloping at break neck speed. The Indians now scatter in all directions. The heroine quickly revives and congratulations follow.

The final scene shows the greaser creeping through the underbrush, and followed by the Indian girl who knocked the glass out of the greaser's hand in the opening scene. The two lovers are resting in a secluded spot. The greaser creeps closer and closer, raises his revolver, takes a steady aim, and is just about to press the trigger when a bullet from the Indian girl's pistol drops him in his tracks. The Indian girl now approaches the two lovers and shows her gratitude to our cowboy hero for his kindness to her and her old father.

SOURCE: *Film Index*, July 7, 1906, p. 9.

DOCUMENT No. 22

Edison Film
"Life of a Cowboy"
13 mins.
Pastor's

A long and interesting moving picture is "Life of a Cowboy" shown at Pastor's. It covers a wide range of subjects and the locale seems to be really the Western plains. The picture runs from a Western mining camp barroom to the arrival of a stage coach at the ranch with "tenderfeet" abroad, for whose delectation trick lariat throwing is introduced, followed by the holding up of the coach by Indians, the abduction of a young girl, the chase by the cowboys through pretty woods and rolling fields to the recapture of the girl, and the tragic finale where an Indian girl shoots a murderous bad man silently crawling up on the lover of the white girl. The series is so melodramatic in treatment that it acted on the audience like a vivid play.

SOURCE: *Variety*, January 19, 1907, p. 9.

The tension between narrative and spectacle in the opening scenes is not resolved. The story is frequently interrupted by the tricks and specialties of the hired rodeo group. Neither camera framing nor staging offers many clues to distinguish actions central to the narrative from inessential ones. The hero barely stands out from other cowboys. While the size of the figures was consistent with theatrical conventions, the absence of dialogue reduced the amount of information that could be communicated to the audience. As a result, the characters are difficult to identify even as stereotypes, and their actions lose significance. One essential aspect of *Life of a Cowboy* is the sudden shift to a chase format two-thirds of the way into the film. The first section lends itself to the showman's narration, whereas the second half, through the redundancy of the chase, achieves a level of clarity that makes this unnecessary. To the unaided spectator the film seems to discover its story partway through. Porter's ability to present a clear narrative is also burdened by the complexity of the story. An otherwise simple action triangle in which the cowboy hero and the "greaser" villain fight for the desired woman is burdened by an elaborate subplot involving themes of temperance and Indian gratitude.

Life of a Cowboy. Scene 1: the tourist is made to dance to six-guns. Final scene: the Indian maid kills the "greaser," who was about to shoot the cowboy hero and his lover.

One of the earliest film westerns, *Life of a Cowboy* owed much to the theater, and it was doubtlessly based on a play, which has so far eluded identification. Its production was encouraged by the general popularity of western subjects, particularly David Belasco's *The Girl of the Golden West*, which opened on November 14, 1905, at the New York Theater.[73] The play was still running when Porter shot his film on Staten Island, May 2–10, 1906. Like *The Train Wreckers* and *The Great Train Robbery*, proper society confronts the outcasts—in this case Indian bandits led by a Mexican. Unlike those two films with their outlaws and posses, this 1906 picture has a courageous and daring hero, who saves the girl and earns her love.

The cowboy hero, a pivotal figure reluctant to conform to the demands of civilized society, lives on the frontier, where civilization meets its opposite. Making the English tourist dance to the music of six-guns or dragging him around the yard recalls not only the dance scene in *The Great Train Robbery* but the antics of the terrible kids. The West is a place where time is told by the sun rather than the clock—a refuge like the romanticized memories of childhood where life has not yet been regimented.[74] Cowboys, not miners, are western heroes. The cow*boy* is impulsive, undisciplined, and not completely socialized. Thus his final acceptance of responsibility at the film's conclusion makes the story very satisfying for audiences who fantasize a release from the regimentation of daily life but still must accept it. Unlike the world of baseball, the frontier is not timeless but receding, disappearing. The presence of (white) women is a sign of its passing. The cowboy's romance turns him out of this unstable, idyllic world like Adam's bite from Eve's apple. The demise of the naughty boy films and the rise of the western occurred at the same time. The greater complexity of the western replaced the narrow, inter/intratextual redundancy of the bad boy genre while addressing similar feelings precipitated by social and economic changes in American life.

Kathleen Mavourneen (May and June 1906) and *Daniel Boone* also utilize complex story lines.[75] Both were adaptations of popular nineteenth-century stage melodramas not unlike *The Miller's Daughter* and its reworking of *Hazel Kirke*. All three plays served as staples for traveling repertory companies. In the process, they were freely adapted, often as a way to avoid copyright infringement. These theatrical reworkings also cultivated the creative aspirations of the troupe and, furthermore, attracted audiences already familiar with the basic story line but ready to be entertained by new variations on a familiar theme.

Kathleen Mavourneen is set in rural Ireland, where Kathleen's happiness is threatened by the unbridled ego of Captain Clearfield, the landlord villain who controls both the local judiciary and a band of robbers. Clearfield's lust for power, wealth, and sex is pitted against the villagers and their hero, Terence O'More, whose courageous actions save the village and Kathleen. It is only when the landlord is defeated that the villagers feel safe to dance and the couple can wed. Again family assumes a central position in Porter's story. Kathleen's childhood family is little more than a memory as the film begins: her father is old and in debt to Clearfield; her mother is dead. O'More not only rescues Kathleen from the villain but, through marriage, renews the family for another generation. While the family's future is threatened by Clearfield's megalomania, it is not capitalism or wealth that the story rejects so much as rapacity.

Kathleen Mavourneen suggests that power is in the wrong hands and must be reclaimed by the people, although the setting is in the past and on the other side of the Atlantic. The conflict and O'More's triumph occur at a distance, within a framework of bittersweet nostalgia for a life without such heroes, a life that many immigrant spectators had left behind. The film's resolution differs from the final equilibrium in *The Ex-Convict*, where the gap between rich and poor is bridged by the recognition of family. Since Clearfield has no comparable source of redemption, only his demise restores peace. The social structure, however, does not change. Here the problem is one of aberrant individualism and does not imply a fundamental critique of social relations. Rather it expresses a simple, Christian longing for human dignity and happiness.

Edison promotional material called it "the first and only Irish picture" and listed its cast to emphasize the film's ties to legitimate theater.[76] None of these were actors with whom Porter continued working, and it seems likely that he hired a theatrical company to make the film. At least some of the names are pseudonyms: Captain Clearfield was said to be played by H. L. Bascom, the name of the actor who originally played this role at the Boston Theater in 1867.[77] Much of Porter and McCutcheon's Irish melodrama was shot as if the audience could understand the absent dialogue exchanged between the various characters. Likewise the collaborators used conventional theatrical blocking in most of their scenes, notably in the opening, for which the expansive landscape was treated as a stage. With nine major characters in the film, audiences would

Kathleen Mavourneen. Terence O'More rescues Kathleen; returning to the village, the lovers pause as the church bells toll the Angelus.

have had difficulty sorting out the narrative unless they already knew the play and/or received assistance from missing intertitles or a lecture. The only easily understood sequence is the chase between the villagers and the soldiers (scenes 5–8). As in *Life of a Cowboy*, the chase relies on representational principles that differ from those used in other sections of the film.

One way to facilitate comprehension was with the exhibitor's judicious use of sound effects, as with scene 15:

> Recently a film was seen in which a young couple were coming across a field. They stopped suddenly and stood with bowed heads for a few seconds, then proceeded on their way, much to the mystification of the audience. But when the same picture was shown at another theater, the mystery was solved; for a second before they stopped a church bell tolled as they seemed to hear it they stood with lowered heads. The realism was pretty and very touching—it made a hit and occasioned comment among the audience.[78]

But sound effects could not solve the problem of narrative clarity by themselves. *Kathleen Mavourneen* and other ambitious Edison projects challenge Nicholas Vardac's assertion that stage melodrama could be readily adapted to silent film because dialogue was an inessential part of the play.[79] The script for one widely disseminated version of the play is not only wordy, but speech provides crucial information and the story line. In this it is not unlike *Hazel Kirke*. This suggests that the absence of words was strongly felt by producers, exhibitors, and viewers and made comprehension of films much more difficult. Despite these drawbacks both *Kathleen Mavourneen* and *Life of a Cowboy* were commercial successes that spectators found attractive, even if somewhat obscure in their narratives.

The preceding analysis only touches on Porter and McCutcheon's full-scale reworking of the *Kathleen Mavourneen; or St. Patrick's Eve* story line.[80] In the play, the landlord character is an aristocrat named Bernard Kavanagh, and Clearfield serves as his underling. In fact, most of the play—act 2 through act 5, scene 2—is actually Kathleen's dream. In act 1, Kavanagh's offer to marry Kathleen is immediately followed by a similar offer from Terence O'More, her childhood friend and lover. Kathleen is torn between becoming a lady or being true to herself. Uncertain which to choose, she falls asleep. In her nightmarish dream (which is not revealed to be a dream until the end of the play), she has married Kavanagh, who becomes bored with her ways and attempts to have her murdered. Terence intervenes and kills him—only to be caught and sent to the gallows. When she awakes, Kathleen knows what she must do. The play thus has much greater psychological subtlety than the film, which avoids the dream construction. The good-versus-evil conflict is in her mind and projected onto the characters. Kavanagh is not without ambiguity, but he is decent enough in "real life," even though he acts despicably in her dream. The play's suggestion of class solidarity is tempered, if not undercut, by strong "know your place" assumptions.

A more extensive comparison of play and film would scrutinize many potentially significant variations: Kavanagh and his sister are completely absent from the film; Clearfield and the lesser villains only exist in the play during Kathleen's dream; two new characters are added for the film (Danny Kelly and Dugan). Other minor characters are dropped, and one (Kitty O'Laverty) assumes an entirely different role. A crag in the play is replaced by a cave, and the film eliminates a scene providing comic relief. Porter concludes his adaptation with a marriage, whereas the play ends with the villagers dancing a jig—the second-to-last scene in the film. Familiarity with the play would have been of only limited help to spectators trying to follow the motion picture story.

The play *Daniel Boone: On the Trail* did not have nearly as wide currency as *Hazel Kirke* or *Kathleen Mavourneen*. Moreover, although many narrative elements and specific tricks were carried over to the *Daniel Boone* film, the adaptation involved substantive changes. In the "original," an archetypal villain cannot win Boone's daughter in marriage and so leads the Indians in an attack on the white settlers in hopes of realizing his ambition by force. Porter and McCutcheon completely deleted this character from the film, turning the good-versus-evil theme into one of civilization versus savages (although Boone is befriended by a "good" Indian maid). Another important character, a black slave used for comic relief, was also expunged. This was consistent with a more general pattern of adaptation: all three plays contain scenes and characters for comic relief that were subsequently eliminated in the films.

According to Van C. Lee, films such as *Daniel Boone* required an accompanying lecture to be understood:

> Think of such subjects as *A Trip Through Switzerland*, *Daniel Boone* or even *The Passion Play*, being thrown on the screen with not one word of explanation. Might just

as well imagine that the public was invited to pay their nickels to see merely an "invention" via a machine that can throw upon a sheet pictures which can actually move with life motion, as certainly the majority would not, any further than that, understand what they see.[81]

Daniel Boone, nonetheless, was frequently shown without a lecture. *Variety* reviewed the film under such circumstances and noted, "There are interesting moments in the story of frontier Indian fighting but the clearness of the story is clouded by a mass of superfluous matter."[82] Although Porter and McCutcheon presented elaborate narratives that aspired to the sophistication of theatrical dramas, they remained dependent on the traditional lecture to explain what was happening on the screen.

Robert K. Bonine and the Production of Actualities: 1906–1907

Although fiction films were the Kinetograph Department's principal product, the Edison Manufacturing Company still continued to produce a significant number of actualities during 1906 and the first half of 1907. Here a simple division of labor was generally observed. Porter's filmmaking energies were directed almost exclusively to the production of acted "features," while Robert K. Bonine traveled around the country and to the new U.S. territorial possessions, where he took actuality subjects. His films were sold primarily to traveling motion picture exhibitors then taking refuge in the travelogue, old-time stereopticon lecturers finally incorporating films into their programs, and exchanges servicing vaudeville theaters retaining a residual interest in travel scenes and news topicals. Hale's Tours and similar shows also provided a significant market during 1906.

Shortly after the earthquake in San Francisco on April 18, 1906, Bonine went to the West Coast and filmed the remains of the destroyed city, including *Panorama Russian and Nob Hill from an Automobile* and *Dynamiting Ruins and Rescuing Soldiers Caught in the Fallen Walls*. Thirteen short subjects were put on sale, and film exchanges and exhibitors were informed that "any selection of subjects may be joined together. Every film is provided with an Edison announcement plainly describing each scene and greatly adding to the interest and value of each picture."[83] The earthquake's news value was such that Edison sold between twenty-two and sixty-eight copies of these films, in many cases to exchanges that rarely purchased news films.

After photographing the San Francisco devastation, the Edison cameraman traveled south and filmed *Flora Fiesta, Los Angeles* on May 22, 1906. The San Francisco disaster had created concern about dangerous earthquakes in Southern California and the week-long festival was designed to refurbish the city's image. A quarter of a million people reportedly attended the flower fete "in perfect May weather, beneath an amorous sun, tempered by deliciously cool winds from the sunset sea." According to the *Los Angeles Times*, the 250,000 saw the most memorable sight of their lives, and "the day was, from every point, the greatest in the city's history."[84] Bonine was probably hired by local businessmen who wanted the parade filmed for promotional purposes. If so, their efforts were not notably successful, since Edison sold only three copies in the next nine months.

After completing his obligations in Los Angeles, Bonine returned to San Francisco, where he received an invitation for a Hawaiian film trip. On May 28th, he cabled the Hawaiian Promotion Committee that he would come.[85] Three days later he left for the islands, where he had earlier taken films for the Biograph Company. His original intention was to travel on to Japan, but Hawaii lured him into a protracted stay: he did not head back to the mainland until August 14th.[86] Cooperating with, and probably subsidized by, the islands' local railroad company and their promotional committee, he photographed a series of short films under the rubric *Scenes and Incidents Hawaiian Islands*. Subjects included *Hawaiians Arriving to Attend a "Luau" or Native Feast*; *Shearing Sheep, Humunla Ranch, Hawaii*; and *Panoramic View of Waikiki Beach, Honolulu*.[87] On his way back home, Bonine filmed in Yellowstone National Park during the late summer.[88] Sales for Bonine's Hawaiian subjects averaged ten to twelve copies over the next six months. *A Trip Through the Yellowstone* was offered as a 735-foot feature and sold twenty-one copies; some of these must have circulated among nickelodeons that were short on product and/or looking for respectable "educational" subjects that might appeal to middle-class patrons and local authorities. While individual scenes of Yellowstone were sold in 75- to 140-foot lengths, only one or two copies were generally purchased.

With Bonine away on his trip, Porter almost certainly was needed to take *Scenes and Incidents, U.S. Military Academy, West Point* and films of local sporting events such as *The Vanderbilt Cup* and *Harvard-Yale Boat Race*. These sold between three and eight copies. On July 31, 1906, he also filmed *Auto Climbing Contest*, which took place at Crawford Notch, New Hampshire. It was sponsored by the Bay State Automobile Association and photographed for Percival Waters at the request of the Keith organization. Alex T. Moore subsequently indicated that these subjects were acknowledged money losers and only made to please important customers.[89] Such films found their way into theaters on special occasions, but were ill suited to the rental system that had sprung up, since topicality limited the period over which an exchange could realistically expect to recoup its investment.

In March 1907, four months after President Roosevelt's trip to the Panama Canal, Bonine accompanied Alfred Patek, former managing editor of the *Denver Times*, and Frank Webster, another Denver newspaperman, to Panama, where he took films and slides of the Canal Zone under their supervision. Scenes

Robert K. Bonine's films of Hawaii.

showing life on the isthmus and the canal's construction included *Panorama of Old French Machinery*; *U.S. Sanitary Squad Fumigating a House*; and *"Making the Dirt Fly."* [90] Once again Bonine took a number of slides and films about a specific subject around which exhibitors could construct programs.

Bonine's travel films were used by exhibitors to celebrate nature both as natural beauty and natural resource. With one group of films, those on Hawaii, the photographer himself became an exhibitor, presenting his own program at several venues, including the Orange Camera Club in May 1907.[91] His Hawaiian travelogue showed the picturesque quality of this overseas territory, acquired at the beginning of the Spanish-American War. Such programs made America's distant possessions seem more concrete and desirable by featuring Hawaii's exotic, unspoiled scenery and its modest contribution to the U.S. economy.

A similar program on the Panama Canal was given by Alfred Patek, who had supervised Bonine's photography in the Canal Zone. Using fifteen Bonine films and two hundred slides (many, but not all, taken by Bonine on the same trip), he presented his program in Denver on April 23, 1907. According to one review, Patek's lecture combined "an intelligent and comprehensive review of the great canal work, past, present and future with pictures that explain better than words all the phases of governmental work in Panama and the life of the natives and the Americans who are carrying on the tremendous undertaking of our Government."[92] Such a program retrospectively justified President Roosevelt's sponsorship of Panama's 1903 secession from Columbia, which had enabled the United States to build the canal. (A treaty in 1904 guaranteed Panama's independence, while the United States acquired sovereignty over the Canal Zone in perpetuity.)[93] The Bonine/Patek films pointed toward the canal's completion, when it would be an economic and military asset. At a time when isolationist feelings were still strong, these pictures, like those of Hawaii, buttressed the principles of American imperialism.[94]

As with his Hawaii films, Bonine's scenes of Yellowstone showed Americans the natural beauty of their country and underlined the necessity of protecting it from short-sighted exploitation. One set of films was used by E. C. Culver, a veteran stage driver who had spent twenty years in Yellowstone National Park. Culver spent the off-season giving illustrated lectures sponsored by the U.S. Department of the Interior and the Yellowstone Park Transportation Company (his previous presentations had used only stereopticon slides).⁹⁵ Like most travelogues, they were designed to spur tourism and to turn nature, exempt from exploitation as natural resource, into a commodity of a different form.⁹⁶ Unlike Porter's and James Smith's earlier films of New York slums and quotidian events or Abadie's films of Europe and the Middle East, Bonine's actualities affirmed the expansionist ambitions of Roosevelt and big business. They supported the president's actions, which Porter often burlesqued.

With Edison giving nonfiction films a low priority, Bonine decided to leave the company's employ. Before he left in mid May 1907, he may have taken one other "series of about 20 motion pictures." These were shot at the Walkover Shoe Plant in Brockton, Massachusetts, for the George Keith Company.⁹⁷ The Walkover Shoe Company later distributed these films as a way to promote its products.⁹⁸ Pushed to the periphery of the motion picture business by the popularity of fiction films, Bonine became embittered. In June, shortly after he left, the cinematographer expressed his unhappiness to a Hawaiian friend:

> You can't imagine the great demand there has been for moving picture films within the past year, due of course to the great number of cheap picture shows springing up all over the country, but the demand is all for "comedy" or, in other words, anything of a subjective nature, and it was the demand for this class of work that kept the place so busy and held my Hawaiian subjects back so long.
>
> This part of the business is handled in a separate department in New York where they can secure the "talent" or actors, costumes, scenic painters, etc., but the developing and finishing is all done here at the factory. My intention was to quit with the Edison company on my return last fall, but I did not want to leave the Hawaiian subjects until they were finished and the work completed, so I remained on until several weeks ago on finishing up my Panama canal subjects.
>
> I have resigned my position now and am making preparations to make a western trip some time quite soon and on over to the islands sometime in July, so am looking forward to seeing you again and giving you an opportunity to see the pictures I made last summer.
>
> I have purchased a set of my Hawaiian scenes and a complete projecting apparatus with the object of giving some exhibitions and [plan to] make a number of other scenes which I was unable to get last summer as I will be much better equipped this time and able to make and finish the work, complete and exhibit it before leaving the islands.
>
> My Hawaiian plate negatives were all put away in storage, as I was unable to do anything with them and just at present I am pushing my Panama negatives for lantern slide purposes, there being a temporary demand for them owing to a number of Senators and M.C.'s having been down there this past winter.⁹⁹

Bonine's Hawaiian trip was part of a world tour, during which he took films for the U.S. government.[100] He eventually settled in Hawaii, where he continued his film and photographic activities until he died in Honolulu on September 11, 1923.[101] His departure from Edison virtually ended the company's activities in nonfiction filmmaking.

11 As Cinema Becomes Mass Entertainment, Porter Resists: 1907–1908

Edwin Porter and the Edison Manufacturing Company found themselves operating within a dynamic, rapidly changing industry. The year 1907 was a key turning point in cinema's history as pressures created or magnified by the nickelodeon boom transformed screen practices on almost every level. Finally, by mid 1908, cinema had become a form of mass communication: "a process in which professional communicators use mechanical media to disseminate messages widely, rapidly and continuously to arouse intended meanings in large and diverse audiences in attempts to influence them in various ways."[1] Such a transformation involved changes in the methods of representation, film production, exhibition, reception, and distribution. Yet Porter barely participated in this process. As a result, his standing and the standing of his films were on the wane. Thomas A. Edison, in contrast, began to assume a new and more powerful role, using litigation victories on his motion picture patents as the basis for this renewed influence.

The End of the Nickelodeon Frontier

The nickelodeon boom was coming to an end by late 1907. Towns in most parts of the country had at least one motion picture theater. Nickelodeon managers were operating within a competitive environment that required them to show more and newer films and to change programs more frequently. Expenses therefore rose. Since most of these improvements made the shows last longer, fewer patrons could be admitted. Since admission remained at five cents, box-office grosses declined. With expenses increasing and revenues decreasing, many small theaters could not seat enough customers to survive. Economies of scale, upgrading and expansion of facilities, and elaboration of exhibition practices

Thomas A. Edison in 1906.

became necessities for many showmen. Larger theaters spread operating expenses over more seats and were able to offer a superior show at a lower cost per customer.

A brief, sharp depression, started by a financial panic in October 1907, intensified competition and the process of rationalization both within the moving picture field and between different parts of the amusement industry. By late

November *Film Index* reported: "All must admit that there has been a stringency in the moving picture field as far as patronage is concerned. It would be an extraordinary thing had that field alone withstood the 'squeeze.' Every line of business in the country has felt it to a more or less severe extent and none more so than the theatrical."[2] Vaudeville houses in big cities drew fewer customers, reducing their profitability. In New York, Keith & Proctor responded by converting many of its vaudeville theaters to moving pictures.

Manhattan's downtown section became a center for motion picture exhibition. William Brady acquired the 1,200-seat Alhambra Theater on Fourteenth Street and reopened it as a motion picture house, the Unique, at the end of 1907.[3] People had predicted that this change would adversely affect neighboring vaudeville and burlesque houses. These expectations proved correct. By late June not only Keith's Union Square Theater but the Dewey, acquired by William Fox, and Pastor's had been converted to motion picture shows. On a single block between Broadway and Third Avenue on Fourteenth Street, there were five picture houses. Competition was so intense that *Variety* called it "the Battle of 14th Street." To attract patronage, Pastor's offered a four-reel, one-and-a-quarter-hour program. Unable to compete, the Miles Brothers closed their Fourteenth Street storefront theater at the end of June.[4] Across the country, managers were using films to replace vaudeville or fill a house that would have otherwise been dark.

Opportunities for safe investments by small-time entrepreneurs were giving way to competition and big business not only among exhibitors but among the film exchanges as well. By December 1907 Carl Laemmle had opened exchanges in Evansville, Indiana; Memphis, Tennessee; and Council Bluffs, Iowa.[5] Less than a year later, he had six offices outside Chicago.[6] William Swanson bought out his partner, James H. Maher, and opened a new exchange in New Orleans in September 1907; a third Swanson exchange was started in St. Louis two months later.[7] Similar moves were made by other prominent renters.

By the end of 1907, a web of film exchanges stretched across the country. Subsequent growth for these companies was no longer based on the exploitation of new territories. Superior service, aggressive promotion, and/or lower prices were needed to maintain a competitive position and to win customers away from rival businesses. During the general financial panic, however, prices were slashed relentlessly. One trade journal called it a "renters' panic":

> From reports of progress from all over the country it is very evident that something must be done now, as regards the competition among film renters. The best of things do at times outgrow their usefulness, and the healthy influence of competition has been worn threadbare in this case; it is no longer the healthy competition which is said to be "the life of the trade," but a menacing, detrimental scramble for all that is within reach, without regard for the ordinary ethics of a self-respecting commercial man.
>
> Yes it is a panic. Why is it that a renter sends emissaries around the showmen

soliciting business, not at any fixed price but at any price at all, just so it is lower than the other man's?[8]

Less efficient exchanges operated at a loss or cut corners. To avoid purchasing new prints, they sent exhibitors "junk"—worn-out prints that should not have been screened. Short on cash, they sometimes paid film manufacturers with bad checks.[9] Some unscrupulous renters—notably the 20th Century Optiscope Company—made or purchased illegal dupes, depriving the original producers of significant revenue.[10]

Although established producers continued to make good profits throughout the fall of 1907 because of the continued shortage of films, they felt uneasy about the future. As a new generation of successful renters looked for growth opportunities within the industry, they followed the leads of Vitagraph, Kalem, and Essanay by moving into production. William H. Goodfellow, owner of the Detroit Film Exchange, started the Goodfellow Manufacturing Company. In St. Louis, Oliver T. Crawford, who owned several exchanges and many theaters, moved into production. His company's first film was of the International Balloon Races in October. Comedies and dramatic films were to follow shortly.[11] The Actograph Company was taking actualities by August and was ready to make fictional subjects three months later. One of the enterprise's assets was the dog Mannie, which had starred in many previous Edison films.[12] Looking toward the future, established producers realized that unregulated competition assured eventual overproduction, falling prices, and lower profits.

Established motion picture manufacturers were caught between aspiring production companies on one hand and Edison litigation on the other. If the validity of Edison's patents was upheld, they, too, would be treated as upstarts. After Edison's partial victory against Biograph in March 1907, the inventor's lawyers reactivated a suit against William Selig and began to build a case against Vitagraph. Edison hired George E. Stevens away from Vitagraph, where he had worked as a stage manager between October 1906 and April 1907. Stevens provided Edison's lawyers with evidence that proved Vitagraph had been using the infringing Warwick camera and had subsequently converted to the Demeny beater camera made by Gaumont in an attempt to circumvent Edison's patents.[13] Six years later, Smith was to recall, "We were very perturbed and disturbed over the fact that they had gotten this evidence and shortly after that suggestions were made to us that we could get together with the Edison Company and pay a license, the probability was that some sort of agreement could be reached, whereby we could proceed with our business in a state of peace and security, with the assurance that we would be no further disturbed in the development of the art, and the investment of our money."[14] Smith's sentiments were echoed by George Spoor and other producers.[15] When an injunction was entered against Selig on October 24, 1907, it was clearly time for the manufacturers to reach an agreement with Edison.[16] Such an agreement, moreover, could provide the basis for an association that might regulate aspects of the industry for the benefit of its members.

The Formation of the Association of Edison Licensees and the Film Service Association

The "general dissatisfaction with conditions" led to a meeting of manufacturers in New York on November 9, 1907. George Spoor and William Selig attended from Chicago, as did the leading New York producers and importers.[17] A week later, this group and owners of many of the country's leading film exchanges gathered in Pittsburgh "to discuss matters of vital importance for the regulation and improvement of existing business conditions."[18] The renters met among themselves and formed the United Film Service Protective Association "for the purpose of working in cooperation with the manufacturers, importers, jobbers and exhibitors of the films and accessories to improve the service now furnished the public, to protect each other in the matter of credits and all other conditions affecting our mutual welfare, and in general to take such action as will be appropriate to improve conditions of the trade."[19] They adopted a platform that prohibited exhibitors from subletting or "bicycling" prints among several theaters, a practice that wore out their goods and reduced the number of paying customers. To assure themselves adequate profits, they established a minimum rate for service. To make it more difficult for new exchanges to begin, they eliminated sale of second-hand film. Prints were to be retired after a designated period of time and returned to the manufacturer. To prevent small or new exchanges from joining the association, an initial membership fee of $200 was imposed and thereafter raised to $5,000 with a waiting period of one year before the newcomer's membership could be activated.

The renters planned to form an alliance with a separate, but coordinated, organization of manufacturers; this group would marginalize if not eliminate nonmember competitors. Although the renters came to ready agreement at the Pittsburgh convention and subsequent meetings in Chicago and Buffalo, the manufacturers and importers encountered much greater difficulties, for Edison was determined to take control of any organization that might emerge. While the producers recognized that Edison's patents could provide a valuable underpinning for the organization, the terms had to be negotiated. *Moving Picture World* later reported: "It is claimed that the motives which led to the combination of interests between the manufacturers were 'ninety-nine parts commercial and one part legal, the legal aspect being only a stepping stone to accomplish the prime object of placing the business on a substantial footing for the ultimate benefit of all concerned.' "[20]

Edison and Gilmore decided to offer licenses to only seven manufacturers and to exclude importers like George Kleine, Isaac Ullman, and Williams, Brown & Earle. Licenses were designated for Biograph, Vitagraph, Lubin, Selig,

Pathé, Méliès, and Kalem. The inclusion of Kalem was supposed to mollify Kleine. Essanay was viewed as a backup: if Biograph failed to join, Spoor and Anderson would be given a license. Biograph was the source of much difficulty. Since its motion picture patents had been recognized by the courts, it wanted this to be reflected in the new organization. This Edison refused to do. After much hesitation, Biograph finally refused to join, thus enabling Essanay to receive a license.[21] Edison executives planned to permit these seven licensed manufacturers to operate if they paid a penny-per-foot royalty on the film they used. While this tribute was acceptable to American manufacturers, Pathé Frères insisted on only half that amount. Edison held a legal advantage, but Pathé held the upper hand commercially. Without Pathé's participation, no association was possible. Pathé had its way.[22]

A formal agreement, effective March 1st, was finally reached at the conference of film renters and manufacturers in Buffalo on February 8th and 9th. *Variety* noted that "the American moving picture trade was organized into a compact, cohesive system of manufacture and distribution which, it is promised, will revolutionize the business."[23] This was accomplished through the mutual support of the Association of Edison Licensees (the production companies) and the renamed Film Service Association (the renters): they were conceived of as allied, equal, and independent organizations. Film Service members agreed to purchase films only from the Edison licensees, while the licensees were to sell only to the members of the Film Service Association (FSA). Several exchanges faced difficult choices. O. T. Crawford, the Actograph Company, and the Miles Brothers ceased their production activities and joined the FSA. Mannie, the Edison dog, did not return to the screen. William Goodfellow, however, kept his exchange out of the combination so he could continue his filmmaking activities. Renters were further prohibited from purchasing a manufacturer's business or license, a rule that was later tested in the case of the Méliès company.[24]

To strengthen the position of the licensees, the Edison Company signed an agreement with George Eastman. This required the licensees to buy all their raw stock from Eastman Kodak; in return, Eastman would not sell to newcomers, including American manufacturers outside the trust, with the sole exception of Biograph. Vitagraph was unhappy that Eastman had not limited his sales to European competitors as well. In a letter to George Eastman marked "strictly confidential," J. Stuart Blackton argued that "the only reason which could induce me to accept a license and permit Edison to make an enormous profit with the royalty would be that in doing so I would thereby keep the foreign competition out of the market."[25] With George Eastman providing the best, and for practical purposes the only, film for motion pictures in America, this agreement greatly strengthened the position of the licensees by raising barriers to aspiring domestic producers.

Licensed renting activities were concentrated in approximately 120 exchanges owned by 60 renters. Some of these were latecomers that were allowed to join the FSA rather than side with the opposition forming around Biograph. Renters were required to buy at least $1,200 worth of film each month. Vitagraph expected this last requirement to increase its sales by at least forty reels of film per month.[26] It also eliminated smaller exchanges that were a potential threat to more established bureaus. Exchanges were not allowed to rent to exhibitors showing unlicensed films or to undercut the schedule of minimum prices. Violation of these and other rules meant fines or expulsion from the FSA. Some restrictions—for instance, one that prohibited businessmen from acting as both renters and exhibitors—were met with skepticism and never enforced.

The Edison licensees also introduced a formal release system. During the fall, some manufacturers had marketed a new film each week but without specifying the precise day of delivery. Now individual manufacturers released a picture on a given day of the week—every week. Pathé, increasing its production rate to five reels of film per week, released films on Mondays, Tuesdays, Wednesdays, Fridays, and Saturdays. Vitagraph at first released on Thursday and later Tuesday.[27] Edison shipped prints of a new film every Thursday.[28] Others sought the most advantageous position. Designed to maximize sales, the release system ensured a steady, predictable flow of new subjects to the exchanges and then on to the exhibitors.

Although the nickelodeons were suppose to receive better service in the form of newer prints, they were the losers under the new arrangements. The announced increase was expected to force some theaters to raise their admission fees to a dime. Others would be forced to close. In Philadelphia, Harry Davis's general manager observed, "while the new agreement entered into by the manufacturers of films would probably force a number of small places out of existence, it would prove beneficial to the larger concerns."[29] Their rental costs rose as manufacturers and renters were organizing to take a higher proportion of industry revenues. Although barriers were created to deter people from entering production and distribution, no deterrent prevented them from entering the exhibition field. The agreements would initially eliminate some marginal theaters and encourage economies of scale, but the producers' goal was to maximize the number of rentees and the corresponding volume of sale. At the top, the Edison arrangement was monopolistic in intent; at the bottom, free enterprise would reign.

Laying out rules that regulated the principal components of the industry, the Association of Edison Licensees and the Film Service Association prohibited marginal film practices. The production of industrials, advertising films like those Edison made for Walkover Shoes, and special comedies like those made for Lew Dockstader was apparently no longer permitted. Local actuality subjects could not be made or handled by members of the Film Service Association, pushing nonfiction filmmaking even further to the margins.[30] Sales of films to schools, hospitals, and amateur exhibitors would continue only under severe restrictions: films had to be at least one year old and under 200 feet in length.[31] Independent activities by exhibitors such as Lyman Howe, Burton Holmes, and Robert Bonine were theoretically banned; practically they continued in a legal twilight.

The Biograph Association of Licensees

The Association of Edison Licensees and the Film Service Association had limited ability to implement their desired regulations because important enterprises stayed outside the combination. The American Mutoscope & Biograph Company and George Kleine were not given the opportunity to join the Edison combination in a capacity commensurate with their economic or legal positions. They formed an opposing organization based on Biograph's productions and patents and Kleine's European imports and chain of exchanges. Italian "Cinès"; Williams, Brown & Earle; and the Great Northern Film Company were also given Biograph licenses to import films from abroad.[32] Altogether they offered a "regular weekly supply of from 12 to 20 reels of splendid new subjects."[33] Furthermore, Biograph announced its intention to license local domestic producers. Although it did not follow up on these threats, companies like Goodfellow Manufacturing operated in cooperation with the Biograph group.[34] The resulting "film war" was waged simultaneously on the legal front through the courts, on a commercial front through pricing and marketing strategies, and on the production front through the efficient manufacture of popular films.

On the legal front, Edison sued Biograph and the Kleine Optical Company in March for infringing on a film patent, reissue no. 12,192, that had not previously been tested in the courts.[35] To strengthen its position, Biograph acquired the "Latham loop" patent from the E. & H. T. Anthony Company for $2,500 and used it to bring countersuit against the Edison Company and its various licensees.[36] Lengthy discussions in the trade were devoted to the value of the Latham loop, which Frank Dyer regarded "as so unimportant as not to warrant serious consideration."[37] George Kleine and Biograph's Harry Marvin, in contrast, insisted the loop was essential for making films over 75 feet in length.[38] Biograph also formed an alliance with the Armat Motion Picture Company on March 21st, thereby gaining access to its patents covering motion picture projection.

"We were engaged in bitter commercial strife," Harry Marvin later explained. "We did what all people do under those circumstances. We fought the best we knew how. We belittled the possessions of our enemies, and we magnified our own possessions."[39] Between March 16th and April 30th, the Edison Company brought suit against thirty theater owners in the Chicago area and six in the Eastern District of Missouri (St. Louis) and the Eastern District of Wisconsin (Milwaukee) for showing films produced or imported by the Biograph licensees.[40] William T. Rock, a longtime believer in patent litigation as an effective commercial weapon, was delighted. "Why, man, all they have to do is to draw up a general complaint, print fifty or a hundred copies and file suits in as many cities of the Union," he told a reporter. "This can be done at very little expense, but look at the thousands of dollars that will have to be spent by the other side in engaging lawyers and defense for all these suits."[41] Kleine, identifying the Biograph licensees as "independents," observed that these suits were attempts to drive users of independent films into the Edison circle by questionable methods. He appealed to "the characteristic feeling of stubbornness in the average American which prompts him to resent such an attempt to compel him to violate his principles of independence."[42] Accepting the argument that such actions constituted harassment, the courts prevented Edison from bringing additional suits against Kleine's customers until the principal suits were resolved. To maintain the balance of anxiety, Biograph and Armat initiated legal action against William Fox's Harlem Amusement Company and a chain of twenty Chicago theaters in late May.[43] Many companies that had joined the Edison association thinking it would bring legal peace were disappointed when the warfare intensified and the uncertainty remained.

On the commercial front, the Edison licensees and Film Service Association cut prices 20 percent to maintain their competitive position. Unaffiliated exchanges were also allowed to join the FSA at the old $200 rate[44] even as the renters' return of old films to the producers was quietly deferred.[45] While able to consolidate their initial advantage, the Edison affiliates could not eliminate the opposition. In an interview, I. W. Ullman of Italian "Cinès" admitted that his company had experienced "the *forced* shrinkage in our market, beginning March 2, 1908, of upwards of 75 per cent."[46] Reports reaching Frank Dyer at the Edison office, however, document the resurgence of the independents in some areas of the country. Writing in late April, Laemmle reported that "there is no denying the fact that the Independents are getting stronger day by day." He enclosed a letter from his manager in Evansville, Indiana, predicting that "this whole section is going to the independents within the next ten days if something is not done and done mighty quick."[47] The independents moved rapidly to establish their own nationwide network of film exchanges. George Kleine, who sold his Kalem Company shares to avoid conflicting interests, opened new branches until he had offices in twelve key cities.[48] Williams, Brown & Earle inaugurated a Philadelphia exchange much against their will; nonetheless, it soon proved profitable.[49] A small group of established exchanges also went over to the independents.[50]

The exclusion of many European and select American producers from the Edison ranks resulted in a serious dearth of subjects. A New York critic visited ten nickelodeons in his neighborhood and found that nine were showing the same first-run films.[51] This was particularly notable along Manhattan's Fourteenth Street, where the Unique, Dewey, Pastor's, and Union Square theaters were "determined to have none but the newest and latest films obtainable from the Edison side."[52] The same pictures were shown in all four theaters. In July the Unique jumped over to the independents to secure fresh subjects. Other large theaters in New York and Brooklyn made a similar switch at about the same time.[53] The *Dramatic Mirror* reported:

> Changes of service have been made both ways by theatres in different parts of the country, and such changes are bound to occur from time to time so long as the field is divided into two camps. Neither side is turning out enough new subjects to supply the entire market, and managers who do not want to give the same pictures as their neighbors, or who think they can get better service by changing, will change. In the long run the best output of subjects will prove the most profitable—that is, providing patent litigation does not wipe out one side or the other.[54]

Since the independents helped to satisfy the nickelodeons' desire for product diversity, the Edison group found it difficult to push them from the field using strictly commercial methods.

The extent to which independent films were available in the New York area was suggested by Edison's industrial spy, Joseph McCoy, who saw 515 films while visiting 106 different storefront theaters in June. Of these films, 57 had been made by the independents and the rest by Edison licensees; however, McCoy saw 133 of them at the Elite Theater in Newark, New Jersey, which showed only licensed films. Disregarding this theater, the independents provided about 15 percent of the films that McCoy saw. Of these 57 films, 15 were made by Biograph, 13 by Italian "Cinès," 11 by Gaumont, 10 by Urban-Eclipse, and 8 by Nordisk. In contrast, the Edison Company alone supplied 45 of the films viewed by McCoy.[55] Despite their small share of the film business, the independent or non-Edison combination made it difficult for the Film Service Association to maintain discipline within its ranks. Expulsions for violations would not put the guilty exchanges out of business but send them into the opposition camp, further strengthening the Biograph licensees and weakening the Edison position.

The Edison group was internally disorganized, with considerable animosity existing between rival FSA exchanges. Despite its recently exposed duping activities, the 20th Century Optiscope Company proclaimed its own determination "to live up to the rules and regulations in every way." It accused the Yale Amusement Company—its principal competitor in Kansas City—of price cutting and asked the manufacturers to make an example of it by stopping its supply of films.[56] A. D. Plintom of the Yale Amusement Company insisted on his own integrity and called the "Twentieth Century people . . . very unscrupulous in their methods."[57] William Swanson, who was on the FSA executive

board, complained that "here in Chicago the kikes have organized among themselves" to the detriment of the business. He characterized three or four renters—
whom he was responsible for organizing into a local association—as vultures,
blood suckers, thieves, and price cutters.[58] Swanson was clearly jealous of
Laemmle's success. The Standard Film Exchange informed Dyer that Swanson's
animosity toward them had existed before the formation of the association and
invited "close scrutiny of our business methods at any and all times."[59] The
Yale Amusement Company accused Swanson of illegally opening a branch office
in Kansas City and severe price cutting as he attempted to win a toehold in his
new territory.[60] Other exchanges also opened unauthorized branch offices.

By June 1908 the situation had become serious enough for Thomas Edison
to intervene publicly. Claiming that he was "for the first time taking a personal
interest in the strictly commercial side of the business," he put the full weight
of his authority behind the venture. In an interview with *Variety*, he announced,

> I am aware of some of the restlessness and minor dissatisfactions among the dealers.
> This is a natural condition. No big movement was ever perfected without experiment.
> That's what we are doing now—experimenting. And I may say we are experimenting
> to some purpose.
>
> What we want to see is a system of business in which everybody is satisfied, ev-
> erybody making money and getting a full return upon his investment of brains, money
> and labor. This is the goal toward which we are working. If the progress at times seems
> slow, it is none the less sure, and our arrival there is a matter of a very short time. This
> is a great organization. It cannot be administered haphazard[ly]. Each movement must
> be carefully considered.[61]

The Association of Edison Licensees was likened to an invention that would be
improved through constant tinkering and experimentation. Now that the Wizard himself had intervened, the problems would be solved to everyone's satisfaction.

Edison was already enjoying financial benefits from the new organization.
Beyond the Edison Company's impressive film-related profits of $410,959 for
the 1908 business year, the inventor was receiving additional monies from his
licensing arrangements. Lubin sent Edison $3,200 in royalties for the period
between February 1st and June 20th.[62] Essanay paid approximately $6,000
during the first year, Pathé $17,000 or $18,000.[63] Edison's total royalty for the
first year approximated $60,000.[64] Yet Edison and association members real-
ized that the imperfect nature of the "trust" prevented the organization from
operating effectively. Many considered an alliance of Biograph and Edison interests as the only way to achieve the associations' original goals.

The new Bronx studio.

The Edison Manufacturing Company
Opens Its Bronx Studio

Gilmore's belated decision to increase the rate of film production in response to the demands of the nickelodeon era coincided with the hiring of James Searle Dawley on May 13, 1907.[65] A playwright, Dawley had been working for the Brooklyn-based Spooner Stock Company as its stage manager. His adaptation of Ouïda's *Under Two Flags* and his musical comedy *Aladdin and His Magic Lamp* were performed by the Spooner Company during the theatrical season.[66] Another one of his plays, *On Shanon's Shore*, had been copyrighted by the Spooners.[67] Dawley was in charge of renting films that were shown between acts of the stock company's plays, a job that took him to Waters' Kinetograph Company, where he eventually met Porter. As the theatrical season came to a close, Dawley was looking for employment. After an interview, the studio manager offered him a job at $40 a week.[68] Dawley joined Porter's staff but did not give up the theater: over the next year and a half, he was to complete at least four plays.[69]

Filming *A Country Girl's Seminary Life and Experiences* inside Edison's new studio in March 1908. Next page, a frame from the film.

Two weeks after Dawley joined the Edison staff, Wallace McCutcheon left the Kinetograph Department. The reasons for McCutcheon's departure are unknown, but Porter's salary had been increased from $40 to $50 in March while his remained unchanged. By October 1907 McCutcheon was back working for Biograph.[70] Although Dawley arrived during the making of *Cohen's Fire Sale*, he remembered Porter's next film, *The Nine Lives of a Cat* (July 1907), as "my first picture." It was also the last subject to be made before the filmmakers moved into their new studio.

Edison executives had recognized that they needed a new studio soon after fiction narrative films became the company's dominant type of film production. Joseph McCoy, who found a site for the new structure, recalled:

> In 1904–5 the Edison Company decided to build a moving picture studio in New York and it was up to me to select a suitable location. I looked at all the vacant places that real estate dealers had listed in Manhattan, but their prices were all too high. I then went over to the Bronx and selected about twelve locations. Mr. Dennison was Secretary of the Company at the time and a photographer. He took photographs of the locations I selected to show to Mr. Gilmore. Moore, Porter and Pelzer visited all the

locations and selected the ground for the studio at 198th Street and Oliver Place, 100 × 100, property owned by Frederick Fox and Company, real estate dealers.

I called to see Fox about buying the property. Fox said he would sell the property for $13,000. I wanted a ten day option on the property at that price. He assured me that the price would be no higher. A couple of days later he telephoned me that his price on the property would be $15,000. I took the matter of the increased price up with Mr. Gilmore. Gilmore, Moore, Pelzer and Ed. Porter looked the location over carefully. As the price of $15,000 was lower than the other locations, Mr. Gilmore said "Take it at the price of $15,000."[71]

This 100' × 100' plot of land on the north side of Oliver Place and the east side of Decatur Avenue near Bronx Park was purchased for $15,000 on June 20, 1905, from the City of New York.[72]

The studio was to be built using reinforced concrete and Edison Portland Cement. Agreements to complete the studio by the spring of 1906 were signed with several contractors just before Christmas 1905. Delays followed. Serious work did not begin on the studio until summer, at which time the studio's completion was announced for the fall at an anticipated cost of $50,000.[73] (The actual cost was $39,557 — not including land.)[74] Construction continued over the next year, however, taking much of Moore and Porter's time. As Dawley recalled in his hesitant, scrawled memoirs:

I had the pleasure of watching [the big studio in the Bronx] being built and help [put] into working [order]. What a huge place it seem[ed] to Porter and I after working in our former place, a[n] old abandoned photographic studio on the top floor of the building with a sky light roof. Every time we started to take a picture we would have to run out on the roof next door and see if the sun would pass over a cloud . . . our 21st street studio was about the size of a large office room.

Our Bronx studio seemed like a whole floor in comparison but before 2 years were out, it seemed to be to[o] small.[75]

Porter and his colleagues moved into their new headquarters on July 11, 1907, although much of the work was unfinished.[76] Heating and ventilation were not completed until October 15th. A roof had to be redone by mid December. The studio was near enough to final completion for publicity photographs to be taken on March 14, 1908, during the making of *A Country Girl's Seminary Life and Experiences*.[77] "The Edison studio is said to be one of the finest and largest of its kind in the world," reported the *Dramatic Mirror*. "The building itself is 60 by 100 feet, built of concrete, iron and glass. The scenic end of the studio, corresponding to the stage in a theatre, except that it is not raised, is 60 by 60 feet and 40 feet high. Here the scenes for film productions that cannot be made with natural outdoor backgrounds are painted and set."[78] With work continuing until June or July, the fitting out of the new studio was largely Porter's responsibility. This included custom designs for everything from lighting equipment to a mechanized developing setup for negatives (which he personally operated). The studio emulated Edison's laboratory, with all likely materials and gadgets close at hand (see document no. 23).

DOCUMENT NO. 23

EDISON CO.'S NEW STUDIO.

On a hillside near Webster avenue, the Bronx, New York, the Edison Manufacturing Company has erected a unique building, entirely of one piece, like a rockhewn temple. The material is concrete, with a roof of glass over the larger portion of the building. This odd looking structure attracts the attention of every passerby, while comments upon its probable use are varied and often ludicrous. Some are sure it is an electric power house, although the glass roof is puzzling; others think it is a dynamite factory built to avoid danger from explosion and fire.

Construction on the building commenced in the summer of 1906; its concrete walls, floors, roofs, ceilings and window casings, all molded in the soft mixture which was used thousands of years ago by the ancient builders, were put up before winter set in. An inspection of this method of house building will convince any one that Mr. Edison is right in using concrete for a photographic studio. Not to mention economy in cost, the hardness is that of rock itself, and therefore neither dampness, frost, nor gnawing rodents can affect it. Dust is minimized, and the floors and walks can be cleaned, washed or swept like a stone house. Again it is hermetically air proof and cold proof, while in the summer the heat penetrates slowly.

All these considerations are of great value to photographers and the building of a moving picture. The building extends for 100 feet along Decatur avenue; it is 60 feet wide and 35 feet high—an imposing object seen from Webster avenue.

This studio is in two parts, distinct, but standing on a common basement story. On the south side stands a plain oblong office building, three stories high, containing offices, dressing rooms, chemical laboratories, darkrooms, tankrooms and drying halls, with other necessary compartments. This faces a glass court. These two parts are connected by a sort of open hall, or atrium, directly open to the stage in the studio.

The main entrance to the offices on the avenue side opens into an entrance hall or reception room for visitors, neatly furnished. On the left is the door of the loading and chemical washrooms, which can in a moment be turned into a darkroom by simply switching off the light and shutting the door. Here a faint red light burns, and the photographer can "load" the eight inch circular boxes holding the blank films. Many other details of the work are done here also. On the right of the reception room a door leads into the main office. It is a neatly kept room, with the usual desks and office furniture, and on one side is a library shelf of books, including history, romance, adventure, travel, fairy tales—books from which particular information is gathered for constructing plots for the pictures.

Passing through the offices one comes out into the main hall or atrium before mentioned, whence a full view of the stage is obtained, of which more anon. Opposite the doors of the dressing rooms are seen, and these are four in number. Each dressing room is fitted up as in a theater, with makeup stands and tables, long wall mirrors, wash basins and even shower baths, while the windows are given plenty of light—more, probably, than many an actual theater room can boast. Every convenience and necessity is provided, except, indeed, easy chairs, for there is no lounging whatever in the Edison studio. A busier place would be hard to find.

Down under the main floor is a long, roomy place of great interest— the property room. Yes, there is even the property man here, for the numerous costumes, paraphernalia and necessaries of the work are legion and must be carefully taken stock of. Mr. W. J. Gilroy is property man, and has many interesting features to show one down in the 60 foot long property room. Among other articles are 18 Springfield rifles and a small armory of other weapons, toys, Roman togas, fairy costumes and lay figures, eagles, and so on. Although not yet a year old, the property room is already filling up.

Upstairs, on the second floor, are certain mysterious rooms, where uninitiated persons are not admitted, although it is to be guessed that they are for experimental work and secrets of the trade. On the third floor, however, are some highly fascinating rooms, the developing and drying chambers, photographic darkroom and chemical laboratories.

E. S. Porter, chief photographer and superintendent, is eminently fitted for the responsible position he holds. His ingenuity is constantly exercised; inventiveness and practical method, so necessary to the building of motion pictures, are at his finger ends.

The scenes painted under Mr. Stevens' direction by the scenic artists, are in distemper—that is, they use only blacks, browns and whites, with the varying shades of these, as photographs do not take color as color, but only suggest it. Houses or block scenery are built up and the stands and wings constructed as in a theatre, only with much more attention to details and naturalness. For the camera, unlike the eye, can not be easily deceived. "Staginess" is avoided and realism is in every case given place over "effect." Scenes indoors can be taken at any time, now that the new and wonderful artificial daylight has been introduced at the studio.

Much of the apparatus for controlling this light is the device of Mr. Porter himself, and the strength of the violet rays capable of being thrown from any part of the stage on any other part is almost beyond belief. Equal to a thousand of the ordinary arc lamps, the light concentrated on the stage by the reflectors is in photographic effect calculated at the following intensity: Taking the arc street light at its usual power of one thousand standard candles, the studio light equals one million candle power. Such a light in violet rays, is not glaring, but is like daylight diffused.

The electrical equipment of the whole building is perfect and interchangeable, and especially so these mysterious stage lights. An ordinary theater switch box, with spider boxes and the usual maze of connections, is used. Electric motors of different sizes come handy for mechanical effects, and so there can be produced any sort of scene whatever, even a water scene.

A water scene? Certainly; and the mystery is explained when we examine the floor of the stage. This floor, 55 × 35 feet, is built in square sections, which can be lifted away, one by one. Beneath is discovered a great tank, the full size of the stage and 8 feet deep. The floor and beams are so arranged as to render the formation of a pond, a fountain or lake, or even the seashore, easy according to the number of sections of floor taken up.

A film several hundred feet long would hardly go into a photographer's developing tray, except in Brobdingnag, the giant's country; so special apparatus is used in development. The finest equipment probably in the world is here at the Edison studio. Up on the third floor is a mysterious room, which at first glance looks like some new kind of Turkish bath, there being six porcelain tubs ranged down its length. These are as large as bathtubs, much like them in appearance, but have apparatus around which would disconcert anything but a chameleon. Underneath each is a gas jet series for heating, and at each end are axles, cranks and motors. The latter are compact little devices which are used to turn the axles aforesaid. Now the other side of the room contains several huge drums, hollow and open ended, like cylinders. Mr. Porter who himself conducts the important process of developing, places one of the cylinder drums on the axles of the first tank. This contains the developer and the bottom of the drum dips into the fluid. Then a negative is unwound, all light having been excluded by double curtains at the window and a red light turned on along the falls. The several hundred feet of film is wound carefully on the drum, which is kept in motion until the pictures on the negative begin to "come up." The red light burns magically, lighting dimly the great revolving drum, like a hall of necromancy. The light comes from curious conical devices.

After development the drum is lifted into a tank of water, warmer than blood heat, and from there at once lifted over to number three tank, where the hypo clears the pictures. While the first drum is on its way down the room from tank to tank a second and third are started after it, each bearing many hundreds of tiny pictures. The series of tanks contain: No. 1, developer; No. 2, warm water; No. 3, hypo; Nos. 4 and 5, water—the bathing is to wash clean the films of hypo—and No. 6, glycerin and water, to render the films pliable in handling.

Behind the developing room is a large chemical dark room and laboratory, and outside these rooms is the drying hall, where films are reeled off on great seven-foot high wooden drums, which each holds a thousand feet of film. Here there must be no dust, as that would settle on the pictures and look like pieces of coal in magnifying the scenes on a screen. So the advantage of stone floors, walls and ceilings becomes manifest. Even the too high speeding of the rollers is avoided to prevent currents of dust carrying air.

The drying is followed by careful inspection and brushing off, and then

Stage Struck and *A Race for Millions.*

the films are reeled into their boxes again, ready for shipment to Lewellyn park, where they are developed into positives and prepared for market.

SOURCE: *Film Index*, November 28, 1908, p. 4.

One of Dawley's responsibilities in the new studio was to keep payroll records for actors. These records, as well as some of Dawley's later statements, have led some historians to credit Dawley as author and director of many Edison films of which Porter was in fact producer, (co)scriptwriter, cameraman, editor, and lab technician. While the nature of their collaboration makes attribution of sole authorship inappropriate, Porter retained the dominant role. Dawley was "stage manager" or "stage director" and responsible for blocking and acting. Dawley not only worked under Porter but had little involvement with filmic elements such as camerawork and editing. Porter's former collaboration with McCutcheon provides a comparable model for the relationship between these two men, with one essential difference. In the beginning Dawley was learning about motion pictures and deferred to his studio chief and cameraman more readily than his predecessor. Dawley acknowledged that Porter knew what he wanted, and it was the new employee's job to help him get it. Films such as *Rescued from an Eagle's Nest* thus continued Porter's previous work in both subject matter and treatment. The two only worked together for a year, after which Dawley was given his own production unit to head. During Dawley's first year, it seems more appropriate to attribute the films that Porter supervised, shot, and edited primarily to the veteran rather than the novice. If this was not the case, Dawley rather than Porter would have taken the blame for the Kinetograph Department's subsequent difficulties.

Stage Struck (July–August 1907) was the first film to be made in the new Edison studio. It starred Herbert Prior as an impoverished thespian who helps three sisters escape the farm for a career on the vaudeville stage. The exteriors

for *Stage Struck* were shot around New York City—at Coney Island and probably in the Bronx. Two scenes utilized the expanded possibilities offered by the
new studio. One set created a concert garden where the thespian and three
sisters performed on a substantial stage while the girls' parents sat at a table in
the foreground viewing the performance. For another set, a "Human Roulette
Wheel" was constructed and used in a chase sequence as the farmer tried to
capture his wayward daughters. The wheel was not essential to the story, but
Porter could not have filmed this indoor amusement either at Coney Island,
where the lighting was inadequate, or in the old studio, which was too small.
Porter next used the studio to create a western locale for *A Race for Millions*
(August–September 1907). A car was driven on stage, again something that had
been impossible at the old Twenty-first Street rooftop. The studio became a
plaything as Porter and his associates explored its many fascinating possibilities.

Once in the new studio, the Kinetograph Department responded to the demand for more films. For the remainder of Porter's tenure, the rate of production increased. In August 1907 the studio staff averaged two films per month;
by February and March 1908 they were producing at twice that rate and releasing a new film each week. In some cases, these films were very short. *Playmates* (February 1908) was only 360 feet long. Within a few months, however,
the production staff produced close to a reel of film per week—often of more
than one subject. The whole approach to filmmaking shifted. Until February,
distribution was determined by the production schedule. When a film was completed, it was readied for release and copies were then sold to the various exchanges. With the release system instituted by the licensees, this arrangement
was reversed. The rate of production was dictated not by Porter's needs but by
the distribution system.

Dawley's records show that the number of days in active production (for
which actors were hired) increased substantially over this period, while the average number of shooting days per film decreased only slightly. Less time was
devoted to preproduction, and work on each film became more concentrated.
The studio rarely hired players who had other acting commitments during a
production. In June 1907 the Edison payroll ledger listed four men as making
negative film subjects: Porter at $50 a week, J. Searle Dawley at $40, and
William Martinetti and George Stevens at $20 a week each. They were assisted
by staff members in other payroll categories, like William Gilroy, who received
$15 a week. When the group moved into the new studio, Henry Cronjager was
hired at $20 a week as Porter's assistant cameraman.[79] In September Martinetti
left and was replaced by the set designer Richard Murphy.[80] With staff size and
rate of production moving upward, Porter's salary was raised to $65 a week.

By late 1907 the Kinetograph Department was casting a group of actors with
increasing regularity. Receiving $5 a day each, they derived a significant portion
of their income from the studio. Edward Boulden appeared in eight films be-

tween September 1907 (*Jack the Kisser*) and March 1908 (*The Cowboy and the Schoolmarm*), and returned subsequently after a few months' absence. A Mr. Sullivan performed in *The Trainer's Daughter* (November 1907) and ten other films over the next six months. William Sorelle, who also made his first documented Edison appearance in *The Trainer's Daughter*, acted in more than twenty films over the next year. John (Jack) Frazer appeared in *Stage Struck* (July 1907) and then joined the Edison staff in September at $18 a week. His baby daughter Jinnie appeared in *The Rivals* (August 1907); in her next performance, she was stolen by a mechanical eagle in *Rescued from an Eagle's Nest* (January 1908). Jinnie Frazer continued to appear in Edison films whenever an infant was needed.

Some of the actors had worked for Porter as early as 1903. Boulden had been the shoe clerk in *The Gay Shoe Clerk*. Phineas Nairs, who played the detective in *The Kleptomaniac* (1905), was steadily employed at the Bronx studio after *Fireside Reminiscences* (January 1908). John Wade, who had been tarred and feathered in *The "White Caps"* (1905), appeared in *Stage Struck* and five other Edison films. Gordon Sackville, who had acted for Porter as early as 1904, appeared in *Tale the Autumn Leaves Told* (March 1908) and *Nero and the Burning of Rome* (April 1908). He later appeared in Porter's first production for Rex, *The Heroine of '76*.[81] Other actors had worked with Dawley in the Spooner Stock Company; among these were Harold Kennedy, Augustus Phillips, and Jessie McAllister. Laura Sawyer, who would become one of Edison's leading players, made her first appearance in *Fireside Reminiscences*.

A number of actors maintained a loose association with the Edison Company. Kate Bruce appeared in five films over ten months, Miss Francis Sullivan in four, and a Mr. Elaxander in five. Others were associated with the company for two or three films and then moved on, among them D. W. (Lawrence) Griffith. Griffith had been an extra in at least two Biograph films in late 1907 before winning a starring role in Porter's *Rescued from an Eagle's Nest*. He then worked as an extra at Biograph in mid January before returning to Edison in a similar position for *Cupid's Pranks* (February 1908).[82] As his connection with Biograph developed and the "film war" heated up, the actor severed his ties with the Edison Company. Herbert Prior appeared in *Stage Struck* and *Nellie, the Pretty Typewriter* (February 1908), then moved on to Biograph. He eventually returned to Edison in late 1909 as a full-time stock company actor.[83]

The development of an informal stock company grew naturally out of the increased rate of production and enabled Porter and his colleagues to work with actors who were more or less familiar with Edison procedures and whose abilities were known in advance. Films were no longer treated as discrete, individual productions: there was little time for casting calls. This was only one aspect of the Edison Manufacturing Company's hesitant move toward a studio system. Under Porter, there were some department heads: a prop man, an art director,

The Devil.

and a stage manager in charge of the actors. Yet Porter also retained complete control over photography, editing, and developing—over all the filmic elements. A division of labor was only partially and unevenly instituted. Many of the gains in the rate of production were accomplished not by increased efficiency but by increased personnel. Edison's rising production level, moreover, was only part of a larger phenomenon occurring throughout the industry. This general increase undermined the representational system that had been established in the period before the nickelodeon.

Narrative Clarity: 1907–1909

The explosion in film production meant that reliance on the spectator's prior familiarity with a story was becoming rapidly outmoded. A textbook demonstration was offered by Arthur Honig, who analyzed the viewer's reaction to Porter's *The Devil* (September 1908). This critic had already witnessed Henry Savage's play of that title when he saw Porter's adaptation. He not only used the play as an aid to following the film's narrative, but imagined the spoken lines and judged the acting and sets in relation to the play. For a modest nickel, Honig happily recalled the Savage production. While pleased with the film, this writer was also accompanied by "an intelligent friend" who had never seen the play. The friend started asking Honig questions about the story line, forcing him into the role of personal narrator. Without the necessary frame of reference, the friend's enjoyment of the film was spoiled.[84] Like Honig, the *Dramatic Mirror* felt that "the Edison players did remarkably well, although to appreciate the pictures one must have seen the original play or read the story."[85] The average nickelodeon viewer did not have this special knowledge, however, and was at a loss to understand the narrative.

While the moving picture world increasingly avoided relying on an audience's prior knowledge of the story, Porter continued to depend on it. Such reliance was fatal, however, in two respects. First, since only a limited number of stories had wide circulation in American popular culture, it limited available narratives unacceptably. There were just not enough stories to go around. Second, the craze or hit on which a story was based often had a more limited audience than the film that emulated it. Narrow, specialized audiences for such films were undesirable and created problems for renters and exhibitors who served a mass audience. Porter and his contemporaries continued to use simple stories and variations on a single gag as the basis for their film narratives, but these were also incapable of providing an overall solution to the problem. As a group, these films were too lacking in diversity and too limited in the kinds of subject matter they could portray.

As the rate of production increased in 1907–8, the only way to achieve product diversity was through the use of more complex, unfamiliar narratives. As this happened, audiences often found it difficult to follow what they saw on the screen. *Variety* remarked of one film:

> This reel offends against the most important of the elements of motion photography—following it involves a decided mental strain. Moving picture subjects, we take it, should be selected first of all for their directness, simplicity and ease of adequate exposition. As little as possible should be left out to the unaided imagination of the spectator. The story, the whole story and nothing but the story should appear on the illuminated sheet. In this subject an effort has been made to tell a complicated and intricate allegory.... When it is all over the spectator asks himself what it is all about. That's enough to mark the best picture, mechanically, ever made a failure.[86]

In a fictitious exchange between two moviegoers, one declares, "I guess they have exhausted all of the old subjects and have nothing else to show us than pictures we cannot understand." Her friend agrees, "Yes, they are at the end of their rope."[87] These complaints were common. People "do not want to sit in a dark room, yawning and asking their neighbors, 'What do the pictures mean?' " *Moving Picture World* observed.[88] The problem of narrative clarity could be solved either (1) by producing self-sufficient work that could be understood without assistance from the exhibitor or the audience's special knowledge of the material, or (2) by facilitating audience understanding through a lecture or behind-the-screen effects and dialogue. Porter's work was aligned with this second alternative.

The Lecture

The lecture, always an important strategy in the exhibitor's repertoire, was the focus of renewed interest by early 1908. In January *Billboard* reported: "Many moving picture houses are adding a lecturer to their theatre. The explanation of the pictures by an efficient talker adds much to their realism."[89] W. Stephen Bush, a former traveling exhibitor and a frequent contributor to *Moving Picture World*, considered the lecture "a creative aid to the moving picture entertainment." Bush, who often lectured at church functions, approached cinema as a traditionalist who wanted to instruct as well as entertain. He condemned the uneducated exhibitor who showed a Shakespearean play on film without a lecture and "bewildered his patrons, who might have been thrilled and delighted with a proper presentation of the work."[90] Bush prepared and offered to sell special lectures, with suggestions as to music and effects, for every feature turned out by the Edison licensees.[91] He was probably the anonymous reviewer who felt that Porter's *The Devil* "is a fine production and if given with a lecture yields little to the real play."[92] Likewise, *Colonial Virginia* (made in May 1907 and eventually released by Edison in November 1908) needed "to be presented with a lecture for the spectators to fully understand and appreciate the scenes that are presented."[93]

Bush argued that a nickelodeon's addition of a skilled lecturer would more than offset the additional salary costs by increasing patronage and turnover. "Why do so many people remain in the moving picture theater and look at the same picture two and even three times?" he asked. "Simply because they do not understand it the first time; and this is by no means in every case a reflection on their intelligence. Once it is made plain to them, their curiosity is gratified, they are pleased and go."[94] In an article entitled "The Value of a Lecture," Van C. Lee claimed surprise that "the managers are just awakening to the fact that a lecture adds much to the realism of a moving picture." Like Bush he asked his readers, "Of what interest is a picture at all if it is not understood?"[95]

Bush's and Lee's viewpoints were substantiated by considerable evidence. James H. Flattery, a humorist and elocutionist who had been in the Ed Harrigan Irish Comedian Company, lectured at the Novelty Theater on Third Avenue in New York City with great success, large crowds packing the theater each night.[96] The Casino Company, which owned a half dozen theaters, tried out a lecturer in its three Detroit houses and then added "talkers" in its three Toledo, Ohio, venues.[97] The lecture, however, encountered serious obstacles. A film fan in Augusta, Georgia, tried to convince local managers to add a lecture and found that they were reluctant to increase their expenses.[98] Some exhibitors lacked

Left: *Spook Minstrels*. Right: Vesta Victoria sings "Waiting at the Church."

access to plot synopses and often did not entirely follow the stories themselves. Furthermore, talented lecturers were difficult to find. General reliance on lectures was unlikely, given the rapid turnover of subject matter, the exhibitor's narrow profit margin, and the substantial number of films that were intelligible without such aid. In seeking to apply traditional strategies of screen presentation to this new form of mass exhibition, Bush and Lee failed to acknowledge the many obstacles that prohibited its broad application.

"Talking Pictures"

The technique of giving live dialogue to screen characters has a long history. In the mid 1890s Alexander Black changed his voice when he endowed the characters in his picture plays with speech. Starting as early as 1898, Lyman Howe's success was "largely due to his well trained assistants who render the dialogue behind the screen."[99] Having become familiar with this procedure at the Eden Musee while projecting *The Opera of Martha*, Porter photographed a minstrel performance, *Spook Minstrels*, late in 1904. *Spook Minstrels* opened on a vaudeville bill at Harry Davis's Grand Opera House in Pittsburgh on January 9, 1905.[100] A month later, it reached New York City's Circle Theater, where it was reviewed:

> A distinct novelty on the bill was the first appearance of Havez and Youngson's *Spook Minstrels*, in which moving pictures are used in a novel way. The pictures show a minstrel company going through a performance, and as the various numbers are presented the songs, jokes and dances are given by men who stand behind the screen and follow the motions of the men in the picture very accurately. The act is original and novel and was highly appreciated. The performers who do the work and who later on appeared before the curtain and sang some additional songs are G. Dey O'Hara, Charles Bates, Leon Parmet, Parvin Witte and Charles Smith.[101]

Songs included "Will You Love Me in December as You Do in May," "In Dear Old Georgia," and "My Octoroon Lady."[102] The act continued to appear at such vaudeville houses as Keith's Union Square Theater, where "the singing of the quartette won unbounded acclaim."[103] The film remained popular for many years. In the fall of 1908, it was being shown as a special at the Bijou Theater in Providence, Rhode Island, along with a regular motion picture program.[104]

The same principle was used when Porter filmed a version of *Waiting at the Church* for the Novelty Song Film Company in January 1907. Vesta Victoria was brought to Edison's Twenty-first Street studio and photographed as she sang "Waiting at the Church" in a wedding gown that was part of her smash vaudeville act. Afterwards, in another costume, she sang "Poor John," a song that was to be that season's hit. At least some of the prints were tinted. According to one announcement, "In 'Poor John' she wears for a costume a bright red satin dress with trimmings of green satin ruffles, a short box coat of imitation ermine with a small cap and tiny muff of the same."[105] In the company's theaters a singer stood behind the screen and sang synchronously with the picture, leaving the audience with the impression of having witnessed an amazingly lifelike performance from Vesta Victoria.

After playing the films in their theaters for several months, the Novelty Song Film Company sold copies to fellow exhibitors:

5 & 10¢ THEATRES—NEW, NOVEL—A TRADE BRINGER.

> We have a proposition in films that we believe will interest you. We are ourselves operating several five and ten cent theatres, and found that there was a great demand for novelties, particularly films to be used in connection with the singer. We posed Vesta Victoria (probably the highest salaried and best known performer in America to-day), singing her two most successful songs, "Waiting at the Church" and her latest hit "Poor John." This film is about 400 feet long and is unusually clear and lifelike.[106]

Even prior to this announcement, purchases were made by Waters' Kinetograph Company.[107] Keith's organization was headlining Vesta Victoria in its vaudeville theaters and wanted the films shown in its film houses too. When they reached Keith's Nickel Theater in Manchester, New Hampshire, promotional blurbs claimed that the films had been taken at its Boston vaudeville house the previous week. While the singer behind the screen usually imitated Vesta Victoria as closely as possible, in some instances the comedic songs were further burlesqued. At Keith's Nickel Theater in Lewiston, Maine, "Poor John" and "Waiting at the Church" were sung alternately by Mr. and Mrs. Harriman Frost.[108] A male voice in combination with Victoria's diminutive figure simply added to the song's hilarity.

Thomas Edison's expressed wish to preserve operatic performance from the passage of time with a combination phonograph/kinetoscope was implemented

A company of performers who delivered dialogue behind the screen for *Uncle Tom's Cabin.*

in a more practical and profit-oriented form. Audiences could be given the illusion of seeing Vesta Victoria, while management only had to pay an unknown performer to sing. Likewise a quartet could give the illusion of being a large troupe. In both cases, cost efficiency plus the novelty of the illusion was the secret of success.

Although Lyman Howe used sound imitators behind the screen in the 1890s, this only became a heavily promoted part of his exhibitions in August 1907, when his "Moving Pictures That Talk" played at Ford's Opera House in Baltimore for four weeks. Trained assistants "yelled orders when the marines attacked the land force, made noises like the popping of guns and the booming of cannon, and helped the figures on the canvas to carry out the proper amount of conversations at suitable times."[109] The exhibitions attracted immense crowds despite adult admission fees of between 25¢ and 50¢. Lubin, who found it expedient to close and refurbish his Baltimore film theater during Howe's run, soon placed actors behind the screen in his Philadelphia theaters. It was reported that Lubin's manager "has a well-known dramatist that writes plays around the pictures and then as they are thrown on the screen a company of actors play the parts, speaking the lines to suit the action of the pictures. This is one of the most novel ideas ever sprung in this section and is making an enormous hit."[110]

By spring "talking pictures" had become a hit in New York, playing at Charles E. Blaney's Third Avenue Theater. Each Saturday Blaney's "dramatist" selected films from the manufacturer's latest productions and wrote the lines.[111] That May talking pictures were presented on Marcus Loew's People's Vaudeville Circuit "using the best dramatic talent available."[112] A large studio was set up in Loew's offices on University Place. Out of this may have come the Humanovo Producing Company, owned by Adolph Zukor and Marcus Loew and run by Will H. Stevens.[113] In a mid-1908 interview Stevens explained how he worked:

> "I have to scratch through a great many films," said he, "to find those that will stand interpretation by speaking actors behind the curtains. I started with Adolph Zukor, who is the proprietor of the companies. We now have twenty-two Humanovo troupes on the road, each consisting of three people. Each company stays at a theatre one week and then moves on to the next stand, traveling like a vaudeville act and producing the same reel of pictures all the time. They travel in wheels, so that a theatre has a change of pictures and company each week. It requires about four days to rehearse a company. First I select a suitable picture; then I write a play for it, putting appropriate speeches in the mouths of the characters. I write off the parts, just as is done in regular plays, and rehearse the people carefully, introducing all possible effects and requiring the actors to move about the stage exactly as is represented in the films, so as to have the voices properly located to carry out the illusion.[114]

New York–based Len Spenser, a "pioneer" in supplying singers and operators to moving picture managers on a systematic basis, added a department in his agency that furnished trained, competent actors to do the talking behind the screen.[115] The Actologue Company, owned by the National Film Company of Detroit and the Lake Shore Film and Supply Company of Cleveland, had eight groups of actors on the road in July and fifteen in September.[116] The Toledo Film Exchange also had four companies for its "Talk-o-Photo" enterprise.[117] William Swanson had ten traveling through Texas and another eight in the Denver area during November.[118] O. T. Crawford's Ta-Mo-Pics (Talking Moving Pictures) were playing in his theaters to immense audiences in November. Most actors, however, wanted to be more than a disembodied voice and saw these jobs as a stopgap. In late August many of the skilled performers left the Humanovo Company in preparation for the new theatrical season. Stevens was forced to hire amateurs and dramatic students.[119]

Many five-cent theaters improvised their own form of talking pictures, with inevitable variation in exhibition quality and effectiveness. "The possibilities of this sort of thing with trained actors and painstaking rehearsals are admitted," remarked the *Dramatic Mirror*, "but the manner in which the idea was carried out in the houses visited by THE MIRROR representative was grotesque and a

Most of *College Chums* was ideally suited for use of actors behind the screen.

drawback to the pictures themselves. The odd effect of the voice of a 'barker' trying to represent several voices, some of them women and children, and in one case a dog, may be amusing as a freak exhibition, but can hardly add to the drawing power of the house."[120] Such makeshift efforts remained popular throughout the summer and fall.

Talking picture companies used an unusual number of Edison films. When the Humanovo played for two weeks at the Maryland Theater in Baltimore, three of their four films were made by Porter: *College Chums* (November 1907), *A Suburbanite's Ingenious Alarm* (December 1907), and *Fireside Reminiscences* (January 1908).[121] Half of the Actologue Company's films appear to have been Edison products, including *College Chums*, *The Gentleman Burglar* (May 1908), and *Curious Mr. Curio* (May 1908).[122] Porter's filmed version of Ferenc Molnár's *The Devil* was particularly suited for this mode of exhibition. As the *Dramatic Mirror* observed, "films of this kind may often serve as excellent vehicles for talking companies behind the curtain, and in this respect The Devil, as produced by the Edison people, offers unusual advantages."[123] In fact, the theatrical paper felt that the absence of such aids placed the film's accessibility in jeopardy. Talking pictures not only added "verisimilitude to the scene to an almost incredible degree" but made the story more intelligible.[124] "The dialogue helps the less intelligent to fully understand the plot, for no matter how skillfully worked out, there are always passages which require something more than mere pantomime to fully explain the situation."[125] Porter's films, in particular, benefited from such treatment. The filmmaker did not so much abandon his reliance on the audience's prior knowledge as accommodate these pictures to the exhibitor's intervention. As with *The Devil*, unaccompanied screenings of Porter's films could often be appreciated by those who knew the necessary referents.

These "talking pictures" reached their peak by the end of 1908, when the practice, then widespread, began to lose some of its popularity in houses relying on untrained personnel.[126] In January, Stephen Bush, an earlier supporter of the practice, criticized it as "unnatural" — but only to endorse his favorite use of voice, the lecture.[127] Although his criticisms were immediately disputed by others, talking pictures gradually declined as a box-office attraction. Lyman Howe, however, kept impersonators behind the screen until his road shows closed in 1919.

Talking pictures were not a part of cinema's new mass communication system. They suffered from lack of standardization, and since the practice of adding behind-the-screen dialogue was never universally adopted, producers had to assume that actors would not be behind the canvas and seldom made films specifically for this purpose. As the new, more self-sufficient representational system developed, ancillary dialogue became less and less necessary. Moreover, the nickelodeons' customary daily change of program precluded sufficient time for rehearsal. Nor were many people up to performing twenty or more times a day. With specialty services, the additional expense of hiring and transporting actors had to be compensated for by a higher admission price. Although middle-class audiences could afford to pay for the increased enjoyment offered, the practice was never a realistic option for storefront theaters that charged a nickel and depended on working-class patrons.

Talking pictures were part of an emphasis on greater illusionism that, although common in the history of the screen, was particularly intense during the early nickelodeon era. Hale's Tours was first introduced in the spring of 1905 and became a fad by the following year. (Adolph Zukor's capitalization on talking pictures was not so coincidental, given that his initial involvement in cinema had been through Hale's Tours.) Pathé's coloring processes using stencils and the slightly later Smith/Urban Kinemacolor process, with its first public showings in late 1908, achieved startlingly naturalistic effects. Earlier uses of hand coloring, in contrast, had customarily heightened the fantastic elements of fairy-tale films like *Jack and the Beanstalk* and *Ali Baba and the Forty Thieves*. These attempts to expand the perceptual range to include sound, color, and bodily sensation further heightened the illusion of film as a transparent medium. The popular conception of film was shifting from cinema as a special kind of magic lantern to cinema as a special kind of theater.

Illusionism and theatricality were parallel currents in cinema that converged with "pictures that talk." As one enthusiast wrote, "The illusion of life which it is the mission of moving pictures to present to the best of its ability, must always be incomplete, from the impossibility of adequately combining sound with sight, but there is no reason why the complete illusion should not be sought after, to a much greater degree than at present, by the means of stage effects."[128] The rise of talking pictures reveals much about the changes occurring within the institution of the screen during this period. It coincided with a new influx of theatrical directors like J. Searle Dawley, D. W. Griffith, and Sidney Olcott (who worked for the Kalem Company). It occurred at a time when cinema was taking over vaudeville and legitimate theaters and when a theatrical newspaper like the *Dramatic Mirror* had begun to review films. It was one of several converging elements in 1907–9 that defined film as a kind of theater—superior to the traditional stage in some respects (diversity of locale) though deficient in others (sound, color, and three-dimensional limitations). The move toward heightened realism in cinema, however, remained subservient to the narrative requirements of entertainment and the need for an efficient mode of exhibition that kept down the showman's expenses. Strategies to achieve a superrealism were abandoned or remained a specialty service because they either limited the filmmaker's freedom to tell a story or increased admission fees—or both. Intertitles were an extremely artificial representational strategy, but because they were an inexpensive and extremely effective way to clarify a narrative—whatever the exhibition circumstances—they quickly became standard industry practice.

Intertitles

By 1908 cinema was already perceived as "a language that is universal. No matter what may be the tongue spoken by the spectator, he can understand the pictures and enjoy them."[129] This "language" centered on the gesture of the actors, their rendering of the narrative, and other pro-filmic elements rather than the filmic "grammar" of Lev Kuleshov, Vsevolod Pudovkin, and later theoreticians. The filmmaker utilized this universal language to construct a narrative that could be understood by audiences with the support, where necessary, of a lecture, dialogue, or intertitles. The more successfully a story was rendered, the less this crutch was needed. Intertitles put this verbal accompaniment in the hands of the production company. Each subject became a complete work in itself, guaranteeing, in principle at least, the intelligibility of a company's films. This allowed for a uniformity of information that was central to an industry based on mass production and consumption.

As noted in chapters 8 and 9, Porter had incorporated intertitles into his films with some frequency between mid 1903 and the end of 1905, but then virtually abandoned the practice in 1906–7. Although the industry's only trade journal had urged film producers to use intertitles on a regular basis in September 1906, Porter ignored such requests. With demands for intertitles becoming more urgent, Porter returned to their use on a consistent basis with *Fireside Reminiscences* (January 1908). Intertitles were indicated in *Moving Picture World* synopses for this and subsequent Edison films through *The Army of Two* (October 1908). These, however, were usually quite brief. For example, *Fireside Reminiscences* has three intertitles: "Parted by a Brother," "Three Years Later," and "Reconciliation." Although these did not adequately explain the story in itself, they provided valuable guideposts when the spectator recalled the popular song, "After the Ball," which provided the key narrative referent. In many cases, these guideposts were considered inadequate. One exhibitor complained: "I think that half of the time the theater manager himself does not understand the picture as it is projected on the canvas. If some film manufacturer would make every one of his film subjects explain themselves as they pass through the machine he would soon have all the business he could attend to. If instead of having a few words of explanation on his film about every 100 feet, as most of them do, they would have these explanations come in at every 20 or 30 feet (or at every place in the film wherein an explanation was necessary), then the theater manager would have no use for a lecturer."[130]

The use of adequate explanatory titles at the beginning of each scene had the strong approval of the *Dramatic Mirror*, whose film reviewer, Frank Woods, did not hesitate to demand more elaborate titles if they seemed necessary to assure an intelligible story. Edison's *Romance of a War Nurse* (July 1908) was strongly criticized because it "is not as clearly told in the pictures as we would like to see. . . . love wins in the end and all are reconciled though how they do it and what was at the bottom of the story we must confess our inability to discover." It was suggested that "The Edison Company would do well in producing complicated dramatic stories of this kind if it would insert printed descriptive paragraphs at the proper points in the films so the spectators might gain a knowledge of what the actors are about."[131] *The Devil* was faulted for this reason. "In producing this film an attempt is made to make it intelligible by inserting descriptive paragraphs, but these are not numerous enough to be of much assistance."[132] Edison's *Ingomar* (September 1908) was criticized along similar lines.[133] In contrast, Griffith's use of titles contributed to the clarity of his films and received occasional praise.[134]

A Rigorous Linear Temporality

The motion picture industry was moving toward a relationship between film production and exhibition in which the showman acted as a businessman-programmer who simply presented the completed, self-sufficient works of the production companies.[135] To the extent that Porter resisted this trend, he was part of the old guard. His continued commitment to a mode of representation associated with the pre-nickelodeon era is perhaps most apparent in his refusal to abandon a conception of temporality that was being jettisoned by his contemporaries. An exhaustive retrospective of films made in 1907–8 organized by Eileen Bowser at the Museum of Modern Art displayed a remarkable shift in the depiction and organization of time. In the early months of 1907, Porter's *The "Teddy" Bears* and *Lost in the Alps* reflected the state of cinematic storytelling. Shots were still discrete units, overlapping action was frequent, temporal repetition common, and the narrative loosely constructed. By mid 1907 the most advanced production companies began to observe a linear structure. This involved two phases.

In the first phase, retrogressive elements like overlapping action were eliminated. In Vitagraph's *The Boy, the Bust and the Bath* (July 1907) or Pathé's *The Doings of a Poodle* (1907), there is rapid cutting between proximate spaces and, in many instances, a strong suggestion of a seamless linear temporality across shots. This, however, is not made explicit by techniques such as a match cut on action. In these films the consistent forward movement of time, often in conjunction with intertitles, greatly facilitated the viewer's effort to comprehend the narrative, particularly once the systematic nature of this representational approach became apparent to the spectator. This system subsequently provided the framework within which the mode of representation associated with the classical Hollywood cinema was to be constructed.

During the second phase, this linear framework was made explicit as new representational strategies, based on this reorganization of temporality, were developed. Pathé's popular *The Runaway Horse*, made in late 1907, explicitly acknowledged a linear temporality through its use of parallel editing. At this stage, however, the procedure served as the basis for a series of tricks:

shot 1. man with scrawny horse and cart arrives outside city apartment building.

shot 2. man goes up stairs.

shot 3. outside the apartment building, the very scrawny horse begins to eat a bag of oats on display at the neighboring store.

shot 4. man goes up the stairs.

shot 5. man goes into family dining room and makes a delivery.

shot 6. outside, the horse is eating—less oats in the bag.

shot 7. family dining room, delivery man talks to man and woman.

shot 8. delivery man goes down the stairs.

shot 9. delivery man stops to talk to concierge.

shot 10. outside, the horse is eating, much less grain in the bag.

shot 11. man says good-bye to concierge.

shot 12. delivery man comes outside—the horse attached to cart is strong, healthy and well-fed. The delivery man and cart quickly leave as the owner of the oats comes out and gives chase.

By cutting back and forth between two lines of action, Pathé's director, Ferdinand Zecca, was able to manipulate the size of the bag of oats and substitute a dashing steed for a scrawny nag without having to resort to stop action. There is a rigorous advancement in time and a rapid alternation between activities in two spaces. Nothing so extensive happens in other available films made in late 1907 or early 1908, but Biograph's *Old Isaacs, the Pawnbroker* (written by Griffith and directed by McCutcheon in March 1908) cuts away from a sequence in which a girl is visiting the offices of the Amalgamated Association of Charities to her sick mother at home—and then back again to the offices.[136] McCutcheon (and Griffith) conveyed a strong sense of linear temporality by showing simultaneous events in a parallel rather than successive manner, stopping short, however, of the rigorous *a-b-a-b* structure that is the paradigm for parallel editing.

Surviving films from late 1907–early 1908, while limited, nonetheless suggest that *The Runaway Horse* and *Old Isaacs, the Pawnbroker* preceded the period when strategies of parallel editing or matching action were readily executed by filmmakers and accepted by spectators. This moment seems to have come in the summer of 1908 around the time Griffith was making *The Fatal Hour* (July 1908). *The Fatal Hour* shows a last minute rescue in which the forward march of time becomes the subject of the film: unless she is rescued, a pistol mounted on a clock will shoot the heroine when the minute hand reaches twelve. The *Dramatic Mirror* described *The Fatal Hour* as "a wholly impossible story, with a series of inconsistent situations, and yet the wild drive to the rescue while the clock slowly approaches the hour of twelve, brings a thrill that redeems the picture."[137] Cutting back and forth between the rescuers and the advancing clock, the editing creates an emotional intensity that far exceeds that of *Lost in the Alps*, which has a similar rescue but lacks a structure based on cross-cutting and the pressure of time moving inevitably forward. Porter's clock was, in fact, painted pasteboard and shows the same time throughout.[138]

In pictures like *Life of an American Fireman* and *Lost in the Alps*, time was primarily altered through pro-filmic manipulations—that is, through the contraction of action occurring off-screen. In *The Fatal Hour*, time was accelerated by filmic manipulation through cross-cutting. Griffith was able to move the clock forward whenever he cut to the rescue party (just as Zecca greatly reduced the sack of oats whenever he cut to the driver in the apartment house). Both types of temporal manipulations (filmic and pro-filmic) appear frequently in Griffith's films of 1908—as one might expect of this transitional period—but Griffith increasingly elaborated on the former and gradually eliminated the latter.

Griffith's films from the summer and fall of 1908, particularly *Betrayed by a Handprint* (August 1908) and *The Guerrilla* (October 1908), give an increasingly strong impression of matching action from shot to shot. By *The Lonely Villa* (April 1909), the Biograph director was matching action in most situations with comparative ease. These procedures specified a rigorous linear temporality. The shot ceased to be a discrete unit and became completely subservient to the narrative and linear flow of events. Action now moved across shots, not within them. Linear temporality, parallel editing, and matching action encouraged a more efficient narrative structure. The dances, rodeo tricks, and peripheral incidents common to so many films of the pre-1907 period disappeared or were pushed into the background. Nor was this surprising. When a story was already known, telling the story was not that central. The ways in which a filmmaker elaborated on the story and introduced novelty features determined its success. With new, unfamiliar stories, that changed. In the terminology of Sergei Eisenstein, filmmakers had begun to edit on the dominant (orthodox montage), to make editorial choices that emphasized the drama of the narrative.[139]

In many cases, as Tom Gunning has shown in his impressive study of D. W. Griffith's career at Biograph, the new linear framework enabled that filmmaker to articulate moral judgments with unprecedented intensity.[140] Despite a radically different representational system, Griffith's ideological perspective had much in common with Porter's own outlook. This similarity is not very surprising, since both filmmakers were recently impoverished members of the old middle class, even if one came from a family of small-town merchants and the other from a family of once well-to-do, but subsequently modest, farmers. Adopting a linear narrative structure, however, enabled Griffith to articulate this viewpoint with greater specificity and explicitness. In *The Kleptomaniac* (February 1905), Porter showed first the story of Mrs. Banker and then the story of the poor mother. In *The Song of the Shirt* (October 1908), Griffith contrasted the predicament of the poor seamstress and her employer throughout the film by repeated juxtapositions of their simultaneously unfolding stories. Griffith was able to express the same moral outlook as Porter, but with greater impact, by operating within the new system of representation and production.

From late 1907 onward, directors at Pathé, Vitagraph, Biograph, and elsewhere were developing strategies that provided the basic framework for classical narrative cinema. By mid 1908 much cinema practice had finally acquired the basic attributes of mass communication. Five criteria offered by Melvin DeFleur and Everette Dennis were being fulfilled:

1. The film industry was using professional communicators throughout its ranks. This had not always been the case. Prior to 1904, for example, production personnel often appeared in front of the camera (a practice that Porter never entirely abandoned). Even in later films, like *Daniel Boone*, Porter had to depend on actors who lacked professional motion picture experience. By 1907–8 Edison and other production companies were increasingly relying on a group of actors who had professional experience in the film industry.

2. The film exchanges and the new release system ensured that films were disseminated in a relatively rapid and continuous way.

3.   The nickelodeons ensured that these films reached relatively large and diverse audiences.

4.   The proto-Hollywood representational system ensured that members of the audience interpreted the films in such a way that their meanings were more or less parallel to those intended by the filmmakers.

5.   As a result of experiencing these films, audience members were influenced in some way. From the very first moving pictures, spectators were, of course, usually entertained and occasionally informed. By mid 1907, however, the scale was different and a cause for societal concern.[141]

The cinema was not automatically a system of mass communication. In 1908, important industry practices such as "talking pictures" remained outside this system. Yet the inauguration in 1908 of both regular, frequent releases and the new mode of representation meant that substantial segments of the motion picture industry had become part of a mass communication system. Porter, however, resisted many of these developments, particularly in the shift toward a mimetically consistent, self-sufficient, linear narrative structure.

Edison Features: 1907–1908

The continuity of Porter's representational system in the face of changes within the moving picture world can be seen in surviving Edison films and the criticisms of this work by contemporaries. *A Race for Millions* (August 1907) ends with a shoot-out between the hero and villain. This western interweaves studio-constructed exteriors with carefully selected locations. Many scenes use theatrical blocking with spatial and temporal condensations. Although a theatrical antecedent seems likely, it has yet to be located. *The Trainer's Daughter; or, A Race for Love* (November 1907), however, has a plot similar to Theodore Kremer's *A Race for a Wife*, in which the victor of a race between the hero and villain wins the bride.[142] Unless familiar with *A Race for a Wife* or aided by the exhibitor, spectators were likely to find the complex, unlikely story obscure. The film has no intertitles. Scenes were photographed primarily in long shot, sometimes making identification of characters difficult. This is particularly true in the case of the villain, who wears two different costumes during the course of the brief film. The significance of the second scene, in which the trainer's daughter offers herself as the ultimate stake, is not apparent unless one reads a plot summary (see document no. 24). The film's credibility and character motivation were undermined by the choice of a Miss DeVarney, who was plain and in her mid forties, to play the romantic lead. In contrast to later cinematic practice, Porter evidenced little interest in making the trainer's daughter an attractive woman who would be a suitable object of Jack's desire.

The first and last scenes from *The Trainer's Daughter*, which survive only as stills.

DOCUMENT NO. 24

The Trainer's Daughter

SYNOPSIS OF SCENES.

The trainer's cottage—The Lovers meet—The owner of the Delmar Stable and the Trainer come upon them unexpectedly—Jack is given to understand that his suit for the daughter's hand is not favored by the trainer.

The exterior of the racing stables—Jack has one horse entered in the coming race for the Windsor Cup—Delmar also has a horse entered in the same race—Jack and Delmar lay a side wager on the winner—The money is placed in the Trainer's hands—The Trainer's daughter overhears the wager—They both seek her favor—She enters the wager by giving her heart and hand in marriage to the winner.

Jack instructs his Jockey—The Jockey tries out Jack's horse—Delmar notes the time—Discovers his own horse has no chance against Jack's—Delmar bribes the stable boy to dope the horse—The Jockey overhears the plans.

The racing stables at night—The Jockey arrives in time—Delmar and the stable boy prepare to dope the horse—The Jockey stops their plans—The fight—The blow—The Jockey down and out—They hide in a deserted house—The escape.

The color room the following day—The hour for the race has arrived—The Jockeys leave for the mount—Jack's Jockey missing—Delmar triumphs—No one to ride the horse—The Jockey staggers in—The story—The villainy of Delmar exposed—The Trainer's daughter decides to ride in the Jockey's place.

The call to the post—The Girl appears dressed in Jack's colors—The mount—The parade—The gong—They are off—The race—The trainer's daughter is riding for something more than victory now—The home stretch—Neck and neck with Delmar's horse—Under the wire—The Trainer's Daughter wins.

SOURCE: *Moving Picture World*, November 30, 1907, p. 639.

Porter's next film, *College Chums* (November 1907) was loosely based on a well-known play, Brandon Thomas's farce-comedy *Charley's Aunt*. A *Variety* reviewer remarked:

> Here's a comedy reel involving a comedy idea which has long been worked to death in burlesque, nothing less than what is called in the profession "seminary stuff." The subject is well enough handled and a variety of fairly humorous incidents is shown. By far the best feature was a mechanical trick scene. A young man and his sweet heart are shown in an altercation over the telephone. Both are seen in small circles at the upper corners of the field of vision, the rest of the sheet being occupied by housetops. As each speaks the words marshal themselves letter by letter in the air and travel across the intervening space. When the quarrel waxes hot the words meet in the middle of the scene and fall to the ground in a shower of letters. The story has to do with a young man who proposes and is accepted by the heroine. She sees him flirting with another girl and without confronting him at the time calls him up on the telephone, telling him the engagement is off. He declares that the other girl is his sister. She declares that she will call on the supposed sister at once. And so the young man's college chum is forced to disguise himself to represent the mythical sister. The sweetheart calls and the bogus girl and she grow entirely too chummy for the taste of her fiance. The girl's father further complicates matters by starting a flirtation with the counterfeit "sister"—a rather far fetched incident even for farcical purposes—and out of these intricacies the humor grows. The reel registered casual approval at the Fifth Avenue.[143]

The last two-thirds of the film is located in the young man's living room: this lengthy, single "shot" was actually photographed in several takes, with the actors exiting and reentering so that Porter could photograph the scene in sections. Actors behind the screen often brought this section of the film to life with quick repartee. This filmed-theater approach, for which the camera is a passive recorder, differs sharply from the animated trick scene that maximizes filmic manipulation and artifice. Here Porter supplied the words, using the technique of animated titles he introduced in 1905. As in the past, Porter juxtaposed various mimetic procedures for a syncretic, rather than internally consistent, mode of representation.

A Suburbanite's Ingenious Alarm (December 1907) was lauded as "another well constructed comedy. . . . The film has a good, up-to-date application and is very well-presented."[144] Its slapstick humor centers around a commuter's attempts to find a foolproof way to wake up in the morning. He "tries the old

Using animated titles in *College Chums*.

dodge of tying a rope to his foot to be awakened by."[145] Again Porter tells a
simple story using a widely recognized situation. Overlapping time and action
are employed as the scene moves between the interior and exterior of the commuter's home.

Porter's next film, *Rescued from an Eagle's Nest* (January 1908), is well
known because it features D. W. Griffith in his first major film role. He plays
a father who battles an eagle as he rescues his child from the bird's nest. The
story for this family-centered drama was taken from a famous incident that the
Eden Musee had enshrined in wax (see document no. 25). The film displays all
the characteristic qualities of Porter's work. Rather than cut between parallel
lines of action, Porter used temporal overlaps. Studio sets for exterior scenes
were interwoven with outdoor locations. Despite the obvious abilities of a newly
hired scenic artist, Richard Murphy, a precocious critic found the film "a feeble
attempt to secure a trick film of a fine subject. The boldness of the conception
is marred by bad lighting and poor blending of outside photography with the
studio work, which is too flat; and the trick of the eagle and its wire wings is
too evident to the audience, while the fight between the man and the eagle is
poor and out of vision. The hill brow is not a precipice. We look for better
things."[146] The reviewer demanded a consistently rendered visual world, with
an emphasis on credibility that was not always valorized within Porter's representational system. Similar criticisms were to become more frequent in the
months ahead.

Rescued from an Eagle's Nest concludes with a re-united nuclear family, their embrace cheered on by friends.

DOCUMENT NO. 25

No. 8 THE EAGLE'S NEST

This artistic group pictures a scene and incident which occurred in the Adirondack Mountains a few years ago. An eagle stole a little child and carried it to its nest high among the crags of the mountains. The father and neighbors pursued and battled with the eagle. After a long fight the eagle was killed and the child rescued. The greatest care has been taken in the coloring of the group, and the light and shadows are so perfect that at first view visitors think they are in the mountain tops witnessing a real battle.

SOURCE: Eden Musee, *Catalogue* (New York, 1901), p. 4.

Fireside Reminiscences (January 1908) is a family-centered "society comedy drama" that evokes the story line of the well-known song "After the Ball."[147] In this song, a man explains to his niece why he is single and has no children. One night when he and his sweetheart were at a ball, he found her in the arms of another man. He abandoned her without waiting for an explanation, and she

The husband reflects in *Fireside Reminiscences*.

eventually died as a result. After learning the man was her brother, he remained faithful to her forever. The ways in which Porter altered this story were consistent with earlier adaptations that add new family-centered elements. The lover is turned into a husband who sees his wife embracing her brother. Without waiting for an explanation, he banishes her from the home. Three years later the husband sits by the fire and recalls his past life in a series of dream balloon images: his wife, he and his wife embracing, their wedding, his wife and child, the moment he threw her out of the house, and his wife on the cold streets at night. This reminiscing is framed by a larger narrative. In fact, his wife is outside the house as he conjures up these images. She is brought inside, and their child acts as a catalyst for reconciliation. The family triumphs over the stern, misguided father, who finally sees the error of his ways and is quickly forgiven.

Surviving fragments of *Cupid's Pranks*, completed on February 10, 1908, but not released in time for Valentine's Day, make use of the charming, naive iconography of Valentine cards and similar illustrations. Filmed inside the studio except for matted shots of the New York skyline, Murphy's elaborate sets added an important element of spectacle. In this light comedy, Cupid brings two lovers together, arranges for their car to break down and turns back the hour hand of a clock to extend their meetings—all in the interest of love. After the couple fight and reconcile, they are finally married, with Cupid looking on approvingly. Many of these scenes are introduced by intertitles that make the story more

Cupid's Pranks.

"WHEN THE HUNTING SEASON OPENS"   COPYRIGHT, 1900, BY LIFE PUBLISHING CO.

14,005—Detroit Publishing Co.

Porter utilized widely available iconography like this for *Cupid's Pranks.*

concrete and guide the spectator. In some instances, they mask or "solve" problematic spatial/temporal transitions between shots.

Only a few fragments of Porter/Edison films made after *Cupid's Pranks* survive. Our understanding of Porter's work therefore depends on reviews in trade journals. Fortunately, these became increasingly common. *Variety*'s occasional film reviews commenced in 1907. The *Dramatic Mirror*, beginning with its issue of June 13, 1908, published systematic reviews of all films released during the previous week, a policy partially motivated by competitive pressures from *Va-*

Tale the Autumn Leaves Told.

Nero and the Burning of Rome.

riety. The *Mirror* reviews, written primarily by Frank Woods, offered carefully reasoned judgments that strongly supported the emerging, more modern representational practices. By late September, *Moving Picture World* responded with its own section of film reviews. Many of these were written by W. Stephen Bush, who remained sympathetic to Porter's approach.

Porter's work generally received strongly favorable comment during the first six months of 1908. *Animated Snowballs* was "a good interesting comedy run" that was well liked by the audience seeing it with Sime Silverman of *Variety*. Sime offered a few muted criticisms: the narrative was temporarily forgotten to show an accomplished figure skater, and the realism of the chase was ruined by the premise of a gouty old man successfully pursuing two young boys on figure skates. Nonetheless: "Some novel effects are shown. Snowballs roll uphill, and men also turn somersaults up the same incline. The opinion that the film is being reversed in the running is dissipated by some attending circumstances. It is not possible for a layman to figure out how it has been accomplished."[148]

After viewing *The Cowboy and the Schoolmarm* (March 1908) at Keith's, one correspondent called it "a specially good film" and reported, "We never saw an audience so affected by a picture show as when the cowboy on the gallop picks up and rescues the kidnapped school teacher."[149] Another referred to *Tale the Autumn Leaves Told* (March 1908) as "Edison's masterpiece."[150] For each scene, the frame had a different mask cut in the shape of a leaf. Thus the title was cleverly and visually transposed. *Nero and the Burning of Rome* (April 1908) likewise received much favorable attention. One unhappy critic excluded only this Porter film from a more general lament. "This subject is spectacular, contains many elements of human interest and possesses the dignity of history," he explained.[151] *Bridal Couple Dodging Cameras* (April 1908) was called "a really novel comedy subject" and "one of the best comedy reels the Edison people have ever turned out."[152] *Skinny's Finish* (May 1908) was "in the best Edison style and should prove popular for some time to come."[153]

Porter's *The Blue and the Gray; or, the Days of '61* (June 1908) garnered the highest praise. "No film that has been issued by any company in a long time can be classed with *The Blue and the Gray* for consistent dramatic force, moving heart interest and clearly told story," declared the *Dramatic Mirror*.[154] *Moving Picture World* felt it was "one of the few film subjects that deserves a long run and which the public will pay to see more than once."[155] *Variety* agreed, calling it "a commendable moving picture."[156] This story of North and South had many familiar narrative incidents that were often utilized by the popular press and theater. Two West Point classmates end up on opposite sides of the war. The Union officer hides his old friend and his sister's true love from his commander. When both are discovered, the Union officer is sentenced to be shot. The sister wins a pardon from the great reconciler, Abraham Lincoln, and arrives with the reprieve as her brother is about to be executed.

Despite the familiar incidents, *Moving Picture World* felt this "masterly production of thrilling interest ... could be made clearer by more explanatory titles."[157] *Variety* found the impersonations of Grant and Lincoln somewhat less than credible and the sister's pleading with Lincoln for a pardon too brief to convey the complexity of the situation and therefore unrealistic. The *Dramatic Mirror* questioned its temporal construction:

> In only one point does the construction of this story appear faulty and that is when the young officer has been stood up to be shot and the command of "fire" is about to be given, the scene is shifted to Washington where the girl is pleading with President Lincoln. The spectator is thus asked to imagine the firing squad suspending the fatal discharge while the girl rides from Washington to the Union Camp. It would have been better if the Washington scene had been inserted somewhat earlier.[158]

Although this successive presentation of two separate lines of action was typical of Porter's earlier chase and rescue films, the reviewer already assumed that linear temporality provided the proper basis for cinematic construction and perceived Porter's customary methods of narrative construction as awkward.

Love Will Find a Way (June 1908) was commended as an "excellent comedy film, since it is based on a central idea which is humorous in itself."[159] With *Pioneers Crossing the Plains in '49* (June 1908), "Edison has given us a very good film in this story of pioneer days. The scenery is excellent and the picture artistic." Nonetheless, the reviewer felt "the film could have been improved in the battle with the indians by the 'pioneers' displaying more judgement in defending themselves instead of standing aimlessly in the open to be shot down like sheep."[160] *Honesty Is the Best Policy* (May–June 1908) had an excellent story and theme, but its effectiveness was spoiled by "faulty construction and the introduction of incidents that have nothing to do with the development of plot."[161] Ironically, the innovations that many historians have attributed to Porter based on the modernized version of *Life of an American Fireman* — parallel editing and matching action — were the very procedures that Porter had the greatest difficulty executing. Porter's work was becoming more and more out of step with the emerging mode of representation.

The Kinetograph Department
Forms Two Production Units

Frank Dyer replaced William Gilmore as vice-president of the Edison Manufacturing Company in June 1908, while Charles H. Wilson was made general manager. Dyer was particularly disturbed by Edison's paltry share of the American film market. Joseph McCoy's June 1908 survey of theaters indicated that the company provided less than 10 percent of their films. In contrast 35 percent of the films were supplied by Pathé (see table 5). In response, Dyer's new regime

Table 5.   Survey of Films Shown in New York Area Theaters Visited by Joseph McCoy, June 1908: Tabulated by Producer.

Pathé	177
Vitagraph	82
Edison	45
Essanay	42
Lubin	40
Kalem	32
Selig	26
Méliès	14
Total Licensed Films	458
Total Unlicensed Films	57
Total films seen	515

SOURCE: Joseph McCoy, report, June 1908, NjWOE. McCoy's addition was inaccurate and has been corrected for purposes of this analysis.

quickly established a second production unit in the studio. Former Biograph employee Fred Armitage was hired as a cameraman at $40 per week beginning in late June or early July 1908. He began to work with Dawley, who was likewise making $40 per week, while Porter operated his own unit with assistance from Cronjager, the newly hired James Cogan ($35 per week), and others. Production again doubled and studio personnel responsible for negative production expanded to at least eleven. Porter's salary was soon raised another $10 to $75 per week. At the Edison factory in West Orange, Charles Wilson ordered the Kinetograph Department to enlarge its release print capabilities: "Mr. Moore is now furnishing us with 2,000 feet of negative film per week, and work of enlarging the film dept. at factory should be pushed with all possible despatch, so that we can handle this amount weekly. As it is at present, our factory limit is about 100,000 feet per week, whereas with 2,000 ft. of negative, we should have factory capabilities of 200,000 ft."[162] Actor Justus D. Barnes (the outlaw leader in *The Great Train Robbery*) was hired on a full-time basis in late July. Actress Francis Sullivan likewise joined the staff in late October. Although both may have had additional duties, this was the beginning of Edison's permanent stock company.

Porter was becoming a de facto studio executive. This move toward a multiunit system of production remained tentative, however, in that Porter continued to head the first unit and run the studio. Each unit was still organized on a collaborative basis. Dawley and Armitage were paid the same amount, and treated as equals—although Dawley always enjoyed Porter's ear. In fact, collaborative working methods continued to operate across units. As Dawley later explained, Porter "would contact me on the phone when I was working on location and say 'Dawley you better come back to the studio at once, I'm all

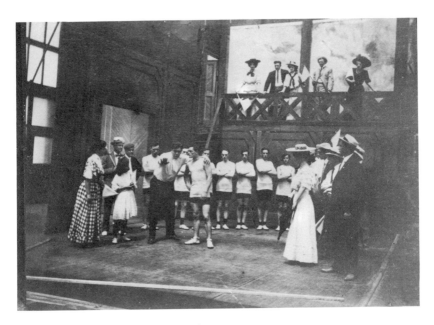

The Little Coxswain of the Varsity Eight.

balked up on this directing stuff. I just can't make it work out the way I want.' "[163] Here Porter's dependence on collaborative working methods continually impeded efficient management based not only on separate production units but on a clear chain of command and responsibility. At a time when Griffith, who had assumed the position of director at Biograph, was producing over two films a week, two production units at Edison struggled to maintain the same output with much less critical success.[164]

The first two Edison films to receive strong negative criticism in the *Dramatic Mirror* were the first films made under the new two-unit system, Dawley and Armitage's *The Boston Tea Party* and Porter's *The Little Coxswain of the Varsity Eight* (both July 1908). *The Boston Tea Party* was "marred by the obscurity of the opening scenes."[165] A review of *The Little Coxswain* elaborated on the lack of narrative coherence (see document no. 26). Because the film was not based on a well-known play or story, Porter's critics had no ready framework for understanding. If the synopses had been turned into a lecture or if actors behind the screen had illuminated the "numerous conversations and altercations" with dialogue, spectators would have been less disoriented.

Document No. 26

The Little Coxswain of the 'Varsity Eight (Edison).—We have hitherto noted a failing of certain Edison films, that they lacked clearness in the telling of a picture story. This drawback was not present in The Blue and The Gray, but it was evident in The Boston Tea Party reviewed last week, and it is more than ever apparent in The Little Coxswain of the 'Varsity Eight. This film needs a diagram to interpret it, without which the various movements of the actors are, for the most part, meaningless to a spectator of average intelligence. It goes without saying that such a fault is a serious one with any film and should be carefully guarded against. More particularly do we look for the Edison Company to be free from criticism along this line, because the name Edison should stand for the best the world over. The coxswain, it appears, sold the race, or tried to, to a scoundrel who bet heavily that the crew would lose; but the perfidy was discovered, a little girl was substituted as coxswain and the crew won. Further than this the film tells us nothing that is understandable. Young men and girls appear to be having numerous conversations and altercations, there is a card game and somebody gives one of the girls a bank check for some purpose or other, but who they are and what it is all about we are unable to discover without reference to the synopsis of the story sent out by the Edison Company, which, however, is not available to the audience generally. It is especially regretable that the story is so badly told, because the film gives an excellent picture of the preparations for the race, the race itself and the scene following the victorious finish.

SOURCE: *New York Dramatic Mirror*, July 25, 1908, p. 7.

Although enthusiasm for Edison films was declining somewhat by mid 1908, the pictures still received as much praise as Griffith's Biograph productions. With *Tales the Searchlight Told* (July 1908), Porter returned to Coney Island:

> By representing a rustic visitor ascending a searchlight tower at Coney Island, where he secures a telescope and looks through it wherever the light is directed, the Edison Company has invented a novel way of presenting a series of interesting views of Coney Island, taken from elevated points. All the chief sensational features of the great resort are presented, and a series of night views are shown, the weird effect of the electric illuminations as reproduced on the film, being truely startling. The pictures close with views among the bathers on the beach in which a number of comedy situations are introduced.[166]

Like *How the Office Boy Saw the Ball Game*, the film recycled actuality footage using point-of-view masks. In this case, the shots were taken from *Coney Island at Night*.[167] At the same time, the device of a country rube visiting Coney Island to see the sights recalls *Rube and Mandy at Coney Island. A Comedy in Black and White* (Porter, August 1908) was a silhouette film "produced in a particularly interesting and attractive manner. The story has to do with the calls of two lovers on a certain lively belle, whose father objects

A Comedy in Black and White.

to the visits. The action is amusing, but the chief charm of the picture is the unique style of the photography."[168] When Porter relied on simple narratives, embellished with special photographic effects, his films still garnered favorable comment.

The Face on the Barroom Floor (Porter, July 1908) was chosen as "feature film of the week" by the *Dramatic Mirror*:

> The subject is of such high class and is handled in such an able and original manner that it at once commands attention. The old-time popular poem, "The Face on the Barroom Floor," is the basis for the picture. Verses from the poem are thrown on the curtain at intervals in the film and between the verses scenes illustrating the story are given. A barroom is shown and it is the real thing. The ruined artist, reeling and in rags appears, and after being treated to a drink tells his story to the deeply interested men in the barroom. As he is telling of his downfall and the cause, the scenes he is relating appear as if in a vision in the large mirror over the bar. Then he draws the face of his faithless wife on the floor and falls dead.[169]

As with *The Night Before Christmas*, selected lines served as intertitles to help spectators maintain a conscious correspondence between poem and picture and to facilitate their understanding of the film.

Reliance on an audience's prior familiarity with the story, increasingly out-moded by the nickelodeons, was further weakened when Harper Brothers won

Shooting titles for *A Comedy in Black and White*.

a court case against the Kalem Company for producing a film version of *Ben Hur* (December 1907) without permission of the copyright owners.[170] Henceforth motion pictures were subject to copyright restriction as dramatic productions, curtailing the free borrowing of song lyrics, stage plays, and comic strips that had been an important element in early film production. Subsequent films continued to have antecedents, but they were disguised in many instances to protect the filmmakers, thereby undermining the audience's ability to use the original story as a trot. The Kinetograph Department paid little attention to these new restrictions when they purchased the idea for *The Face on the Barroom Floor* from a scenario writer. After the poem's original author, H. A. D'Arcy, demanded compensation, Edison lawyers informed him that he had inadequately protected his poem by failing to indicate it was copyrighted.[171]

Edison executives did not have to worry about copyright with another poem-based film, *The Bridge of Sighs* (Dawley and Armitage, October 1908). Written by the Englishman Thomas Hood (1799–1845) shortly before his death, the poem describes a young suicide who throws herself into the river and drowns. Having no well-developed narrative, the poem lent itself to a reworking of themes expressed in *The Miller's Daughter* (1905). A country lass runs off to the city with a man who uses her and then abandons her. Her situation becomes more and more desperate. Finally, penniless and without hope, she throws herself off the "Bridge of Sighs." Instead of being rescued by a faithful lover, she dies. The *Dramatic Mirror* declared the film to be "one of the most effective moving picture productions we have seen in a long time. Lines of the poem are thrown on the screen between various scenes, adding to the effectiveness, but if they had been omitted the picture story would still have been complete and powerful so well is it arranged and acted."[172]

Porter shot *Ex-Convict No. 900* (July 1908) as Dawley was making *The Bridge of Sighs*. A meticulous remake of his earlier *The Ex-Convict* (1904), the picture was nevertheless heavily criticized. "The story of this film resembles to a considerable extent a well-known vaudeville sketch, which may account for the lack of clearness with which the pictures are made to tell the story. As THE MIRROR has frequently pointed out, when motion picture actors follow in detail a stage drama they usually fail to get the story out to the spectators. In this film, also, the action in a most critical scene is pictured in so much dim obscurity that one finds it difficult to tell what is going on. The plot, itself, is a good one, although none too well handled in this instance."[173]

The basic story for *The New Stenographer* (Porter, November 1908), had been used in earlier films like Biograph's *The New Typewriter* and *The Story the Biograph Told*. (In 1911 Vitagraph remade the film under the same title; it undoubtedly had many vaudeville antecedents, too.) The plot revolves around two partners' employment of an attractive secretary and the subsequent discovery by one man's jealous wife. The *Mirror* declared this one to be "a very amusing and a particularly well acted comedy."[174]

Several Porter/Edison films continued to offer variations on a simple premise. *Fly Paper* (Porter, June 1908) recalls *The Terrible Kids*. Two bad boys have a fine time covering people with flypaper until they are caught and plastered with the sticky material by their victims.[175] The troublemakers were no longer allowed to go free. *Ten Pickaninnies* (Porter, August 1908) recalls the childhood rhyme "Ten Little Indians." Each scene was introduced by a couplet, beginning with

> Ten little Darkies eating Melon fine.
> Farmer catches one leaving but Nine.[176]

"A clever idea is carried out in this series of ten scenes," felt Frank Woods, who later wrote the screenplay for *The Birth of a Nation*.[177] In Dawley and Armitage's *The Lover's Guide* (September 1908), a young man uses a how-to manual to facilitate his courtship of women; a series of disastrous incidents result. *Moving Picture World* approved: " 'Lover's Guide' is not what can be called as high standard work as 'Ingomar' of the same manufacturer, but is better received, as the audiences can understand and follow the plot. It is an amusing, well produced, comic picture with some good photographic effects."[178]

Other Edison films continued to tell simple stories that were easy for audiences to follow. *When Reuben Comes to Town* (Porter, July 1908) elaborated

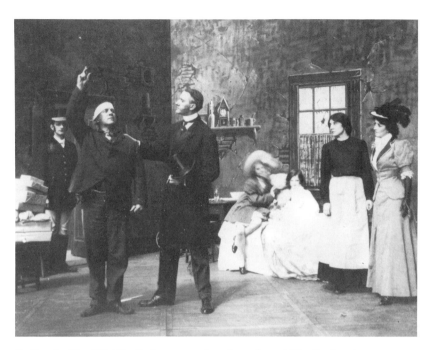

Ex-Convict No. 900. The final scene reprises the ending of *The Ex-Convict.*

on the basic idea for *Another Job for the Undertaker* (1901) and Vitagraph's *The Haunted Hotel* (1906), allowing plenty of opportunities for film tricks. A farmer checks into a hotel, where all sorts of bizarre incidents take place. He is attacked by huge bedbugs and robbers. By the conclusion, he is delighted to get home alive. *Buying a Title* (Porter, August 1908) was "slightly reminiscent of a popular vaudeville sketch."[179] A wealthy man wants his daughter to marry a foreign count, but she prefers her American sweetheart. The father is outwitted, and the count suffers a beating. It was declared a clever, clean-cut comedy that was much appreciated by the audience that saw it at the Keith & Proctor's Union Square Theater.

Although *Wifey's Strategy* (Porter, August 1908) was not a particularly complicated story, it was criticized from two different perspectives. A husband disapproves of his new wife's culinary abilities and decides to hire a cook. The wife disguises herself and manages to get the job. The disguised cook makes life miserable for the husband until the ruse is exposed and the couple are reconciled. *Variety* felt it was an old idea, suggesting that "the producers are suffering from a paucity of original plots." Nonetheless, it was "well laid out and acted and amused."[180] The *Dramatic Mirror* disagreed, finding the idea clever, but "so poorly handled that the Edison Company must feel just a little bit ashamed to take the money."[181] Again, familiarity facilitated spectators' appreciation, while its absence led to confusion and criticism.

One Porter film with a narrative of more than usual complexity, *Heard over the 'Phone* (August 1908), was praised by the *Mirror* as a particularly novel subject:

> Heard Over the 'Phone is the story of a family living in the suburbs, near Scarsdale evidently. The father, after discharging his hostler for brutal treatment of a horse, goes to business, leaving his wife and child alone. The hostler, in revenge, enters the house to rob. The wife observing his approach, calls her husband over the phone, but she is attacked by the robber, drops the phone and is murdered, the sounds of the conflict and tragedy being carried to the ears of the horrified father at the other end of the wire. The acting of this picture is good, and photographically it is especially artistic.[182]

The film was based on *Au téléphone*, a play by André de Lorde, which was first presented in Paris in November 1901 at the Théâtre Antoine. An English version, *At the Telephone*, opened in New York City during October 1902 as a curtain raiser.[183] Subsequent revivals were likely: the play offered a challenging role to the male actor, who conveyed the wife's murder through his changing expression as he listened on the telephone. In March 1908 Pathé released the film *A Narrow Escape* in the United States; it was based on the same play but substituted a last minute rescue for the bloody ending. Six months after the release of *Heard over the 'Phone* and a year after the release of *A Narrow Escape*, Griffith made *The Lonely Villa*, which was indebted to the Pathé film.[184]

The differences in narrative structure between *Heard over the 'Phone* and *The Lonely Villa* are typical of the different representational systems used by Porter and Griffith. Information about the Edison film is scarce, but Porter apparently showed two actions—the husband at the office and the murder at home—simultaneously with a split-screen technique. Griffith, of course, cut back and forth between husband, wife, and robbers in a way that built suspense.

Pocahontas (Porter and Will Rising, September 1908), based on a play produced by Will Rising and originally given at the Jamestown Exposition, was reviewed approvingly in the *Dramatic Mirror*, which favored films of an instructional or "elevated" nature:

> This is a creditable attempt to tell in picture narrative the story of John Smith, Powhatan, Pocahontas and Rolfe, the story ending with the marriage of Rolfe and Pocahontas. Historical subjects, such as this one, should be encouraged not only because they are interesting but also for their instructive value. The different episodes are well selected, the scenery is excellent, and the acting above the ordinary. One or two points in the costuming and stage settings are open to question, historically, notably the use of Navaho blankets and the manner of dressing the hair of the Indians, but the general character of the production is of such high order that we need not be too exacting in this respect.[185]

Heard over the 'Phone. The despairing husband appeared in the darkened left portion of the screen.

Sime Silverman at *Variety* did not share this educational bias and criticized the film much more severely:

> "Whoever stage managed that picture made a bum of it," said one evidently "wise" person at the Manhattan Wednesday evening. While the opinion may have been slangy, it strikes home. "Pocahontas" is the historical story involving John Smith and John Rolfe, Pocahontas' husband. History will probably tell if the Indians were in the habit of shaking hands in the 16th century as a token of friendship. Somebody said they had a "pipe of peace." And the Indians in "Pocahontas" look like Chinese ballet girls must appear, if they have ballet girls in China. Also the Colonists who were at Jamestown in history—and the picture—resemble a crowd of Hebrew impersonators. "Pocahontas" could only be saved by proclaiming it a comedy subject. It is a pity the waste of time this picture caused, for it is rather elaborately laid out. The Edison Company produced the series.[186]

Surviving fragments of the film affirm Silverman's strongly negative reaction.

By early fall 1908, *Mirror* assessments of Biograph and Edison films had shifted, reflecting a more general change in the overall film industry. During the first week in November both companies released films based on the popular William DeMille play *Strongheart*, which focused on an Indian's attempt

She.

to integrate himself into white society. Griffith's *The Call of the Wild* (September 1908) found special favor. Remarking on the popularity of Indian stories for motion pictures, the *Mirror* declared that "none . . . can be truthfully said to excell the latest Biograph offering in the particular elements that go to make up a successful moving picture story."[187] *A Football Warrior* (Dawley and Armitage, October 1908) was complimented for its elaborate detail, but the *Mirror* found its story line somewhat obscured by excessive shadow and the extreme distance between actors and camera.[188] A mid November overview of Edison productions observed:

> Edison pictures are noted for elaborate scenic productions and the artistic beauty of the scenes, whether natural or painted interiors, but these results are sometimes secured at the expense of clearness in telling a picture story. Important action taking place in artistic shadow or at a distance which permits of a beautiful and extended view may, and usually does, weaken the dramatic effect. This criticism is not always true of Edison pictures, as there are frequent occasions when art has been attained without loss of lucidity. Edison subjects are also nearly always of striking character with novel effects.[189]

In contrast Biograph films were distinguished by a closer camera, which showed actors in "heroic size" and enabled them "to convey the ideas intended with utmost clearness."[190]

The *Mirror* critic felt that *She* (November 1908), the Kinetograph Department's adaptation of Rider Haggard's novel and the subsequent nineteenth-century stage play, "might have been more comprehensible if the adapter had not undertaken to tell so much, but, on the other hand, there would not have have been so many spectacular scenes with sumptuous settings if the story had been curtailed."[191] Reviewing *The King's Pardon* (Porter, November 1908), the same critic noted, "There is doubtless an interesting story which this picture is meant to tell, and it has the advantage of elaborate scenic surroundings and fairly capable acting, but the arrangement of the scenes and action fail to give us a clear, connected narrative, and we are constantly in doubt as to the trend of the story."[192] The issue of linear temporality was again raised; the critic suggested that "a scene showing the preparations for the hanging inserted between the scenes showing the ride to the prison with the pardon, would have added interest to the conclusion."[193] Far more comfortable with pre-nickelodeon narrative constructions, Bush remarked that "among the scenes deserving special praise is the ride of the King's messenger."[194] By late 1908, however, cross-cutting was recognized as a significant editorial procedure that could add credibility and excitement to the narrative. Porter's failure to utilize it was becoming a consistent basis for criticism.

Cinema and Society

The rapid expansion of nickelodeon exhibitions precipitated a crisis not only over *how* a story was to be cinematically represented but over *what* was to be presented in the theaters. This latter problem created sharp tensions between the moving picture world and the larger society. As Robert Sklar has pointed out, it was as mass entertainment that the cinema and its subject matter became deeply disturbing to the traditional guardians of American culture.[195] Its increasing presence in American life led many reform groups, newspaper editors, and government officials to demand censorship or even outright prohibition of films. They attempted to limit the nickelodeons' impact by Sunday closing, sometimes harsh fire regulations, and exorbitant licensing fees for theaters.

By September 1906 Chicago papers were publicizing and supporting a crusade against the nickel theaters. The clergymen who initiated the attack claimed that moving pictures "inflame the minds of the younger generation, seriously diverting their moral sense and awakening prurient thoughts which prepare the way for future sin."[196] In New York the police began to apply the Sunday blue laws against the use of a drop curtain to moving picture shows by claiming the screen was such a curtain.[197] *Views and Film Index* responded in a manner that would typify the motion picture industry for years to come. First, its columnist argued that showing a burglary in which the culprit was captured or killed discouraged the impressionable viewer from becoming a burglar himself. Most of the films were therefore wholesome. Second, he maintained that the motion picture industry was reforming itself and improving its offerings, that "a comparison of the conditions today with what it was only a few years ago will testify that it has become an art, and is going higher and higher every day."[198]

Vituperative attacks against nickelodeons reached new heights in the spring of 1907. Lubin's *The Unwritten Law*, a reenactment drama focusing on Harry K. Thaw's murder of his wife's former lover, the architect Stanford White, was the hit of the season in many cities. But in Houston, Worcester, and other locales, police stopped showings of the film.[199] The *Chicago Tribune* reiterated the belief that five-cent theaters "make schools of crime where murder, robberies and hold-ups are illustrated. The outlaw life they portray in their cheap plays tends to the encouragement of wickedness. They manufacture criminals to infest the streets of the city. Not a single thing connected with them has influence for good. The proper thing for the city authorities to do is to suppress them at once."[200] Small-town newspapers soon followed the lead of large city dailies. Even in New York City, the nation's film capital, motion pictures were under assault. Theater owners were occasionally arrested for showing films depicting murder and suicide.[201] A July report from Police Commissioner Theodore Alfred Bingham urged Mayor George Brinton McClellan to revoke the nickelodeons' licenses and asserted that the suppression of cheap shows would improve city conditions.[202] *Moving Picture World* asked: "When will this persecution cease? The owners of these places have done all in their power to improve them, have obeyed unjust exactions in many instances and are trying to comply with public sentiment as never before."[203]

Although these attacks posed a direct threat to the entire film industry, the Edison Company was particularly vulnerable to such crusades. Reform ministers and press representatives spoke for—or at least to—prospective purchasers of Edison records, phonographs, batteries, and cement houses. Unrestrained hostility could harm the inventor's reputation and tarnish the image of other Edison products. Some of the best-known Edison films from the pre-nickelodeon era were films of crime (*The Great Train Robbery* and *The Train Wreckers*). Several films from 1905–6 showed juvenile delinquency in a sympathetic light (*The Little Train Robbery* and *The Terrible Kids*). *Cohen's Fire Sale* showed a Jewish merchant defrauding an insurance company. William Swanson nonetheless maintained that "in the case of the Edison films one never gets a picture 'off color' among them."[204] The Kinetograph Department tried to avoid improper subjects that might have seriously offended sensibilities. As pressures from reformers mounted, top Edison executives, including the inventor himself, began to screen completed films.[205] Yet, as the *Dramatic Mirror* and other publications noted with surprise, what was acceptable on the stage was not necessarily so in movie houses (a reversal from the days when *The Passion Play* could be shown on the screen but not on the stage).[206] *College Chums* (November 1907) offered bawdy humor that had been "worked to death in burlesque." Nonetheless, the Edison film's play with homosexuality, transvestism, and infidelity was not so trite in the nickelodeons, which reached a wider audience in terms of age (children), gender (unescorted women), socioeconomic background (lower classes), ethnicity (recent immigrants), and geography (rural areas).

By late October 1907 Edison advertisements began to announce that "Edison films depend entirely for their success upon their cleverness. They are never coarse or suggestive."[207] Edison soon appeared to side with critics of the nickelodeons. On the cover of *Moving Picture World*, a photograph that portrayed

Playmates.

Edison as the stern father accompanied his signed statement: "In my opinion, nothing is of greater importance to the Success of the motion picture interests than films of good moral tone. Motion picture shows are now passing through a period similar to that of vaudeville some years ago. Vaudeville became a great success by eliminating all of its once objectionable features, and, for the same reason, the five-cent theatre will prosper according to its moral attitude. Unless it can secure the entire respect of the amusement-loving public it will not endure."[208]

The industry was caught between the desire to make sensational films that would sell and the need to make films that would avoid the wrath of authorities who might interfere in their business. More than most companies, Edison tried to accommodate its critics. Sentimentality was frequently indulged. *Playmates* (February 1908) is about a child and her faithful companion, a dog, which is dressed in a costume and given a pipe. When the child gets sick, the dog informs the parents and stays with the bedridden girl. When the doctor proclaims the child's case to be hopeless, the dog prays (!) and effects a miraculous cure.[209] A reviewer called it "a well produced and touching story, which called for many exclamations of 'fine, sweet,' etc. . . . The only fault with this film is that it is too short, as an audience is never tired of such a charming subject."[210] Many pictures, for instance *A Suburbanite's Ingenious Alarm* and *Bridal Couple Dodging Cameras*, were fluffy, innocent comedies. Others, like *A Sculptor's*

In *The Gentleman Burglar*, the beloved father in the portrait dies a hunted and forgotten criminal—as his daughter looks on.

Welsh Rarebit Dream (January 1908) and *The Painter's Revenge* (May 1908), presented inoffensive film tricks. When a release like *The Gentleman Burglar* (April 1908) dealt with crime, it had a heavy moral overlay. A gentleman burglar abandons his wicked ways, marries, settles down, and starts a family. He is blissfully happy until an old confederate blackmails him. The gentleman burglar tries to steal the needed money from his father-in-law, but is discovered and turned out. He returns to his old haunts and quarrels with a friend, killing him. He goes to prison, escapes, and returns to his family, only to discover that his child no longer recognizes him. When he realizes that his wife has married her old suitor, the shock kills him. The truth is kept from the wife, "who never knows that the man she loved was nothing more than a common thief."[211] Certainly even the most conservative critic had to acknowledge that this film contained an unequivocal message: "Crime does not pay."

"Hangings, murders and violent deaths in any form should be barred from the sheet," Edison declared in a mid-1908 *Variety* interview.[212] Yet his company frequently placed these controversial narrative elements in a historic or patriotic setting to diffuse controversy. The tactic often worked: schoolchildren at Public School 188 in New York City were escorted to the local Golden Rule

Patriotic violence in *A Yankee Man-o-Warsman's Fight for Love* seems to have met with approval.

Theater on Rivington Street to see *The Midnight Ride of Paul Revere* (October 1907), in which British soldiers kill the tollgate keeper's daughter.[213] *A Yankee Man-o-Warsman's Fight for Love* (January 1908) included a three-round fight between an American and a British sailor, with "several good knockdowns."[214] Because violence was used to defend American honor, it was apparently acceptable. *Nero and the Burning of Rome* could show the decadence and cruelty of the pagan emperor and still be shown in an occasional church. Even Edison felt comfortable endorsing it as "one of the most interesting [pictures] that has come to my notice."[215]

These efforts to place sensationalistic actions in an acceptable context did not always work. After *Nero and the Burning of Rome* was shown in his church, Rev. E. L. Goodell protested: "There was nothing in the moving pictures of scantily clad women that could appeal to the innocent mind of a child, but there was a great deal in the pictures of bloodshed that caused terror."[216] With *The King's Pardon* showing one robbery, two brutal murders, and "a sensational finish of a man standing on the gallows and the executioner adjusting the black cap and the rope," *Moving Picture World* remarked, "We are once more again going back to highly sensational films."[217] Despite its debt to the stage and the artistic opportunities it gave the lead actor, *Heard over the 'Phone* must have been controversial. Its portrayal of a helpless father, unable to protect his family from a wanton criminal, completely violated norms of desirability. The basic story for *The New Stenographer* (November 1908), the man's employment of an attractive secretary and the subsequent discovery by his jealous wife, had been done often in earlier films. Now the subject had become too hot to handle. One critic said he had to pinch himself to be sure he wasn't dreaming when he saw the manufacturer's trademark.[218]

Attacks by newspapers and government organizations did not abate during 1908. Formal censorship of films was established in several cities including Chicago, Detroit, Cleveland, Omaha, Nebraska City, and Butte.[219] New Jersey passed a law that forbade children under sixteen years of age to attend movies unless accompanied by a parent.[220] Sunday shows were prohibited in many places including, briefly, New York.[221] Licensing fees were imposed or raised by city, county, and state governments. Coordinated action by motion picture exhibitors, renters, and producers was needed to protect the industry's interests. Industry self-regulation might eliminate the most provocative films while still leaving enough bite to draw patrons to the theaters. Moreover, national, state, and local motion picture organizations were needed to lobby against excessive restrictions and do battle in the courts. The desire for such organizations had encouraged the formation of the Edison combination. Instead, the film war divided the industry and made effective action against anti–motion picture forces more difficult. Here, too, incentive existed for a reconciliation between the Edison and Biograph interests.

12 Edison Lets Porter Go: 1908–1909

Porter and the Edison Manufacturing Company found themselves increasingly at odds during 1908–9 until finally they parted ways. The filmmaker later explained that he had left to make more money elsewhere. The real truth, however, was that Edison fired Porter because his methods of motion picture production and of telling film narratives were thwarting the company's commercial efforts. If Noël Burch has aptly described Porter as a Janus figure facing toward both past and future, in the late 1890s and early 1900s the filmmaker was primarily looking forward. Now he was resisting a new approach and steadfastly looking the other way. While pursuing long-standing commercial strategies such as licensing and patent infringement suits, Edison and his corporate executives simultaneously sought to adapt to changing industry practices. Porter's refusal to accommodate made his departure inevitable.

Edison and Biograph Begin to Negotiate

By June 1908 it was becoming clear that Edison and his licensees would be unable to drive the Biograph association from the field. Many film people, particularly exhibitors, viewed the rivalry as desirable. "It is well that there are two competing elements in the field," *Moving Picture World* asserted. "It simplifies the question of providing separate programs to theaters which are in close proximity to each other and it gives the manager the opportunity of making a distinct change if he is subjected to treatment which is injurious to his business."[1] The Association of Edison Licensees had eliminated little competition. Although it had forced a few renters to abandon their aspirations to become producers, the organization had failed to exclude unlicensed European producers from the marketplace. The warfare between Edison and Biograph had even provided a space where some new producers—for example, the Goodfellow Manufacturing Company and the New Jersey–based Centaur Film Company—could operate.[2]

The Edison-Biograph rivalry made discipline within the ranks of the Film Service Association difficult to enforce. Some theaters still rented programs through subletters and showed films by both associations—practices that had been forbidden. Exchanges undercut the rental rates with increasing frequency. In mid June, William Swanson informed Frank Dyer that two of the largest dealers in Chicago would withdraw from the association if action was not taken against violators of the agreement.[3] When Laemmle's income from his Evansville office fell from $1,000 to $500 per week, the renter asked Dyer to come up with a solution. Laemmle hinted that he would find his own solution if Dyer could not provide one.[4] Tally's Film Exchange in Los Angeles also threatened to go its own way.[5] If Edison interests could not eliminate their opposition, it was only a question of time before licensed producers and FSA exchanges broke off on their own.

Biograph and its licensees were also unhappy with the state of affairs. Unlike Edison, Biograph was not receiving royalties for its sponsorship of importers. Its goal was to survive and then work out a financial arrangement with Edison. The Kleine Optical Company encountered many expenses in opening up offices across the country, yet faced a restricted market for its goods. The litigation and commercial rivalry that had plagued the American industry for ten years continued unabated and seemed to hurt almost everyone. While in opposite camps, Pathé and Gaumont let both sides know that they were displeased with the state of affairs and urged a reconciliation.[6]

On July 11th, shortly after assuming charge of Edison's film business, Dyer lunched with Harry Marvin and Jeremiah J. Kennedy of Biograph and discussed peace terms.[7] A week later, George Kleine came to New York and met with the Edison vice-president.[8] By the end of the month, negotiations had proceeded far enough for Edison executives to outline terms (see document no. 27). In early August *Variety* reported: "It seems to be the general impression among the leaders of the motion picture business that a settlement of the fight now on is but a question of days, weeks or months."[9]

DOCUMENT NO. 27

Proposed Scheme

(1)   Biograph Company to come in as Licensee under Edison patents the same as others.

(2)   Kleine to be recognized as Licensee, limiting importation to 5,000 feet of new subjects per week for entire list of foreign manufacture as advertised, including Gaumont. In case any foreign manufacture[r] drops

Frank L. Dyer.

out, the amount of film imported to be correspondingly reduced in proportion to his importance as shown by Kleine's output since February 1st,
1908.

(3)   Other Biograph licensees to be taken in (Williams, Brown & Earle,
Italian Cines and Great Northern Film Company) on same basis as Kleine,
the number of feet of new subjects to be based on amount of film put out

since February 1, 1908, but not to exceed a total of 2000 feet per week.

(4)   Royalties of present licensees and new ones above contemplated not to be increased.

(5)   All licensees to be licensed under Edison, Biograph & Armat patents, and royalties under Biograph and Armat patents to be collected preferably from exchanges who in turn will exact them from exhibitors. Royalties to be based on charge for rental service but not to exceed an average of $2.00 per week.

(6)   All projecting machines now in use to be licensed under all patents, and name-plate attached, limiting use of machines to licensed films. All projecting machine manufacturers to put on similar licensed plates.

(7)   All films to be leased for a limited period and restricted to use with licensed machines.

(8)   Cameraphone Company, Gaumont, or any other concern now making or contemplating making, talking pictures to be licensed, but limited to talking pictures and not to sell or lease films separately. Royalties to be ½ cent per foot and $5 per week or less for each machine.

(9)   Contract limited to two years, but to be extended from year to year until expiration of last patent.

(10)   Expenses for litigation to be borne by respective interests, each defending or prosecuting its own patents.

(11)   Expenses for litigation based on price-cutting or violation of license agreements to be borne pro rata by all licensees, up to $25,000. per year.

(12)   Price of film, net, to exchanges not to be reduced below nine (9) cents per foot, except by unanimous vote of all licensees. All votes to be on basis of running feet of new subjects.

(13)   All film to be bought from Eastman Company, who will collect film royalties.

(14)   Question of licenses to machine manufacturers and number of licensees, to be taken up and concluded after film situation is settled.

SOURCE: Addendum to communication from Frank Dyer to H. N. Marvin, July 29, 1908, NNMoMA. The term *talking pictures* in point 8 refers to films shown synchronously with phonograph recordings.

As the next step, licensed manufacturers met with Kleine, Edison, and Biograph interests. The substance of these negotiations was never reported, but the licensed manufacturers apparently insisted on substantial changes. The licensors (Edison and Biograph) had planned to include almost every European producer in the new arrangement—but limit their future participation in the American market to current (mid-1908) levels. This would have coopted virtually all the opposition. The licensed manufacturers, however, wanted to restrict the scope of imported films and increase available supply by expanding their own production capacities.[10] They also wanted to increase their profits by raising the price for films. To further these goals, Biograph abruptly revoked the license of Italian "Cinès," and Edison licensees raised their prices from 9 to 11 cents per foot, effective September 1st.[11]

Agreement between the parties was close enough for the Motion Picture Patents Company to be incorporated in New Jersey on September 9th. Each company was searching for ways to maximize its position in the future combine. Pathé announced plans to open its own rental concern, following the examples of Vitagraph, Lubin, and Kleine, who had their own exchanges. This led to such strong protest among their regular customers that the offer had to be withdrawn.[12] Léon Gaumont visited New York in mid September and entered the negotiations.[13] An agreement was soon reached between Kleine and Gaumont that would allow Kleine to sell 2,000 feet of new Gaumont subjects each week.[14]

Negotiations encountered snags in October. "All talk of merger has dwindled to an extent that not even a whisper is audible in authentic circles," it was reported.[15] The licensed producers seemed to be the principal stumbling blocks. Articulating a viewpoint shared by his colleagues, one company representative "considered that group of manufacturers well able to cope with the demand [for films] for years to come, therefore he would not see the necessity or wisdom of taking in any other manufacturers."[16] Many of these manufacturers worried that additional reels of film supplied by the former independents would reduce their own sales.[17] Adding two weekly releases from Biograph and three through Kleine would increase the number of licensed subjects by approximately 40 percent. Licensed renters, in contrast, were extremely anxious to gain access to a more diverse product line, particularly since many of their customers wanted these films. The potential licensors were not unsympathetic to the renters' position and were ready to incorporate as much of the opposition within their ranks as possible, if only as a way to increase royalties. Offering itself as an impartial observer, *Moving Picture World* urged the two sides to reconcile their differences for the benefit of the industry.[18]

Griffith's filmmaking activities at Biograph had a somewhat contradictory impact on these negotiations. The high quality of his pictures generally strengthened Biograph's position. Theaters and renters wanted its films. Yet this success discouraged flexibility by Edison-licensed manufacturers. Even while denied access to FSA exchanges, Biograph increased sales per film from 30+ to 50+ prints between September and December 1908.[19] Some Edison licensees had been selling as many as 100 prints per subject. If Biograph entered the licensed ranks, its sales would double again, and previously licensed manufacturers seemed likely to suffer.

Edison and Dyer were ready to strike a deal with Biograph's Harry Marvin and Jeremiah Kennedy, except for the recalcitrant producers. According to Terry Ramsaye, Kennedy ended the long negotiations by threatening "to bust this business wide open" and give a Biograph camera to anyone who wanted it.[20] It was a clear signal to the manufacturers: reach an agreement or competition will be even more extensive. Negotiations began to move forward again. On November 18th the Film Service Association postponed a December membership meeting because "it will be necessary for the association members to meet the manufacturers early in January to consider new business arrangements."[21] While the final details were hammered out, the way for a new agreement was being cleared. On December 1st the manufacturers notified the renters that their relationship would fundamentally change in sixty days. Until then, licensed manufacturers could only terminate their relationship with an FSA exchange if it violated the contract. In the future they could simply terminate the contract with ten days' notice.[22] Whatever the terms of the new combination, renters had little choice but to accept them. When new snags materialized in early December, Edison made additional concessions to the licensed manufacturers. After more than five months of negotiations, agreement was finally reached.

Motion Picture Patents Company Agreements

The Motion Picture Patents Company (MPPCo) was owned equally by the Edison and Biograph companies, with a few shares going to the directors as required by law.[23] Dyer, vice-president of the Edison Manufacturing Company, was elected president and George F. Scull, another Edison lawyer, was elected secretary. Harry Marvin and Jeremiah Kennedy were elected vice-president and treasurer respectively. The MPPCo was formed with the recognition that the patents controlled by Biograph and those controlled by Edison were of equal importance in the eyes of the courts. Each company agreed to deposit its shares of stock with the Empire Trust Company, which acted as trustee, and instructed it "not to release, transfer or return the said certificates so deposited without the consent of" both parties and Thomas Armat.[24]

The Edison Manufacturing Company, the American Mutoscope & Biograph Company, the Armat Motion Picture Company, and Vitagraph Company of America assigned their patents to the MPPCo in return for certain guarantees on the morning of December 18, 1908. That afternoon the MPPCo signed agreements with nine producers and importers: the Kleine Optical Company, Biograph, the Edison Company, and the original Edison licensees, excepting the Méliès company. The Méliès concern was denied a license because it had come under the control of Max Lewis, a Chicago renter, in violation of earlier Edison licensing agreements.[25] Over his objections, Kleine was only allowed to import three reels of film per week, two to be supplied by Gaumont and one by Urban-Eclipse. Gaumont was selected because it owned the patents to the Demeny camera and might have provided independents with a non-infringing apparatus if left outside the trust (the status of the Demeny camera had yet to be tested in

Executives of film companies newly licensed by the Motion Picture Patents Company gather at the Edison Laboratory on December 18, 1908. First row (left to right): Frank L. Dyer, Sigmund Lubin, William T. Rock, Thomas A. Edison, J. Stuart Blackton, Jeremiah J. Kennedy, George Kleine, and George K. Spoor. Second row: Frank J. Marion, Samuel Long, William N. Selig, Albert E. Smith, Jacques A. Berst, Harry N. Marvin, Thomas Armat(?), and George Scull(?).

the courts).[26] Urban-Eclipse was probably included because Charles Urban controlled G. Albert Smith's kinemacolor process. Other European firms were considered too weak to effectively confront the power of the MPPCo and were entirely excluded.

Based on the MPPCo's control of essential patents, interlocking agreements were made with the moving picture manufacturers and importers, film exchanges, exhibitors, Eastman Kodak, and various projector manufacturers.[27] These not only assured the collection of royalties in different areas but further concentrated power in the hands of the film producers and importers who were the keystone of the contractual system. The nine companies could only lose their licenses if they acted in gross violation of the agreements and ignored specific warnings for a protracted period of time. Their right to a license was effectively assured. Moreover, additional licenses could only be granted with majority approval of the already licensed manufacturers. They still paid royalties to the licensor on raw stock, but the amount was lower than under the old agreement. Royalties remained 5 mills (½¢) per foot for firms buying less than 4,000,000 feet of raw stock each year, but were 4.5 mills per foot for manufacturers purchasing from 4,000,000 to 6,000,000 feet, 4 mills per foot if between 6,000,000 and 8,000,000 feet, 3.75 mills if orders totaled between 8,000,000 and 10,000,000 feet, and only 3.25 mills per foot if a company exceeded 10,000,000 feet per year. The Edison Manufacturing Company, however, did not pay a licensing fee on raw stock. A minimum pricing schedule for films leased to exchanges continued as before. List price was 13¢ per foot and standing orders were 11¢ per foot—figures that assured a healthy profit margin for most producers. The licensed manufacturers had no restrictions on the quantity of their releases. Only Kleine was limited to three reels of film per week.

The MPPCo signed an agreement with Eastman Kodak on January 1st, superseding the one previously in effect between the raw stock supplier and the Edison licensees. Under this reciprocal arrangement, licensed producers and importers would only purchase film from Eastman, and Eastman in return would only sell 35mm motion picture film to licensed manufacturers, excepting a small percentage of film set aside for experimental and educational purposes. As it had done for the previous six months, the Eastman Kodak Company collected MPPCo royalties on raw stock as it was purchased by the licensed manufacturers. This arrangement made it more difficult for independent moving picture producers to operate effectively and secured Eastman's position by turning major users into long-term customers. The company also agreed to supply raw stock for a maximum cost of 3¢ a foot for unperforated film and 3.25¢ for perforated. Such an arrangement reduced commercial uncertainty for both parties.

Film exchanges were given until January 20th to sign contracts with the MPPCo. These were to go into effect on February 1st. Almost all the renters from the Film Service Association and a few major "independent" exchanges were given the opportunity to become licensees. The Toledo Film Exchange was not offered a license because its checks had often bounced; the Chicago Film Exchange because of its attempt to acquire the Méliès license; Adam Kessel's Empire Film Company probably because it was bicycling prints; and Harstn & Company because its purchases were too small under the old system.[28] In the earlier agreements between the FSA and the Association of Edison Licensees, manufacturers and renters met, at least nominally, as equals. This was no longer the case. The MPPCo offered renters a license that could be unilaterally revoked with or without cause after fourteen days' notice. As one trade journal remarked: "The position of the renter . . . is not an enviable one. He might work up a large business, the tenure of which is determinable by a fortnight's notice at the discretion of a possibly irresponsible person. Thus, the sword is always suspended over the head of the renter. Not a reassuring state of affairs to an ordinary business man."[29] The MPPCo and the manufacturers, rather than the FSA, established rules and punished the violations of rental exchanges.

Many of the regulations established by the FSA were enforced with new rigor. Again licensed exchanges could only acquire films from licensed manufacturers, just as licensed manufacturers could only deal with licensed exchanges. Film was no longer sold outright but leased. A film or some substitute had to be returned to its original manufacturer seven months after it was acquired. Films could also be recalled by the manufacturer after an exchange violated the licensing agreement. Each branch owned by a renter was now treated as a separate exchange, while the minimum amount of film that an exchange had to purchase was increased to $2,500 per month, double the old figure. Nor could film be shuffled back and forth between exchanges run by the same owner. This eliminated a number of small exchanges and branches, but increased overall demand. It also encouraged a steady, year-round flow of films through the system. The release system was refined: a film could not be shipped from an exchange before 9 A.M. on its release day. A minimum rental schedule was again established, this time determined by the manufacturers. Moreover, a licensed exchange could only rent to a theater that was licensed by the MPPCo. Violations resulted in fines and eventual suspension. As a result, renters found their activities highly regulated and restricted.

Exhibitors were a new and important revenue-generating element in the MPPCo's agreements. The key patents for exhibition were controlled by Thomas Armat, whose attempts to license exhibitors in the 1890s and early 1900s had failed after receiving insufficient judicial support. The MPPCo now asserted that Armat's patents, in combination with others under its control, allowed it to license exhibitors for the use of its members' various inventions. Each exhibitor was required to pay the MPPCo $2 a week per theater, irrespective of its size or profitability. Compulsion was not so much legal as commercial. In practice, a license simply gave the exhibitor the right to use licensed films rented from licensed exchanges. Exhibitors who showed unlicensed films without paying the $2 were not challenged for patent infringement. An exhibitor could not, however, present licensed and unlicensed subjects at the same time. When this was attempted, the MPPCo instituted replevin suits and repossessed its films. The power of the MPPCo over the exhibitor was based on its control of product rather than on potential legal action for patent violation. Originally the exchanges were expected to collect the theaters' royalties for the MPPCo. When the renters protested, however, the MPPCo agreed to assume that role.[30] The problem of coordinating exhibitors and exchanges proved so awkward and unsatisfactory, however, that the original plan was reinstituted within a few months. While renters paid no direct royalties, like Eastman they were given the task of supervising another branch of the industry. Royalties from exhibitors alone were expected to total more than $500,000 a year during the first year of operations.[31]

Incidental to this series of interlocking agreements was the licensing of ten projector manufacturers, who were charged a royalty fee of $5 per machine.

Three of the licensees—Vitagraph, George Spoor & Company, and the Armat Motion Picture Company—were inactive. Several others were licensed film manufacturers, including the Selig Polyscope Company, the Lubin Manufacturing Company, the Edison Manufacturing Company, and Kleine's Edengraph Company (manufacturer of the Edengraph projector, which descended from the machine Porter had used and refined at the Eden Musee). Licensing arrangements excluded some small equipment manufacturers and raised barriers to entry into the field. The MPPCo forced the Viascope Company out of business by court action.[32] Licensed projectors were, in theory, only to be used with licensed films, but no mechanism was set up to assure that this would be the case. Perhaps more important, the manufacturers agreed to sell their machines for at least $150 each, assuring an adequate profit margin for everyone concerned. Since profits from projector sales represented a large portion of Edison motion picture profits, the financial value of this arrangement cannot be ignored.[33]

Royalties came from three different areas of the industry (exhibitors, film producers, and equipment manufacturers) and were divided in the following manner:

1. Net royalty figures to be derived by (a) subtracting Vitagraph royalties, $1 per projecting machine manufactured, from total machine royalties, (b) deducting 24 percent from gross exhibitor royalties for distribution to motion picture manufacturers and importers other than Biograph and Edison, and (c) deducting general litigation expenses from film and other royalties

2. Net royalties to be paid for distribution (a) to Edison in an amount equal to "net film royalties," and (b) to Biograph two-thirds and to Armat one-third of the remainder, up to an amount equal to "net film royalties"

3. Any balance after the division indicated above to be paid to Edison, Biograph, and Armat on a basis of one-half, one-third, and one-sixth respectively[34]

The Edison Company maintained its prominence in the new corporation, which its vice-president headed. Edison received the largest portion of the royalties, and the company's products were protected from price wars and other forms of competition it considered undesirable.

Commercial Warfare Within a New Framework

The MPPCo agreements were used as a weapon by licensed producers who wanted to reassert their authority and solidify their dominance of the industry. The renters, the group that had most clearly challenged the producers' commercial hegemony, were forced to assume a subordinate capacity. While rental rates assured them adequate revenues, exchanges had become a convenient intermediary between producers and exhibitors. Astute observers already foresaw the day when the production companies would take over distribution by forming their own exchange.[35] The principal opposition to the MPPCo, therefore, came from renters and was centered in Chicago. In a letter to exhibitors, Max Lewis and his Chicago Film Exchange vehemently protested the new arrangements: "We have not and will not sign the outrageous agreement offered to the Film Exchanges, and we positively refuse to connect ourselves with any movement intended to take the profits from you and others who have worked night and day and made the motion picture industry what it is today."[36] D. B. Baker announced: "The Globe Film Service is not going to sign any such contract as that presented by the Motion Picture Patents Company which is all one-sided. And we are certainly going to continue in business." Baker claimed to have a motion picture projecting machine and camera that operated without a sprocket or loop and used principles not covered by the MPPCo patents.[37]

Many renters who took a license were also unhappy. To show his displeasure, Carl Laemmle submitted his license application after the January 20th deadline. This was grounds for exclusion. Although Laemmle was indicating his readiness to strike out independently, the application was accepted. Realizing that "in unity there is strength," Swanson proposed the formation of a Motion Picture Service Company that would purchase as many exchanges as possible and then use its economic clout for the "improvement of rental conditions" and "co-operation with manufacturers for mutual benefit."[38] The organization's purpose was to challenge the power being accrued by the licensed producers. William Swanson, considered a radical in the old FSA, was promptly elected president of the new Film Service Association. Laemmle was elected vice-president. The organization had little power, but the choice of officers indicated the mood among its members. Although the renters recognized that they had to sign with the MPPCo if they wished to continue profitable operations, many voiced hopes that an effective, independent opposition would emerge.[39]

Exhibitors were likewise outraged by the MPPCo's demand for a $2 a week royalty. In Philadelphia 160 of the city's 185 exhibitors organized an association to combat the MPPCo. They contended that "the latest move of the Trust in compelling them to sign an agreement which doubles the rental price and the charging of $2 weekly royalty and the stringent conditions in regard to the licensing of exhibitors" threatened their businesses.[40] A screening of unlicensed films in Chicago was attended by 400 angry showmen, and "it certainly looked as if there wasn't a licensed showman in Chicago."[41] Vaudeville manager Percy Williams refused to take out a license and challenged the Patents Company in the courts. "I have no intention," remarked Williams, "of laying myself open to any royalty demands this moving picture combination chooses to make. I have no assurance that the $2 week fee now exacted will not be shortly advanced."[42] "How paying $100 per year to the film trust would protect me in any way or increase my business I am unable to see," protested a less prominent midwestern exhibitor.[43] In a full-scale revolt, an estimated 80 percent of the country's motion picture theater managers disapproved of the new arrangement and were ready to join the independents.[44]

Opposition coalesced around several different groups. By early February John J. Murdock, vice-president and general manager of the Western Vaudeville Managers Association and a group of Chicago film men formed the International Projecting and Producing Company.[45] Murdock moved into the void created by Kleine's alliance with the MPPCo. Within a month he had reached agreement with twenty-seven companies in England, France, Germany, Italy, and Russia. The International Projecting and Producing Company claimed to have forty reels of new material available each week, from which it proposed to select twenty-five to thirty reels for release.[46] During late February and March the company showed films in key cities to enlist exhibitors and film exchanges in the independents' cause. In addition, several established film importers, including the Great Northern Film Company and Isaac Ullman's Film Import Trading Company, continued their independent activities.

The Columbia Phonograph Company, Edison's old rival, which had been quiescent in motion picture affairs since C. Francis Jenkins' departure in 1896, again became active. Columbia acquired the patent rights for a camera made by Joseph Bianchi, a former recording expert for the company. Claiming the camera operated on a principle completely different from Edison and Biograph apparatuses, Columbia indicated that it intended to move into production.[47] An alliance between the International Projecting and Producing Company and Columbia was soon being discussed.[48]

The main opposition was to come from a group of Chicago and New York exchange men. Some of these, like the Empire Film Exchange and Chicago Film Exchange, were denied a license. But at the end of February the MPPCo cancelled the licenses of William Swanson's three exchanges.[49] Swanson had been a thorn in the new organization's side, and when the opportunity arose, the MPPCo demonstrated its power and self-confidence by expelling the president of the new FSA.[50] Within a month ten additional exchanges had joined the independents, including those conducted by Robert Bachman and Eugene Cline.[51] On April 12th America's largest renter, Carl Laemmle, informed the MPPCo that he was surrendering his license.[52]

Nonetheless, by early May 75 percent of theaters nationwide were licensed. In many eastern localities licensed theaters exceeded 90 percent of the total. The percentage fell further to the west, and the areas around Chicago were nearly evenly divided, but in the Far West and in the South the MPPCo carried the day. Throughout the country virtually all the leading houses were licensed.[53]

The protracted film war between the independents and the MPPCo is outside the scope of this study. It is merely important to note that the formation of the MPPCo failed to eliminate competition outside the trust as its members had hoped. The terms Dyer and his associates offered many renters and exhibitors alienated important elements in the film world. Once again there were defectors, and once again a new competitive environment emerged. Many renters, Young Turks who had represented the most dynamic elements of the industry, refused to accept the dominance and regulation of the industry's somewhat older and more established producers. By mid 1909 Carl Laemmle had started the Independent Motion Picture Company, while Adam Kessel and Charles Bauman of the Empire Film Exchange had started the New York Motion Picture Company.[54]

Despite the continued existence of the independents, the Motion Picture Patents Company was able to implement many of its goals and policies. It organized and coordinated all phases of the motion picture business on a systematic, contractual basis, maximizing control and profits in the hands of a select group of producers/owners. The combination did not, however, transform the industry into a thoroughly rationalized modern system. Licensing arrangements permitted an ambiguous relationship between licensee and licensor. Edison's problems with Vitagraph in the late 1890s continued in the MPPCo's dealings with producers, renters, and exhibitors. These groups served their own interests, not those of the licensor. While the MPPCo hoped to control the industry through legal intimidation and by controlling the supply of films, the best it could do was regulate those members who, for the moment at least, saw the alternative as less desirable. The industry had changed radically in ten years, but Edison's attempts to dominate it remained basically the same. The system of management was decentralized, yet depended on the consensus of diverse interests.

Although the MPPCo seemingly assured Thomas Edison of a prominent role in the motion picture industry for many years to come, it also limited the extent to which his company could ever again dominate the industry or dictate terms to rivals. Yet Dyer was able to enhance Edison's reputation or at least avoid any further tarnishing of his "biographical legend." MPPCo policies helped to make motion pictures respectable entertainment for the middle classes. To assure acceptable film subjects, the organization cooperated in the setting up of the National Board of Censorship early in 1909. In theory at least, it also policed licensed houses. Any theater that did not comply with fire laws, that was not clean and as light as proper film projection allowed, was threatened with revocation of its license.[55] MPPCo executives hoped to create an atmosphere in which the film business could be safely and profitably conducted. Likewise, these policies were designed to portray the MPPCo as a benign trust that should not be sued for violation of antitrust laws by the government. This last goal eluded Dyer and the MPPCo, although the others were largely achieved.

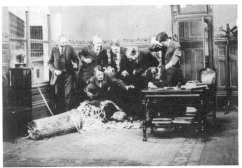

The Tale the Ticker Told.

The Porter/Edison Films in Disfavor

As Edison executives were seeking to secure their commercial future through license-related agreements, Edison films were frequently and stridently criticized for their failure to present clear, enjoyable, and effective narratives. The *New York Dramatic Mirror*, which championed the storytelling methods of Griffith, felt that *The Lovers' Telegraph Code* (Porter, November 1908) contained "the foundations for a capital comedy ... although the full possibilities of the situation appear to have been overlooked or awkwardly handled in the construction."[56] *Miss Sherlock Holmes* (Porter, November 1908) was "an inconsistent and complex story, none too easy to follow, although it is admirably mounted and fairly acted."[57] *The Old Maids' Temperance Club* (Porter, November 1908) started out "in promising style" but became "flat."[58] One of the most devastating reviews was directed at *The Tale the Ticker Told* (Dawley and Armitage, December 1908):

> This film is a confused, unintelligible series of scenes in which a will, an heir and an heiress, two rivals for a woman's hand, a hunting trip, a bad broker and a good broker, a trip in automobile down Broadway, a scene in the Stock Exchange and a suicide in a broker's office are so mixed up without connection or reason that we can make little headway in figuring out what it is all about. Somehow we divine that one of the rivals puts up a job on the other, gets the worst of it and kills himself. The photography is all right and the scenic qualities are fine, but the story is in an unknown picture language and if one can't understand the story what is the use of all the acting? The tale that this ticker told needs translation.[59]

A Persistent Suitor (Porter, December 1908) "would have been infinitely more humorous if it had been logically and consistently constructed, and if many opportunities for comedy had not been overlooked or carelessly handled."[60]

Positive reviews reiterated the Edison films' usual basic weaknesses by noting their absence. With *An Unexpected Santa Claus* (Porter, December 1908), "The Edison Company continues to produce films that are clearly told picture stories, in pleasing contrast to a number issued from the same studio last fall."[61] For *Turning Over a New Leaf* (Dawley and Armitage, December 1908), Armitage's "camera has been placed closer to the actors than was formerly the Edison practice, thus making identity of the different characters more apparent to the spectators."[62] *Where Is My Wandering Boy To-night?* (Dawley and Armitage, January 1909)

> comes as near to the point of perfection in every essential particular as any subject ever produced by an American company. It lacks every fault that has been apparent heretofore in so many Edison productions. The story, the first and most important consideration in every picture, is simple, consistent and interesting though trite. The characters are introduced distinctly, and their identity is clearly maintained throughout. The scenes follow each other naturally and each tells its part of the story and no more. The acting is done with great feeling, but without being overdrawn. There is not a gesture or movement that appears to be wanting and there is not one too many. The photography is even, and the camera is placed sufficiently close to the actors to make each character always recognizable. Finally the scenic backgrounds are in the usual artistic taste of Edison pictures. In short, the picture is a model that the Edison forces would do well to follow in future work.[63]

This flurry of positive reviews suggests that the Edison films had been bad enough for the *Mirror* critic to mute many previous criticisms. Certainly this was the case with *Moving Picture World*, which was careful not to criticize the Edison Company's productions lest its executives withdraw their advertising—along with the advertising of affiliated licensees—as they had done once before.

Edison executives were frustrated by the quality of their films and wanted to find more qualified personnel. In a letter to the managing director of the Edison Manufacturing Company in Europe, Thomas Graf, Frank Dyer confessed:

> In our moving picture business we are very badly handicapped for the lack of skilled camera operators and stage directors. The business has developed to such enormous proportions that it seems to be very difficult to get a good man. Camera men may be found, but to get a good competent stage director, a man with sufficient originality to get up and direct the acting of a picture, seems to be almost hopeless. This is especially true in the case of trick and eccentric pictures. It occurs to me that such a man might be found in Paris, either out of employment or who might be willing to take a better position in this country. The leading manufacturers are there and they must have educated a good many men. I would like to get a first-class man in every respect, one of good intelligence, full of ideas and capable of having them worked out, and especially a man familiar with getting up trick pictures and startling and original effects. For a really good man we could pay $75.00 per week and traveling expenses from

By 1909 film dryers at the Orange, New Jersey, plant had gotten larger to handle increased capacity.

Paris, with a guarantee to pay expenses back if unsatisfactory. . . . Time is very essential, as we are being handicapped every day by this defect.[64]

Dyer's letter reveals the depths of his unhappiness and his limited insights into the problem. Like Porter, he did not recognize that the crucial problem involved the construction of narratives that could be readily understood by the spectator.

The commercial basis for Dyer's unhappiness is evident in the superficially impressive figures for film sales during the 1908 business year. Film sales increased 170 percent over the previous business year, from $205,243 to $554,359; profits, however, only increased 97 percent to $230,383. This occurred because the number of productions completed between February 1, 1908, and January 31, 1909—seventy-four in all—quadrupled (increasing expenses), even as the number of prints sold on a per-film basis fell sharply, particularly late in the year as quality declined and the number of films offered by competitors increased.

Dyer and Wilson, unable to locate a foreign director who would solve their production problems, reorganized the Kinetograph Department in January 1909. Porter ceased to make his own productions by mid month and continued solely as studio manager and head of negative production.[65] Dawley, given a raise to $45, began to make $5 more per week than Armitage. Harry C. Matthews was hired as a stage director at $40 per week and teamed with Henry Cronjager ($25 per week). The director and cameraman no longer received identical wages—an indication that competent directors were not only harder to find but that they were assuming principal responsibility for productions. These two units were based at the Bronx studio, while a third unit was formed (for which George Harrington, William Moulton, and Henry Schneider were hired) and sent to the Twenty-first Street studio to make short comedies.[66] Porter was thus put in a strictly management position.

Dyer introduced a director/unit system of production. The cameraman no longer worked with the *stage* director but for the *film* director. There was nothing automatic about this shift. Although the photographer and stage director had different responsibilities, they could have easily retained co-equal status. And yet, the director needed to be in closer consultation with the studio head than the cameraman. Story and script, actors and sets—all the "non-filmic" elements—were his responsibility. We know, for example, that Porter collaborated with Dawley on the script for *The Star of Bethlehem* (March 1909). The move to a multi-unit production system with a supervising producer thus encouraged the emergence of the director as unit head. An efficiently run studio with a well-established hierarchy as well as clear lines of authority and accountability required the implementation of the director system.

The reorganization of production occurring in the industry at this time was primarily a move from the collaborative system to a director-unit system rather than, as Janet Staiger has suggested, from a cameraman system to a director system.[67] Such a shift had occurred at Vitagraph early in 1907, where there were three collaborative teams: J. Stuart Blackton, Albert E. Smith, and Jim French (their senior employee) each acted as cameraman for one of the units and worked closely with stage directors (including William Ranous). A reorganization took place when Smith left for Europe. French was charged with managing the studio operations. Blackton assumed the role of production head and oversaw the work of the three directors, and the three directors had cameramen in their charge. The shift to a director-unit system came about because a military-type model of command facilitated the management of a large and growing studio.

The shift at Vitagraph gives us insight into the transition occurring two years later at Edison's Bronx studio. While documentation is scanty, the Edison Company was in the midst of a tortuous transitional phase: the director-unit system was emerging but not yet fully established. Moreover, Porter, who felt awkward handling actors, was not adept at giving orders and delegating authority, a necessity for any manager who hoped to run a multi-unit studio successfully. In short, he was still committed to a collaborative mode of work. Moreover, he was unhappy with the frenetic pace of production necessitated by the mass entertainment system. The studio manager "always believed that the bane of the producer was the turning loose of so many reels a week, on certain days, regardless entirely of surrounding circumstances." This did not allow "sufficient time to do those things which ought to be done and to avoid those things which ought not to be done."[68]

The extent of this shift to the director-unit system can easily be exaggerated. The cameraman retained a large amount of authority. He developed the negative and still edited the picture. On the other hand, the increased rate of production resulted in the creation of a script department. In late January 1909 Stanner E. V. Taylor, who had scripted Griffith's *The Adventures of Dollie*, was hired at $35 a week to form it. While Alex T. Moore remained as manager of the Kinetograph Department (still making $100 per week), he was increasingly squeezed between Porter on one hand and Wilson on the other. Negative film production, of course, was only one of many departments under Wilson. These also included equipment manufacturing, the production of release prints, and sales.

While Porter concentrated on his job as studio head, Edison films continued to be greeted with frequent complaints. A few films received mild praise, but most were strongly criticized. *Drawing the Color Line* (January 1909) "is very well carried out, although it might have been made stronger if the different situations had been properly led up to."[69] *Pagan and Christian* (Dawley, January 1909) was "a beautifully elaborate production that may find more popularity in lecture course entertainments than in regular picture houses." Made at the height of the censorship crisis in New York City, the film dealt with a commendable theme, but "the story is somewhat obscure in its details and drags in the action."[70] *A Bachelor's Supper* (Dawley, February 1909) was criticized for "the unnatural manner in which the story is worked out."[71] *The Saleslady's Matinee Idol* (Dawley, February 1909) was condemned because "the producers do not appear to have realized the value of their best scenes—at least they have failed to make the most of them and have introduced other scenes that are either confusing or inconsistent." The critic again emphasized the absence of effective intercutting: "If short scenes had alternated back and forth between the stage and the balcony, showing the progress on the stage and the effect on the balcony audience concurrently, the effect would have been greatly increased."[72] This is precisely what Griffith did in *A Drunkard's Reformation*, which he began to film a few days after this review appeared.

The criticisms leveled at the Edison films were applied to productions by other companies as well. After listing several specific failings in a potentially excellent production, a review of Selig's *Love and Law* concluded, "A few titles would have cleared up some of the obscurity, but care in construction, to make sure that the story would be conveyed easily to all spectators, would have been better."[73] With *The Castaways*, Vitagraph was chided because "the scenes of the story are disconnected and give the impression of being hastily strung together."[74] Many films, however, received a positive response. Biograph continued to enjoy the most frequent kudos, but Woods often praised subjects like Kalem's *The Girl at the Mill* and used them to illustrate his points—in this instance that "it is the simple, uncomplicated story, if well told, that gives the best results in moving pictures."[75]

The dissatisfaction with Edison productions came from many quarters. In early February, Jonathan M. Bradlet, who had written several scenarios for the Edison Company, wrote Frank Dyer a polite letter outlining a few criticisms of specific films:

> It appears to me, that in several of your productions, the studio does not pay enough attention to the distribution of the light. For instance in "KING'S PARDON" the top light is entirely too strong, it is difficult to see the features of the Judge sitting at the high bench, while the faces of the other persons, sitting below the Judge, in a less strong light, are visible.
>
> Your studio grows a little careless in the details, for instance, in "UNDER THE NORTHERN SKIES" the supposed murdered man is a too willing corpse. He steadies himself on his legs and gently passes his arm over the shoulders of the man carrying him away.
>
> You would be surprised to see how the spectators pay some attention to these little details. When a man is supposed to be dead, they want him to appear dead and not to help himself.
>
> With these two cases you can ask Mr. Porter to put more care.[76]

In a postscript to his letter, Bradlet voiced sympathy for Porter's predicament. "I do not blame Mr. Porter but the foolish exhibitors refusing to show repeaters and forcing the Manufacturers to produce too much," explained Bradlet. "If repeaters could be shown you would sell more copies; as there would not be such a tremendous demand for new subjects, the producers would have more time to take care of the details of the new productions." But other companies operated under the same constraints with better success. When an Edison sales representative went on a business trip, he wrote the home office, "I can sell machines but film is out of the question. Our films are being roasted everywhere, particularly the short subjects at 21st St Studio and you know they are not what they should be."[77]

By late February, Edison executives were thoroughly disenchanted with Porter and the films he was producing. Some of these faults can be seen in a surviving fragment of *The Uplifting of Mr. Barker* (Dawley, February 1909).[78] The actors are heavily made up and their exaggerated gestures often have no clear meaning. This acting style may have been encouraged by a distant camera that reduced the actors to quite small proportions in the frame. The sets and actors are presented frontally, the lighting is flat and the performers seem more like cartoon characters than real people. Scenes are often drawn out. Even the

The Uplifting of Mr. Barker.

surviving fragment supports the *Dramatic Mirror*'s suggestion that "a pair of shears judiciously used on the film would have improved it."[79] In one scene at a society ball, Mr. Barker fights with his daughters' two escorts and pushes them into a fountain. How this comes about is unclear and there is a long exchange between the three that is impossible to decipher even after repeated viewings. The *Mirror*'s critic may have been generous when he said the film is "funny only in spots."[80]

Films that were completed but not yet released would receive even more negative assessments. *The Landlady's Portrait* (Matthews, February 1909) was "a mixed-up 'comic' without point or story and we must confess our inability to find in it a single excuse for a laugh."[81] *A Bird in a Gilded Cage* (Matthews, February 1909) was "greatly weakened by faulty construction, aimless action and the omission of necessary connecting scenes or subtitle."[82] *The Colored Stenographer* (Matthews, February 1909) was condemned because "there is in this subject so much aimless action, having no apparent connection with the story, that a really good comedy idea is obscured and weakened. We can liken it only to a writer who starts out to tell a certain tale and who continually digresses to tell little side stories of no interest, and only calculated to draw attention away from the main issue."[83] *Mary Jane's Lovers* (Matthews, February 1909) was "another good comedy idea weakened by bad handling."[84] *A Midnight Supper* (Matthews, February 1909) was "certainly not the kind of work the Edison company should be offering to the public," and *Love is Blind* (Matthews, February 1909) was "not much better handled" and "whatever point there is to the subject is lost in the hurried action."[85] Edison films were being constantly attacked for the incoherence of their narratives.

Porter Is Demoted

Frank Dyer and other Edison executives screened and approved all completed productions prior to distribution: they were well aware of their films' continued deficiencies. By late February, as Dyer prepared to expand the Kinetograph Department to four production units (three in the Bronx), he concluded that a new head of negative production was needed. On February 26th he accordingly removed the maker of *The Great Train Robbery* from his position as studio manager. John Pelzer, manager of sales, was temporarily placed in charge of the studio. Porter was sent on a trip to Savannah, Georgia, with James White who had been rehired in December 1908. The reunited makers of *Life of an American Fireman* filmed *A Road to Love; or, Romance of a Yankee Engineer in Central America* (March 1909), a film that was "pleasing notwithstanding the apparent carelessness with which it was produced."[86] After his Georgia sojourn, Porter judiciously stayed away from the Bronx studio, making *The Doctored Dinner Pail*, a comedy trick film in the French style, at East Orange during mid March.

Meanwhile, Dyer had located a new studio chief, his friend Horace G. Plimpton—a carpet dealer.[87] On Saturday March 27th, Wilson announced that Plimpton would become manager of negative production (for $100 a week) and John Pelzer would return to his duties as manager of sales. Edwin Porter would act as photographic expert under Plimpton's direction. Alex T. Moore resigned—or was dismissed. Later characterized by some as lazy, Moore was not needed at Edison and did not continue in film production. A memo was circulated to various departments elaborating on these changes:

3/27/09

TO ALL DEPARTMENTS:

Regarding the attached notice, in order that there may be no conflicting authority between the respective departments, it is to be understood that Mr. Plimpton will have entire charge of and be responsible for the production of all negatives until they are turned over to the Orange factory for printing.

Mr. Porter, acting under Mr. Plimpton's directions, will give such advice regarding negative production and questions relating thereto as his experience may suggest, and

A Road to Love; or, Romance of a Yankee Engineer, made by Porter and White outside the studio system in March 1909.

will do such other special photographic work as may be possible; and when requested by Mr. Weber, shall investigate and make any recommendations concerning the Orange plant and our machines and output. He will act solely as a consulting and advisory man.

Mr. Pelzer, as Manager of Sales, will confine himself to the selling end of the business, and Mr. Farrell shall act as his assistant. Mr. Jameson [*sic*] will be the foreman of the Printing and Developing Plant.

It is hoped that all departments will co-operate cheerfully and in a friendly spirit to advance and improve the quality of Edison pictures.

Frank L. Dyer
Vice-President[88]

Although Dyer and Wilson thus reduced Porter's role to that of consultant, he retained his substantial salary of $75 a week.

Under Horace Plimpton, the Bronx studio continued to expand, and its production procedures were increasingly systematized. A unit-director system with clear lines of authority emerged. In March 1909 Plimpton added a third unit at the Bronx studio, with Maurice George Winterbert St. Loup ($60 per week) as director and Otis M. Gove ($35 per week), who had earlier worked at Biograph, as cameraman.[89] In May, St. Loup was let go, and William F. Haddock ($40 per week) replaced George Harrington at the Twenty-first Street studio. In early June a fourth director, Ashley Miller ($40 per week), and a fourth cameraman,

Staff at Edison's Bronx studio, ca. 1909–10. The four directors sit in front (Ashley Miller on left, Dawley with cigar).

C. L. Gregory ($25 per week), were hired. The number of production units had quadrupled in the space of a year. This was made possible by the enlargement of the Bronx studio, a process begun in 1908 and completed by mid 1909. All regular production was eventually centralized in the Bronx.

During most of his time at Edison, Porter had served simultaneously as cameraman, director, studio manager, film editor, negative developer, and equipment designer. By mid 1909 the Kinetograph Department had developed a highly specialized and hierarchical structure. Under Plimpton were four directors (Dawley, Haddock, Miller, and Matthews) and four cameramen (Cronjager, Armitage, Gove, and Gregory). Plimpton created a camera department headed by Armitage, who coordinated or reassigned such tasks as negative development and editing.[90] It was not until late January 1910 that Edison hired its first film editor—Bert Dawley, J. Searle Dawley's brother. Following Plimpton's arrival, additional actors were hired on a full-time basis, including William Sorelle, Edward Boulden, John Steppling, Herbert E. Bostwick, and Laura Sawyer. The stock company was well established, and the basic elements of the studio system were in place.

Although publicity coming from the MPPCo and the Edison Company continually emphasized the increasing expense of their films, documentation suggests differently. Edison executives kept precise accounts for each film, totaled the expenses of each director, and compared the results on a monthly basis. The average negative cost varied from $1.28 per foot for Dawley in June 1909 (inflated by the cost of one film, *The Prince and the Pauper*) to $.30 per foot for Haddock in October. The average cost per negative foot was $.508 (just over $500 to produce a one-reel film) for June–October 1909, a reduction of 37 percent over the cost of a negative foot for 1906 ($.81).[91] Moreover, the average cost per negative foot declined over the course of the June–October period. By mid 1909 Plimpton had set up rigorous cost controls and other forms of accountability by director. If their units performed poorly either as to production costs or production results, the directors were chastised. If the problem persisted, they were replaced—as Matthews was replaced by Frank McGlynn in August 1909.[92] Despite these efforts to control costs and improve quality, the Edison Company's performance remained disappointing. Although the number of Edison productions increased almost threefold from 1908 to 1909, film sales increased only 22 percent from $554,359 to $675,306. Fewer prints of more subjects were being sold. With film profits remaining virtually unchanged at $234,798, much more energy was being used to attain the same financial results.

The Edison studio was operated like a factory. Creative personnel made templates or negatives of selected subjects as inexpensively as possible. This process involved the highly coordinated efforts of many specialists (actors, set designers, cameramen), who worked with several separate units, each of which was the responsibility of managers (the directors). These unit managers reported to and worked with one head supervisor (Plimpton). The negative was developed and a positive copy of each film was assembled by the camera department (headed by Armitage). The picture was screened for quality control in West Orange by a select group of executives—including, in principle at least, Thomas Edison. Once approved, multiple copies were printed up and assembled according to specification in West Orange by low-paid workers. Clearly the cinema had undergone a radical transformation from the days, just ten years earlier, when each exhibitor selected his own one-shot films and ordered them in a way that satisfied his own sense of authorship. By mid 1909, Edison executives were applying many principles of scientific management to film production.[93]

Porter's situation after his demotion was a delicate one. Above and beyond its formal regulation of the industry, the MPPCo provided a framework within which licensed manufacturers reached informal or secret understandings and acted in concert. Manufacturers agreed not to hire personnel away from other licensed producers, nor to hire those that had been discharged for "justified reasons" or simply left. Sidney Olcott, for instance, was dismissed by Kalem in April of 1909 because, according to Frank Marion, "he had a notion that all the manufacturers were clamouring for his services and was therefore beyond all criticism from us." "I don't know that you have a notion of taking him on, but if so I trust you will appreciate that it would have a very bad effect on the discipline of our establishment," Frank Marion told Dyer. "I suppose this can come well within the defines of our mutual understanding as to employees."[94] Dyer, who desperately needed just such a director, nonetheless reassured Marion by return mail. Olcott, Dyer acknowledged, would be useful, but "the belief that they can leave us at will" could not in any way be encouraged.[95] In the case of Olcott, the director was properly chastened and soon rejoined Kalem in his old capacity. Directors, actors, and other production personnel had to look beyond Edison-affiliated producers for an increase in salary, recognition, or a more sympathetic employer. These restrictions applied to Porter, too.

Porter's continued Edison employment at a good salary may have been designed to discourage him from leaving and joining the independents. Although newly formed independent companies would have benefited from Porter's years of experience, the veteran filmmaker may have been reluctant to join them too precipitously, since their future was so unpredictable. Rather Porter spent his next six months at Edison working on a series of miscellaneous projects. Some of his time was devoted to testing film stock—particularly a nonflammable stock developed by Eastman Kodak. "After making several tests of the new Eastman negative and positive film, we find the speed, quality and action during the course of operation is about the same as our present film," he concluded. "The texture of the stock is much harder and not so flexible and do not think it will stand the wear and tear as our old, but this can only be determined by time."[96] Porter's reservations about the new Eastman stock soon proved accurate. When the nonflammable film was put on the market, renters protested that it wore out very quickly and they could not recoup their costs. Porter, moreover, may have devoted some time to refining the projecting kinetoscope. Although kinetoscope sales for 1908 had declined 18 percent from the previous year to $341,848, they still represented almost 40 percent of the Edison Manufacturing Company's film-related business.

Porter also made a handful of films outside the studio system. In May he directed a comedy, *The $10,000 Painting*, shot by Armitage and released on June 25th as *An Affair of Art*. For whatever reasons, this film was not well received. "Oh, Great Edison, what horrors are perpetuated in thy name!" commented the *Dramatic Mirror*. "This picture is pretty nearly the worst excuse for comedy we have ever seen on a screen."[97] In August, Porter was sent out west for two months (what better way to keep him away from the independents!); he filmed a "fruit industrial" and *Bear Hunt in the Rockies* in Marble, Colorado. *Bear Hunt*, his last Edison film, was released on January 11, 1910, and received a generally warm reception:

> This fine film has educational as well as some dramatic value. It depicts with fidelity what appears to be a real bear hunt in the Rocky Mountains. The natural scenery is superb, and the bear is a sure enough bear. A considerable party sets out on the hunt on horseback, and with pack horses conveying their camp material. In the party are

two ladies—actor ladies evidently, as they fail at times to conceal their professional training. One of them goes fishing, and is having luck, when a bear appears. She pretends to be frightened and starts to run, but in front of the camera comes the fatal desire to pose, and we realize that the danger from the bear is mere pretense. When she arrives at the camp she again poses, facing the camera, while she tells her experience to those standing behind her. The dogs are now called, and the bear is pursued, treed and shot. We are mercifully spared a scene showing the details of butchering. Later a cub is roped, and led home by the party. Taken as a whole, the film is decidedly entertaining.[98]

Porter's last Edison film recalls one of his first—*Terrible Teddy, the Grizzly King*—and one of his favorites—*The "Teddy" Bears*.

Although Porter and White were permitted to operate outside the studio system with minimum resources, they remained only as relics of a bygone era. Porter's methods of production and representation were at odds with developments both at Edison and in the industry as a whole. This awkward situation did not endure. Perhaps Porter was in contact with the increasingly active independents, or was finally judged expendable. In any case, on November 10th Horace Plimpton notified others that Edwin S. Porter and his assistant William J. Gilroy were being dismissed.[99] A few days later they were off the payroll. Though considered America's leading filmmaker in the era before the nickelodeon, Porter had been fired.

13 Postscript

Although Porter and the Edison Company went in different directions, their subsequent activities involved numerous parallels as well as significant contrasts. Many industry figures believed that Porter's filmmaking days were over, but this did not prove to be the case. After leaving Edison, Porter found employment among the independents. He worked briefly with Will Rising who was head of production for the Actophone Company. Actophone, however, was quickly prosecuted by the Motion Picture Patents Company and eventually went bankrupt.[1] Porter then formed the Defender Film Company with Joseph Engel, a theater owner, and William Swanson, the well-known independent distributor and exhibitor, who had first met Porter in the 1890s.[2] This New York–based company began to release subjects on June 10, 1910. Little is known about Defender, and much of that is contradictory. Trade journals paid it surprisingly little attention. A report in *Moving Picture World*, however, mentioned that Defender's pictures were originally made by the World Film Manufacturing Company of Portland, Oregon—a company earlier put out of business by a studio fire.[3] These releases were expected to continue until the new Defender studio was completed. Yet Arthur Miller, who was hired by Porter as an assistant, recalls working on the company's first subject: *Russia, the Land of Oppression*.[4] Miller's account, however, contains puzzling gaps—for example, he never names any of the actors appearing in these films. Perhaps Porter shot a handful of Defender productions while most releases were supplied by old World Film Company negatives, or he may have simply added a few scenes to some otherwise completed productions. Was *Wild Bill's Defeat* (released October 6, 1910) shot in Oregon or on Staten Island, where Porter did most of his

The Rex symbol. Frame suffers from nitrate decomposition.

location work? Not one Defender film is available to answer these questions.

Defender films were strongly criticized in trade publications. After viewing *Russia, the Land of Oppression*, Frank Woods wrote:

> In this first release of a new company we find the photography far from satisfactory and the story disconnected and without a discoverable plot. The oppression of the Jews in Russia forms the basis for the film, and when the soldiers enter the synagogue they all pause and pose while the camera pictures the anguish of the Jews. Then we see the refugees entering America, through the Castle Garden, and the film ends with an actor and actress making senseless grimaces at close view as if to indicate how happy they are in the land of the free.[5]

A Cowboy's Courtship (released September 8th) "is not a story at all; it has no plot."[6] *The Cattle Thief's Revenge* was "morally crooked because it leaves the villain triumphant," while *A Schoolmarm's Ride for Life* (released September 29th) was "necessarily more or less blighted by the impossibility of the plot."[7] Excepting the acting, which received occasional praise, these Defender films were condemned in a manner that recalls the harsh comments on earlier Edison films.

Defender stopped releasing in November 1910. Perhaps it was considered best to disassociate Porter's own productions from those made by a defunct firm. Or if the productions were made by Porter, his continuing problems may have forced the partners to reorganize their company.[8] In any case, Porter, Engel, and Swanson now formed the Rex Motion Picture Manufacturing Company, which began to release films in February 1911. By then Porter had already completed more than twenty productions at the Rex studio at 573 Eleventh Avenue in New York City.[9] This unusually extensive backlog was undoubtedly designed to free Porter from the pressure of the weekly release schedule.

The first Rex production, *Heroine of '76*, starred Gordon Sackville, who had acted for Porter as far back as 1904.[10] The film was made for a modest sum but the results were hailed as "a remarkably good picture … and is bound in respect of its patriotic theme, to be popular all over the United States."[11] Even the *Dramatic Mirror* was enthusiastic, remarking that the story was "told with clearness and precision, and aside from a certain nervous haste to be over a situation which will doubtlessly wear off, is well acted. Great care in detail is displayed in costume and setting."[12] The company's third release, *By the Light of the Moon* (March 1911), was a silhouette film that revived a technique Porter had used almost three years earlier with *A Comedy in Black and White* (August 1908):

> The film is a real novelty in modern pictures and is interesting and attractive as well. It is an excellent example of what Mr. Porter can do with a camera in a studio by the manipulation of light and trick effects in which branch of the art he has few if any peers in the world. The characters are seen in black silhouette moving in front of backgrounds that are illuminated by a representation of silvery moonlight. The effect is striking, the story is a pleasing little farce, telling of the love of two young people, the interruptions from a tramp, the objections of the girl's parents, and the elopement of the couple in an aeroplane pursued by the father in an automobile. The elopers reach the parson's house and are married before papa arrives. The picture is good enough to stand alone without the ridiculous introduction of the ballet that marches out carrying banners that spell out the name of the firm.[13]

It also provided the *Dramatic Mirror* with an opportunity to profile the director in a laudatory article, the first such career profile.[14]

At Rex, Porter returned to his former production methods. Once again he outfitted the new studio to his specifications and had charge of every detail of the production process. Soon he developed a Rex stock company, which featured Phillips Smalley, his wife Lois Weber, and Cleo Ridgely. Smalley also worked closely with Porter and directed the actors, assuming the position held earlier by Dawley and McCutcheon. Weber wrote many of the scenarios. Porter's collaborative approach to filmmaking proved itself effective, as Rex films quickly established an excellent reputation. "The success that has been achieved by the Rex Company in the Independent field is not difficult to understand," Woods remarked. "It proves again the fact that it is quality of the dependable, consistent kind that counts. The Rex Company started in making good pictures and has kept it up with much more than average uniformity."[15]

Only one surviving Rex film, *Fate* (released July 16, 1911), can be definitely attributed to Porter and it is a reworking of his earlier *The Gentleman Burglar* (May 1908).[16] Reviews suggest it was an unexceptional Rex production (see document no. 28). Nonetheless, the picture has a coherent, understandable narrative. By mid 1911 Porter had simplified his storytelling methods and eliminated antiquated elements that had been so harshly criticized in his Edison films. Gone were narrative digressions and overlapping temporality. Yet other elements of his earlier approach were developed and found favor in some circles.

One critic praised Rex productions for photographing actors in full shot, maintaining enough distance between the camera and the actors so the frame did not exclude the actors' feet. Readers were urged to "study their work for consistent and praiseworthy effort to keep the full figure on the screen."[17] The veteran filmmaker did not, however, enrich this reduced system of representation with techniques, such as parallel editing, that Griffith and others were finding so strikingly effective.

DOCUMENT NO. 28

Fate (Rex, July 6).—This story seems to depend too much on its titles for its development, rather than the subsequent action. The result is oftentimes shown without the events leading up to it, making rather a "jumpy" story, that might have been better blended by different treatment and handling of characters. It deals with a gentleman burglar, who marries a respectable girl and changed his manner of life. A former pal turned up, demanding money. He stole it from his father-in-law's desk, evidently was caught and ordered from the house. He is then implicated in a murder and convicted. He escapes after five years, commits a burglary on his wife's room, where she lives as a wife of a former lover. Discovered by his child, he shoots himself and his identity is kept secret by the other man. It is not always quite natural in its deductions and movements. Some parts left out would have benefited others.

SOURCE: *New York Dramatic Mirror*, July 12, 1911, p. 25.

The popularity of Rex films gave Porter renewed credibility. A year after the company's debut, the studio chief reaped kudos from a trade press that was only beginning to acknowledge the role of individual filmmakers. As one journalist described him:

He may be rightfully considered the dean of all producers. His work to-day—the work of an artist and mechanical genius—is by no means a matter of inspiration but the result of long experience in a profession to which many are called, but few are chosen. To be a great producer in these days a man must first be born an artist. Whether or not he be a trained artist, the essence of art must be born with him. There never has been a training school for motion picture art and the successful producers in that line have been obliged to train themselves in the school of experience. A great producer must also be a born mechanic in order to successfully cope with the marvels of photography and the engineering ability required for great scenic conceptions. . . . It is safe to say that there is no living man who knows as much about the making of a moving picture as Edwin Porter. Through the medium of Rex pictures we know his artistic ability. He is capable of preparing a first-class film picture in the manuscript. With his story in hand he undertakes the scenic arrangements and rehearsals with the absolute confidence of a master. With his familiar cry of "stand-by" he takes his place at the camera and turns the handle while directing the play. He knows his camera inside and out; in fact, he builds them himself. He knows electricity and stage lighting to the ultimate of perfection. When the negative has been exposed Mr. Porter becomes a photographer and follows it through the developing process and there is none who knows the work better than he. He is the absolute master of his trade from beginning to end and is perhaps the best qualified man to be in charge of a motion picture studio there has ever been.[18]

Porter's reputation thus enjoyed a powerful resurgence within the film industry. The Rex pictures he produced justified the now atypical way he went about making films. Collaboration and nonspecialization remained, for him, two sides of the same coin—two dimensions of the filmmaking process.

The veteran producer and his business partners used their enhanced standing to expand commercially. In January 1912 Rex commenced distributing two subjects each week.[19] Porter's films with Weber and Smalley were released on Thursdays, and pictures starring Marion Leonard and produced by her husband, the former Porter/Edison scenario chief Stanner E. V. Taylor, appeared on Sunday. In May, Porter and Rex were instrumental in the formation of the Universal Film Manufacturing Company, ultimately controlled by Carl Laemmle.

Edison Filmmaking Revives

Edison films gradually recovered from their low point at Porter's departure: by 1910–11 they were often considered the equal of any then being produced.[20] This meant more natural acting and clearly told stories. Nothing indicates this improvement better than *The Passer-by* (June 1912). With a flashback structure, an elderly man (played movingly by Marc McDermott) recalls his life and the crucial moments when it intersected with the woman he loved but was never able to marry. The remarkable film frames the flashbacks with camera moves toward and away from the speaker's face. Edison films were exceeded in popularity only by Biograph's, at least among MPPCo-licensed producers. As quality improved at Edison, so did the rate of production. Output increased to three reels per week beginning November 1, 1910, four per week beginning August 1, 1911, and five reels commencing September 23, 1912.[21]

Consistent with the practices of such production companies as Kalem, and to a lesser extent Biograph, Edison frequently sent small groups of actors and production personnel to distant locations. On January 19, 1910, Horace G. Plimpton dispatched a crew to Cuba, where Dawley directed Laura Sawyer in love stories such as *The Princess and the Peasant* and *A Vacation in Havana*, the latter doubling as a travel picture.[22] Since cold weather and a crowded studio hampered efficient work and novel scenery boosted interest in the Edison pictures, the additional expense seemed justified. Later that year Dawley traveled to the Rocky Mountains in Canada. In 1911 and in 1912 he again headed to Cuba and the Rocky Mountains on filming expeditions.[23] Director Ashley Miller took several Edison stars to London in July 1912. These trips were made in lieu of creating a studio on the West Coast (i.e., Hollywood), something that many production companies were doing by 1911–12.

Edison's profits from filmmaking fluctuated between $200,000 and $230,000 between 1908 and 1911. In about April 1911 film activities were shifted from the Edison Manufacturing Company to a new corporate entity, Thomas A. Edison, Inc. That year domestic film sales averaged 40 prints for each of 178 pictures released.[24] Foreign sales in many instances approached, and occasionally exceeded, domestic sales. The lure of overseas distribution had become significant. Because British exchanges only bought films on an individual basis (rather than placing a standing order for many weeks as in the United States), sales could fluctuate from less than ten for some American-oriented subjects to more than one hundred for a melodrama such as *The Switchman's Tower*.[25] The impact was noticeable. Edison stopped making films about American history and focused on European events, instead. *The Charge of the Light Brigade* (1912) was shot by Dawley in Cheyenne, Colorado, using American soldiers but costumes reputed to have been shipped from England.[26] Whether or not true, the English praised this spectacle and placed an unprecedented print order. Edison executives considered the British market in hiring English cartoonist Harry Furniss and purchasing rights to stories. Sales in Australia, South Africa, and South America had also become an important area of concern for Edison executives. This sensitivity to the foreign market was in marked contrast to the pre-1909 period, when Edison showed little interest in overseas sales.

In the fall of 1911 Edison made a few multireel subjects (*The Three Musketeers* and *Foul Play*) that were early premonitions of the longer, full-length films that would soon dominate the industry. In 1912 this interest shifted and the company introduced the first "serial," *What Happened to Jane* (released July 26, 1912). Each 15-minute film was "complete in itself," but the star (Mary Fuller) and a larger narrative bound the episodes together. This was prepared in conjunction with the *Ladies' World* magazine, which published corresponding accounts of Jane's adventures. This tie-in proved exceedingly popular and was much imitated, both at Edison and throughout the industry. At that very moment, however, Edwin Porter was involved in a somewhat related, but ultimately more far-reaching, development—the rise of the full-length feature film.

Edwin S. Porter and the Formation of Famous Players

While still at Rex, Porter was also pursuing other plans. In July 1912 he, Daniel Frohman, and Adolph Zukor acquired the American rights to *Queen Elizabeth*, a three-reel feature starring Sarah Bernhardt, and marketed it through their newly formed Famous Players Film Company. At a time when the American film industry was still seeking the mantle of respectability, Bernhardt's name generated laudatory coverage in newspapers that customarily mentioned moving pictures only if the editors wanted to condemn them.[27] *Queen Elizabeth* played to standing room only on the Loew circuit and in other theaters.[28] As Porter became more involved with Famous Players, he spent less time at Rex. Phillips Smalley and Lois Weber assumed greater responsibility, including the direction of many Rex films, until they left in September. That October Porter sold his shares in Universal for a substantial sum.[29]

By the fall of 1912 Famous Players was moving to film plays with top American theatrical stars. Bernhardt set the example, Daniel Frohman provided ties to the theatrical world, Porter the expertise in film production, and Zukor the business acumen and much of the financing. Late that year, after hastily converting an old armory on West Twenty-sixth Street into a picture studio, Porter shot *The Count of Monte Cristo* with James O'Neill. Again he pursued a collaborative approach, working with Joseph A. Golden, who had written scenarios and produced films at Biograph, Centaur, and Nestor.[30] When the Selig company preemptively released a competing feature based on the same story, Famous Players sued and delayed distribution of its picture for almost a year.[31] In any case, this remarkable record of late-nineteenth-century theatrical technique may not have been dynamic enough to launch the company's new line of original productions. O'Neill's acting style and the sets were incompatible with popular conceptions of realism and had become old-fashioned, even in the theater. When finally released late in 1913, *The Count of Monte Cristo* received little attention even in the trade press. Not surprisingly, the Porter-Golden collaboration was not repeated.

The first Famous Players production to be distributed, *The Prisoner of Zenda*, featured matinee idol James Hackett in a film version of his well-known theatrical vehicle. Production began in December 1912 and encountered initial difficulties. As Adolph Zukor recalled, Porter gave the actors little direction beyond the marks that they had to hit in order to remain within camera range. After Hackett saw his performance on screen, he assumed a more active interest in shaping the project. The initial shooting was redone as "he began to help Porter map out the action."[32] And so a collaborative relationship once again emerged. The results were considered electrifying, and as one reviewer remarked, "We owe much of the excellence of this production to the harmonious working of masters on the speaking and silent stage."[33]

The Prisoner of Zenda, released in February 1913, was "more the visualization of the novel on which the play was based than a reproduction in moving pictures of the play itself." Four acts were transformed into over a hundred scenes. Location scenes and interiors were integrated in a way that gained applause from members of the theatrical profession who attended a preview. They found the film "unexpectedly successful," although some critics considered Por-

"Rudolf witnesses Rupert's escape from Antoinette's room after the murder of Duke Michael"—The Prisoner of Zenda

A postcard used to promote *The Prisoner of Zenda*.

ter's camera to be too distant from the actors.[34] A modern viewing of the film likewise shows Porter and Hackett in full control of their mise-en-scène. *Moving Picture World* remarked, "With this four-act [i.e., four-reel] film the producers have leaped to the pinnacle of moving picture fame at one gigantic bound."[35] A large-scale marketing campaign began, with Edwin's youngest brother, E. M. Porter, the chief representative in Pittsburgh.[36]

The Prisoner of Zenda enabled Famous Players to acquire the services of such leading actors as Minnie Maddern Fiske and Lillie Langtry. Benjamin (B. P.) Schulberg, who had been put on the payroll back in late 1912, headed publicity and script editing—jobs he had performed effectively for Porter at Rex.[37] J. Searle Dawley left the Edison organization in the summer of 1913 and became Porter's collaborator. Actors and production personnel who had worked with Dawley and/or Porter soon found their way to the Famous Players' studio—including actors John Steppling and John Gordon, writer Jim Cogan, and set designer Richard Murphy. Laura Sawyer, who had become an Edison star, joined her old colleagues in August.[38] However, the most important individual attracted by the new company was Mary Pickford.

Porter directed Pickford's first feature, *A Good Little Devil*, which was shown to admiring exhibitors in early July. It was based on David Belasco's theatrical production of that name and had Pickford as one of the leads. *Moving Picture World*'s praise was somewhat qualified. "That [the play] is one of Mr. Belasco's big successes is, alone, enough to make people want to see [the

Tess of the D'Urbervilles, starring Minnie Maddern Fiske.

film]. We think it as good, almost, as any fairy picture could be and, in the past, fairy pictures have been very popular, especially with children and their mothers."[39] In his memoirs, Zukor more forthrightly explained his reasons for postponing the film's release for nine months. Belasco had offered to help with the direction of the film, and Famous Players eagerly accepted. Publicity surrounding Belasco's involvement, particularly his agreement to appear in the film, heightened still further the company's already considerable prestige. Belasco's supervisory role backfired, however, for he limited the filmmakers' ability to adapt the play to motion pictures. Nonetheless, Zukor achieved one additional goal with *A Good Little Devil*: he signed Pickford to a one-year contract.

Porter had directed three films for Famous Players, and in two cases the results were somewhat problematic. Dawley joined Porter in directing the company's fourth effort, *Tess of the D'Urbervilles*, which featured Madame Fiske in an adaptation of her stage vehicle of that name. The risks were particularly high since Fiske had the right to destroy the negative if it did not meet with her satisfaction. The film, however, delighted her, in part because Porter's soft photography (and lack of close-ups) shed years off the middle-aged actress's appearance. The picture relied more closely on the book than the play, gener-

In the Bishop's Carriage, with Mary Pickford.

ating a large number of scenes. *Tess of the D'Urbervilles* was called "a revelation" and "glorious surprise," and Dawley was labeled "a master of photoplay arrangement."[40]

Porter and Dawley then directed Mary Pickford in *In the Bishop's Carriage*. Although purportedly based on the play of that name, it was, in fact, adapted by B. P. Schulberg from the original novel. Pickford plays a young thief who turns from a criminal life to become a successful stage actress. Although a former accomplice comes back to haunt her, she ultimately escapes his threatening grasp. Upon its debut, the film was promptly declared "a winner" and proved to be a highly successful showcase for Pickford's talents.[41] Porter and Dawley went on to co-direct Mary Pickford's next film, *Caprice*. "Mr. Porter has directed the whole with an admirable attention to detail and an artist's eye for beautiful scenes," the *New York Telegraph* later announced.[42] Pickford's acting and the blend of romance with comedy likewise received strong endorsements. Afterwards Porter remained in charge of the key Pickford unit, while his protégé was assigned to his own production group. Dawley was soon directing such pictures as *Chelsea 7750*, a detective thriller starring Laura Sawyer (Dawley also wrote the scenario).

Although Famous Players had been producing a feature film a month, these were stockpiled—as had been done at Rex. The company finally began to market its films systematically in September 1913, announcing that it would release three pictures at regular intervals each month, or "30 Famous Features" (most were four to six reels or 60 to 90 minutes each) per year—an unprecedented number and a return to the regular release schedule that Porter had disliked.[43] Beginning with *Tess of the D'Urbervilles* (September 1st) and *In the Bishop's Carriage* (September 10th),[44] Famous Players Film Company became the first film producer in the world to regularly release full-length feature films. Famous Players effectively launched a new era of motion picture practice.

Porter took Pickford to California for several months of filming in November 1913.[45] There they made at least two films under makeshift conditions. In the first, *Hearts Adrift* (released February 10, 1914), the Pickford character was cast away on a desert island. Although some critics praised the picture for its star's performance and for its dramatic photography, *Variety* contended that Famous Players had "slipped some cogs in this feature and the movie followers will no doubt pick flaws right and left."[46] *Tess of the Storm Country* (1914), one of Pickford's most successful films, came next. *Variety* declared: "Little Mary comes into her own and her work in this five-part movie production so far o'ershadows her work in the other films there's no comparison."[47] *Moving Picture World* told the trade that the picture "possesses the qualities that make for success."[48] Despite widespread accolades and a box-office bonanza (the film was so successful that Pickford would later remake it), *Tess of the Storm Country* shows a director who had not fully adopted contemporary American techniques of storytelling. The camera always remains at a distance and fails to make effective use of Pickford's enchanting and expressive face.

Tess of the Storm Country demonstrates the extent to which Porter and the film industry had moved away from a homosocial way of working and thinking. It was based on a novel by a woman (Grace Miller White), starred a woman, and appealed in large part to female spectators. This is obviously not the entire story (the scenario was by B. P. Schulberg, the direction Porter's), but production companies had developed a heterosocial mode of work that was strongly inflected by the influx of personnel from the theater. Within the industry women asserted a powerful presence in the years immediately prior to gaining the vote. Adolph Zukor found Mary Pickford and her mother astute both financially and in the subtleties of building the actress's career. "America's Sweetheart," moreover, was active behind the camera as well as in front of it. As the president of Famous Players later recalled: "Mary had her hand in everything, writing scripts, arguing with directors, making suggestions to other players. But everyone knew she did it for the benefit of the picture, and her ideas were helpful."[49] Pickford had assumed such a role in the past—at Independent Motion Picture Company she wrote and starred in *The Dream* (1911), directed by Thomas Ince.

Correspondingly, Porter had provided Lois Weber with similar opportunities. Although he was hardly a convert to feminism, working with women on an equal basis did not prove difficult for him. It would not be inappropriate to see Pickford as filling the void left by Porter's more formal collaborators, particularly on these two West Coast films.

After Porter and Pickford returned to New York, the filmmaker took Frederick Thomson as his co-director for *The Spitfire* (released June 20th)—a non-Pickford feature. Although the results were "certainly worthy of a place in any theater," Thomson was supplanted by Hugh Ford, an "international theatrical authority," who had joined Famous Players late in 1913.[50] These two worked together for the remainder of Porter's Famous Players career. Their first film, *Such a Little Queen*, was also Porter's last with Pickford; some of the picture's early scenes may have been shot during their California sojourn. This film likewise received wide acclaim. The co-directors continued to direct "in collaboration" on *The Crucible*, starring Marguerite Clark.[51]

Encouraged by its many successes, the Famous Players Film Company planned to make a series of dramas in Europe. Porter and Ford began this project by filming *The Eternal City* (1914), an eight-reel adaptation of Hall Caine's epic novel. Heavily inspired by the success of such Italian epics as *Quo Vadis* and *Cabiria*, they shot in the Vatican gardens, the Roman Forum, and the Coliseum. World War I soon curtailed their activities, and they finished their production in New York City. Opening at the Lyceum Theatre on December 27, 1914, the film's presentation was handled by S. F. Rothapfel, a showman whose lavish presentations matched the film's ambitions. The *Dramatic Mirror* called it "the finest dramatic work thus far made here or elsewhere" and noted its unparalleled use of spectacle—this just one month before *The Birth of a Nation* opened in New York.[52] *Variety* was almost as enthusiastic. During the course of 1915, another nine Porter/Ford productions were released to generally enthusiastic reviews.

Shortly before his directing career ended, Porter reminisced,

> Looking back upon the past eighteen years in motion pictures—back to the day when no one knew what a motion picture was—and realizing the wonderful strides the industry has taken since then, I am more than impressed. I am thrilled. Artistically and mechanically the motion picture has forged its way forward until today it is recognized as the greatest amusement factor in the world and the greatest educational force in the history of civilization.[53]

Yet Porter's feelings must have been more mixed than he could publicly acknowledge. As feature films of four or more reels became the dominant product of the industry, pressures to standardize production intensified, and large staffs were even more stratified than they had been at the Edison Company. At Famous Players, the veteran filmmaker was considered something of an oddity.

His insistence on photographing productions was proving embarrassing to Adolph Zukor, who increasingly questioned his abilities. "Porter was, I have always felt, more of an artistic mechanic than a dramatic artist," the mogul later remarked.[54] Porter's predicament replayed his Edison experience; the falling out of favor he had suffered with the standardization of one-reel production recurred with features. His final break with Zukor came after the burning of the Famous Players studio at 213 West Twenty-sixth Street on September 11, 1915. Porter remained to supervise the hastened completion of a new studio in northern Manhattan and then left for South America after selling his one-quarter share in Famous Players for $800,000—an immense sum at the time.[55] Independent, small-scale feature production was too risky to attempt on his own. Perhaps because he lacked satisfactory alternatives, Porter retired from filmmaking.

Edison's Motion Picture Business Comes to a Close

Even as Porter enjoyed increasing prosperity in the mid teens, the Edison company encountered an array of problems. A major blow to Edison's motion picture efforts in mid-decade involved the Motion Picture Patents Company. The MPPCo had sued almost all unlicensed domestic film producers between 1909 and 1911. While it enjoyed initial successes against these independents, Carl Laemmle in particular challenged the validity of MPPCo patents in court and eventually won. Meanwhile the MPPCo-licensed film producers started their own film exchange in mid 1910, absorbing many of the rental companies owned by or affiliated with the "trust." The resulting General Film Company then bought out many of the remaining licensed exchanges; and when a renter refused to sell, he found that his license was quickly cancelled. Tactics such as these led the U.S. government to bring an antitrust suit on August 15, 1912. Much damaging evidence was submitted, and on October 1, 1915, the courts found the Motion Picture Patents Company guilty of antitrust violation.[56] Edison and other licensed producers then became liable to pay injured parties triple damages. This defeat was not only a costly financial and commercial setback but a public relations disaster.

Although Edison's motion picture enterprise suffered setbacks in many areas, the principal ones were in the area of filmmaking. The talent of its staff was weakened by the departure of Dawley, Laura Sawyer, and other personnel to the Famous Players Film Company in mid 1913. In March 1914 the Bronx studio suffered a major fire, which disrupted production. Yet Edison's decisive failure centered on its refusal to make a timely transition to full-length feature filmmaking. Edison released only one-reelers throughout 1912 and most of 1913, even as the average number of prints sold per subject fell from 40 to about 30.[57] That August, Edison introduced one two-reeler per week. Sales quickly picked up, halving the previous decline. Feature films (and even two-reelers were sometimes considered features at this stage) were in immense demand while one-reelers were becoming "filler."[58] Nonetheless, Thomas A. Edison, Inc. regularly released four one-reelers and one two-reeler each week through the beginning of 1915.[59] In mid 1914 Edison began to release one three-reel subject a month, but such "features" only became a regular part of Edison's weekly output on March 1st, 1915.[60] By then *The Birth of a Nation* had opened and Famous Players had been regularly releasing pictures of four to six reels for a year and a half. In the fall of 1915 Edison was barely selling 22 prints per subject through the General Film Company—a money-losing proposition. Before the end of the year, Edison had ceased to make one-reelers for regular release.[61]

William Hodkinson, president of Paramount Pictures Corporation, which distributed all the films made by Famous Players, had come to rely on block booking (in which a theater contracted for all its programs over a given year) and arrangements whereby his company received a percentage of the gross receipts. These commercial strategies ensured healthy profits, while the General Film Company's failure to pursue such innovative methods was a major reason for Edison's lack of profitability in the feature area. Finally, in mid 1915, Edison began to have outside distributors handle its features as well as the General Film Company. This included both Paramount and George Kleine.[62] Negative costs were expected to be about $15,000 per five-to-six reel film with the cost of prints adding another $6,000. Profits, it was assumed, would be substantial. The Kleine-Edison Feature Service was inaugurated with the release of *Vanity Fair* on October 6, 1915, starring Minnie Maddern Fiske, the renowned, but aging, stage actress who had already appeared in Famous Players' *Tess of the D'Urbervilles*. Income was disappointing, however, and the picture may have never recovered its cost of $28,676.

The advent of features and World War I (which curtailed foreign markets) destroyed Edison's profitability. The Motion Picture Division would have lost $25,000 during the 1915 business year had it not been for a special $50,000 charge against Edison's foreign division. The following year, it made profits of $2,480 on sales of $566,120. To compensate for the decline in revenues, Edison brought in an efficiency engineer, S. B. Mambert. Mambert was determined to keep expenses down. When filmmaking costs went up from $1.35 per negative foot in May 1915 to $1.71 in June, Horace Plimpton was fired. L. W. McChesney became head of the Motion Picture Division that August, even as Charles Wilson remained general manager of Thomas A. Edison, Inc. Ironically, bureaucratization and petty paperwork proliferated in an attempt to reduce waste. The impact, other than further disruption, seemed small—costs for September rose slightly, to $1.773 per foot. Directors were ordered to work with an exceedingly low (1.33 to 1) shooting ratio, which inevitably hampered production and curtailed quality.[63] The cost of a film more than the potential box-office success of a picture seemed to be foremost in the minds of Edison executives.

Since the second half of 1915, the Edison company had released its films through a variety of organizations, diffusing its identity and often creating minor conflicts between exhibitors, who found their exclusives undermined. The Paramount deal, which had looked highly promising in 1915, progressed slowly and then soured after Adolph Zukor and Jesse Lasky staged a coup and forced Hodkinson's departure in June 1916. Only three features were sold to Paramount. Beginning October 1916, the Kleine-Edison Feature Service was expanded to become the K.E.S.E. Service, involving Kleine, Edison, Selig, and Essanay. Edison also made films for McClure Pictures during 1916.[64]

Edison pictures, irrespective of distributor, appealed to moralistic, middle-class reform groups. Immediate pleasures of the flesh were shown to cause long-term misery. *The Stoning* (released March 25, 1915), for example, warns against premarital sex. It is the story of a naive middle-class girl (played by Viola Dana) who is misled, seduced, and abandoned by a railroad conductor. Though befriended by a virile, reformist minister, she is otherwise snubbed by the community and finally commits suicide. This moralizing tendency was only intensified when America entered World War I in April 1917. As many influential groups called for heightened moral purity and cleanliness, Edison inaugurated a series known as "Conquest Pictures." These programs were meant to provide "cleaner and more wholesome films, which could be exhibited with safety before any member of the family." The results proved disappointing.

Thomas Edison put much of his commitment to innovation in the area of technology. Edison had subsidized several aspiring inventors who claimed to be close to solving the problem of producing color films. They never succeeded, but two products closer to the inventor's concerns reached fruition. The Home Projecting Kinetoscope, often referred to as the Home P.K., and the updated "Kinetophone," which projected motion pictures with synchronous recorded sound in a large theater, looked back to Edison's first caveats. Each, unfortunately, would have a devastating effect on his motion picture enterprise. The Home P.K. was designed for use in homes, churches, and noncommercial venues. Its 21mm strip contained three 5.7mm images across its width; thus each foot of film contained 210 frames. Seventy-seven feet of film provided fifteen minutes of screen time. (This compactness recalls the miniscule images generated by Dickson's cylinder experiments over twenty years before.) People would buy the machine and a few films, which could then be exchanged for new ones at a small cost. The Home P.K. was launched in late 1911 and sold by many of Edison's phonograph dealers. Pictures were taken from the catalog of outdated Edison subjects—with some acquisitions made from other MPPCo-licensed producers. Edison also had personnel make science and educational subjects specifically for the Home P.K. The new motion picture system was complicated to operate and

encumbered by technical deficiencies. Although it represented a major investment of money and energy, the Home P.K. never became very popular.[65]

The kinetophone, in contrast, enjoyed an initial success when it opened in
February 1913.[66] The American and Canadian rights were sold to a company
set up by prominent vaudeville organizations. They embraced the kinetophone
because it gave them a way to differentiate their moving pictures from those
being shown in regular picture houses. Vaudeville theaters therefore made long-
term (three- to six-month) commitments to the machine, with Edison receiving
a rental that varied from $150 to $200 per week. With more than fifty machines
playing these houses, gross income exceeded $10,000 a week. In addition, as
many as a dozen exhibition units toured the country, presenting the novelty in
small-town theaters for a few days at a time. Each reel of film was only six
minutes long, and pictures usually showed mediocre vaudeville acts or scenes
from plays. Although business boomed through the summer, people began to
lose interest. As one of Edison's associates fumed, "The public is interested in
seeing Talking Pictures as a novelty, once or twice, and then they want longer
subjects and first class acting."[67] Although American interest in the kinetophone
novelty seriously faded by the fall of 1913, Edison had also sold kinetophone
rights to various parties throughout the world, including Japan. These organizations started somewhat later and often continued to be viable well into 1914;
the onset of World War I delivered the final blow to these enterprises in many
instances.[68]

With all the technical energy put into the Home P.K. and the kinetophone,
the regular Edison 35mm projectors were not kept up-to-date. In 1909 and 1910
profits from the projecting kinetoscope averaged $135,000 per year, down sub-
stantially from the $200,000 average of the previous two years but still respect-
able. Sales fell 30 percent in 1911 and were declining rapidly by 1912. Within
another two years, this once profitable part of Edison's business had all but
ceased to exist. A half-hearted revival was attempted with the development of
a new model, the "Super-Kinetoscope," in 1915; but it was expensive to manufacture and too highly priced. The revival effort was quickly abandoned, and
with it all attempts to produce motion picture hardware.[69]

Throughout the 1910s Porter had retained his interest in motion picture
technology. In the throes of leaving the Edison Manufacturing Company, he
developed the Simplex projector with Frank Cannock. This machine, promoted
by Richard Hollaman of the Eden Musee, was first sold commercially in 1911.[70]
The rise of the Simplex projector coincided with the decline of the Edison counterpart. Even at Famous Players, Porter had continued to experiment with technological innovations. In June 1915, he and William E. Waddell gave a demonstration of projected stereoscopic moving pictures. As exhibitors would do in
the 1950s, they provided spectators with glasses sporting a red filter for one eye
and a green filter for the other. According to one report, "the audience at the

Astor Theater was frequently moved to applause by the beauty of the scenes which gave one the impression of looking at actual stage settings and not the shadowy figures of the ordinary picture."[71]

When Porter sold his shares in Famous Players, he used some of the proceeds to buy shares in the Precision Machine Company and became its president. Under his supervision, the company's Simplex projector became the industry standard. Again Porter returned to his passion for mechanical invention. In 1917–18 Porter was vice-president, and Dawley secretary-treasurer, of the Sunlight Arc Company, which marketed innovative lights for studio filming. Competition from a major corporation soon proved their undoing.[72] At the Precision Machine Company, Porter developed several pieces of new equipment, for example an inexpensive motion picture camera that exhibitors could use to take local views. These were not notably successful, and when the company merged with the International Projecting Company in 1925, Porter did not become an officer of the new corporation, but slid quietly into retirement.

Porter, once known as Thomas Edison, Jr., was actively involved in the film industry for roughly thirty years—the same length of time as his role model and one-time boss. By the beginning of 1918, Thomas A. Edison was looking to sell the Bronx studio and leave the filmmaking business. In February, thirty years after the "Wizard" had his interview with Eadweard Muybridge, the actors and production staff at the Edison Studios were laid off. On March 30, 1918, Thomas A. Edison, Inc. sold its studio and plant to the Lincoln & Parker Film Company for $150,000 cash and $200,000 in common and preferred stock. Edison's role in filmmaking, as well as his aspirations as a movie mogul, had come to an end. But for this very reason, he could finally become a figure revered and romanticized by all sectors of the motion picture industry. Until his death on October 18, 1931, he helped to shape the public memory in regard to his role as "father of the motion picture industry."[73] Porter, not unlike Edison, continued to tinker in a machine shop during his years of retirement. Yet after losing much of his money in the stock market crash of 1929, the former filmmaker became a recluse and a largely forgotten figure. He lived with his wife in the Taft Hotel, off Times Square, until he died on April 30, 1941, shortly after his seventy-first birthday.[74]

Conclusion

The practices that Porter espoused during his filmmaking career, while ill suited to the structure of Hollywood studios and the representational system that it supported, did not disappear. Even within this Hollywood system, informal collaborations were, and still are, common either at specific stages of production or by personnel performing complementary tasks (producer and director, for example). However, collaboration from the beginning to the end of a project and overlapping responsibilities have been more unusual. Buster

Keaton was one of the rare figures who seemed at ease with this approach—both in his work with Roscoe "Fatty" Arbuckle and later in his features, when he often shared directing credit and maintained a crew of creative collaborators from project to project. William Powell and Emeric Pressburger forged a more formal collaborative team, which flourished in England between 1942 and 1951.

Not surprisingly, the collaborative approach to filmmaking has flourished best outside of a Hollywood-type situation. We often forget that Sergei Eisenstein had a co-director, Grigori Alexandrov, on *October* and *Old and New*. Avant-garde films of the 1920s characteristically relied on a collaborative working method. *Ballet mécanique* was made by Fernand Léger *and* Dudley Murphy. *Un Chien andalou* by Luis Buñuel *and* Salvador Dali, *Entr'acte* by René Clair *and* Francis Picabia. To the extent that these films stand either in opposition to—or as alternatives to—large-scale capitalism, with its character-istic system of organization, we must consider how these films were made as much as the formal alternatives that they espoused.

In recent years, American "Independents" seem torn between two opposing impulses: on one hand collaboration, on the other a conception of the film "artist" that is grounded in nineteenth-century romanticism, one that requires all elements of a film to be subservient to a single vision. Thus many filmmakers have found collaboration a practical and comfortable way to make films. Rich-ard Leacock and D. A. Pennebaker, the Maysles brothers (often with Charlotte Zwerin), Julia Reichert and James Klein: these are some of the many partner-ships of greater or lesser duration. Likewise, it is characteristic of these working relationships that the participants perform a multiplicity of tasks—producing, camerawork, editing—and often distribution as well.

The tradition of independent filmmaking has also been used by individual filmmakers seeking greater freedom from commercial formulas. Stan Brakhage, John Sayles, and Emile de Antonio are some of the many independent film-makers who seek near total control over their filmmaking.[75] Without disputing the often progressive accomplishments of these three filmmakers, it would seem that alternative methods of working have had much to offer. Although collective approaches to filmmaking, such as those practiced by Newsreel in the 1960s and 1970s, offer a more radical approach to the organization of work than the pairings mentioned above, their theoretical attractiveness seems fraught with particular difficulties. Compromise and political infighting, rather than synthe-sis, often seem to be the result. Collaboration at its best can be dialectical—the synthesis of two points of view, two sets of skills, and two personalities that become more than either individual. This was, I believe, how Porter liked to work. It was a way that acknowledged his own strengths and weaknesses.

Independent, avant-garde, or alternative filmmakers have also continued to use some of the representational procedures of the early silent period, albeit within a modernist framework.[76] This was particularly true in the 1920s, for instance with the use of overlapping action in *October*. Chase and magic scenes in many French and American early films were reworked in *Entr'acte*, which also celebrated their peculiar methods of manipulating real time. The repeated shot of a woman mounting a staircase in *Ballet mécanique* likewise recalls those first vitascope projections with their continuous band of film. Jump cuts in *Breathless* and other films by Jean-Luc Godard evoke those in turn-of-the-century creations.

Although contemporary filmmakers such as Ken Jacobs pay explicit homage to early cinema in their work, evoking its affinities with the contemporary avant-garde, Porter's films and filmmaking practices can act as a broader touchstone. Independent cinema is committed to developing alternative, even oppositional, forms of expression and different ways of making cinema (filmmaking, exhibition, and reception), not simply to imitating the dominant, Hollywood-oriented cinema.[77] Given such goals, Porter's resistance to the proto-Hollywood storytelling methods of Griffith and others makes him a significant figure in what has come to be called "our usable past."

Appendixes

APPENDIX A

Edison Manufacturing Company Statements of Profit and Loss: 1893–1911

(Figures rounded off to the nearest dollar)

Year	Film Sales[4]	Film Sales & Inventory	Film Costs	Film Profits	Kineto. Sales
1893–1895[1]	25,882	30,132	17,809	12,324	149,549*[5]
1895–1896[2]	18,616	23,820	19,519	4,302	30,110*[6]
1896–1897	84,771	87,564	63,000	24,564	21,159
					3,317*
1897–1898	75,250	76,864	52,425	24,439	27,186
					1,923*[7]
1898–1899	41,207	42,904	26,800	16,104	15,963[8]
1899–1900	38,991	40,529	27,628	12,901	22,426[9]
1900–1901[3]	49,756	52,575	32,297	20,278	23,033
1901–1902	82,108	97,483	60,049	37,434	34,685
1902–1903	75,695	103,913	75,385	28,528	33,967
1903–1904	91,122	119,087	94,274	24,813	36,651
1904–1905	106,984	135,722	95,973	39,748	51,597
1905–1906	116,829	153,884	93,173	60,660	78,829
1906–1907	191,908	227,999	131,472	96,527	182,135
1907–1908	205,243	244,484	127,571	116,912	418,893
1908–1909	554,359	569,394	339,012	230,383	341,848
1909–1910	675,306	720,738	485,940	234,798	265,761
1910–1911	762,240	815,626	613,377	202,250	275,499

*Figures for peep-hole kinetoscope; all other figures in this column for projecting machines.
[1]1 November 1893 to 1 March 1895.
[2]Business years run from 1 March to end of February for this and subsequent entries.
[3]Combines figures for private and corporate entity.
[4]Sales and Inventory also includes general expenses and depreciation.
[5]Loss on kinetoscope sundries is $441 on sales of $2,426.
[6]Loss on kinetoscope sundries is $717 on sales of $1,170.

Proj. Kineto. Sales & Inv.	Kineto. Costs	Kineto. Profits	Total Sales	Total Costs[10]	Total Profits[10]
155,585*	82,130*	73,455*	268,080	215,122	89,090
30,401*	29,845*	556[6]*	138,343	145,317	24,650
22,570	21,037	1,534	201,266	193,159	36,566
3,623*	4,070*	(447)*			
27,802	22,976	4,826	211,908	205,093	41,018
2,318*	2,720*	(401)*			
17,059	10,861	6,198	217,277	169,406	81,018
24,909	14,854	10,056	277,828	196,515	118,134
25,475	15,018	10,457	283,995	230,104	120,151
36,341	20,870	15,471	438,413	285,762	192,473
37,290	22,774	14,545	458,742	319,280	210,062
40,321	24,684	15,637	421,193	326,634	171,378
55,168	32,848	22,321	353,870	296,919	125,001[11]
82,706	47,897	34,809	430,745	314,538	195,725
195,628	108,400	87,228	641,234	446,213	296,372
445,399	224,776	220,622	887,421	578,966	413,172
371,193	190,616	180,577	1,228,121	785,106	550,289
290,184	151,676	138,507	1,445,888	1,013,826	571,446
294,242	162,089	132,153	1,621,279	1,173,121	589,789

[7]Does not include kinetophone attachments with sales of $193 and profits of $11.

[8]Does not include kinetophone attachments with sales of $50 and losses of $74.

[9]Does not include kinetophone attachments with sales of $576 and profits of $26.

[10]Costs + Profits = Sales & Inventory. Total costs and profits include products such as batteries and fans.

[11]Other balance sheets for 1904–5 give profits of $136,199. Difference in figures involves batteries.

Kleine Optical Company Accounts
(Figures rounded off to the nearest dollar)

Films and Merchandise Purchased from Edison Mfg. Co. from 1899 to 1904

	1899	1900	1901	1902	1903	1904
January		428	2703	1735	3889	2732
February			743	2959	2193	1242
March		600	1303	1757	1255	2089
April		385	1973	1238	3188	1983
May		366	1610	911	2039	3318
June	40	342	1018	1937	3291	3001
July	29	262	1021	1745	3410	2295
August	247	980	1763	1375	2677	391
September	113	836	4338	3397	4012	
October	290	1633	7350	4855	3608	1650
November		347	4343	3509	4432	1252
December	170	1307	4106	697	5977	671
Year total	890	7,451	32,272	26,114	38,974	20,673

Purchases from:			
Vitagraph Co.	Pathé	Méliès	Biograph
1904			
June		1269		
July				
August				
September				
October		2903	62	3196
November		708	418	2545
December		1338	139	2714
Year total		6218	619	8456
1905				
January		997	254	1685
February		897	71	983
March		1556	267	2425
April		1544	52	1598
May		1732	642	2226
June		2350	547	934
July		5292	573	1294
August		2345	1007	1916
September	290	3635	1200	3802
October	1771	1245	258	2062

	Purchases from:			
	Vitagraph Co.	Pathé	Méliès	Biograph
1905 (*continued*)				
November	1688	1168	405	1554
December	1512	2022	2080	1238
Year total	5,260	23,786	7,101	21,716
1906				
January	1365	3087	237	1222
February	2197	1881	242	1950
March	2754	2658	509	1409
April	2497	5392	153	1677
May	6862	4303	745	2176
June	4071	2591	658	2889
July	3619	2677	298	1605
August	2213	1566	217	1531
September	3587	2426	244	1611
October	3139	4799	1191	1652
November	2216	7890	1156	845
December	1138	7754	1455	861
Year total	35,657	47,024	7,106	19,427
1907				
January	2858	6807	141	1164
February	1756	5414	1627	831
March	1934	9455	914	1573
April	3038	10422	1364	1215
May	3499	11007	850	2184
June	3665	10358	3218	1102
July	3492	8525	1458	436
August	2605	8188	456	394
September	1918	10082	653	639
October	4028	7613	1629	755
November	2343	757	836	629
December	1770	468	313	837
Year total	32,906	89,096	13,462	11,758

SOURCE: George Kleine Collection, DLC. These figures are not always mutually consistent, and discrepancies (some explainable, some not) have not been adjusted for in this table. In addition, the following sums were paid to various film manufacturers during 1907:

Vitagraph Company of America	$30,398
Pathé Frères	82,040
Kalem Co. (8 months)	52,548
S. Lubin	1,287
Selig Polyscope Co.	7,369
Essanay Co. (5 months)	3,451
Geo. Méliès	14,987
Edison Manufacturing Co.	23,023
Italian Cinès (2 months)	1,702

From February 1, 1907, to February 1, 1908, Kleine paid $530,280 for imported films for its exclusive agencies.

Credits and Key to Quotations in the Documentary Film *Before the Nickelodeon: The Early Cinema of Edwin S. Porter*

Readers may be interested in a film produced by the author, titled as above. It is available in film and video formats through First Run Features, 153 Waverly Place, New York, NY 10014 (tel: 212-243-0600). The film is also distributed by the Museum of Modern Art, New York. The film was funded in part by the National Endowment for the Arts and the New York State Council on the Arts. A New York–Hollywood Feature Film Production.

The film and the book form a matching pair, so to speak; quotes used in the film also appear in this book, where their source is fully identified. They, along with additional information, are provided for convenient reference below.

Narrator:	Blanche Sweet
Producer/Director/Editor:	Charles Musser (with Edwin Porter)
Executive Producer	Stephen Brier
Screenplay:	Warren D. Leight and Charles Musser
Associate Producer and Photocolorist:	Elizabeth Lennard
Assistant Director:	Rick King
Cinematography:	Rob Issen (stills)
Re-photography:	Suzanne Williamson
Consultants:	Eileen Bowser, Nancy Musser, Robert Rosen, and Robert Sklar
Technical Advisor:	John E. Allen, Jr.
Sound Effects:	Bill Uttley

Quotes	Voices	Reference
Thomas A. Edison:	Jay Leyda	p. 29
Porter's Naval Record:	Robert Sklar	p. 27
The Corbett-Courtney Fight:	Rob Issen	p. 48
Vitascope's Opening Night:	Robert Rosen	pp. 60–61
May Irwin Kiss review:	Mitchell Kriegman	pp. 80, 83
Eden Musee/War Films:	Peter Davis	pp. 132, 135–36
Film as a Visual Newspaper:	D. A. Pennebaker	p. 163
The Capture of the Biddle Brothers:	Milos Forman	pp. 193–94
Terrible Teddy, the Grizzly King:	Warren D. Leight	pp. 169–170
Sampson-Schley Controversy:	Rick King	p. 182
Fighting the Flames:	Tony Potter	p. 521 n. 13
Méliès catalog:	Louis Malle	p. 240
Jack and the Beanstalk Promo:	Robert Altman	p. 205

Quotes	Voices	Reference
Jack and the Beanstalk:	Jim Walton	pp. 202–5
Edwin S. Porter:	Charles Musser	p. 209
Edison Studio:	Michael Peyser	p. 386
Rescued from an Eagle's Nest review:	Grahame Weinbren	p. 410
Edwin S. Porter:	Charles Musser	pp. 450
Adolph Zukor:	Stephen Brier	p. 471

In some cases quotes were combined and/or slightly altered to fit the film and the speaker.

The following complete films appear in the documentary:

Mr. Edison at Work in His Chemical Laboratory (1897)
The Corbett-Courtney Fight (one round) (1894)
May Irwin Kiss (1896)
Wreck of the Battleship "Maine" (1898)
Kansas Saloon Smashers (1901)
The Capture of the Biddle Brothers (1902)
The Finish of Bridget McKeen (1901)
Terrible Teddy, the Grizzly King (1901)
Sampson-Schley Controversy (1901)
The Execution of Czolgosz (1901)
Elephants Shooting the Chutes, Luna Park, Coney Island, No. 2 (1904)
Appointment by Telephone (1902)
Jack and the Beanstalk (1902)
How They Do Things on the Bowery (1902)
Life of An American Fireman (1902–3)

List of Abbreviations
and Primary Sources

Abbreviations for frequently cited periodicals:

Clipper	*New York Clipper*
Film Index	*Views and Film Index*
Mail and Express	*New York Mail and Express*
MPW	*Moving Picture World*
NYDM	*New York Dramatic Mirror*
NYT	*New York Times*

Archival collections, designated by their American
Library symbols

CLAc: Academy of Motion Picture Arts and Sciences, Margaret Herrick
      Library
  1. J. Searle Dawley Collection
  2. William Selig Collection
  3. Charles Clark Collection

CBevA: American Film Institute, Los Angeles, Center for Advanced Film
      Studies
  1. Library

CLCM: Los Angeles County Museum of Natural History
  1. Thomas Armat Collection
  2. Miscellaneous catalogs

CLU: University of California at Los Angeles
  1. Albert Smith Collection
  2. UCLA Film Archive

CU-BANC: University of California at Berkeley, Bancroft Library
  1. Vaudeville Programmes

DLC: Library of Congress, Washington, D.C.
  1. Motion Picture, Television and Recorded Sound Division
     a. Paper Print Collection
     b. AFI Collection
     c. George Kleine Collection
     d. Searchlight Theatre Collection
  2. Manuscript Division
     a. George Kleine Collection
  3. Newspapers and Periodical Division

DNA: National Archives
  1. Motion Picture Section

ICFAR: Federal Archive and Record Center, Chicago, Illinois
  1. Court Cases for the Circuit Court, Northern District of Illinois

ICC: Cook County Clerk's Office, Chicago
  1. Incorporation Records

ICHi: Chicago Historical Society

IaU: University of Iowa
  1. E. F. Albee Collection, Special Collections

MdSuFR: Washington National Record Center, Suitland, Maryland
  1. Court Cases for the Supreme Court, District of Columbia

MH-BA: Harvard Business School, Baker Library, Boston
  1. Dun and Company Collection
  2. Raff & Gammon Collection

NN: New York Public Library
  1. Newspaper and Periodical Collection
  2. Billy Rose Theater Collection

NNHi: New York Historical Society
  1. Bella Landour Collection

NNMoMA: Museum of Modern Art, New York City
  1. Film Study Center
     a. Merritt Crawford Collection
     b. Edison Collection
     c. Film Collections
  2. Library

NNMus: Museum of the City of New York
  1. Theater Collection
  2. Photograph Collection

NNNCC-Ar: New York County Clerk's Office
1. Court Cases for the Supreme Court of New York State
2. Partnership and Incorporation Records

NR-GE: George Eastman House
1. Glenn Matthews/Thomas Armat Collection
2. Film Collections

NjBaFAR: Federal Archive and Record Center, Bayonne, New Jersey
1. Court Cases for the Circuit Court, Southern District of New York
2. Court Cases for the Circuit Court, Eastern District of New York
3. Court Cases for the Circuit Court, District of New Jersey
4. Court Cases for the District Court, Southern District of New York
5. Court Cases for the District Court, Eastern District of New York

NjWOE: Edison National Historic Site, West Orange, New Jersey
1. Legal Files
2. Copyright Files
3. Document Files
4. Edison Manufacturing Company, Payroll Books (1895–1910)
5. Edison Manufacturing Company, Financial Records
6. Letter Books, Thomas A. Edison
7. Edison Laboratory, Financial Records

PP: Free Library of Philadelphia
1. Theater Collection

PPFAR: Federal Archive and Record Center, Philadelphia
1. Court Cases for the Circuit Court, Eastern District of Pennsylvania
2. Court Cases for the District Court, Eastern District of Pennsylvania

PPS: Franklin Institute of Arts and Sciences
1. C. Francis Jenkins Collection

PW-bH: Wyoming Historical and Geological Society, Wilkes-Barre, Pennsylvania
1. Robert Gillaum Collection

Notes

Acknowledgments

1. Portions of chapter 5 appeared in "The Eden Musee in 1898: The Exhibitor as Creator," *Film and History* 11 (December 1981): 73–83 +; an early draft of chapter 6 appeared as "The Early Cinema of Edwin S. Porter," *Cinema Journal* 19 (Fall 1979): 1–38; portions of chapters 8 and 9 appeared in "The Travel Genre in 1903–04: Moving Toward Fictional Narrative," *Iris* 2 (Spring 1984): 61–70; selections from chapters 10 and 11 were reworked for "The Nickelodeon Era Begins: Establishing a Framework for Hollywood's Mode of Representation," *Framework* 22/23 (Autumn 1983): 4–11.

1. Introduction

1. John Fell, "Introduction," in John Fell, ed., *Film Before Griffith* (Berkeley: University of California Press, 1983), pp. 1–5.

2. Terry Ramsaye, *A Million and One Nights: A History of the Motion Pictures Through 1925* (New York: Simon & Schuster, 1926); Gordon Hendricks, *The Edison Motion Picture Myth* (Berkeley: University of California Press, 1961); Gordon Hendricks, *The Kinetoscope: America's First Commercially Successful Motion Picture Exhibitor* (New York: The Beginnings of the American Film, 1966).

3. This attitude is particularly evident in Lewis Jacobs, *The Rise of the American Film* (New York: Harcourt, Brace, 1939), p. 35.

4. Ramsaye, *Million and One Nights*, p. 414; Jacobs, *Rise of the American Film*, pp. 35–37. Gerald Mast, *A Short History of the Movies*, 4th ed. (New York: Macmillan, 1986), still argues that the modernized version of *Life of an American Fireman* is the correct one, suggesting that the paper print copy at the Library of Congress may simply be an unedited version. Mast ignores two similar copies that have been found by the AFI, which make his position untenable. David Cook, *A History of Narrative Film* (New York:

W. W. Norton, 1981) is a noteworthy exception to this stereotyping: faced with new information, Cook revised his section on early cinema in galleys. Kenneth Macgowan, *Behind the Screen* (New York: Delacorte Press, 1965), pp. 111–14, is one of the few to have avoided reductive statements on Porter's role.

5. Georges Sadoul, *Histoire générale du cinéma*, vol. 2: *Les Pionniers du cinéma, 1897–1909*, 3d ed. (Paris: Editions Denoël, 1948), pp. 401, 407–8.

6. Jacques Deslandes and Jacques Richard, *Histoire comparée du cinéma*, vol. 2: *Du cinématograph au cinéma* (Paris: Casterman, 1968), p. 386.

7. Robert Sklar, *Movie-Made America: A Cultural History of American Movies* (New York: Vintage Books, 1975), p. 320.

8. The group who met at the 1978 FIAF Conference included Noël Burch, Tom Gunning, Paul Spehr, Eileen Bowser, Barry Salt, Russell Merritt, Jon Gartenberg, André Gaudreault, David Levy, John Barnes, and myself. These papers were collected in Roger Hollman, compiler, *Cinéma, 1900–1906* (2 vols.; Brussels: Fédération Internationale des Archives du Film, 1982). A preparatory meeting of American scholars at the Museum of Modern Art involved extensive screening of American films by interested scholars, including John Fell and John Hagan, not all of whom were able to travel to England. Then working on a film project in Los Angeles, I was unable to attend this earlier gathering.

9. Besides those mentioned above, scholars writing articles on early cinema during the past ten years notably include Miriam Hansen, Judith Mayne, Lucy Fischer, Martin Sopocy, Paul Hammond, Roberta Pearson, Paolo Cherchi-Usai, Stephen Bottomore, Emmanuelle Toulet, Ben Brewster, Kristin Thompson, Donald Crafton, Aldo Bernardini, Richard Abel, Patrick G. Loughney, and Robert C. Allen. A selection of these articles appears in Fell, ed., *Film Before Griffith*; André Gaudreault, ed., *Ce que je vois de mon ciné: La representation du regard dans le cinéma des premiers temps* (Saint-Étienne: Méridiens Klincksieck, 1988); Thomas Elsasser and Adam Barker, eds., *Early Cinema: Space, Frame, Narrative* (London: British Film Institute, 1990).

10. Michael Chanan, *The Dream That Kicks: The Prehistory and Early Years of Cinema in Britain* (London: Routledge & Kegan Paul, 1980). John Barnes, *The Beginnings of the Cinema in England* (Newton Abbot, England: David & Charles, 1976), focuses on the 1894–96 period. It has been followed, more recently, by Barnes's *The Rise of the Cinema in Great Britain* (London: Bishopsgate Press, 1983).

11. John Frazer, *Artificially Arranged Scenes: The Films of Georges Méliès* (Boston: G. K. Hall, 1979), and Paul Hammond, *Marvellous Méliès* (New York: St. Martin's Press, 1975), are both excellent studies.

12. See, however, David Levy, "Edwin S. Porter and the Origins of the American Narrative Film, 1894–1907" (Ph. D. diss., McGill University, 1983). Levy's hostile attitude to both Porter and the Edison Company limits his study's usefulness. Levy has published two articles drawn from his dissertation which are referred to elsewhere in this book. Robert Allen and Lary May devote substantial portions of their books to the pre-1910 cinema. The ambitious scope of their studies, however, prevents both authors from systematically confronting this period. See Robert C. Allen, *Vaudeville and Film, 1895–1915: A Study in Media Interaction* (Ph. D. diss., University of Iowa, 1977; New York: Arno Press, 1980); Lary May, *Screening the Past: The Birth of Mass Culture and the Motion Picture Industry, 1896–1920* (New York: Oxford University Press, 1980).

13. Historians dealing with the pre-Griffith cinema at first felt it was unnecessary—or impossible—to see the relevant films. They relied on reminiscences and to a lesser extent

on primary source documents. Terry Ramsaye, for example, not only interviewed many figures in the early industry but utilized their scrapbooks, various legal documents, and business records. This approach was continued in a more rigorous manner by Gordon Hendricks, who sifted through large amounts of materials at the Edison National Historic Site and perused pertinent newspapers and journals. A recent textbook by Robert C. Allen and Douglas Gomery, *Film History: Theory and Practice* (New York: Alfred Knopf, 1985), also emphasizes this approach. With the growing availability of films, many scholars have adopted the converse attitude that viewing the films is sufficient to understand the cinema of this period. This is evident, for instance, in Richard Arlo Sanderson, "A Historical Study of the Development of American Motion Picture Content and Techniques Prior to 1904" (Ph. D. diss., University of Southern California, 1961), and Kemp R. Niver, *The First Twenty Years: A Segment of Film History* (Los Angeles: Locare Research Group, 1968). Mast takes this approach throughout his *Short History of the Movies*. The assumption is that the films speak for themselves. They don't. While viewing films is an essential first step, it is necessary to situate them within the moving picture world in which they were made, exhibited, and seen. A careful reading of primary source material is needed to achieve this understanding. While reminiscences and early secondary sources like Ramsaye's *Million and One Nights* often provide important clues, scholars must synthesize a new history from written primary source materials and viewings of the films. Such a synthesis characterizes a number of histories, yet has remained an elusive goal for those examining the first fifteen years of American cinema. Such exemplary histories include Jay Leyda, *Kino: A History of Russian and Soviet Film* (London: George Allen & Unwin, 1960), and David Bordwell, Janet Staiger, and Kristin Thompson, *The Classical Hollywood Cinema: Film Style and Mode of Production to 1960* (New York: Columbia University Press, 1985).

14. Charles Musser et al., *Motion Picture Catalogs by American Producers and Distributors, 1894–1908: A Microfilm Edition* (Frederick, Md.: University Publications of America, 1984).

15. Ramsaye, *Million and One Nights*, p. 439.

16. Kemp R. Niver, *Early Motion Pictures: The Paper Print Collection in the Library of Congress* (Washington, D.C.: Library of Congress, 1985).

17. Société des Etablissements Gaumont to Frank Dyer, 11 October 1909, NjWOE.

18. For example, there were few "outs" (i.e., discarded footage) in the 1890s and early 1900s, whoever was doing the editing.

19. Raymond Williams, "Base and Superstructure in Marxist Cultural Theory," in *Problems in Materialism and Culture* (London: Verso Press, 1980).

20. Distribution is discussed as a process functioning at the interface of film production and exhibition.

21. Harry Braverman, *Labor and Monopoly Capital: The Degradation of Work in Twentieth Century America* (New York: Monthly Review Press, 1974), p. 65.

22. Ibid., p. 72.

23. Janet Staiger, "Dividing Labor for Production Control: Thomas Ince and the Rise of the Studio System," in Gorham Kindem, ed., *The American Movie Industry: The Business of Motion Pictures* (Carbondale: Southern Illinois University Press, 1982).

24. Noël Burch, "Porter, or Ambivalence," *Screen* 19, no. 4 (Winter 1978–79), pp. 91–105.

25. David Montgomery, *Workers' Control in America: Studies in the History of*

Work, Technology, and Labor Struggles (Cambridge: Cambridge University Press, 1979).

26. Madeleine Matz to Charles Musser, June 1984, Washington D.C. Matz is technical expert at the Division of Motion Pictures, Broadcasting and Recorded Sound at the Library of Congress.

27. Like many other young film students I found Noël Burch's *Theory of Film Practice* (New York: Praeger, 1973) to be a liberating way to look at cinematic representation. Burch's emphasis on temporal and spatial relationships between shots provides a framework for grappling with the otherness of early cinema. Annette Michelson's often phenomenological approach to film analysis, the work in representational theory by Russian Formalists, and Soviet film theorists have all been influential in this respect. It is hardly surprising, therefore, that the rigorous approach of David Bordwell and Kristin Thompson to questions of filmic representation has also been exceedingly valuable.

28. Special knowledge—for instance, familarity with the actor or the story being adapted—could enhance viewers' pleasure in this post-nickelodeon phase, but it was not usually essential. Certain exceptions, particularly in the realm of comedy and burlesque, continued.

29. Tom Gunning, "The Cinema of Attraction[s]," *Wide Angle* 8, no. 3/4 (1986): 63–70.

30. Macgowan's *Behind the Screen* offers an intelligent version of this approach.

31. John Fell, *Film and the Narrative Tradition* (1974; Berkeley: University of California Press, 1986).

32. Henry V. Hopwood, *Living Pictures: Their History, Photoduplication and Practical Working* (London: Optician and Photographic Trades Review, 1899), p. 188.

33. Athanasius Kircher, *Ars magna lucis et umbrae* (Rome, 1646) describes and illustrates the process of projecting images. Kircher's text indicates that explaining the technical basis of projection to spectators was a necessary precondition for screen entertainment. See Charles Musser, "Towards a History of Screen Practice," *Quarterly Review of Film Studies* 9, no. 1 (Winter 1984): 59–73.

34. The terms *homosocial* and *heterosocial* are used by Kathy Peiss, *Cheap Amusements: Working Women and Leisure in Turn of the Century New York* (Philadelphia: Temple University Press, 1986), who explores the ways nineteenth-century leisure was largely segregated by sex. As dance halls and motion picture theaters replaced the saloon in the early twentieth century, single-sex, or "homosocial," amusement gave way to "heterosocial" entertainments where the sexes intermingled more freely.

35. Ibid; Roy Rosenzweig, *Eight Hours for What We Will: Work & Leisure in an Industrial City, 1870–1920* (Cambridge: Cambridge University Press, 1983).

36. This study assumes that mass entertainment uses a form of mass communication and, for heuristic purposes, relies on the definition found in Melvin L. Defleur and Everette Dennis, *Understanding Mass Communication* (Boston: Houghton Mifflin, 1981), p. 11.

37. See Hannah Segal, "A Psychoanalytic Approach to Aesthetics," in *Collected Papers on Psychoanalysis* (New York: Bruner-Mazel, 1951).

38. Burch, "Porter, or Ambivalence," p. 93.

39. Robert C. Allen, "Motion Picture Exhibition in Manhattan, 1906–1912: Beyond the Nickelodeon," in Fell, ed., *Film Before Griffith*, pp. 162–75.

40. Braverman, *Labor and Monopoly Captial*, pp. 403–9.

41. Douglas Gomery is a leading proponent of this approach, which he has discussed in a series of articles on the coming of recorded sound. See id., "The Coming of the Talkies: Invention, Innovation, and Diffusion," in Tino Balio, ed., *The American Film Industry* (Madison: University of Wisconsin Press, 1975), pp. 193–94.

42. For a further discussion of this issue see Charles Musser, "American Vitagraph: 1897–1901," *Cinema Journal* 22, no. 3 (Spring 1983): 4–46, as well as Gomery's response and my reply in *Cinema Journal* 22, no. 4 (Summer 1984): 58–64.

43. Robert Conot, *A Streak of Luck: The Life and Legend of Thomas Alva Edison* (New York: Seaview Books, 1979), provides insight into Edison's career as a businessman, although the staff of the Thomas Edison Papers have found many inaccuracies in its details.

44. "Dupes" are films printed from duplicate negatives struck from a positive projection print. Since internegative or interpositive stock had not been developed, there was a significant falloff in quality. Dupes were usually made from competitors' films that were unprotected by copyright. This saved the cost of making an original negative and enabled the duper to enjoy the rewards from film sales without paying the original producer. George Kleine defined "dupes" at some length: see chapter 8.

2. Porter's Early Years: 1870–1896

1. Porter's childhood and youth have been little examined. Biographical capsules have him growing up in Pittsburgh, consistently misstate the number of siblings, never specify his father's occupation, and generally provide an inaccurate and incomplete picture of his formative experiences.

2. William B. Spies, *The Pennsylvania Railroad: Its Origins, Construction, Condition, and Connections* (Philadelphia: The Passenger Department, 1875), p. 220.

3. U. S. Department of Commerce, Bureau of the Census, *Ninth Census of the United States, 1870; Tenth Census of the United States, 1880; Twelfth Census of the United States, 1900*. The census report of 1900 lists Mary Clark Porter as having eight children, seven living. A sibling, who probably was born shortly after Edward, must have died in infancy. *Connellsville* [Pa.] *Courier*, 23 August 1905.

4. Id., *Seventh Census of the United States, 1850; Eighth Census of the United States, 1860*.

5. R. G. Dun and Company, credit ledgers, Pennsylvania, vol. 66: pp. 2 and 356, Baker Library, Harvard Business School (MB-H); J. C. McClenathan et al., *Centennial History of the Borough of Connellsville, Pennsylvania* (Connellsville: Connellsville Area Historical Society, 1906; reprint, Connellsville Area Historical Society, 1974), p. 322.

6. *Connellsville Courier*, 26 July 1889.

7. *Connellsville Courier*, 15 April 1892.

8. McClenathan et al., *Centennial History*, pp. 488–89. In 1871 Samuel Porter also helped to found the Yough National Bank of Connellsville, which soon was the oldest bank in town.

9. *Tenth Census of the United States, 1880*.

10. John W. Jordan and James Hadden, eds., *Genealogical and Personal History of Fayette County* (New York: Lewis Historical Publishing Co., 1912), 2: 385.

11. *Keystone Courier*, 22 June 1883.

12. *Keystone Courier*, 12 October and 21 December 1883, 22 February 1884, and 15 August 1885.

13. Porter Reilly, Edwin Porter's godson, to Charles Musser, New York City, January 1979.

14. Ibid.; Lewis Jacobs, who interviewed Porter for his *Rise of the American Film*, to Charles Musser, 1983.

15. *Connellsville Courier*, 17 April 1896.

16. *Connellsville Courier*, 27 February and 15 May 1891 and 24 November and 23 December 1892.

17. *Keystone Courier*, 11 June 1880 and *Connellsville Courier*, 18 August 1893.

18. *Keystone Courier*, 9 July 1880.

19. *Keystone Courier*, 24 February 1882.

20. *Connellsville Courier*, 30 May 1889.

21. *Keystone Courier*, 2 January 1885.

22. *Connellsville Courier*, 30 August 1889.

23. The Great Railroad Strike of 1877; *Keystone Courier*, 7 November 1879 — lasting less than one day and won by the cokers; January 1880 — won by the cokers; February 1883 — won by the operators; January–February 1886 — won by the cokers reestablishing their union; May–June 1887 — won by the cokers; August 1889 — won by the cokers; February to May 1891 — won by the operators (i.e., Henry Frick). See also Jon Amsden and Stephen Brier, "Coal Miners on Strike: The Transformation of Strike Demands and the Formation of a National Union," in Robert Rotberg and Theodore Rabb, eds., *Industrialization and Urbanization* (Princeton: Princeton University Press, 1981), pp. 137–70.

24. *Keystone Courier*, 29 January 1886.

25. Herbert Gutman writes about similar situations in "Two Lockouts in Pennsylvania, 1873–4," in *Work, Culture and Society* (New York: Vintage Books, 1977), pp. 321–43.

26. *Keystone Courier*, 16 February 1883.

27. *Keystone Courier*, 23 February 1883.

28. *Keystone Courier*, 29 January 1886.

29. *Connellsville Courier*, 18 September 1891.

30. *Connellsville Courier*, 22 May 1891.

31. *Connellsville Courier*, 26 June 1891.

32. Jacobs, *Rise of the American Film*, p. 41.

33. *Keystone Courier*, 16 April 1880.

34. *Keystone Courier*, 17 December 1880.

35. *Keystone Courier*, 16 and 23 December 1881.

36. Ibid.

37. "Edwin S. Porter," *Moving Picture World* (henceforth *MPW*), 7 December 1912, p. 961.

38. *Keystone Courier*, 17 August 1883. The census indicates the two were not closely related. The families did, however, live nearby: Thomas Porter's house was no. 205 and Byron Porter's no. 208 in the local 1880 census. Fragmentary evidence suggests that the two families helped each other out. Byron Porter made his living representing the Terra

Cotta Casket Company in 1886, a job he may have gained through Porter & Bro. Byron's son George went on an extensive fishing trip with Ed Porter.

39. *Keystone Courier*, 8 October 1886.

40. *Keystone Courier*, 26 July 1886.

41. Photographs of a fishing trip attended by Ed Porter, but not by Byron or his son, resulted in a small show at the photographer's art gallery (*Connellsville Courier*, 22 August 1890).

42. *MPW*, 22 April 1911, p. 878.

43. *Keystone Courier*, 19 January and 15 December 1882; 17 and 31 August 1883; 12 September and 26 December 1884; 4 and 31 December 1885; 19 March, 9 April, 26 May, 19 November, and 17 December 1886; 14 January, 8 April, 17 May, 28 October, and 4 November 1887; 15 February 1888; *Connellsville Courier*, 26 October, 1 November, and 28 December 1888; 8 March 1889; 29 January 1892.

44. *MPW*, 7 December 1912, p. 961.

45. *New York Clipper* (henceforth *Clipper*), 4 April 1914, p. 3.

46. "Edward Franklin Albee," *National Cyclopedia of American Biography* (New York: James T. White & Co., 1932), 22: 53; clipping of Albany (New York) newspaper, 19 May 1940, theater files, Albany Public Library.

47. *Courier*, 28 September 1888.

48. *Keystone Courier*, 5 September 1884; 22 May, 4 and 31 December 1885.

49. Alan Trachtenberg, *The Incorporation of America: Culture and Society in the Gilded Age* (New York: Hill & Wang, 1982), p. 143.

50. *Keystone Courier*, 6 March 1885 and 16 March 1888; *Connellsville Courier*, 7 October 1892.

51. *Keystone Courier*, 24 December 1886. See Charles Musser with Carol Nelson, *High-Class Moving Pictures* (Princeton: Princeton University Press, 1991) for a more elaborate treatment of church-sponsored cultural events.

52. *Keystone Courier*, 4 January 1884.

53. *Keystone Courier*, 18 December 1885 and 9 July 1886.

54. *Keystone Courier*, 25 November and 17 December 1886.

55. *Keystone Courier*, 12 December 1884.

56. Francis G. Couvares, *The Remaking of Pittsburgh: Class and Culture in an Industrializing City, 1877–1919* (Albany: State University of New York Press, 1984).

57. Tony Keefer to Charles Musser, June 1981.

58. Trachtenberg, *Incorporation of America*, pp. 64–67.

59. *MPW*, 7 December 1912, p. 961.

60. Ibid.; *Keystone Courier*, 23 September 1887.

61. *Connellsville Courier*, 27 September 1889, 21 February and 7 March 1890.

62. U. S. Patent Office, patent no. 451,798, Charles H. Balsley, Jr. and Edwin M. Porter, Current-Regulator for Electric Lamps, granted 5 May 1891.

63. *Connellsville Courier*, 15 May 1891.

64. *Connellsville Courier*, 12 February 1892.

65. *Connellsville Courier*, 4 March 1892.

66. U. S. Industrial Commission, *Reports*, vol. 15, *Report on Immigration* (19 vols.; Washington, D.C.: 1901–2), pp. 322–25 cited in Thomas Kessner, *The Golden Door:*

Italian and Jewish Immigrant Mobility in New York City, 1880–1915 (New York: Oxford University Press, 1977), p. 62.

67. Connellsville, Pa. *Deed Book*, p. 154, courtesy of Tony Keefer.

68. "Edwin Stanton Porter," in *National Cyclopedia of American Biography* (New York: James T. White & Co., 1943), 30: 407–8. See also Robert Sklar, "Edwin Stanton Porter," in *Dictionary of American Biography* (New York: Charles Scribner's Sons, 1973), pp. 606–7.

69. U.S. Navy Department, enlistment record of Edwin Stanton Porter, National Archives, Washington, D.C.

70. *Connellsville Courier*, 3 July 1896, p. 4.

71. *Cyclopedia of American Biography*, 30: 407.

3. Edison and the Kinetoscope: 1888–1895

1. Although this chapter disagrees with some of Gordon Hendricks's conclusions, it is deeply indebted to his detailed research. The process and framework for the invention of Edison's motion picture system is not dealt with extensively in this volume, but is explored in greater depth in *The Emergence of Cinema*, chapter 2.

2. "Animal Locomotion," *Orange* [N.J.] *Chronicle*, 3 March 1888, p. 5; "Edison's Talking Baby," *New York World*, 3 June 1888, p. 16.

3. Thomas A. Edison, caveat 110, 8 October 1888, filed 17 October 1888, NjWOE. Hendricks, *Edison Motion Picture Myth*, p. 15, provides a useful definition of *caveat* from *Webster's Dictionary* (1888): "A description of some invention, designed to be patented, lodged in the office before the patent right is taken out, operating as a bar to applications respecting the same invention from any other quarter."

4. Edison, caveat 110.

5. "Complainant's Exhibit Work on Kinetoscope Experiment from February 1, 1889, to February 1, 1890," *Thomas A. Edison v. American Mutoscope Co. and Benjamin Keith*, no. 6928, C.C.S.D.N.Y., filed 13 May 1898, printed record, pp. 360–62, NjBaFAR.

6. Charles A. Brown, deposition, 31 January 1900, *Edison v. American Mutoscope Co.*, p. 141.

7. *Orange Chronicle*, 23 May 1891.

8. "The Kinetograph," *New York Sun*, 28 May 1891, p. 1.

9. Charles Batchelor notebook, 18 June 1891, p. 153, NjWOE.

10. "The Kinetograph," *Phonogram*, October 1892, pp. 217–18.

11. J. F. Randolph, deposition, 3 February 1900, *Edison v. American Mutoscope Co.*, p. 159.

12. "Sandow at the Edison Laboratory," *Orange Chronicle*, 10 March 1894, p. 5.

13. Rosenzweig, *Eight Hours for What We Will*, p. 37.

14. "Edison and the Kinetoscope," *Photographic Times*, p. 210.

15. Ramsaye claims, after interviewing Norman Raff, that no Edison peep-hole kinetoscope was shown at the Columbian fair (*Million and One Nights*, p. 85). Hendricks suggests that at least one machine—the model shown at the Brooklyn Institute—was part of the Edison phonograph exhibit (*Kinetoscope*, pp. 40–45). This was advance publicity,

however, and the increasing body of evidence makes Ramsaye's statement more and more compelling.

16. Gordon Hendricks, "A New Look at an 'Old Sneeze,' " *Film Culture* no. 22–23 (1961), pp. 90–95.

17. "Wizard Edison's Kinetograph," *New York World*, 18 March 1894, pp. 21–22.

18. "Sandow at the Edison Laboratory," *Orange Chronicle*, 10 March 1894, p. 5.

19. "A New Bill at Koster & Bial's," *NYT*, 6 November 1894, p. 5.

20. "The Vaudeville Fad," *New York Dramatic Mirror* (henceforth *NYDM*), 27 June 1896, p. 11.

21. Kinetoscope Company, *Bulletin No. 1* [December 1894].

22. "Indians Before the Kinetograph," *Orange Journal*, 27 September 1894, p. 5.

23. Kinetoscope Company to Kansas Phonograph Company, 29 December 1894, vol. 1, p. 172, Raff & Gammon Collection, MH-BA.

24. Kinetoscope Company, *Bulletin No. 1*.

25. Antonia and W. K. L. Dickson, "Edison's Invention of the Kineto-Phonograph," *Century Magazine* 48, no. 2 (June 1894): 212.

26. The Glenroy Brothers being domestic in both appearance and kinship.

27. *Newark Evening News*, 17 July 1894, in Hendricks, *Kinetoscope*, pp. 77–78.

28. J. F. Randolph, deposition, 3 February 1900, *Edison v. American Mutoscope Co.*, p. 161.

29. Alfred O. Tate to Thomas Edison, 13 February 1894, NjWOE; Hendricks, *Kinetoscope*, pp. 50–51 and 132–33.

30. *MPW*, 15 July 1916, p. 399.

31. W. J. Holland to N. C. Raff, 4 July 1894, Bills 1894–96, MH-BA.

32. James H. White, testimony, 9 February 1900, *Edison v. American Mutoscope Co.*, p. 165.

33. Edison Manufacturing Company, cash book no. 2, pp. 72 and 102, NjWOE.

34. Thomas A. Edison and Norman Raff and Frank Gammon, agreement, 18 August 1894, NjWOE; Raff & Gammon Collection, invoices, vol. 1, pp. 10, 14, 23, 40, 60, etc., MH-BA.

35. Edison Manufacturing Company, cash book no. 2, pp. 74 and 114.

36. Edison Manufacturing Company, cash book no. 2, 11 July 1894, received $1275.

37. Thomas Edison to Maguire & Baucus, 3 September 1894, NjWOE.

38. Some Raff & Gammon and Commercial Commerce Company customers may occasionally have paid the Edison Company directly. Moreover, Raff & Gammon reimbursed Colonel George E. Gourand for a large order of kinetoscopes for which they later assumed commercial responsibility.

39. In any case, these payments were much higher than their former salaries. Since Dickson left Edison's employ in April 1895, these figures were more than simple weekly paychecks. This extension of royalties to Dickson and Heise contradicts Hendricks's portrayal of Edison as a parsimonious egomaniac (*Kinetoscope*, p. 30). In fact, Edison routinely extended royalties to his co-inventors and collaborators.

40. Edison Manufacturing Company, cash book no. 2, November 1893–December 1895.

41. "Jack Cushing's Waterloo," *New York World*, 16 June 1894, p. 1.

42. Thomas A. Edison to Otway Latham, 18 August 1894, NjWOE. Hendricks (*Ki-

netoscope, pp. 97–99) argues that the exhibition of *The Leonard-Cushing Fight* was not financially remunerative, but a more ambitious undertaking would seem unlikely if this had been the case. Some level of success must have encouraged the Lathams and induced Tilden to join the group.

43. "Corbett Before the Kinetoscope," *New York Herald*, 8 September 1894, p. 11; *Phonoscope*, March 1898, p. 9.

44. Like many pugilists of the period, Corbett made his living principally on the stage.

45. "Knocked Out by Corbett," *New York Sun*, 8 September 1894, pp. 1–2.

46. Ibid.

47. *Orange Chronicle*, 26 January 1895, p. 5.

48. "In the Kinetographic Theatre," *Orange Chronicle*, 20 October 1894, p. 4.

49. "Miscellaneous Entertainments," *New York World*, 7 June 1894, p. 21.

50. Terrace Garden advertisement, *New York Tribune*, 22 July 1894, p. 11.

51. "In the Breezy Roof Gardens," *New York Tribune*, 24 June 1894, p. 22.

52. For example: "The Wild West," *New York Tribune*, 1 July 1894, p. 14; "Day with the Wild West," *New York Tribune*, 22 July 1894, p. 15.

53. Kinetoscope Company, *Price List of Films*, [May–June 1895], p. 3; Edison Manufacturing Company, *Edison Films*, March 1900, p. 19.

54. "Before the Kinetograph," *Orange Chronicle*, 13 October 1894, p. 5.

55. "Before the Kinetograph," *Orange Journal*, 18 October 1894, p. 5.

56. "In the Kinetograph Theatre," *Orange Chronicle*, 3 November 1894, p. 7.

57. Kinetoscope Company, *Price List of Films*, p. 4.

58. Kinetoscope Company, *Bulletin No. 1*.

59. "Mr. Dickson to Leave the Laboratory," *Orange Chronicle*, 27 April 1895, p. 7.

60. "The Barnum and Bailey Show," *Orange Chronicle*, 11 May 1895, p. 6; Kinetoscope Company, *Price List of Films*, p. 4.

61. " 'Trilby' Is a Triumph," *New York World*, 16 April 1895, p. 7.

62. "Trilby Visits the Eden Musee," *New York World*, 9 April 1895, p. 3; "Tableaux from 'Trilby,' " *New York World*, 16 April 1895, p. 7.

63. "Kinetoscope Scenes," *Asbury Park Daily Press*, 2 August 1895, p. 1.

64. "Distress Warrant Issued," *Asbury Park Daily Press*, 3 August 1895, p. 1.

65. Hendricks, *Kinetoscope*, pp. 161–69.

66. "Magic Lantern Kinetoscope," *New York Sun*, 22 April 1895, p. 2.

67. Edison Manufacturing Company, labor and materials sub-ledger no. 6, 31 May 1895, p. 252; Ramsaye, *Million and One Nights*, p. 120.

68. "Combining the Phonograph and the Kinetoscope," *Orange Chronicle*, 16 March 1895, p. 7.

69. Kinetoscope Company, *Price List of Films*, p. 1.

70. Ibid.; Kinetoscope Company, invoices, MH-BA.

71. James H. White, deposition, 9 February 1900, *Edison v. American Mutoscope Co.*, p. 175.

72. A connection pointed out to me by Pat Loughney in regard to *The Execution of Mary, Queen of Scots*.

73. Alfred Clark, oral history, ca. 1944, NjWOE.

74. James H. White, deposition, 9 February 1900, and Charles H. Webster, deposition, 9 February 1900, *Edison v. American Mutoscope Co.*

75. Charles Webster, *Edison v. American Mutoscope Co.*

4. Cinema, A Screen Novelty: 1895–1897

1. Thomas Armat, testimony, 10 October 1901, *Armat Moving Picture Company v. American Mutoscope Company and Benjamin Keith*, no. 7130, C.C.S.D.N.Y., filed 31 December 1897, printed record, p. 87, NjBaFAR.

2. Raff & Gammon to Daniel and Armat, 15 January 1896, letter books, vol. 3, p. 197, MH-BA.

3. Armat-Raff & Gammon contract, exhibit, *Armat Moving Picture Co. v. American Mutoscope Co.*

4. Raff & Gammon to Thomas Cushing Daniel and Thomas Armat, n.d. [ca. 26 December 1895], 3:179–81, MH-BA.

5. Ibid.; and Raff & Gammon to Armat, 17 March 1896, 3:367, MH-BA.

6. Raff & Gammon to Thomas Armat, 10 February 1896, exhibit, *Armat Moving Picture Co. v. American Mutoscope Co.*, p. 142.

7. As Raff & Gammon wrote to Armat, "We have heard from it [the phantoscope] two or three times to-day, and some people seem to think that he has a machine which is an improvement of the 'Vitascope,' or are afraid that it will develop into one. Can you not choke him off, or take the machine from him?" (Raff & Gammon to Thomas Armat, 4 March 1896, 3:279, MH-BA.)

8. Raff & Gammon to Armat, 5 March 1896, 3:289–90, MH-BA.

9. In film studies, the idea of a biographical legend has been developed in David Bordwell, *The Films of Carl-Theodor Dreyer* (Berkeley: University of California Press, 1981); see also Conot, *Streak of Luck.*

10. As preparations for the vitascope were getting under way, Edison had once again demonstrated his powerful hold on the press. At the beginning of March, his "perfection" of Wilhem Roentgen's recently discovered x-rays had made front-page news.

11. Raff & Gammon to Armat, 5 March 1896, 3:289, MH-BA.

12. "Magic Lantern Kinetoscope," *New York Sun*, 22 April 1895, p. 2.

13. Norman C. Raff to Thomas Armat, 21 March 1896, 3:390, MH-BA.

14. P. W. Kiefaber to Raff & Gammon, ca. 28 May 1896, MH-BA.

15. "Lifeless Skirt Dancers," *New York Journal*, 4 April 1896, p. 9.

16. Raff & Gammon to E. Kuhn, 18 April 1896, 2:258, MH-BA.

17. Raff & Gammon to J. H. White, 10 April 1896, 2:135, MH-BA.

18. Raff & Gammon to Albert Bial, 7 April 1896, 2:108, MH-BA.

19. James White, testimony, 9 February 1900, *Edison v. American Mutoscope Co.*

20. "Edwin S. Porter," *MPW*, 7 December 1912, p. 961; Niver, *First Twenty Years*, p. 16.

21. "Wonderful is the Vitascope," *New York Herald*, 24 April 1896, p. 11.

22. "Edison's Vitascope Cheered," *NYT*, 24 April 1896, p. 5.

23. "Amusements," *New York Daily News*, 24 April 1896, clipping, MH-BA.

24. "Edison's Vitascope Seen," *New York Journal*, 24 April 1896.

25. *New York Herald*, 24 April 1896, p. 11.

26. Ibid.

27. Raff & Gammon, *The Vitascope* (New York: n.d. [March 1896]).

28. "The Vitascope at Keith's," *Boston Herald*, 19 May 1896, p. 9.

29. Saengerfest Hall, programme, 30 August 1896, clipping, MH-BA.

30. Robert C. Allen, "Vitascope/Cinématographe: Initial Patterns of American Film Practice," in Fell, ed., *Film Before Griffith*, pp. 144–52.

31. Raff & Gammon to W. E. Gilmore, 25 March 1896, 3:408, MH-BA.

32. *New York World*, 26 April 1896, p. 21.

33. *New York Herald*, 10 May 1896, p. 6F.

34. Raff & Gammon to P. W. Kiefaber, 6 May 1896, 2:474, MH-BA.

35. "Herald Square 'Vitascoped,' " *New York Herald*, 12 May 1896, p. 9.

36. *Boston Herald*, 26 May 1896, p. 7.

37. *Boston Herald*, 23 June 1896, p. 9.

38. "Navarre's Great Race," *Brooklyn Eagle*, 24 June 1896, p. 5.

39. *Brooklyn Eagle*, 28 June 1896, p. 5.

40. John F. Kasson, *Amusing the Millions: Coney Island at the Turn of the Century* (New York: Hill & Wang, 1978).

41. "Bergen Beach," *Brooklyn Eagle*, 21 June 1896, p. 23.

42. "The Theatrical World," *Philadelphia Record*, 19 July 1896, p. 11.

43. *Boston Herald*, 4 August 1896, p. 7.

44. Ramsaye, *Million and One Nights*, p. 257; *New York World*, 12 September 1896, p. 14. Ramsaye claims that several films, such as *The May Irwin Kiss* were filmed at this studio when they were, in fact, photographed at the Black Maria. On the other hand, Blackton's claim to have visited the Orange studio when appearing in these three films (meeting Edison, etc.) is almost certainly myth. Our knowledge about this studio is, for the moment, very limited.

45. *New York Mail and Express* (henceforth *Mail and Express*), 15 September 1896, p. 5, and 19 September 1896, p. 10.

46. *Edison Films*, March 1900, p. 36; *New York World*, 11 October 1896, p. 14.

47. Vitascope Company, certificate of incorporation, 5 May 1896, NNNCC-Ar.

48. Raff & Gammon to Thomas Armat, 17 March 1896, 3:368, MH-BA. While using some of the same research, my conclusions again differ from those of Robert C. Allen ("Vitascope/Cinématographe," pp. 146–52). Allen suggests that Raff & Gammon's states rights approach to marketing was antiquated and that vaudeville circuits such as Keith's were discouraged from using the vitascope because they operated in different states and were therefore forced to deal with different entrepreneurs while the Lumière Agency with its cinématographe serviced their needs from a centralized source. Yet Keith's acquired the vitascope for its Boston and Philadelphia theaters. In each case, this acquisition was done by the local theater manager, who was responsible for booking his own acts until the spring of 1898 (*NYDM*, 12 March 1898, p. 19). In other words, Keith's did not have a centralized system as Allen assumes. Allen also asserts that the reasons for Raff & Gammon's choice of a states rights system were never clearly thought out or articulated. Yet Raff & Gammon further elaborated on the advantages of this system in other parts of this letter. Allen's *Vaudeville and Film, 1895–1915*, however, does not impose this interpretation on his data to the same extent and is often perceptive in articulating the problems faced by Raff & Gammon and the owners of vitascope exhibition rights.

49. Norman Raff to William Gilmore, 10 April 1896, 2:137–38 and 140–54, MH-BA.

50. Conot, *Streak of Luck*, p. 317.

51. For a broad overview, see Ramsaye, *Million and One Nights*, pp. 251–80; Allen, *Vaudeville and Film, 1895–1915*, pp. 81–109; and Musser, *Emergence of Cinema*, pp. 109–32.

52. Raff & Gammon to Charles Balsley, 1 April, 3:471, MH-BA.

53. Raff & Gammon to J. R. Balsley, 4 April 1896, 2:42, MH-BA; Raff & Gammon to A. F. Rieser, 4 April 1896, MH-BA.

54. Not only is this trip referred to in the following news article, but the lack of correspondence suggests that this deal was closed in person.

55. *Connellsville Courier*, 20 March 1896.

56. R. G. Dun and Company, credit ledgers, 66:187, MH-BA; McClenathan et al., *Centennial History*, p. 417.

57. McClenathan et al., *Centennial History*, pp. 248–50.

58. *Connellsville Courier*, 10 April 1896.

59. Raff & Gammon to Thomas L. Tally, 4 April 1896, 2:58, MH-BA.

60. Raff & Gammon to Charles Balsley, 11 April 1896, 2:161, MH-BA.

61. Raff & Gammon to R. S. Paine, 22 April 1896, 2:272, MH-BA.

62. Raff & Gammon to J. R. Balsley, 18 April 1896, 2:320, MH-BA. The mention of clear stock refers to a persistent problem at this time. Edison needed to switch from a semi-opaque stock suitable for peep-show kinetoscopes to a clear base needed for projection. This was a major concern to Thomas Armat, but was not treated with much urgency at the Edison factory. Many of the early subjects, presumably including those the Connellsville group saw in New York, were on the old-type stock.

63. *New York World*, 19 April 1896, p. 14.

64. Raff & Gammon to R. S. Paine, 28 April 1896, 2:331–2, MH-BA.

65. Raff & Gammon to J. R. Balsley, 30 April 1896, 2:391, MH-BA.

66. P. W. Kiefaber to Raff & Gammon, 8 and 9 May 1896, MH-BA.

67. *Connellsville Courier*, 22 May 1896.

68. *San Francisco Examiner*, 24 May 1896, p. 33.

69. "Edison's Wizard Wand on the Stage," *San Francisco Examiner*, 12 May 1896, p. 6.

70. Charles H. Balsley to George Beck, 9 July 1915. Courtesy Lorraine Balsley.

71. *New York Clipper* (henceforth *Clipper*), 6 June 1896, p. 212.

72. "With the Actor Folks," *San Francisco Examiner*, 7 June 1896, p. 34. See also *San Francisco Chronicle*, 7 June 1896, p. 6.

73. Orpheum Theater, programme, week of 8 June 1896, CU-BANC.

74. *San Francisco Chronicle*, 9 June 1896, p. 7.

75. *San Francisco Chronicle*, 14 June 1896, p. 5.

76. *San Francisco Examiner*, 9 June 1896, p. 3.

77. *San Francisco Call*, 7 June 1896.

78. *San Francisco Call*, 9 June 1896.

79. "The Camera Made to Tell a Story," *San Francisco Chronicle*, 9 June 1896, p. 14.

80. "The Illustrated Song Is Now the Latest Novelty of the Stage," *San Francisco Examiner*, 7 June 1896, p. 33.

81. *San Francisco Examiner*, 1 March 1896, p. 31, and 15 March 1896, p. 1.

82. *San Francisco Chronicle*, 14 June 1896, p. 5.

83. *San Francisco Chronicle*, 21 June 1896, p. 8.

84. *San Francisco Chronicle*, 16 June 1896, p. 8.

85. Charles Balsley to E. V. Durling, 22 June 1922. Courtesy Lorraine Balsley.

86. *San Francisco Examiner*, 21 June 1896, p. 20.

87. *Boston Herald*, 19 May 1896, p. 9.

88. *San Francisco Chronicle*, 25 June 1896, p. 14.

89. "Local Theater Bills," *San Francisco Chronicle*, 26 July 1896, p. 5.

90. *Los Angeles Herald*, 12 July 1896, p. 12.

91. Albert F. McLean, Jr., *American Vaudeville as Ritual* (Lexington: University Press of Kentucky, 1965).

92. Navy Department, "Enlistment Record of Edwin Stanton Porter."

93. *MPW*, 27 October 1917, p. 587.

94. *NYDM*, 15 March 1911, p. 34; Edwin S. Porter, testimony, 20 June 1907, *Armat Moving Picture Company v. Edison Manufacturing Company*, no. 8303, C.C.S.D.N.Y., Court, NjBaFAR.

95. *Los Angeles Times*, 5 July 1896, p. 8.

96. *Los Angeles Herald*, 5 July 1896, p. 14.

97. Ibid.

98. *Los Angeles Herald*, 5 July 1896, p. 15.

99. *Los Angeles Herald*, 12 July 1896, p. 12.

100. *Julius Cahn's Official Theatrical Guide* (New York, 1896), p. 181.

101. *Los Angeles Herald*, 7 July 1896, p. 4.

102. *Los Angeles Times*, 7 July 1896, p. 6.

103. *Clipper*, 25 July 1896, p. 325.

104. *Worcester* [Mass.] *Telegraph*, August 1896, clipping, NjWOE.

105. *Los Angeles Herald*, 8 July 1896.

106. *Los Angeles Times*, 10 July 1896, p. 6.

107. *Los Angeles Herald*, 14 July 1896; *Los Angeles Times*, 12 July 1896, p. 1.

108. *Los Angeles Times*, 12 July 1896, p. 21.

109. Tom Gunning, "The Cinema of Attraction[s]," *Wide Angle* 8, no. 3/4 (1986): pp. 63–70.

110. *Los Angeles Times*, 14 July 1896.

111. Holland to Norman Raff, 23 September 1896, MH-BA.

112. *Los Angeles Herald*, 25 July 1896, p. 10; and *Los Angeles Times*, 25 July 1896, p. 12.

113. *Los Angeles Times*, 26 July 1896, p. 12.

114. Charles Balsley to MPW, 30 October 1911, courtesy Lorraine Balsley.

115. Thomas Armat, testimony, 11 August 1911, *Motion Picture Patents Co. v. Carl Laemmle*, no. 5–167, D.C.S.D.N.Y., filed 10 February 1910, p. 602, NjBaFAR.

116. George Pratt, "Firsting the Firsts," in Marshall Deutelbaum, ed., *"Image": On the Art and Evolution of the Film* (New York: Dover, 1979), p. 21.

117. Purdy and Kiefaber to Vitascope Company, 6 July 1896, MH-BA.

118. *Clipper*, 11 July 1896, p. 296.

119. "The Cinematographe," *Mail and Express*, 25 July 1896, p. 8; *Pittsburgh Dispatch*, 13 September 1896, p. 21.

120. *New York World*, 23 August 1896, p. 15.

121. Raff suffered from nervous collapse in August and was unable to work for some time. Holland to Frank Gammon, 11 and 18 August 1896, MH-BA.

122. Holland to Raff, 14 and 26 September 1896, MH-BA.

123. Raff & Gammon to C. W. Walters, 26 March 1897, 4:102, MH-BA; see also Edison Manufacturing Company, cash book no. 3, 1895–97, NjWOE.

124. Holland to Raff, 3 September 1896, MH-BA.

125. Edmund McLoughlin to Raff & Gammon, 4 August 1896, MH-BA.

126. Edison Manufacturing Company, cash book no. 3, 24 September 1896, p. 199.

127. Purdy and Kiefaber to Vitascope Company, 6 July 1896, MH-BA.

128. E. F. Albee to Kiefaber, 29 July 1896, incoming letters, 1896–P. W. Kiefaber, MH-BA.

129. *Connellsville Courier*, 17 July 1896. Unfortunately Terre Haute newspapers do not survive from this era.

130. Rieser to Vitascope Company, 19 October 1896, MH-BA.

131. Charles Balsley to *MPW*, 30 October 1911. The general chronology of this chapter as it relates to the Connellsville group is outlined in this letter.

132. *Indianapolis Sentinel*, 13 September 1896, p. 5.

133. *Indianapolis Journal*, 13 and 15 September 1896.

134. *Indianapolis Journal*, 18 October 1896, p. 10.

135. *Indianapolis Sentinel*, 18 October 1896, p. 13.

136. *Indianapolis Sentinel*, 20 October 1896.

137. *Indianapolis Sentinel*, 25 October 1896, p. 6.

138. *Clipper*, 31 October 1896, p. 559.

139. Charles Balsley to *MPW*, 30 October 1911.

140. "Out of the Past," *Connellsville Courier*, 5 November 1965. Courtesy Tony Keefer.

141. "Amusements," *New York World*, 11 October 1896, p. 15.

142. *Clipper*, 17 October 1896, p. 522.

143. Gordon Hendricks, *The Beginnings of the Biograph: The Story of the Invention of the Mutoscope and the Biograph and Their Supply Camera* (New York: Beginnings of the American Film, 1966), pp. 39–49.

144. *Phonoscope*, November 1896, p. 16.

145. McLoughlin to Raff & Gammon, 10 October 1896.

146. *Clipper*, 19 September 1896, p. 462.

147. *Clipper*, 7 November 1896, p. 595. *Phonoscope*, January–February 1897, p. 3. Ramsaye (*Million and One Nights*, p. 342) incorrectly refers to the International Film Company's machine as a projectoscope.

148. *Clipper*, 26 September 1896, p. 480; 31 October 1896, p. 554; 14 November 1896, p. 595; *Phonoscope*, December 1896, p. 13.

149. Edison Manufacturing Company, cash book no. 3, 26 September 1896, p. 200.

150. Rieser to Vitascope Company, 9 November 1896, MH-BA. See also *Clipper*, 28 November 1896, p. 624, for Edison advertisement offering to sell films directly to customers. Vitascope entrepreneurs were contractually obligated to acquire their films and supplies from Raff & Gammon.

151. James White, testimony, 9 February 1900, *Edison v. American Mutoscope Co.*, p. 174.

152. "The Projectoscope Will Do," *Harrisburg Daily Telegraph*, 30 November 1896, p. 1.

153. "A Great Attraction," *Harrisburg Daily Telegraph*, 5 December 1896, p. 4.

154. Maguire & Baucus, *Preliminary Circular*, 16 February 1897.

155. Edison Manufacturing Company, statement of profit and loss, 1 March 1896 to 1 March 1897, NjWOE.

156. Ibid.

157. Edison Manufacturing Company, cash book no. 3, October 1896–February 1897.

158. *Phonoscope*, December 1896, p. 16.

159. "Pictures Taken at a Gallop," *Newark Daily Advertiser*, 14 November 1896, p. 2.

160. *Wilkes-Barre Leader*, 3 December 1896, p. 2.

161. "Hammerstein's Olympia," *Mail and Express*, 20 October 1896, p. 4.

162. "Vitascopic Pictures," *Orange Chronicle*, 26 December 1896, p. 7.

163. *Harrisburg Daily Telegraph*, 16 December 1896, p. 4.

164. "Local Projectoscope Views," *Harrisburg Daily Telegraph*, 24 December 1896, p. 1.

165. *Harrisburg Patriot*, 13 January 1897, p. 5.

166. Ibid.

167. "Injunction Refused," *Harrisburg Daily Telegraph*, 13 January 1897, p. 1.

168. Although the Lumière cinématographe was able to act as a camera, printer, and projector, negatives taken by local operators were not developed in the United States as commonly assumed.

169. Maguire & Baucus, *Fall Catalogue*, 1897, p. 10.

170. F. M. Prescott, *Catalogue of New Films*, p. 12.

171. Ibid.

172. Maguire & Baucus, *Fall Catalogue*, 1897, p. 13.

173. Ibid., p. 10.

174. Edwin S. Porter, testimony, 20 June 1907, *Armat Moving Picture Company v. Edison Manufacturing Company*, no. 8303, C. C. S. D. N. Y., filed 28 November 1902, NjBaFAR. Porter states he was running a machine by Kuhn and Webster. If so it was a projectograph, not a projectoscope as he states in his testimony.

175. *Phonoscope*, March 1897, p. 7.

176. Ramsaye, *Million and One Nights*, pp. 342–46.

5. Producer and Exhibitor as Co-Creators: 1897–1900

1. Niver, *Early Motion Pictures*, provides an extensive catalog of these films.

2. "Summer Horse Show," *Mail and Express*, 12 August 1897, p. 3. It is possible that White left for the West Coast in June, altering the specifics of this account accordingly.

3. After the initial development of the kinetograph, camera technology was never an Edison strong point. Since the inventor was opposed in principle to the sale of camera technology, his mechanical experts never had the opportunity to develop such equipment.

4. *Edison Films*, March 1900, p. 20.

5. Promotional blurbs and advertisements for these tours appeared in endless news-

papers from the period. See, for example, "Mexico and California," *Orange Chronicle*, 27 January 1900, p. 4. Many tourist packages involved the very hotels and stopping points that White filmed on his journey (for example, "Grand Mid-Winter Tour to California," *Brooklyn Eagle*, 29 January 1899, p. 21).

6. Although these films may have been taken by White and Blechynden, this seems unlikely. Wright's presence in Seattle was reported while White's was not. The Edison Company also advertised these films separately from the other films White took on the trip (*Edison Films*, March 1900, pp. 14–22 and 38).

7. "The Indians," *Denver Post*, 4 October 1897, p. 3, and "Golden Cripple," *Denver Post*, 5 October 1897, p. 8; *Denver Republican*, 6 October 1897, clipping, NjWOE.

8. *Edison Films*, March 1900, p. 17.

9. "The 'Coptic' Arrives at Last," *Japan Weekly Mail*, 26 July 1898, p. 216.

10. *Phonoscope*, October 1898, p. 14; Gorham & Company (Hong Kong) to the Edison Laboratory, 17 May 1898, and clipping, NjWOE.

11. "Honolulu in Kinetoscope," *Hawaii Gazette*, 10 May 1898, p. 8, and 13 May 1898, p. 3. See also Hawaii Film Board, *Souvenir Program* (5 February 1977).

12. *Phonoscope*, October 1898, p. 14.

13. "Making Vitascopic Pictures of the Ambulance," *Orange Chronicle*, 9 October 1897, p. 7.

14. "First Ambulance Performance," *Orange Chronicle*, 19 February 1898, p. 8.

15. "Gattling Gun Company A," *Orange Chronicle*, 27 November 1897, p. 5.

16. "Gattling Gun Company A," *Orange Chronicle*, 11 December 1897, p. 5.

17. *War Extra, Edison Films*, 20 May 1898, pp. 10–11.

18. The date of filming has yet to be firmly established. It was not copyrighted until 16 December 1898, and yet the film includes a notice indicating it was copyrighted in 1897. Moreover, the film does not show up in Edison catalogs.

19. Hendricks, *Edison Motion Picture Myth*, pp. 130–37.

20. *Thomas A. Edison v. Charles Webster and Edmund Kuhn*, nos. 6795 and 6796, C.C.S.D.N.Y., filed 7 December 1897, NjBaFAR.

21. *Thomas A. Edison v. Maguire and Baucus, Limited, Joseph D. Baucus et al.*, nos. 6797 and 6798, C.C.S.D.N.Y., filed 7 December 1897, NjBaFAR. Maguire & Baucus concentrated their energies in England, where their Warwick Trading Company became a prominent firm.

22. *Thomas A. Edison v. Siegmund Lubin*, no. 50, October Sessions, 1897, C.C.E.D.P., filed 10 January 1898, PPFAR; *Thomas A. Edison v. American Mutoscope Co. and Benjamin Keith*, no. 6928, C.C.S.D.N.Y., filed 13 May 1898, NjBaFAR.

23. "A Moral Wax-Work Show," *NYT*, 1 January 1884, p. 3; "Scenes and Figures in Wax," *NYT*, 29 March 1884, p. 4.

24. Eden Musee American Company, *Eden Musee Catalogue* (New York: 1896), p. 2.

25. "Trouble in the Eden Musee," *New York Herald*, 11 April 1894, p. 9; "A Visit and a Chat with Mr. Rich. G. Hollaman, of the Eden Musee," *MPW*, 22 February 1908, p. 131; *New York Tribune*, 20 December 1896, p. 10, and 15 June 1897, p. 1. Ramsaye incorrectly suggests that the Lumière cinématographe opened at the Eden Musee and Keith's Union Square Theater at the same time—June 29, 1896 (*Million and One Nights*, p. 263).

26. *Mail and Express*, 26 December 1896, p. 12.

27. "Edison at the Eden Musee," *Mail and Express*, 6 February 1897, p. 17.

28. "New Cinematographe at the Musee," *Mail and Express*, 20 February 1897, p. 17. See also Deslandes and Richard, *Histoire comparée*, 2:129–31 on the Cinématographe Joly in France. Eberhard Schneider, deposition, 11 February 1900, *Thomas A. Edison v. Eberhard Schneider*, nos. 7124 and 7125, C.C.S.D.N.Y., filed 21 December 1898, NjBaFAR.

29. *Mail and Express*, 23 February 1897, p. 7.

30. *Mail and Express*, 13 April 1897, p. 7. It is possible that the American cinematograph was a new machine, but it was not treated this way in the press. Schneider still owned the projector and provided the exhibition service, but did not own its newly designated "American Cinematograph" trade name.

31. *Mail and Express*, 1 May 1897, p. 14.

32. This information is based on a survey that appeared in Charles Musser, "Another Look at the 'Chaser Period,'" *Studies in Visual Communication* 10, no. 4 (Fall 1984): 24–44. Since that study was published more exhibitions in New York City theaters have been identified. These alter certain details but not the central argument.

33. *New York Tribune*, 15 June 1897, p. 1; *Mail and Express*, 15 June 1897, p. 7, and 26 June 1897, p. 10. Deslandes and Richard, *Histoire comparée*, 2:23. Presumably the cinématographe was then owned by an independent exhibitor.

34. *NYT*, 31 August 1897, p. 11C.

35. *Mail and Express*, 31 August 1897, p. 5.

36. "Edwin S. Porter," *MPW*, 7 December 1912, p. 961. Beadnell was able to promote not only the Eden Musee but himself in the *Mail and Express*, which at one point stated, "No man in the advertising world has been so well-known and so highly esteemed as Mr. Beadnell" (16 January 1899, p. 4). At the testimonial dinner given in Beadnell's honor and described in this article, James White sang a solo and joined in a duet. Porter may have been there.

37. An advertisement for this company appears in the *Brooklyn Eagle*, 29 January 1899, p. 21. Schneider, who did not control the name "American Cinematograph," went on to call his service the German-American Cinematograph Company.

38. Ramsaye, *Million and One Nights*, pp. 345–46.

39. *Phonoscope*, August–September 1897, p. 9.

40. Ramsaye, *Million and One Nights*, p. 346; *Halifax* [Nova Scotia] *Morning Chronicle*, 27 September 1897, p. 6.

41. Porter was one of several exhibitors showing these films in Canada ("Canada," *NYDM*, 18 September 1897, p. 8; 25 September 1897, p. 10; 2 October 1897, p. 9; 9 October 1897, p. 8; 30 October 1897, p. 9; and 6 November 1897, p. 11).

42. *Halifax Morning Chronicle*, 28 September 1897, p. 8.

43. Wormwood was performing at Harry Davis's Avenue Theater (*Pittsburgh Post*, 14 November 1897, p. 16).

44. *Mail and Express*, 5 October 1897, p. 5.

45. *Mail and Express*, 16 October 1897, p. 14.

46. "Danger in X-rays," *Phonoscope*, January–February 1897, p. 15; *Clipper*, 3 April 1897, p. 84.

47. Edwin Porter, unused deposition, ca. 1907, legal files, NjWOE; Ramsaye, *Million and One Nights*, p. 348.

48. "Crowds at the Musee," *Mail and Express*, 5 February 1898, p. 5; and *Mail and Express*, 5 March 1898, p. 12.

49. See Zdenek Stabla, *Queries concerning the Horice Passion Film* (Prague: Film Institute, 1971) and Kemp Niver and Bebe Bergsten, *Klaw & Erlanger Present Famous Plays in Pictures* (Los Angeles: Locare Research Group, 1976) for information about *The Horitz Passion Play*, filmed in Horitz, Bohemia.

50. *MPW*, 22 February 1908, p. 132.

51. Ramsaye, *Million and One Nights*, p. 371, gives some members of the cast and a generally informative account of this program.

52. While the *Mail and Express* (19 February 1898, p. 15) gives the projection speed at twenty frames per second, a surviving print indicates that thirty frames per second would have been necessary if movements were to be natural.

53. "Scenes of Bible Subjects," *New York Tribune*, 29 January 1898, p. 9.

54. The Morse *Passion Play* was scheduled to open on December 7, 1880, but its producer, Henry E. Abbey, withdrew it at the last moment ("Mr. Abbey's Decision," *NYT*, 28 November 1880, p. 7).

55. *Phonoscope*, March 1898, 2:3, p. 7.

56. *New York Tribune*, 29 January 1898, p. 9.

57. *Mail and Express*, 5 February 1898, p. 15.

58. *New York World*, 1 February 1898, p. 9.

59. *Mail and Express*, 5 February 1898, p. 15, and 19 February 1898, p. 15.

60. "Ober-Ammergau's Passion Play," *NYT*, 12 December 1880, p. 5; *New York Tribune*, 12 December 1880, p. 2.

61. *Edison Films*, July 1901, p. 5.

62. Cecil M. Hepworth, *Animated Photography—The ABC of Cinematography*, 2nd rev. ed. (London: Amateur Photographer Library, [1900]).

63. C. Francis Jenkins, *Animated Pictures* (Washington, D.C.: by the author, 1898), pp. 89–90.

64. Ibid.

65. See Macgowan, *Behind the Screen*, pp. 87–92.

66. *Mail and Express*, 26 March 1898, p. 15.

67. "Correspondence," *NYDM*, 26 March 1898, p. 7, and 9 April 1898, pp. 4–6.

68. *Edison Films*, July 1901, p. 5. Although earlier Edison catalogs (e.g., *Edison Films*, May 1900, p. 2) advertise the films as only available in a set of twenty-two scenes (one having been dropped since the program's debut), exhibitors did not always show all scenes and almost certainly insisted on selective purchases. These practical realities are evident in the 1901 catalog.

69. Lubin advertisement, *Clipper*, 28 May 1898, p. 932, and Sigmund Lubin, *The Passion Play* (Philadelphia: ca. 1904); Selig Polyscope Company, *Films of the Passion Play* (Chicago: ca. 1903).

70. *Thomas A. Edison v. Eden Musee American Company Ltd. and Richard G. Hollaman, individually and as President of said Company*, nos. 6845 and 6846, C.C.S.D.N.Y., filed 7 February 1898, NjBaFAR.

71. *New York Herald*, 6 February 1898, p. 7C.

72. Only one Musee advertisement mentioned the biograph. David Levy, however, has argued that the Musee was able to acquire a sufficient quantity of 35mm films to satisfy

spectators. He may be right, but descriptions such as those in the *Mail and Express*, 5 April 1898, p. 7, suggest that these films were taken by Biograph cameramen.

73. *Clipper*, 19 March 1898, p. 42.

74. *New York Journal*, 14 March 1898.

75. "Patriotism at Theaters Shows No Diminution," *New York World*, 8 March 1898, p. 4. See also, "Chicago Enthusiasts," *New York World*, 24 February 1898, p. 3.

76. *New York World*, 27 March 1898, p. 15.

77. *Mail and Express*, 5 April 1898, p. 7.

78. *Clipper*, 9 April 1898, p. 99.

79. F. Z. Maguire to William Gilmore, 20 April 1898, NjWOE.

80. "Yellow Journalism," Alfred Henry Lewis, *New York Journal and Advertiser*, 7 April 1898, p. 6.

81. Paley to Edison Manufacturing Company, 12 March 1898, NjWOE.

82. *War Extra: Edison Films*, 20 May 1898, pp. 5–7.

83. Advertisement, *Clipper*, 30 April 1898, p. 153.

84. F. Z. Maguire to William Gilmore, 20 April 1898, NjWOE.

85. *Phonoscope*, October 1898, p. 15.

86. "Bill Paley, the 'Kinetoscope Man,'" *Phonoscope*, August 1898, p. 7.

87. *Mail and Express*, 19 April 1898, p. 7.

88. *Mail and Express*, 7 May 1898, p. 14.

89. *Mail and Express*, 21 May 1898, p. 14. Paley apparently retained close ties to the Musee and took films for its exclusive use. The Library of Congress Paper Print Collection, therefore, may offer only a portion of his wartime output.

90. Traveling exhibitors generally did not respond to this opportunity as quickly as their urban counterparts. Most small-town residents did not have the opportunity to see Paley's films until the fall of 1898.

91. The two Proctor theaters, Keith's Union Square, Pastor's, the Central Opera House, Huber's 14th Street Museum, and the Eden Musee.

92. *MPW*, 7 December 1912, p. 961. Porter's interview is a little ambiguous on this point. He suggests not only that these were machines that he and Beadnell manufactured (presumably along with Frank Cannock) but that they had operators, and therefore a complete exhibition service in these houses. The Eden Musee offered its services as a film exhibitor to outside parties, suggesting that Hollaman may have had some kind of special arrangement with Porter and his associates.

93. For a full account of American Vitagraph Company's activities as an Edison licensee see Charles Musser, "American Vitagraph, 1897–1901," *Cinema Journal* 23, no. 3 (Spring 1983): 4–46. A major revision of this article will soon be published in English.

94. "Eden Musee," *Mail and Express*, 11 June 1898, p. 14.

95. "Eden Musee," *Mail and Express*, 25 June 1898, p. 14.

96. *Mail and Express*, 16 July 1898, p. 18.

97. *Mail and Express*, 9 July 1898, p. 16.

98. *New York Tribune*, 7 August 1898, p. 10B.

99. *Mail and Express*, 27 August 1898, p. 12.

100. *Mail and Express*, 17 September 1898, p. 14.

101. *Mail and Express*, 1 October 1898, p. 12, and 1 November 1898, p. 5.

102. *Brooklyn Eagle*, 20 November 1898, p. 18.

103. See Musser with Nelson, *High-Class Moving Pictures*, pp. 86–93.

104. For example, Proctor advertisements, *New York World*, 21 August 1898, p. 13.

105. *Clipper*, 4 June 1898, p. 238, and 18 June 1898, p. 270.

106. Proctor's Pleasure Palace, programme, week of 11 July 1898, Harvard Theatre Collection.

107. "Last Week's Bill, Pleasure Palace," *NYDM*, 19 November 1898, p. 20.

108. *New York Tribune*, 4 December 1898, p. 8B; *Mail and Express*, 20 December 1898, p. 7.

109. *New York Tribune*, 8 January 1899, p. 12B.

110. *New York Tribune*, 1 January 1899, p. 10B.

111. *New York Herald*, 6 February 1898, p. 7C. Gilmore to Paley, 7 March 1898, mentions this film, indicating it had already been completed.

112. *New York Tribune*, 15 January 1899, p. 12B.

113. *Edison Films*, March 1900, p. 2.

114. Albert Eaves and Rich Hollaman, receipt, 19 July 1899, NjWOE.

115. These were named after the Théâtre Robert-Houdin, which was owned and operated by the Parisian magician turned filmmaker.

116. *Mail and Express*, 8 April 1899, p. 11. Erik Barnouw, *The Magician and the Cinema* (New York: Oxford University Press, 1981) deals extensively with those magicians who used cinema in the 1890s. Lucy Fischer, "The Lady Vanishes: Women, Magic and the Movies," in Fell, ed., *Film Before Griffith*, pp. 339–54.

117. Porter, unused deposition, circa 1907, NjWOE.

118. The veriscope's wide-screen format also matched the boxing ring.

119. *Clipper*, 9 September 1899, p. 571.

120. *Clipper*, 23 September 1899, p. 609.

121. *Clipper*, 9 September 1899, p. 571.

122. Ibid.

123. "Palmer-M'Govern Bout Off Until To-morrow," *New York Evening Journal*, 11 September 1899, p. 8.

124. *Clipper*, 23 September 1899, p. 620. As was the case throughout this period, Sigmund Lubin enjoyed modest, but certain, financial gains by taking motion pictures of fight reenactments.

125. *Mail and Express*, 23 September 1899, p. 17.

126. *Edison Films*, March 1900, p. 7. One might speculate on the makeup of these crews: James White, William Heise, Charles Webster (a recently hired Edison employee), Albert E. Smith, J. Stuart Blackton, and William Paley. Perhaps Alfred C. Abadie and William Jamison, who worked for the Edison Manufacturing Company. Porter is another obvious possibility, although he never made such a claim.

127. *Mail and Express*, 30 September 1899, p. 13.

128. *Mail and Express*, 3 October 1899, p. 7.

129. *Mail and Express*, 28 October 1899, p. 15.

130. Lewis Jacobs reports that Porter began working for Edison as a handyman, totally ignoring his role as an exhibitor in the 1890s; he also indicates that Porter had been working as a cameraman for Edison during much of this period (*Rise of the American Film*, p. 36). These incorrect claims may have encouraged Kemp R. Niver to attribute several Edison films from the 1898–1900 period to Porter, including *The Cavalier's*

Dream, Elopement on Horseback, The Astor Tramp, and *Storm at Sea (Motion Pictures from the Library of Congress Paper Print Collection 1894–1912* [Berkeley: University of California Press, 1967], p. 361). As the evidence presented in this chapter suggests, Ramsaye offers a much more credible chronology of Porter's career.

131. *Clipper*, 7 October 1899, p. 652.

132. *Clipper*, 4 November 1899, p. 756.

133. *New York World*, 24 December 1899, p. 3E.

134. Porter, unused deposition, ca. 1907, NjWOE. An advertisement in the *Clipper* (11 August 1900, p. 535) from Frank Bowland in New York City, asked Edwin Porter to "communicate with me at once," suggesting that Porter was then on the road.

135. William H. Swanson, "The Inception of the 'Black Top,' " *MPW*, 15 July 1916, p. 369. Swanson's dating is off, but other parts of his description merit some credibility.

136. As of December 8, 1899, the Edison Company had sold 973 projecting kineto-scopes (James H. White, testimony, 9 February 1900, *Edison v. American Mutoscope Co.*, p. 165). See appendix A for additional figures.

137. *NYDM*, 22 October 1898, p. 22.

138. Maguire & Baucus, *Edison Films*, 20 January 1897; *War Extra: Edison Films*, 20 May 1898; *Clipper*, 23 July 1898, p. 348. See Lubin advertisements in the *Clipper* for this period as a source of competitive pressure.

139. *New York World*, 5 November 1899, p. 8E, 12 November 1899, p. 5E, and 19 November 1899, p. 6E; *Clipper*, 21 April 1900, p. 184.

140. *Thomas A. Edison v. Eberhard Schneider*, nos. 7124 and 7125, C.C.S.D.N.Y., filed 21 December 1898, NjBaFAR.

141. Thomas Edison and Thomas Crahan, contract, 14 March 1899, NjWOE.

142. "Making Pictures of the Klondike," *Orange Chronicle*, 28 October 1899, p. 6; *New York Press*, 30 October 1899, and *Newark* [N.J.] *Call*, 29 October 1899, clippings, NjWOE.

143. I am also grateful for information about Bonine's early life from Robert Darrah and Kenneth Nelson. See Kenneth Nelson, "A Compilation of Information About Robert Kates Bonine, 1862–1923, with an Examination of His Early Years in Photography and Film" (M.A. thesis, Rochester Institute of Technology, 1987).

144. Thomas Edison and Thomas Crahan, contract, 14 March 1899, NjWOE. Al-though the 35mm films were to be Edison's exclusive property, the failure of the large-format camera must have altered this agreement.

145. Thomas Edison to John Ott, n.d. [ca. November 1899], NjWOE.

146. *Moving Picture News*, 4 February 1911, p. 11. Schneider provided this infor-mation to denigrate Edison's patents and so it requires some interpretation.

147. The American Scenic Company, *Artistic Glimpses of the Wonder World* (Thom-as Crahan, 1900), NjWOE.

148. Thomas Crahan, Klondike Exposition Company, and Thomas Edison, contract, 18 June 1900, NjWOE.

149. *Phonoscope*, October 1898, p. 14; William Heise, testimony, 9 December 1902, *Armat Moving Picture Co. v. Edison Manufacturing Co.*

150. "Fake Pictures," *Phonoscope*, July 1900, p. 9.

151. Niver, *Early Motion Pictures*, p. 170.

152. *Edison Films*, March 1900, p. 29.

153. Ibid., p. 44.

154. Ibid., p. 30.

155. Ibid., p. 3.

156. Ibid.

157. "How the Bowery Tramp Got into Society," *New York World*, 25 November 1894, p. 25.

158. *Edison Films*, July 1901, p. 13.

159. *Edison Films*, March 1900, p. 3.

160. Biograph made *The American Soldier in Love and War* in 1903. Although its plot is somewhat similar, it was not a simple remake.

161. The Edison Company gained access to Smith's device when American Vitagraph became a licensee in the summer of 1898.

162. "Our Foreign Correspondence," *Phonoscope*, July 1900, p. 9.

163. William Alfred Higginbotham to Herbert Serious, New York Public Library, 3 November 1982. Susan Kemplar kindly brought this to my attention.

164. "Our Foreign Correspondence," *Phonoscope*, July 1900, p. 9. This was one of several efforts to show motion pictures with recorded sound at the Paris Exposition. See Emmanuelle Toulet, "Le Cinéma a l'Exposition Universelle de 1900," *Revue d'Histoire Moderne et Contemporaine* 33 (April–June 1986): 179–209.

165. Warwick Trading Company, *Bioscope and Warwick Films, Supplement* (September 1900), p. 149. "The first section comprises a close-view of the base of the chimney showing the lighting of the fire for burning the props which support the column. Next is shown a view from a distance, showing the fierce burning of the props."

166. See Charles Musser with Carol Nelson, *High Class Moving Pictures*, pp. 105–9, for a programme that structured eight of these films into a sequence and an analysis of Howe's use of these films.

167. *Moving Picture News*, 4 February 1911, p. 11. White intended to buy a group of negatives taken by Schneider in Europe but ruined many of them using the bad hypo.

168. *Thomas A. Edison v. Frederick M. Prescott*, nos. 7275 and 7276, C.C.S.D.N.Y., filed 9 June 1899, NjBaFAR. Perhaps to fill this hole, James White engaged Charles Webster, his former partner, to sell projecting machines and films at Edison's New York office. Charles H. Webster, deposition, 9 February 1900, *Edison v. American Mutoscope Co.*

169. Kleine Optical Company, "Films and Merchandise Purchased from Edison Mfg Company from 1899 to 1904," n.d., Kleine Collection, DLC.

170. *James H. White and John Schermerhorn v. Percival Waters*, Supreme Court, New York County. The entire case focused on the nature of this partnership.

171. White, testimony, 4, 5, and 6 May 1910, *White and Schermerhorn v. Waters*, p. 99.

172. Conot, *Streak of Luck*, passim.

173. *Thomas A. Edison v. George Huber*, no. 7224, C.C.S.D.N.Y., filed 28 April 1899, NjBaFAR.

174. *New York World*, 19 November 1899, p. 5E.

175. Harry Marvin to Thomas Edison, 27 March 1900, NjWOE.

176. Ramsaye, *Million and One Nights*, p. 384.

177. Edison Manufacturing Company, journal, 1900–1911, p. 8, NjWOE. The Edison

Manufacturing Company produced not only films and projectors but batteries, fan motors, the Phonoplex, gas engine spark coils, and x-ray apparatus.

6. The Production Company Assumes Greater Control: 1900–1902

1. "Edwin S. Porter," *MPW*, 7 December 1912, p. 961. The fact that Beadnell's business at 5 Beekman Street in 1900 was terminated and he was working the following year as a manager at 16 Warren Street supports Porter's reference to a conflagration (New York City directories, 1900 and 1902).

2. Edwin Porter, testimony, 17 February 1911, *Motion Picture Patents Company v. Carl Laemmle and Independent Moving Picture Company of America*, no. 7-151, D.C.S.D.N.Y., filed 27 March 1911, NjBaFAR.

3. Ibid.

4. *Clipper*, 2 March 1901, p. 24.

5. Edison Manufacturing Company, investment ledger, p. 20, NjWOE.

6. Edison Manufacturing Company and Hinkle Iron Company, contract, 12 October 1900, NjWOE. This building has since been torn down and replaced by a New York Savings Bank.

7. Edison Manufacturing Company, investment ledger, p. 20; E. E. Hinkle to William Simpkin, 12 January 1901, NjWOE.

8. Percival Waters, deposition, 25 May 1912, *James H. White and John Schermerhorn v. Percival Waters*, Supreme Court for the County of New York, NNNCC-Ar. This deposition describes the situation in 1906. Waters may have only occupied the front half of the top floor at first. The rent would have been somewhat less, but the basic arrangment was the same.

9. *MPW*, 7 December 1912, p. 961.

10. Bordwell, Staiger, and Thompson, *Classical Hollywood Cinema*, pp. 116–17. As we have seen, various methods of organizing film production were practiced before 1907, including the multi-unit production of actualities (as with the Dewey celebration). The question is which method, if any, was dominant.

11. James White to Dyer, Edmonds and Dyer, 10 January 1901, legal files, NjWOE.

12. Jacobs, *American Film*, p. 36.

13. Robert C. Allen, "Contra the Chaser Theory," *Wide Angle* 3, no. 1 (1979), pp. 4–11; repr. in Fell, ed., *Film Before Griffith*, pp. 105–15.

14. *Leslie Weekly*, 6 July 1899, cited in Kemp Niver, *Biograph Bulletins: 1896–1908* (Los Angeles: Artisan Press, 1971), p. 46.

15. Harry Marvin, request for stay of injunction, 23 July 1901, *Edison v. American Mutoscope Co.*

16. *Clipper*, 23 February 1901, p. 1160.

17. *New York Journal and Advertiser*, 6 February 1901, p. 16, and 7 February 1901, p. 3.

18. "Ninth and Arch Museum," *Philadelphia Record*, 24 February 1901, p. 13. Possibly, Lubin showed his own remake (mentioned below) even at this early date.

19. Lubin's film is described in *Clipper*, 9 March 1901, p. 24. The Biograph film,

Carrie Nation Smashing a Saloon, was photographed on 10 April 1901. Its realism was increased by the inclusion of an actual mirror. The Biograph film survives in the Paper Print Collection; the Lubin film is presumed lost.

20. "Eleventh Street Theatre," *Philadelphia Record*, 17 February 1901, p. 13.

21. *New York World*, 12 May 1901, p. 2 (comic section).

22. *New York Journal and Advertiser*, 2 February 1902, pp. 1A and 1B.

23. Tom Gunning makes this point in "The Non-Continuous Style of Early Film (1900–1906)," in Holman, comp., *Cinema, 1900–1906*, pp. 219–29. Gunning's analysis is extremely useful, but I find his term *non-continuous* an unfortunate one. Filmmakers of this period had their own concept of continuity. While differing from the post-Griffith concept, it is nonetheless valid. Catalogs from the period, for instance, sometimes refer to films being in "continuous scenes."

24. *New Haven Journal Courier*, 30 October 1899, p. 3.

25. *Edison Films*, July 1901, p. 77.

26. Ibid., p. 72.

27. Niver, *Motion Pictures from the Library of Congress*, p. 94. See also Niver, *First Twenty Years*, pp. 16–17.

28. Noël Burch, *Correction Please: A Study Guide* (London: Arts Council of Great Britain, 1980), provides a provocative analysis of a similar explosion film.

29. *Edison Films*, July 1901, p. 76.

30. John Barnes, *Optical Projection*, p. 32, attributes the invention of dissolving views to Henry Langdon Childe in 1836–37.

31. Hepworth, *Came the Dawn*, pp. 35–36.

32. *Edison Films*, July 1901, p. 51.

33. One might speculate on Porter's frequent use of trained animals. This (and perhaps even the Porter-Mosher relationship) may have owed something to Porter's travels with Wormwood's Dog and Monkey Circus.

34. *Edison Films*, July 1901, p. 51.

35. F. M. Prescott, *Catalogue of New Films* (New York: 20 November 1899), p. 4. See Sigmund Lubin, *Complete Catalogue of Lubin Films* (January 1903), pp. 21–22, for description. The film itself can be seen in the *Before Hollywood* series (American Federation of the Arts).

36. Certainly Lubin cannot simply be dismissed as an imitator as in Ramsaye, *Million and One Nights*, pp. 377 and 419.

37. The English filmmaker G. A. Smith did this with some frequency in such films as *Let Me Dream Again* and *Grandma's Reading Glass*. His efforts were widely imitated, particularly by Ferdinand Zecca, the chief filmmaker at Pathé Frères in France.

38. *Clipper*, 13 April 1901, p. 160.

39. *Clipper*, 13 April 1901, p. 147. The Edison Company's long-standing relationship with Buffalo Bill dated back to the fall of 1894, when *Broncho Busting* and other films were photographed at the Edison laboratory.

40. *Edison Films*, July 1901, p. 80.

41. See Rachel Low and Roger Manvell, *The History of British Film, 1896–1906* (London: George Allen & Unwin, 1948), pp. 104–5, for a description of *Robbery of a Mail Coach*. Sadoul suggests that *Robbery of a Mail Coach* was a model for *The Great*

Train Robbery (*Histoire générale*, 3d ed., 2:407–8). The holdup of a stagecoach was such a popular situation and portrayed so frequently in different forms of popular culture that its use at a given time or place probably did not have any single antecedent.

42. A few of these were later copyrighted: *Japanese Village* on 31 July 1901 and *Esquimaux Village* on 9 August 1901.

43. *Clipper*, 1 and 8 June 1901, pp. 312 and 336. This supplement does not survive, but extensive descriptions can be found in *Edison Films*, July 1901, pp. 3–7.

44. *Clipper*, 8 June 1901, p. 336; *Edison Films*, July 1901, p. 91.

45. *Edison Films*, July 1901, pp. 86–88. It is possible, though unlikely, that some of these are dupes of competitors' pictures.

46. 110 *Federal Reporter*, pp. 660–64.

47. 110 *Federal Reporter*, pp. 664–65.

48. H. J. Collins, depositions, 2 August 1901 to March 1902, *Edison v. American Mutoscope Co.*, NjBaFAR.

49. Sigmund Lubin, testimony, 11 March 1914, *United States of America v. Motion Picture Patents Company*, no. 889, September sessions, 1912, D.C.E.D.P., printed record, p. 3046; Jacob Blair Smith, testimony, 20 May 1902, *Thomas A. Edison v. Siegmund Lubin*, no. 36, April sessions, 1902, C.C.E.D.P., filed 25 February 1902, PPFAR.

50. Thomas Armat to Thomas A. Edison, 15 November 1901, NjWOE.

51. Howard W. Hayes to William Gilmore, 31 July 1901, NjWOE.

52. "How Moving Pictures Are Made in Pittsburgh for Amusement, Practical and Scientific Purposes," *Pittsburgh Post*, 9 December 1906, p. 4G.

53. Notes on newspaper reproduction, Charles Hummel Collection. That Abadie, a cameraman, acted in this film emphasizes the ways in which production personnel assumed many different roles, avoiding specialization.

54. Judith Mayne, "Uncovering the Female Body," in Leyda and Musser, eds., *Before Hollywood*, p. 65.

55. Tom Gunning, "Cinema of Attraction[s]," p. 64.

56. "Dime Museum," *Philadelphia Record*, 1 May 1898, p. 16. In this instance, Charmion appeared on the same bill with Little Egypt.

57. The making of *The Tramp's Miraculous Escape* and *The Photographer's Mishap* is described in the *Photographic Times-Bulletin*, November 1902, pp. 525–26.

58. F. M. Prescott, *Catalogue of New Films* (New York, 1899), p. 4.

59. *New York Journal and Advertiser*, 24 July 1901, p. 16.

60. In an interview eleven years later, Porter recalled serving under Admiral Schley. Rhetorically asking himself, "What did I think of Schley?" Porter responded, "He was a very fine man" (*MPW*, 7 December 1912, p. 961).

61. *Clipper*, 10 August 1901, p. 552.

62. "Spanish Fleet's Destruction," *Utica Observer*, 15 March 1899, p. 8.

63. For instance: "Sampson Says Officers Must Be Gentlemen. No Promotion for Sailors," *New York Journal and Advertiser*, 25 February 1901, p. 1.

64. Kleine Optical Company, *Complete Illustrated Catalogue of Moving Picture Machines, Stereopticons, Magic Lanterns, Accessories and Stereopticon Views* (Chicago, June 1902), p. 108.

65. A technique of set construction often found in life-model lantern slides and the films of Georges Méliès.

66. *Clipper*, 31 August 1901, p. 583.

67. San Francisco Orpheum, programme, 26 November 1899, San Francisco Historical Society.

68. *Edison Films*, September 1902, p. 12.

69. *Clipper*, 14 September 1901, p. 624, offers a listing of photographed subjects, many of which were never actually offered for sale. They include *President McKinley at the Stadium, President McKinley Walking on the Exposition Grounds, President McKinley at the Niagara Power Plant,* and *President McKinley Entering the Temple of Music.*

70. "Kinetoscope Scenes in Buffalo Tragedy," *New York World*, 10 September 1901, p. 3. In *Moving Picture News*, 2 April 1910, Smith claims to have photographed McKinley the day before he was shot.

71. *Edison Films*, September 1902, p. 12. These films were copyrighted as: *Arrival of McKinley's Funeral Train at Canton, Ohio; Taking President McKinley's Body from Train at Canton, Ohio; President Roosevelt at Canton Station; Panoramic View of the President's House at Canton, Ohio; Funeral Leaving the President's House and Church at Canton, Ohio;* and *McKinley's Funeral Entering Westlawn Cemetery, Canton.*

72. Searchlight Theater, programme, 13 October 1901, DLC; Lyman Howe Moving Picture Company, programme, 22 November 1901, Robert Gillaum Collection (PWbH). Appropriate sections of both programmes are reprinted in Musser with Nelson, *High-Class Moving Pictures,* forthcoming.

73. *Oswego* [New York] *Times*, 20 November 1901, clipping, NjWOE.

74. This statement is extrapolated from purchases made by George Kleine; Kleine Optical Company, "Films and Merchandise Purchased from Edison Mfg. Co. from 1899 to 1904," Kleine Collection, DLC.

75. L. J. Marcy, *Marcy's Sciopticon: Priced Catalogue of Sciopticon Apparatus and Magic Lantern Slides,* 6th ed. (Philadelphia, ca. 1878), p. 32:

OUR DEPARTED HEROES. Dissolving chromotrope. Arranged for dissolving effect, for two lanterns on two slides. One slider exhibits the National colors in Cromatic effect, with black center for the one lantern. The other, intended for the other lantern, contains on a movable slider five life-like portraits of distinguished heros who lost their lives for the preservation of the union.

76. *Edison Films*, September 1902, p. 17.

77. Although Porter took credit for this film in his interview with George Blaisdell (*MPW*, 7 December 1912, p. 961), it seems likely that James Smith and James White were also involved.

78. *Edison Films*, September 1902, p. 22.

79. Ibid., p. 90.

80. *Clipper*, 16 November 1901, p. 832.

81. For example, "Chic Paree," *The Phonoscope*, November 1896, p. 10.

82. "Execution of Czolgosz," *NYT*, 15 October 1901, p. 11; "Begging to See Czolgosz's Death," *New York Journal*, 22 October 1901, p. 1.

83. *New York World*, 29 October 1901, p. 3. Other amusement centers took similar actions. The Eden Musee placed Czolgosz's wax look-alike in its Chamber of Horrors electric chair, and "a museum keeper in a large city telegraphed an offer of $5,000 for either the body or the garments of the murderer" (ibid.).

84. *Clipper*, 16 November 1901, p. 832.

85. Iris Barry, note in collection of Edison material, n.d., NNMoMA. In France, Pathé Frères did not have the same hesitations: they recreated the assassination and offered it for sale (*Films Pathé* [Paris: Compagnie Générale des Phonographes, Cinématographes et Appareils de Précision, May 1903], p. 63).

86. *Edison Films*, September 1902, p. 91.

87. Other examples include Bamforth's *Kiss in the Tunnel* (ca. 1900), Williamson's *Fire!* (1901), and Méliès' *Bluebeard* (1901).

88. *Clipper*, 16 November 1901, p. 832.

89. *New York World*, 29 October 1901, p. 3.

90. "Assassin Czolgosz is Executed at Auburn," *NYT*, 30 October 1901, p. 5.

91. Thomas Edison to T. Cushing Daniel, 14 December 1901, Edison letter book, 5 September 1901 to 3 March 1902, p. 224, NjWOE. Edison's letters indicate a comparative disinterest in moving pictures relative to the phonograph and other business undertakings. They also reveal a frequent shortage of funds for various business schemes. He never devoted the money or attention that might have made his film business comparable to Pathé's in France and Europe.

92. *Clipper*, 19 October 1901, p. 748.

93. James White, testimony, 4 May 1910, *White and Schermerhorn v. Waters*, printed record, p. 108.

94. *Newark Advertiser*, 1 November 1901, clipping, NjWOE.

95. "Tammany 'Grafts' Pictured," *New York Tribune*, 8 October 1901, p. 2.

96. "A Stereopticon Explosion," *NYT*, 15 October 1901, p. 2.

97. *Clipper*, 23 November 1901, p. 586. See Ramsaye, *Million and One Nights,* pp. 404–5, for a greatly exaggerated account of this deal's importance to the film industry. Some commissioned films have survived in the George Kleine Collection (DLC), corroborating White's assertion that they provided an important source of income.

98. James White, testimony, 4 May 1910, p. 108.

99. "The Films That Failed," *Phonoscope*, May 1899, p. 14.

100. *San Francisco Chronicle*, 16 November 1901, p. 9.

101. *New York World*, 16 November 1901, p. 2.

102. James White, testimony, 4 May 1910, pp. 107–8.

103. Kleine Optical Company, *Complete Illustrated Catalogue,* June 1902, p. 99.

104. *Clipper*, 7 December 1901, p. 880.

105. Edison Manufacturing Company, *Edison Films*, September 1902, p. 4.

106. "100 Automobiles in Parade," *New York World*, 17 November 1901, p. 2.

107. Perhaps Edwin Porter returned East after helping White make films in British Columbia.

108. R. W. Paul, *Catalogue for 1901/02 Season* (London, 1901), offers the following description:

The Countryman's First Sight of the Animated Pictures

This amusing novelty is a representation of an animated photograph exhibition and shows the stage, proscenium and screen. The first picture thrown on the screen is that of a dancer, and a yokel in the audience becomes so excited over this that he climbs upon the stage, and expresses his delight in pantomime as the picture proceeds. The next picture (within the picture) is that of an express train, which rushes towards the yokel at full speed, so that he becomes frightened, and runs off at the wings. The last scene produced is that of the yokel himself, making love to a dairy-maid, and he becomes so enraged that he tears down the screen, disclosing the machine and operator, whom he severely handles. Length 50 ft.

109. See still in *Films Pathé*, May 1903, p. 38, or Sadoul, *Histoire générale*, 3d ed., 2:186.

110. *Edison Films*, September 1902, p. 104.

111. Ibid., p. 93.

112. "Cash for Chicago ticket to Porter," James White to Percival Waters, 25 November 1902, exhibit 4A, *White and Schermerhorn v. Waters*. The invoice does not specify the purpose or date of this trip, but *Prince Henry* was the only film taken in Chicago during the period.

113. *Edison Films*, March 1902, p. 92.

114. Pathé produced a very similar film, *Love-Sick*, which the Kinetograph Department may have copied (*Films Pathé*, May 1903, p. 26).

115. *Albany Evening Journal*, 20 May 1901, p. 10.

116. *Albany Evening Journal*, 24 May 1901, p. 10; *Clipper*, 25 May 1901, p. 292.

117. Germain Lacasse avec la collaboration de Serge Duigou, *L'Historiographe: Les Débuts du spectacle cinématographique au Quebec* (Montreal: Cinémathèque Québécoise, 1985), p. 33.

118. Robert C. Allen, "Contra the Chaser Theory." Allen demonstrates that many historians referred to this situation without the evidence to back it up. I challenge his conclusions in "Another Look at the 'Chaser Period.' "

119. Judge Wallace, opinion, *Thomas A. Edison v. American Mutoscope & Biograph Company*, 114 *Federal Reporter*, p. 934. An appeal to the Supreme Court was turned down on 2 June 1902. Edison then paid court costs of $2,618.65.

120. *Clipper*, 22 March 1902, p. 92.

121. *Clipper*, 29 March 1902, p. 110.

122. *Clipper*, 29 March 1902, p. 109, and 12 April 1902, p. 156.

123. *Thomas A. Edison v. Siegmund Lubin*, no. 36, April sessions, 1902, C.C.E.D.P., filed 25 February 1902, PPFAR.

124. *Clipper*, 5 April 1902, p. 140.

125. Payroll records indicate that this announcement lacked any basis. It could only be seen as a belated announcement of Smith's addition to the staff almost a year before.

126. *East Orange Gazette*, 24 April 1902, clipping, NjWOE.

127. Howard Hayes to William Gilmore, 22 August 1902, NjWOE.

128. James White was in Europe during the making of both *Appointment by Telephone* and *Jack and the Beanstalk*.

129. *Edison Films*, September 1902, p. 122.

130. Prescott, *Catalogue of New Films*, 1899, pp. 18–19. These films are not listed consecutively. One wonders if this suggests that the films could be shown as part of the same program but not actually juxtaposed. One could imagine the showman telling his audience, "And now we return to the gay young man with those wicked intentions." In the earlier films, the typewriter conspires with the wife while in the Porter film the discovery is by chance.

131. Arthur S. White was hired in November 1900 as a replacement for Charles Webster, who apparently decided to try his luck as an exhibitor.

132. Edwin S. Porter, deposition, 20 October 1902, *Thomas A. Edison v. Arthur D. Hotaling*, no. 8317, C.C.S.D.N.Y. This deposition, which was not submitted to the courts, is located in legal files, NjWOE.

133. E. J. Hobsbawm, *The Age of Revolution* (London: Weidenfeld & Nicolson, 1962), pp. 319–25, for a discussion of the fairy tale during the early nineteenth century.

134. Bruno Bettelheim, *The Uses of Enchantment: The Meaning and Importance of Fairy Tales* (New York: Knopf, 1976), p. 194.

135. Vardac, *Stage to Screen*, pp. 181–82.

136. *Edison Films*, September 1902, p. 116.

137. Another view on this problem is taken by Barry Salt, *Film Style and Technology: History and Analysis* (London: Starword, 1983), pp. 53 and 55.

138. *Clipper*, 24 May 1902, p. 301.

139. *Clipper*, 12 July 1902, p. 444.

140. William Gilmore to William Pelzer, 29 July 1902, NjWOE.

141. *Clipper*, 12 July 1902, p. 444.

142. *Jersey City Journal*, 2 June 1902, clipping, NjWOE.

143. *Clipper*, 24 May 1902, p. 301.

144. *Edison Films*, September 1902, p. 113.

145. *Chautauqua* [N.Y.] *Daily Assembly Herald*, May to September 1902.

146. Walter Parker to Thomas A. Edison, 17 November 1908, NjWOE. These films may also have been taken by William Wright or possibly the Miles Brothers.

147. *Denver Post*, 9 and 10 October 1902. The same carnival that White filmed in 1897. The contest was won by M. T. Sowders of Buffalo Bill's Wild West Show amidst charges of fraud.

148. A. C. Abadie to Iris Barry, 11 January 1936, NNMoMA.

149. Arthur White, statement, 10 November 1939, Merritt Crawford Collection, NNMoMA.

150. *Clipper*, 4 October 1902, p. 712.

151. "Reminiscences of Edwin S. Porter, or the History of the Motion Picture," *NYT*, 2 June 1940, p. 4J.

152. *Edison Films*, February 1903, p. 8.

153. André Bazin, *Jean Renoir* (New York: Simon & Schuster, 1973), pp. 87–89.

7. A Close Look at *Life of an American Fireman*: 1902–1903

1. *Newark Evening News*, 15 November 1902, p. 1B.

2. Ramsaye, *Million and One Nights*, p. 415. Eileen Bowser, ed., *Film Notes* (New York: Museum of Modern Art, 1969), p. 3, and other publications cite Arthur White as the star of *Life of an American Fireman*. This can be traced to an interview with Arthur White from the 1940s in which he takes credit for many of his brother's accomplishments (*Motion Picture Herald*, 12 February 1944, p. 28). In fact, James White seems to have remained in the film.

3. "White-Dede," *NYT*, 1 December 1902, p. 9.

4. *New York Herald*, 8 March 1903, 14E, see ad for Circle Theater; Keith's Union Square Theater, programme, week of 13 April 1903, PP.

5. *Reading* [Pa.] *Eagle*, 10 April 1904, p. 4.

6. Both lectures and all twelve images are reproduced in Charles Musser, "Bob the Fireman," *Les Cahiers de la Cinémathèque* 29 (Winter 1979): 147–51.

7. "Last Week's Bill/Keith's Union Square," *NYDM*, 3 October 1896, p. 19.

8. *Edison Films*, September 1902, pp. 66–67.

9. Selig Polyscope Company, minutes, 18 December 1900, p. 9, CLAc.

10. S. Lubin, *Catalogue No. 3: New Films* (Philadelphia, 1902), p. 8.

11. Georges Sadoul, *Histoire générale*, 3d ed., 2:400–401.

12. A reproduction of this painting can be found in Linda Nochlin, *Realism* (Harmondsworth, England: Penguin Books, 1971), p. 136.

13. *History of Coney Island* (New York: Burroughs and Co., ca. 1905), pp. 12–13; Biograph Bulletin no. 27, 11 August 1904, reprinted in Niver, *Biograph Bulletins*, p. 119.

14. Couvares, *Remaking of Pittsburgh*, pp. 45–50. The concept of "plebeian culture" was developed by E. P. Thompson, "Patrician Society, Plebeian Culture," *Journal of Social History* 7 (1974): 382–405. Such cultural activities engaged different social classes on an egalitarian basis with the center of gravity in the lower classes.

15. *Edison Films*, February 1903, p. 2.

16. Erich Auerbach, *Mimesis*, trans. Willard Trask (Princeton: Princeton University Press, 1953), p. 114.

17. Gerard J. Brault, trans., *The Song of Roland* (University Park, Pa.: Pennsylvania State University Press, 1978), pp. 145–47.

18. Ibid., p. 137.

19. Jean Rychner, *Chanson de geste: Essai sur l'art des jongleurs* (Geneva: E. Droz, 1955), p. 25.

20. This particular parallel was suggested to me by Brian Winston.

21. Rychner, *Chanson de geste*, p. 37.

22. Sergei Eisenstein, "Dickens, Griffith and the Film Today" in *Film Form: Essays in Film Theory*, ed. and trans. Jay Leyda (New York: Harcourt, Brace & World, 1949), pp. 199–255.

23. *Theatre Magazine*, May 1913, pp. 156, 158, and viii. George Pratt kindly brought this statement to my attention.

24. Ramsaye, *Million and One Nights*, pp. 414–15.

25. Jacobs, *Rise of the American Film*, p. 35.

26. Sadoul, *Histoire générale*, 3d ed., 2:397.

27. Jean Mitry, *Histoire du cinéma*, vol. 1 (Paris: Editions Universitaires, 1967), p. 237.

28. Jay Leyda has suggested that William Jamison, who made the original copyright photographs for *Life of an American Fireman* while working for the Edison Company and later worked at the Museum of Modern Art, may have been responsible for this modernized version.

29. Macgowan, *Behind the Screen*, pp. 113–14.

30. Mast, *Short History of the Movies*, 2d ed. (Indianapolis: Bobbs-Merrill, 1976), p. 42. His reference to *Last Year at Marienbad* alludes to Robert Gessner, "Porter and the Creation of Cinematic Motion," *Journal of the Society of Cinematologists* 2 (1962): 1–13.

The most recent edition of Mast's book unfortunately does not revise this section based on current scholarly work, perhaps because the DLC version does not fit into his historical framework.

31. Deslandes and Richard, *Histoire comparée*, 2:385.

32. For a detailed comparison of the two versions, see Charles Musser, "The Early Cinema of Edwin Porter," *Cinema Journal* 19 (Fall 1979): 29–31; and André Gaudreault, "Detours in Film Narrative: The Development of Cross-cutting," *Cinema Journal* 19 (Fall 1979): 39–59.

33. In 1908, the Amusement Supply Company still devoted many pages of its catalog to programs for which the exhibitor integrated slides and films.

8. Story Films Become the Dominant Product: 1903–1904

1. *Phonograph Monthly*, **March 1903, p. 5.**

2. Gilmore to Edison, 27 August 1903, NjWOE.

3. Gilmore to Edison, 2 March 1903, NjWOE.

4. *Animated Photo Projecting Company v. American Mutoscope Company and Benjamin Keith*, no. 7130, C.C.S.D.N.Y., NjBaFAR. On patent no. 586,953.

5. Thomas Armat, testimony, 2 December 1913, *United States v. Motion Picture Patents Co.*, printed record, p. 2184.

6. *Armat Moving Picture Co. v. Edison Manufacturing Co.*, no. 8303, C.C.S.D.N.Y., filed 28 November 1902, NjBaFAR. Armat claimed Edison did not resume sales of projectors until June 1903. Thomas Armat, testimony, 2 December 1913, p. 2180.

7. Thomas Armat to Gilmore, 11 April 1903, NjWOE.

8. Charles W. Luhr, testimony, 27 June 1907, *Armat Moving Picture Co. v. Edison Manufacturing Co.* When describing the principle of the intermittent mechanism, Armat's patent simply indicated that the period of rest (when the film was stationary in front of the light source) had to be more than the period of change (when the film frame was being moved forward). This half-shutter made the period of rest equal to the period of change and, hypothetically at least, avoided Armat's patent.

9. Howard W. Hayes, argument, *Edison v. Lubin*, no. 36, April sessions, 1902, PPFAR.

10. Sigmund Lubin, answer, *Edison v. Lubin*, no. 36, April sessions.

11. *Edison v. Lubin*, 119 *Federal Reporter*, p. 993.

12. *Orange Chronicle*, 14 February 1903; *Edison Films*, May 1903.

13. Frank Dyer, deposition, *Thomas A. Edison v. American Mutoscope and Biograph Company*, no. 8289 and 8290, C.C.S.D.N.Y., filed 7 November 1902, NjFAR.

14. 122 *Federal Reporter*, p. 240.

15. When Blackton and Smith were sued in 1898 and Arthur Hotaling in 1902, they either settled out of court or fled the court's jurisdiction.

16. Hayes to Gilmore, 22 April 1903, legal files, NjWOE.

17. Copyright files, NjWOE. References for the remaining years of this study will emphasize production dates taken from these files rather than the copyright date.

18. For example, Keith's Union Square Theater, programme, 16 February 1903, PP.

19. *Clipper*, 21 and 28 March 1903, pp. 108 and 132.

20. *Clipper*, 11 April 1903, p. 168.

21. Gilmore to White, quoted in letter, Gilmore to White, 3 December 1903, NjWOE.

22. Gaston Méliès, *Complete Catalogue of Genuine and Original Star Films* (New York, 1903), p. 5.

23. *Clipper*, 12 September 1903, p. 680, a review of Méliès' *La Royaume des fées* [*Fairyland*] shown at Keith's Union Square Theater.

24. Balshofer indicates that Lubin, at least, continued to dupe Méliès productions into 1905–6 (Fred Balshofer and Arthur C. Miller, *One Reel a Week* [Berkeley: University of California Press, 1967], pp. 5–9).

25. A selection of these Porter/Smith films were integrated into the lantern show *Lights and Shadows of a Great City, New York* (Kleine Optical Company, *Complete Illustrated Catalogue of Moving Picture Machines, Stereopticons, Magic Lanterns, Accessories and Stereopticon Views* [Chicago, 1903], p. 139). This program combined sixty-one slides with nine films and a lecture by Rev. W. T. Elsing. The films were used, in effect, to revitalize an increasingly antiquated form. Five of the nine films were actualities, including *Panoramic View of the Brooklyn Bridge, River Front and Tall Buildings* (© as *Panorama Waterfront and the Brooklyn Bridge from East River*), taken by Porter on 9 May. One, *Dancing on the Bowery*, was staged on the streets, and the remainder were comedies, including Blackton and Smith's *Burglar on the Roof*. The program consisted primarily of hard-edged documentary slides, some taken by the renowned photographer Jacob Riis, but "comics" were interspersed for relief. Though *Lights and Shadows* was standardized by the distributor, exhibitors could introduce their own variations and refinements. With its slides and films gathered from disparate sources, the program juxtaposed diverse mimetic techniques, creating a synthetic mode of representation.

26. Sklar, *Movie-Made America*, p. 26.

27. See Harry Birdoff, *The World's Greatest Hits: "Uncle Tom's Cabin"* (New York: S. F. Vanni, 1947); Thomas F. Gassett, *"Uncle Tom's Cabin" and American Culture* (Dallas: Southern Methodist University Press, 1985).

28. Biograph Bulletin no. 5, 14 May 1903, reproduced in Kemp Niver, *Biograph Bulletins, 1896–1908* (Los Angeles: Artisan Press, 1971), p. 82.

29. Mast, *Short History of the Movies*, 4th ed., p. 38.

30. Burch, "Porter, or Ambivalence," pp. 96–98.

31. *Dorothy's Dream* was offered for sale in *Edison Films*, February 1903, p. 6, as *Mother Goose Nursery Rhymes*. The description noted that "the title of each of the above subjects is included in the film and same can therefore be run without announcement slides."

32. Although, as Miriam Hansen has pointed out, many American theatrical classics were translated and performed in immigrant theaters.

33. Kleine Optical Company, *Complete Illustrated Catalogue*, 1903, p. 157; Jacobs, *Rise of the American Film*, p. 42.

34. Howard Lamarr Walls, *Motion Pictures, 1894–1912* (Washington, D.C.: Library of Congress, 1953), p. 86.

35. N. D. Cloward to Frank Dyer, 28 July 1903, legal files, NjWOE.

36. Howard W. Hayes to J. R. Schermerhorn, 1 September 1903, legal files, NjWOE.

37. *Clipper*, 5 and 12 September 1903, pp. 668 and 704.

38. Edison Manufacturing Company, *Uncle Tom's Cabin* (1903), p. 5; Sigmund Lubin, *Uncle Tom's Cabin* (Philadelphia, 1904).

39. On Coney Island, see Kasson, *Amusing the Millions*.

40. *Edison Films*, October 1903, p. 12.

41. Ibid., p. 19.

42. *Clipper*, 14 November 1903, p. 920.

43. *Clipper*, 6 June 1903, p. 358. The film was copyrighted 30 May 1903 as *The Manicure Fools the Husband* and also sold as *Don't Get Gay with Your Manicure*. This one-shot picture is described in Niver, *Early Motion Pictures*, p. 199. Lubin also made *Don't Get Gay with Your Manicurist* (*Clipper*, 13 June 1903, p. 379).

44. American Mutoscope & Biograph Company, *Picture Catalogue* (November 1902), p. 51.

45. *Edison Films*, May 1903, p. 19.

46. *Edison Films*, October 1903, p. 20.

47. *Kuleshov on Film: Writings of Lev Kuleshov*, ed. and trans. Ronald Levaco (Berkeley: University of California Press, 1974), pp. 52–54.

48. Interpolated close-ups occurred with some frequency in early cinema. The procedure, occasionally employed in lantern shows, was adopted by filmmakers with comparative ease. In Edison's *Looping the Loop at Coney Island* (made in late 1902 or early 1903) the second shot "gives a still closer view of the cars as they leave the circle and go shooting out towards the camera, the different expressions of fear, pleasure and excitement on the passengers' faces being clearly discernible" (*Edison Films*, February 1903, p. 15). Another line of development, evolving through studio/acted films, was indebted to the Englishman G. A. Smith. Smith employed the close-up in connection with point-of-view shots in which an optical instrument acted as a mediating device, as in *Grandma's Reading Glass*. His *Mary Jane's Mishaps* (1903) did without the point-of-view motivation: the woman's facial expressions, shown in close-up against a plain background, periodically interrupt the narrative executed in far shot. (*Mary Jane's Mishaps* was duped in West Orange before Porter made *The Gay Shoe Clerk*; while both appear in Edison's October 1903 catalog, the Smith film has an earlier "code word.")

49. *Edison Films*, October 1903, p. 8.

50. Ibid., p. 16.

51. William Selig, for example, urged exhibitors to interlace a program of his travel films with a selection of comedies (Selig Polyscope Company, *Special Supplement of Colorado Films* [1 November 1902], p. 3).

52. *Wilmington* [Del.] *Every Evening*, 9, 10, and 11 July 1903, p. 3.

53. *Wilmington Every Evening*, 21 and 22 August 1903; many but probably not all the films taken for Cloward were subsequently copyrighted.

54. Biograph Bulletin no. 6, 1 June 1903, reproduced in Niver, *Biograph Bulletins*, p. 83. Biograph announced the removal of its offices from 841 Broadway to 11 East Fourteenth Street in *Clipper*, 17 February 1903, p. 1124.

55. *Clipper*, 17 October 1903, p. 820.

56. See Biograph Bulletins nos. 10–13, reproduced in Niver, *Biograph Bulletins*, pp. 93–107, and *Clipper* for this period.

57. "Engagements," *NYDM*, 3 October 1903, p. 9. George Pratt kindly brought this piece of information to my attention.

58. For an illustrated supplement on the Essex County Park system, see *Orange Chronicle*, 9 April 1898.

59. For Anderson's claim to joint direction, see "2 Survive Great Train Robbery," *New York Herald Tribune*, 9 October 1961, p. 13, cited in Levy, "Edwin S. Porter and the Origins of the American Narrative Film," p. 29. For Cameron, see *Theatre News*, 22 September 1938, p. 2. For Smith, see *Moving Picture News*, 2 April 1910, p. 11. Barnes and Anderson can be identified by pictures. Ramsaye (who gave Barnes the wrong first name) adds Frank Hanaway as a bandit and Mae Murray as a dancer in the dance hall scene (Ramsaye, *Million and One Nights*, pp. 417–18).

60. *Clipper*, 7 November 1903, p. 896.

61. This copy is made available through the Museum of Modern Art, courtesy of David Shepard.

62. *Mail and Express*, 22 December 1903, p. 6; *Clipper*, 6 January 1904, p. 113.

63. Macgowan, *Behind the Screen*, p. 114.

64. George N. Fenin and William K. Everson, *The Western: From Silents to Cinerama* (New York: Bonanza Books, 1962), p. 47.

65. Sklar, *Movie-Made America*, p. 338.

66. Jacobs, *Rise of the American Film*, p. 43.

67. Gaudreault, "Detours in Film Narrative: The Development of Cross-Cutting," pp. 39–59; David Levy, "Reconstituted Newsreels, Re-enactments and the American Narrative Film," in Holman, comp., *Cinéma, 1900–1906*, pp. 243–60.

68. Neil Harris, *Humbug: The Art of P. T. Barnum* (Boston: Little, Brown, 1973), pp. 72–89.

69. American Mutoscope & Biograph Company, production records, Biograph Collection, NNMoMA.

70. *Clipper*, 12 December 1903, p. 1016.

71. George C. Pratt, *Spellbound in Darkness: A History of the Silent Film* (Greenwich, Conn.: New York Graphic Society, 1973), pp. 38–39.

72. *Clipper*, 24 October 1896, p. 544. William Martinetti brought *The Great Train Robbery* play to Porter's attention (Ramsaye, *Million and One Nights*, p. 416).

73. *Brooklyn Eagle*, 13 October 1896, p. 11.

74. *Clipper*, 12 December 1903, p. 1016.

75. "Outlaws Rob Station," *New York Tribune*, 23 November 1903, p. 1.

76. David Levy, "The Fake Train Robbery," in Holman, comp., *Cinéma, 1900–1906*.

77. Biograph Bulletin no. 33, 10 October 1904, reproduced in Niver, *Biograph Bulletins*, p. 132.

78. Kleine Optical Company, *Complete Illustrated Catalog of Moving Picture Machines, Stereopticons, Slides, Films* (Chicago, November 1905), p. 207.

79. Wolfgang Schivelbusch, *The Railway Journey: Trains and Travel in the 19th Century* (New York: Urizen Books, 1980), pp. 25–27.

80. John L. Stoddard, *John L. Stoddard Lectures* (10 vols.; Boston: Balch Brothers Co., 1907).

81. Schivelbusch, *Railway Journey*, p. 59.

82. *Mail and Express*, 21 September 1897, p. 2.

83. See note 51 above.

84. Sigmund Lubin, *Complete Lubin Films*, January 1903, p. 34. This basic gag had newspaper antecedents. See "A Tunnel Mystery," *New York Journal*, 31 March 1898, p. 12.

85. Advertisement, *New York Herald*, 24 January 1904, magazine section, p. 16.

86. *Kansas City Star*, 28 May 1905, p. 7B. See Raymond Fielding, "Hale's Tours: Ultra-Realism in the Pre-1910 Motion Picture," in Fell, ed., *Film Before Griffith*, pp. 116–30.

87. *Clipper*, 28 April 1906, p. 287.

88. The important function of this shot has been misunderstood by historians since Lewis Jacobs, who saw it as an extraneous trick, unconnected to the film's narrative.

89. The Hale's Tours exhibitor may have stopped his effects machines at various points in the film when the viewer was not looking at images from the perspective of a passenger. See Will Irwin, *The House That Shadows Built* (Garden City, N.Y.: Doubleday, Doran, 1928), p. 104.

90. Ibid., pp. 105–6.

91. Joseph McCoy, oral history, ca. 1934, p. 24, NjWOE; James White to William E. Gilmore, 22 March 1904, NjWOE.

92. Percival Waters, deposition, 25 May 1912, *White and Schermerhorn v. Waters*, p. 2.

93. Joseph McCoy, oral history, p. 24.

94. *Clipper*, 19 March 1904, p. 88.

95. The *New York Herald*, which ran Outcault's strip, claimed that "R. T. Outcault's humorous ideas have been augmented by James Gorman, and between them they have written a bright book, with catchy songs, which have been set to music by several well-known composers" ("Buster Brown on the Stage," *New York Herald*, 26 December 1903, p. 9). Other newspapers were less appreciative. One called it the poorest vehicle that Master Gabriel, the well-known midget who played Buster, had ever had (clippings, Robinson Locke Collection, vol. 192: pp. 5, 6, 13, and 23, NN).

96. *Richard F. Outcault v. Edison Manufacturing Company and Percival Waters*, no. 8743, C.C.S.D.N.Y., filed 6 May 1904, NjBaFAR.

97. Frank Dyer to J. R. Schermerhorn, 10 May 1904, NjWOE. Outcault's friendship with Edison was only temporarily strained. By 1905 he was again visiting the West Orange Laboratory (*Phonograph Monthly*, November 1905, p. 5).

98. *Edison Films*, July 1901, pp. 57–60.

99. *Edison Films*, July 1906, pp. 29–30.

100. *Clipper*, 9 April 1904, p. 160.

101. Chicago Projecting Company, *Catalog of Stereopticons, Motion Picture Machines, Lantern Slides, Film Accessories and Supplies for the Optical Projection Trade*, no. 120 (1907), p. 212.

102. "New York Show," Keith's Booking Office, reports, 31 October 1904, 3:204, IaU.

103. Kinetograph Department, film sales, 1904–6, NjWOE. This indicates that these

films were purchased from Armat. Armat received such films "in kind" from Burton Holmes as part of their licensing arrangement.

104. For example, *New York Journal*, 23 April 1904, p. 2, and 2 May 1904, p. 3.

105. *Edison Films*, July 1906, p. 29.

106. Ramsaye, *Million and One Nights*, pp. 434–39.

107. *Washington Star*, 19 May 1904, p. 1.

108. *Washington Star*, 21 May 1904, p. 7.

109. Ramsaye, *Million and One Nights*, p. 439. Some time after the ruckus dissipated, Dockstader also announced that the film survived.

110. "How Elephants Shoot the Chutes," *New York World*, 15 May 1904, magazine section, pp. 6–7.

111. It is the Biograph film that appears in the documentary film *Before the Nickelodeon*.

112. Descriptions of these films can be found in Niver, *Biograph Bulletins, 1896–1908*.

113. Frank Dyer to William Gilmore, 21 July 1904, NjWOE.

114. Charles Pathé to Edison Import House, 1 July 1904 (in house translation), NjWOE.

115. Frank Dyer to William Gilmore, 21 July 1904, NjWOE.

116. Alex T. Moore to James White, 10 October 1904, NjWOE.

117. Joseph McCoy, oral history, p. 24, NjWOE.

118. Joseph McCoy to Dyer's office, report, November 1904, NjWOE.

119. For the 1903 calendar year, Kleine had purchased $38,974 of Edison goods, while Edison sales for its 1903 business year were $127,773.

120. Gilmore to George Kleine, 15 February 1904, NjWOE.

121. Kleine to Gilmore, 2 April 1904, NjWOE.

122. Gilmore to Kleine, 15 August 1904, NjWOE.

123. Kleine to Gilmore, 20 August 1904, NjWOE.

124. Gilmore to Kleine, 24 August 1904, NjWOE.

125. *MPW*, 6 December 1913, p. 1129.

126. George Kleine to Several Good Customers, 11 October 1904, George Kleine Collection, DLC.

127. *Clipper*, 15 October 1904, p. 796.

128. The copyright files at NjWOE indicate that Waters almost invariably received the first print of a given subject.

129. Albert Smith, testimony, 14 November 1913, *United States v. Motion Picture Patents Co.*, PPFAR.

130. Biograph Bulletin no. 28, 15 August 1904, in Niver, *Biograph Bulletins*, p. 121.

131. Percival Waters, memorandum re: Marion Conversation, 1 December 1904, legal files, NjWOE.

132. *Clipper*, 15 July 1905, p. 530, and 22 July 1905.

133. Waters, memorandum re: Marion Conversation, NjWOE.

134. Bill of complaint, *American Mutoscope & Biograph Company v. Edison Manufacturing Company*, no. 10-221, C.C.D.N.J., filed 12 November 1904. Note: Many cases

for this district were destroyed by a fire, including records of this case. Printed records survive in legal files, NjWOE.

135. Delos Holden, Frank L. Dyer, and Melville Church, points for defendant in opposition to complainant's motion for preliminary injunction, 19 December 1904, *American Mutoscope & Biograph Co. v. Edison Manufacturing Co.*

136. Delos Holden to Melville Church, 28 and 30 November 1904, legal files, NjWOE. Some historians—for instance, Kemp Niver and David Levy—have suggested that Porter thought of each scene as an individual film, basing this conclusion on Edison copyright practices. This shift in copyright practice was done for legal reasons only—most of the films were sold in only one length (Niver, *First Twenty Years*, pp. 85, 87, and 90; Levy, "Edison Sales Policy and the Continuous Action Film, 1904–1906," in Fell, ed., *Film Before Griffith*, pp. 207–22).

137. Delos Holden to Melville Church, 29 November 1904, legal files, NjWOE. McCutcheon insisted the cartoon never existed.

138. Edwin S. Porter, affidavit, 3 December 1904, "Defendant's Affidavits in Opposition to Complainant's Motion for Preliminary Injunction," *American Mutoscope & Biograph Co. v. Edison Manufacturing Co.*, no. 10-221, pp. 7–10.

139. Allen, *Vaudeville and Film*, p. 217; see also id., "Film History: The Narrow Discourse," in Ben Lawton and Janet Staiger, eds., *Film: Historical-Theoretical Speculations: The 1977 Film Studies Annual (Part Two)* (Pleasantville, N.Y.: Redgrave Publishing Co., 1977), pp. 9–17. Allen compounds his error by arguing that fiction films were somehow cheaper to produce than actualities. In fact, the gradual nature of this shift only occurred because actualities were usually much cheaper to produce.

140. The case of the Edison Company in 1906 shows the fallacy of statistical analyses that simply rely on copyright data. Thomas Edison copyrighted forty films in 1906; twenty-nine of these were actuality films taken by Robert K. Bonine in Hawaii. Bonine's films were from 75 to 770 feet in length, totaling 3,700 feet of negative. In contrast, ten fiction films by Porter were copyrighted during the 1906 calendar year, varying in length from 60 to 1,000 feet, and totaling 6,815 feet (all but one was a "feature"). In 1906 one Porter film, *Dream of a Rarebit Fiend*, sold 192 copies, or 90,240 feet, while all of Bonine's Hawaii films only sold 29,060 feet. *Dream of a Rarebit Fiend* had three times the commercial value of the twenty-nine Bonine films.

141. *East Orange Gazette*, 16 February 1905, clipping, NjWOE; "Moving Picture Exhibition," *Orange Chronicle*, 25 February 1905, p. 5.

142. Edison Manufacturing Company, film sales, 1904–6, NjWOE.

143. For *How a French Nobleman . . .* , Porter apparently employed the chase extensively for the first time (its use having been adumbrated in *The Great Train Robbery*). Subsequently he made his own original chase films. *From Rector's to Claremont*, made on New York City streets and in Central Park, shows a rube chasing after a stagecoach in a vain attempt to regain his seat. It was made for a client, possibly in late summer 1904. (Without correlating information, any attribution regarding this film, which is in Paul Killiam's collection and which he dates as 1903, is highly speculative. It underscores the limitations on any close reading of Porter's work because of this "hidden" body of sponsored films.) Porter's chases in this and succeeding films, however, frequently feel mechanical and obligatory. They lack the originality and distinctive detail that make various Pathé and Biograph farces amusing and memorable. The simple and finally boring rep-

etition of the rube and the stagecoach contrasts with Biograph's accumulation of idiosyncratic pursuers over the course of *The Lost Child.*

144. Lyman Howe Moving Picture Company, programme, 30 August 1905 at Casino in Vandergrift, Pennsylvania, Robert Gillaum Collection, PWb-H.

145. *Clipper,* 13 August 1904, p. 574. Ramsaye reverses the pattern of imitation, claiming *The Bold Bank Robbery* was modeled after *The Capture of the "Yegg" Bank Burglars,* which he calls *The Great Bank Robbery* (Ramsaye, *Million and One Nights,* p. 419).

146. *Clipper,* 15 October 1904, p. 789.

147. Only in one instance, the burglary in the bank and the patrolling of the streets by the outside Yeggs (scenes 6 and 7), are simultaneous actions shown in successive scenes.

148. Nitrate prints were usually struck immediately after the paper print was made. Although David Levy argues that Edison did not sell two different versions of *The Capture of the "Yegg" Bank Burglars* because it was not noted in Edison sales records, these records do not appear so detailed as to provide decisive evidence either way (Levy, "Edison Sales Policy and the Continuous Action Film, 1904–1906," in Fell, ed., *Film Before Griffith,* p. 220).

149. *Edison Films,* July 1906, p. 33.

150. *Clipper,* 12 November 1904, p. 895. A synopsis of *Parsifal* can be found in *Edison Films,* July 1906, pp. 50–53.

151. Kleine Optical Company, *Complete Illustrated Catalog of Moving Picture Machines, Stereopticons, Slides, Films,* November 1905, p. 271.

152. "Parsifal," ca. 1946, an anonymous note acquired courtesy of Bebe Bergsten.

153. *New York World,* 22 December 1903, p. 1.

154. "Music and Drama," *New York Tribune,* 24 May 1904, p. 7.

155. Copy of contract accompanying H. L. Roth to Frank Dyer, 24 January 1905, legal files, NjWOE.

156. Edison Manufacturing Company, accounting invoices, legal files, NjWOE.

157. Edison Manufacturing Company, film sales 1904–6, NjWOE.

158. *Clipper,* 5 November 1904, p. 872.

159. Janet Staiger's discussion of the tension between standardization and differentiation is particularly applicable to the Edison Company's commercial conduct (see Bordwell, Staiger, and Thompson, *Classical Hollywood Cinema,* pp. 96–112).

160. Gilmore to Frank Dyer, 17 October 1904, legal files, NjWOE.

9. Articulating an Old-Middle-Class Ideology: 1904–1905

1. William J. Gilroy, deposition, 18 September 1902, legal files, NjWOE.

2. Ramsaye, *Million and One Nights,* p. 421; Jacobs, *Rise of the American Film,* pp. 45–47; Vardac, *Stage to Screen,* pp. 184–85; Macgowan, *Behind the Screen,* p. 120; Everson, *American Silent Film,* p. 40; Sklar, *Movie-Made America,* p. 27.

3. Background for an understanding of the Progressive movement is provided by Gabriel Kolko, *The Triumph of Conservatism: A Re-interpretation of American History* (New York: Free Press of Glencoe, 1963), and Richard Hofstadter, *The Age of Reform from Bryan to F.D.R.* (New York: Knopf, 1955).

4. *Clipper,* 3 December 1904, p. 968.

5. *NYDM*, 12 September 1903, p. 16.

6. *New York World*, 1 September 1903, p. 4. Two years later Hilliard went on to play the male lead in David Belasco's hit play *The Girl of the Golden West*.

7. "Robert Hilliard and Vaudeville—Keith's," *Philadelphia Record*, 29 September 1903, p. 3.

8. Walter Rauschenbusch, *Christianity and the Social Crisis* (New York: Macmillan, 1907), and David Graham Phillips, "Algrich, the Head of It All," *Cosmopolitan Magazine*, April 1906, excerpted in Richard Hofstadter, ed., *The Progressive Movement, 1900–1915* (Englewood Cliffs, N. J.: Prentice-Hall, 1963), pp. 79–83 and 108–12.

9. Robert Hunter, *Poverty* (New York: Macmillan, 1904) excerpted in Hofstadter, ed., *Progressive Movement, 1900–1915*, pp. 55–56.

10. Kleine Optical Company, *Complete Catalogue*, November 1903, p. 221.

11. Everson, *American Silent Film*, p. 40.

12. Once again two lines of action that occurred simultaneously are shown in successive "acts." Ramsaye, however, offers a modernized description of the subject in which "the two stories ran through the film neck and neck" (*Million and One Nights*, p. 421).

13. *New York World*, 2 June 1896, p. 1.

14. This film narrative exactly parallels an earlier account of "White Cap" activity in a turn-of-the-century newspaper. In the newspaper account, the tar clogged up the man's pores and he eventually died.

15. *Clipper*, 7 October 1905, p. 847.

16. *Pittsburgh Post*, 27 August 1905, p. 9.

17. "Among the Dramatists," *NYDM*, 29 July 1905, p. 4; and "Gossip," 19 August 1905, p. 4.

18. Albert Bushnell Hart and Herbert Ronald Ferleger, eds., *Theodore Roosevelt Encyclopedia* (New York: Roosevelt Memorial Association, 1941), pp. 45 and 587.

19. Kenneth Macgowan and William Melnitz, *The Living Stage* (Englewood Cliffs, N.J.: Prentice-Hall, 1955), p. 393.

20. Harlowe R. Hoyt, *Town Hall Tonight* (Englewood Cliffs, N.J.: Prentice-Hall, 1955), p. 40. The following analysis relies on Steele MacKaye, *Hazel Kirke* (1880; New York: Samuel French, 1912).

21. *Edison Film, Life of an American Policeman*, December 1905.

22. "Burglar Kills Police and Wounds Second," *New York World*, 21 March 1904, p. 3.

23. A roundsman was responsible for making sure the policemen were on the job, a position eliminated in today's world of two-way radios and patrol cars.

24. See Nochlin, *Realism*, pp. 150–99.

25. *Connellsville Courier*, 26 June 1885.

26. "Experiences of Boys as Tramps," *New York Tribune*, 1 May 1904, illustrated supplement, p. 5.

27. E. W. Hornung, *Raffles* (New York: Charles Scribner's Sons, 1901), and *The Amateur Cracksman* (New York: Charles Scribner's Sons, 1902).

28. *Edison Film, The Watermelon Patch*, October 1905.

29. It is difficult to agree with claims that the first ten years of American cinema offered a kind of primitive, nonracist innocence. Thomas Cripps sees this "fall" from grace occurring with the introduction of editorial techniques (*Slow Fade to Black: The Negro in American Film, 1900–1942* [London: Oxford University Press, 1977], pp. 8–19). Al-

though editing, as already shown, existed from the beginning of the post-novelty period, the racist underpinnings were frequently intertextual.

30. See "The Chicken Thief," Biograph Bulletin no. 39, 27 December 1904, reproduced in Niver, *Biograph Bulletins*, pp. 140–43.

31. *Edison Film, The Watermelon Patch*, October 1905.

32. *MPW*, 8 June 1907, pp. 216–17.

33. This film was copyrighted by Biograph on 9 June 1904.

34. Edwin Porter to the Edison Company, 6 July 1905, in *Stolen by Gypsies* copyright envelope, NjWOE.

35. *New York Sun*, 15 August 1905, cited in *Clipper*, 2 September 1905, p. 716.

36. These animations were shot in reverse motion and upside down, beginning with the final title and proceeding to chaos. The results were then used tail first to give the desired effect.

37. *Clipper*, 27 May 1905, p. 368.

38. Edwin Porter, affidavit, 3 December 1904, *American Mutoscope & Biograph Co. v. Edison Manufacturing Co.*, no. 10-221.

39. *Edison Films*, July 1906, pp. 36–37.

40. "The Whole Damm Family Staged," *NYDM*, 8 July 1905, pp. 12–14.

41. *Edison Films*, July 1906, p. 40.

42. Niver, *Biograph Bulletins*, p. 231; American Mutoscope & Biograph Company, programme, [1905], CLCM.

43. *Clipper*, 1 July 1905, p. 488.

44. "On a Good Old Trolley Ride," © 26 March 1904, written by Jos. C. Farrell, music by Pat Rooney.

45. *Edison Films*, July 1906, p. 36.

46. Ibid., p. 66.

47. Olympia Park was north of Connellsville between Irwin and Greensburg, Pennsylvania. The *Connellsville Courier* acknowledged the filmmaker as the creator of *The Great Train Robbery* and reminded everyone that Edward was "better known as 'Betty' Porter" when a child (*Connellsville Courier*, 22 August 1905, p. 8). I am again indebted to Tony Keefer for this information.

48. *Edison Films*, July 1906, p. 66.

49. *Boarding School Girls*, copyright envelope, NjWOE.

50. *Clipper*, 23 September 1905, p. 793.

51. *Billboard*, 7 December 1907, p. 16.

52. "Dockstader's Minstrels," *Birmingham* [Alabama] *Age*, 14 March 1906, p. 8.

53. *Clipper*, 22 April 1905, p. 235.

54. *Clipper*, 30 December 1905, p. 1163.

55. George H. Keyes to Edison Manufacturing Company, 14 July 1905, legal files, NjWOE. These figures reveal characteristic costs and arrangements when actuality films were made for private clients.

56. Frank Dyer to John W. Kelly, 30 August 1905, NjWOE.

57. *Edison Films*, July 1906, p. 91.

58. *Clipper*, 22 July 1905, p. 564.

59. *Edison Films*, July 1906, p. 98.

60. Ibid., p. 40.

10. Elaborating on the Established Mode of Representation: 1905–1907

1. *Variety*, 23 December 1905, p. 3. The reference is to Porter and McCutcheon's *The Train Wreckers*.

2. *MPW*, 30 November 1907, p. 629.

3. *Film Index*, 5 May 1906, p. 11.

4. *Film Index*, 6 October 1906, pp. 3–4.

5. *Film Index*, 6 October 1906, p. 3. This article indicates that Bowery film theaters drew most of their patrons from the Lower East Side and that Italians from this area were important moviegoers, contrary to Robert C. Allen's assertions in "Motion Picture Exhibition in Manhattan 1906–1912: Beyond the Nickelodeon," in Fell, ed., *Film Before Griffith*, pp. 162–75. The paucity of nickelodeons in many of these Italian neighborhoods can be explained by information that Allen provides but misinterprets. The fact that these Italian neighborhoods had heavy concentrations of single males who would repatriate does not mean that these men forsook the movies, but rather suggests that they were free to travel to the motion picture theaters outside their neighborhoods, to the entertainment districts.

6. There is an extensive literature on nickelodeons and their audiences. This includes Sklar, *Movie-Made America*, pp. 18–32; Garth Jowett, *Film and the Democractic Art* (Boston: Little, Brown, 1976), pp. 30–50; Russell Merritt, "Nickelodeon Theaters 1905–1914: Building an Audience for the Movies," in Balio, ed., *American Film Industry*, pp. 59–82; Judith Mayne, "Immigrants and Spectators," *Wide Angle* 5, no. 2 (1982): 32–40; Miriam Hansen, "Early Silent Cinema: Whose Public Sphere?" *New German Critique* 29 (Winter 1983): 147–84; Rosenzweig, *Eight Hours for What We Will*, pp. 191–220; Robert Sklar, "Oh! Althusser! Historiography and the Rise of Cinema Studies," *Radical History Review* 41 (Spring 1988): 11–35. My own research in this area can be found in *The Emergence of Cinema: The American Screen to 1907* (New York: Scribner's/Macmillan, 1990), pp. 415–47.

7. *Film Index*, 1 December 1906, p. 3.

8. *Billboard*, 18 May 1907, p. 43.

9. *Clipper*, 7 October 1905, p. 842.

10. *Billboard*, 16 June 1906, p. 26.

11. Carl Laemmle, "This Business of Motion Pictures" (unpublished manuscript, ca. 1935), p. 41, CBevA.

12. *Billboard*, 6 October 1906, p. 22.

13. Greater New York Film Rental Company, certificate of incorporation, filed 25 March 1907, NNNCC-Ar.

14. *Billboard*, 11 May 1907, p. 8.

15. *Clipper*, 23 September 1905, p. 795. For a filmography and an account of Vitagraph's activities subsequent to this date, see Jon Gartenberg, "Vitagraph Before Griffith: Forging Ahead in the Nickelodeon Era," *Studies in Visual Communication* 10, no. 4 (Fall 1984): 7–23.

16. *Clipper*, 19 January 1907, p. 1266. Kalem Company, certificate of incorporation, filed 2 May 1907, NNNCC-Ar.

17. Peerless Film Manufacturing Company, certificate of incorporation, filed 29 April 1907; name changed on 9 April 1907, ICC.

18. Edison Manufacturing Company, statement of profit and loss, NjWOE.

19. *Film Index*, 24 November 1906, p. 6.

20. Edison Company, Film Sales 1904–6, NjWOE.

21. *Film Index*, 25 April 1906, p. 6.

22. Edison Company, Film Sales 1904–6, NjWOE. The discrepancy of $3,000 between this figure and the one cited in Edison Manufacturing Company, statement of profit and loss, may be accounted for by the rental of studio space and other miscellaneous activities.

23. John Hardin to William Gilmore, 16 October 1906, NjWOE. The $.1027 per foot cited in the previous paragraph is lower than Hardin's $.12 per foot owing to jobber and agent discounts.

24. *Clipper*, 13 January 1906, p. 1207.

25. *Edison Films*, July 1906, pp. 70–71.

26. *Clipper*, 10 March 1906, p. 94.

27. "Edwin S. Porter," *MPW*, 7 December 1912, p. 961.

28. One potential exception was *Honeymoon at Niagara Falls*, for which the Edison company offered to sell discrete scenes; no one, however, took advantage of the offer.

29. Edison Manufacturing Company to Colonial Virginia Company, Inc., bill no. 27,045, 17 May 1907, attached to Alex T. Moore to Frank L. Dyer, 13 August 1908, NjWOE. Edison bought the film back for $150 in 1908 and to release it through normal channels.

30. Alex T. Moore, deposition, 13 May 1912, *White and Schermerhorn v. Waters*, NNNCC-Ar. There was some disagreement over the extent and nature of this expansion. Porter was not overtly unhappy with the arrangements, but his facilities were far from satisfactory.

31. William Gilmore to Thomas Graf, 31 December 1906, NjWOE.

32. Patent reissue no. 12,037 for the Kinetograph and reissue no. 12,038 for Kinetoscopic Film. Reissue no. 12,038 was reissued again on 12 January 1904 as patent reissue no. 12,192.

33. *Thomas A. Edison v. American Mutoscope and Biograph Company*, nos. 8289 and 8290, C.C.S.D.N.Y., filed 7 November 1902, NjBaFAR; *Thomas A. Edison v. Selig Polyscope Company*, no. 26,512, C.C.N.D.I., filed 7 November 1902, ICFAR; *Thomas A. Edison v. Siegmund Lubin*, nos. 24 and 25, October sessions 1902, C.C.E.D.P., filed 6 November 1902, PPFAR.

34. *Thomas A. Edison v. William Paley and William F. Steiner*, no. 8911, C.C.S.D.N.Y., filed 23 November 1904; *Thomas A. Edison v. Compagnie Generale des Phonographes, Cinematographes et Appareils de Precision and J. A. Berst, doing business under the name Pathe Cinematograph* Co., no. 8912, C.C.S.D.N.Y., filed 23 November 1904; *Thomas A. Edison v. Georges Melies and Gaston Melies*, no. 8913, C.C.S.D.N.Y., 23 November 1904; *Thomas A. Edison v. Eberhard Schneider doing business as American Cinematograph Co. and German-American Cinematograph and Film Co.*, no. 8914, C.C.S.D.N.Y., filed 23 November 1904, NjBaFAR.

35. *Thomas A. Edison v. American Vitagraph Co.*, no. 9035, C.C.S.D.N.Y., filed 13 March 1905, NjBaFAR.

36. George W. Ray, decision, 26 March 1906, 144 *Federal Reporter*, pp. 121–28.

37. 151 *Federal Reporter*, pp. 767–74. Biograph was using the same Warwick 35mm camera as everyone else until it constructed and used a 35mm camera covered by its original patent.

38. See Charles Musser et al., *A Guide to Motion Picture Catalogs by American Producers and Distributors, 1894–1908, A Microfilm Edition* (Frederick, Md.: University Publications of America, 1985), pp. 34–44.

39. Ramsaye, *Million and One Nights*, pp. 468–69.

40. Lawrence F. Karr, "Introduction," in Rita Horwitz, *An Index to Volume 1 of "The Moving Picture World and View Photographer"* (American Film Institute, 1974).

41. Charles Pathé, *De Pathé Frères à Pathé cinéma* (Nice: 1940; Premier Plan, June 1970), p. 62.

42. F. Croydon Marks to William Gilmore, 13 April 1907, NjWOE.

43. Ibid.

44. Marks to Pathé, 21 May 1907, NjWOE.

45. Pathé to Marks, 22 May 1907, NjWOE. A franc was then approximately equal to 20¢.

46. Gilmore to Pelzer, 28 May 1907, NjWOE.

47. *New York World*, 29 November 1906, p. 2. This helps to explain such anachronisms as the use of a repeating rifle in a drama supposedly set in the late eighteenth century. Lest Lawrence's memory seem too faulty, the stage production was described as an eastern melodrama "set with gigantic and wonderous picturesque scenery, and in noise, excitement and movement can almost be compared with a wild west show."

48. Although *Daniel Boone: On the Trail* was copyrighted in 1906, internal evidence strongly suggests that the script placed on deposit had been in circulation for many years.

49. "Edwin S. Porter," *MPW*, 7 December 1912, p. 961.

50. *Edison Films*, July 1906, p. 70. A tinted print of this film can be seen through Paul Killiam.

51. Maurice Horn, ed., *World Encyclopedia of Comics* (New York: Chelsea House Publishers, 1976) pp. 223–24.

52. Translated from a Pathé catalog quoted in Sadoul, *Histoire générale*, 3d ed., 2:306–8.

53. The self-sufficiency of the narrative may explain why *Dream of a Rarebit Fiend* has been included in so many standard histories. Unfortunately its canonization—and our ignorance of its antecedents—has also limited our insight into the cinema of this period.

54. *Film Index*, 23 June 1906, p. 9.

55. Amusement Supply Company, *Amusement for Profit* (Chicago: 1907), pp. 266–70; Eileen Bowser, "Preparation for Brighton—the American Contribution," in Hollman, comp., *Cinema 1900–1906*, p. 10, discusses other examples of this genre.

56. *Film Index*, 23 June 1906, p. 9.

57. *New York World*, 1 May 1905, illustrated supplement.

58. Adrienne Harris, "Women, Baseball and Words," *PsychCritique* 1, no. 1 (1985): 41.

59. Ibid., p. 51.

60. Charles Lovenberg, United Booking Offices, *Reports*, 3 September 1906, 6:96, Albee Papers, IaU.

61. *Film Index*, 4 August 1906, p. 9.

62. "Edwin S. Porter," *MPW*, 7 December 1912, p. 961.

63. *MPW*, 6 April 1907, p. 86. For a description of the film see *MPW*, 16 March 1907, p. 31.

64. Peter Bull, *The Teddy Bear Book* (New York: Random House, 1970), offers a useful collection of memorabilia from this period. Contemporaneous newspapers, however, provide many contradictory accounts about the origins of the craze.

65. *Variety*, 9 March 1907, p. 8.

66. The film was a huge hit and caused "much fun in the big cities," according to one prominent exhibitor, who recommended it especially for women and children. The exhibitor published a detailed description of the film that only identified the Teddy Roosevelt character as the girl's father (*Lewiston Evening Journal*, 6 May 1907, p. 2, and 8 May 1907, p. 2).

67. *New York World*, 22 October 1907, p. 1.

68. *New York American*, 27 January 1907, comic section; 17 and 24 February 1907, comic section; and others from this period. The strip, however, does not appear to have been running when Porter actually made the film (see *New York American*, 4, 18, and 25 August 1907).

69. *Film Index*, 10 November 1906, p. 8.

70. Alan Trachtenberg, "Photography/Cinematography," in Jay Leyda and Charles Musser, eds., *Before Hollywood* (New York: American Federation of the Arts, 1987), pp. 73–79.

71. Clement Greenberg, "Avant Garde and Kitsch," in Bernard Rosenberg and David Manning White, eds., *Mass Culture: The Popular Arts in America* (Glencoe, Ill.: Falcon's Wing Press, 1957), p. 98.

72. *Film Index*, 1 September 1906, p. 16.

73. Raymond D. McGill, *Notable Names in the American Theatre* (Clifton, N.J.: James T. White, 1976), p. 26.

74. Film companies sometimes rediscovered the West's rejection of regimentation, to their dismay (see, e.g., "Essanay Cowboys Refuse to 'Punch the Clock' So It Goes," *New York Telegraph*, 26 October 1913, p. 5E).

75. The surviving print at the Museum of Modern Art lacks scenes 9 and 10 as described in the *Film Index*.

76. *Clipper*, 25 August 1906, p. 712, listed the cast:

Kathleen	Kitty O'Neal
Terence O'More, Kathleen's Lover	Walter Griswoll
Captain Clearfield, An Irish Landlord	H. L. Bascom
Dugan, Clearfield's Willing Tool	W. R. Floyd
David O'Connor, Kathleen's father	E. M. Leslie
Father O'Cassidy, The Parish Priest	N. B. Clarke
Danny Kelly, Friend of Terence	J. McDovall
Kitty O'Lavey, An Odd Irish Character	Jeannie Clifford
Black Rody, The Robber Chief	C. F. Seabert
Red Barney	D. R. Allen
Darby Doyle	D. J. McGinnis
Dennis O'Gaff	W. F. Borroughs

77. Despite Ramsaye's assertion (p. 442), William Ranous did not act in this film.

78. *Film Index*, 13 October 1906, p. 3.

79. Vardac, *Stage to Screen*, pp. 24, 42–43.

80. *Kathleen Mavourneen; or St. Patrick Eve* (Clyde, Ohio: Ames Publishing Co., n.d.).

81. Van C. Lee, "The Value of a Lecture," in *MPW*, 8 February 1908, p. 91.

82. *Variety*, 1 June 1907, p. 10.

83. *Clipper*, 26 May 1906, p. 384.

84. *Los Angeles Times*, 23 May 1906, p. 2B.

85. "The Scenes of Hawaii," *Hawaiian Gazette*, 29 May 1906, p. 6. Ken Nelson graciously brought these *Hawaiian Gazette* articles to my attention.

86. "Many Scenes of Hawaii Secured," *Hawaiian Gazette*, 27 July 1906, p. 6.

87. *Honolulu Bulletin* cited in *Film Index*, 15 September 1906, p. 4.

88. *Billboard*, 10 November 1906, p. 15.

89. *New York World*, 1 August, 1906; Alex T. Moore, deposition, 13 May 1912, *White and Schermerhorn v. Waters*. Waters, however, claimed that Bonine rather than Porter took these films.

90. Most of the films that Bonine took in 1906–7 survive in the George Kleine Collection, DLC.

91. *MPW*, 1 June 1907, pp. 199–200.

92. *MPW*, 4 May 1907, p. 137.

93. This treaty was subsequently revised in 1978.

94. Bonine and Patek's lectures were part of a tradition of educational entertainment that was often sponsored by civic groups, churches, or "refined institutions." Similar subjects were dealt with by a range of traveling lecturers such as Burton Holmes and Dwight Elmendorf. See Charles Musser with Carol Nelson, *High-Class Moving Pictures*.

95. "In the Yellowstone," *Oswego* [N.Y.] *Palladium*, 23 May 1906, p. 4; *MPW*, 17 March 1907, p. 41.

96. Trachtenberg, *Incorporation of America*, pp. 17–19.

97. *MPW*, 13 July 1907, p. 295.

98. Walkover Shoe Company, catalog, ca. 1908, NjWOE.

99. *Film Index*, 16 July 1907, p. 8.

100. *MPW*, 5 October 1907, p. 487.

101. *MPW*, 13 February 1909, p. 176.

11. As Cinema Becomes Mass Entertainment, Porter Resists: 1907–1908

1. Melvin L. Defleur and Everette Dennis, *Understanding Mass Communication* (Boston: Houghton Mifflin, 1981), p. 11.

2. *Film Index*, 30 November 1907, p. 3.

3. *MPW*, 4 January 1908, p. 8.

4. *Variety*, 13 June 1908, p. 11, and 4 July 1908, p. 11.

5. *Billboard*, 14 December 1907, p. 17.

6. Laemmle Film Service, letterhead dated 2 October 1908, NjWOE.

7. *Billboard*, 21 September 1907, pp. 28 and 33; and 23 November 1907, p. 20.

8. *Film Index*, 9 November 1907, p. 3.

9. J. Stuart Blackton to George Eastman, 11 February 1908, document no. 0035, Albert Smith Collection, CLU.

10. *Thomas A. Edison v. 20th Century Optiscope Co.*, no. 28,863, C.C.N.D.I., filed October 1907, ICFAR.

11. *Film Index*, 17 August 1907, p. 4; *Show World*, 2 November 1907, p. 110; *Film Index*, 23 November 1907, p. 6.

12. *Film Index*, 7 September 1907, p. 6; *Billboard*, 7 December 1907, p. 74. The Actograph Company was owned by Edward M. Harrington, Frederick L. Beck, and Norman H. Mosher (Actograph Company, certificate of doing business under an assumed name, 12 June 1907, NNNCC-Ar).

13. George E. Stevens, deposition, [May 1907], legal files, NjWOE.

14. Albert E. Smith, testimony, 14 November 1913, *United States v. Motion Picture Patents Co.*, p. 1714.

15. George Spoor, testimony, 10 March 1914, *United States v. Motion Picture Patents Co.*, p. 2987.

16. Defendants' exhibit no. 164, docket of Dyer & Dyer for *Thomas A. Edison v. Selig Polyscope Co.*, in *United States v. Motion Picture Patents Co.*, p. 3131.

17. *Billboard*, 16 November 1907, p. 16.

18. *MPW*, 16 November 1907, p. 592.

19. *MPW*, 23 November 1907, p. 609.

20. "The Platform of the Association," *MPW*, 15 February 1908, p. 111.

21. William T. Rock to Albert Smith, 31 January 1908, document no. 0032, CLU. Even at the date of this letter, Biograph was still seriously contemplating joining the Edison group.

22. J. A. Berst, testimony, 18 November 1913, *United States v. Motion Picture Patents Co.*, p. 1772.

23. "Film Renters Meet in Convention," *Variety*, 15 February 1908, p. 10.

24. See *George Melies Company v. Motion Picture Patents Co. and Edison Manufacturing Company, and George Melies and Gaston Melies*, no. 5826, C.C.D.N.J., filed 21 May 1909, NjBaFAR, printed record at NjWOE.

25. Blackton to George Eastman, 11 February 1908, document no. 0035, CLU.

26. William Rock to Albert E. Smith, 11 February 1908, document no. 0037, CLU.

27. William Rock to Albert E. Smith, 21 February 1908, document no. 0046, CLU.

28. Edison advertisements, *Billboard*, 4 April 1908, p. 27, and 11 April 1908, p. 38.

29. "Organization Expected in Philadelphia," *Variety*, 22 February 1908, p. 10.

30. See William Swanson to Frank Dyer, 29 September 1908, and H. H. Buckwalter to Frank Dyer, 29 September 1908, NjWOE, in regard to an attempt by William Bullock to take pictures in Colorado and Cleveland, Ohio, for local distribution. Some exceptions did occur. Although the Miles Bros. worked out an arrangement with Kalem to photograph American warships on the West Coast (*Variety*, 4 April 1908, p. 12), such arrangements were cumbersome and not generally practiced.

31. Frank Dyer to Sigmund Lubin, 7 April 1908, NjWOE.

32. "Biograph Co. Licenses Three Manufacturers," *Variety*, 22 February 1908, p. 10, and "Biograph Company Defines Its Position in the Fight," *Variety*, 14 March 1908, p. 12.

33. *MPW*, 22 February 1908, p. 130.

34. *Variety*, 22 February 1908, p. 10; "Detroit Takes a Hand in the Fray," *MPW*, 28 March 1908, p. 264.

35. *Edison Manufacturing Co. et al. v. George Kleine*, no. 28,990, C.C.N.D.I., filed 6 March 1908, ICFAR; *Edison Manufacturing Co. v. American Mutoscope & Biograph Co.*, no. 2-169, C.C.S.D.N.Y., filed 16 March 1908, NjBaFAR.

36. Harry Marvin, testimony, 15 and 16 January 1913, *United States v. Motion Picture Patents Co.*, pp. 123–24, and 146; *American Mutoscope & Biograph Co. v. Essanay Mfg. Co.*, no. 29,109, C.C.N.D.I.; *American Mutoscope & Biograph Co. v. William N. Selig*, no. 29,110, C.C.N.D.I., ICFAR. Suits against the Edison Company and other East Coast concerns were apparently initiated in the U. S. Circuit Court for the District of New Jersey, for which incomplete records are available.

37. "Statement Given Out by the Edison Company," *Variety*, 14 March 1908, p. 13.

38. *Variety*, 14 March 1908, p. 12.

39. Harry N. Marvin, testimony, 16 January 1913, *United States v. Motion Picture Patents Co.*, p. 123.

40. Exhibit no. 164, *United States v. Motion Picture Patents Co.*, p. 3092.

41. "Interviews with F.S.A. Members and Others," *MPW*, 28 March 1908, p. 260.

42. *Show World*, 28 March 1908, p. 9.

43. *American Mutoscope & Biograph Co. v. Aaron J. Jones et al.*, no. 29,107, C.C.N.D.I., ICFAR.

44. "Editorial," *MPW*, 7 March 1908, p. 12.

45. "The Future Should Be Taken Care Of in the Present," *MPW*, 19 September 1908, p. 211.

46. "Chats with the Interviewer," *MPW*, 4 April 1908, p. 288.

47. Carl Laemmle to Frank Dyer, 27 April 1908, accompanied by letter from B. R. Craycroft to Laemmle, 26 April 1908, NjWOE.

48. "Long Buys Kleine Out," *Variety*, 25 April 1908, p. 14; "Editorial Notes," *MPW*, 23 May 1908, p. 456.

49. "Trade Notes," *MPW*, 29 February 1908, p. 159, and "Philadelphia," *MPW*, 18 April 1908, p. 347.

50. Among the exchanges that joined the independents were: Goodfellow's Detroit Film Exchange, the Cut Rate Film Exchange, the Cincinnati Film Exchange, C. J. Hite & Co., the Cleveland Film Exchange, and the Southern Film Exchange (*Billboard*, 29 February 1908, p. 33, and 14 March 1908, p. 53; "Quits Association," *Variety*, 28 March 1908, p. 13, and "Association Cuts Off Deserters' Line of Retreat," *Variety*, 4 April 1908, p. 12).

51. *MPW*, 4 April 1908, p. 283.

52. "Opposing with Same Pictures," *Variety*, 21 March 1908, p. 14.

53. "Another Flop to Independents," *Variety*, 25 July 1908, p. 13, and "Went Over to the Independents," *NYDM*, 18 July 1908, p. 7.

54. "An Alleged Scare," *NYDM*, 1 August 1908, p. 7.

55. Joseph McCoy, report, June 1908, NjWOE.

56. William Hodkinson to Offield, Towle and Linthicum, 10 April 1908, NjWOE.

57. A. D. Plintom to John Hardin, 18 April 1908, NjWOE.

58. William Swanson to William Gilmore, 9 May 1908; Swanson to Dyer, 18 June 1908, NjWOE. While such anti-Semitism continued to manifest itself within the industry, it was frequently put aside in the interests of commercial alliances.

59. Standard Film Exchange to Frank Dyer, 28 June 1908, NjWOE.

60. Plintom to Dyer, 6 November 1908, NjWOE.

61. " 'A Square Deal for All' is Thomas Edison's Promise," *Variety*, 20 June 1908, p. 12.

62. Statement, 1908, NjWOE.

63. George K. Spoor, testimony, 10 March 1914, *United States v. Motion Picture Patents Co.*, p. 2988; J. A. Berst, 18 November 1913, *United States v. Motion Picture Patents Co.*, p. 1729.

64. This figure is estimated using proportions derived from Joseph McCoy's June 1908 survey.

65. See above, pp. 335–36. J. Searle Dawley, memoirs, n.d., CLAc, confirmed by Edison Manufacturing Company, payroll ledger, NjWOE.

66. *Brooklyn Eagle*, 11 December 1906, p. 4, and 23 December 1906, p. 5C.

67. Among Dawley's plays were *Little Miss Sherlock Jr.*, © 10 July 1900; *The Land Beyond the Firelight*, © 15 December 1900; *At Old Fort Lookout*, a western military drama in several acts, © 13 October 1902; and *On Shanon's Shore*, © Mary G. Spooner, 22 October 1906. In addition, Dawley co-wrote *Dreamland's Gateway, or the Land of Nod*, © J. de Cordova, 9 October 1902.

68. Article in *Movie Weekly*, n.d., courtesy of Mark Wannamaker.

69. *The Girl and the Detective; or, My Little Detective*, a play in four acts © Charles E. Blaney; *Countess Du Barry*, a historical drama, © Edna May Spooner, 24 April 1908; *Daughter of the People*, a drama in four acts, © 5 June 1808; and *The She Devil*, adapted from the English translation of Ferenc Molnár's *Der Teufel*, © 28 September 1908.

70. *MPW*, 12 October 1907, p. 502.

71. Joseph McCoy, oral history, NjWOE.

72. Edison Manufacturing Company, investment ledger, NjWOE. Fox may have been acting as agent for the city: McCoy's recollection, however, is accurate on other details. Edison also purchased an adjoining 20' x 100' plot on 25 October 1907 for $4,000.

73. *Film Index*, 16 June 1906, p. 5.

74. Edison Manufacturing Company, general ledger, 1900–1911, pp. 50–51.

75. J. Searle Dawley, memoirs, n.d., CLAc.

76. Edwin Porter, draft of affidavit for equity no. 28,863, *Thomas A. Edison v. 20th Century Optiscope Co.*, ca. October 1907, legal files, NjWOE.

77. J. Searle Dawley, payroll books, CLAc. This was the only day the actors appearing in the still were hired.

78. "A Model Studio," *NYDM*, 14 November 1908, p. 12.

79. Edison Manufacturing Company, payroll ledger, indicates that Cronjager was hired 1 July 1907, shortly after Bonine's departure. He appears in the production photograph of *A Country Girl's Seminary Life and Experiences* turning the crank.

80. Richard Murphy would later follow Porter to Rex and Famous Players. In 1919, when he went to the British Famous Players–Lasky Studio, he was accompanied by his

assistant, William Cameron Menzies (*MPW*, 2 August 1919, p. 667; I thank Russell Merritt for bringing this to my attention).

81. *MPW*, 16 December 1911, p. 908.

82. Eileen Bowser, "Griffith's Film Career Before *The Adventures of Dollie*," in Fell, ed., *Film Before Griffith*, pp. 367–73.

83. Dawley, payroll notebook, CLAc; Edison Manufacturing Company, payroll ledger, NjWOE. Dawley's books were for those actors hired on a per day basis. The Edison ledger was for those working on staff.

84. "Edison's Devil," *Film Index*, 3 October 1908, p. 4.

85. *NYDM*, 19 September 1908, p. 9.

86. "The Flower of Youth," *Variety*, 15 February 1908, p. 11.

87. *MPW*, 26 September 1908, p. 232.

88. "Whither Are We Drifting," *MPW*, 10 October 1908, p. 276.

89. *Billboard*, 25 January 1908, p. 17.

90. "Lectures on Moving Pictures," *MPW*, 22 August 1908, pp. 136–37.

91. W. Stephen Bush advertisement, *NYDM*, 9 January 1909, p. 9.

92. *MPW*, 3 October 1908, p. 253.

93. *MPW*, 21 November 1908, p. 398.

94. *MPW*, 22 August 1908, p. 137.

95. "The Value of a Lecture," *MPW*, 8 February 1908, p. 93.

96. *MPW*, 11 January 1908, p. 23.

97. *Billboard*, 7 March 1908, p. 29.

98. *MPW*, 22 February 1908, p. 143.

99. "The Successful Exhibitor," *MPW*, 16 May 1908, p. 431; and *NYDM*, 14 November 1908, p. 11.

100. *Pittsburgh Dispatch*, 8 January 1905, p. 4D.

101. *NYDM*, 25 February 1905, p. 18. George Pratt generously provided much of this information about *Spook Minstrels*. See also *Film Index*, 13 October 1906, p. 3; and *MPW*, 7 September 1907, pp. 421–22.

102. *Detroit Free Press*, 4 February 1906, p. 6D.

103. *Clipper*, 25 March 1905, p. 126; *Pittsburgh Post*, 30 January 1906, p. 4; and *Cincinnati Commercial Tribune*, 7 January 1906, p. 22.

104. *NYDM*, 19 September 1908, p. 9.

105. *Manchester* [N.H.] *Union*, 22 April 1907, p. 8.

106. *Clipper*, 20 April 1907, p. 246.

107. Ibid.

108. *Manchester Union*, 22 April 1907, p. 8; *Lewiston Evening Journal*, 16 April 1907, p. 2.

109. "Pictures at Ford's," *Baltimore Sun*, 6 August 1907, p. 9.

110. *Billboard*, 15 February 1908, p. 7.

111. *Billboard*, 25 April 1908, p. 41.

112. *Clipper*, 16 May 1908, p. 350.

113. Humanovo Producing Company, consent to increase stock, 12 November 1909, NNNCC-Ar. When Loew became a part-owner is not clear.

114. "Twenty-Two Humanovo Companies," *NYDM*, 18 July 1908, p. 7.

115. *NYDM*, 13 June 1908, p. 10.

116. *MPW*, 4 July 1908, p. 9, and 12 September 1908, p. 195.

117. *MPW*, 25 July 1908, pp. 64–65.

118. *MPW*, 31 October 1908, p. 352.

119. "How Talking Pictures Are Made. A Scarcity of Picture Actors," *MPW*, 22 August 1908, p. 138.

120. "Alleged Talking Pictures," *NYDM*, 6 June 1908, p. 6.

121. *Baltimore Sun*, 31 May 1908, p. 1, and 7 June 1908, p. 1. The fourth film was Selig's *The Two Orphans*.

122. *MPW*, 4 July 1908, p. 9. See also "Motion Picture Notes" in *NYDM* for this period. *College Chums* was probably the most frequently used film for talking pictures. Tom Gunning and I wrote dialogue for and performed with the film at the Collective for Living Cinema, New York City, 29 April 1979. It was the high point of the evening.

123. *NYDM*, 19 September 1908, p. 9.

124. *Film Index*, 17 August 1907, p. 3.

125. *MPW*, 16 May 1908, p. 431.

126. *MPW*, 28 November 1908, p. 419.

127. *MPW*, 23 January 1909, p. 86.

128. *Film Index*, 7 August 1907, p. 3.

129. "Moving Pictures as a Profession," *NYDM*, 12 September 1908, p. 9.

130. *MPW*, 22 February 1908, p. 143.

131. *NYDM*, 5 September 1908, p. 8.

132. *NYDM*, 19 September 1908, p. 9.

133. *NYDM*, 26 September 1908, p. 9, and 10 October 1908, p. 8. Both films were based on plays.

134. See "Barbarian Ingomar," *NYDM*, 24 October 1908, p. 8; and "Song of the Shirt," *NYDM*, 28 November 1908, p. 8.

135. Recent research by Richard Koszarski indicates that many projectionists in the 1920s continued to play an editorial role by cutting down their film programs to fit within a designated time-slot (Richard Koszarski, *An Evening's Entertainment: The Age of the Silent Feature Picture, 1915–1928* [New York: Scribner's, 1990]). This does not seem to have been a common practice during the nickelodeon era, however.

136. Bowser, "Griffith's Film Career Before *The Adventures of Dollie*," in Fell, ed., *Film Before Griffith*, p. 371.

137. *NYDM*, 29 August 1908, p. 7.

138. Thomas Robert Gunning, "D. W. Griffith and the Narrator-System: Narrative Structure and Industry Organization in Biograph Films, 1908–1909" (Ph.D. diss., New York University, 1986), pp. 145–54.

139. Sergei Eisenstein, "The Filmic Fourth Dimension," in *Film Form*, Leyda, ed. and trans., p. 64.

140. Tom Gunning, *D. W. Griffith and the Origin of American Narrative Film* (Urbana: University of Illinois Press, forthcoming). This is a revision of Gunning's dissertation, cited in a previous note.

141. Defleur and Dennis, *Understanding Mass Communication*, p. 6. In their discussion of motion pictures, however, Defleur and Dennis fail to analyze the cinema in light of their definition (see pp. 208–37). Moreover, Defleur and Dennis neglect certain aspects of mass communication that have been the focus of this study and seem particularly

important. Mass communication, for example, requires more than professional communicators. It usually depends on an organizational structure that utilizes specialization and hierarchy.

142. Vardac, *Stage to Screen*, p. 57. The play opened at New York's New Star Theater in November 1904 and was soon burlesqued by the Vitagraph Company in its film *A Race for a Wife* (November 1906). Available prints of *The Trainer's Daughter* lack the first and last shots, although these sections were restored by adding copyright stills and catalog descriptions.

143. *Variety*, 29 February 1908, p. 12.

144. *Variety*, 16 May 1908, p. 11.

145. "Last Week at Maryland," *Baltimore Sun*, 9 June 1908, p. 9.

146. *MPW*, 1 February 1908, p. 71.

147. *Baltimore Sun*, 7 June 1908, p. 1. The reference to the song was brought to my attention by Tom Gunning. This song is performed by Joan Morris and William Bolcom on their record *After the Ball* (Nonesuch, H-71304). The complete lyrics are reprinted in the accompanying notes.

148. *Variety*, 21 March 1908, p. 15.

149. *MPW*, 11 April 1908, p. 312.

150. *Billboard*, 25 April 1908, p. 6.

151. Hans Leigh, "Exhibitors Are Not Satisfied with Their Bill of Fare," *MPW*, 23 May 1908, p. 454.

152. *Variety*, 9 May 1908, p. 11.

153. *NYDM*, 13 June 1908, p. 10.

154. *NYDM*, 20 June 1908, p. 6.

155. *MPW*, 20 June 1908, p. 526.

156. *Variety*, 20 June 1908, p. 13.

157. *MPW*, 20 June 1908, p. 526.

158. *NYDM*, 20 June 1908, p. 6.

159. *NYDM*, 4 July 1908, p. 4.

160. *NYDM*, 11 July 1908, p. 7.

161. *NYDM*, 27 June 1908, p. 5.

162. C. H. Wilson to Mr. Weber, 24 July 1908, NjWOE.

163. J. Searle Dawley, memoirs, CLAc.

164. Compare reviews of Edison and Biograph films from this period in the *NYDM* and *Variety*.

165. *NYDM*, 18 July 1908, p. 7.

166. *NYDM*, 15 August 1908, p. 7.

167. These night scenes are in the Museum of Modern Art Collection and labeled *Tales the Searchlight Told*. The original 1905 intertitles had been removed.

168. *NYDM*, 12 September 1908, p. 9.

169. *NYDM*, 1 August 1908, p. 7.

170. *Harper & Bros. et al. v. Kalem Co. and Kleine Optical Co.*, no. 2-160, C.C.S.D.N.Y., filed 6 April 1908, NjBaFAR. This ruling was augmented by copyright legislation signed by President Theodore Roosevelt in the closing days of his administration. See *NYDM*, 20 March 1909, p. 3.

171. A. T. Moore to Frank Dyer, 25 July 1908, and Frank Dyer to H. Anthony D'Arcy, NjWOE.

172. *NYDM*, 24 October 1908, p. 8. Griffith also made use of this method with *Song of the Shirt*.

173. *NYDM*, 24 October 1908, p. 8.

174. *NYDM*, 28 November 1908, p. 8.

175. *MPW*, 25 July 1908, p. 67.

176. *MPW*, 3 October 1908, p. 263.

177. *NYDM*, 10 October 1908, p. 8.

178. *MPW*, 24 October 1908, p. 318.

179. *NYDM*, 3 October 1908, p. 8.

180. *Variety*, 26 September 1908, p. 12.

181. *NYDM*, 26 September 1908, p. 9.

182. *NYDM*, 12 September 1908, p. 9.

183. *NYDM*, 11 October 1902, p. 16. Tom Gunning brought information about the de Lorde play to my attention.

184. Jay Leyda often showed this Pathé film in his Griffith classes in conjunction with *The Lonely Villa*.

185. *NYDM*, 10 October 1908, p. 8. The play was probably *Pocahontas* by Tecumtha, © 7 June 1906.

186. *Variety*, 3 October 1908, p. 11.

187. *NYDM*, 7 November 1908, p. 8.

188. *NYDM*, 7 November 1908, p. 8.

189. "Earmarks of the Makers," *NYDM*, 14 November 1908, p. 10.

190. Ibid.

191. *NYDM*, 21 November 1908, p. 8.

192. *NYDM*, 5 December 1908, p. 8.

193. Ibid.

194. *MPW*, 5 December 1908, p. 448.

195. Sklar, *Movie-Made America*, p. 30.

196. *Film Index*, 22 September 1906, p. 3.

197. *Film Index*, 15 September 1906, p. 6.

198. *Film Index*, 22 September 1906, p. 3.

199. *MPW*, 20 April 1907, p. 102; and Rosenzweig, *Eight Hours for What We Will*, pp. 205 and 207.

200. *Chicago Tribune*, 10 April 1907 cited in *MPW*, 20 April 1907, p. 101.

201. *MPW*, 25 May 1907, p. 179, and 14 March 1908, p. 214.

202. *MPW*, 20 July 1907, p. 312.

203. Ibid.

204. *Billboard*, 24 August 1907, p. 5.

205. J. Pelzer, memos, 16 and 23 June 1908, NjWOE; when this practice began is uncertain.

206. "The Merry Widower," *NYDM*, 29 August 1908, p. 7.

207. *Clipper*, 26 October 1907, p. 1005.

208. *MPW*, 21 December 1907, p. 677.

209. *MPW*, 7 March 1908, p. 190.

210. *MPW*, 19 December 1908, p. 501.

211. *MPW*, 16 May 1908, p. 443.

212. *Variety*, 20 June 1908, p. 12.

213. *Film Index*, 30 November 1907, p. 3; *Clipper*, 9 November 1907, p. 1066.

214. *Variety*, 22 February 1908, p. 11; *MPW*, 1 February 1908, p. 82.

215. *Variety*, 20 June 1908, p. 12.

216. Newspaper article, reprinted in *MPW*, 5 December 1908, p. 444.

217. *MPW*, 5 December 1908, p. 448.

218. *MPW*, 28 November 1908, p. 422.

219. *MPW*, 21 September 1908, p. 524; 7 September 1907, p. 422; 7 December 1907, pp. 645–46; and 14 December 1907, p. 665.

220. *MPW*, 2 May 1908, p. 392.

221. *Variety*, 23 May 1908, p. 12.

12. Edison Lets Porter Go: 1908–1909

1. "Legitimate Competition," *MPW*, 13 June 1908, p. 507.

2. "New Film Factories," *MPW*, 29 August 1908, p. 155.

3. William Swanson to Frank Dyer, 18 June 1908, NjWOE.

4. Carl Laemmle to Frank Dyer, 6 May 1908, NjWOE.

5. T. L. Tally to Dwight McDonald, 26 August 1908, NjWOE.

6. Harry N. Marvin, testimony, 15 January 1913, *United States v. Motion Picture Patents Co.*, p. 11.

7. Ramsaye, *Million and One Nights*, p. 471.

8. Hector J. Streyckmans, testimony, 8 July 1913, *United States v. Motion Picture Patents Co.*, p. 965.

9. "Fight Settlement Expected," *Variety*, 8 August 1908, p. 10.

10. "Moving Picture Peace Strongly Rumored About," *Variety*, 15 August 1908, p. 11.

11. "Italian Cines Out," *Variety*, 15 August 1908, p. 11; "Advance in Price of Films," *MPW*, 22 August 1908, p. 135.

12. "Pathe Will Not Invade Rental Field," *MPW*, 12 September 1908, p. 191.

13. "Settlement Talk Going On," *Variety*, 19 September 1908, p. 11.

14. Léon Gaumont and George Kleine, memorandum of agreement, 23 September 1908, NNMoMA.

15. "The Renters and the Rumored Merger," *MPW*, 17 October 1908, p. 295.

16. "Association of Film Manufacturers," *MPW*, 14 November 1908, p. 375.

17. "The Film Service Problem," *MPW*, 21 November 1908, p. 395.

18. *MPW*, 14 November 1908, p. 375.

19. American Mutoscope & Biograph Company, sales records, 1908–9, NNMoMA.

20. Ramsaye, *Million and One Nights*, p. 472.

21. "Postpone Convention till Film Peace Pact Is Made," *Variety*, 21 November 1908, p. 13.

22. "Among the Renters," *MPW*, 5 December 1908, p. 443. Sixty days' advance notice was required for any contractual changes between FSA members and the Edison-licensed manufacturers.

23. For more information on the Motion Picture Patents Company, see Janet Staiger, "Combination and Litigation: Structures of U.S. Film Distribution, 1891–1917," *Cinema Journal* 23 (Winter 1984): 41–72; Robert J. Anderson, "The Motion Picture Patents Company" (Ph.D. diss., University of Wisconsin, Madison, 1983); Gunning, "D. W. Griffith and the Narrator-System."

24. These agreements and related documents were published in *United States v. Motion Picture Patents Co.*, pp. 16–145.

25. A new agreement was to be made with Gaston Méliès on 20 July 1909. See *George Melies Co. v. Motion Picture Patents Co., et al.*, printed record, NjWOE.

26. Hector J. Streyckmans, testimony, *United States v. Motion Picture Patents Co.*, pp. 966–67.

27. Ralph Cassady, Jr., "Monopoly in Motion Picture Production and Distribution, 1908–1915," *Southern California Law Review* 32 (Summer 1959): 325–90, provides a useful overview of the Motion Picture Patents Co. An abridged version of this article appears in Gorham Kindem, ed., *American Movie Industry*, pp. 25–67.

28. William Selig to Frank Dyer, 21 January 1909; Motion Picture Patents Company, "Meeting Held January 26, 1909," NjWOE.

29. "The Conditions of License," *MPW*, 23 January 1909, p. 85.

30. "Manufacturers Assume Control of All Moving Pictures," *Variety*, 16 January 1909, p. 13.

31. Approximately 5,000 theaters were licensed during the first year, with each paying $104 per year.

32. *Motion Picture Patents Co. v. Viascope Manufacturing Company*, no. 29,514, C.C.N.D.I., filed 28 September 1909, ICFAR.

33. This agreement was apparently enforced; $150 was the lowest figure cited after 1 May 1909 in *MPW*. Most advertisements, moreover, stopped citing prices as a way to entice prospective purchasers (see, for instance, *MPW*, 22 May 1909, p. 661). This suggests that competition by pricing was reduced, if not eliminated.

34. Cassady, "Monopoly in Motion Picture Production and Distribution: 1908–1915," p. 332.

35. For example, William Swanson in *Show World*, 6 March 1909, p. 6.

36. Chicago Film Exchange to Exhibitors, 18 January 1909, NjWOE.

37. *Show World*, 23 January 1909, p. 3.

38. "To Handle Huge Volume of Film," *Variety*, 16 January 1909, p. 12.

39. "The Position of the Independents," *MPW*, 16 January 1909, p. 59.

40. "Independents Promise to Supply 25 Reels Weekly," *Variety*, 30 January 1909, p. 13.

41. "The Independent Protective Association," *MPW*, 30 January 1909, p. 116.

42. "Williams Refuses to Sign," *Variety*, 6 February 1909, p. 13.

43. "An Exhibitor's Protest," *MPW*, 6 February 1909, p. 149.

44. "Observation by Our Man-About-Town," *MPW*, 20 February 1909, p. 195.

45. *Show World*, 6 February 1909, p. 3. Capt. L. A. Boening, former treasurer for

William Swanson & Co., was treasurer, while Hector J. Streyckmans, business manager of the trade journal *Show World*, became secretary.

46. "The International Projecting and Producing Company," *MPW*, 20 February 1909, p. 197.

47. "Columbia Co. Will Soon Make Film Announcement," *Variety*, 13 February 1909, p. 12; Ramsaye, p. 497.

48. "Columbia and Murdock Cos. Plan Mutuality Scheme?" *Variety*, 20 February 1909, p. 12.

49. "Exchange Licenses Cancelled," *MPW*, 27 February 1909, p. 233.

50. "W. H. Swanson and 'Our Man About Town,' " *MPW*, 13 March 1909, pp. 308–9.

51. "Eugene Cline Also Out," *Variety*, 13 March 1909, p. 13; *Show World*, 27 March 1909, pp. 8 and 11.

52. Carl Laemmle to MPPCo, 12 April 1909, NjWOE.

53. "Strength of the Two Film Factions," *NYDM*, 1 May 1909, p. 39.

54. *MPW*, 5 June 1909, pp. 740 and 871; 3 July 1909, p. 22.

55. *NYDM*, 3 April 1909, p. 13.

56. *NYDM*, 21 November 1908, p. 8.

57. *NYDM*, 12 December 1908, p. 6.

58. Ibid.

59. *NYDM*, 19 December 1908, p. 6.

60. *NYDM*, 9 January 1909, p. 9.

61. *NYDM*, 2 January 1909, p. 8.

62. *NYDM*, 2 January 1909, p. 8.

63. *NYDM*, 23 January 1909, p. 7.

64. Dyer to Graf, 14 December 1908, NjWOE.

65. Copyright records, NjWOE.

66. Fragmentary documentation leaves the historian somewhat confused on this point. Production records indicate that these employees were at the old studio, and yet only films shot by Armitage and Cronjager were then being copyrighted and released. Were Cronjager and Matthews also at the Twenty-first Street studio, in which case there were only two units, or were the films at the Twenty-first Street studio being treated differently from those made in the Bronx?

67. Bordwell, Staiger, and Thompson, *Classical Hollywood Cinema*, pp. 92–127. This suggests certain modifications in Staiger's model, some of which have already been discussed. There are significant differences in organization between a single-unit production company and one with multiple units, but these differences occur for the cameraman system as well as the collaborative system. Certainly the director-unit system did not emerge out of a director system as Staiger suggests. If anything, the problems of management in multi-unit companies encouraged the emergence of the director as a key figure. Staiger's principal reasons for this shift—cost savings and the lack of personnel trained in all areas of production—are important to consider when accounting for these changes, but they are not the only ones.

68. "Edwin S. Porter," *MPW*, 7 December 1912, p. 962.

69. *NYDM*, 23 January 1909, p. 7.

70. *NYDM*, 30 January 1909, p. 16.

71. *NYDM*, 20 February 1909, p. 16.

72. Ibid.

73. *NYDM*, 30 January 1909, p. 16.

74. *NYDM*, 23 January 1909, p. 7.

75. *NYDM*, 30 January 1909, p. 16.

76. M. Bradlet to Frank Dyer, 3 February 1909, NjWOE.

77. Jack Farrell to John Pelzer, 20 April 1909, NjWOE.

78. This fragment is at the George Eastman House. The film's story appealed to American chauvinism. A rich American tries to introduce his daughters into English society. He becomes disenchanted with European nobility and telegraphs two American boys to come over and rescue his girls from the aristocratic "monkeys." Perhaps because the *Moving Picture World* reviewer watched the film with an audience that gave "vent to its enthusiasm," he declared it "one of the best films to come out within the past month" (*MPW*, 27 February 1909, p. 237).

79. *NYDM*, 27 February 1909, p. 13.

80. Ibid.

81. *NYDM*, 6 March 1909, p. 12.

82. *NYDM*, 13 March 1909, p. 16.

83. *NYDM*, 20 March 1909, p. 13.

84. Ibid.

85. *NYDM*, 27 March 1909, p. 13.

86. *NYDM*, 15 May 1909, p. 15.

87. Ramsaye, *Million and One Nights*, p. 496.

88. Frank Dyer to all departments, 27 March 1909, NjWOE.

89. St. Loup may have been the sought-after European director. He had previously directed films for Théophile Pathé.

90. Horace G. Plimpton to Frank L. Dyer, 18 August 1911, NjWOE.

91. Edison Manufacturing Company, accounting sheet by film and director, [June–October 1909], NjWOE.

92. Matthews continued to work as a director into the 1910s (*New York Telegraph*, 30 November 1913, p. 2E).

93. See Janet Staiger, "Dividing Labor for Production Control: Thomas Ince and the Rise of the Studio System," *Cinema Journal* 18, no. 2 (Spring 1979): 16–25.

94. Frank Marion to Frank Dyer, 26 April 1909, NjWOE.

95. Dyer to Marion, 27 April 1909, NjWOE.

96. E. S. Porter to H. G. Plimpton, 17 June 1909, NjWOE.

97. *NYDM*, 3 July 1909, p. 15.

98. *NYDM*, 22 January 1910, p. 16.

99. Horace Plimpton to Frank Dyer, 10 November 1909, NjWOE.

13. Postscript

1. Ramsaye, *Million and One Nights*, p. 492; *Motion Picture Patents Co. v. Actophone*, no. 5-105, C.C.S.D.N.Y., filed 24 December 1909, NjBaFAR. Edison was granted a preliminary injunction in this case on 12 January 1910.

2. "The Inception of the 'Black Top,' " *MPW*, 15 July 1916, p. 368.

3. *MPW*, 30 July 1910, p. 239.

4. Balshofer and Miller, *One Reel a Week*, pp. 43–53.

5. *NYDM*, 18 June 1910, p. 20.

6. *NYDM*, 14 September 1910, p. 34.

7. *NYDM*, 28 September 1910, p. 31, and 5 October 1910, p. 32.

8. Again, Defender executives may have referred to World Film Company negatives in order to throw MPPCo detectives off the track. Moreover, it is hard to imagine Swanson and Engel investing scarce funds in a new studio when Porter was performing so poorly in one he had just built. The mystery is deepened by Budd Schulberg (*Moving Pictures: Memories of a Hollywood Prince* [New York: Stein & Day, 1981], p. 15) who reports that Porter handed a copy of the scenario for *The Schoolmarm's Ride for Life* to his father, Benjamin Schulberg, suggesting that he was its producer.

9. *NYDM*, 15 March 1911, p. 34.

10. *MPW*, 16 December 1911, p. 968.

11. *MPW*, 4 March 1911, p. 463.

12. *NYDM*, 22 February 1911, p. 32.

13. *NYDM*, 8 March 1911, p. 32. Porter's tendency to recycle subjects is evident in the Rex releases, but not in those for Defender, yet another argument against Porter's responsibility for the earlier company's productions.

14. *NYDM*, 15 March 1911, p. 34.

15. "Rex Company Success," *NYDM*, 23 August 1911, p. 20.

16. A print of *Fate* survives at the George Eastman House.

17. "Too Near the Camera," *MPW*, 25 March 1911, pp. 633–34.

18. "The Rex Director," *MPW*, 24 February 1912, p. 674.

19. *MPW*, 27 January 1912, p. 269.

20. The film-related activities of the Edison Manufacturing Company shifted to Thomas A. Edison, Inc. in mid 1911, placing various Edison-owned business ventures under the umbrella of a single corporation.

21. *Kinetogram*, 1 November 1910, p. 2; 1 August 1911, p. 15; and 15 September 1912, p. 17.

22. *Kinetogram*, 1 March 1910, p. 2.

23. "Dawley Goes West," *Kinetogram*, 1 August 1912, pp. 14 and 16.

24. Horace Plimpton to Frank L. Dyer, 24 April 1912, NjWOE.

25. To meet overseas demand in this period, the Edison Company made two negatives and shipped one overseas.

26. *Kinetogram*, 1 October 1912, p. 4.

27. Stephen Bush, "Queen Elizabeth," *MPW*, 3 August 1912, p. 428.

28. "Observations by Our Man About Town," *MPW*, 26 October 1912, p. 326.

29. "E. S. Porter Resigns from Universal," *MPW*, 2 November 1912, p. 441.

30. American Film Institute Data Base.

31. *James O'Neill v. General Film Company*, New York Supreme Court, County of New York, filed 18 November 1912, NNNCC-Ar. The James O'Neill character plays a key role in Eugene O'Neill 's autobiographical *Long Day's Journey into Night*. The play is set in August 1912, immediately before O'Neill made *The Count of Monte Cristo*.

32. Adolph Zukor with Dale Kramer, *The Public Is Never Wrong* (New York: G. P. Putnam's Sons, 1953), p. 84.

33. *MPW*, 1 March 1913, p. 871.

34. *New York World*, 19 February 1913, p. 7.

35. *MPW*, 1 March 1913, p. 871.

36. *MPW*, 12 April 1913, p. 124.

37. "With the Film Men," *NYDM*, 4 December 1912, p. 31; see Schulberg, *Moving Pictures*, for a loving, witty portrait of B. P. Schulberg and his association with Porter at Famous Players.

38. "Laura Sawyer Joins Famous Players," *MPW*, 30 August 1913, p. 465.

39. " 'A Good Little Devil' Shown," *MPW*, 26 July 1913, p. 407.

40. "Mrs. Fiske as Tess," *NYDM*, 10 September 1913, p. 28; J. Searle Dawley, manuscript, CLAc.

41. " 'Little Mary' in Fine Role," *NYDM*, 17 September 1913, p. 28.

42. *New York Telegraph*, 16 November 1913, p. 3E; Dawley also claimed directing credit for *Caprice*—suggesting the continuation of his collaboration with Porter.

43. "Famous Players Co. Makes Innovation," *Pittsburgh Post*, 10 August 1913, p. 4B.

44. The exhibition of this latter film, however, was restricted for a time as the issue of rights was challenged in the courts ("Injunction Against 'In Bishop's Carriage,' " *New York Telegraph*, 21 September 1913, p. 1E).

45. "Mary Pickford with Famous Players," *MPW*, 29 November 1913, p. 1015; *New York Telegraph*, 23 November 1913, p. 2E. She left for California shortly after attending the opening of *Caprice*, at which she was mobbed ("Little Mary Receives Ovation While at Hamilton Theatre," *New York Telegraph*, 16 November 1913, p. 3E). The star had been ill.

46. *MPW*, 21 February 1914, p. 927; *Variety*, 20 February 1914, p. 23.

47. *NYDM*, 25 March 1914, p. 34.

48. *MPW*, 3 April 1914, p. 40.

49. Zukor, *Public Is Never Wrong*, p. 110.

50. *MPW*, 20 December 1913, pp. 1374–5; "Famous Players Sign Ford, Stanhope, Morange," *New York Telegraph*, 7 December 1913, p. 1E. Hugh Ford had been the stage director for Israel Zangwill's hit play, *The Melting Pot* (1909).

51. *NYDM*, 23 December 1914, p. 32.

52. "The Eternal City," *NYDM*, 6 January 1915, p. 26.

53. "Evolution of the Motion Picture," *MPW*, 11 July 1914, p. 206.

54. Zukor, *Public Is Never Wrong*, p. 120.

55. "Porter Sells Famous Players Holdings," *MPW*, 20 November 1915, p. 1468; "Zukor Buys Out Porter," *Variety*, 19 November 1915, p. 21.

56. Cassady, "Monopoly in Motion Picture Production and Distribution: 1908–1915," 325–40; Michael Conant, *Antitrust in the Motion Picture Industry* (Berkeley: University of California Press, 1960), pp. 18–21.

57. W. L. Eckert to Edison, 16 February 1915, NjWOE.

58. L. W. McChesney to Wilson, Maxwell, and L. C. McChesney, 23 October 1914, NjWOE.

59. McChesney to Plimpton, 23 October 1914, NjWOE.

60. Although *My Friend from India* (August 1914), a special, 3½-reel feature distributed by the General Film Company, cost a modest $5,548 to produce, one year later it had yet to yield a profit. Perhaps this helps to explain the delayed shift to features.

61. Stephen B. Mambert, financial executive memorandum no. 3324, 20 November 1915, NjWOE.

62. L. W. McChesney to Charles Wilson, 17 March 1915, NjWOE.

63. L. W. McChesney to Messers Ridgely, Collins, McGlynn, Wright, Ridgwell, Louis, Turbett & George, 9 December 1915, NjWOE.

64. L. W. McChesney, report of recent activities of Motion Picture Division, 5 December 1916, NjWOE.

65. Ben Singer, "Early Home Cinema and the Edison Home Projecting Kinetoscope," *Film History* 2 (1988): 37–69.

66. "At Last the 'Talkies' Are Before the Public," *New York World*, 18 February 1913, p. 6.

67. Miller Reese Hutchinson to Thomas Edison, 25 July 1913, NjWOE.

68. Rosalind Rogoff, "Edison's Dream: A Brief History of the Kinetophone," *Cinema Journal* 15 (Spring 1976): 58–68.

69. L. W. McChesney to J. W. Farrell, 11 May 1916, NjWOE.

70. *MPW*, 15 July 1911, p. 1.

71. "Stereoscopic Films Shown," *NYDM*, 16 June 1915, p. 21.

72. Dawley, manuscript, CLAc.

73. For example by reading and "correcting" Terry Ramsaye's manuscript for *A Million and One Nights*.

74. Porter file, NN; Jack Spears, "Edwin S. Porter," *Films in Review*, June–July 1970: 351–54.

75. Stan Brakhage represents personal cinema at its most extreme. Sayles writes, directs, and edits his own films; Emile de Antonio frequently declares that he makes every cut on his films and that the editor is "just a pair of hands."

76. A number of scholars have explored the relationship between early cinema and the avant-garde, particularly in terms of representation. See Miriam Hansen, "Reinventing the Nickelodeon: Notes on Kluge and Early Cinema," *October* 46 (1988): 179–98; Noël Burch, "Primitivism and the Avant-Gardes: A Dialectical Approach," in Philip Rosen, ed., *Narrative, Apparatus, Ideology* (New York: Columbia University Press, 1986), pp. 483–506; Tom Gunning, "An Unseen Energy Swallows Space: The Space of Early Film and Its Relation to American Avant-Garde Film," in Fell, ed., *Film Before Griffith*, pp. 335–66 and "The Cinema of Attraction[s]: Early Film, Its Spectator and the Avant-Garde," *Wide Angle* 8, no. 3/4 (1986): 63–70.

77. For such reasons, independent or avant-garde filmmaking has contributed extensively to our understanding of early film form. It is safe to say that without the "experimental" cinema of the 1950s, 1960s, and early 1970s, historians would still find it difficult to recognize early cinema's otherwise unfamiliar representational practices for what they were—something quite different than a simplified, rudimentary precursor of a natural, universal "film language."

Credits for Illustrations

Cover: a nickelodeon, photographed in 1909; from the Library of Congress. Tinted by Elizabeth Lennard.

Academy of Motion Picture Arts and Sciences: 467, 468.

Author's Collection: 35, 40, 41 (bottom), 43, 44, 85, 219, 318.

British Film Institute: 206.

Charles Hummel Collection: 54.

Circus World: 137.

Edison National Historic Site: 30, 31, 49, 55, 73, 145, 158, 159, 160, 162, 247, 263, 268, 273, 282, 286, 287, 293, 300, 302, 304, 306, 308, 312, 313, 316, 321, 327, 331, 337, 341, 344, 346, 347, 350, 353, 354 (bottom), 356, 357, 363, 365, 369, 373, 383, 384, 385, 390, 393, 396 (right), 400, 408, 410, 411, 412, 413 (top), 414, 418, 420, 421, 423, 425, 426, 429, 430, 431, 435, 446, 452, 454. Photographer, Joyce Jesionowski: 34, 36, 72, 115, 241, 243, 252, 344.

Federal Archive and Record Center, Bayonne, New Jersey: 134.

Harvard Theater Collection: 398.

International Museum of Photography at the George Eastman House, Film Department: 257, 439. Photographers, Joyce Jesionowski: 51, 52, 66; Paolo Cherci-Usai: 123, 460.

John Barnes/Science Museum: 63

Library of Congress, 94, 95, 98, 100 (bottom), 102, 165, 166, 167, 168 (top), 171, 181 (top), 183, 188, 201, 205, 210, 262, 270, 301, 343, 354 (top). Photographers, Pat

Loughney: 104, 106, 107, 108, 109, 110, 112, 113, 128, 129, 132, 149, 150, 152, 154, 164, 168 (bottom), 169, 175, 181 (bottom), 185, 186, 199, 315; Joyce Jesionowski: 180, 323.

Marc Wanamaker/Bison Archives: 86, 326, 455.

Museum of Modern Art, Film Stills Archive: ii, 65, 96, 224, 448, 466. Film Archive: 41, 97, 170, 248. Photographer, Joyce Jesionowski: 41 (top), 100 (top), 111, 114, 147, 250, 285, 319, 323, 396 (left).

Museum of the City of New York: 61, 62, 116, 352, 413 (bottom).

New York Public Library: 26, 133, 177, 225, 255, 269.

Smithsonian Institution: 33.

Subject and Name Index

Abadie, Alfred C., 176, 179, 249, 251,
252, 275–76, 286, 291, 370, 516n.53;
in Europe and Middle East, 197–98,
209, 234, 240
Acting and Actors. *See also* Reenactments
—development of professional film actors
and stock companies by film manufacturers, 253–54, 260, 391–92, 417,
455, 461, 466–67, 540n.80
—dubbing dialogue behind screen, 138,
396–402
—female impersonators, 55, 169, 171
—methods and styles of: presentational
approach, 8, 189–90, 200, 242, 451,
457–58, 464–65; verisimilar approach,
189–90, 463
—nonprofessional, in films, 146–48; laboratory staff as, 31–33, 254; production personnel as, 148, 187, 212–14,
516n.53
—quality of film performances judged,
415, 422, 424, 427, 447, 451
—theatrical personnel: and filmmaking,
50, 51, *51*, 52, 64, 65, 138, 253–54,
267, 268–72, 364–65, 391–92, 464–
68; as represented in film, 391–92
—vaudeville performers, 39–41, *41, 42,*
43, 50, 55, 64, 65, 69, 169, 173, 179,
321–22, 397
—wild west show and rodeo performers,
50, 51, 174, 275–76, 323, 360–63
Actograph Company, 375, 377
Actologue Company, 399–400

Actophone Company, 459
Actualities. *See also* Film subjects; Reenactments
—versus acted/fiction film, 63, 67, 160,
276, 282–84, 292, 370, 378–79,
528nn.139, 140
—declining appeal of, 195
—inexpensive nature of, 95–96, 108,
109, 284, 368, 528n.139, 531n.55
—relabeling of films, 126, 193
—repertoire of techniques used for, 105,
107, 211; applied to fiction films, 211,
225, 249–50, 259
—subgenres: industrial films, 322, 370,
378, 457, 531n.55; local views, 65–66,
96–98, 251, 284, 378–79, 537n.30;
news films, 67, 68–69, 98, 101,
104–5, 112, 117, 119–20, 126–33,
135–36, 138, 140–41, 142, 143, 154,
161, 175, 176, 184–86, 187, 190,
208–9, 251, 252, 253, 275, 276, 284,
286, 289, 291, 322–23, 367–68; quotidian views, 63, 65–69, 79, 84, 86,
93–96, 101, 102, 105, 106–7, 148–49,
151–52, 161, 208, 251, 267, 276, 291,
323, 324; travel films, 84, 95–96, 97–
98, 108–12, 122, 144, 152–53, 209,
240, 249, 264, 274, 285, 368–71, 457,
506–7n.5
Admission fees (ticket prices): at Eden
Musee, 120; at nickelodeons, 325,
372, 378; at storefronts, 86
Advertisements: for films, *133, 256,* 316,

553

507n.25. *See also* Lumière, Auguste and Louis

Cinematographers. *See* Cameramen

Cinematograph projector (Eden Musee), 118–19, 121, 442. *See also* Eden Musee

Cinematography. *See also* Camera technology; Editing; Special effects
—dream balloons and visions, 174, 200–201, 203, 205, 223–24, 412, *412*
—frames per second, 45–46, 143
—framing, 105, 107; close views, 169, 173, 245–50, 264–65, 304, 318–19, 341, 513n.165, 524n.48; and double exposures, *341*, *342*; establishing/far shots, 297, 362, *363*, 407, *408*, 425, 447, 462, 465–66, 469, 513n.165; point-of-view shots, 345–46; two-shots, 250, *304*
—isolating performers and objects against plain background, 31, *31*, 32, *33*, 114, 246–47, 250, 524n.48
—lighting, 392; arc lights, 191, 388, 475; complaints about, 422, 426, 451; Cooper-Hewitt lights, 388; sunlight, 32, 152
—reverse motion, 176
—silhouettes, 419–20, 461
—split-screen exposures, 192–93
—time-lapse photography, 186
—use of depth, 79, 94, *95*, 95–96, 97, 105

Circuses, 22, 23, 51, 100–101

City versus country, 274–75, 302–3, 305–11, 390–91, 421–22

Clair, René, 476

The Clansman (play), 303

Clark, Alfred, 56

Clark, Harry, 88, 89

Clark, Marguerite, 470

Class:
—class conflict, 18–21, 280–82, 296, 301–2, 305, 307, 317, 327–28, 355
—differences effaced or transcended, 200, 221–23, 311–17, 345–46
—elites: as audiences, 31, 327; as represented in films, 280–82, 296–302
—middle class, 10–11, 23, 24, 292–304, 305–11, 312–17, 327–28, 473; as audiences, 116–17, 327; old versus new, 11, 309–10, 406; as represented in films, 223
—working class: as audiences, 326–27, 355 (*see also* Nickelodeons); as represented in films, 222–23, 280–82, 295–96, 473

Cleveland, Grover, 69

Cline, Eugene, 328, 444

Close-ups, 318–19

Cloward, N. Dushane, 244, 251, 524n.53

Cock fight films, 41, 44

Cody, William ("Buffalo Bill"), 50, 338

Cogan, James, 417, 466

Coke industry, 15, 18–20; strikes, 19–20

Collaborative system of film production, 25, 105, 160–61, 268, 271–72, 449–50, 461–63, 465, 475, 546n.67. *See also* Film production; Working methods
—characteristic of old middle-class ideology, 340
—compared to later studio system, 336–37
—and nonspecialization, 393–94, 463
—specific examples of: Dickson and Heise, 32–34, 105; Porter and Anderson, 253, 525n.59; Porter and Dawley, 383–85, 390–93, 402, 417, 450, 461, 466–69; Porter and Fleming, 160–62, 192; Porter and McCutcheon, 291, 302, 325, 336–40, 349, 360, 364–65, 390; Porter and Smith, 240–41; Porter's later career, 461–63, 465; White and Blechynden, 105–12; White and Heise, 95–101, 105

Colonial Virginia Company, 333

Color images: hand tinted, 41, 62, 254, 397, 401; Kinemacolor, 401; tinted and toned, 331, 397, 401

Columbia Phonograph Company, 45, 71, 89, 444

Comedies, 113–14, 138, 143, 148, 163–74, 179, 189–90, 198–99, 208, 209–11, 245–50, 256, 259, 262–64, 267–72, 274–75, 280–82, 284–86, 287, 303–4, 307, 310, 311–14, 317–22, 332, 342–53, 409–10, 412–13, 415, 423. *See also* Bad-boy films; Tramp comedies

Comic strips, *167*; as conventions in films, 162; provide characters for films, 165, 167, 245, 267–72, 311, 353–54, *354*; as subjects for films, 267–72, *270*, 281. *See also* Political cartoons

Commercial methods: relationship to production and representation, 11–12

Commissioned films, 190–92, 333, 368, 378

Comstock, Laura, 173

Coney Island: as exhibition venue, 67; as film subject, 67–68, 93, *94*, 148–49, 192, 220, 245, 249–51, 275, 276, 321,

Film Title Index

Compositor: auto-graphics, inc.
Text: 10/12 Sabon Condensed
Display: Bookman Light
Printer: Edwards Brothers
Binder: Edwards Brothers